CADOGAN GUIDES

"Designed to offer the educated traveler historical and cultural insights along with practical information. Authors have intimate experience and understanding of the locales they write about."

—*The Traveler* newsletter, Traveler's Information Exchange, Boston, Massachusetts

"Rochelle Jaffe, owner and manager of Travel Books Unlimited in Bethesda, Maryland, attributes [Cadogan Guides'] popularity to both their good, clean-looking format and the fact that they include 'information about everything for everyone'. . . . These guides are one of the most exciting series available on European travel."

—*American Bookseller* magazine

Other titles in the Cadogan Guide series:

AUSTRALIA
THE CARIBBEAN
GREEK ISLANDS
INDIA
IRELAND
ITALIAN ISLANDS
ITALY
MOROCCO
ROME
SCOTLAND
SPAIN
TURKEY
THAILAND & BURMA
TUSCANY & UMBRIA

Forthcoming:
COLOMBIA,
    ECUADOR &
    THE
    GALAPAGOS
NEW YORK
NEW ORLEANS
MEXICO
PORTUGAL
TUNISIA
VENICE

ABOUT THE AUTHORS

ANTONY MASON was born in England, christened in France and went to nursery school in the USA. He has been travelling widely and regularly ever since, hitch-hiking throughout Europe, teaching English in Martinique, digging up the medieval past in Iran, bussing it across South America. Having worked in publishing for ten years, he is now a freelance editor and professional travel writer, a move to independence inspired by sitting on a beach in Bali and wondering if there was any way that he might get paid to do so.

FELICITY GOULDEN, also a confirmed traveller, fell in love with Bali. In 1986 she spent the best part of eight months on the island, during which she stayed with a family of artists in a small village off the beaten track. Subsequently she decided to set up business importing the work of some of the painters and craftspeople she had met. She now travels to Bali twice a year to do her buying—and to refresh her soul.

RICHARD OVERTON happened upon Bali in the summer of 1986. Like many before him—artists, writers, musicians and travellers—his main aim in life was to return to Bali and stay as long as possible. He contrived to do this in 1987 and took up residence with a family in Kuta—Bali's premier beach resort. From this base he set off on his motorbike, notebook in hand, to explore every last village and temple on the island. He plans to stay in Bali and is busy developing his entrepreneurial and diplomatic skills to enable him to do so.

CADOGAN GUIDES

BALI

ANTONY MASON & FELICITY GOULDEN

with Richard Overton

Illustrations by Rob Baker

A Voyager Book

The Globe Pequot Press

Chester, Connecticut

Copyright © 1989 by Cadogan Books
Illustrations copyright © 1989 by Rob Baker
Cover design by Keith Pointing
Cover illustration by Povl Webb
Maps by Thames Cartographic Services Ltd
Series Editors: Rachel Fielding and Paula Levey

Library of Congress Cataloging-in-Publication Data

Mason, Antony.
    Bali / Antony Mason, Felicity Goulden, Richard Overton:
illustrations by Rob Baker
    (Cadogan guides)
    "A Voyager book."
    Bibliography
    Includes index.
    ISBN 0–87106–602–5
    1. Bali Island (Indonesia)—Description and travel—Guide books.
    2. Bali Island (Indonesia)—Civilization.   I. Goulden, Felicity.
II. Overton, Richard.   III. Title.   IV. Series.
DS647.B2M35   1988   88–22735
915.98′60438—dc19   CIP

Manufactured in the United Kingdom

CONTENTS

v

Part IV: Religion, Festivals, Music and Dance *Pages 111–131*

Part V: Badung Regency *Pages 132–186*

Part VI: Gianyar Regency *Pages 187–231*

Part VII: Klungkung Regency *Pages 232–255*

Part VIII: Bangli Regency *Pages 256–272*

Part IX: Karangasem Regency *Pages 273–297*

Part X: Buleleng Regency *Pages 298–323*

Part XI: Tabanan Regency *Pages 324–339*

Part XII: Jembrana Regency *Pages 340–346*

Appendix *Pages 347–367*

Index *Pages 368–372*

LIST OF MAPS

ACKNOWLEDGEMENTS

The authors are indebted to a great many people who have helped them in one way or another in putting this guide book together. To the following, listed in simple alphabetical order, we would like to offer our special thanks: Richard Abraham; Nyoman Adnyana of the Badung Government Tourist Office; Dewa Ayu Oka Ariyani and family; Albert Beaucourt; Tony Bellis; Peggy Buchanan; Wayan Buja; Giusy Cicero; Kurt Debroux; I Made Dendi of Bina Wisata, Ubud; I Gusti Ngurah Rai Girigunadhi; Vicki Ingle; Sjoerd Koopman and Irene Wolters of the Koninklijke Bibliotheek, The Hague; Paula Levey; Myriam Mason; Becky Morris; Tjokorda Oka Pemayun, Director of the Bali Government Tourist Office; Ermanno Re; Dewa Made Santana and family; Ni Nyoman Sarni, Denis and the two Ketuts; Nick and Buzz Stanton; I Ketut Oka Sudana of the Badung Government Tourist Office; I Gusti Agung Ngurah Supartha, Director of the Art Centre, Denpasar; Jimmy Wijaya and family and the staff of the *Bali Tourist Guide*.

PLEASE NOTE

Collecting information in Bali is notoriously difficult, not simply because information services are still in an embryonic state (although rapidly improving), but also because what information is available is frequently contradictory. Often, after checking and cross-checking, we would find not that one contradictory statement was wrong and another right, but that both were right in their own kind of way. As they say in Bali, '*rua bineda*', 'everything has two sides'.

Nevertheless we have made every effort to ensure that the information in this book is accurate at the time of going to press. However, practical details such as opening hours, travel information, visa requirements, standards in hotels and restaurants and, in particular, prices are liable to continual change.

We cannot accept any responsibility for consequences arising from the use of this guide. If, however, you can propose any corrections and suggestions for improvement, please do write to us, so that we can make amendments to the text for the next edition. Writers of the best letters will receive a free copy of the Cadogan Guide of their choice.

INTRODUCTION

Careering along in the back of a crowded pick-up—Bali's main form of public transport—squeezed between a sack of rice, a basket of guavas and a large painting of herons alighting on a riverside nest, the old man opposite may catch your attention with a boyish twinkle in his eye. He leans across, smiles with teeth stained black with betel nut and clove-scented cigarettes, then gracefully extends a scrawny arm towards the swerving screen of landscape framed by the back of the truck—a patchwork of vivid green rice terraces etched on volcanic hills which drop towards the sea far below. 'Bali *bagus?*' he exclaims. Loosely translated: 'Isn't Bali wonderful?'

Yes indeed. This is a land of startling beauty, from the deep blue crater lakes, through Douanier Rousseau ravines of damp green foliage and trailing vines, to shores of white sand or black where the surf of the Java Sea pounds beneath classic palms. Among the rice terraces there are villages where little has changed since the days when warring rajas, were carried around their lands on ornately carved palanquins beneath gold-painted parasols—semi-deified men living in a haze of opium with their 200 wives and glittering courts of painters, carvers, musicians and dancers.

There is a profound stillness in these villages, disturbed only by the scratchy complaint of a great sway-back pig in the undergrowth, or the gentle splashing of a woman standing waist-deep in an irrigation channel, taking her morning bath. A troupe of boys rustle along narrow paths between rice fields carrying sticky-tipped wands on which they trap dragonflies for their supper.

Balinese appreciate the beauty of the country as much as starry-eyed foreigners. It belongs to the gods, on loan only; it is an expression of divinity. In the eyes of the Balinese every mundane event is a part of the eternal drama as gods of good and evil struggle for dominance over mankind. The Balinese have an acute sense of mortality, and they fill the gap between human comprehension and the immensity of the universe with the poetry of myth and inexhaustible creativity. Rice farmers are also carvers of gods and demons, or of cheerful frogs sheltering from the rain under a taro leaf. Their wives prepare the tiered temple offerings of fruit, pink rice cakes and halo of richly scented frangipani blossom. Their daughters are the exquisite *legong* dancers, who will reach the apex of their art at the age of twelve.

In the last twenty years the Balinese have drawn on this exceptional fund of creativity to meet the newest source of mystification: tourism. With nearly one million tourists a year, bringing with them their foraging curiosity, their space-age cameras, roll-on deodorants and wads of money, Bali is having to cope with rapid change. The Balinese have met the challenge with characteristic self-assuredness. Adaptable and imaginative, they have learned to cater for tourists of all budgets, coralling the most rampant tourist development into the south and leaving the rest of the island tranquil and unspoiled. They greet the changes with good humour, appreciative of the benefits they bring, and always ready to laugh at absurdities as their own culture encounters the alien values of the tourist.

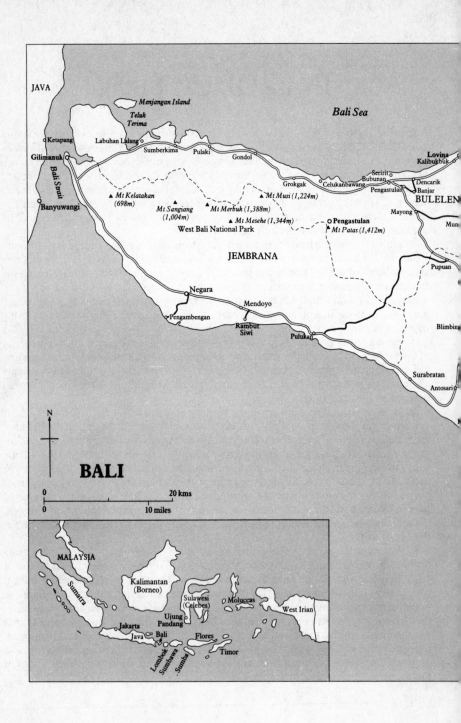

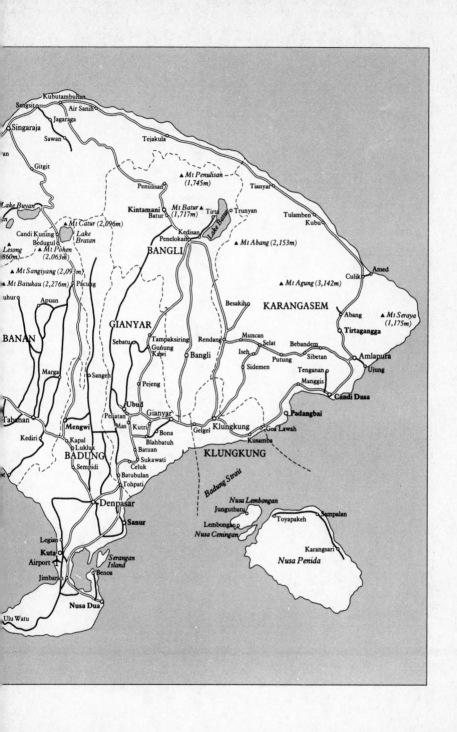

Part I

GENERAL INFORMATION

A cengceng, an instrument from the gamelan orchestra, on its carved wooden base

Essential Geography

At 5,591 sq km (2,159 sq miles), Bali is only about two-thirds the size of Crete. From east to west it measures 140 km (87 miles); from north to south, including the Bukit peninsula, 90 km (56 miles). The backbone of the island is a ridge of volcanic mountains which runs along the east–west axis, six more than 2,000 m (6,560 ft) high, two of which have erupted this century. The highest, most destructive, stands slightly apart from the others in the eastern part of the island. This is Gunung (Mt) Agung, which at 3,142 m (10,306 ft) has a presence that can be seen and felt across the island; it is revered as a holy mountain, the seat of the gods.

Bali has a population of 2.5 million, most of whom live in rural villages in the southern half of the island, where the fertile rice terraces are fed by numerous rivers descending from the central mountains. The capital, Denpasar, is also in the south, with a population of about 85,000.

Bali is an exception in the Republic of Indonesia, for whereas about 90% of Indonesia's 180 million people are Muslim—making it by far the largest Muslim country in the world—Bali's population is almost entirely Hindu.

1

Getting to Bali

By air

The majority of visitors to Bali fly, arriving at Bali's only airport, Ngurah Rai, just to the south of Denpasar.

Indonesia has been successful in restricting almost all air travel to Bali to Indonesian airlines. Besides the government-owned airline, Garuda Indonesia, only three international carriers have direct flights into Bali: Qantas (from Sydney, Melbourne, Perth and Port Hedland, and Brisbane via Sydney); KLM, the Dutch airline (from Amsterdam); and Singapore Airlines (from Singapore). In addition to its reciprocal rights at those towns, Garuda flies direct from London, Brussels, Paris, Frankfurt, Zurich, Vienna and Rome; from Hong Kong, Kuala Lumpur and Manila; and from Los Angeles and Honolulu.

Those who cannot get a direct flight will have to travel to Jakarta and then take an onward flight to Bali. Numerous carriers fly to Jakarta: Garuda Indonesia, of course, but also Swissair, KLM, Qantas, Singapore Airlines, Thai Airways, Cathay Pacific, Malaysian Airline System, China Airways. Note that British Airways do not fly to Jakarta, nor do Panam, TWA or Air Canada. American and Canadian visitors to Bali either have to fly to Los Angeles and take the Garuda flight direct to Bali (stopping at Honolulu and Biak, West Irian), which runs four times a week; or travel to somewhere like Singapore or Hong Kong to connect with an onward flight.

Getting from Jakarta to Bali is straightforward: Garuda's domestic service runs some nine flights a day to Denpasar and the smaller domestic airlines, Merpati, Bouraq and Mandala, all run scheduled services. These airlines also fly into Bali from other destinations in Indonesia, such Yogyakarta and Surabaya in Java, Ujung Pandang and Manado in Sulawesi, or Medan in Sumatra.

If you are flying to Jakarta to take an onward flight to Bali, we advise arranging connecting flights. Jakarta really is not worth a stopover: the airport is 26 km (16 miles) from the city, and the city has very little to offer the tourist besides big international hotels.

It is hard to give anything more than a general picture of the cost of flights to Bali; although airlines quote their published prices, rates offered by travel agents vary widely and it is worth shopping around. The cost of your flight will depend on your route, level of comfort, the flexibility of the ticket, the season when you are travelling, and the discount you can get through your travel agent. For Qantas, the high season is over the Christmas period only (22 Nov–15 Jan); for KLM and Garuda it is 1 Dec–31 Jan and 16 June–30 Sept. The cheap fares in the economy class are called PEX or 'Excursion' and are fairly flexible, but usually limit you to staying between 6 and 45 days in Indonesia. Low season examples (for high season be prepared to pay an extra 15%):

Return fare London to Bali direct, flying with Garuda and booked through an agent, £586. Return fare London to Bali, with KLM, changing at Amsterdam and then direct to Bali, £621.

Return fare London to Jakarta with Garuda, booked through an agent, £512; with KLM, £664.

Jakarta to Bali with Garuda, tickets purchased in Indonesia, around $100 US each way (can be up to 50% cheaper if purchased through an agent with your international ticket).

Return fare Sydney to Bali with Qantas, $782 AUS; the same fare applies from Melbourne and Brisbane. (High season, $889 AUS.)

Return fare Los Angeles to Bali with Garuda, booked through an agent, $1,070 US.

Infants (under 2 years old) usually travel at 10% of the adult fare. Children under 12 travelling in their own seat will usually pay around 70% of the adult fare.

Flights from Europe take approximately 20 hours; from Australia, anywhere between two and seven hours; and from Los Angeles about 14 hours. Jakarta is seven hours ahead of Greenwich Mean Time, and Bali is one hour ahead of Jakarta.

LEAVING BALI

It is important to reconfirm your return flight usually 72 hours before the departure time. You can reconfirm by telephoning or going in person to one of the airline offices in Bali (see p.42), but this can be a trying business. If you are staying at a large hotel, ask reception to do it for you. Make sure they get a confirmation reference number for Garuda flights, without which the airline representatives at the airport may well deny all knowledge.

Note that there is an airport tax of 9,900rp payable by all passengers leaving Indonesia, including infants. Passengers on domestic flights pay an airport tax of 3,300rp.

Overland

Bali is easily accessible from Java: there is a regular ferry service across the Bali Strait from the port of Ketapang (8 km, 5 miles north of Banyuwangi) to Gilimanuk on the western tip of Bali; you can travel by train or bus to Banyuwangi, and by bus from Gilimanuk to Denpasar (there is no railway in Bali).

The overland trip to Bali, however, is not for the faint-hearted. It is only really worth considering if Bali is part of a longer trip through Indonesia, taking in the old Javanese cities of Yogyakarta and Solo, for instance. The travel itself is not much fun, but it is remarkably cheap.

There are regular trains from Jakarta across the north of Java to Surabaya and then on to Banyuwangi; they take about 24 hours if everything goes to schedule, and cost around 30,000rp first or second class (we strongly recommend that you use express trains and travel first class where possible). Trains leave from Kota Station in Jakarta; there's one at 4.30 pm. You have to change trains and stations in the morning at Surabaya; a train leaves from Surabaya Kota station for Banyuwangi at 9.30 am, or you can take the night train at 10 pm. Only second and third class seats are available on this sector.

Buses travel between Jakarta and Denpasar via Surabaya (where you may have to change buses); the journey takes 24 hours or so in all and costs around 32,000rp.

Timetables for trains and buses are not very reliable. You can buy tickets at stations and bus terminals, but this needs some skill and persistence: leave plenty of time, and reserve a seat. The best solution is to buy your ticket in advance through a reputable travel agent, of which there are many in Jakarta. In Bali there is a railway office at Jl. Diponegoro 172, Denpasar. Ask your hotel for advice.

You can get to Yogyakarta via Bandung by train, a journey that will take some 14 hours and cost around 20,000rp. From Yogyakarta you can go by train to Banyuwangi, stopping if you like at Probolinggo, starting point for visits to the great volcano, Mt Bromo. You have to take a bus from Banyuwangi to the port of Ketapang: you can buy a ticket all the way through to Denpasar for around 3,000rp. The ferry to Gilimanuk takes 20 minutes and costs 250rp. Buses mount the ageing ferries on a ramp over the sand, though they have been known to get stuck in the sand and be left marooned as the ferry nonchalantly pulls away.

If you intend to go straight to Bali from Yogyakarta, take the bus all the way: it is much quicker, and will take you right through to Denpasar. There are a number of bus companies operating this route: go for one of the more luxurious, such as Bali Indah, which leaves Yogyakarta for Denpasar at 3 pm and takes 14 hrs. Even the best that money can buy will only cost 17,500rp or so. They offer a ticket direct to Lovina, northern Bali, as well, but the bus does not in fact go there.

For the return journey, buses leave Ubung bus station in Denpasar. Buses to Jakarta, Bogor and Badung leave at 7.30 am; those for Yogyakarta, Surabaya and Malang leave in the late afternoon and evening.

Tour Operators

Many travel companies offer trips to Bali; in fact, just about any tour operator dealing with Southeast Asia will include Bali somewhere in its brochure. Here are some of them: Bales, Hayes & Jarvis, Keith Prowse, Kuoni, Oriental Magic, Saga, Speedbird, Swan Hellenic, Thompsons, Tradewind, Trailfinders. In Australia and the USA, Garuda has its own holiday tour company called Garuda Orient Holidays. Consult a travel agent to help you choose. Many of them offer a lightning flit around the region, and give Bali three days, helping to bring the average stay in Bali for all tourists down to 9.3 days. Three days may be enough for Singapore or Chiang Mai or Yogyakarta, but not for Bali. You simply will not see the best of it. If you want to go to Bali with a tour operator, try to find one that offers at least a week there.

For more independent travellers, especially those on a narrow budget, Trailfinders in London are worth consulting. This is a reliable agency with long experience in this part of the world; they also offer good prices for flights. They are at 42–48 Earls Court Road, London W8 6EJ, tel 01–938 3366, and have opened a new office, with their 'Special Tours' desk, at 194 Kensington High Street, London W8 7RG, tel 01–938 3939.

Those with more money to spend and looking for tailor-made travel arrangements should try Abercrombie & Kent, who have offices in England, the USA and Australia. Their offices are: Abercrombie & Kent Travel, Sloane Square House, Holbein Place, London SW1, tel 01–730 9600; Abercrombie & Kent International Inc., 1420 Kensington Road, Oak Brook, Illinois 60521, tel (312) 954 1944,9; Abercrombie & Kent (Australia) Pty Ltd, 90 Bridport Street, Albert Park, Melbourne 3206, tel (61) 3–699–9766.

Indonesian Tourist Offices Abroad

Unlike most countries trying to encourage tourism as a means of acquiring foreign income, Indonesia has no official tourist board in Britain, and the embassy can only answer questions about visas and other technicalities. The private travel company Indonesian Express (70/71 New Bond Street, London W1Y 9DE, tel 01–491 4469; fax 01–491 7544), can give helpful advice, but their prime function is to promote their own range of tours and travel services.

There is an official Indonesian Tourist Board in the USA: 3457 Wilshire Blvd, Los Angeles, California 90010 , tel (213) 387 2078. There is also one in Australia: 4 Bligh Street, P.O. Box 3836, Sydney 200, tel 232 6044. There is also an Indonesian Tourist Promotion office in West Germany: Wiesenhuttenplatz 26, 06000 Frankfurt/Main 1, tel (69) 233 677. They should be able to provide whatever free information brochures are currently available.

Immigration and Visas

Anyone entering Indonesia must have a passport valid for at least six months after the date of entry. You must also have a return or onward ticket to demonstrate your intention and ability to leave the country at the end of your stay.

You do not need a visa to enter Indonesia if you hold a British, Australian, New Zealand, USA or Canadian passport. Your passport will simply be stamped on arrival with a 'tourist pass' valid for two months.

There are a few exceptions to this simple rule. First, if you are visiting family or friends in Indonesia, you are supposed to have a 'Social Visa', obtained through an embassy or consulate before your arrival (cost in the UK: £5). This is valid for four weeks only, but is renewable once in Indonesia. Secondly, travellers to Indonesia for business purposes should obtain a business visa, which is valid for five weeks, and renewable in Indonesia (cost in the UK: £13). Thirdly, any foreign journalist travelling in Indonesia should have 'clearance', which usually means visa. A final point: the two-month tourist pass is only issued at major airports and seaports, so if you plan to enter Bali through some obscure place, by private yacht or plane, check what regulations apply.

The same rules also apply to citizens of all other EEC countries—except Portugal, whose nationals are not permitted to enter Indonesia at all at present—as well as those of Austria, Finland, Iceland, Japan, Liechtenstein, Malaysia, Malta, Norway, Philippines, Singapore, South Korea, Sweden, Switzerland and Thailand.

Visitors from countries not listed here should contact an Indonesian embassy to check immigration requirements; tourist visas will have to be obtained before arrival in Indonesia, usually valid for 30 days.

In any case all visitors to Indonesia ought to double-check visa requirements with their travel agent or an embassy before departure, as regulations do change, sometimes with little notice.

If you wish to stay longer than two months in Indonesia as a tourist, you have to leave the country and re-enter, as the two-month tourist pass is not renewable and can only be replaced by a fresh one. This can be a nuisance, and expensive, but at least it is reasonably trouble-free. It is standard practice for long-term visitors to Bali to make brief excursions to Singapore, Hong Kong or Australia for this purpose, which passes unquestioned until the habit is noticed by immigration officials. If they suspect that you are becoming more resident than tourist, the rules are liable to become somewhat more arbitrary.

Visas can be renewed in Bali at the Immigration Office in Renon, the administrative suburb of Denpasar: Niti Mandala Complex, Jl. Raya Puputan, tel (0361) 27828, open Mon–Thur 7–1 pm, Fri 7–11 am, Sat 7–12 noon.

Health Requirements

You are not obliged to have any vaccinations or certificates for entry into Indonesia, unless you are coming from an area infected by yellow fever. See see pp.10–13 for general advice about health matters in Bali.

Customs

The regulations are fairly standard. You are allowed to bring in 2 litres of alcohol (although the form that you fill out in the aeroplane asks you declare anything over 1 litre), 200 cigarettes or 50 cigars or 100 gm of tobacco and a 'reasonable amount' of perfume per adult.

There are, however, restrictions concerning cassette recorders, video cameras, personal computers and other technical wizardry. You should be able to import these provided you declare that you are going to take them away with you and fill out all the documents. Video cassettes will be withheld for review. Arms and ammunition and publications deemed pornographic are forbidden, as are Chinese medicines and any publication in Chinese. And any attempt to import narcotics will be met with the full force of Indonesia's severe drugs laws.

Currency Restrictions

You can bring in, or take out, as much foreign currency or travellers' cheques as you like. However, Indonesia restricts the import or export of its own currency, and you can only bring in or take out a maximum of 50,000 rupiah, just enough to get you out of the airport and fed and watered. In fact, it is better to wait until you are in Indonesia to change money; facilities are available at the airport, at hotels and at established moneychangers at most times of the day and night. If you are worried about having enough cash to cover your first few hours, take some US dollars in small denominations, which are readily exchangeable.

Climate

Bali is just 8°5′ south of the Equator, in the Tropic of Capricorn, but because it is a small island, and mountainous, the tropical heat is tempered by coastal breezes and by the comparative coolness of the uplands. The average temperature is 26°C (79°F) in the shade.

There are two seasons: the dry season from about April to September, and the wet season from October to March. Even in the dry season it will rain from time to time, but areas not fed by abundant rivers—particularly the north coast—gradually fade to a leafless amber, only to spring back to life as the wet season unfurls.

The wet season is not a complete wash-out. It usually rains heavily in short bursts interspersed by periods of bright glistening sunshine. But it *can* just rain and rain and rain. When this happens everything comes to a standstill; in the oppressive humidity, people hover disconsolately under shelter, the roads turn to mud and sections of the more remote mountain roads slide down the hillside. This might occur at any time in the wet season, but late January and early February can be particularly bad.

So what is the best time to go to Bali? Many regular visitors favour May, but the climate in the dry season right through to, and often including, October can be very pleasant. But do not be disheartened if you have already booked a holiday that coincides with the wet season: that, too, can be perfectly agreeable. Indeed, one of Bali's two annual high seasons is November to January, coinciding with the Australian Christmas holidays. The other high season coincides with the Australia winter holidays: mid-June to the end of September. Bali is noticeably more crowded in the high seasons, and prices go up. A high point in Bali's festive calendar is March, when Nyepi is celebrated over several days in numerous ceremonies island-wide.

The higher, inland regions of Bali are usually several degrees cooler than the coast. Ubud, for instance, has an agreeable climate that makes it ideal for walking or cycling. More mountainous areas, such as Kintamani and Lake Batur can be decidedly chilly, even at midday: remember to take a light jersey or cardigan.

Daylight begins at around 6 am and night falls swiftly at about 6.30 pm throughout the year.

Currency and Money Matters

The currency of Indonesia is the rupiah. At the time of writing there are about 2,800rp to the pound sterling, or 1,700 to the US dollar, so you end up dealing with thousands of them: it can be difficult at first to gain a sense of the value of anything.

The rupiah comes in coins and notes. The common coins are in 25, 50 and 100 rupiah denominations; but you may also come across 5 and 10 rupiah coins. Notes are printed in 10, 500, 1,000, 5,000 and 10,000rp denominations. The fact that 10,000rp is the largest note printed has awkward consequences. If you go to a bank to change say $300 US, you will come out with over 50 banknotes, time consuming to count, and hard to conceal in a wallet or billfold. The most modern banks now have counting machines which zip through the notes using suction and show the amount on a digital display—totally reliable, it would seem.

That 10,000rp is the highest denomination of banknote may seem irritating to us, but then we are loaded: even the humble backpacker doing Indonesia on $250 US a month is loaded. The average Balinese very rarely deals in such sums. For example, a labourer on a government road project will expect to earn around 2,000rp, maybe 3,000rp in a day. Hotel staff in a good hotel will earn only 100,000rp in a month for an eight-hour day, every day. Meanwhile, they may well serve dinner to a group of four who will spend 100,000rp on a single meal.

These scales of income explain why the 5 and 10rp coins are still in circulation. It also explains why lower-value notes are frequently so scruffy. It is worth hanging on to coins and notes of small denominations, since traders, ticket-sellers, taxi and bus drivers often (genuinely or not) cannot give you change for a 5,000rp or 10,000rp note.

There is really no problem in changing money in Bali. There are plenty of banks in the main resorts and Denpasar, as well as moneychangers who offer very respectable rates, with no hidden commissions; and any of the large hotels will change money. (Note, however, that this becomes increasingly more difficult the further you get from places frequented by tourists.) It is worth shopping around before exchanging large sums—hotels in particular do not always update their rates from day to day, sometimes to your advantage. Although any major foreign currency will be gladly accepted, the US dollar is the most readily welcomed; it is useful also to have some US dollars in currency for emergencies. Travellers' cheques from the major international issuers are readily exchangeable by banks and moneychangers alike at good rates.

Several banks in Denpasar can supply credit card holders with cash (see below). The transaction has to be checked with a central computer which can take a while, so be prepared to wait half an hour or so.

Major credit and charge cards, such as American Express, Access/Mastercard, Barclaycard/Visa and Diner's Club are accepted in all the major hotels, and in some of the middle-ranking hotels. You can also use credit cards for airline tickets and in a few shops.

If you have a lot of rupiah left at the end of your stay you will have to exchange it back into a foreign currency, since you are only allowed to take 50,000rp out of the country. For this you may need the exchange receipts from your transactions into rupiah—so be sure to keep them.

Banks

The main branches of the major Indonesian banks are in Denpasar. Bank Negara Indonesia 1946 (the first state bank) at Jl. Gajah Mada 30, tel (0361) 24050, has the best connections with Britain—its London branch is at 3 Finsbury Square, EC2A 1DL. Bank Ekspor–Impor Indonesia at Jl. Udayana 11, tel (0361) 23511 also has good international connections. Bank Bumi Daya at Jl. Veteran 2, tel (0361) 24143; telex 35101, 35132, also has a reputation for efficiency and reliability. Go to any of these to arrange for transfer of money from abroad.

Bank Dagang Bali on Jl. Gajah Mada, Denpasar, is the Access/Mastercard representative, where you can draw money on account and where you should report a lost card. They also accept Visa cards. This bank also has a branch in Kuta (opposite the Gelael Dewata supermarket on the Denpasar/Sanur exit to the town), offering the same facilities. The Barclaycard/Visa representative is the Bank Duta Ekonomi on Jl. Raya Sanur, tel (0361) 26578. Bank Central Asia on Jl. Thamrin 75 tel (0361) 23438, Denpasar, cashes some Mastercards too (up to $1,000 US per day on Access Gold, for instance).

See p.42 for banking hours.

The American Express representative is at the offices of Pacto Ltd in the Jabaan arcade of the Hotel Bali Beach, Sanur, tel (0361) 88449; or (0361) 88511 Ext. 783. It is open Mon–Fri 8–4, Sat 8–12, closed Sundays and holidays. Card-holders can obtain $700 US worth of American Express travellers' cheques with a personal bank cheque. Lost cards should be reported here, or to the central Indonesian office in Jakarta, tel (21) 587 512.

Tipping

The Balinese really do not expect to be tipped, although in the larger hotels they have become more used to the idea. This can often become tricky because you are likely to be tended to by a fair number of staff over a few days, and it is probably easier to donate something to the staff fund at reception at the end of your stay, if you wish. Otherwise, certain services may call for some extra recognition—a guide, driver, babysitter, for example—but there is no point in insisting. Many Balinese seem to think it a bit humiliating to accept this kind of charity.

Packing for Bali

Dress in Indonesia is relaxed and practical. Cotton shirts and blouses, T-shirts, trousers, shorts and skirts are what you should be packing. Washing and laundry facilities are supplied by all hotels; in even the most modest accommodation you can get someone to do this for you. And you can buy good cotton shirts, shorts, sarongs, straw hats, thongs (flip-flops), bathing costumes for absurd prices (e.g. 5,000rp for a short-sleeved shirt) from beach traders and market stalls. What you cannot buy on the beach you can usually get in Kuta, Sanur or Denpasar, even if the brand-names are unfamiliar.

In other words, travel light; but remember that it can be cold in the mountains, so bring at least one light jersey or cardigan. Also, if you intend to drive or do much walking, bring a pair of stout shoes. Those travelling far afield on motorbikes should consider bringing light-weight protective clothing of some kind.

The Balinese do appreciate elegance, and if you attend a ceremony or a public office, you should dress respectfully. It will make a great difference to how you are treated. For temple ceremonies you should follow Balinese custom (see pp.51–52); for other occasions requiring some formality, a long-sleeved shirt, long trousers or a long dress or skirt, preferably freshly cleaned and ironed, plus proper shoes are required. Note that the further you go from the tourist haunts, the less accustomed the local people will be to shorts or short skirts.

Long trousers and long-sleeved shirts are also some defence against mosquitoes, which are present throughout the island, though not a major pest. Mosquito coils (the sort that burn), and knock-down sprays such as Baygon are widely available, but mosquito repellents in the form of roll-on sticks, towellettes or sprays (Autan, Mijex, Jungle Formula) are worth bringing with you, as is antihistamine ointment.

It is best to bring your own suntan lotion, toothpaste, shampoo and so forth. Tampons are not always available in the shops. For medicines etc., see p.11.

A torch/flashlight is indispensable when staying in lower-priced accommodation. The Balinese go to bed early, and trying to find your way back into a family compound or homestay on a moonless night, through gates and across drainage ditches with all the village dogs at your heels, is not easy.

Other useful items: a sharp penknife for peeling fruit; a compass for walking in more remote parts; a good map of Bali (the map produced by APA Press is probably the best, available from most good travel bookshops but not always available in Bali itself).

Electrical current is usually 220–240 volts.

Lastly, wine is absurdly expensive in Bali, and usually undistinguished—a great pity when excellent Australian wines are just across the water. Bring along your allowance of 2 litres per head if you want to enjoy a little wine with your seafood. Restaurants don't seem to mind if you bring your own bottle; they may charge corkage, but it is still worth it.

9

It is best to bring your own film. Film is available in Bali at reasonable prices, but there is no telling if it has been properly stored.

We would advise using 100 ISO/ASA film for general daylight conditions. Since flash is unwelcome at temple ceremonies, consider bringing some very fast film capable of responding in low levels of light. Note that in daylight conditions the contrasts between light and shade can be intense: light meters will tend to read the brightness of the sky and so underexpose shadow. You need to adjust the reading downwards to compensate (i.e. by 'stopping down' the aperture). Cameras with built-in light meters which adjust the aperture automatically may produce disappointing results if this is not taken into account.

Health

Bali is a comparatively safe place to travel in for two principal reasons. First, the Balinese themselves are sticklers for cleanliness—because their style of food is made of fresh ingredients boiled or fried in piping-hot oil you can eat with reasonable confidence from the simplest restaurants. Secondly, because Bali is a major tourist resort, it can deal with major health problems reasonably quickly and efficiently.

Nevertheless, the climate is a perfect breeding ground for infection, and it is as well to be careful.

Before You Go

Consult your doctor in good time, especially if you are travelling with children. Check that you are up to date with immunizations against polio, typhoid and tetanus. Tuberculosis is still common in Indonesia and if you are staying in Bali for some time, you should check that you are immune. There is only a low risk of cholera in the area, and since the immunization is only 60% effective, it is not generally advised. You only need a yellow fever jab if you are coming from an infected area. Some people take a course of gammaglobulin injections against hepatitis A.

There seems to be some confusion about whether or not Bali is malarial. It is. Unfortunately Indonesian mosquitoes have become resistant to chloroquine, so to cover yourself you should take two sorts of malarial tablets, such as Maloprim and Nivaquine (chloroquine). These can usually be provided in tablets that you take once a week. Begin the course several days before you arrive in Bali, and continue it some six weeks after you leave, since infection can lay dormant for that period.

In Bali

You can stay healthy by taking a few simple precautions. First, take things easy to begin with: the change of climate, diet and time zone, especially after a very long flight, is enough to weaken the best of us. Give your body time to adjust.

And avoid getting sunburn. This seems quite obvious, but it is amazing how many people stay out too long in the sun when they first arrive. For untanned skins, 20 minutes is quite enough the first day; you can double it the next.

Food and Water

Balinese food is perfectly healthy provided it has been freshly prepared and cooked. Avoid raw food such as salad, unless you know it has been washed in good water, and avoid eating in the small restaurants which only serve dishes that have been sitting around for half the day. Wash and peel all fruit carefully.

The Balinese know how concerned Westerners are about water and even the most lowly hotel will provide vacuum flasks of boiled water for drinking. You can trust them: this water will have been properly boiled. Alternatively you can buy bottled water, which is widely available and not expensive. Use boiled or bottled water (not tap water) to clean your teeth.

Ice is a well-known hazard for tourists in foreign climes, and the cautious will avoid it completely. In Bali it is manufactured centrally, from boiled water, and is quite safe when it leaves the factory. It is what happens between the factory and your glass that counts. The large hotels treat ice with the respect it deserves, but smaller bar-owners and shopkeepers are more cavalier. It is not uncommon for the morning delivery to leave a block of ice sitting in the dust beside the road, waiting for the day to begin.

'Bali Belly'

The name suggests that stomach upsets and diarrhoea are common in Bali, which is not really the case. Diarrhoea is not pleasant, but it is nothing to panic about; the change of diet alone may be the cause. Most stomach upsets will clear up of their own accord after three days or so. It is much better to allow your body to deal with any infection in its own time than to reach immediately for proprietary medicines. You must, however, be sure that you have plenty to drink: dehydration can incur more serious risks—particularly in young children. Also you should try to replace the salt in your body. A simple remedy can be a solution of one litre of clean water with $1/2$ teaspoon of salt and 8 teaspoons of sugar. Alternatively, buy packets made up of similar ingredients—called Dioralyte or Electrosol. If you do have to stop yourself up quickly, to take a flight for instance, use a drug containing loperamide, such as Arret or Imodium (manufactured under license in Java). If diarrhoea lasts longer than four days, find a doctor. And if you pass blood, consult a doctor immediately.

When suffering from an upset stomach avoid eating spicy food. Plain boiled rice is what the Balinese would eat, or *bubur*, which is rice cooked in stock with a few vegetables. Bananas are recommended, but other fruit should be avoided.

A Simple Medical Kit

This is really all you need: malaria tablets (see above); aspirin or paracetamol (or other pain-killing pills); Dioralyte or Electrosol, and loperamide (for diarrhoea); sticking plaster; bandage (for sprains); antiseptic cream; antihistamine lotion; sunscreen; moisturizing cream; throat pastilles.

Cuts can easily become infected in this climate, and may take rather longer to heal than in more temperate regions. It is important to keep all wounds clean: apply antiseptic ointment.

For minor illnesses and indispositions you can call upon Balinese wisdom. They have plenty of local remedies which have proven their effectiveness over the centuries. Balinese medicine, with its mixture of herbal cures and massage, is an interesting subject in its own right.

Serious Illness and Accidents

If you become seriously ill in Bali your best bet is to get help through any of the major hotels, such as the Hotel Bali Beach, the Bali Hyatt or any of the Nusa Dua hotels, even if you are not a guest. They have their own listed doctors who are experienced and well-trained, and who can arrange hospital treatment if you need it. You will find that, confronted with illness, the Balinese are very sympathetic and helpful.

Basically, Balinese medics are good at treating the kind of minor illnesses associated with the climate, such as stomach bugs, fevers, minor infections and so on. They are less well equipped to deal with serious illness requiring surgery, or accidents involving broken limbs. For these you really need to go to Singapore or Australia. It is therefore a wise precaution to make sure you are adequately covered by insurance, including provisions to get you 'medi-vacced' by air-ambulance if need be (see Insurance, p.13). When illness or injury has reached this level of seriousness, your consulate should be contacted.

Other Medical Risks

There is one kind of poisonous snake in Bali, called the *lelipis gedong*; it is a green snake with a red tail. The Balinese live in mortal fear of it, which helps its effectiveness enormously, since it does not always inject poison but victims can literally die of the shock alone. Nonetheless, snake bites should be taken extremely seriously. The victim should be moved as little as possible, reassured, and medical attention sought without delay.

Indonesia suffers from rabies. The best advice is to have nothing to do with any of Bali's dogs, especially if it is behaving oddly. Remember that rabies can be transmitted by saliva alone. If you are bitten and worried, first wash the wound very thoroughly, then consult a doctor at once. Your consulate should know where the necessary vaccine is available: you may have to be flown home to get it, but your insurance should cover this.

Monkey bites should also be taken seriously; these can turn into nastily infected sores, and you cannot entirely rule out rabies. The Balinese have their own very effective cures, so listen to them if they offer help. Otherwise seek medical advice.

Be warned that Bali has its fair share of venereal disease. It is difficult to assess the risk of AIDS; with such a continuous turnover of active and promiscuous foreigners, both male and female, those that expose themselves to any risk should act with as much circumspection as they would anywhere else in the world. Condoms are available at pharmacies for 300–500rp each.

Hospitals and Clinics

The Surya Husadha Private Hospital, Jl. Pulau Serangan 1–3, Denpasar, tel (0361) 25249, is specially geared to tourist needs. They offer insurance cover during your stay which costs $10 US for 14 days up to $25 US for 60 days, payable on arrival. Their services are available 24 hours a day.

Sanglah Public Hospital is the main hospital (*rumah sakit*), Jl. Kesehatan Selatan 1, Sanglah, Denpasar, tel (0361) 27911. Facilities are adequate but nursing is left more or less to the family in Indonesia, so aftercare is generally poor by Western standards.

Dr. Indra Guizot, Jl. Pattimura 19, Denpasar, tel (0361) 22445, 26445, offers emergency medical treatment.

The standard fee for a consultation with a doctor is around 5,000rp, plus however many thousand rupiah are required for prescriptions.

Emergency ambulance, tel (0361) 27911. Public ambulance service, tel (0361) 118.

Balinese Massage

Massages on Kuta beach became a byword for sybaritic pleasure among travellers in the 1970s. The masseuses are still there in plenty, despite numerous attempts to regulate and restrict them. Now each massage lady has a number, proudly displayed on a peaked cap, and all avid beach-goers have their favourites. Massage is also offered at Sanur, Candi Dasa and Ubud.

Massage plays an important role in Balinese healing, and some practitioners are highly experienced. The beach ladies, however, offer little more than a rub-down with coconut oil—still pleasurable and good value at 2,000rp or so for half an hour. Sand and massage do not go well together: brush yourself down well, and check your masseuse's hands before she starts (it is something they often overlook).

Insurance

You would be wise to insure fully for your travel, whatever your budget. Travel insurance will cover you against cancellation due to unforeseen eventualities, compensating for a lost holiday. It will also cover for lost baggage, and theft. Most of all it covers for medical expenses, and many travel insurance packages offer the services of such operations as Europ Assistance to sort out travellers' medical problems abroad. Once contacted, they will see that you are given proper treatment, or flown to wherever you can get it ('medi-vacced'), by air-ambulance if necessary. They will also guarantee hospital fees.

Remember that unless you are totally incapacitated and a company such as Europ Assistance has had to step in, you actually have to pay for treatment, and then claim back the costs from the insurance company.

Theft

Alas, this is not paradise. Security in Bali is probably considerably better than almost any other place, but you should not drop your guard. Money and valuables have a habit of disappearing from hotel rooms, especially in the tourist south, but also in more modest tourist haunts of Ubud and Candi Dasa. Use the safe deposit facilities of your hotel if they have them; or those offered by the various banks and moneychangers. Failing this, just be circumspect, and keep your valuables out of temptation's path.

For loss of credit cards, see the section on banks above (p.8). If you lose your passport you will have to apply for a new one through your consulate, a process that can take up to a week (see the section on consulates below, p.42). If you lose your money and much else, you will probably want to claim against your insurance, which means that you will need to have proof that the theft has been reported to the police. Tell your hotel manager what has happened and see if he can smooth the path. Otherwise you will simply have to go to the nearest police station and do what you can.

Kuta had a bad reputation for street crime in the 1970s, but this has now been largely cleaned up. Robbery with violence is rare. However, there are two notorious ways that tourists are robbed, besides theft from hotels. One is from the front baskets of hire bicycles: cyclists putting their money and documents in them provide easy prey for thieves on motorbikes. The other involves an old trick in crowded *bemos*, the small buses and wagons that provide most of the public transport. Smiling faces will offer to help the victim by placing luggage at the far end of the compartment, whereupon it will be casually covered by a coat or rug, or even a painting. With more smiling faces, the victim will be distracted while his, or her, bag is rifled. So in *bemos* keep your luggage with you.

Accommodation

One of the pleasures of travelling in Bali is the accommodation. There is every grade of hotel and lodgings that you can imagine, from the extremely luxurious, with every Western comfort, to the most basic room in a family compound. Furthermore, accommodation in Bali is not expensive compared to Europe, for instance, or the Caribbean.

At the top of the range are the big hotels, belonging to the big multinational hotel groups: the Nusa Dua Beach Hotel, the Bali Sol, the Bali Hyatt and so forth. Most of these hotels are superbly designed, incorporating tropical gardens into the grand architectural plan. You can spend anywhere between $70 US and $120 US a night for a double room in such places, or $1,200 US a night for the island's most luxurious hotel suite.

Only one hotel in Bali is high-rise, the dreary Hotel Bali Beach in Sanur, built in 1965. The lesson was learnt: after this no hotel could be built above the height of a palm tree, about four storeys high. The newer international hotels, some of which have 700 rooms, have all the expected facilities such as telephones, television, air-conditioning, lifts, swimming pools and numerous restaurants to cater for every international taste. They also bring in cultural shows to give their guests a taste of Bali. They are relaxing and pleasant, but virtually indistinguishable from any other such hotel in a tropical climate.

There are several smaller hotels, also in this price bracket, which offer what to our minds is a much more rewarding experience. You stay in Balinese-style accommodation, usually thatched cottages, decorated with wood-carvings and Balinese paintings, with your own verandah surrounded by a luxuriant and beautifully tended garden. Service is exceptional, and the hotels have most of the facilities associated with the international hotels. The Bali Oberoi in Kuta is the largest in this bracket. The Tandjung Sari in Sanur is perhaps the most famous example. And Kupu Kupu Barong in Kedewatan, near Ubud is the most recent addition to this distinguished league.

There are a fair number of good, smallish hotels which offer similar accommodation at around $60–$70 US per night: cottages in Balinese style set out in a garden compound, with swimming pools, restaurants and so forth, such as La Taverna in Sanur, Poppies Cottages in Kuta, or the PanSea Puri Bali in Jimbaran—delightful, though lacking just that special touch of pampered exclusivity of the next grade up.

After these come the mass of middle-ranking hotels which cost from $25 to $40 US per night for a double room. These again will usually offer cottages in a garden compound, swimming pool and restaurant; most will have air-conditioning, certainly fans. They are good value, and perfectly pleasant, but because they tend to cater for the package-tour operators they lose some of the personal charm which is the essential ingredient of Bali's most lovely hotels.

But personal charm is not short in much of Bali's budget accommodation, which can cost anywhere between 7,000rp ($4 US) per night for a double room and $25 US; 15,000rp ($8 US) is a common price. Accommodation of this kind is usually laid out on the same principle as a Balinese family compound: an enclosed area containing a number of cottages where aunts and uncles, grandparents and cousins live with their own families, dogs and chickens. Indeed, some of these 'hotels', especially the cheaper ones, are still family compounds, very much lived in by the family, where you simply occupy one of the buildings. This is why you will often find that they are called 'homestays'. The other term used to describe cheaper accommodation of any kind is *losmen*, an Indonesian word derived from the French *logement*. Homestays and *losmen*s can be found in the tourist resorts of the south, and they are the most usual form of accommodation elsewhere on the island, in the towns and the tourist havens such as Ubud, Candi Dasa and Lovina.

Homestays and *losmen* tend to provide fairly basic but clean accommodation: a room with a bed or two beds and a table, with bathroom attached. You will invariably have a verandah on which you can sit to have your breakfast (often included in the price), surrounded by a garden. In fact, apart from the lack of facilities such as telephones, room service and air-conditioning (some will have fans), these tiny hotels can offer almost as much as smaller up-market hotels of the resorts, but for as little as one tenth of the price. In the small, family homestays you will be treated with kindness and interest, where you are to some extent guests of the family. You will be kept informed of local events, temple ceremonies, cock fighting, and be encouraged to join the fun. The more expensive ones—increasing numbers of which are now purpose-built, but in traditional Balinese style—will be staffed by people more conscious of running a hotel.

Note that it is now against the law to stay with an ordinary family in their house for any length of time. You must register at the local police station, where you will be given a permit lasting two days only. This can be extended once only, for a further two days.

Prices

Note that Bali's higher-grade hotels always quote prices in US dollars, while the cheaper accommodation is quoted in rupiah. We have followed the same pattern in this book and have not attempted to convert quoted prices, in view of fluctuating exchange rates. Indeed all prices are constantly under review and depend on exchange rates and demand.

Hotel accommodation, of course, forms part of the numerous package deals to Bali. Such deals can be amazingly competitive, and are well worth investigating if you plan to stay in one hotel for most of your stay.

The prices given in this book are those quoted by the hotels themselves and are what these hotels would charge you on a nightly basis if you booked as an independent traveller. They are as accurate as they can be as we go to press, but are intended more to establish a scale of rates. In the past few years they have tended to rise at a rate of about 10–15% per annum.

Different prices for single and double accommodation will be quoted by most hotels, but by and large all rooms are double rooms. Single guests simply have exclusive use of a double room and usually pay less for it, although some hotels will charge a room price, regardless of the number of occupants. Double beds are a rarity in Bali: most hotels provide two single beds in a double room, although often these single beds are quite wide.

The more expensive hotels—any in the bracket of $25 US upwards in fact—will probably be quoting prices exclusive of the standard 15.5% government tax and service charge (5.5% tax and 10% service charge), although some quote inclusive prices. It is well worth checking this, as these charges can make a considerable difference to your bill. The cheaper hotels, homestays and *losmen*s, especially those that quote in rupiah, do not normally charge tax and service.

By and large breakfast is not included in the prices quoted by the larger hotels, but check when making a booking. It is, however, often included in the price of the cheaper homestays and *losmen*s, and the more delightful the *losmen* the more delicious and generous will be their breakfast.

Bathrooms

Indonesia has the perfect answer to bathing in a tropical climate. It is called the *mandi* and consists of a small tank like a kind of very deep basin, usually completely tiled, plus a scoop, usually a plastic object shaped like a saucepan. You fill the *mandi* with water from the tap suspended over it, strip off, and then, standing beside the *mandi*, you dowse yourself in copious scoops of water. Then you rub soap all over your body, before rinsing with more scoops of fresh water.

You only need to do this once at the end of a hot and dusty day to become a devotee. *Mandi*s are not supplied by hot water, but by water from a shaded tank which is deliciously cool. Take a *mandi* at round 5 pm, before the evening chill sets in. This is when the Balinese head down to the rivers and public bathing places for their communal bathing, part of the day's round of pleasures.

Sadly, we have to say that traditional *mandi*s have become a threatened species. The large hotels, and the new ones with pretensions, will proudly show you their 'Western-style' bathrooms, complete with bathtub and high-pressure shower, beloved by many a tourist but disheartening for the *mandi* aficionados.

*Mandi*s were traditionally built in a semi-open space where you could freely slosh around plenty of water with a degree of privacy. Sometimes, therefore, the *mandi* is little more than a shelter with a tiled runaway, overlooking its own little garden, which adds another dimension to its delights. The pleasures of this arrangement have been recognized by hotel builders, and many hotels, from *losmen*s to the more expensive accommodation, have what we call 'garden bathrooms'—half open to the elements, but quite private, and often with all the Western-style fittings.

Booking

The large international hotels, as well as the medium-sized ones, will all take bookings, either made personally in writing or by telex, or indeed by telephone (but get written confirmation), or through travel agents.

Booking in advance for the smaller hotels and *losmen*s, is somewhat more difficult. You can try writing to them using the addresses given in this book (where we do not give an address just write to the name of the hotel, the village, the town, the regency, Bali,

Indonesia), but this does not necessarily elicit a response, or the one you want. The London-based Bali Booking Agency (8 Ferdinand Street, London NW1 8ER, tel 01–267 0296) has been set up to fill this gap, specializing in accommodation in small family hotels and private houses.

You can negotiate to some extent the price you pay for accommodation, although your success will depend on the demand. If the hotel is half empty, bargain hard! The larger hotels will be paying a commission of 10% (or more) to travel agents who arrange accommodation on behalf of their clients. If, therefore, you make a booking personally, your hotel may be willing to give you a 10% reduction, or 25% if the published room rates are inclusive of the 15.5% tax and service.

Noise

The trouble with traditional-style accommodation in Bali is that it is exposed to traditional levels of noise. Most Balinese go to bed early and villages are usually quiet by 8 pm—except for the odd television—unless there is a ceremony afoot, in which case most people will be up all night. Cocks are no respecters of sleep and will crack open the day at around 4 am, just before dawn.

The cocks wake up the little birds, which, unlike our melodious blackbirds and starlings, tend to stick to a single note. The household will now stir, clear the nasal tubes demonstratively, rattle around in the kitchen, feed the impatient pigs, chatter, and prime the motorbike.

Moral: go to bed early and get up early. Dawn is truly a lovely part of the day in Bali, cool and beautiful. But you must be prepared to have it thrust upon you.

Food

There are hundreds of places to eat in Bali, ranging from the itinerant noodle seller ('*Bakso! Bakso!*') to the international hotel cuisine of Sanur and Nusa Dua; but most are at the more modest end of the range.

The fertility of Bali's soil and the range of climates at different altitudes mean that there are plenty of fresh fruits and vegetables throughout the year. Many restaurateurs send someone up to the hill-town markets, such as Bedugul, every day to buy fresh food. Beef, pork, goat and duck are freely available, while Bali's small, free-range chickens (now, unfortunately, becoming rarer), have a flavour which is famous throughout Indonesia. Fish are caught daily by fleets of outriggers all around the coasts.

Most restaurants will serve Indonesian and Chinese food, though in the tourist resorts you can also get European, Mexican and Japanese food. It is, however, quite difficult to find Balinese food.

Apart from some notable exceptions, few restaurants have outstanding cuisine. The large hotels cater for all tastes, but the food tends to be bland, that of the tourist restaurants even blander. In our view the best food is usually to be found in the more modest, family-run restaurants—the *warung* or *rumah makan*—where love has gone into the food and not the decor. A *warung* may be little more than a stall with a few benches, although the larger ones will have tables and chairs and a separate kitchen. A *rumah makan*—literally 'house for eating'—will be slightly larger, and probably more impersonal.

The price of food in Bali varies hugely, but even the most expensive restaurants are comparatively cheap. The weekly Balinese buffet or *rijsttafel* at the Tandjung Sari hotel in Sanur, one of the best meals you can have on the island, costs \$25 US (£15 UK) per head. Dinner in up-market restaurants may cost 20,000rp (\$11 US) per head, while in Ubud it would be difficult to spend more than 12,000rp for an excellent meal in the best restaurants. But in yet more modest places you can eat very good Indonesian food, including soup, fish, prawns, meat dishes and dessert for 5,000rp per head—and a perfectly satisfactory rice-based lunch might cost as little as 1,000rp. All these sums are fairly unbelievable to the average Balinese earning perhaps 3,000rp a day. They do not tend to eat in restaurants at all, but they will happily frequent their favourite night-market stand, or the itinerant noodle man, and be well satisfied with a dish of rice with a spicy sauce and a glass of tea for 200rp.

Traditionally, Indonesians eat with their fingers or with a spoon rather than with knives and forks—and not with chopsticks, by the way.

Indonesian Food

There are many classic Indonesian dishes which, when well prepared, are quite delicious. Rice (*nasi*) is the mainstay, but noodles (*mie* or *bakmi*) are also widely used. Fried rice (*nasi goreng*) is a simple but tasty preparation, flavoured by vegetables and a small amount of meat or fish. *Nasi campur* is boiled rice with vegetables, meat or fish, often accompanied by an egg and *krupuk*, feather-light rice- or cassava-flour crisps flavoured with prawns or fish.

The distinctive spicy qualities of these dishes come from the use of chillies, soy sauce (*kecup*, of the same origin as our word ketchup), ground peanuts, garlic, ginger and *laos* or galingale (a ginger-like root), coconut (milk, flesh and oil), tamarind, cloves, nutmeg and cinnamon, turmeric, lemon grass, and dried fish or prawns. A chilli-based sauce called *sambal* is a typical accompaniment, for those who want something even hotter.

Apart from the rice and noodle dishes, Indonesia is famous for its *gado gado* and *sate*, both of which depend upon a spicy peanut sauce. *Gado gado* consists simply of steamed, or raw, vegetables coated with this sauce. *Sate* is a kind of small kebab cooked over a charcoal fire and served on its bamboo stick—mostly beef, pork, chicken and fish, though the Balinese are more likely to go for goat or even turtle *sate*.

Other dishes worth looking for include fried chicken (*ayam goreng*), fish wrapped in a banana leaf and steamed (*ikan pepes*), Chinese-style stir-fried vegetables (*capcai*), fried bananas (*pisang goreng*). There are also excellent chilli-hot dishes from the Minangkabau region of Sumatra, around Padang; *makan Padang* ('Padang food') has spread throughout Indonesia and is on the menus of many restaurants serving good Indonesian food, as well as in the specialist Rumah Makan Padang. *Rendang*, dry-cooked spicy beef with coconut, is a particularly mouth-watering speciality.

Another feature of Indonesian eating is the Chinese restaurant. In most of these the food is little different to that offered by Indonesian restaurants, and only a pale shadow of what is available in Hong Kong, although often equally heavy-handed with the monosodium-glutamate.

Local fish is excellent. Tuna is always good. The local *kakap* (sea perch or barramundi) comes in several qualities: *warung*s tend to serve very small *kakap*, tasty but very

18

bony. Crab, lobster, prawns and shellfish are worth looking out for in the coastal resorts. Be careful with shellfish, since this a notorious source of food poisoning, although Balinese shellfish is probably no more dangerous than, say, French or Italian.

Indonesian soups (*soto*) are also good. However, the Balinese cannot get used to the pattern of presenting three-course meals to Westerners, and if you order soup, or any other kind of starter, it is liable to come with your *ayam goreng*. If you want a hot dessert, order it after you have finished your main course and put up with the wait, unless you like cold banana pancake.

The king of Indonesian feasts is the *rijsttafel*, invented by the Dutch: literally 'rice table', it consists of a huge variety of delicious specialities, usually served as a buffet. You take a spoonful from each, and go back as many times as you like. It is a good way of getting to know the full scope of Indonesian cooking. Several hotels offer a weekly *rijsttafel*.

The main difference between Indonesian and Western cooking is the almost complete absence of milk and wheat. Cheese, butter, milk (long-life or tinned) and yoghurt, and flour for baking, are imported specially for Western visitors. The Balinese say that Westerners smell of milk and are faintly derogatory about it; the Balinese smell of coconut oil.

Long-term residents often complain, after their initial enthusiasm, that Indonesian food is limited and monotone. (Thailand still holds the Southeast Asian crown.) But for the short-term visitor to Indonesia, the food is exotic, fresh, nourishing and delicious. *Selamat makan!* (*Bon appétit!*)

For a glossary of Indonesian food and dishes, see pp.358–61.

Balinese Food

There are a few occasions when you can eat excellent Balinese food, and one or two restaurants specialize in local dishes adapted, a little, to accommodate Western tastes and sensibilities. At temple ceremonies you can eat specialities such as the delicious *sate Bali* (ground pork mixed with spices and shredded coconut, massaged on to little skewers and cooked over an open fire). And if you are lucky enough to be invited to a wealthy family's celebration, such as a tooth-filing ceremony, the food you are offered will be excellent and quite authentic.

However, Balinese food is not to everyone's taste, and some of their culinary treats can turn the unadventurous Western stomach. Eyes and claws, fat and gristle, unnamed pieces of animal intestine, even pig's balls, turn up as specialities. Fresh chicken's or pig's blood is mixed with finely chopped chilli and vegetables to produce *lawar*, a favourite Balinese dish with a flavour something like the French blood sausage or *boudin noir*. Nothing is wasted; even the bones are ground up for sauces. Dragonflies are caught by children using a long wand with a gluey tip and are deep fried, as are the tiny fish from the ricefields, lured by the light of paraffin lamps at night. Such things provide valuable protein to a family's diet of rice, vegetables and *sambal*. It may be a healthy diet, but the chilli content alone often makes these dishes unpalatable to the rest of us.

A few Balinese dishes, however, are acceptable and widely available. Smoked duck (*betutu bebek*) is wonderful; it is cooked very slowly in a kind of underground earth oven and it usually has to be ordered a day in advance. *Babi guling*, often wrongly translated as roast suckling pig, is actually young pig coated in spices and roasted whole on a spit over a fire of coconut husks, similar to the Italian *porchetta*. It can be found at specialist *warung*s in most districts. Frogs' legs, too, are good—as in France, they taste rather like a delicate form of chicken.

Desserts are not really a feature of Indonesian eating: pieces of fruit might be offered to round off a meal, but fried bananas can turn up at any time of the day. There is, however, one truly splendid Balinese sweet dish: black rice pudding. Black rice is a strain of rice that, literally, has a black husk. This is boiled and served with a sweet sauce and perhaps some fresh fruit. At its best, this sauce will be made of coconut milk sweetened by palm sugar, and served so that an island of slightly salted black rice will be surrounded by a pool of white—visually spectacular and quite delicious.

Foreign Food

Italian pizzas and pasta, Japanese *sushi*, Mexican chicken with chocolate, toast and marmalade, vegemite sandwiches—it's all here. You can bring whatever tastes you like to Bali, and have a fair chance of being satisfied. However, few of the restaurants offering such fare provide anything better than an adequate imitation of the real thing. After all, if the menu offers 'Chicken Gordon Blue', you cannot really hope to get chicken *cordon bleu*.

One valued heritage of the hippy trail is the way in which it spawned a kind of hybrid cooking with its own distinctive merits. Good salads, banana and carrot cake, yoghurt and other health foods, as well as snacks such as 'jaffles' (a kind of toasted sandwich) and so forth are served by many little bars and restaurants in a relaxed and informal atmosphere. Several small restaurants have taken this one step further and have come up with excellent menus of delicious, fresh, original food which is neither Indonesian, nor Balinese, nor Western, but something of a mix of all of them.

One problem is getting the Balinese to appreciate the expectations of a foreign clientele. One restaurant owner in Ubud described the long and difficult process of training his staff to meet and maintain the required standards. His perseverance paid off; his restaurant is now always busy, even in the quiet season, and has expanded rapidly without losing its quality of good 'home cooking'—fresh produce, no suspect additives, thrifty prices, prepared with interest and concern. It is the best of this kind of cooking, and can be found in a few restaurants in Kuta and Candi Dasa, as well as Ubud.

Fruit

Cheap, widely available, and with a huge range, fruit is one of the great pleasures of the Balinese table. Most tropical fruits are represented: bananas, mangoes and pineapples of course, but also papayas (or pawpaws), guavas, lychees, avocados. There are also fruit associated with more temperate climates, such as apples, oranges (usually with rather greener skins than we are used to, and of mixed quality), mandarin oranges, lemons, watermelons, an outsized ancestor of the grapefruit called *jeruk Bali* or pomelo, and surprisingly perhaps, grapes, mainly black, which are grown in abundance along the north coast.

All tropical fruit tastes best when picked mature and eaten fresh. This is particularly true of bananas, which are delicious in Bali, fresh or fried. Keep a look out for the small, orange-tinted *pisang mas* (literally, golden banana), which has a particularly delicate flavour.

There are other delights which may be less familiar, such as mangosteens—small, round fruit with a thick, cardboardy skin over segments of white, fragrant flesh clustered around the pips. Beware of the juice in the skin, however, which stains badly. Rambutans are little, red fruit covered in fine spikes (the name derives from *rambut* meaning hair); peel off the skin to reveal firm and delicately scented flesh, with a taste similar to that of a lychee. There is also a form of passion fruit or granadilla called a *markisah* or *anggur Bedugul* (literally, Bedugul grape, after the mountain village of that name). Beneath the khaki-green skin, lies a pool of tiny seeds covered in spawn-like jelly, with quite sharp, almost citrus flavour. The sapodillo or *sawo* (*sabo* in Balinese), much prized in Bali, is a small, round fruit with a smooth, greenish-brown skin; the flesh has the texture of an apple, but a curious flavour reminiscent of caramel. Huge tamarind trees line the main

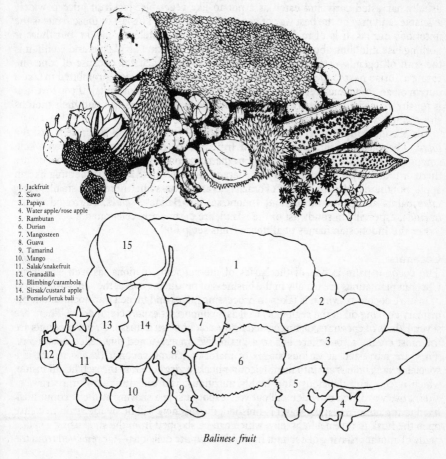

1. Jackfruit
2. Sawo
3. Papaya
4. Water apple/rose apple
5. Rambutan
6. Durian
7. Mangosteen
8. Guava
9. Tamarind
10. Mango
11. Salak/snakefruit
12. Granadilla
13. Blimbing/carambola
14. Sirsak/custard apple
15. Pomelo/jeruk bali

Balinese fruit

21

roads along the coast of northern Bali, producing prodigious quantities of bean-like pods. The black, tarry flesh inside these crisp pods is widely used in cooking, but can also be sucked from the large seeds, more as a kind of tangy sweet than a food. Note, however, that tamarind is a well-known cure for constipation.

A couple of fruits have flavours so delicate that they are prized more for their refreshing, watery qualities than their taste. The starfruit or carambola is one of these. Oblong in shape, it has deep ridges running the length of its yellow, waxy skin; slice it to reveal a perfect five-pointed star. The delicate flavour of the water apple, or rose apple, justifies its common names. This is a small fruit with purplish skin and an exaggerated pear shape, and crisp flesh that is the perfect antidote to too much chilli sauce.

A group of fruits are distinguished by their peculiar, warty appearance. The smallest, and the wartiest, is the custard apple or soursop, which has sweet, milky-white flesh. The jackfruit (*nangka*), by contrast is outlandishly large, a great pillow of a fruit that hangs strangely from the main trunk of the tree. This can be eaten as a fruit when mature, but is usually harvested early and eaten as a potato-like vegetable. Jackfruit juice is widely available, and may be the best way of consuming this fruit. The last of these fruits is the notorious durian. It is of middling size, as large as a canteloupe melon, but there is nothing else middling about it. With a smell something akin to bad eggs and vomit, it is the stuff of legends—stories about office blocks being evacuated because of someone eating a durian next to the air-conditioning intake, and so forth. It is prohibited to take a durian on an aeroplane. Yet many people hold it to be the 'king of fruits'. If you love it, it is for the exquisite complexity of its taste, but many Westerners will find their mouths situated too near their noses to appreciate it.

We put forward another, more modest candidate for the king of Balinese fruits: the *salak*. These curious little pear-shaped fruits are covered with a hard, brown skin composed of prickly scales, giving rise to the common name of snakefruit. Inside are three or four waxy segments harbouring large pips. They have a taste something like an apple, but there is also the flavour of brazil nuts and citrus somewhere. The small, jungly *salak* palms are grown throughout Indonesia, but Balinese *salak*s, cultivated in the uplands, especially in southeast of the island, are particularly celebrated.

For the Indonesian names of all these fruits see p.360.

Coconuts

The coconut palm is one of the basics of the economy, national as well as village. Coconut plantations are usually in the business of producing copra, the semi-dried meat of mature coconuts, which is taken to processing plants and turned into coconut oil, the primary cooking oil of the region, as well as an important export commodity. There are several kinds of coconuts, distinguished by the colour of their husks. Green coconuts are the most common, but there is also a distinctive orange-toned one called *kelapa mas*. They are harvested at various stages of maturity. Young coconut (*kelapa muda*) is a special treat; a hole is cut into the thick outer husk to give access to the rich liquid inside, which is cool and delicious, and highly nutritious; you can drink it with a straw, or alternatively a skilled provider will cut you a spout using a shaving of the coconut husk fixed to the hole. When the water is finished, the machete will be swung again to cleave open the husk to reveal a light jelly, which can be scooped from the shell using a spoon made of another shaving of coconut husk. This is quite delicious—far removed from the woody chunks of coconut that you get at home. It is held to be quite pure, and babies are weaned on it.

In due course, the solids in the water of the young coconut will build up into the familiar layer of hard, white flesh. This is used widely in Balinese cooking, and you will often see women grating slabs of coconut meat on primitive graters made of bamboo or pierced metal sheets. This grated coconut meat is also used to make coconut milk, an important ingredient in cooking (the natural juice inside a coconut is coconut water). This is made by infusing grated coconut in boiling water, then straining and pressing out the moisture until the meat is left as a dry, tasteless powder, fit only for the pigs.

Every part of the coconut palm is valued: trunks will be used as timber, the fronds are used as a roofing material and for basket work, and the fibrous husks are used as fuel.

Drink

Hot Drinks

Balinese coffee (*kopi Bali*) is said by many to be the best in Indonesia. Drunk black, strong and sweet, rather like Turkish coffee but in tall glasses, it has punch as well as fine flavour. *Kopi Java* has a somewhat different flavour along the same lines. *Nescafe* will get you instant coffee of some kind, which you only need to try once.

Tea (*teh*) is brewed everywhere and is always cheap, but of variable quality. It is best drunk weak, without milk (should you be offered any), and is a good alternative to water as an accompaniment to meals. *Teh jahe*, tea with lumps of ginger floating about in the bottom of the glass, is also refreshing, and said to be a good cure for colds and chills. Ask for it with honey and lemon.

Other hot drinks, which are also surprisingly refreshing on a hot day, are made with fresh orange or lemon. *Jeruk* is the generic term for citrus fruit; ask for *jeruk panas* (literally, hot citrus) for hot orange, and *jeruk nipis panas* for hot lemon.

Cold Drinks

Freshly milled fruit juices of pineapple, papaya and banana are available in most places catering for tourists—rich, thick and delicious. You need, however, to consider how these are prepared, and whether or not you want to trust the ice. The thinner home-made lemon or orange cordials are similarly good, as of course is freshly-pressed orange juice.

Bottled drinks are available everywhere: Sprite, Coca-cola, Fanta are all bottled locally and are quite safe. In smaller *warung*s and food stalls they may, however, not be cold; ask if they are *dingin* if this is important to you.

For a change, you might look out for Balinese bottled drinks: *salak* juice is bottled in Denpasar under the brand name of 'Indah'; and there is also a spicy fizzy-drink called 'Temulawak'.

Alcoholic Beverages

You can buy any sort of alcohol you like in the bars of the tourist havens, and in the large supermarkets down south. All foreign bottled alcohol is comparatively expensive. Equivalent Indonesian spirits are much cheaper, but watered down versions of the real thing.

Beer costs about 1,500rp for a large bottle, more in some places, and the cost of a couple of beers with a meal can easily equal what you spend on the food. Nonetheless, for foreigners this is very much the standard accompaniment to spicy Indonesian food; it is widely available and good. There are Indonesian brews such as Anker and Bintang, and others such as Beck and Carlsberg which are brewed in Indonesia under licence but which are usually more expensive.

The Balinese generally do not drink much alcohol, although sometimes some will drink a great deal and become the object of hilarity. There are two principal Balinese drinks: *brem*, a rice wine which is usually rather sweet and liquorous; and *tuak*, which is newly fermented palm wine or toddy made from juice that pours forth from tapped palm flowers. *Brem* is available in bottle form—try the white version in Ubud, sweet and delicious. *Tuak* is less commonly found, although there is a notorious '*tuak* bar' in central Kuta. In north Bali a sweet sherry-like wine is made from the grapes grown in terraces along the coast.

Arak seems to be a traders' generic term for any liquid empowered to send you to oblivion. In Bali this is usually the distillate of *tuak*, and shares nothing with the Middle Eastern *arak*, which is flavoured with aniseed. The quality of *arak* varies considerably and is usually disappointing, although one or two bars have brought it to a wonderful, spicy perfection. It is ferociously strong and takes you unawares: many bars refuse to stock it at all, claiming that it causes too much trouble.

Kretek

Smell a 'Gauloise' cigarette, and you think of Parisian cafés and can almost hear an accordion. In Indonesia you smell *kretek*, a scent even more evocative and compelling.

At least 80% of all Indonesian cigarettes are *kretek* cigarettes, that is, flavoured with crushed cloves. The world *kretek* is said to imitate the crackling noise made by the grains of cloves as they burn. As in virtually all 'third world' countries, cigarettes are very cheap and smoked almost universally by men. It is interesting that although Indonesia is the world's largest producer of cloves, it is also a net importer of cloves simply in order to provide for this industry.

Western smokers are divided: some will smoke *kretek* happily, others cannot abide them. Even non-smokers cannot be indifferent: the scent of *kretek* anywhere in the world will conjure up memories of Indonesia.

Betel Nut

Betel nut, a mild form of stimulant and digestive which comes from a vine of the pepper family, is part of a regular ritual among many of the older generation of Balinese. They will carefully make up a 'betel nut chew', of powdered lime, tobacco and the betel nut itself, wrapped up in a *sirih* (pepper) leaf rather like rolling a cigarette. The chew, known generally as *sirih*, will then be lodged in the mouth for as long as it takes to dissolve, mixing with the saliva to produce a blood-red juice which is ejected from time to time in a well-aimed jet, an effect that is extremely alarming on first encounter.

The practice of chewing *sirih* appears to be dying out, which is good for Balinese teeth. Betel nut stains the teeth black, and the lime wears away the enamel—a broad grin from a confirmed betel chewer, male or female, can haunt you forever.

Getting around in Bali

Road Lore

Bali's compact geography lends itself to a good, efficient road transport system. Denpasar is Bali's heart, the network of main roads its main arteries, and road traffic its life blood. As you would expect, the closer to the heart, the more frantic and congested the traffic. However, west of Tabanan, north of Ubud, east of Klungkung, and south of Kuta the roads become quiet and pleasant and are a joy to use.

In recent years roads in Bali have been considerably improved by the central Indonesian government; many have been resurfaced and the busier routes are being widened at last. Many people return from Bali with horror stories about the roads and crazy Balinese drivers, but such criticism usually derives from a lack of understanding of the way Asian roads work. Here are a few ground rules:

In the first place, roads are not just for motorized vehicles and pushbikes: they are also the legitimate preserve of pedestrians, mobile food stalls; pony traps, farmers herding their ducks to the ricefields, cattle; school or army jogging outings; religious processions—and of course the dogs, chickens and pigs for which the road is just another place in which to run, fight, play and sleep.

Everything moves at its own pace, so there is a continuous need to overtake. This means swerving out into the oncoming lane to pass the slower mover. As this is constantly happening in both directions, a sort of perpetual weaving pattern emerges, into which a driver must harmonize. Thankfully, traffic in Bali rarely moves at any great pace.

Buses, *bemo*s and other forms of public transport stop wherever and whenever someone wishes to get on or off, and they are forever pulling over to one side of the road or pulling back into the traffic without any thought for what is behind.

What a Westerner would consider a 'near miss' is considered normal passing distance in Asia; as long as you pass with an inch to spare, that is fine. When you realize how often this occurs, you begin to appreciate the fine judgement of the people who use these roads day in, day out, and it is the want of this judgement that scares Westerners.

Of course, in such conditions accidents do happen: people lose concentration or do something silly just as anywhere else in the world, and Bali has its fair share of maniac drivers too. Many of them are Westerners, much to the irritation of the Balinese. But if you abide by the rules, your chances of having an accident are no greater than they are at home. If you can drive in any congested city, you can drive in Bali.

Note that in Indonesia you drive on the *left*—the same as in Britain and Australia; which gives Americans, Canadians and Europeans an added disadvantage.

Hiring a Car or Motorbike

If you still feel capable of tackling Balinese roads you can take advantage of the comparative cheapness of car and motorbike hire.

Having your own transport in Bali gives you freedom to explore, set your own pace, be you own boss, and enjoy Bali to the full. Many of Bali's wonders are difficult to reach by public transport.

It may be stating the obvious, but it is vital to give a motorbike or car a thorough check before hiring it. Check that the horn works (essential, as you are expected to sound the horn when overtaking); check the brakes, lights (particularly the brake lights), mile-ometer/odometer, fuel gauge. If it is a four-wheel drive vehicle, check that it is not in four-wheel drive.

Remember, too, that high speeds are inappropriate. A maximum of 45–50 km per hour for a motorbike, or 60 km per hour for a car is quite sufficient. In the mountains the roads are frequently so tortuous that anything but a crawl would be silly. The only 'big' road is the bypass from Batubulan and Tohpati through Sanur and on to the airport. People usually put their foot down here, but as the signpost puts it, '80 km MAX BUT . . . BETTER LATE THAN END IN THE HOSPITAL'.

Signposting has recently improved in Bali. If you are unsure of the direction ask someone '*Kemana* name-of-the-place?' Take a good map with you (such as the APA map). It is, however, quite hard to navigate by night, when the signposts are not easily visible and there are few people about to ask, quite apart from the additional hazards of unmarked roadworks and stray villagers weaving about on bicycles without lights. Many of the major towns operate one-way systems, but all of these are small enough to zip round in a matter of minutes—all, that is, except Denpasar, where life is altogether more confusing. No Entry signs (the standard international sign) are not always very well sited, so watch out for oncoming traffic in both lanes! Some No Entry signs have another sign below it saying *kecuali* or *kec.*—which means 'except'—followed by the exception permit-ted (*kecuali sepeda*, except bicycles; *kecuali sepeda motor*, except motorbikes). At certain traffic lights, in particular those on the Sanur bypass road, there are signs saying *belok kiri, jalan terus*, which means if you are turning left, ignore the red light (in other words it is a kind of filter). Most signs are easily enough understood.

Just about anywhere that you choose to park, especially near an established tourist venue, a *parkir* will want to give you a parking ticket for 50rp or 100rp. In fact *parkir*s serve a very useful job of keeping parking well organized, as well as offering some security to your vehicle while you are away from it.

Car Hire
First, you will need a valid International Driver's Licence. These are available to anyone in possession of a standard driving licence from 'contracting states', which is to say most countries (ask any major motoring organization; in Britain, for example, the AA will issue them for a fee of £2.50).

There are numerous car-hire agencies in Kuta and Denpasar, some in Sanur and Ubud, and many of the hotels have their own arrangements. To a certain degree you will pay for what you get, anything from a wreck to the newest jeep. The large hotels and more reputable agencies will supply reliable cars, and will provide you with as genuine insurance as you can hope to find in Bali (see 'Insurance' below). They can also be relied upon to get you out of trouble—and it is worth paying for these advantages.

Car hire in Bali really means jeep hire: the remoter roads demand a high wheelbase. At the top of the range are the small Suzuki jeeps with air-conditioning, cassette recorder, and good road handling. Hire will be about 30–35,000rp per day; 160–180,000rp per week. Older models without air-conditioning will be slightly cheaper.

Next are the Toyota jeeps, which usually cost upwards of 25,000rp per day, or

130–150,000 per week. The old Volkswagen jalopies occupy the the low end of the range and cost 20,000rp per day, or 100,000rp per week.

Minibuses are available for groups travelling together, at 35–45,000rp per day. They can take up to eight people comfortably.

Note that you should always travel with your driving licence and the vehicle registration documents. It is a legal requirement. Police road-blocks are common, especially on the approaches to Denpasar.

Motorbike Hire

As with hire cars, the quality of motorbikes for hire varies considerably. It is this, and the rental period, that will dictate the price. All the models are 90, 100 or 125cc and range from trial bikes to automatic Honda Astreas. A good bike will cost about 7,000rp per day, 40,000rp per week and 140,000rp per month in the low season. An 'old clunker' will cost 4,000rp per day, 25,000rp per week and 90,000rp per month. In the high season, add a further 10% to all these prices. Petrol consumption may play a part in your costings. An old, beaten-up Binter might do 20 km per litre, whereas a Honda Astrea should do well over twice this.

Come to Bali armed with an International Driving Licence if you intend to hire a bike here; if you do not have one, you will have to pass a test in Bali (see below).

Additional points to note:

On a motorbike you will be exposed to the sun, and bare arms, legs and faces burn quickly and without you noticing. Lobster-red thighs are a traditional hazard. Use a good sun-cream—or cover up.

Many trucks, buses and *bemo*s emit the foulest fumes, covering your skin with a layer of black grime. You are advised to wear a scarf over your nose and mouth, particularly when driving in Denpasar. Sunglasses are a must.

You will collide with insects, some of which are large enough to be quite painful. At dusk and just after nightfall insects abound, but you can't wear your sunglasses then, a good reason for not driving fast or doing any long journeys after dark.

The rainy season can be particularly hazardous. If it rains, find shelter in a *warung* and sit it out.

Punctures are a natural occurrence, but fortunately you will rarely be far from someone who can fix them (look for signs saying 'Presban', or 'Servis' or 'Bengkel'). The normal cost will be somewhere between 600–1,000rp.

Helmets are compulsory. In small villages, even around Ubud, you see locals without helmets, but they probably have good friends in the constabulary.

ACQUIRING A BALINESE MOTORBIKE LICENCE

If you fail to bring an International Driving Licence, you can acquire a temporary licence for 11,000rp, valid for one month in Bali only, as follows:

Stage 1. Once you have negotiated the hire of your bike, the bike owner will take you to the Denpasar Police Office, which opens at 8 am (closed Thur and Sun); arrive as early as possible! On the way into Denpasar you stop off and have your photograph taken (the licence requires four photographs). Once at the Police Office you are required to take a 20-question multiple choice examination. Your bike owner will give you a piece of paper with all the answers on (the official in attendance pays little attention).

27

Stage 2. Wait. Wait some more. The bikes of all the prospective candidates are lined up in front of the test circuit, but the tests do not begin until everyone has completed Stage 1. There may be from 30 to 80 tourists taking tests on any one day, so a wait of an hour and a half for Stage 2 is not unusual.

Stage 3. The practical test requires you to zigzag around four cones and do a figure of eight twice. That's it. Do not hit any of the cones; do not put your feet down; stay inside the outer line of the figure of eight—and you are through!

Stage 4. Wait another hour while you are fingerprinted, your passport details are taken, and while you fill in several forms. You then receive a licence.

If you fail, you can come back the next day.

Insurance

Insurance is the grey area of car and motorbike hire. Many owners will simply tell you not to worry, and offer the hope that they will sort things out if you have an accident. You can do better than this, but not much. Some rental agencies, and indeed all of the better ones, offer insurance which will cover you against accidental damage. For cars, this is usually included in the hire price; for motorbikes, expect to pay 12–14,000rp per week; 30–35,000rp per month. You should watch out for the 'excess' (the first, however-many dollars of the costs of repair for which you are responsible). Some agencies will stipulate $500 excess, which is too much; ask for this to be reduced to $200 US and alter the documents accordingly.

This insurance may include third party cover, but its real value is in covering you against returning to your hire agency with a damaged vehicle. The problem of third party cover is that it depends upon a system of establishing liability, which simply does not exist in Indonesia. If you damage someone else's vehicle you must hope that they are similarly insured (unusual), or negotiate your way out of it. If possible, call in the help of your hire agency; you may be able to reclaim any compensation you have to pay from the insurance cover (unlikely). Try to establish whether you are covered against such an eventuality when you hire the vehicle (it is not easy to get a straight answer to this kind of hypothetical question).

If you injure a Balinese in an accident, you may be expected to pay compensation, regardless of whose fault the accident is. An accident involving injury is really the worst thing that can happen to you if you are driving in Bali: friends or relatives of the injured could exploit you for as much as they possibly can to cover medical costs, distress, loss of income and so on. They have, after all, no other system of insurance or compensation to cover such mishaps. You are likely to find little of the Balinese grace and charm in such incidents; instead, resentfulness and anguish. Try to stay calm; get the police, who should be able to find someone who speaks English. If necessary, get in touch with your consulate. Your travel insurance should cover you for personal liability, but the kind of informal settlement that is often required in these circumstances will not provide you with the necessary paperwork.

Fuel

Indonesia is a major oil-producing country, one of the benefits of which is comparatively cheap petrol (*bensin*), about 450rp per litre, which is around 2,000rp per Imperial gallon, 1,700rp per US gallon. Proper petrol stations, run by the government-owned petrol company Pertamina, are few and far between outside the south of the island. Bear this in mind as you set out for a long journey. Fill up when you can—on account of their rarity, the forecourts are often packed with a line of waiting buses and *bemo*s.

However, most villages have ramshackle shops (look for the signs saying 'Premium' or 'Socar'), where you can buy *bensin* from a drum, at a slightly higher price. This is usually pretty low-grade but will keep your vehicle running.

Bicycles

Bicycles can be hired for as little as 1,500rp per day in most of the tourist havens and provide an excellent way of seeing the countryside, particularly around Ubud, where the climate is rather cooler than at the coast. Generally the minor roads are calm and peaceful, although you may have to negotiate large potholes and some steep hills. You can take bicycles on some of the public transport, so a good ploy is to motor to an uphill destination, then bicycle down.

The key to happy cycling is a good bike, which is not always so easy to find. Balinese bikes tend to be robust and rudimentary, but are subject to no end of abuse. Check the brakes, both front and back; check that the wheels are not buckled and that the tyres are healthy. The bike is likely to be equipped with dynamo-powered lights; check that these work if you are planning to cycle late in the day. A reflector is also important, especially since with dynamo lighting, the lights go out when you are stationary. A bell is a valuable accessory too, so you can signal your presence to other road users, particularly pedestrians. Check that you are supplied with an effective lock so you can be confident of leaving the bike unattended when you go to visit places of interest. Give the bike a spin before you rent it, and go on a modest trip first time out, before you take on a major excursion.

A number of people do extensive bicycle tours of Bali; you do not really need any special equipment for this, but you must be even more sure of your bike. Hire a bike with a carrier at the back, on to which you can strap a light bag for your (minimal) belongings with elasticated hooks. Do not be tempted to cycle with a backpack: you will very quickly become aware of the disadvantage of this. Remember to cover up well to avoid sunburn, and wear a good pair of shoes, or trainers, for cycling.

Be modest in your goals. Although a bicycle will travel at approximately 20 km (12 miles) per hour, you will find that about 30 km (18 miles) is a lot of cycling in a day, especially in this heat and terrain.

Lastly, a warning to all cyclists: do not carry valuables openly in the front basket. They are liable to be snatched by thieves on passing motorbikes (see 'Theft', pp.13–14).

Public Transport

A trip to Bali without at least a few journeys by public transport would not be complete. Since few people in Bali have their own private vehicles, public transport remains a key factor in the economy. Here you will come face to face with the warmth, humour, colour and easy sociability of daily Balinese life. After an hour of sitting with your knees under your chin next to an old man chain-smoking *kretek* and a car-sick child, with the ancient bus pounding over a switch-back road in the heat of the day, with all windows closed (as the Balinese seem to prefer it), you may find your enthusiasm waning. But it cannot be denied: public transport is cheap, and very much a part of the 'Indonesian experience'.

Buses cover all the main 'inter-town' routes, and Denpasar is the central terminal. All the main routes, as well as all the minor passable ones, are also covered by *bemo*s.

There are several sorts of *bemo*. The older kind are little trucks with covered back, usually without windows but with the rear end open, and with benches lining either side. The minibuses (often called 'Colts' after the Mitsubishi Colt which provided the prototype) are the newer generation, variable in size and generally with more and better seating, but rather less adaptable for carrying chickens, bolts of cloth, sacks of rice, baskets of fruit plus seventeen people to the market.

The route that they cover is displayed on the side of some *bemo*s and across the windscreen of buses—for example: 'Tegal, Kuta, Tuban, P.P.', where P.P. stands for *pulang pergi*, which basically means 'and back again'. Other *bemo*s are not named, so check your destination before you get in.

There are four main bus and *bemo* terminals in Denpasar: Ubung, Kereneng, Tegal and Wangaya. Ubung serves the west and north of Bali, including the route via the Gilimanuk ferry to Java. Kereneng serves the east of Bali. Tegal serves Kuta and Nusa Dua. Wangaya serves a route north via Sangeh. There is another small bus station called Suci, which serves points south, including Benoa Port.

Around Denpasar, and in the other larger towns, you can travel by *tiga roda*, the strange three-wheel hybrid of scooter and *bemo*, notable for its contribution to the greenhouse effect. This, however, is the best way to get from one station to another, usually for 250rp. More ecologically sound, and romantic, is the *dokar*, anachronistic pony traps that dodge awkwardly in and out of the traffic and the fumes in most of the major towns. These are very much a working means of transport, and are not there for the pleasure of tourists. Indeed the contrary: *dokar* drivers will be rather surprised if you patronize them. Prices are negotiable, but should be on a par with the *tiga roda*s. The origin of the term *dokar*, incidentally, is the English 'dogcart', a horse-drawn cart which earnt its name from a compartment used for carrying gun dogs.

Official prices for *bemo*s are published, but are hard to come across, quickly out of date, and considered an affront by any *bemo* driver. Observe how much the Balinese are paying, and try to follow suit. You pay the driver, or the person who acts as conductor, whose skill is to exploit every last square centimetre of space. They are almost bound to ask you to pay at least 50rp to 100rp above the going rate, sometimes considerably more if you look the generous sort. You can always ask the price before you board, which is usually enough to inspire moderation.

Here are a few official fares, believed to be correct at the time of going to press (use for a comparative scale rather than a tool for bargaining, please!). These prices are for *bemo*s unless otherwise stated—buses only operate on the main routes and make slower progress, which is why they are cheaper.

Tegal	to Kuta	250rp
	to Legian	300rp
	to the airport	300rp
	to Nusa Dua	350rp
Kereneng	to Ubud	400rp
	to Gianyar	600rp
	to Klungkung	800rp

	to Bangli	800rp
	to Padangbai	1,125rp
	to Singaraja	2,250rp; bus 1,500rp
	(via Kintamini)	
	to Candi Dasa	1,300rp; bus 800rp
	to Amlapura	1,600rp; bus 1,000rp
Ubung	to Tabanan	450rp
	to Singaraja	1,500rp
	(via Bedugul)	
	to Singaraja	2,100rp
	(via Tabanan)	
	to Negara	1,600rp
	to Gilimanuk	2,400rp; bus 1,700rp
Wangaya	to Sangeh	400rp

Buses and *bemo*s run throughout the network of roads in Bali, for example from Singaraja across the north of the island. In a town you should pick up a bus or *bemo* at a bus station, but elsewhere you can flag one down just about anywhere. Indeed if you are standing at the end of the road, or walking, they will customarily honk at you and slow down to see if you want a ride.

Look after your bags in public transport; on certain routes, particularly Denpasar–Ubud, friendly looking thieves will relieve the unwary of their valuables (see 'Theft', pp.13–14).

Note that public transport does not run all day and night; on most routes it stops in the late afternoon. The last *bemo* from Ubud to Denpasar, for instance, leaves at around 5 pm. On more rural routes the last *bemo* may be as early as 2 pm.

Language

There are at least two different languages spoken in Bali today—Bahasa Indonesia, the official language of the Republic of Indonesia, and Bahasa Bali, the traditional language of the people. The use of the two languages tells you a lot about the dual allegiances of the Balinese. Bahasa Indonesia is the language of formal education, at least above the third grade, of books and commerce, of government and officialdom. Bahasa Bali is the language of Balinese religion and culture, of *adat*, which is the social and traditional law, of local drama and folklore, of the family and the *banjar*. It is the language of gossip and banter, of allusion and intimacy, of the home and the marketplace and the temple. Bahasa Bali is seldom seen written down outside the traditional *lontar* books (texts inscribed on thin strips made from the fronds of *lontar* palms), and because it is composed of several different languages and intricately bound up with local custom, it is extremely difficult to learn with any fluency.

English is the most common foreign language, although the older people often speak Dutch as a memento of their days as a colony. The young people who make a living from tourists are starting to learn Japanese too, reflecting the way that the Japanese have now supplanted Americans as the richest tourists and source of the best business opportunities.

31

In Kuta you will invariably be addressed in special Kuta–speak: Bahasa Campur (mixed-up language), a kind of hybrid Indo-Aussie with optional additions from any language you choose thrown in.

Bahasa Indonesia

The Indonesian language comes from the ancient *Melayu*, first widely used in Sumatra in the 12th century. From Melayu the Malay language was derived, which became the lingua franca among sailors and traders of Southeast Asia for several centuries. It was used by the Dutch for purposes of government and adopted by a generation of nationalist-conscious young poets in the 1920s, such as Effendi, Yane and Pane. In 1928 the All Indonesia Youth Congress urged the development and adoption of a single national language as a political tool. It was a proposal of immense importance in the bid to unite the far-flung islands of the archipelago into a single nation. It is estimated that there are more than 250 ethnic groups and 300 languages and dialects within Indonesia: as a shared language of Asian origin, Bahasa Indonesia was an essential instrument in the struggle for independence. In the 1950s, as the Republic established itself throughout the islands, the language was extended and adapted for all the modern needs of a newly emergent nation.

The basics of Bahasa Indonesia are surprisingly easy to learn. In this way it suits the needs of the myriad different cultures for whose people it is a second language. It is written in the Latin script but there are no tenses or genders, and no definite articles. Spelling is phonetic and the basic sounds are easy to master. It has been built into a modern international language by adding prefixes and suffixes to the root words, and so there is a vast difference between basic *bahasa pasar* (market language) and the sophisticated language of news reportage and literature. But that need not trouble the traveller: you will be able to get by quite well enough with English and a smattering of Indonesian words and phrases.

Bahasa Indonesia has taken words from numerous sources besides Melayu: from Sanskrit and Tamil, Arabic, Chinese, Portuguese, Dutch and English. From Portuguese traders came *mentega* (butter), *keju* (cheese), *sepatu* (shoe), *pesta* (festival or feast) and *gereja* (church). If you become close with a family the children often call you *om* or *tante* , which are Dutch for uncle and aunt. Many Dutch words have been dropped as being too redolent of the colonial past; *babu* (maid) is an obvious example, but words like *asback* (ashtray) have also gone out of fashion, to be replaced by the Indonesian *tempat abu*. Technical language and the language of industry borrow heavily from English/American, e.g. *ekonomi, rekomendasi* and *adaptasi*. The Indonesian/Malay language has also donated some words to international usage: orang-utan is from *orang* meaning man, and *hutan*, forest—so literally, 'man of the forest'.

Bahasa Indonesia can be wonderfully onomatopoeic, musical and picturesque. *Layang-layang* means kite, and *cemplung* means to drop into the water (note that 'c' is pronounced 'ch'). From *mata* meaning eye, and *air* meaning water comes *mata air*, a spring; *air mata*, tears; *matahari* (literally, 'eye of the day') is the sun; *mata sapi* (literally, 'eye of the cow') is a fried egg; *main* means play, which gives *main mata*, a flirt; while *mata-mata* is a spy. *Bunga uang* (literally, 'flower of money') means bank interest. Perhaps because of its basic simplicity and poetry, direct translations of everyday statements can be oddly moving.

In Bali you need seldom be shy about making mistakes in Indonesian; people are more concerned to understand you than to note grammatical niceties, and anyhow local people themselves use the language with more gusto and dramatic licence than precision. They appreciate and applaud your beginner's efforts with the cry *'Pintar sekali!'*('Very clever!') and fall about laughing in the most gratifying way at your feeble attempts at a joke in their language.

Pronunciation

Pronunciation is not difficult because of the phonetic spelling—except for the hard 'c', pronounced 'ch'. People often compare the vowel sounds with Italian, which may help you.

VOWEL SOUNDS

a as in the 'a' of father but shorter. Examples: *apa* (what), *daftar* (list), *tanda* (sign).

 e 1. as in the 'a' of sofa. Examples: *ke* (to), *empat* (four), *emas* (gold).

  2. as in the 'e' of pet. Examples: *enak* (delicious), *ember* (bucket), *heran* (surprise).

  3. as in the 'a' of make. Example: *sen* (signal).

 i as in the 'ee' of feet, but shorter, almost to the 'i' in pit. Examples: *itu* (that), *minum* (drink), *pagi* (morning).

 o 1. as in the 'oa' of coat, but shorter. Example: *kopi* (copy).

  2. as in the 'o' of soft. Examples: *kopi* (coffee), *toko* (shop), *kotor* (dirty).

 u as in the 'u' of put. Replaces the old Dutch *oe* spelling as in *boekoe*, now *buku* (book). Other examples: *susu* (milk), *guru* (teacher), *tuan* (sir).

DIPHTHONGS

These occur only in an open syllable.

 ai something between the 'ie' of pie and the 'ay' of pay. Examples: *pantai* (beach), *sampai* (until).

 au as in the 'ow' of how. Examples: *saudara* (brother), *kalau* (if), *hijau* (green).

Note that vowel sounds invariably receive equal stress, unlike in English. Words of three or more syllables have a slightly stronger stress on the penultimate syllable, e.g. *kecelākaan* (accident), *pengucāpan* (pronunciation), Denpāsar.

Double vowel sounds are common in Indonesian. Some are separated by a glottal stop; for example *keadaan* (situation) is pronounced *ke-a-da-an*, *keenam* (sixth) is pronounced *ke-e-nam*, and *daerah* (area) is pronounced *da-e-rah*.

Other double vowels have a glide between them, e.g. *lain* (another), *haus* (thirsty), *siap* (ready), *bioskop* (cinema), *uang* (money) and *kueh* (cake).

CONSONANTS

Most of these are as in English, except the following:

 c, as noted above, is always pronounced like the 'ch' of cheese. It replaces the old Dutch-Indonesian 'tj' which is still sometimes seen, for example in Hotel Tjampuhan in Ubud. Examples: *kaca* (glass), *mencuci* (to wash).

kh is an unvoiced 'k' sound, as if clearing the throat. Example: *akhir* (end).

g is always hard, as in girl, never soft as in gem.

j replaces the old Indonesian 'dj' and is pronounced as in jump. Examples: *jalan* (road), *meja* (table).

h should always be sounded, especially at the end of words, where its presence gives a totally different meaning. Examples: *mudah* (cheap)/*muda* (young); *bawah* (under)/*bawa* (bring); *guruh* (thunder)/*guru* (teacher).

ng as is pronounced as the 'ng' of singer, not as in finger (which is reproduced as *ngg*). Examples: *dengan* (with), *uang* (money).

ny replaces the Dutch-Indonesian 'nj', pronounced as in canyon. Examples: *tanya* (to ask), *nyonya* (Miss), *nyoman* (third-born child).

w is pronounced somewhere between 'v' as in vane and 'w' as in wane (hence sometimes Java is spelled Jawa). Examples: *lawar* (Balinese vegetable dish), *sawah* (ricefield).

The final *k* or *t* is sometimes cut very short indeed, so as to be almost unvoiced. Examples: *bapak* (father), *anak* (child); *ketut* (fourth-born son), *barat* (west).

Lastly, you might note that the Indonesians are, it seems, quite incapable of producing an 'f' sound, which barely exists in their alphabet. Hence French comes out as *Perancis*; and Felicity comes out as Golicity, or even Electricity.

Grammar

1. There are no definite articles, so that *buku* means 'a book' or 'the book', but *ini* (this), *itu* (that), and *satu* (one) are commonly used to identify. Thus: *buku ini* = this book (here); *buku itu* = that book (over there); *satu buku* (abbreviated to *sebuku*) = one book. *Satu ratus* is similarly abbreviated to *seratus* = one hundred.

Plurals are often indicated by repeating the noun if it is not clear from the context: *buku-buku* = books. (Note that this makes transliterating plurals of Indonesian words in an English text somewhat problematic. We refer to *losmen*s, *warung*s and *bemo*s in this book—a compromise to avoid confusion.)

2. In the absence of verb tenses, time is indicated by some key adverbs, of which the most commonly used in Bali are:

sudah = already (finished); e.g. *saya sudah makan* = I have already eaten.

belum = not yet; e.g. *saya belum makan* = I haven't eaten yet.

akan = will; e.g. *saya akan makan* = I will eat. This is often replaced by the idiomatic *mau*; e.g. *saya mau makan* = (literally, I want to eat) I am going to eat.

sedang = in the process of; e.g. *saya sedang makan* = I am eating (now at this minute).

masih = still; e.g. *saya masih makan* = I am still eating.

3. Pronouns can be very confusing in Bali. The traditional Balinese way of putting things always avoids a direct 'I' or 'you', so that Wayan will tell John, '*Wayan mau bertemu teman John*' = (literally, 'Wayan wants to meet John's friend') 'I'd like to meet your friend'. The word *saya* for 'I' is perfectly acceptable now, but 'you' still requires some careful handling. When addressing a man older than yourself, it is polite to use *bapak* (father), usually shortened to *pak*; and for an older woman, *ibu* (mother), usually shortened to *bu*. For example, 'I want to come with you (male/female) to the temple' =

34

'Saya mau ikut bapak/ibu ke pura.' For an equal, *abang* (older brother) and *kakak* (older sister) are fine; for someone younger *adik* (younger brother or sister) is useful. If you are close friends, use *kamu*, which is like our old English thou, or the French 'tu'. *Saudara-saudara* (literally, 'brothers and sisters') is a formal option for the plural 'you'. As a foreigner you may find *tuan* (sir or Mr), *nyonya* (Miss) and *nona* (Madam or Mrs) being used for a respectful *you*, e.g. *'Apakah tuan mau makan sekarang?* = 'Do you want to eat now?'

If you get totally confused just resort to *anda* on all occasions where 'you' is required. This is a modern Indonesian attempt to avoid all the difficulties of the traditional language. It is very bland, mostly used for advertising and government announcements and not at all respectful, but everyone will know what you mean at least.

Other pronouns (used also as possessive adjectives) are as follows:

saya = I, my and mine

dia = he, she, his, hers, its. This is often abbreviated to the suffix *nya*, e.g. *namanya* = his, her or its name.

kami = we (excluding the person you are speaking to)

kita = we (including the person you are speaking to)

mereka = they

4. The basic word order follows the subject–verb–object pattern. For example: *saya makan pisang* = I eat a banana. Adjectives generally follow the noun, as *saya makan pisang goreng* = I eat fried banana. Exceptions to this rule are the adjectives *semua* (all), e.g. *semua orang* (everyone); *banyak* (much/many), e.g. *banyak sepeda* (lots of bicycles) or *banyak hujan* (much rain); and *sedikit* (a little or few), e.g. *sedikit rumah* (a few houses) or *sedikit haus* (a little bit thirsty).

For a traveller's vocabulary of Bahasa Indonesia, see pp.350–63.

Bahasa Bali

Bahasa Bali is the real native language of the island, spoken in homes, temples and markets. Indonesians from other islands often express surprise at the extent to which Bahasa Bali dominates communication. Outside the towns people over 45 have only limited Indonesian; few have had much formal schooling. There is no doubt that the strength of Bahasa Bali contributes to the survival of the culture, the sense of identity as well as the Balinese way of seeing things. It is used as a sort of private language within which all matters Balinese can safely be discussed, criticized, exclaimed upon and, frequently, joked about. It is as fundamental to the survival of the self-respect of the Balinese and their unique culture as Bahasa Indonesia is to the success of the government of the Republic of Indonesia.

Bahasa Bali is not one language but four, each using a different set of vocabulary; one even has a different structure. The origin of this phenomenon is caste, the rigid Hindu social structure based on inherited class which still persists (see pp.103–4). Which language is used will depend on the social situation of speaker and audience, caste as well as social relationships. Traditionally one language is used to address those of lower caste than yourself (Basa Rendah), one to address people of the same level (and usually age)

(Basa Lumrah, or Biasa); one is used more formally amongst people of higher caste or better education (Basa Alus); there is also a separate language (Basa Singgih) which is used exclusively to address people of high caste and social standing, for religious occasions and for certain dramas.

This 'highest' language is closely related to Kawi, the written Sanskrit-based language of Bali's most ancient and holy texts. You hear it in the chant of the temple priests of Brahmana caste and in the shadow puppet performances, used by the noblest characters. It is often mixed with Basa Alus, either in directly addressing someone of high standing, or in talking about them. When speaking of yourself respectfully you might use Basa Alus, if humbling yourself you might use Basa Rendah.

All categories survive and are used, but there is currently a move to a more egalitarian language. 'Basa Mider' is a sort of mixed, intermediate language, borrowing vocabulary from the higher Basa Alus and the baser Basa Biasa. Alternatively Balinese will use a kind of mixed Balinese and Indonesian language, especially with other Balinese they do not know, to avoid the social embarrassment of getting caste distinctions wrong. Fewer and fewer ordinary Balinese speak more than a few words of the 'high' language, so they now tend to address high-caste priests in Bahasa Indonesia.

Vocabulary

Here are a few words of Bahasa Bali which you might encounter when you are with a family, or recognize in place names. Caste levels are only indicated where two words are given for the same meaning, or where caste is a consideration in the meaning. It is fairly rare for words to be quite different in all languages simultaneously; the middle and high languages share much of their vocabulary, and the low language shares much with Bahasa Indonesia: for instance, *ambara*, the word for 'sky' or 'heaven', is common to middle and high languages, whereas the low equivalent, *langit*, is also a Bahasa Indonesia word. The word for a stomach, however, is *perut* in Bahasa Indonesia, *basang* in low Balinese, *wanduk* in the middle language, and *weteng* in the high language.

The *b* in Indonesian is often replaced by *w* in Balinese, so that *batu* (stone) is *watu* in Bahasa Bali. Hence the great raja called Batu Renggong is often spelt Watu Renggong. The *b* sound often persists as a *w* sound, especially among the villagers.

ambara	sky or heaven (middle–high)
alit	small (middle–high)
anom	girl, maiden (middle–high)
ayu	pretty (high)
banten	offering
banteng	cow (the original wild deer-like cows)
becik	good, fine
belog	stupid (as in the comic folklore story of Pan Belog)
biang	mother
bogbog	nonsense
cenik	small (low)
danu	lake
destar	headcloth (middle–high)
dija?/ring dija?	where?
edan	mad, crazy

griya	Brahmana house (high priest's house)
jegeg	pretty (low–middle)
jero	in
jungjung	carry on head (as in village Jungjungan)
kaja	seawards (the opposite to *kelod*)
kangin	to the right of the *kaja–kelod* axis
karya	make, work
kauh	to the left of the *kaja–kelod* axis
kebo	buffalo (as in Pura Kebo Edan, Crazy Buffalo Temple; and Kebo Iwa, the monster of Gunung Kawi fame)
kelod	mountainwards (in the direction of the holy Mt Agung)
kenken kebara?	how (are you)? (this is the most usual greeting in Balinese)
kerta	(Brahmana) judge
kija?/lunga kija?	where to?
labuhan	harbour
lalang	grass (as in Labuhan Lalang)
larapan	token, small gift
lelawah	bat (creature) (as in Goa Lawah)
mapandes	teeth-filing (middle–high)
marga	road (as in the village of Marga)
medal	go out (as in *pemedal*, door, gate)
misan	cousin
naga	serpent, snake
napi?	what?
ngaben	cremation
niki/puniki	this, this way
nika/punika	that, that way
ngomong-ngomong	talk/chatter
nusa	island
padang	grass
paksi	bird
pamit	equivalent to the Indonesian *permisi*, asking permission
pan	father (as in Pan Belog)
puput	ended, finished (middle–high Balinese word, as in *puputan*)
pura	temple
puri	palace
purnama	full moon
puspa	flower (high)
rangda	widow (as in Rangda dramas)
rauh	arrive(d) (as in Dang Hyang Bau Rauh, the name given to Nirartha, a holy priest from Java; it means 'Holy man newly arrived').
ring jero	inside (in the home)
semer	well (water)

simpang	visit (you are sometimes invited to *simpang* in the villages; the Bahasa Indonesia equivalent is *mampir*)
suci	clean (i.e. holy, pure, as in *air suci*, holy water)
surya	sun
sweca	merciful
taru	wood
tasik	salt, sea, seawards (high) (Tasik Madu is the mythological Sea of Honey)
tengan	right (direction) (as in Tenganan)
tilem	new moon
tirta/toya	(holy) water (middle–high) (as in Tirta Empul, Toyahbunkah)
togog	statue
udeng	headcloth (low)
wangsa/bangsa	caste
wau/bau (sometimes *wawu*)	fresh, new (medium–high)
yeh	(holy) water, river (low) (as in Yeh Pulu)

'*Kenken kebara?*' or '*Napi orti?*' means 'How are you?/How are things?', to which the common reply is '*becik*', meaning fine. You also hear '*Lunga kija?*' ('Where are you going?'), or the Bahasa Indonesia equivalent '*Kemana?*' This is a standard greeting or acknowledgement rather than nosiness, and should be answered by the name of the place you are heading for.

SPELLING OF NAMES

The fair number of variant spellings in both Indonesian and Balinese result from efforts to transliterate the spoken word into the Roman script. A number of places have more than one spelling. A common variant is the shortened 'e' in the first syllable; thus the village of Krambitan may also be spelt Kerambitan. The old Dutch spellings sometimes still persist (as in Hotel Tjampuhan in Campuan). Other discrepancies: Samprangan can be spelt Samplangan; Tahingan can also be spelt Tihingan, or even Tiyingan; certain names are sometimes written as two words, sometimes one: Toya Bungkah or Toya-bungkah, for instance. We have attempted to follow the current local usage, and give variants where confusion may arise.

Government

Indonesian Government: 'Unity in Diversity'

Indonesia must be a strong contender for the title of the most scattered and disparate nation on earth. The fact that it is ruled under one flag with a reasonable sense of cohesion is a considerable achievement. It is governed with a strong arm from the capital, Jakarta, and the main instruments of rule are the army and the bureaucracy. The head of government is the President, who has wide-ranging executive power. He presides over a cabinet of ministers of his own appointment and is directly answerable to the large upper house, the Consultative Assembly. This non-elected Assembly meets periodically to consider constitutional affairs and general policy as well as to appoint the President for five-year terms. The main legislative body is a separate parliament of elected representatives.

The electorate of Indonesia does not have a great deal of choice: by far the most important party is the government party, Golkar, which enjoys the full participation and support of the army. The old Communist Party has been outlawed since the traumatic coup of 1965, which saw the demise of Indonesia's first president, Sukarno, and the sudden rise of President Suharto. Since that time political opposition has been skilfully outmanoeuvred by the government party, including various Islamic movements which have long exerted pressure to Islamicize Indonesia's institutions.

To pronounce unfavourably upon Indonesia's system of government by saying that it is not a Western-style democracy would be to apply a model that is simply inappropriate. The foundations of the pyramid of power in Indonesia are still very much the local community, in Bali's case the *banjar*, in which all members will have a say in issues affecting that community's interests and welfare. Decisions are made on the basis of consensus, which involves discussion until the resolution takes account of all the various interests on the basis that a simple majority vote could leave unrepresented the wishes of any large minority. It is, however, a ponderous mechanism and the full deliberations of the community are often bypassed in the interests of getting things done: the weakness of the system is its vulnerability to factionalism and graft. Nonetheless the sense of responsibility to a community provides an ever-present backdrop to Indonesian politics.

On a national level the army plays a key role; both Presidents Sukarno and Suharto had military backgrounds. The army is present throughout the archipelago, but you will not be aware of its significance in Bali—unless there is a crisis or a disaster, when army manpower is called upon as the main agent of the administration.

You are more likely to gain a feel for the political climate through the press and media, both of which come under the direct control of the government. Television, which now reaches almost all parts of the nation, is probably the central government's most powerful tool in promoting a sense of nationhood. The *Jakarta Post* is best of the three English-language papers published in Jakarta. It is well-written and informative, sometimes decidedly quirky, but gives an interesting view of both world and domestic events from an Indonesian stance. It cannot, however, disguise the constraints under which it operates. The censor still has formidable powers, although he now operates with slightly more stealth than in the past when foreign journals and magazines such as *Newsweek* and *Time* would frequently appear on the streets with offending articles carefully rollered out by hand in black ink. In a way, though, that practice shows that the government is willing to admit there are problems and that there is dissent. What certainly is not tolerated, however, is criticism—especially scurrilous criticism or mockery—of its institutions or those in power.

The national philosophy of Indonesia has been summarized in the 'Pancasila': the Five Principles. These are: (1) the belief in one God; (2) a just and civilized humanity; (3) the unity of Indonesia; (4) the belief in democracy through consultation; (5) social justice for all. Note that the first principle specifically does not state which God, an important issue for Bali, as well as other non-Islamic islands. But it has to be one God, which is why the Balinese are at pains to demonstrate that Hinduism is essentially monotheistic.

Beneath Indonesia's coat of arms, which shows the mythological Hindu bird Garuda bearing a shield decorated with the five symbols of Pancasila, are the words *Bhinneka Tunggal Ika*, meaning 'Unity in Diversity'.

Provincial Government

Indonesia is divided into 27 provinces, of which Bali forms one. Each province has its own legislative assembly, which will nominate a governor, who, if approved, will then be formally appointed by the president of the republic.

Bali is divided into eight *kabupaten*. They are: Badung (the main town of which is Denpasar, also capital of Bali, and which contains the main tourist resorts of Kuta, Sanur and Nusa Dua); Gianyar (the main town of which is also called Gianyar); Bangli (main town: Bangli); Klungkung (main town: Klungkung); Karangasem (main town: Amlapura); Buleleng (main town: Singaraja); Jembrana (main town: Negara); and Tabanan (main town: Tabanan). These *kabupaten* more or less follow the same boundaries as the old rajadoms that existed when the Dutch took control of the whole island in 1908. The Dutch ruled Bali through the rajas, assisted by a 'controleur', a high-ranking officer of the Netherlands East Indies civil service. The rajadoms then became known as regencies, and *kabupaten* is still usually translated as regency, a practice that we have followed. At the head of each *kabupaten* is an appointed official called a *bupati*.

Each *kabupaten* is divided into districts called *camat* or *kecamaten*, under a *Pak camat*. They comprise a number of villages centring upon a small town, usually a market town. The villages themselves are called *desa*, or *dusun*, run by a *kepala desa*, the village headman (also called *perbekel* or *lurah*), who has the job of coordinating the interests of the lowest and most important strata of Balinese public life, the *banjar*, of which there are a number in every *desa*, each headed by a *klian*. The workings of the *banjar* are discussed under Balinese Topics (see pp.100–1); it is enough to say here that all affairs that affect the community—road-building, tourist development, the implementation of government health policy, as well as religious affairs—will send ripples of discussion and consultation throughout the different levels of this structure, all of which will be accompanied by a great show of diplomacy, deference and respect. At its best this is archetype for democratic socialism; but it is also an excellent tool for frustrating unwelcome proposals while giving every indication of cooperating.

Public Offices and Business Hours

Basic business hours of public offices in Bali are 8 am–2 pm Monday to Thursday, 8 am–11 am Friday, with sometimes a shortened day (8 am–12.30 pm) on Saturday; closed Sunday. Museums, art centres and libraries tend also to be closed on Mondays, but may be open on Sundays.

Remember that you should dress respectfully (clean long trousers, shirt and proper shoes for men; dress, or blouse and skirt, for women) when visiting any goverment office or police station. The same applies to certain extent to other public offices, such as banks, where if you want respectful and efficient treatment, you should dress for it.

Immigration Office

Most visitors travel on two-month tourist visas, which cannot be extended. Visitors from countries where the tourist visa is not obtainable, holders of business, study or social visas will need to go to the immigration office if they wish to extend their visas. The main one is in the Niti Mandala Complex, Jl. Raya Puputan, Renon, Denpasar, tel (0361) 27828; open Mon–Thur 7 am–1 pm, Fri 7–11 am, Sat 7 am–12 noon. There is also an immigration office at the airport which deals with foreign nationals based in places to the south of Denpasar.

Tourist Information Offices

Bali is not strong on tourist offices; see details under 'Tourist Information' for each major town. The Badung Government Tourist Information Office in Denpasar (see p.141) is really the only government-run office that can provide travellers with tourist information in its true sense. The general opening hours of the government-run tourist information offices are Mon–Thur 8–2 pm, Fri 8–11 am, Sat 8–12.30 pm; closed Sun.

A useful monthly paper, the *Bali Tourist Guide*, published in Denpasar, contains details about what is on and where to go, plus snippets of information—written in its own inimitable English—about Balinese life and culture. It is free, available from the airport, hotels and tourist offices.

Directorate of Nature Conservation and Wildlife Management (PPHA)

This body administers the national parks of Bali. If you want a permit for visiting West Bali National Park (Taman Nasional Bali Barat)—to dive at Menjangan Island, for example, if you are travelling independently—you need to apply here. The office is outside Denpasar, just to the north of the bypass in the direction of Benoa Port. If you are using public transport, take a *bemo* going to Benoa and ask for the Kampong Suwang turn-off, then walk 400 m (400 yards) till you see the office on your left. The address is Jl. Suwung 40, P.O.Box 320, Denpasar.

Post Offices

Post offices are open Mon–Thur 8–2 pm, Fri 8–11 am, Sat 8–12.30 pm; closed Sun. Go to a post office to buy stamps in bulk, and to post awkward letters and packages that need to be weighed, or registered. Stamps in more modest quantities can be bought in the larger hotels and in many of the shops selling postcards and stationery. Hotels and shops advertising 'postal service' will also post letters.

Poste Restante facilities are available in Kuta, Denpasar and Ubud. Remember that post within Indonesia can be slow; allow two weeks for airmail delivery from Europe or the USA. The post from Bali to the West is quicker, usually less than a week.

Telephone Offices

These are run by a government agency called Perumtel, with offices scattered about the island. Most follow normal business hours, although the office in the airport compound is open 24 hours a day. A better alternative is to make calls through the larger international hotels. Few private individuals have their own telephones outside Denpasar and the south.

Telephoning out of Bali other than through the major international hotels has always been a headache. Even in the Denpasar main office you can wait over two hours for a connection, with no guarantee of a clear line at the first try; and if you have to make a special trip to town, telephoning can easily consume your entire day. A modern direct-dialling system is being installed on the island, but so far it is only in use at the airport telephone office. Make your international calls from here. Note that if you want to make a collect call (i.e. reverse the charges), you have to take your turn with the operator. Avoid it. Elsewhere, the inefficiency of the current system is liable to turn any user into an abusive and frantic maniac, but the Perumtel staff are quite immune to abuse.

Banking Hours

Times vary from bank to bank, but are usually open Mon–Fri, 7.30 or 8 am; close at 12.30 pm or 1pm for an hour of *istirahat* (literally, 'relaxation'); then reopen until 2.30 or 4pm. Cash desks may not be open after 2 or 3 pm, and will certainly be closed at least one hour before the bank closes. On Sat: open until 12 noon or 1 pm, cash desks close at 11 am or 12 noon. It is best to go to a bank between 8 and 11 am. Dress respectfully.

For details of the services provided by individual banks, see pp.7–8.

Airline Offices

The main office of Garuda Indonesia is at Jl. Merpati 61, Denpasar, tel (0361) 22028, 27825, but they also have offices at Hotel Bali Beach, Sanur (tel (0361) 88511 and ask for Garuda) and at the Kuta Beach Hotel (tel (0361) 51179 (direct line), or 51361/2 and ask for Garuda). Office hours are 7.30–4.30 Mon–Fri, 1–5 Sat, closed Sun and holidays.

Qantas has an office at Hotel Bali Beach, Sanur, tel (0361) 88331/2/3, open 8.30–4 Mon–Fri, 8.30–12.30 Sat, closed Sun and holidays.

Singapore Airlines also has an office at Hotel Bali Beach, Sanur (tel (0361) 88511, and ask for Singapore Airlines), open 8.30–1 and 2–4.30 Mon–Fri, 8.30–1 Sat, closed Sun and holidays.

KLM similarly has an office at Hotel Bali Beach, Sanur (tel (0361) 87460 (direct), or 88511 and ask for KLM), open 8–12.30 and 1.30–4.30 Mon–Fri, 8–1 Sat, closed Sun and holidays.

Two other airlines maintain offices at Hotel Bali Beach, Sanur: Cathay Pacific, tel (0361) 88576; and Malaysian Airlines System, tel (0361) 88511 and ask for MAS.

Bouraq Indonesia Airlines has offices at Jl. Sudirman 19A, Denpasar, tel (0361) 24656/23564.

Merpati Nusantara Airlines has offices at Jl. Merpati 57, tel (0361) 22864/25841.

Consulates

Consulates provide an invaluable service to tourists in difficulty: if you lose your passport, or all your money; if you have an accident; or if you are involved in any incident that becomes a police matter you should contact your consular representative for advice.

There is no **British** consulate in Bali, but the Australian Consulate handles the affairs of British citizens and refers to the British Embassy in Jakarta, or the British Consulate in Surabaya. Lost passports can only be replaced through the British Embassy in Jakarta, which takes about a week. (British Embassy in Jakarta, tel (21) 330904.)

The **Australian** Consulate is at Jl. Raya Sanur 146, Tanjung Bungkak, Denpasar, tel

(0361) 25997/8; open 8–2 Mon–Fri. At weekends you can leave an answerphone message on the 25997 number. Lost Australian passports can be replaced by a one-month identity card if you are returning direct to Australia; this will take four working days to arrange. (Australian Embassy in Jakarta, tel (21) 323109.)

The Australian Consulate will also handle the consular affairs of citizens of **Canada** and **New Zealand**. (Canadian Embassy in Jakarta, tel (21) 584031; New Zealand Embassy in Jakarta, tel (21) 357924/5.)

The US Consular Agency is at Jl. Segara Ayu 5, Sanur, tel (0361) 88478; open 8–4 Mon–Fri, but a consular representative is available 24 hours a day for emergencies. Lost passports can be replaced through the US Consulate in Surabaya, a process that takes 4–5 working days. (US Embassy in Jakarta, tel (21) 360360.)

OTHER CONSULATES AND HONORARY CONSULS
Japanese Consulate, Jl. Raya Sanur 124, Tanjung Bungkak, Denpasar, tel (0361) 25611.
Italian honorary consul, Jl. Padanggalak, Sanur, tel (0361) 88372/25858.
Swedish and **Danish** honorary consul, Hotel Segara, Sanur, tel (0361) 88408.
Swiss consular representative, Swiss Restaurant, Jl. Legian, Kuta, tel (0361) 51735.
West German honorary consul, Jl. Pantai Karang 17, Sanur, tel (0361) 88535.

What to Do in an Emergency

In the case of serious accident, illness, theft involving the loss of passports or significant amounts of money or valuables, or any other major complications, you will usually find the Balinese extremely helpful. The only exception might be if you cause injury to a Balinese (for motor accidents see p.28).

If you are staying at a major hotel, get the hotel to help. If necessary, contact the consulate, or coopt a reliable fellow traveller to contact your consulate on your behalf. Alternatively go, or send someone, to one of the major hotels to ask for their advice or help; if you have stayed in any of the major hotels go to that one and plead with them to help you as a past client. For ambulance services, see p.13. In cases involving the police, ask for someone who can speak English: the police can usually find someone to act as interpreter.

Sports

The Balinese are not avid sportsmen. Soccer, *sepakbola*, is played on school pitches and is Bali's most popular team sport, although it is not played with the dedication you find in, for example, South America. Badminton, *bulu tangkis*, is probably the national sport, and when Indonesia vies with China for the world title, the nation's wellbeing hangs on every news bulletin. Volleyball, *bola voli*, and basketball, *bola basket*, are also popular, as is table tennis: the community hall (the *bale banjar*) is often the home of a table and focus of youthful gatherings in the late evenings. There is also a form of self-defence, *pencak silat*, unique to Indonesia, around which numerous clubs have been formed, emerging en masse from time to time to pound around the roads in a military sort of way.

Sunday is Indonesia's official day for rest and sport, when families head for the beach to walk, wade and wallow, or join a game of soccer or volleyball. At 9 am on Sunday instructions are given at the start of a nationwide sports broadcast on television and performed with typically Balinese languor.

While watersports attract flocks of tourists, the local population generally hold the sea in awe; the shores are the haunts of evil spirits, and subject to strong taboos, and the sea is the home of the merciless god Baruna, who regularly claims his victims. Comparatively few people make their living from the sea. The taboos do not seem to prevent the Balinese going into the sea, however, sometimes as part of the early morning washing ritual, or flocking to it on Sundays, but you will rarely see a Balinese swimming. In Sanur, for instance, low tide—too shallow for swimming—is the favoured hour, when families can wallow almost fully clothed in the idle pools of water and chat. A small number of Balinese nonetheless have become highly skilled surfers, whilst others practise scuba-diving, snorkelling and windsurfing as a profession.

Kite-flying is a popular Balinese pursuit. Competitions are keenly contested and judged in a typically Balinese way not only on flying skills, but on aesthetic beauty. Similar criteria are the deciding factor in the riotous annual bull-races in Negara and near Singaraja.

But there is one 'sport' that is a truly consuming passion, for Balinese men at least: cockfighting. Hours are spent preening the cocks; family fortunes are consumed at the cockpit. (See under 'Balinese Topics', p.109.)

Surfing

For many, a holiday in Bali means surfing. This is a world of its own, and we are grateful to Chris Hines, an experienced surfer and frequent visitor to Bali, for the following guide to one of the island's greatest attractions.

Ever since the early 1970s Bali has had a reputation for being home to some of the best surfing waves in the world. For the inexperienced surfer, the beachbreaks of Kuta and Legian are ideal, providing a variety of clean, fast waves. For competent surfers who have never experienced reef surfing, Kuta Reef or Canggu will provide a good first taste. If you are an experienced surfer looking to stretch your limits and thrills beyond belief, the tubes of Padang Padang leave nothing lacking.

Equipment
Although there are a growing number of surf shops in Kuta and Legian, the prices tend to be high, so you are best advised to take your own. If you are only taking one board, settle for something around the 6 ft 6 in (2 m) mark. This will handle the beachbreaks and some of the reefs. If you are in Bali to get some big surf and really stretch yourself, take a big wave gun, something over 6 ft 10 in (2.10 m). You will need that extra length to catch the wave and make it down the face. Three-finned thrusters are the go. Take two leashes of good quality (you are quite likely to break one), a pair of bootees for foot protection over the coral, and a singlet or T-top for protection not only against the reef but also the sun. Take plenty of waterproof sun block and zinc—being in the water on the Equator is a pretty hot business—and plenty of tropical blend wax for the board.

If you have not got a board bag with shoulder strap, wrap your board in bubble wrap for the trip there and buy a board bag on arrival. You will need the shoulder strap for getting around to some of the breaks. Although there are places in Kuta and Legian, and even one at Ulu Watu, where you can get dings (holes) repaired, you are well advised to take a small kit anyway. Even if you do not use it, the locals will love you if you leave it with them when you head for home.

Surf

Right, enough of all that. Let's go surfing! Depending on your ability, you have several choices.

For the inexperienced surfer, the beachbreaks of Kuta and Legian are perfect. They produce fast snappy waves with some clean tubes. Basically, the further north you go the larger the waves. So walk the beach until you find something you like the look of and *get in there*. Some of the locals who hang out and surf here have a really high standard of surfing. Treat them with a bit of respect or you will find it hard to get waves.

If you fancy something a bit more testing, or maybe you have never surfed a coral reef break before, at the southern end of Kuta Bay is Kuta Reef. This is a good left-hander breaking over coral. It is surfable at all stages of the tide except dead low. You can get a ride out there on one of the outriggers (*prahus*) for around 1,000rp per surfer. The wave itself is a fast take-off but a fun wave. The close proximity of the coral flashing by under the water can be a bit alarming. Take it easy at first. Observe what the waves are doing, and the surfers. Avoid getting caught to the left of the peak. When you wipe out (fall off), try to fall flat as this will reduce your chances of hitting the reef. After you have wiped out, do not try to stand up. Lie back on the board and paddle out to the right towards the deeper wave.

For the competent surfer, Bali's most famous spot is without a doubt Ulu Watu. Even if you are not a surfer, it is well worth a visit. Situated on the southwest corner of the Bukit Peninsula, it is about a 30-minute ride or drive from Kuta. Then it is a 3 km (1³/₄ mile) walk or ride down a track that winds through fields to the break itself. The set-up at Ulu is stunning. As you approach it you will catch a glimpse of grinding left-handers steaming past the cliffs. On the edge of the cliffs are a row of huts where you can get shade, drinks, food, a massage and even a place to sleep.

The wave itself is a series of left-hand reefs which break depending on swell size. The most frequently surfed are the Peak and Inside Corner. The Peak is a big drop and then a race down a pitching wall. The Inside Corner is a super-fast hollow left that freight-trains away below the cliff. On bigger swells the Outside Corner to the South and even the Bommie, a coral *bombora* behind the Peak, may work. If you arrive and they are working, *it is big!*

As with any unknown surf spot, before going in have a chat with some of the surfers; find out what's what. Assess the situation and then, if you feel up to it, head down to the cave. If you can go out with someone, so much the better. At high tide the waves rush into the cave, so timing is a key. Chances are you are going to get swept down the line to the right before you have made it out beyond the breaking waves. When coming in, head for the cave. If you miss, go back out and around, then try again. As always, give the place, the surf and the surfers some healthy respect. This is not the same as paddling out at your local beach break.

The ultimate challenge for any surfer visiting Indonesia has to be Padang Padang. Just north of Ulu, this wave is another ballgame all together. It is a super-hollow, fast, shallow, left-hand reef break. It is a tube, full on, do or die. If riding left-hand tubes is not your strong point, switch to spectator mode, or the chances are you will get a severe grating on the reef. If you have handled Padang Padang and want to go further in your pursuit of the ultimate thrill, get on a plane to Hawaii.

If you would like something a bit mellower, to the north of Legian is Canggu. The reef here is covered with sand and there is a left and a right. A couple of huts provide refreshments. Best to go by bike, as the track in has some of the wildest axle-eating pot-holes around. Medewi, further north again, is a mellower left-hander consisting of a big drop then a peeling wall.

During the wet season the east side of the island works best; Sanur has a good right-hand reef break with hollow tubes. Out through the up-market hotels of Nusa Dua there is a series of right-hand reefs. Here you can again get a boat to take you out.

If you fancy a bit of an extended jaunt, head for the small island of Nusa Lembongan, where you will find the aptly-named right reef break, Lacerations.

The rest will unfold as you get there. A few words on safety. Take it easy. Know your limits and stretch them cautiously. Too many people end up ruining their holiday by coming off a bike on the way to the surf or getting dragged across a reef. Take plenty of antiseptic and cover any cuts immediately. Try to ensure that there are no small bits of coral stuck in the wound. Having said all that, do not be paranoid. For the vast majority of surfers, visiting Bali is a trip of a lifetime, with hot water and perfect waves.

Snorkelling

Plenty of hotels will provide basic snorkelling equipment so there is really no need to bring your own. The best reefs, mainly accessible by outrigger, are found at Sanur, around Candi Dasa, and at Lovina. You can fix up a trip at any of these places, either with a fisherman or with one of the diving clubs (see below). If you have never been snorkelling, do try it: shallow water receives the most sunlight and therefore you are likely to see as much colourful and fascinating sea-life as a scuba-diver, if not more.

Scuba-diving

This is a remarkably underdeveloped sport in Bali. The diving is not exceptional, but there are some good sites. The best, however, are away from the main tourist resorts and require rather exhausting boat or overland journeys to reach them. When the specialist diving facilities are completed in Labuhan Lalang, in the West Bali National Park, giving direct access to the good diving off Menjangan Island, the status of Balinese diving will begin to reflect its merits.

Only one hotel in Bali provides full diving facilities. This is the Hotel Club Bualu in Nusa Dua, tel (0361) 71310/1, which has instructors affiliated to P.A.D.I. (Professional Association of Diving Instructors). Here you can do a six-day diving course leading to a P.A.D.I. certificate, as well as partake in their numerous excursions, and they have a full selection of well-maintained equipment.

Other diving clubs include the Paris Diving Academy, Jl. Imam Bonjol 234, P.O. Box 1116, Denpasar, tel (0361) 24952; telex 35222 JANTOUR DPR; fax: (0361) 72009; and the Bali Dive Sports Club, Jl. Danu Tamblingan 9, Semawang, Sanur, with a beach-side office next to the Bali Hyatt Hotel on Jl. Duyung, Sanur, tel (0361) 88582. These offer instruction courses to novice divers, but are not qualified to issue certificates of any international value. If you have a certificate, or have dived before and know what you are doing, these clubs are fine.

All the diving clubs offer excursions to the main diving spots in Bali. Prices depend on the number of people in the party and will include transport, a lunch box, equipment plus two tanks of air and the services of a dive guide. Prices quoted below are for one person only, travelling with a diving club on an excursion from the south of the island, and are given to show the scale of fees.

The best diving is around Menjangan Island (Pulau Menjangan) in the northwest ($140 US). This is also furthest from the south, but shore-based diving facilities are being developed at Labuhan Lalang as part of the project to open up the West Bali National Park to visitors. Note that you need a parks permit to dive here, which will be organized by your diving club. If you are travelling independently get a permit from the parks office listed under 'Public Offices' above. Alternatively, you should be able to get one at the office at Teluk Terima or Labuhan Lalang, but it would be a pity to travel this far and be disappointed. There is accommodation at Teluk Terima and Labuhan Lalang. The main dive is a spectacular drop-off, 5–40 m (16–130 ft), accessible from the beach or by boat.

Another famous dive is at Tulamben in the northeast of the island, where you can see the coral-coated wreck of the American merchant ship, the *Liberty*, which sank here during the Second World War ($85 US). This dive is accessible from the beach and ranges from 3–30 m (10–100 ft). There is accommodation at Tulamben.

There is good diving off the island of Nusa Lembongan to the southeast of Bali ($145 US). To get here you need to take a 2-hour boat trip. The coral rises from a sandy floor and has produced some interesting grottos at 3–20 m (10–65 ft).

Other dives include: Gili Toapekong ($85 US), a small island off the coast near Candi Dasa, with a well-furnished drop-off of 13–40 m (40–130 ft); Padangbai ($80 US) for coral and fish at 3–20 m (10–65 ft); Amed ($85 US) in the northeast of the island for coral and sponges at 3–33 m (10–100 ft), accessible from the beach; Singaraja ($85 US) in the north of the island for coral and fish at 3–30 m (10–100 ft). Reefs off Nusa Dua and Sanur ($35 US or less), have some good stands of coral, sponges and a range of fish.

Serious divers will want to bring much of their own equipment, especially wet-suit tops to keep off the chill of long deep dives. Equipment available locally should be thoroughly checked before use.

Waterskiing

You can waterski from Sanur, Kuta, Nusa Dua and Benoa which have all the necessary equipment. The best waterskiing, however, is on Lake Bratan in the middle of the island, where Indonesia's National Waterskiing Championships and certain international championships are held. Lake Bratan has 100 hp boats, jumping ramps, plus all the usual facilities. Expect to pay around $10 US per 15-minute round.

Sailing and Wind-surfing

The local outrigger fishing boat is known as *jukung* or *prahu*. *Jukung*s look about as flimsy as those water-skimming insects called waterboatmen, and they are nearly as agile. The main hull is made of a single hollowed tree-trunk. Small *jukung*s are just wide enough to seat one person; passengers have to sit in a line, one behind the other. The bow of the boat is carved with the happy-looking *gajahmina* figure: this is the mythological elephant fish, one of the deities of the seas. Parallel with the hull are the two floats, one on either side, made from a large piece of bamboo, containing a number of airtight chambers. They are attached to the main hull by two curving pieces of wood. The sail is a single triangle of canvas or nylon, often brightly coloured, stretched between two bamboo poles, the apex pointing downwards.

These boats have virtually no draught, so can skit across the reefs to the open seas, where they will travel extraordinary distances. Despite their lightweight construction, they are extremely stable.

You can take a *jukung* out for a sail with its owner for about 10,000rp an hour or less. *Jukung* owners will also offer fishing trips in these boats, or their motorized equivalents.

More familiar kinds of sailing are available at the beachside watersports clubs at Kuta, Sanur, Nusa Dua and Benoa. Dinghies and lightweight catamarans can be rented out for around $10 US per hour. Wind-surfing (or board-sailing) equipment is also available from these places for as little as $5 US per day. Bali now has its own board-sailing championships held in July (for details apply to The Bali Open Board-sailing Regatta, c/o Hotel Segara Village, Sanur—see listing under Sanur for details). These clubs also have facilities for parasailing (a cross between waterskiing and parachuting—do check the harness properly!) and rent out water bikes (sort of marine scooters).

For those who want to tackle the high seas in style there are also a few large yachts available for charter, or for day-cruises. The *Sri Dewi* does various four-hour trips from its base in Benoa Port, one in the morning leaving at 8 am, another in the afternoon leaving at 1 pm, for $23 US per head. The ketch, *Golden Hawk*, built in New Zealand in 1880 and described as 'the oldest continuously operating vessel in the world', can be rented for around $750 US per day for up to 80 people if you want to throw a party; you can do three- and five-day excursions through the islands for around $300 US or $525 US per head, inclusive of all meals, for groups of 8–12 people. A useful address in this field is the Bali International Yacht Club, Jl. Pantai Karang 5, Sanur (tel (0361) 88391; telex 47319 FINAS; fax: (0361) 7993530) which organizes a variety of trips; it also provides a full set of harbour services at Benoa Port, including documentation, for foreign yachts arriving in Bali.

Golf

There are two proper golf courses in Bali—although both the Bali Hyatt Hotel in Sanur and the Club Méditerranée also have some golfing facilities. There is a modest 9-hole course at the Hotel Bali Beach, Sanur (see Sanur listings for details), which is perfectly good for a joyous hack around a seaside links. But for the committed golfer there is the first-class course in the hills above Lake Bratan at the Bali Handara Country Club (see pp.310–13 for details). This has been beautifully designed in the lush crater of an extinct volcano, and sown with imported grass to provide perfect fairways and greens. It is a lovely setting and is claimed by some to rank among the best 50 golf courses in the world.

Equipment is available for hire at both these courses, but keen golfers will, of course, want to bring their own clubs.

Tennis

A fair number of the larger hotels have tennis courts, most available to residents and non-residents alike. The Hotel Bali Beach, Sanur, for example, has two clay courts for $4.25 US per hour. You can usually hire rackets from the hotels, but tennis balls are often in short supply, so if you plan to play much tennis bring your own.

Running

Since 1987 Bali has held its own annual 10 km (6.25 mile) 'marathon', usually in October, attracting contestants from all over the world, particularly Japan—although it is intended more as a fun-run than as an opportunity for record breaking. The course leads around the Bukit Peninsula in the south of the island. Prizes are modest: woodcarvings for the winners, commemorative T-shirts for those who finish, lunch at the Nusa Dua Beach Hotel, and so forth. (For details, write to the Bali Tourism Promotion Board (Diparda), Jl. Raya Puputan, Renon, Denpasar.)

On an equally light-hearted note (if running in this tropical heat can ever be called that) the Bali Hash House Harriers have weekly fixtures. Participants—foreigners and Balinese, men and women—have to run through a chosen piece of landscape (or even townscape) on a kind of paper chase: the 'hares' lay a trail and the 'hounds' follow. The object of 'hashing' is less to take hard exercise than to have a jovial runabout with various fun-loving characters, and then to consume quantities of liquid refreshment.

The Hash House Harriers have their origin in a group of like-minded expatriates in Kuala Lumpur just before the Second World War who were looking for a way to counteract enormous colonial lunches; there are now around 700 branches throughout the world. The Bali branch was founded in 1977 by Victor Mason, the owner of the Beggar's Bush Pub in Ubud. The motto is 'per ardua ad bintang dua' (to decipher, look under the 'Drink' section on p.24). Announcements of their coming fixtures (normally on Mondays) are posted in most of the larger hotels, but since these are virtually impossible to understand except by the initiated, ask around. Otherwise write to P.O. Box 476, Denpasar. Information about how to get to a meet seems to be part of the hunt.

Climbing Bali's Mountains

Mountain climbing in Bali is more a matter of hiking and needs no special equipment beyond stout shoes, a flashlight with spare bulbs and batteries, a water bottle, and a sweater or warm jacket. None of the hikes need take more than a day.

The most popular climbs are Mt Batur (1,717 m, 5,632 ft)—the easiest, and Mt Agung (3,142 m, 10,306 ft)—the most spectacular and the most difficult. You can also climb Mt Abang (2,152 m, 7,060 ft), Mt Batukau (2,276 m, 7,467 ft), and several lower peaks of the ridge of mountains through the West Bali National Park.

49

Mt Batur

Start your hike inside the old Batur crater. You can stay overnight at Tirta or Toya-bunkah, by the hot springs. There are a number of trails to the foot of the climb. Several of them have signs, and it is not hard to find your way. After walking for about an hour you come to the foot of the steeper part. From here it is a further 1–2 hours, on a cindery slope with no trees to clutch on to, to the edge of the crater.

Mt Agung

You can climb the holy mountain from the villages above Selat or from Besakih. You need a guide for the trip from Besakih; make arrangements in the village (note that you cannot actually reach the crater from this direction). From Sebudi or Sorga, the trail is much more straightforward to follow, and takes less time. It is still a good idea to use a guide though. It is possible to sleep overnight at a small temple called Pura Pasar Agung, to the north of Sebudi, so that you reach the crater in the early morning. The climb takes 4 hours at least from the last houses on the side of the mountain to the crater rim. The view into the smouldering crater is like nothing on earth. Looking back to south Bali, there is a wonderful panoramic view.

Mt Abang

Start the trail at the entrance to the protected forest, just east of Penelokan. You need permission from the PPHA authority at Denpasar to enter (see p.41). The trail is slippery and overgrown right up to the peak but you can see through the trees out over the lake. The climb takes 5–6 hours from the road and back.

Mt Batukau

You start this climb from Pura Batukau. You need a guide, the trail is slippery, and it is overgrown all the way. Not recommended.

West Bali National Park

Get information from the authorities at the PPHA office for the trails to follow, starting out, for example, from the Christian village of Blimbingsari in Jembrana. Walks take you along the paths that lead around these western mountains clad in relatively undisturbed forest.

Horse Riding

It used to be possible to hire horses on Kuta beach, but sadly there were too many occasions when inexperienced riders lost control of their mounts and unsuspecting sunbathers got trampled on. Now the only place still offering horse riding is the Bualu Hotel in Nusa Dua (see pp.179–80), with only two horses available for 13,000rp per hour, plus 3,000rp if you need an instructor. You need to give a day's notice, and rides start at 8.30 am, with the last rides at 4 pm.

Kite-flying

Kite-flying is a true Balinese sport with a long history. As with most things Balinese, it has a religious significance: beautiful, graceful kites are believed to please Rare Angon, the shepherd god, lord of animals, and to enlist his protection against pests. Competitions are fiercely contested by the *banjar* communities, who will work together to produce a kite more graceful, more extravagant than that of their neighbours. Some kites are enormous, complete with papier-mâché figures of the gods, and require a dozen or so men to fly them, accompanied by the strains of a *gamelan* orchestra. Alternatively, kites are provided with their own musical instrument, a kind of aeolian hummer made of rattan and wood called a *guangan*. Smaller, fighting kites provide entertainment for boys in the villages: the lines are armed with a sharp edge to sever the opponent's line.

Kite-flying has now been given a further impetus by the Badung Government Tourist Office with a biennial International Kite-Flying Contest, held in fields between Sanur and Tohpati in July, August or September. Kite enthusiasts come from all over the world. Kites are judged on the basis of design, colour and shape, and their performance in the air. There are two main categories: traditional kites and 'new creations'. For details, apply to the Badung Government Tourist Office (see p.141).

Etiquette and Taboos

The French traveller and writer Jacques Chegaray came to Bali in the early 1950s and stayed for several months in the village of Bentuyung, just to the north of Ubud. His account of this experience was unfortunately translated into English as *Bliss in Bali: The Island of Taboos*. In fact there are very few taboos in his book: it is easy to exaggerate this aspect of Balinese life. There are, however, certain rules of behaviour which the foreign visitor should heed.

The most important of these are to do with temples and temple ceremonies. Whenever you visit a temple you should dress respectfully (not beach shorts and a T-shirt) and, most important, you should wear a temple sash or *selendang*, tied around the waist like a belt. These can be hired at the entrance to most large temples, but it makes more sense to buy one and take it on your travels. They need not cost more than 1,000rp and can be bought in the market or any clothing shop.

For temple ceremonies you should pay rather more attention to how you look. Both men and women should wear sarongs and a temple sash. Men should wear a buttoned shirt, and—if you really want to do things properly—the cloth headdress known as a *destar* or *udeng*. Women should wear a long-sleeved blouse, or, even better, the Balinese long-sleeved jacket called a *kebaya*. Thongs or sandals are acceptable footwear. Anyone in your hotel or *losmen* would be delighted to show you how to put these clothes on properly. Make sure you shower before a ceremony; being inappropriately dressed will cause a certain amount of offence, smelling bad will cause rather more.

If you go to any ceremony attended by a number of tourists, you will be surprised how many people fail to observe this code of practice. Overweight foreigners, getting in the way with their cameras, drop-shouldered, paunches out, decked in lurid T-shirts, Bermuda shorts and trainers provide a sad reflection on the worlds we represent. The Balinese are tolerant and polite, and the rude traveller is probably too thick-skinned to notice. By contrast if you take the trouble to dress properly for a temple ceremony you will be treated with respect and even warmth.

You should not take flash photographs at temple ceremonies. The Balinese will not mind you taking long-exposure shots with a tripod, and even do so themselves, but they will not like flash—even though they do not usually say so. This applies to temple dancing as well, and particularly to trance dancing, for which flash is deemed to be not only distasteful but potentially dangerous to the participants.

Do not walk in front of people praying. Do not sit on parts of the temple architecture, and on no account climb on the walls, for instance to take photographs. By raising yourself above the heads of participants and particularly any priests or shrines you will cause grave offence.

There are taboos which forbid certain people from entering a temple at all. Women during menstruation are considered to be *sebel* or ritually unclean—hence the awkwardly worded signs at temple entrances. Similarly, anyone who has had a recent bereavement is considered *sebel* until three days after the cremation or burial.

Outside the temple there are one or two points of etiquette worth mentioning. As elsewhere in Southeast Asia, a person's head is considered more or less sacred, whereas the feet, by contrast, are considered base. You should not pat a child on the head, or ruffle up someone's hair in jest, or lean over someone's head to reach something in a shop, say. If the only place to sit in someone's room is on the bed, do not sit on the pillow. Similarly, do not use your feet to point, or to draw someone's attention when sitting on the ground. Strictly you should not even show the soles of your feet.

In a restaurant, or when eating with a family, it is considered offensive to blow your nose, or to pick your teeth without covering your mouth with your other hand. The Balinese will not share food from the same plate, or drink from someone else's glass.

On just about any occasion, from the inauguration of a business to a simple family visit, the guests will bring a gift of some kind. You can do the same—bring a gift of fruit or cake, or something for the children. There is very little ostentation in the giving of gifts; but remember that the left hand is considered unclean and gifts—or indeed anything you pass to someone else—should be given or received with the right hand.

Nude and topless bathing and sunbathing is considered offensive, but you would not guess it by looking at the beaches of Kuta and Sanur. The Balinese, of course, are glimpsed naked all over the island as they take their open-air baths in rivers and streams. But this is for the purpose of bathing, where the sexes are clearly segregated. You should never stare at people bathing, and certainly not attempt to photograph them.

Incidentally, you will see older women in the villages going about their daily work with bare breasts. This was common practice for women of all ages until the 1930s. The Dutch began the move towards covering up in the late-19th century, enforcing the use of the *kebaya* in the northern parts of the island where they held sway in order, apparently, to protect the moral wellbeing of their soldiers. This process continued as the Dutch took control of the entire island in 1908, and was reinforced after independence by the mainly Muslim central government in Jakarta.

You can wear just about anything you like in the tourist zones, but should be increasingly conservative as you go into more remote parts. Dress respectfully to visit government offices (see p.40).

As mentioned in the section on 'Language' above, the Balinese are inquisitive and will want to know about your life. There are two questions which require diplomatic, answers whatever you really think. When you are asked 'Are you married?', it is better to answer 'Not yet' (*belum*) than suggest that you may never wish to marry—an idea that is quite alien to the Balinese way of thinking. Better still, of course, to be able to say that you are married—and have at least two children. Also, if you are asked what religion (*agama*), it will not be appreciated if you say you have none; it is better to say Christian (*agama Kristen* or *agama Nasrani*), or Muslim (*agama Islam*) than nothing at all.

Where a Woman can Travel Alone

In a list of the best places in the world for the woman traveller, Bali must come very close to the top.

Relationships between men and women are remarkably harmonious; there is plenty of evidence of gross inequality, but women are certainly not downtrodden. In general you get the feeling in Bali that men do like women and enjoy their company—in private if not in public. There is no sign of overt aggression towards women, nor is there any cultural institution resembling machismo. You can travel to any part of the island as a woman on your own and never be afraid, or feel under pressure from any man.

Balinese think it odd for a woman to be on her own, but they are good humoured and tolerant towards this and other odd aspects of tourist behaviour. People talk to you easily, men and women alike. On other islands it is not unheard of for a single woman traveller to be abused, even stoned, but no such thing was ever reported in Bali. Outside the main tourist resorts, where people want your custom and your money whatever your gender, men may be curious and want to know where they stand with you, but they are not intrusive. They are genuinely friendly for the most part. You can tell anyone, anywhere that you wish to be alone, and so long as you are polite about it—the Balinese cannot stand bad manners of any sort and will not treat you with respect if you are rude—your wishes will be immediately respected. There is no need to feel threatened by the casual physical closeness that is part of Balinese life. Of course here, as anywhere else, it is possible for touching to have sexual overtones, in which case you need to make your feelings known immediately and directly if you do not like it. But it is not usual.

In the tourist resorts there are plenty of lads-about-town, the 'cowboys' as they are derisively called by other Balinese: the Balinese equivalent of a beach-bum, looking for a Western woman with money. With their uncharacteristic swagger and muscle-clad triangular chests, they have a fairly well-established clientele. They can be extremely charming but will almost certainly expect you to pay for them in return for their company. They would not normally go to a tourist bar or restaurant, so if that is where you take them, you pick up the tab. They are following the tradition of guides and drivers that operates throughout the East: personal service is not to be confused with friendship.

Women who are understood to be looking for romance are treated with the usual Balinese good manners and disinclination to disappoint. Remember that, for a Balinese, family obligations far outweigh in importance any transitory pleasures with you. Do not be deceived by a Western style of dress and manners. The pull of the community has survived all sorts of changes, and you can be sure it will survive you. If he loves you and leaves you quickly it is because he is expected back in the village, in the family compound. It does not do a Balinese any good in the community to get a reputation for hanging around with Westerners except for business purposes. Passion has its place in the Balinese order of things, is allowed for and thereby contained within firm boundaries.

The best preparation for a single traveller of either sex is to learn some Indonesian. It transforms the most uneasy of situations into a friendly, relaxed one. A few minutes of polite conversation (What's your name? Where do you come from? Excuse me, I can't speak Indonesian), followed by a moment's brief pause before you excuse yourself (*'Permisi'*) are absolutely essential. Anything more abrupt than this makes people profoundly uneasy, and that is when misunderstandings occur.

Useful phrases for women travellers include: *'Saya senang sendiri'*, 'I like to be alone'; *'Maaf, sekarang saya tidak mau omong-omong'*, 'Excuse me, I don't feel like conversation'; *'Saya mau lihat-lihat seorang saja'*, 'I want to look around by myself'; *'Maaf, saya belum bisa bijara Bahasa Indonesia'*, 'Sorry, I can't speak Indonesian'; *'Saya tidak bisa mengerti'*, 'I don't understand'; and, as a last resort, *'Pergi!'*, 'Go away!'

Travelling with (Young) Children

Bring the children with you! Travelling with children in Bali is sheer delight. The Balinese adore children, and infants and babies are held in something like a state of grace, next to sacred. You will have no problems finding willing babysitters; if you go to the beach, women who should be out earning a crust for the family by selling shirts and offering massages will drop everything to take your child by the hand or in their arms, sit with them, play with them, and then bring them back to you, expecting nothing in return but the pleasure it gives them to be entrusted with their company. It is almost as if you do the Balinese an honour by bringing your children to their island.

In Bali, having children is really the most important part of adult life for men and women. Couples travelling without children will be asked how long they have been married, then how many children they have; if you have been married a number of years and have no children, the inquirer will look concerned. If you say you don't know if you can have children, you will be offered deep sympathy and all kinds of advice, including as to which *dukun*s (native doctors) have a proven record in this field. Not having children is considered tragic, and life for a Balinese couple faced with childlessness must be even more painful here than it is in the West. To compensate, a couple will often informally adopt the child of a sibling.

You can take a baby to Bali as young as you dare. We took a nine-month-old baby who had a whale of a time. The worst of it was the 18-hour flight from Europe, coupled with the disorienting effect of the complete change in hours, from which he needed several days to recover, and as many fairly sleepless nights. All of which suggests that if you are going to take children to Bali and must endure a long flight, you should be planning a reasonably long trip to make it worth while. We met a number of other parents travelling with young children: none expressed any reservations other that those that we have listed here, and all expressed the pleasures of travelling in Bali with children.

The larger hotels all have cots of some kind, but the Balinese do not really go in for cots and the design may well leave something to be desired—for instance the bars may be too far apart. Outside the tourist south, however, cots are hard to come by. You may be able to create something out of bamboo furniture, or you may have to sleep with the baby in your bed. Older children can sleep on mattresses on the floor, but keep a look out for ants, which can deliver a sharp sting.

High chairs are only available in the larger hotels: Balinese infants are fed on their mother's lap.

Most things are available in the supermarkets in the south of the island, including bottled baby food. Disposable nappies/diapers are also available but very expensive (14,000rp for 18), so you would be wise to bring your own supply. The Balinese do not use such things.

Travelling about in Bali can be hard on young children. The roads can be rough, the suspension of the transport rudimentary, and there are no such things as child seats or even rear safety belts. What you achieve will really depend on the hardiness of the children, but of course the further up country you go the more rapturous will be the welcome.

Walking in Bali can be one of the great pleasures, but there are few road surfaces, let alone pavements, that make walking with a pushchair much of a pleasure. If your child is of carryable age, take a carrying frame for walks. Pushchairs, however, do have their uses, if only at the airport. They can also double up as highchairs where there are none.

All the larger hotels will have babysitters (sometimes advertised as 'baby sisters'), costing around 3,000rp per hour. The babysitter will normally be a member of staff, or the wife of a member of staff, keen to increase her income. Babysitters do rather like to see the baby awake, so you may have to depart for the restaurant, leaving the baby in the babysitter's arms. In our experience the babysitters of all ages had unusual natural gifts and were able to put the baby to sleep with a gentle lullaby. In smaller *losmens* there will always be someone in the family, or from a neighbouring family, who will be delighted to watch over your child when you go out to eat in the evening. Tell them where you are going if they need to come and find you: you can have complete trust in them. Away from the tourist south, in Ubud for instance, you should be able to find a *pembantu*—a local person who will act as a nanny and look after the children during the day if you so desire, for around 5,000rp a day.

Be ready to answer questions about your children: how old, boy or girl, how many teeth, and so forth. (See the Indonesian vocabulary at the end of this book.)

Balinese children are remarkably placid. They seldom cry and the Balinese become rather concerned if a Western child starts screaming its head off. This is something we just have to grin and bear: we cannot hope that the effects of Bali rub off that much.

Children's health

The main concern of any parent bringing children to Bali will be health. Ask your doctor what immunization is advisable prior to departure: this will depend on the child's age, but medical wisdom dictates that all children should be protected against polio, tetanus, and tuberculosis, the full course of which can take several weeks, so do this well in advance. To protect children against malaria, you may need chloroquine in a syrup form and a paedriatric formulation of Maloprim, which in Britain at least is not available over the counter.

You must be very wary of diarrhoea: infants and babies can dehydrate and fade fast, so it is essential to recognize the problem swiftly and to provide plenty of fluids. If in any doubt, get hold of a doctor.

Cleanliness is very important. Do make sure that children wash their hands thoroughly before eating. For babies, bring sterilizing tablets so that you can clean bottles and drinking cups regularly. A supply of baby wipes, or similar wet tissues is useful for children of all ages.

Children should be strongly discouraged from touching animals in Bali, and because there may be infected excrement almost anywhere, they should keep their shoes on as much as possible.

Note also quite a few common tropical plants contain poisonous sap—the dieffen-bachia, or 'dumb cane', for instance. Bear this in mind if children start to play amongst foliage, or if infants start to eat it.

Beware of the sun: children are blissfully unaware of it and can suffer frightful burns which will keep them, and you, awake all night. Bring a good sunblocking cream with you, as well as waterproof sun tan lotion, and a cream for soothing sunburn. Try to keep hats on their heads.

Mosquitoes can be a pest; you may feel that knock-down sprays and burning mosquito coils are unsuitable ways of protecting sleeping infants and babies. Citronella-based repellents are kinder, but the best answer is a mosquito net which you can tuck in all around the cot or mattress. They are not easy to find in Bali, so bring one with you. Failing this, get one of the special anti-mosquito plugs which you can now buy in Bali's supermarkets. These are plugged into a light socket, cost around 5,000rp and take small disposable cartridges (10 for about 1,000rp), which respond to heat and give off an imperceptible and non-toxic insect repellent.

Lastly, take out an insurance policy that includes full 'medi-vac' facilities. See also pp.10–13.

Food and Drink for Children

Balinese food is by and large clean and healthy. Obviously the same *do*s and *don't*s apply to children as to adults. Take extra care with water, and it would be as well to bring some water purifying tablets so that you can be sure of a clean supply of water in case of illness.

For babies and infants, ask for *bubur*, which is a tasty and healthy sort of rice porridge, flavoured with a little chicken and vegetables—the standard food for young Balinese children. Fresh fruit is excellent; the jelly-like flesh of young coconut (*kelapa muda*) is particularly recommended for babies.

Flora and Fauna

Bali is distinguished in the world of Natural History for being on the very cusp of the Wallace Line. The deep channel between Bali and Lombok marks the southern extremity of the border separating the animals of Asia and those of Australasia. This at least was the conclusion of the great British naturalist Alfred Russel Wallace (1823–1913), author of *The Malay Archipelago: A Narrative of Travel with Studies of Man and Nature* (1868). 'The great contrast between the two divisions of the Archipelago is nowhere so abruptly exhibited as on passing from the island of Bali to that of Lombock,' he wrote. 'In Bali we have barbets, fruit-thrushes and woodpeckers; on passing over to Lombock these are seen no more, but we have an abundance of cockatoos, honey-suckers, and brush-turkeys, which are equally unknown in Bali, or any island further west.' It would be wrong to conclude that the two islands are like chalk and cheese—the contrasts are more a question of shading—but the Wallace Line played an important role in the development of Wallace's theories of biogeography and evolution which coincided with those of his older contemporary, Charles Darwin (1809–82).

The naturalist's view will be rather different to the tourist's, and to the latter it will be the plant life of Bali that is the most striking. In colder lands we carefully tend our potted houseplants—coleus, poinsettia, monstera, dracaena, bird's nest fern and foliage begonia. In Bali's rich soil and humid climate these plants seed themselves casually at the roadside and have to be pruned back with machetes.

There are plenty of animals, to be sure, from iridescent dragonflies and singing frogs to monkeys and doe-like cows, but you would not come on safari to Bali to see them. The island has only one animal which is unique to it, the rare *Leucospar rothschildi*, known variously as 'Rothschild's quackle' or 'Rothschild's mynah' or 'white starling', and in Bali as *jalak putih*. You can go and search for them in the West Bali National Park, or you may occasionally see one as a caged bird: there are said to be only about 200 left in the wild. There was once a Balinese tiger, but this appears to have been hunted to extinction in the 1930s.

The descriptions, below, have been limited to those plants and animals that you are likely to come across without going out of your way.

Flora

Flowering shrubs and trees play an important role in Balinese life. Not only do the Balinese love to decorate themselves, and statues, with a fresh flower, but flowers are also used in religious rituals and ceremonies. The most treasured are the sweetly smelling flowers of certain trees.

The *cempaka* is a large kind of magnolia which bears a white flower throughout the year, similar in shape and size to the flower of the garden magnolia, but more spindly and ragged. The flower has a deliciously sweet scent and is much prized for temple offerings ceremonies, as a result of which they are constantly harvested and it is quite rare to see *cempaka* trees in bloom.

Not so hard to find is the wonderful frangipani, which is widely used as an ornamental tree in gardens and temple compounds. The Indonesian name is *kamboja*, and the term 'cambodia tree' is frequently found in older texts. The Balinese name is *bungan jepun*. There are two types, both of which have clusters of smallish five-petalled flowers which twist out from the centre to form an open bell. One sort has white flowers with yellow centres, or pink flowers, and leaves with rounded tips; the other sort has smaller, even sweeter smelling flowers, either white with orangey-pink centres, or pink and with a more pronounced screw-like formation, and leaves with pointed tips. The latter will drop its leaves gradually as the dry season progesses, leaving the tree naked except for clusters of flowers at the tips of its branches—a rather peculiar sight. Frangipani has a fragrance that might justifiably be called heavenly. The flowers are used in offerings, in the crowns of the *legong* dancers, and are held in the hand during prayers.

Another notable flowering tree is the flame tree or flamboyant (*flamboyan* in Indonesian), which produces stunning clumps of scarlet flowers towards the end of the dry season and long dangling pods thereafter. A more delicate and less spectacular cousin is the poinciana, called *kempang merak* in Indonesian. This produces little cup-shaped flowers on spindly stems, red, pink or orange with long, whiskery stamens. They are often kept to about head height to line the road in villages.

Hibiscus is now familiar throughout the world, especially since plant breeders succeeded in producing a pot-plant version for temperate climates. Hibiscus can grow into quite big bushes, lavishly dotted with exuberant flowers in red or orange, their long pistils waving the pollen in the wind. In the Caribbean creole, hibiscus is called *choublac* because the buccaneers used the staining flower to blacken their boots; in Indonesian, it is called the 'shoe flower' (*kembang sebatu*)—maybe for the same reason.

Many of Bali's ornamental trees and shrubs have been imported, by Arab and Indian traders, and by Europeans in more recent centuries. The bougainvillea originally came from Brazil but is now widespread throughout the tropical and subtropical world. And justly so: with its massive drifts spreading over walls and balconies, this plant is one of the delights of warmer climes. The vivid clusters of mauve, red, pink, orange or yellow are actually not flowers at all, but coloured bracts around tiny white flowers. Bougainvillea always has a papery freshness—hence its Balinese name, *bunga kertas* or 'paper flower'. Another impressive flowering shrub is the datura or 'handkerchief tree' which has large drooping, trumpet-shaped flowers, usually white or orange-pink.

Take a trip to the lovely flower market in the lakeside hill-village of Candi Kuning to see the large numbers of flowers, familiar and unfamiliar, which are cultivated in Bali. These include canna lilies, gardenias, roses, heliconia and cock's combs, as well as the humble marigold. Orchids are grown commercially and can be seen in the nurseries on the Sanur road out of Denpasar and at Blahbatuh.

A number of trees have religious significance, the foremost being the banyan, called *waringan* in Indonesian, originally imported to the region by Indian traders. This is a member of the fig family, and has many of the features of the *Ficus benjamina* which is widely used as a house-plant: comparatively small, deep-green leaves and a whitish look to the bark. The banyan, however, can be massive. It towers from a tangle of trunks formed by the invasive aerial roots; and from the thicket of branches hangs a huge cloak of foliage. Banyans are often found outside temples, and large banyans are unmistakable landmarks. They will be dressed up in the familiar black-and-white chequered cloth (*kain poleng*), and adorned with decorative parasols. Small shrines are often constructed in their branches, high above the ground. The banyan has been associated with Hinduism since time immemorial: it is said that if you fold a banyan leaf in half across its central axis, it looks like a *candi* or shrine. Another similar member of the fig family is a tree called *pule*, also deemed sacred; its wood is used to make masks for the *rangda* figure, the embodiment of evil. The *kepuh* tree, from the kapok family, is the traditional tree of the cemetery, and said to be a favoured haunt of evil spirits. Another holy tree is the *dadap*, a tall and spindly member of the *Erythrina* family; leafy branches of this tree will be seen at cremations, and are also used to mark the screen in *wayang* puppet plays performed at temple ceremonies for the benefit of the gods.

Fauna

With the high population density of Bali, much of its fauna is domesticated. Lumbering sway-back pigs scratch and honk in their concrete compounds, or you may see them looking mournfully out of rattan baskets on their way to market. The cows (*banteng*) of

Bali are beautiful, gentle creatures, all soft-brown curves and dewy eyes that really belong in the world of Disney. These are said to be indigenous, and there is supposed to be a wild form in the West Bali National Park. Unlike India, Bali has no taboos about eating beef, and these cattle are raised for a flourishing export market. A more robust kind of cattle, the water-buffalo or ox, armed with thick, curving horns, is used to plough the rice terraces, and is also harnessed to little buggies for the bull-races of Negara.

The prettiest birds in Bali come in cages. The bird market in Denpasar will demonstrate the range of birds available, and the enthusiasm of collectors. You will occasionally come across cockatoos, macaws and parrots of various kinds, but smaller, brightly coloured tropical birds are common. Cages are sometimes hoisted up on high bamboo poles, where the birds will spend the day enjoying the kind of views they might have had if they were free. Turtle doves in particular get this treatment, and every now and then are let out with whistles and bells attached and make an eerie kind of music as they wheel about.

A charming sight in Bali is the duck herder, marching his chattering brood down the road to the rice field to spend the day dabbling in the water for food. The herder seldom needs to use his big stick, which he plants at the corner of the rice field and the ducks will never stray far from it.

And then there are the dogs: moth-eaten, scabrous, with short coats and piggy tails, this must be the bottom line of dogdom, the lowest common denominator of mongrelization. They pad around the villages, scavenging, sniffing, procreating and baring their fangs in vicious fights with rivals. Their relationship to people is casual, but in return for the honour for being claimed, a dog will spend the night howling in order to protect the family compound. The greatest compliment a Balinese can accord a dog is to dress it up and take it off to a temple ceremony to be sacrificed. Otherwise dogs are tolerated as any living being, part of the great hierarchy of life and rebirth but definitely somewhere near the bottom. Furthermore, they invite denigration by eating the offerings put out for evil spirits, suggesting that they might be possessed by them.

There is no shortage of insects in Bali, as the dogs well know. There are the mosquitoes, of course, and ants of all sizes that will blaze a trail across your bathroom floor by night. There are fireflies, dragonflies, chirruping crickets and butterflies. There are spiders, some as big as a hand, but none dangerous. Even more alarming, but also harmless, are the large black beetles the Balinese call *beduda*, which occasionally find their way into the *losmen* rooms at night. Once trapped inside the room, they fly blindly around, whining furiously and crashing into the walls. Once the *beduda* lands on its back it is completely helpless and will die. It is not a pleasant creature, but it cannot hurt you—other than by giving you the fright of your life. You may also meet the odd cockroach—harmless—or, very occasionally, a scorpion. Scorpions bite, in case you did not know, and their poison will make you sick for about 24 hours.

Your friends against the smaller intrusive insects are the geckos. There are two main kinds, both with onomatopoeic names. The smaller, daintier kind is the *cikcak*, which darts nervously around the walls and ceilings on its pudgy toes, gesturing with little flicks of its tail, in search of its dinner. *Cikcak* is not really a very good imitation of its call, which is more like the chuckle of a small bird. *Toke* (pronounced 'tokay'), however, is a good description of the noise made by the larger gecko. *Toke*s can be as large as 30 cm (1 ft) long from tip to tail and have deep orange spots. They tend to hide behind mirrors in hotel rooms, from where in the very early morning they will gurgle briefly and then sing out a resonant 'tock-ay, tock-ay, tock-ay . . .' up to a dozen or so times before lapsing back into silence. It is apparently good luck if they give 9 'tock-ays' in a single breath. They also live in the palm-thatch roofs of bungalows, and let you know this by dropping black cigar-shaped pellets on to the bed. We mention all this because they can scare a visitor on first encounter. Do not be alarmed, they are quite harmless.

The only seriously dangerous land animal is the green viper, known locally as *lelipis gedong*, recognizable by the red colouring in its tail. The *ular sawah*—the snake of the ricefield— is brown in colour and completely safe.

You should be wary of the little grey monkeys that inhabit a number of temples and forests around the island. They occupy a semi-sacred position, recalling the monkey army of Hanuman in Hindu mythology. This seems to have gone to their heads: although some troupes are friendly enough, others are positively aggressive. Treat mothers with young with particular caution.

Bali's sealife offers no particular threat, although you should watch out for urchins. Snorkellers and divers will see a wide range of colourful coral fish: damselfish, kingfish, queenfish, parrotfish, butterflyfish, angelfish, trunkfish, pufferfish, sergeant majors, green wrasse, grouper and tangs, moray eels, squid and lobster. There are sharks in these waters, but the Balinese show no concern about them, either because they stay in deep water, or because those that divers do come across are harmless whale sharks—the largest of all fish, but which restrict their diet to plankton.

Arts and Crafts

The creativity of the Balinese people is legendary. Once all their creative energy was devoted to honouring their gods with temple decorations and temple ceremonies, or to pleasing the local rajas. Now tourism and export business have replaced royal patronage, but honouring the gods is still a serious occupation. A major portion of the daily life of Balinese families is devoted to preparation of offerings, decorations and performances for temple ceremonies and the life-cycle rituals. For all their beauty and intricacy, offerings and decorations may last but two or three days. The impact of a cremation ceremony or an *odalan* (the annual temple festival), with several nights of festivities, depends on all the preparations and the performances, which are done without significant financial reward or individual recognition. Music and dancing, arts and crafts, are deemed to belong to everyone. Excellence and beauty enrich the craftsman and his community in a way that has nothing to do with commercial gain or individual status.

Furthermore, in Bali the concepts of craftsmanship on the one hand and of art on the other, are blurred. Precision and skilled application of age-old techniques are what earn esteem; there is no such word as 'artist', only 'paint worker' or 'wood worker'. There is nothing of the Western view of art as a means of self-expression.

But the Balinese are quick to learn. They understand Western commerce well enough to know how to adapt their skills to satisfy the tourist and export markets. It was back in the 1930s that paintings first of all, then woodcarvings, became not only a means of decorating temple buildings and palaces but also a way of supplementing income by creating individual pieces to sell to the newly arrived Europeans. This change of attitude was encouraged by Western artists living in Bali at that time, notably the German painter and musician Walter Spies and the Dutch painter Rudolf Bonnet (see pp.190–91), who saw the potential in Balinese painting both as a style of great interest in the world at large, and as a means of bringing the financial benefits of tourism to the people themselves. But they were also keen to see that Balinese artists maintained their integrity. Walter Spies, for instance, who was actively promoting Balinese art to the outside world, refused an order for hundreds of identical wood statues, wanting to preserve the artistic value of individual pieces.

Things have moved on since then. The depressing rows of identical bare-breasted ebony women lining the shelves of some of the large tourist shops may make you feel that it has been all downhill. To some extent, though, the Balinese have been able to have it both ways: indifferent craftsmen make a tolerable living in bearable working conditions by catering for indifferent buyers, while individual pieces of real merit have a good market too. The only people really miserable about the state of Balinese crafts today are those who want a work of art at a knockdown price. Meanwhile at the cheaper end of the market, the constant input of new ideas and adaptation of old ones produces lively, amusing designs of all sorts, evidence of genuine creativity, though of a more prosaic kind.

Crafts which are not suitable for the tourist market have remained largely unchanged. These include temple decorations, prepared mainly by women. The ornamental hanging called *lamak* is woven from palm leaves into hundreds of different designs, both figurative and purely decorative. They last only 24 hours before they dry and curl at the edges, but they are true masterpieces. The simple daily offerings and the elaborate mountains of fruit, sweets and cakes for temple *odalan* are also works of art in themselves. An astonishing variety of materials are pressed into use to worship the gods and to celebrate life, including pig fat and intestines.

Stone Carving

Wherever you go in Bali, the skill of the stone carvers is evident. Richly carved temple gateways, such as the distinctive *candi bentar* (the split gate), elaborate stone friezes and grotesque statuary come to seem as natural a part of the Balinese landscape as the rice terraces and the outlines of palm trees against the sky and the mountains. The island is a kind of treasure trove of decorative imagery and motifs and absurd mythological characters. In the temples, representations of gods and demons, serpents and sacred animals and formal floral decorations cover every available stone surface. Amongst the familiar figures telling the endless story of the battle of good and evil forces, are lively, comical, contemporary scenes which continue the Balinese tradition of art as comment on everyday life. There is nothing stale or frozen about the art of temple carving. No two temples are alike, and yet the same themes are endlessly repeated.

The themes have something in common with the medieval tradition of decorative carving, with its comical, grotesque figures and saintly icons. Carving varies from region to region, and according to the function of the particular temple. In the south the most common material is the soft *paras* volcanic rock. In the north, where the temple carvings are even more exuberant and outrageous than those of the south, a pinkish sandstone is

Boy Dancer

used. The northern temples of Sangsit, Jagaraga and Kubutambahan are famous for the humour of contemporary scenes showing bicycles, aeroplanes and motor cars.

Even individual stone carvings are usually too heavy for tourists to take home, so remain as examples of pure Balinese invention. Roadside shops in Batubulan and Kapal are good places to see the full variety of statuary, from mythological or religious sources, from the natural world, or in the modern civic style apparently favoured by the government. These are almost all produced for the domestic market, for decorating family temples and gardens, and carved from a grey volcanic stone which is almost as soft as plaster, though rather more durable.

Paintings

Paintings were the first artistic product to catch the attention of European and American markets. Classical '*wayang*' style painting, such as can be seen on the ceiling of the Kerta Gosa (Court of Justice) in Klungkung, is still produced in the village of Kamasan. It is called '*wayang*' because the style of the figures (with bodies set mainly at three-quarter view, heads in profile), their iconography and positioning, and the stories told by the paintings resemble that of the *wayang kulit* shadow puppet shows. Painted cloth rectangles around 80 × 60 cm (33 × 24 in) depict scenes from Balinese folklore, from the Ramayana and Mahabharata Hindu epics, or astrological themes. A traditional pictorial Balinese calendar is painted in this style.

Wayang painting is produced according to strict conventions. There is little room for individual experimentation. The predominant colours are red, shades of ochre, and black, with touches of blue and green. Traditionally these colours came from natural dyes: black from volcanic soot, white from bones, red from the Chinese *kencu* dye, ochre from a kind of clay called *atal*, blue from indigo. Today artificial dyes may be used. The cloth is treated with a rice paste to give it body, and polished with a smooth shell to give it its characteristic sheen. Paintings can cost from 10,000rp upwards, depending on their quality. They are sold by women on the streets of Ubud, and in the art shops of Kuta and

Denpasar, as well as in Kamasan itself. The same kind of painting is used to decorate other objects, such as coolie hats, to sell to tourists.

In the 1930s Walter Spies and Rudolf Bonnet settled in Ubud and joined with local painters and the influential raja of Ubud to form a society known as Pitha Maha, devoted to encouraging young artists. For the first time in Bali painting was considered to be something other than a matter of beautifying temples and palaces. Paintings could be put on canvas and sold—and indeed some soon began to fetch high prices in the European and American market. Instead of epic narrative scenes from Hindu mythology, painters began to depict single scenes and images of local, daily life. Nonetheless, they still used 'traditional' methods.

'Traditional' refers to the style of the painting rather than the subject matter. The Balinese artist will start by drawing out the design carefully, following strict rules of composition and design, before colour is added. Once again the aim of the 'traditional' artist is to create something of beauty and harmony according to established principles, rather than make a statement or express individual experience. For this reason imitation is not despised as it would be in the West: it can be an honour rather than a threat. It is common for the work on a painting to be shared between several painters: one contributing the basic design, one deciding the colours, another doing the fine shading. Signatures are now *de rigueur*, but this custom was developed purely to please the market. The most famous early painters in this traditional Balinese style are Lempad, Sobrat, Kebot, I.B. Nadra and Ida Bagus Made. Later the Australian artist Donald Friend encouraged Balinese painters to take their imaginations one step further: Ida Bagus Rai from Sanur began painting his splendid sea scenes full of strange beasts and birds.

Painting suffered a setback with the onset of the Second World War. Not till the 1950s did a new impetus take place, in Penestanen, just outside Ubud, where the Dutch painter Arie Smit encouraged young boys to paint from life and from fantasy. 'The Young Artists', as they were called, produced vivid canvases using modern bright colours. Many of the comic motifs seen in contemporary painted woodcarvings, such as the frogs in human clothes, or using the huge *keladi* (taro) leaves as umbrellas as the Balinese will, come from these paintings.

Today you can find paintings which depict anything from mythological scenes to Rousseauesque jungles, or scenes from everyday life in Bali. Prices vary enormously, from 15,000rp for a standard 60 × 45 cm (24 × 18 in) painting of herons, to $800 US for something by an established artist with a reputation in Jakarta. Those who are painting now and commanding most respect and the highest prices can be seen in the galleries of Agung Rai and Agung Raka in Peliatan and Mas.

Some painters have stepped right outside Balinese traditions, producing work based on Western values of individual self-expression and personal creativity. Artists from all over the world have been attracted to Bali for the past 50 years; some have left a legacy of paintings in Ubud's galleries, some are painting here still.

If you are thinking of buying a painting in Bali, you would be well advised to look first at the range of work displayed in the main museums and galleries, for instance in Denpasar's Abiankapas Art Centre, and in Museum Puri Lukisan and the galleries of Ubud, where much of Bali's painting is produced. Here you will get an idea of the numerous styles available, and the prices. When buying a painting, look for good quality canvas and imported paints, such as acrylic or gouache, which keep their colour best.

63

Woodcarvings

Some of the liveliest and freshest ideas among Bali's arts and crafts are to be found in woodcarvings. There are plentiful supplies of fast-growing local woods in Bali, a renewable resource on which this industry depends. Small family-based workshops abound, in the villages of Mas, Pengosekan, Nyuhkuning, Peliatan, Tegallalang, Pujung and Sebatu and in Ubud, where apprenticeships and the work itself fit into a pattern of community life.

The subject matter can be drawn from well-established themes and mythological characters, or it might come from new design ideas brought in by exporters specially to cater for their own markets. As we have seen, copying is not taboo, and indeed there is very little truly original work. No one knows where the first wooden banana tree was made, or by whom, but the concept has a wit that seems distinctively Balinese and the world is now thick with them. Peliatan, Pengosekan and Tegallalang are the places to go for outrageous painted wooden flowers, frogs, and carved and painted mirror frames; Batubulan and Sebatu for antique style masks and mythological creatures; Mas for modern style masks and unpainted polished wood figures.

If you buy woodcarvings, especially large pieces, from the villages remember that the wood may not be properly seasoned, or may have absorbed the moisture from the humid climate to such an extent that it will shrink and crack in air-conditioned or centrally-heated rooms. Even carvings from the more expensive galleries may not be immune to this problem if a soft wood, rather than ebony or teak, has been used.

Masks

Masks have a special place among woodcarvings as part of a long tradition and are an important part of dance dramas. The encapsulation of expression in these masks is a special skill, often achieved with great economy. *Topeng* is Indonesian for mask, and also the name given to masked dancing, which requires the dancer to portray the character represented by the mask, an old man say, complete with posture and gesture. Masks may be grotesque or finely carved and painted, according to the character. For the large, elaborate and awesome masks of Rangda the witch, horse or goat hair is used for her long tresses, and bone for her teeth, while the best Barong masks (the good dragon-like character) have gold-painted leather decorations.

The best masks are to be found in the village of Mas. For the production of the smooth-surfaced Japanese-style modern dance masks, a light, strong wood is used, a local member of the balsawood family. Although the masks copy a basic design, each one has its separate identity, unique to its carver, and no attempt is made at complete uniformity. Many layers of paint are used to get a perfect finish.

Textiles

Textiles are another area of craftsmanship that has taken new directions in response to Western interest. There are a number of techniques of dyeing and weaving which you will come across in Bali, of which the following are the principal ones.

Batik

Batik dyeing is not strictly a Balinese craft: it is native to Java, from whence come all the traditional batik sarongs that are made up into Western clothes and sold in Kuta. The batik process has been adapted by the Balinese, however, to make bright designs of flowers and birds for dresses, children's clothes, cushion covers and so on. It is a dye-resist method in which hot liquid wax is applied to the cloth before dyeing. The principle is simple: liquid dye will not penetrate the areas of cloth covered in wax, so whatever shapes are drawn in wax in the cloth will remain undyed.

Wax may be applied by a brass 'cap', a kind of printing block which is dipped in a bath of hot wax and then stamped on the cloth to make a repeating pattern. But the very best batik, *batik tulis*, is entirely hand drawn using the brass pen called a *canting* to apply fine lines of wax. When the pattern has been imposed in wax on the cloth, the cloth is plunged into a dye-bath. Later, the wax is washed out of the fabric with hot water. The process may now be repeated, with a further waxing and a new colour dye-bath, as often as needed to create the required pattern and colours.

Traditional Javanese batik is usually in variations of blue (from the indigo plant) and brown (made from root bark). Beware of fabric sold as *batik* but which is actually machine or screen printed in factories; there is more and more of this about, as the genuine batik from central Java becomes increasingly difficult to obtain. Because of lack of investment in new workshops, the batik industry in Solo, the centre of traditional batik in Java, has shrunk in the last few years to a quarter of the size. You can tell real batik from screenprinted by the depth of the colours (real batik is much richer), the appearance of the pattern on both sides of the cloth (the batik process allows the dye to penetrate right through the fabric, screen printing remains on the surface), and the regularity of the pattern (there will always be variation in waxing and dyeing of real batik). Real batik is also distinguished by the hair-like trails of colour where the dye has penetrated cracks in the wax: look especially at the selvedge. Expect to pay 8,000rp for a batik sarong done with a brass 'cap', or 25–40,000rp for a good quality *batik tulis* sarong. The very best cost much more than this.

Ikat

Ikat, known in Bali as *endek*, is a traditional Indonesian type of hand-weaving with its own distinctive qualities. In Bali its most celebrated form it is still practised by two or three households in the village of Tenganan: the 'double *ikat*' or *gringsing* cloth of Tenganan is held to have sacred and protective properties, and is used in temple rituals in many Balinese villages.

Ikat is an Indonesian word meaning to bind or knot. In straightforward *ikat* the warp (vertical threads on the loom) is stretched on a frame before weaving commences. The weft threads are bound according to a certain pattern, and then dyed. The bound areas resist the dye, although some dye seeps under the binding, which contributes to the characteristic blurred edge of *ikat* designs. The cloth is then woven on a loom with plain warp (vertical) threads. A weaver makes about 2 m (2 yards) of cloth in a day.

In 'double *ikat*' both warp and weft threads are dyed by this painstaking process, and must then be woven so exactly that the patterns coincide. It takes several months to complete even one narrow scarf of double *ikat*.

Some Balinese *ikat* or *endek* is made of pure silk, usually imported from Ujung Pandang (Sulawesi), but most is 100% cotton. Some cotton is grown locally, especially in the eastern isles, but the best is imported from the U.S.A. Cotton *endek* can be given a silky texture by treating the cotton with a clay-based solution, a process called 'mercerization' which was developed in England in the Industrial Revolution.

You can buy simple *endek* sarongs quite cheaply at markets throughout Bali; these are usually simple two-tone pieces in blue and white, or deep red and white. Some of the best designs are made in the village of Sampalan Tengah, just east of Klungkung, where they sell pure silk *endek* for 25–30,000rp per metre. You can also buy '*mesres*', as mercerized *ikat* is called, off the roll at 8–10,000rp per metre. There are also several weaving centres on the road into Gianyar from Ubud—this is where the tour buses call. Another good place to try is Singaraja: go to the weaving centre behind the Gedong Kirtya library.

Songket

Songket is another type of fabric produced in Bali's cottage industries, though the main centre of production is Sumatra. The distinctive effect of *songket* is achieved by the supplementary weft technique, where extra threads are introduced at the time of weaving by means of special wooden heddles on the loom, which raise the vertical warp threads in a particular pattern. The supplementary weft is then introduced to make a contrasting decorative pattern on the cloth. In Bali the process is called *tenun* [weaving] *cag-cag*, and here the extra weft threads are almost always gold or silver. The effect of all the gold decoration is sumptuous.

Songket has a special place in ceremonies of all kinds. It is used, for instance, for the over-sarong cloth (*saput*) worn by men dressed for temple ceremonies, and for the *selendang* cloth which is wound round the torso of *legong* dancers. Common motifs are geometrical shapes of flowers, birds or animals, on a plain purple, green, blue or red background. One piece can cost anything from a few thousand to several hundred thousand rupiah. Cheaper pieces do not last long as the gold or silver thread tends to fray.

Basketwork

Basketwork is one of the essential crafts of Bali: look at any typical market place and you will see that not only are the main containers made of woven palm fronds and bamboo, but also the matting partitions and sunscreens. Some of the market baskets are as beautiful as those in the tourist shops.

The unusual big brown, black and white patterned baskets seen in Sukawati and Ubud are made from the leaf of the *lontar* palm and dyed with natural dyes. Places to buy are Sukawati (in the small shops near the market) and Ubud. Prices for a good basket will range anywhere from 5,000rp to 30,000rp. Note that some of those on sale in Bali are imported from Lombok.

The village of Bona is particularly famed for another kind of basketwork, producing not only baskets but palm-leaf hats, mats, bags and purses. These are now being made in bright, artificial colours as well as from traditional natural dyes. A simple palm-leaf 'panama' hat will cost a mere 3,000rp.

Bamboo

Almost adjoining the village of Bona is Belega, where wonderful chunky bamboo furniture is made to a high standard. A massive sofa with cushions will cost around

$300 US, a bargain compared to bamboo furniture abroad—shipping costs can double the actual cost of the exported product.

To prevent the transmission of plant diseases the import of bamboo is subject to restrictions in various countries, including Australia. The bigger furniture makers can treat their furniture and supply you with the necessary certificate, which should then be attached to the shipping documents. Shippers will be able to advise on this. An additional problem of taking bamboo to a less humid climate is that it can crack along the grain, making it not only unsightly, but dangerous.

Silver

Celuk is the silversmiths' village, where households have grown rich on the proceeds of the tourist trade. Tour buses come to any of a dozen big establishments on the main Denpasar road, but there are plenty of smaller places on the back roads towards the village of Singapadu where prices are more reasonable. Good designs are also to be found in Ubud and Kuta, though many of these are mass produced in Denpasar. The silver is imported but good quality and does not tarnish quickly like that used in Java. Most products are in sterling silver, which is composed of 92.5% silver and 7.5% other metals, usually copper; this is why people in the shops talk about '925' if you ask. Many of the semi-precious stones used are native to Indonesia. Among the most commonly used are garnet, amethyst, onyx, turquoise and lapis lazuli. The transparent stone is zircon. You can also find opals—from Java or Australia—rose quartz, topaz, agate and green malachite. The gold decoration is 18 carat.

Most of the silver-only work is remarkably cheap, especially considering the delicacy of the hand-crafting that goes into it. It is one of Bali's best buys. Designs are both traditional and modern, often witty if not plain outrageous.

Other Carvings

Bone, horn, coconut husk and shell are other materials used for intricate traditional-style carvings. Some little bone carvings from Tampaksiring resemble Japanese ivory netsuke, but are a fraction of the price. Of course the workmanship is not as fine as the collectors' pieces, but they make good presents nevertheless. Tampaksiring, Klungkung and Bangli are all good places to find this kind of carving. A small Rangda or Buddha figure 8 cm (3 in) tall might cost you 5,000rp.

Shadow Puppets

The leather puppets featured in Balinese shadow puppet shows (*wayang kulit*, see pp.130–31) are made in the village of Puaya, near Sukawati, and in Peliatan. Cowhide is punched out and painted to make the familiar profiles of Ramayana characters. The lace-like decoration of the characters' clothes and headgear is quite beautiful. Somehow these puppets capture the mystery of Indonesia and the cultish practices associated with Hindu Bali and Java. *Wayang kulit* puppets cost from 7,500–10,000rp upwards.

Ceramics

Red clay pottery is widely used for household containers in Bali: it is brittle and treated as disposable. Nonetheless it has a rough-and-ready handmade charm to it. Visit Kapal, north of Denpasar, to see this kind of pottery being thrown on foot-operated wheels. You might like to buy a traditional *sate* stand, like a miniature barbecue. The fired clay is highly resonant and is made into little figurines used as wind-chimes.

Glazed pottery is also produced on the island in two workshops that have brought in modern techniques and designs from abroad. Pottery from Pejaten is quite widely promoted, with celadon-style work as their main line. The other pottery, in Sanur, is noted for its simple forms, matt-glazed and usually decorated with understated motifs, such as tiny model frogs. Interesting new designs are emerging on to the market slowly. Go to Rumah Manis at the north (Seminyak) end of Jl. Legian in Kuta to see some of the best.

Lontar Books

The old religious stories and strictures of Bali's traditional (*adat*) laws are inscribed on long, rectangular strips made from the fronds of the *lontar* palm. The inscriptions, often illustrated with fine line drawings, are highlighted with lampblack or the black oil of the *kemiri* nut; the 'leaves' are then bound together rather like a fan. This is still very much a living art, and numerous villages still have *lontar* clubs where people of all ages study the ancestral texts. Genuinely old *lontar* books are very valuable indeed; the main archives are at the Gedong Kirtya library in Singaraja, the *lontar* library of Udayana University Literature Faculty in Denpasar, and the Hindu Dharma religious institute in Denpasar. A number of *lontar* scribes produce work for sale, which can be found at some considerable price in Denpasar's art shops; other scribes produce one-off works of poetry or philosophy for posterity alone.

Kris making

The sacred, bejewelled daggers of the East, with their unusual blades or undulating curves, have found their way into many a tale of Oriental mystery. '"Why look at it?"' cried G. K. Chesterton's Father Brown, holding out the crooked knife at arm's length, as if it were some glittering snake . . . "Don't you see that is has no hearty and plain purpose? It does not point like a spear. It does not sweep like a scythe. It does not *look* like a weapon. It looks like an instrument of torture."' And indeed there is something about all that intricate and rich decoration combined with the savage curves of the blade that does make a *kris* send shivers down the spine. A *kris* is part of a Balinese man's traditional dress, worn tucked into the band round his sarong, behind his left shoulder blade. The decorated hilt protrudes above the shoulder, as you can see in the photos of the rajas earlier this century, or in Balinese dance dramas. As the traditional weapon, a *kris* represents a man's power, and that of his ancestors. A raja's *kris*, stuck in a tree, could stand in for him at the wedding ceremony of his lesser wives. The *kris* is the most treasured heirloom any family can have: to lose it or to sell it would be to invite disaster. Like King Arthur's sword, certain *kris*es are believed to carry magical power, bestowed by the gods, and make their possessor invincible in battle. This is not something unique to Bali: the *kris* has an important status in Java and elsewhere in Indonesia, and in Malaya.

The art of *kris*-making is still alive, though increasingly rare. *Kris*-makers have a special place in Bali's caste system; each stage of the elaborate production process is part of a sacred ritual, and involves ceremonies and sacrifices. Thin sheets of rare metal are applied one at a time, and then filed down to make the characteristic wavy edge, revealing the several layers of different coloured metals. The length of the process plus the value of the jewelled handles adds to the mystique.

It is still possible to buy a *kris*, though really good ones cost hundreds or thousands of dollars. Try the top floor of Sukawati art market for some cheaper versions.

Gamelan Instruments

The craft of casting the bronze *gongs*, the instruments that make up the most character-istic of the *gamelan* sounds, is highly skilled, yet carried out in conditions that cannot have changed for half a millennium. Go to the village foundry at Blahbatuh, in Gianyar regency, or to Tihingan west of Klungkung town, or the village of Sawan near Jagaraga, east of Singaraja, to see smiths at work in their traditional forges. The muted colours of the flickering firelight on the bare brown skins and old batik sarongs of the ring of men at work, the sparks from the hand-held anvil and the bronze of the *gamelan gong*s as they are painstakingly hammered into shape, all make a memorable scene, like something out of an Old Master painting. Finished *gamelan* instruments can be seen in a Denpasar showroom, U.D. Gema Kencana in Tohpati.

Parasols, Fans, Headdresses

The delicate fabric parasols—of gold painted cloth, fringed and tasselled—which are carried in processions in Bali are now primarily decorative, although in the days of the royal courts they were used to denote rank. You can buy these, especially in the village of Paksebali, near Klungkung.

More robust and practical parasols are decorated with bright flower and bird motifs, on a black or white background, popular among tourists and found in most of the art markets. Pay a visit to the parasol man just by the turning to Petulu, outside Ubud, to see the process of production. Other ceremonial paraphernalia and dancers' costumes are also produced for this same market. Fans, such as those seen in some of the dances, are decorated in a manner similar to the parasols, and come in all sizes, some huge and purely ornamental—look for them in Sukawati.

Antiques

There are occasionally genuine antiques to be found in Bali, including antique carved wood furniture. Most often, though, the furniture is reassembled in Batubulan from several cannibalized old pieces, so it is not 'antique' in the collectors' sense of the word. Indonesians in general do not have our reverence for old things, and there is a thriving and skilled market in the recreation of old carvings (which are then left to accumulate authentic cobwebs). Such is their success, you would need to be an expert to find the real thing. Our advice is, enjoy your 'antique' woodcarving for its special decorative or humorous charm, and do not concern yourself too much with its actual age.

Shopping

You should be able to buy almost anything you need in Bali: the large shops and supermarkets of Denpasar carry more or less the full range of Western requirements. As you go out into the remoter parts of the island the shops become increasingly rudimentary. Small villages may have no shop at all.

You should go to the markets for a true flavour of Balinese life; yet more exotic are the night markets (*pasar malam*) which can be found in most larger towns, including Kuta, selling food and snacks and all kinds of cheap local goods (not handicrafts). Some will close at 11pm, whilst others continue their hubbub right through night. They open late—around 10am—and close around 7 or 8pm. There is rarely anyone awake in the early afternoon—even the assistants doze on a mat behind the counter.

In Denpasar the shops open around 7.30am and close around 6pm, except for the big supermarkets, which stay open late (see p.145).

Here are a few things, besides crafts, which you can buy in Bali at remarkable prices: cotton clothes, especially shirts, shorts and beachwear in wild holiday colours; lightweight zip-up travelling bags in *ikat* cloth or bright patchwork, and shopping bags and lightweight backpacks in a similar style; flimsy but imaginative shoes; patchwork bedcovers; batik tablecloths; paper kites; pirated watches and sunglasses; cheap cassette tapes...

Supermarkets, pharmacies, hotel shops and the like will have fixed prices, but in the tourist shops, beach markets or village markets you will be expected to bargain, and sometimes you must bargain very hard. Tourist shops in the main tourist haunts are liable to quote starting prices three or four times what you should be paying; but elsewhere on the island you may find that you are quoted prices that are disarmingly honest. There are no hard and fast rules, and you are bound to pay over the odds until you have a feel for the true value of things.

Bargaining

Bargaining will always be a painful experience to the Westerner: no matter what splendid deal you have achieved after protracted negotiations, the fact that the vendor is willing to sell at that price makes you think that you must have paid too much. Then you will meet someone who has paid considerably less for exactly the same thing, from the very same shop. You cannot really win: all you can do is think to yourself, as calmly as you can with three Balinese beach girls holding on to your arm saying pitifully 'No bisnis today', what the value of the object is to you. This may bear no relation to the price that is quoted. It does not matter: give it a go. The key is to do your bargaining in good spirit, so when the response to your opening bid is that you will bring ruin of the vendor's entire family, laugh. Some people get quite aggravated, which is a mistake. Bargaining is fun—take your time.

It is sometimes possible to reach prices by bargaining that really are rock bottom. For whatever reason, a shopkeeper may occasionally let something go cheaply, so when you walk out with your bargain you do not always have to feel that you have paid too much.

Shipping

Most art shops and enterprises selling goods for export will have contacts with local shipping agents. These will provide a reliable service, and will handle the packing and necessary documentation. Shipping by sea costs around $40 US per 10 kg; allow about three months for your consignment to reach its destination. Air cargo is very expensive: around $15 US per kilo, but has the merits of speed. You can send large parcels through the post office, but really you are better off going to a shipping agent or 'postal agent', who are cheaper and can do the packing for you. Mark documents 'for personal use only' or 'samples'. If you send more than 20 of any one item you are liable to be judged a trader by the customs authorities and your consignment may then not only attract VAT plus import duties ranging from 5% to 25%, but require documentation from the Indonesian end for clearance. Goods may be impounded while you contact your shippers back in Bali, and meanwhile you foot the storage costs. Certain goods, such as leather, always require clearance from the Indonesian authorities. Check with your shipping agent.

Weights and Measures

1 kilogram = 2.205 lb
1 litre = 1.76 Imperial pints
        = 2.11 US pints
1 centimetre = 0.39 inches
1 metre = 39.37 inches
        = 3.28 feet
1 kilometre = 0.621 miles
1 hectare = 2.47 acres

1 lb = 0.45 kg
1 Imperial pint = 0.56 litres
1 US pint = 0.47 litres
1 Imperial gallon = 4.54 litres
1 US gallon = 3.78 litres
1 foot = 0.305 metres
1 mile = 1.609 kilometres
1 acre = 0.404 hectares

A Quick Guide to the Best in Bali

Six Day-trips from the South

These suggestions assume that you will be starting out from a base south of Denpasar—in other words from Sanur, Kuta and Nusa Dua—and that you have your own transport. They involve a fairly full day, but with time for leisurely stops. Use the index to find full details of places listed.

1. Tirta Empul and Ubud

Early morning drive to Gunung Kawi (rock temple); on to Tampaksiring (holy springs and temple); across to Sebatu (exceptional temple, wonderful views on the way); lunch at Ubud; afternoon in Ubud (Museum Puri Lukisan, paintings, craftshops, walk to Monkey Forest, or swim); Mas (carver's village); back to base.

2. Pejeng and the Ayung River
Early morning start to Goa Gajah (cave temple); on to Yeh Pulu (rock carving); on to Pejeng (three great temples); on to Pura Pengukur Ukuran and Goa Garba (temple off the beaten track); to Ubud for lunch; visit Museum Neka; walk from Campuan to Penestanan and Sayan (views down the spectacular Ayung river); return to base.

3. Klungkung, Besakih, Penelokan
Early morning start to Kutri (temple with view); on to Tihingan (*gamelan*-founding village) and then Klungkung (famous painted ceiling of Kerta Gosa, old court of Justice); early lunch at Klungkung then on to Bukit Jambul (wonderful views); on to Besakih (Bali's most holy temple); on to Penelokan, to see Mt Batur and the crater lake, with views of Mt Agung and Mt Abang; return south via Bangli (Pura Kehen) and back to base.

4. Mengwi, and Lake Bratan
Early morning start to Mengwi (beautiful temple); on to Bedugul and Candi Kuning on Lake Bratan (flower market, lakeside temple, botanical gardens); lunch at Bedugul, or at Bali Handara Country Club; return to base by same route, taking detour to visit Marga (Independence struggle memorial).

5. Pura Luhur and Tanah Lot
Take packed lunch or picnic; early morning start to Kapal (temple); on to Tabanan (agricultural museum); on to Pura Luhur Batukau (remote, jungly temple); on to Jatuluwih (spectacular views); picnic here; back down to Tabanan and on to Pejaten (pottery); late afternoon, head for Tanah Lot (seaside temple) for sunset; back to base.

6. Denpasar and Bukit
To Denpasar in cool of the morning (Museum Bali (closed Mon), Pura Jagatnata, Abiankapas Art Centre, Badung market). Now you have a choice: if you are staying in Sanur go to Nusa Dua (unreal hotel complex) and swim with spectacular view of the volcanoes to the north; lunch here, or in Bualu; or go on to Benoa and eat there; in the late afternoon head across the Bukit peninsula to Ulu Watu (cliff-top temple) for the sunset; then go to Kuta for some Kuta experience. If you are staying in Kuta, leave Denpasar to go to Sanur to get a flavour of it, then go to Nusa Dua/Benoa for lunch and a swim and on to Ulu Watu for the sunset. If you are staying at Nusa Dua, leave Denpasar to get a glimpse of Sanur, lunch at Wayan's Warung (you need the change) and relax on the beach; head across the Bukit to see Ulu Watu at sunset, then go to Kuta and eat at the night market.

Three Three-night Excursions

These trips assume that you have your own transport and are starting out from the south, and are prepared to sleep in less-than-three-star accommodation.

1. Karangasem

DAY ONE
Travel via Klungkung (famous painted ceiling in old court of justice, Kerta Gosa) and Goa Lawah (temple in bat cave) to Padangbai (small port); lunch here, then go on to Balina Beach or Candi Dasa, whichever will be your chosen base.

DAY TWO
Visit Tenganan (traditional village) in the morning; do as little as possible for the rest of the day.

DAY THREE
Early start to Amlapura (charming old palace); then on to Ujung (decrepit old palace, but spectacular coastal views); return northwards to Tirtagangga (old water palace); swim in pools and lunch here; after lunch drive across to north coast for exceptional landscape and views of Mt Agung; return to hotel.

DAY FOUR
Early start to Bebandem (small market town); you now follow the road that leads through Sibetan, Putung, Duda, Iseh, Sidemen—a road of breath-taking beauty; lunch at Sidemen; on to Klungkung; pause at Sidan (grotesque carvings) and then return to base.

2. Ubud

DAY ONE
Gentle trip up to Ubud to find the perfect accommodation; lunch; relax; walk in the rice fields.

DAY TWO
Walk to Museum Puri Lukisan and Museum Neka (paintings); Penestanan and Sayan; lunch in Ubud; late afternoon, go to Petulu to see herons; evening, go to a dance performance.

DAY THREE
Walk (or drive) to Goa Gajah (cave temple); on to Yeh Pulu (rock carving); on to Pejeng (three great temples); late lunch in Ubud; afternoon, relax; late afternoon, go over to Kedewatan to watch sunset over Ayung river gorge.

DAY FOUR
Drive to Gunung Kawi (rock temple) and Tirta Empul (holy springs and temple) via rough road through Gentong and Kendran; on to Sebatu (exceptional temple and views); return to Ubud for a late lunch at your favourite restaurant; return to base via the waterfall at Tegenungan.

3. The North

DAY ONE
Early start to head over the mountains, either via Kintamani (spectacular views of crater

73

BALI

lake) (bring packed lunch or eat in a tourist restaurant); or via Bedugul and Candi Kuning (flower market, lakeside temple, botanical gardens) (lunch here); go to Lovina to find accommodation; relax.

DAY TWO
Morning on the beach; lunch in Lovina; in the afternoon drive to the Singsing waterfall, Buddhist monastery and Banjar Tega hot springs; return to hotel.

DAY THREE
Early start to Singaraja and on to Sangsit (temple with carvings); inland to Jagaraga (temples with famous carvings), back down to Kubutambuhan (another temple with famous carvings); then on to Yeh Sanih (fresh water springs); swim and lunch here; in the afternoon take a leisurely drive to Tejakula (market town) to get a flavour of the quiet north; return to hotel.

DAY FOUR
The object today is to get back to base in the south. Either take the alternative of the outgoing routes above; or drive to Pengastulan and take the mountain road via Blimbing to Antosari (pretty road). Or drive around the western tip of the island as follows: early start to Pengastulan and on to Pulaki (beautiful seaside temple); then on to Labuhan Lalang and Teluk Terima (shrine of Jayaprana); lunch here; then on to Gilimanuk (spectacular views of eastern Java); back down to Negara (pretty road) to Rambut Siwi (beautiful seaside temple); then down the coast to Tabanan and Denpasar and back to base (a long day but perfectly feasible).

Tour Agencies

There are innumerable tour agencies in all the main resorts, which organize trips around the island. We recommend in particular **Jan's Tours**, Jl. Nusa Indah 62, P.O. Box 26, Denpasar; tel (0361) 23076; fax (0361) 24595; telex 35222 JANTRS.

Other reputable agencies include: **Golden Kris**, Jl. Raya Sanur 58, P.O. Box 108, Denpasar; tel (0361) 25850/27769; telex 35187 GKRIS; **Nitour**, Jl. Veteran 5, P.O. Box 21, Denpasar; tel (0361) 24233/22593; telex 35111 NITDPR; fax (0361) 24233; and **Pacto**, Jl. Tanjung Sari, Sanur, or P.O. Box 52, Denpasar; tel (0361) 88096/88240; telex 35110 PACTO; fax (0361) 88240.

HELICOPTER TOURS
Finally, **P.T. Bali Avia** offer helicopter flights over Bali at US $87.50 for a half-hour flight, or $175.00 for an hour, with a minimum of four passengers. You can plan your own route, and there is a free pick-up service from hotels in Nusa Dua, Sanur, Kuta and Denpasar areas. Bali Avia are at Jl. Sepinggan 17, Bandara Ngurah Rai, Tuban 80362, Denpasar; tel (0361) 51257; telex 35308 KUTA.

Part II

HISTORY

Rice terraces

As cloud cloaks the slopes of Mount Agung, obscuring its hard outline against the sky, so myth hangs over Balinese history. To the Balinese, history is largely an oral tradition, or a story to be found in *lontar* books, and written in the opaque, poetic language of kawi. This is sufficient for their needs: the Balinese have an irreverence for historical fact, preferring the quality of the story to the criteria of truth.

We will try to confine ourselves here to a factual history in the Western form; elsewhere, we will show how, in Bali, history is entwined with myth, a tradition that surfaces in dance-dramas, puppet shows and story-telling, and in the legends attached to historical sites, temples and their accompanying ceremonies.

Prehistoric Times–AD 1293: from Bronze Age to Hinduism

Little is known about the earliest forefathers of the Balinese, other than the fact that they were part of a great movement of people which slowly worked its way through Southeast Asia from southern China from about 3000 BC. A distinctive 'Malay' race was created as they displaced and mingled with local groups whose ancestors were of the same stock as the Australian Aboriginals. Archaeological remains in Bali date from the 'Bronze Age' in the early part of the first millennium BC; they include spear and axe heads and other implements, as well as massive stone sarcophagi. Both bronze and iron were in use when the first Indian and Chinese traders began to visit the area in the 2nd and 3rd centuries AD, and it is probably at about this time that the Balinese began to turn their hands to growing rice in flooded paddy fields.

A map of modern Bali shows how rice cultivation has affected where and how people live. A chain of volcanic mountains stretches like a massive yoke across the shoulders of

75

Bali's body. Beneath is a throng of bustling villages, occupying less than a quarter of the total land area. Here, in these well-watered foothills, are the main areas of rice cultivation. This is the economic heartland, where the richest and most influential kingdoms were to rise. By comparison, the mountains to the north—barely passable until the 19th century—are sparsely inhabited, and the northern coast is but a thin strip of cultivable land, at the mercy of a long dry season. This, and the fact that Bali has few natural harbours offering safe anchorage, the fact that the Balinese are generally not a sea-faring people and look to their own island rather than to the outside world, and the fact that they long had the reputation of being fearsomely warlike and keen on converting visitors into slaves, help to explain how the island largely escaped the attentions of predators.

The early kingdoms of Bali became aware of Hinduism and Buddhism, either directly through Indian traders, or, more probably, through contact with Hinduized Java. Hinduism, in a form which also combined Buddhist concepts, arrived in Southeast Asia in the 2nd or 3rd century AD. It offered a well-structured political and legal organization; it had a distinguished intellectual and literary tradition; and it could be easily grafted onto existing groups of local gods without its new adherents having to renounce these first.

By the 9th century AD, Hinduism had reached Bali. Stone inscriptions dating from this period are still to be found, among them that on the early 10th-century stone pillar in its modern-day pit behind the Pura Belanjong in the southern part of Sanur (see page 167). This records in Sanskrit (the ancient language of India) and in old Balinese the military successes of a king of the Warmadewa dynasty, and marks the beginning of modern Balinese history, when the empires of Hinduized Java began to play a decisive role.

In the late 10th century, Bali was conquered by the Javanese king Dharmawangsa. His sister, Princess Mahendradatta, married the Balinese king, Udayana, at a time when the island appears to have undergone important changes in both its religious and political life. A high priest from Padangbai by the name of Kuturan instituted a number of fundamental reforms: he is credited with the introduction of the caste system, and with the unification of Balinese religion under the Hindu Trinity (Brahma, Shiva and Vishnu). The son of Udayana and Mahendradatta, Prince Erlangga (or Airlangga), was educated in Bali and Java, and was appointed ruler of Kediri (eastern Java) from 1019 to 1042, while his brother, Anak Wangsa, reigned under his authority in Bali, thus founding a political and cultural link between Bali and Java which was to continue over the next five hundred years.

The degree to which Bali was subjected to Javanese rule from one decade to the next depended upon the comparative strength of the central Javanese powers. In 1284 a Javanese king of the Singasari dynasty, Kertanegara, reconquered Bali for a short period, but before the century was out there arose a powerful and unifying Balinese dynasty, centred on Pejeng, which appeared to show little allegiance to Java.

1293–1550: Gajah Mada and Majapahit Rule

The year 1293 marks the foundation of the Majapahit empire in Java, which was to last for over 200 years and witnessed the full flourish of Javanese Hindu culture before it was swamped by the rising tide of Islam. These were the times of one of the great figures of Balinese history: Gajah Mada, prime minister and generalissimo of the growing Majapahit empire. In 1343 he conquered Bali anew, removing the last of the Pejeng dynasty and bringing the island into the sphere of an empire that now included Java, Sumatra and Borneo.

The new ruler of Bali was a nobleman appointed by Gajah Mada, Sri Dalem Kapakisan. He ruled from a royal palace (*kraton* in Javanese; *puri* in Balinese) which was the centre of political, religious and cultural activity. Kapakisan's palace was in a place called Samprangan, just outside the modern town of Gianyar, but within a few generations Samprangan was abandoned in favour of a new site at Gelgel, south of modern Klungkung. I Dewa Ketut, grandson of Kapakisan, is thought to have been responsible for this move as part of a strategy of usurping power from his brother, who was considered too degenerate to rule—something of a recurring tradition among Balinese royal families.

Since the chronicles of this time relate only to the activities of the court and ruling families, little impression can be gained of what the *people* of Bali felt about this new influx of Javanese overlords. By this time, Bali was more or less Hinduized, and the form of government before the Majapahit invasion probably differed little from what followed from it. Where the intervention of the Majapahit in Bali is significant, however, is in the degree to which the new ruling elite was now tied to Java. The Majapahit Empire was undergoing a cultural renaissance, and the royal courts of Bali followed these trends avidly. The achievements of the Majapahit Empire, in both religion and the arts—dance, music, literature, painting—filtered through all levels of society. To this day most Balinese, especially high caste Balinese, consider the Majapahit to be a crucial part of their ancestry; Gajah Mada is considered a hero, not an alien oppressor. Within a few decades of Gajah Mada, the Majapahit Empire began a long process of disintegration, an increasingly important factor being the rise of Islam.

Islam came to Southeast Asia with the Arab and Gujarati traders around the middle of the 13th century. Marco Polo noted its presence in Sumatra in 1292. When the ruler of the great trading empire of Malacca announced his conversion in the mid-15th century, Islam could claim to have spread its net from Malaya and Sumatra across the seas to Mindanao, an island in what was shortly to become the Philippines.

In Java a number of small kingdoms, newly converted to Islam, converged to create the Mataram Empire; they exerted increasing pressure on the Majapahit Empire and eventually caused its collapse in 1515. This was the signal for large numbers of Majapahit rulers and their families to cross the narrow straits to Bali, where they hoped to preserve their traditional ways of rule and caste. The result was that suddenly Bali became the principal heir to mainstream Javanese Hindu culture; after a couple of decades of adjustment, it was about to enter its 'Golden Age'.

1550–1601: The 'Golden Age' and the First Europeans

In 1550 a new king, Batu Renggong, ascended the throne at Gelgel, taking on the traditional title for this role, Dewa Agung, literally 'Great God'. Military successes led to control over the buffer state of eastern Java, Blambangan, and added the islands of Lombok and Sumbawa, to the east of Bali, to Bali's domain. Batu Renggong also

77

presided over a great cultural flourish that followed the exile of the Majapahit courts to Bali. This period also coincided with the work of Nirartha (also known as Bau Rauh, or Bheggawan Dwijendra), one of the great historical figures of Balinese religion. His mission was to try to hold back the floodgates of Islam; he came to the court of Gelgel from Java in about 1550. He is credited with being the author of part of the chronicle *Usana Bali*, recording the island's mythological history, and his name is associated with a number of important temples, notably Pulaki, Rambut Siwi and Ulu Watu.

Batu Renggong's son, Raja Bekung, maintained the élan of his father's court into the next century before decline set in under his son, Di Made Bekung. But before this time a new ingredient had begun to flavour the broth of Southeast Asia, momentarily sending a waft of its particular odour beneath the noses of the Balinese: Europeans.

The Portuguese were the first European traders in this region, pushing further along the route around the Cape of Good Hope to Ceylon, India and beyond, in search of the riches of the Orient. Spices were the main attraction; they had previously been brought to Europe overland across the Middle East by Arab traders, who sold them to Mediterranean merchants. Spices were not only used to flavour food, they were also essential in the preservation of meat in countries which had to slaughter much of their livestock before winter and keep the meat fresh through to the spring. Spices were also held to have valuable medicinal qualities. Europeans knew that the spices came from the Orient, and they were determined to seize the trade by going to its source. They were to find pepper in southern India and cinnamon in Ceylon, but for nutmeg and cloves they had to go deep into the islands of Southeast Asia to the Moluccas (now Maluku). By 1527, the Portuguese had control of the Moluccas, an achievement not without bloodshed, including the destruction of 'infidel' Malacca in 1511 and numerous skirmishes with Spanish rivals, as well as with uncooperative natives.

Then came the British and the Dutch. By the end of the 16th century, Bali had been noted by both, but at that time it failed to arouse their interest. It was not, after all, a spice island. The expedition led by Portuguese navigator Ferdinand Magellan, the first to circumnavigate the world (from west to east, in 1519–22), passed by Bali and named it Java Minor, though Magellan himself had met his death in the Philippines. It is likely that Sir Francis Drake set foot on the island in 1580, and Thomas Cavendish in 1585.

In that same year, 1585, a Portuguese ship was wrecked off the Bukit; its five survivors were regarded by the Dewa Agung as a gift from the sea-god Baruna. They were well treated and given Balinese wives, but prevented from leaving the island.

The Dutch first entered these waters in 1597, under the tattered flag of Cornelis de Houtman, whose expedition limped towards Bali in three ships, the crew of 89 men being survivors of all kinds of savagery, sickness and mutiny from an original complement of 249. They assembled in the bay off Padangbai and stayed for a month or so, doing remarkably little. Cornelis de Houtman himself seems to have left ship only once to negotiate the return of three Balinese hostages, taken on arrival as a cautionary measure. However, four of his crew made a short but historic excursion ashore, during which they visited the palace of the Dewa Agung (at this time Batu Renggong's son, Raja Bekung) at Gelgel. They also met a survivor of the Portuguese wreck, Pedro de Noronha, who declared himself content with his lot and not at all inclined to leave his wife and family.

The Dutchmen were lavishly entertained, first at Kuta, where troops were being assembled to launch an expedition to Blambangan, and later at Gelgel. The Dewa Agung had 200 wives as well as a collection of dwarfs, whose growth had been deliberately stunted to represent a gnarled mythological figure called Sangut, who often adorns the handles of sacred *krises*. The power and wealth of the Dewa Agung was represented by his extensive retinue and bodyguard, who accompanied him wherever he went in a shimmering display of jewellery, gold-painted parasols, lances and banners.

The Dutchmen attended an audience with the Dewa Agung and presented him with gifts that included an elegant mirror and a rifle. But the Dewa Agung was especially fascinated by a map of the world and he questioned his visitors closely about the Dutch King, his military strength and his methods of governing. At the end of their stay, two of these Dutchmen, Emanuel Roodenburg and Jacob Claaszoon, jumped ship in order to enter the service of the Royal Court, but their companion, Arnoudt Lintgens, returned to Holland where he published a glowing report of his experiences in Gelgel.

Another four years passed before the Dutch reappeared on Bali's shores, this time under the leadership of Jacob van Heemskerck, who was the first in a long line of his countrymen to stake a claim on the island. Using the services of Emanuel Roodenburg as interpreter, Heemskerck persuaded the Dewa Agung to enter into a trading agreement and to proclaim Holland and Bali to be in some way mystically united. The Dewa Agung signed a letter to the King of Holland to this effect, though clearly without any appreciation of how this would be interpreted in that country. Over the next two centuries the Dutch made some attempts to establish a trading post in Bali, but with little success. However, the document that van Heemskerck had managed to coax out of the Dewa Agung in 1601 remained the basis for their claim over the island for ever after.

1601–1795: Unquiet Isolation

Bali was now to enjoy 250 years with only minor disturbances from the covetous Europeans, a period in which its inhabitants were able to consolidate a culture which was already unique to the region. Isolation, however, had its drawbacks: energies that the ruling families might have used for fending off common enemies from outside were now devoted to a ceaseless stream of squabbles amongst themselves as the island split into some eight separate rajadoms.

Decline set in with the rule of Dewa Agung Di Made of the Gelgel dynasty, the son of Raja Bekung (who entertained Cornelis de Houtman's men). Under him, Bali lost control of Blambangan, Lombok and Sumbawa. Until then the Dewa Agung was acknowledged as the *Susuhunan* (emperor) of Bali by all the lesser rajadoms. The ruling families throughout the island had been established by the Gelgel royal palace: they were all relatives of one kind of another of the Dewa Agung, intermarried and cross-related, providing fertile ground for intrigue and power-broking.

In the latter part of the 17th century Di Made's son moved the royal palace from Gelgel to a new site in neighbouring Klungkung, apparently because the misfortunes that had befallen his father had been ascribed to a curse upon the old palace. But it was already too late: by the end of the 17th century the Dewa Agung was *Susuhunan* in name alone. His kingdom had already been divided by the emergence of the rajadom of Gianyar under Dewa Manggis Kuning in 1667. Thence onward the real power in Bali shifted from one rajadom to another, but never returned to Klungkung, although successive Dewa Agungs always commanded traditional respect as the senior raja and religious leader.

In the late 17th century it was Buleleng to the north that became the dominant rajadom, through the manoeuvrings of a charismatic raja named Gusti Pandji Sakti, who brought not only neighbouring Karangasem and Jembrana, but also Blambangan in eastern Java, under his control. His territory was further extended when Gusti Panji Sakti was usurped in 1711 by his son-in-law, Gusti Agung Sakti, raja of Mengwi, thereby creating a powerful joint rajadom of Buleleng-Mengwi that was the main force in Bali for the next three decades.

From the 1650s onwards Karangasem started to take a direct interest in Lombok, which, since the decline in power of the Dewa Agung, had begun to convert to Islam. When the Raja of Lombok started to oust the Hindu Balinese, Karangasem intervened and managed, in the course of half a century, to gain complete control over the island; it installed a group of four puppet rajas, who ruled over the majority (mainly Muslim) Sassak people through an élite of Balinese.

Throughout this period, from the foundation of Batavia (now Jakarta) in Java in 1619, through to the end of the 18th century, the Dutch were building their empire in Java and establishing a series of trading posts in Sumatra, south Borneo, Macassar and the Moluccas. In a manner similar to that of the British in India, the traders led the way, and imperial government followed in their footsteps. These were heady days for adventurers and fortune-seekers, who carved out little empires for themselves making up the laws as they went along, trading and mingling with people of all nations, marrying locally, settling, amassing great wealth, and losing it through misfortune, greed and bloodshed. In 1602, the Dutch traders organized themselves into the Dutch East India Company, but Bali had little participation in this trade, the Dutch being either disinclined or too high-minded to involve themselves with Bali's principal commodities: opium and slaves. It left these to Chinese and Arab merchants, and to the Bugis traders based in Makassar (now Ujung Pandang) on the southwestern tip of the Celebes (now Sulawesi).

Originally, the use of opium in Bali was confined to the raja and the royal courts, and was associated with religious rites. Later, in the 19th century, its use spread to the people, many of whom would smoke small quantities daily. Since this opium came primarily from India and mainland Southeast Asia, it had to be traded, usually by the Chinese.

The Chinese brought with them the currency of southern China, the *kepeng*, a small round coin with a square hole in the middle. The Balinese did not have their own coinage, and so used the *kepeng* when they were not simply exchanging goods by barter. Thus the Chinese found themselves in the position of being both traders and bankers, and they earned fortunes by trading *kepeng*s at vastly inflated exchange rates. *Kepeng*s could be strung on a thread and traded by weight. Like virtually everything in Bali, they were soon to earn a religious status which they have kept to this day: *kepeng*s still play an important role in the cremation rituals. Incidentally, this coin was known as 'cash' by British traders and is the origin of that term in our language; they borrowed the word from the Portuguese term *cas*, which they in turn had lifted from the Tamil to apply generally to local coinage.

As for slaves, this was one of the prime sources of income for the Balinese rajas.

Balinese slaves were much prized: the men were said to be nimble and hardworking, and the women graceful and compliant. Thousands of them were shipped to Batavia to work in Dutch households; others were taken yet further afield. The rajas controlled this trade, and received all the income from it. The slaves were generally people who had caused some offence or who threatened to be a burden on society: it was considered a quite acceptable duty of the raja to ensure that such people did not impede the good health of the rest of the community.

Bali featured on Dutch maps of the 17th and 18th centuries, but only on the fringes. There were the Balinese slaves and former slaves in Batavia; there was a fair number of Balinese in the Dutch colonial army, recruited through the rajas in return for a bounty. There were also the odd niggling problems which reminded the Dutch that Bali remained an untamed and virtually unknown quantity within their sphere of influence— such as the continuing friction between Bali and the Islamic Mataram Empire in eastern Java, which erupted in warfare from time to time throughout the 17th century. In 1717–18 the Balinese raided Mataram, causing widespread destruction on the mainland and the neighbouring island of Madura, and succeeded in bestirring the Dutch to assist in their expulsion. But the Dutch went no further; they had their hands full with rebellious kingdoms nearer Batavia.

In the 1750s a series of bizarre events in Bali led to the final decline of power of the Dewa Agung and to the rise of a new star, Karangasem. At this time the Raja of Karangasem was an eccentric ascetic who took his role as spiritual leader of his people to a degree that eclipsed his position as head of the government. He spent his days in such deep meditation that he neglected to control his bowels. Persuaded to emerge briefly from his private and insanitary world to pay a visit to the Dewa Agung in Klungkung, he so disgusted his hosts that they arranged for his assassination on his journey back to Karangasem.

The murdered raja's three sons then assembled an army and marched on Klungkung to avenge their father's death. They spared the Dewa Agung, but established their freedom from his authority. The eldest son, Raja Gusti Gede Karangasem, then went on to conquer Buleleng, where he installed one of his brothers as raja; the other brother became raja of Lombok.

It was then that Bali's isolation came to a close. Repercussions of momentous events thousands of miles away in Europe began to be felt on its shores and the island began to move slowly but surely into a world that few of its inhabitants had ever known to exist.

1795–1846: Dutch Solicitations

For the last decade of the 18th century, in the wake of the French Revolution of 1789, Europe was in turmoil. In 1795 Holland was overrun by the French Revolutionary Armies; Britain was at war with France, and thus effectively at war with the new rulers of Holland and its overseas possessions.

The turn of the 19th century found Java and the Dutch possessions under the rule of a Governor-General appointed by Napoleon; he was an unpopular figure, soon to be disposed of by the British, who were determined to protect their interests in Southeast Asia and India from the French. The Dutch possessions then came under the control of an outstanding young British administrator, Thomas Stamford Raffles, who was

Lieutenant-Governor of Java from 1811 to 1816. Raffles filled his role with character-istic diligence, visiting much of his territory, studying the culture and history of the people. In doing so, he visited Bali, but for a few days only. He introduced a number of reforms, many of which were widely welcomed. However, one of these was the abolition of the slave-trade—good for the slaves, but not for the rajas. Goaded by this affront to their purses, in 1814 the Rajas of Buleleng and Karangasem launched yet another attack on Bali's traditional punch-bag, Blambangan, but returned home when confronted by a show of force by the British under Major-General Nightingale off Buleleng.

At the end of the Napoleonic Wars, Britain and Holland became allies once more and in 1817, in an act of goodwill that infuriated Raffles, Britain returned Java and the other former Dutch possessions to the rule of Holland. These lands, previously ruled by the Dutch East Indies Company, were now taken over by the Netherlands Indies Govern-ment. No sooner had the Dutch returned to Java than they sent a mission to Bali to try to bolster their claims to the island, it being well known that the British were on the look-out for a major trading post to pair with Penang, in Malaya, which they had acquired in 1791. Bali was temptingly placed in the archipelago, right on the trade routes between Southeast Asia and the new British colony in Australia.

For the moment, the Dutch had a propaganda advantage: the rajas were still fulminat-ing over their loss of income brought about by the end of slave-trading, and Bali was in a state of turmoil.

Raffles therefore turned elsewhere, and in 1819 founded Singapore in a perfect, but swampy position on the southern tip of Malaya. In 1824 the British and Dutch settled their differences in a treaty that carved Malaya and Indonesia neatly in two. A line was drawn through the Straits of Malacca: north of the line was to be a British sphere of influence, and south of it, Dutch. The British gave up settlements in Sumatra, and the Dutch handed Malacca to the British.

There then followed a series of expeditions by the Dutch to Bali, each more assertive than the last. The Dutch object was not only to bind the rajas to exclusive trading agree-ments that would give them a toehold on the island, but also afford them the right to protect this trade with an administration, and with garrisons. In exchange, they offered the rajas that defence and protection which would come from being associated with the Dutch Empire. In a word, the Dutch desired sovereignty. The Balinese wanted some of the things that the Dutch offered, but they were vigorously protective of their right to rule themselves. The tactic of the Balinese rajas was therefore to be courteous and welcoming at times, and totally uncommunicative at others—a maddening situation for the colonial power.

The Dutch gained paltry rewards from these attempts. Trading continued as before, mainly through Buleleng but also through Kuta, the old port of the Badung rajadom. It was there that they set up a trading post under an agreement negotiated in 1826 with the Raja of Badung by a Dutch agent. One of the main purposes of the Kuta station was to recruit Balinese soldiers to help the Dutch in their continuing fight against the remnants of the Mataram Empire on Java; when this war came to a close, the need for soldiers vanished and the resident Dutch agent, denouncing Kuta as unhealthy and unfriendly, left in 1831 having achieved virtually nothing in the way of trade.

Why the Dutch were so unsuccessful with trade in Bali is curious in the light of the extraordinary success of the first major European figure in Balinese history: the Danish trader Mads Lange. Mads Lange arrived in Bali in 1839, having left Lombok in a hurry. In Lombok he and his three brothers had built up a substantial trading business with the support of the family of the Rajas of Karangasem. The power of this family was represented in Lombok by the daughter of the raja, who took the rank of Cokorda (the head of a high-caste family). Her rival in Lombok, the Raja of Mataram (a town in Lombok), was supported by Mads Lange's English rival in trade, a merchant adventurer called George King. The two sides clashed in 1838; victory went to Mataram, but not before the Raja had been killed and the Cokorda had died in a *puputan*—a suicidal fight to the death when the only alternative is defeat.

With the tables thus turned, Mads Lange fled Lombok and sailed for Kuta, where he had established a trading station as early as 1836.

Survivors of the wreck of the *Overijssel*, a Dutch ship carrying machinery for sugar refining which went aground off Serangan Island in 1841, stayed in comfort at Mads Lange's house and were able to compare his prosperous enterprise with the desolate Dutch trading station next door that had opened up following negotiations with the Raja of Badung in 1838. The *Overijssel*, however, was yet another example of a wreck plundered by the Balinese, despite vigorous protestations by the Dutch over this practice. The Balinese believed that it was their god-given right to dispose of the survivors and contents of wrecks as they wished. It was a more lucrative business than ever now that the seas were filled with ships trading through the islands from mainland Southeast Asia to Australia, to Europe, and to the USA. Many of these vessels were Dutch, and many more were Chinese, Javanese, Bugis and Arab vessels flying under the Dutch flag. It was therefore particularly galling to the Dutch to feel at once responsible and impotent when ships which they were supposed to be protecting ran aground in Bali and were stripped of their goods. To add to their woes, pirates—mainly from Makassar—were now using Bali as a haven and the British were becoming increasingly irritated by the threat to their shipping in waters claimed by the Dutch. If the Dutch could not put their house in order, so the argument ran, the British might just have to do it for them.

So back went the Dutch, contracts in hand, to the rajas of Bali who, as always, laid before their suitors mere mirages of hope. It was now the turn of the Raja Kesiman of Badung to be courted for, unlike all the other rajas, he did express some inclination to open Bali up to Western influence—especially if he could do so at the expense of his rivals. For receiving Dutch delegations in 1838 and 1839, the Raja of Badung earned himself a bronze cannon. Unbeknown to him, it had been deliberately miscast by the Dutch to prevent any danger of being used effectively against themselves. Meanwhile, the Dewa Agung in Klungkung had requested a rhinoceros, which the Dutch agreed to provide. It was sent, at great expense and trouble, with the agent who was to open up the new Dutch trading station at Kuta by agreement with the Raja of Badung, who was, needless to say, greatly discomfited to see what a prestigious gift the agent had brought for his rival.

At this point H. J. Koopman, one of the Netherlands Indies Government's most gifted negotiators, entered the scene. In 1841, as a result of pressure to make good the losses over the wreck of the *Overijssel*, the Raja of Badung agreed, rather surprisingly, to accept the terms of the treaties which the Dutch had been proposing. Koopman then went to the Dewa Agung and managed to persuade him to accept a similar treaty, giving the Dutch a monopoly of trade, and agreeing that Bali should be considered part of the Netherlands

Indies Government. Koopman also succeeded in making a military agreement with the Karangasem family to help them regain control in Lombok.

What Koopman had not done was to spell out in the treaty with the Dewa Agung that the rajas of Bali were to desist in practising their traditional reef rights over shipwrecks—a condition that the Governor-General of the Netherlands Indies insisted must be included in all contracts. By the time Koopman had travelled backwards and forwards between Bali and Batavia, and to Lombok, to finalize these negotiations, the Balinese rajas were beginning to have second thoughts. Koopman, no doubt exasperated, went into retirement. At last, in 1844, the Dutch Commissioner arrived in Buleleng to set the seal on these treaties.

He was greeted by defiance, for at this point one of the great heroes of Balinese history emerged: Gusti Ketut Jelantik, younger brother of the Rajas of Buleleng and Karangasem. 'Never while I live,' goes his famous statement, 'shall the state recognize the sovereignty of the Netherlands in the sense in which you interpret it. After my death the Raja may do as he chooses. Not by a mere scrap of paper shall any man become the master of another's domain. Rather let the *kris* decide.'

The Dutch scurried back to Java—to set about preparing an invasion.

1846–1850: The First Three Dutch Military Expeditions

The First Dutch Military Expedition against Bali arrived off Buleleng in 1846 with 58 ships and 3,000 men, including a landforce of 1,700, of whom 400 were Europeans; the rest were troops recruited from the other islands. The enemy was the Raja of Buleleng and his ally, the Raja of Karangasem, who were supported by the Dewa Agung—but not, however, by the Rajas of Badung or Tabanan. Other rajadoms sat on the fence, whilst Lombok, now in control of sworn enemies of Karangasem, was itching to give the Dutch a hand. Indeed, George King made a special trip to Java to assist in the preparations of the expedition.

The Dutch announced what they wanted: all could be conveniently settled if the Raja of Buleleng accepted the treaties drafted over 1841, 1842 and 1843; the Raja would have to pay the cost of the Dutch expedition and permit the building of a garrison in Buleleng, to which reparations could be made in instalments.

Jelantik, in the meantime, had been busy arming his forces and fortifying both Buleleng and Jagaraga, which lies in the hills some 10 km (6.25 miles) from Buleleng. The British in Singapore had proved very obliging in supplying weapons.

The Dutch troops had little trouble in taking Buleleng under a salvo from the ships offshore; they then set about razing Buleleng, along with the neighbouring royal capital, Singaraja. Meanwhile, the Balinese had repaired to Jagaraga. The Dutch, who had lost only 18 men in this first encounter, prepared for a final battle.

At this point Mads Lange stepped in, setting off towards Jagaraga on horseback with a Balinese assistant and a servant, claiming that he could bring affairs to an amicable conclusion. Much to the Dutch surprise, he returned unharmed, with news that the Balinese had agreed to sue for peace. Negotiations then took place in Buleleng, attended by the Rajas of both Buleleng and Karangasem, at which the Balinese agreed to all the Dutch demands, including the payment of reparation—a massive sum to be disbursed over ten years. The Dutch sailed away, leaving a garrison of 200 men.

What the Dutch had not bargained for was the total disinterest of the Balinese to carry out the terms of this settlement. Not only did they refuse to pay the money demanded of them, they also boycotted the garrison, leaving them wretched and hungry and inducing several to desert.

The Second Dutch Military Expedition against Bali, with 20 ships and a landforce of 2,400, of which 775 were European, appeared at Buleleng in 1848. Quickly destroying the coastal village of Sangsit, the Dutch headed into the hills towards Jagaraga, where a rude shock awaited them. Jelantik had laid a careful ambush on the approaches to the town, and had assembled a force of 16,000 backed by 25 cannon. The Balinese had 1,500 rifles; those who were not so armed had lances and sharpened bamboo poles. Poorly equipped compared with the Dutch, they had the advantage of a huge weight of numbers and a terrifying ferocity. The Dutch advance was soon brought to a halt, their troops took to their heels and fled back to their ships, leaving 264 dead. This famous victory cost the Balinese 2,000 lives.

The Third Dutch Military Expedition—100 ships and 5,000 troops, including 187 European officers, as well as 3,000 sailors, 273 cavalry horses and 3,000 labourers— arrived in 1849, and quickly found their feet in the familiar surroundings of Sangsit, Buleleng and Singaraja. Then came an anti-climax when the Balinese asked for peace negotiations. The Dutch readily agreed, requesting the Balinese leaders to present themselves at the Raja's palace of Singaraja with however many men they believed necessary to ensure their safety. The Raja of Karangasem and Jelantik duly appeared, with 12,000 men, all attired in the splendid ceremonial *baris* (or warrior) costume.

The peace terms were quite conciliatory compared with Dutch demands during the First Military Expedition. All that was now required of the Balinese was to return to Jagaraga and disarm. In two days, the Dutch would arrive to take formal control of the rajadom.

The Balinese returned to Jagaraga, and promptly set about doing everything possible to fortify the stronghold against the Dutch advance, putting up barricades and digging trenches on all the approaches. When the Dutch arrived at the perimeter they were confronted by Jelantik and his 15,000 men, armed with 2,000 rifles. The Dutch reply was a night attack, successful and comparatively economic. The Dutch lost 33 men; the Balinese lost thousands, amongst them Jelantik's wife, who marched towards the invaders with other women of the royal family to meet their deaths in another *puputan*. Jelantik and the Rajas of Buleleng and Karangasem fled deeper into the hinterland while the Dutch returned to their ships and headed back to Java, leaving a strong force to secure the newly conquered lands.

The Dutch now decided to push home this success with a campaign to conquer the heartlands of Bali from the south, seeking to punish the Dewa Agung for his support of the northern rajadoms. With Buleleng now in their control, and Karangasem in turmoil aggravated by 4,000 troops supplied by the Raja of Lombok, the Dutch landed at Padangbai in May 1850 to complete the business. They advanced quickly on Kusamba, where they destroyed a particularly sacred temple—a demoralizing blow to the Balinese. At this point the Raja of Karangasem, feeling that the tables had now turned irrevocably against his line, carried out a *puputan* which brought an honourable end to the lives of his wives and children. By falling to their Lombok allies, Karangasem was now effectively in the Dutch sphere of influence.

Meanwhile the Raja of Buleleng and Jelantik had assembled a force of over 30,000 in the Dewa Agung's capital of Klungkung, ready to fight to the death. But the Dutch troops were suddenly attacked by dysentery. As they reeled about Kusamba in their sickness, the half-sister of the Dewa Agung, Dewa Agung Isteri, the effective ruler of Klungkung, accompanied by the Raja of Gianyar, led a night attack on the Dutch forces, causing numerous casualties and fatally wounding the general in command. The Dutch staggered back to their ships, but before they could set sail there came news that the Lombok troops, who were still marauding around the eastern end of the island after their victory in Karangasem, had succeeded in ambushing and killing the Raja of Buleleng and inducing the suicide, by poison, of Jelantik.

The Dutch therefore changed their plans and prepared for a final push on Klungkung. Here Mads Lange once again intervened, in the most daring of his exploits. Seeing how the situation was developing, he called upon the Raja of Tabanan to raise an army and to march on Klungkung. With this show of strength, Mads Lange persuaded the Dewa Agung to sue for peace and to let him negotiate a truce with the Dutch. This he did, riding out to meet the Dutch forces as they came towards Klungkung; he managed to impress upon the Dutch that if they did not accept the Dewa Agung's offer of peace the Raja of Tabanan would join forces with the Dewa Agung and they would fight to the death. The Dutch took the point. Enough was enough—for the time being at least. It was Mads Lange's finest hour, and he presided over lavish celebrations to mark this reconciliation between foes.

1850–1904: Regents and Controleurs

It would be wrong to suppose that the Dutch achieved their control of Bali entirely against the wishes of the Balinese, or that they were always heavy-handed. In the last decades of the 19th century they proceeded with caution and often with reluctance. They brought stability to the north, after years in which it had been devastated by strife; they introduced a system of justice that removed the worst excesses of the traditional forms of Balinese law, which frequently involved blindings and other forms of mutilation; they put an end to slavery, buying the freedom of all slaves in Jembrana and Buleleng over the next 35 years; and they also decreed that *suttee*—the Hindu practice whereby widows joined their husbands on the funeral pyre—was illegal. All these things can be claimed to be interference with traditions, but not all traditional ways could be said to be of benefit to ordinary Balinese people.

The Dutch governed through regents, who were almost always members of the royal family, usually the incumbent raja—unless he proved incompatible with Dutch intentions, in which case he was removed and not always replaced, as in the case of Buleleng, which survived with no regent from 1872–1882. The regent used a traditional structure of power, administering through local hereditary leaders called *punggawas*, often powerful characters in their own right. These *punggawas* proved frequently to be a thorn in the flesh of both the regents and the Dutch, and indeed the next two Dutch Military Expeditions against Bali, the Fourth in 1858 and the Fifth in 1864, were sent to stamp out the flames of revolt fanned by rebellious *punggawas*. Neither of these Expeditions was as significant as the first three, but the latter did succeed in creating a hero for Buleleng out of *punggawa* Ida Made Rai.

The regent was 'assisted' by a Dutch administrator called a controleur. The controleurs answered to a Resident who looked after Dutch affairs in Bali and Lombok, and who, from 1882, was stationed at Buleleng, which was to remain the capital of Bali until after the Second World War.

The controleurs were often outstanding administrators and, furthermore, sympathetic to the Balinese and keen observers of their unique culture. One such man was the first controleur of Buleleng, P.L. van Bloemen Waanders. But Dutch colonialism was not philanthropic: the Balinese soon learnt that the Dutch administration cost money, paid for by increased taxes on virtually every activity, including trade and agriculture, and collected through agents of the regent. The Dutch also closed in on the opium trade, turning it into a state monopoly whereby only appointed Dutch agents could legally trade in the drug. In principle, this move was designed so that the Dutch could control the abuse of opium, which had become a serious problem, but in the meantime, they stood to gain an enormous profit. Before long, Bali's Dutch administration was paying its own way very handsomely.

Thus was the scene in Buleleng, and the quiet kingdom of Jembrana, whose fortunes were tied to Buleleng. Meanwhile, in the south, business was proceeding as usual. Whilst the southern rajadoms—Mengwi, Tabanan, Badung, Bangli, Klungkung and Gianyar—found cause to scrap with all, or some of the others, it was the rajadom of Gianyar which was causing the worst conflict. Since its creation in the mid-17th century under the rule of the Dewa Manggis dynasty, Gianyar had been at perpetual loggerheads with the Dewa Agung of Klungkung, out of whose territory Gianyar had been forged; Gianyar's boundaries, furthermore, still contained enclaves owing allegiance to the Dewa Agung. By the 1880s the cauldron was bubbling, especially after the Dewa Manggis VII misguidedly decided to pay a visit to the Dewa Agung with his family to try to patch things up. Not for the first time in Klungkung, the response was a classic act of treachery: the Dewa Manggis and his family were imprisoned by the Dewa Agung, who then proceeded to carve up Gianyar and apportion it between himself and the Raja of Bangli. The Raja of Karangasem, assisted by soldiers from Lombok, then decided to realize a tenuous claim to Gianyar, at which point the Dewa Agung, feeling threatened, invited the Raja of Mengwi to seize Gianyar. This was the signal for Badung to invade Mengwi and to share the spoils with neighbouring Tabanan, thus wiping out the Rajadom of Mengwi in all but name for the rest of history.

In 1889, two of Dewa Manggis's sons managed to flee their prison and make their way back to Gianyar, where they called upon the help of a powerful *punggawa*, the Cokorda Sukawati of Ubud. Together they raised sufficient support to place the second son, Dewa Gede Raka, back on the throne of Gianyar in 1892. He ruled amidst continuing turbulence through the decade, but finally decided that the only way to bring stability to his domain—and indeed to his claim to it—was to enlist the help of the Dutch, who so far had been reluctant to intervene. Bending the ear of the Raja of Karangasem, who by this time had established a somewhat eccentric but trusted relationship with the Dutch, and with the help of the persuasive powers of the Cokorda Sukawati, the Raja of Gianyar was able to win over Dutch resistance. In 1900 he became not just Regent, but Viceroy of Gianyar, and the Dutch moved in.

Needless to say, the Dewa Agung found this highly provocative, and spent the opening years of the present century making a nuisance of himself to his neighbours in every possible way.

1904–1908: *Puputan*

In May 1904 a Chinese schooner, the *Sri Kumala*, sailing from Borneo under the Dutch flag, ran aground off Sanur, where local people exercised their god-given rights and stripped the wreck of its contents, apparently with the approval of the Raja of Badung. The owner of the schooner submitted an exaggerated claim to the Dutch authorities, who, exasperated by the incident, scaled it down to more reasonable proportions and presented it to the Raja of Badung with an ultimatum. The Raja, supported by the Dewa Agung and the Raja of Tabanan, loftily refused to have any truck with the claim. The Dutch already had reason to quarrel with the Raja of Tabanan, who with plenty of advance publicity and against vigorous Dutch protestations, had permitted two widows of his recently deceased father to commit *suttee* at their husband's cremation, causing the Dutch great embarrassment internationally. It was time for the Dutch to put an end to such disrespect.

So it was that the Raja's refusal to pay 7,500 florins—not an exceptional sum for the exchequer—provided an excuse for the Dutch to launch their last attack on Bali: the Sixth Military Expedition. In September 1906 a fleet carrying three battalions of infantry and two batteries of artillery arrived off the coast of Badung. This force consisted mainly of troops of the KNIL (*Koninklijk Nederlandsch–Indisch Leger*), men recruited from other Indonesian islands, particularly the Moluccas, under the command of Dutch officers, and assisted by numerous 'coolies'. On 14 September, after a bombardment, they landed at Sanur beach.

They met almost no resistance and marched towards Denpasar. There, they were greeted by an ominous emptiness—just the sight of a pall of smoke rising from the Raja's *puri*, and the insistent beat of *kulkul*s (wooden bells).

As the Dutch took up their positions around the *puri*, the gates were thrown open and a crowd of people, dressed in white and bedecked in their jewels and finery, poured forth, led by the Raja, borne aloft in his litter by four servants. At a stone's throw from the Dutch, the procession halted. A priest raised the Raja's *kris* and stabbed him through the heart. It was the signal for the rest of the court to turn their knives upon their children and themselves or else to throw their bodies suicidally upon the Dutch. Women, it is reported, mockingly threw jewels at the troops before succumbing. Other accounts suggest that some of the Dutch tried to intervene to prevent the massacre; yet others paint a picture of the Dutch mowing down the people before scrabbling amongst them for their jewels.

Whatever the details, the result was a sickening slaughter of some 600 Balinese, the most effective and pungent use of the tradition of *puputan*. The Dutch were left virtually unscathed, but numbed at the pride and despair that this act represented.

But the Dutch were not yet finished. From the Raja's palace they proceeded to the subsidiary royal palace of Pemecutan, a suburb of Denpasar, where a similar scene was enacted, though on this occasion the troops showed more restraint.

From thence the invading forces moved on to Tabanan. There, the Raja and his eldest son resisted the pleadings of the high priest to carry out a *puputan* and went instead to treat with the Dutch, offering their services as regents. At Denpasar, however, they were cast into prison and told that they would be exiled to Madura or Lombok. At this, the Raja and his son committed suicide; the Dutch exiled all the Raja's family to Lombok and their splendid palace was destroyed.

The savagery of these occasions must have sickened many of the Dutch themselves, especially those who had served with the Balinese over the past half-century. They now called a halt to their advances, after putting on a show of strength in Klungkung which impressed the Dewa Agung sufficiently to restrain the powerful *punggawa* of Gelgel, who was sorely provoked. The Dewa Agung was submissive, agreeing to most of the Dutch demands that left him with few powers other than those solely affecting his kingdom. The Dutch, however, wished to control Klungkung and Bangli as they now controlled the rest of the island.

On 1 January 1908 they enforced their opium monopoly throughout the island, causing much resentment in those areas that still considered themselves autonomous. Agents of the opium monopoly set up shop in Gelgel near Klungkung, but were soon embroiled in violence which resulted in the death of three of them. Troops were sent to bring the culprits to justice, but they were sent packing by a fierce resistance organized by the *punggawa*, and which resulted in heavy casualties on both sides. The *punggawa* then took refuge with the Dewa Agung in Klungkung, expecting the success of his action to be answered by a naval bombardment.

It was. Gelgel was virtually demolished, and a large force marched into Klungkung unopposed. The troops set up their artillery in the square before the palace gates and began sporadic firing to goad their opposition into surrender.

The palace gates opened and the Raja, dressed ominously in white, walked forward in front of 200 of his retinue, men, women and children. At some distance from the guns, the Dewa Agung drew his sacred *kris* and thrust it into the ground. This action, he had been advised by his priests, would cause the ground to split asunder and engulf his enemies, if the gods so favoured him.

He was shot in the knee. Falling, he was shot again and killed. Six of his wives surrounded him and, drawing their *krises*, plunged them into their hearts. Other members of the family followed suit; others launched themselves at the Dutch guns which cut them down in a blaze of fire.

In this way, the Dutch won dominion over the last independent rajadoms of Bali.

1908–1941: 'Ethical' Colonialism and Sympathetic Visitors

On that day in Klungkung, 18 April 1908, the Majapahit empire drew to a close—but its final despairing gesture was not in vain. The sacrifice at Klungkung, and those that preceded it, brought home to the Dutch the very special nature of Balinese temperament. In the years that followed, the colonial administrators reverted to the broadly paternalistic policies they had pursued before the events of 1906.

Thus, Bali was never subjected to the worst abuses of the colonial agricultural policy, which elsewhere led to vast plantations geared only to producing commodities for export. True, there were some plantations in the north of island, which produced copra and coffee, but only on a modest scale.

The authorities did not encourage missionaries. At various times in the 19th century small numbers of them had been at work in the island, but with little success. One incident in the 1860s set the tone: after months of trying, one missionary made a single conversion, a man who changed his name to Nicodemus. The missionary left the island and the convert lapsed into Hinduism; the missionary's two successors then exerted such pressure on Nicodemus that he eventually cracked and killed one of them, for which he was executed. The second missionary was sent home and the missionary society in question was instructed to stay away. By the 1930s, an American fundamentalist sect called the Christian and Missionary Alliance was becoming more successful, and although their efforts were frowned upon, conversions to both Protestantism and Catholicism snowballed, and today there are some 100,000 Christians in Bali.

The Dutch, furthermore, were not keen to encourage tourism which from an early date they viewed with distrust: the Balinese had to be protected from casual visitors who brought bad influences of foreign ways. However, tourists began to appear at a rate of 100 per month in the 1930s, most of them under the auspices of the Dutch steamship company, KPM (Koninklijke Pakketvaart Maatschappij), which organized tours and built the Bali Hotel in Denpasar, reached by travelling over the mountains from Bali's main port and capital, Buleleng.

Bali was now becoming highly sought after by those in the know. A book called *Insel Bali* (The Island of Bali), published in Germany in 1920 caused something of a sensation. This contained photographs by Gregor Krause, who had worked as a doctor in Bangli between 1912 and 1914. The world was suddenly presented with quite startling images of Balinese life, from the village market to temple ceremonies; and, perhaps most evocative of all to the buttoned-up, post-war Europe and USA of the 1920s, a series of pictures of men and women bathing naked in cascading streams.

Visitors to Bali with a genuine desire to probe its history and culture were tolerated by the Dutch authorities since such interests broadly coincided with their own. The Dutch were now busily building schools and roads, setting up clinics and making headway against the scourges of leprosy and smallpox, administering justice, restoring historic monuments and fostering the work of distinguished scholars in their researches into Balinese culture. But the spotlight of Balinese history through the 1920s and 1930s was focused on the comparatively few European and American painters, writers, musicians, film-makers and anthropologists who came and stayed on the island. Many have left their mark, and some have had a profound influence.

The German musician and painter Walter Spies was one of the key figures of this period. He settled in Ubud in 1927 and helped bring about the renaissance in Balinese painting that is a feature of life in Ubud today. Others include the Dutch painter Rudolf Bonnet; the Mexican painter Miguel Covarrubias, whose book *The Island of Bali*, published in 1937, is still the classic study of the island's culture; the German author Vicki Baum, who wrote a semi-fictional account of the events of 1906 in her novel *Das Ende der Geburt* (A Tale from Bali), published in 1937; the American musician Colin McPhee who wrote his account of setting up home in *A House in Bali* (first published in 1944); his wife, Jane Belo, an anthropologist who wrote a number of studies of Balinese culture; the American anthropologist Margaret Mead and her husband Gregory Bateson; and the American dancer Katherine Mershon.

This was a period of peace, prosperity, and constructive cultural exchange. The Dutch were criticized for poor standards of education, for exploiting the lower caste's traditional obligations of free labour to their raja, for the burden of higher levels of taxation, as well as petty administrative restrictions. But, as a subject race under a colonial regime, the Balinese were reasonably contented with their lot. In 1938, the Dutch introduced reforms that returned some of the powers of the controleurs to the rajas—the so-called *Zelf Bestuurs Regelen*, 'Rules of Self Government'.

But as the 1930s drew to a close, the whole world was about to change.

1941–1949: The End of Dutch Colonialism

On 7 December 1941, the Japanese bombed the US naval base of Pearl Harbor in Hawaii, making their intentions of military expansion graphically clear. With astounding speed they swept through Southeast Asia, taking Singapore in February 1942. The Dutch army deserted their posts in Bali (for which they subsequently faced courts-martial) and joined the throngs of civilians and army personnel in Java who were anxious to flee to Australia. On 18 February the Japanese appeared off the shore at Sanur and captured Bali without a fight before moving on to Java and Sumatra, which fell on 9 March.

The Japanese invasion had a significant effect on the people of Indonesia, as indeed on all the colonized nations of the Far East. Suddenly, the ruling European nations were shown as vulnerable: the scent of liberation was in the air. 'Asia for the Asians' was the cry. However, the Japanese did not style themselves as liberators: they were occupation forces and made it clear that they wanted to rule in much the same way as the Dutch. Indeed, to the Balinese there was little to choose between them and the Dutch, although towards the end of the war Japanese food requisitions became increasingly demanding and resulted in widespread hardships. When Japan surrendered on 14 August 1945, its forces laid down their arms and left, but not before they helped to sow the seeds of the conflict which was about to ensue by endorsing Indonesia's declaration of independence, on 17 August 1945, with Sukarno as its first president.

Bali slumbered for six months, largely equivocal to the overtures made to it by the nationalist movement in Java which had included Bali in the new republic. Java was, after all, a Muslim country, and a traditional adversary. For many Balinese the prospect of joining a nation dominated by Java, and a Muslim Java at that, was unappealing. However, not all Balinese felt this way: one, a young officer in the nationalist army called Ngurah Rai, took the opportunity of the political lull to organize a force to defend Bali in the nationalist cause with weapons surrendered by the Japanese.

The Dutch returned to Indonesia in early 1946, ready to stake their claim to all the territories which had been theirs. The nationalist Indonesians took a different view and in Java fought tooth and nail against the Dutch, who were aided somewhat reluctantly by the British. But in Bali and in other parts of Indonesia, the Dutch were able to slip back into their former colonial seats; they returned to the island in March 1946, virtually unopposed.

But the clouds of dissent could not be ignored. A small but determined guerrilla force, led by Ngurah Rai, took to the hills, emerging from time to time to broadcast their war cry *'Merdeka atau mati!'*—'Freedom or death!'. Nine months later, after futile negotiations, the Dutch took the offensive and in November 1946 succeeded in pinning down Ngurah Rai's force near the village of Marga in the foothills of Mt Batukau in Tabanan. What followed was, to all intents and purposes, the last *puputan*: Ngurah Rai's men fought to the death, and all 97 of them were killed.

The Dutch in Bali were now left in peace, and were able to govern through rajas who broadly supported their intentions. These intentions had now been tempered with the political reality of the other islands of Indonesia: the Dutch, who now only had control of the islands to the east of Java, created the Republic of East Indonesia comprising 13 separate districts, of which Bali was one. The administrative capital was Makassar, in south Sulawesi. In 1948 Bali became an autonomous state within this republic.

In the post-war atmosphere of European reconciliation, and in recognition of the changed and chastened circumstances of colonial rulers, the Dutch set about the task of building their new republic with a sense of enlightenment. Bali was now to see a revitalized administration which placed the interests of the Balinese people first. The capital was moved to Denpasar, more central to the main concentration of population; the controleurs were replaced by district officers, with a considerably more benign role, while the main political power was vested in a joint council of the rajas.

Critics of the Dutch interpreted all this as simple window-dressing. In any case, Balinese cooperation with the Dutch cooled rapidly when, in 1947 and 1948, the Dutch launched a series of attacks on nationalist strongholds in Java and Sumatra—the so-called 'Police Actions', which caused outrage throughout the world. As a result, the USA threatened to withdraw its support from the Netherlands in its plan for European post-war reconstruction, and at the Round Table Conference in the Hague in 1949, the Republic of the United States of Indonesia (RUSI) was formed, uniting Java and Sumatra with the Republic of East Indonesia. Sukarno was president, but official head of state was Queen Juliana of the Netherlands. Bali was represented at this conference by the Raja of Gianyar, Ide Anak Agung Gede Agung, one of the leading negotiators in the integration of the Republic of East Indonesia into the new republic.

1949–1965: A Descent into Tragedy

Indonesia was now independent, and set forth its own course in the world. In 1956, it relinquished its relationship with the Dutch crown. In 1963, the Dutch were forced out of Irian Jaya, thereby losing their last toehold in this massive archipelago which had once been theirs.

In Bali, the years after independence were not happy ones. For a start, Sukarno's administration rapidly trod a path to economic chaos, with increasing levels of graft and corruption. Martial law was imposed in 1957 after a series of military coups in the islands, and in 1959 parliament was abolished. Sukarno, a charismatic figurehead, rode a dangerous troika comprised of the military, the Nationalist Party (the PNI), and the increasingly powerful Communist party (the PKI). From 1961 to 1964 inflation was running at over 100 per cent as the economy faltered and Western investment was shunned or was withdrawn. In 1963, Indonesia launched a disastrous war against Malaya in an effort to disrupt the formation of the Malayan Federation, condemned by Sukarno as being the creation of British 'neo-colonialism'.

Bali lived in the shadow of these events, affected by the deteriorating economy, and by the increasingly tarnished political structure. In Bali, as elsewhere, villages were dividing up into factions as the PKI and the PNI vied with each other for allegiance, whilst publicly proclaiming their common goals. Land reforms in 1960 reduced all private ownership to 7.5 hectares (19 acres); many large landowners in Bali submitted to this freely, only to find that the land thus released was not redistributed fairly. Traditional hierarchies with the villages were crumbling, and with them the structures that supported the religious and cultural fabric of Balinese society. To add to this, Bali suffered from political and economic neglect by Jakarta: after all, whilst Java had suffered great privations during the fight for independence, Bali had readily accepted the benefits of renewed colonial rule. In addition, Bali was Hindu. Bali was suspect.

It did, however, receive one special form of attention from President Sukarno. Sukarno was in fact half Balinese: his mother was Balinese, his father Javanese. He harboured an affection for Bali and would visit the island frequently, often accompanied by large entourages which would be lodged in the modern palace that incongruously looms over the ancient and especially sacred temple of Tampaksiring. These visits became an increasing source of resentment, for they made big demands on the local population, who were expected to provide food, entertainment and gifts of art for the distinguished visitors, as well as to line the streets in adulation. The story goes that government agents would shoot the pigs and dogs in the villages lying on the route to Tampaksiring in order that the good Muslims in the President's cavalcade were not offended by the sight of them; there are tales of debauchery in which local Balinese girls were the victims. Whatever the truth of such allegations, they demonstrate a tide of resentment rising in Bali towards the mid-1960s.

The Balinese, ever looking for signs in the firmament, saw that something was deeply amiss in the land, and that events were coming to a head. The gods were surely displeased. In 1962, widespread damage was caused by a plague of unusually voracious and plump rats which the Balinese were unwilling to kill until suitable propitiations had been made by the high priests. By that time it was too late: the crops were devastated, leaving many families with three months' supply of rice to last half a year.

In February 1963, Mt Agung, Bali's sacred mountain and the abode of the gods, stirred from the slumber in which it had lain for at least 300 years, and began spewing forth smoke and ash. At the foot of the mountain, at Bali's holiest temple, Besakih, the 'mother temple', preparations were under way for Eka Dasa Rudra, a ceremony of great importance in the Balinese calendar and which takes place only once in every 100 years, marking a complete purification of the island. The religious authorities disputed whether the correct, auspicious day had in fact been computed, and as Mt Agung rumbled beneath the slopes above Besakih, local opinion favoured calling off the ceremony.

By this time, however, the ceremony at Besakih had become an item in the itinerary of delegates to an international conference of travel agents in Jakarta. They were to be flown in from Java to watch the spectacle, and Sukarno himself was to attend. So the ceremonies went ahead, beginning on 8 March. Now Mt Agung was in the full throes of eruption, shooting mud and rock into the sky and turning the landscape grey with ash. The travel agents witnessed the ceremony, held in a tense atmosphere and without the expected company of Sukarno, and then flew home. On 17 March, Mt Agung blew up, sending rivers of molten rock all over eastern Bali, destroying entire villages on the higher slopes of the mountains and wiping out whole communities which, because they knew no other way, refused to abandon the homes of their ancestors. The roads to

Klungkung were blocked for weeks. Refugees, bereaved and starving, wandered the countryside; 2,000 people are believed to have died, and a further 100,000 were made homeless. The extent of this tragedy was not widely broadcast by the Indonesian government and, when foreign aid did eventually arrive, its distribution was erratic and inefficient. The area affected by the eruption was to suffer for many years to come, and some villages have never recovered. Many of those made destitute had to leave Bali to start new lives in other islands, thereby forming part of Indonesia's controversial 'transmigration' policy which aims to redistribute its population more evenly through its territories.

This was not the end of Bali's troubles. On 30 September 1965 an attempted military coup in Jakarta by leftist factions of the army and airforce was foiled, but not before six leading generals, together with a hapless lieutenant mistaken for another general, had been tortured to death and their bodies dumped in a well. This incident caused widespread revulsion, which was then whipped into a frenzy of revenge. The Communists were made to take responsibility for the attempted coup. What followed was a massive blood-letting that engulfed the whole of Indonesia, and Bali was in the thick of it. No family was spared the carnage: brothers turned on each other, uncles killed nephews, whole communities disappeared by night and bodies were found savaged at the roadside or floating in the rivers. The large Chinese community, traditionally the object of resentment as the money-lenders and for their control of business, was decimated. No one knows the figures; some say that 40,000 people died in Bali, others estimate the figure at more than twice that. It is a horror that still haunts people today.

Sukarno continued in power after 1965, but more or less as a figurehead, widely respected for the part he played in Indonesia's independence, as indeed he still is today. But it was Suharto who now held the reins and in 1968 was elected President of the Republic, ushering in a new era during which, with the benefits of oil wealth and constructive foreign investment, Indonesia has prospered. Sukarno died in 1970.

1965—present: Prosperity and Tourism

The late 1960s saw the arrival of a new group of visitors to Bali: a generation of rootless and happy-go-lucky travellers in search of alternatives to Western materialism. Bali was on the 'hippy'-trail—for Australians on the way to enlightenment in India, for Europeans who had been overland to India and were still searching. This was the foundation of a new lease of life for Kuta, which provided the kind of warm hospitality, cheap accommodation and easy charm that attracted the budget traveller. Other parts of Bali soon followed suit—Ubud, Lovina, Candi Dasa. In recent years the average tourist has become someone of greater wealth, demanding ever higher standards of comfort. New hotels, new resorts have been developed and still more are being planned, involving local and national government and the multi-national hotel industry. Bali received nearly one million foreign visitors a year in the late 1980s, and two million a year are projected for the next decade.

Tourism has been the dominating theme in the last two decades of Bali's history. It is clear that Bali is currently undergoing a more dramatic period of change and adaptation than it has ever previously experienced.

Part III
BALINESE TOPICS

Massaging a fighting cock

Towards the mountains

It is a measure of the self-sufficiency of the Balinese as an island race that their main system of orientation is entirely their own. Directions are either *kaja*, 'towards the mountains', or *kelod*, 'towards the sea'. Thus larger villages may well be divided into two sections, for example Pujung Kaja and Pujung Kelod.

The mountains, and especially Mt Agung, are the seat of the gods, and so *kaja* is associated with holiness; they are also the source of the water that feeds the rice terraces, the life-blood of so many Balinese. Temples will almost always be oriented along this same axis, with the holiest shrines towards the *kaja* end. The opposite of *kaja* is considered base. In a village family compound, the family temple will be in the *kaja* position, the kitchen and the rubbish heap on the *kelod* side. The Balinese will much prefer to sleep with their heads towards the mountains, their feet—the baser part of the human body in more sense than one—to the sea.

Apart from the spiritual implications of this sense of orientation, it is a practical solution. The mountains are always visible, the most obvious landmark. A people who, for whatever reason, have largely shunned the sea, do not need a navigator's knowledge of the compass. But by the same token, because this system of orientation only has relevance in Bali, the Balinese easily lose their sense of direction when abroad.

The Village Home

Most people in Bali live not in a house but in a family compound called *pekarangan*, a walled area often filled with an abundance of flowering shrubs and trees and containing

95

a number of small bungalows, each with its own verandah, and each designated to members of the extended family. The simplest, rural compounds are very rudimentary. Walls may be made of woven bamboo partitions or wattle, the roofs thatched with palm-fronds (*atap*), which has to be renewed every eight years or so. The floors may be just trodden earth. Moving up the scale, the pattern changes little, but the cottages are more solid—these days often built of concrete or clay brick and with glazed windows—and may perhaps be adorned by traditionally carved and gilded woodwork, and roofed in *alang-alang* grass, which can last for 50 years. Even palaces or *puri*s, the traditional homes of the ruling elite, differ only in the elaboration of detail, but may not be much larger than the homes of ordinary villagers.

The Balinese explain that the family compound is laid out like the human body. The head, in the *kaja* position, is the family temple (*sanggah kemulan*), the kitchen (*paon*) the feet. In the traditional, well-to-do compound the body will contain not only the living quarters, but also certain pavilions, or *bale*s, reserved for ceremonial occasions: the *bale gede* for tooth-filing ceremonies, weddings and rituals connected with cremation; the *bale gedong* which is reserved for the wedding night after formal marriage celebrations, and is where family treasures and archives are kept; and the *bale dauh* for clan meetings, and for the use of guests. These may be splendidly decorated, jewels of painted and gilded carving.

The family members themselves are likely to sleep in the most unpretentious, unadorned *bale*s, although these are a little more sophisticated these days. Whereas the older beds were simply wood platforms, on which the bamboo mat was rolled out and covered with a sarong, modern fashion has introduced mattresses and bedcovers, and some kind of cupboard is usual for clothes and schoolbooks, and maybe a radio.

A comparative lack of personal possessions—and almost total lack of privacy—is common to Balinese dwellings of all strata of society. Most possessions are shared, so that you will see the same pair of shoes, sarong or T-shirt doing the rounds of the family. The notable exception is that new Balinese status symbol: the motorcycle. These are the prized possessions of the sons—and often daughters—of the family, and jealously guarded.

Everything has a human scale: all proportions in a traditional Balinese home are based on the physical measurements of the head of the household at the time of construction, all of which are carefully calibrated by a priest, the smallest unit being the length of his thumb from knuckle to nail.

So if this is true of the villages, what of the towns? The Balinese do have their own form of internationalized urban architecture, small-scale apartment blocks, suburban villas. But the temples still are there—on the roof. It is surprising to what extent the basic model of Balinese family life, the family compound, still exists in the towns—tranquil, green oases in contrast to the plate-glass windows and concrete shopfronts, the fetid storm drains and the roar of traffic which are the more familiar attributes of Asian cities.

Leaves from a Balinese Kitchen

In family compounds outside the towns traditional and rudimentary kitchens are still preferred for the flavour of food cooked over wood. These dark, ramshackle and unprepossessing shelters contain little but a brick fireplace, a selection of large black-ened pots, ceramic water containers, and a few bamboo utensils. Crude graters and knives are made from recycled bits of metal stuck in wooden handles. The chopping block is a big cross-section of a tree trunk, with remains of bark attached. Spices and peanuts are ground in shallow stone mortars. A small shrine honours Brahma, the god of fire and so of kitchens.

Everyday eating in the family compound is a mundane matter. The basic food is of course rice, to which a strong *sambal* or chilli sauce is invariably added, along with whatever titbits of fish, meat and vegetables are around. Local vegetation such as a certain kind of palm leaf is often used for 'greens', and you get coconut with everything. Meals are totally informal. Members of the family wander in and eat when they are hungry, though you find people congregate in the central compound around 11–11.30 am for the main meal. Balinese food is best eaten with the fingers from a banana leaf. Afterwards water is scooped from the *mandi* and poured over everyone's hands with some ceremony, and then thick, strong Balinese coffee will be served, black and sweet.

Come feast times, however, cooking and eating become a major event. As with other things Balinese, when the occasion is right things happen with panache. Whereas everyday cooking is the women's province, cooking for a feast is a matter for the men. Rows of men toil away at the chopping blocks and spice-grinding duties, up at crack of dawn so that the food is fresh. There will be whole pig roast on a spit, several varieties of *sate*—especially the delicious *sate Bali*, made of ground pork, spices and coconut—and *lawar*, the Balinese dish of vegetables mixed with fresh animal blood. On more lavish occasions, the range of food will be impressive, and the Balinese, normally so frugal, will show themselves to be a nation of secret trenchermen.

Children of the Gods

Until fairly recently, almost all Balinese babies were born in the home using traditional methods of childbirth. The husband delivered the child himself, assisted by a male midwife who supported the mother in a crouching position. Older women of the village, family and friends lent moral support, and most of the village, including young children, hovered around the door. Childbirth was a community affair. Today, most babies are born in local clinics, although traditional childbirth is still practised in remote villages. Nonetheless, from the day of its birth, a Balinese child is a child of the whole community, which will support it and nurture it in an atmosphere of exceptional warmth and stability.

Each stage of a Balinese child's life is marked by ritual. Indeed, ceremonies begin after the third month of pregnancy, and husbands still follow the taboo which forbids them from cutting their hair throughout the wife's pregnancy. After the delivery there is a ceremony in which the afterbirth is buried in a coconut shell outside the family house. After 42 days another ceremony is held for the child; then another is held after 105 days to mark the baby's first half year of the Balinese 210-day year; and another when the child is a year old, *pawetonan*, at which the baby is presented to the ancestral temple.

Children are gifts of the gods, cosseted, but somehow not spoilt. Boys are the cause of particular celebration and pride, but girls are not the cause of disappointment or rejection as in many Asian cultures. Only one type of baby is unwelcome: boy-and-girl twins, who are held to have committed incest in the womb; and elaborate rituals are performed to cleanse not only the children, or just the family, but the whole community, which feels itself blighted by this rare misfortune. Boy-and-girl twins of high-caste families are, however, welcomed, a tradition that harks back to the Pejeng dynasty in which several generations of rulers are said to have married twin siblings.

Balinese babies are not allowed to touch the ground until the *pawetonan* ceremony, and in practice will be constantly carried around in the arms of one or other member of the family rather longer than this. The reasoning is that if the baby is allowed to crawl around on the ground its animal nature will predominate over its spiritual one.

Fathers are just as much concerned with the upbringing of their children as mothers, and are often more demonstrative. It is part of the general pattern of village life in Bali, maintained even now by the home-based workshops of the handicrafts industry, that husbands do not go out to work—except to the ricefields—and so play an integral part in the daily home routine. Often it is the father who carries the new baby around all day, shows it off to visitors and, at an incredibly early age, takes it to see the dramas and dances performed in the village. A small child will often be seen leaning against its father's shoulder as he plays the *gamelan*, or paints or carves at home, absorbing his skills without earnest study.

Once it can walk, a child is free to roam the compound in the company of brothers, sisters, cousins, aunts, uncles, or grandparents, any of whom will be as ready as its parents to watch and rescue should harm threaten. Relationships are formed within a firm social pattern; young children take on responsibilities and become self-sufficient at a very tender age. They are close to the natural world. Pregnancy, birth, marriage and death are not much mystified, even though they are celebrated with great pageantry.

The amount of time a child spends with its peers rather than with its parents is probably crucial to its development as a fully socialized member of the Balinese community. The spirit of cooperation is a fundamental part of family life. The level of awareness and attentiveness to others is very high, and this underlies the institutions of Balinese life. The 'special relationship' between parents and child is not quite the same way as in the West: a child is not so emotionally dependent on its parents, nor is it under so great a pressure to fulfil the emotional needs of its parents. The child learns to do as others do, and not to ask questions. To the Balinese way of thinking, the great Western 'why?' is just bad manners, being awkward. There is great security in this, although the other side of the coin is that, generally speaking, the Balinese are reluctant to step away from what is familiar.

Balinese children do not have toys in the Western sense. A wheel to push around on the end of a stick is about it (good quality toys are some of the best presents you can take with you). We met a French couple travelling with a beautiful, blonde two-year-old daughter. Yes, they said, the Balinese loved to see her, but she was persistently eclipsed by her doll, which the Balinese found irresistibly fascinating.

In place of toys Balinese children use make-believe, drawing on the movements and gestures of the dances and dramas. You even see solitary children suddenly make a stylized move, or break into a dance pattern to an imaginary audience. There are also many games involving imitations of animals, with wonderfully onomatopaeic names: *meong-meongan* (a vicious cat, *meong*, traps a rat); *jaran teji* (two horses fighting); *jangkrik-*

jangkrikan (crickets) and so on. Take time to watch the children at play, so they are not aware of your gaze: you will be entranced.

Love, Sex and Marriage

In this, the most romantic environment possible, with warm tropical nights, sweet-scented flowers and the distant strains of *gamelan* music, the Balinese are in some ways comically practical about their sexual affairs. It is a fact that children reared close to nature are wiser about such matters than their city-bred fellows, and the Balinese are usually sufficiently close to the struggle for survival to make very cool, level-headed decisions before giving way to the demands of the heart or flesh. Once the decision is made, however, the thing is done with dramatic flourish. Style is everything, whether it is a matter of a runaway marriage or the rage of a jealous lover.

Courtship is traditionally brief, a matter of exchanging looks and innuendoes. Because Balinese society is so close and has such a firm, shared base—not to mention a total lack of privacy—people are generally more finely tuned to each other than any outsider can ever hope to be. No doubt that is the origin of oriental inscrutability: people are so quick to read each others' minds and know their intentions, you need to become a master of your expressions to preserve some private space. The Balinese complain that Westerners, by contrast, are too exaggerated, unsubtle, insensitive and blustering. Balinese women who find Western boyfriends, on the other hand, say that the Balinese men are too unromantic, not demonstrably affectionate, and assume too much.

Sexual affairs are carried on with discretion. No one seems to object so long as there is no fuss. It is a matter of quick and silent liaisons in the quiet of the countryside, or even in the home, with everyone apparently pretending not to see. Adulterous couples who can afford it use Denpasar hotels; the people of Denpasar go to Ubud for the same reason. If an affair results in pregnancy, and the partners are unmarried, then there will be a marriage, but there is no shame implied in this—as indeed in many rural societies where the ability to produce offspring is a critical factor in marriage.

Couples begin to pair off in their early twenties. There are two sorts of marriage in Bali. The more formal kind, typical of high-caste families but also dependent on village tradition, is called *mapadik*, in which the family of the groom will plead with the bride's family for her hand in marriage. The bride's family will raise all manner of objections, until the groom's family have pleaded five times, each occasion being marked with great ceremony and the presentation of suitable gifts. At last the bride's family will agree (if they are so inclined), and marriage will be arranged. Prior to the day, the bride will be kept indoors for three to five days where she will undergo a purification ritual in the company of women considered adept in these matters, who sing chants in a prescribed manner. The marriage itself is a lavish affair, a great show of hospitality and status, attended by priests. The bride will go to live with her husband's family, spending the wedding night in the *bale gedong*.

All this can be devastatingly expensive. A much cheaper, and more widespread solution is *ngorod*, marriage by elopement. When a couple, after their secret trysts, decide they want to get married, the man, usually with the help of his friends, will arrange to carry off his bride to some hideaway. When this information is leaked to the parents of the bride, there will be uproar; even if they know exactly what is going on, they have to display the greatest disapproval. After one night of elopement, the couple will be discovered, the families placated (one hopes) and the marriage sealed by a temple ceremony. It is a wonderfully Balinese solution: highly dramatic and entirely practical. Subsequent to the marriage, the couple will usually have the Balinese 'honeymoon', when they stay together undisturbed for a week in a quiet place, brought food by family and friends so they do not even need to go out to eat.

These days men will have only one wife, or at least one official wife, although polygamy was widely practised until a quarter of a century ago. You will come across old people with polygamous marriages, and hear of other, younger families where polygamy is clearly being practised in an informal way. Divorce is simple, handled by the local *banjar*; the woman returns to her parental home, leaving any children in the care of her husband's family. It is rare, and the ease of divorce is more an acknowledgement that some marriages become intolerable for both parties.

In making love, the Balinese are no doubt as diverse as any other race, but they are characteristically precise, fastidious, graceful, effortless and demanding. In a film shown in Bali about the life of Matahari, the beautiful woman spy born in Java, there was a scene in which a fat German diplomat makes love to the heroine. Often scenes involving sex are greeted with silent fascination, but the unfortunate German's efforts, his noisy protestations of passion and lumbering sexuality were greeted with screams of laughter and hoots of derision by the young male audience. The scene was just about as far as you could get from the silent and elegant erotic style of the Balinese.

The Bonds of Community: *Banjar* and *Adat*

Within each village, *desa*, are a number of smaller communities which make up the basic unit of Balinese life—the *banjar*s. In many respects the *banjar* is more important even than the family in maintaining the continuity of Balinese life.

The *banjar*s are run by a large representative committee of young adults, who will join either on marriage, or on the birth of their first child, at which point their parents will step back. Men, women and children are considered to be members of the *banjar*, but usually only husbands attend the meetings. There are elected officials, but decisions are taken by consensus. The visible life of the *banjar* revolves round the *banjar bale* (community building) and the village temples. Meetings are normally held once every 35 days or so to discuss the full range of issues affecting the community: building, planning, education, police matters, relations with other administrative bodies, the schedule of temple ceremonies and cock fights, the work of the *gamelan*, and problems affecting individuals and families.

Within the *banjar* countless different groupings operate: clubs or associations called *sakehe* based on age, sex, kinship, caste or social interests. An important one is the *sakehe teruna*, the youth club. Any new fad, such as a new dance or pastime, is likely to become the focus of a group of like-minded people. Because of the looseness and diversity of the groupings, everyone has a chance to shine at something, to make a valued contribution and earn respect and status. No doubt the endless possibilities for social recognition are part of the secret of success of the *banjar*. Little emphasis, however, is placed on individual achievement: people are much more concerned with the status of the *banjar* as a whole, and there is lively competition between *banjar*s.

It is remarkable that even the wildest youths are not rejected by their communities. Social commitments are expected of them just like anyone else, and they honour them, but there is no attempt to impose the sort of tight control of dress or behaviour or personal inclinations that typify the Western 'generation gap'. On a personal level there seems to be a kind of enjoyment of differences and good humour in the face of idiosyncracies. Everything is commented on, in the most personal terms, but nothing that does not endanger the life of the community or threaten its religious rituals is actually forbidden.

The deliberations of the *banjar* and the code of behaviour within the community are governed by *adat*—traditional and social laws which have been inherited and passed down through centuries of relatively undisturbed community life.

Adat varies in detail from village to village, though the essence is recognized throughout Bali. The laws are written down in old *lontar* leaf books and often stored in the *pura desa*, the central village temple, in the safekeeping of a specially appointed *banjar* member.

Adat dictates the offerings, clothing, prayers, timing and basic organization for every kind of temple or life-cycle ceremony. It determines the way the *banjar* operates—who meets when and for what purpose. It determines the distribution of labour in the village. It affects the ways in which people relate to each other, what happens when an offence is committed by one member of the *banjar* against another, or by a member against the community as a whole. It is a powerful force in Balinese life, in many ways more powerful than civil law. Like civil law, *adat* prescribes the means to punish misdemeanour, but it also provides a firm code of behaviour and, by appealing to the cohesive instincts of the community, seems to contain anti-social behaviour in a way that civil law cannot.

Rice

For over two thousand years, the exceptional fertility of Bali's volcanic soil has provided at least two abundant rice harvests a year, establishing a strong economic base as well as comfortable leisure hours during periods between planting and harvesting. The combination of stable communal life, economic assurance and leisure has allowed the Balinese to develop their exceptional creative gifts.

Rice is the single most important product of Bali, although in fact it only accounts for a quarter of the land under cultivation. The glorious rice terraces (*sawahs*) which are such a spectacular feature of the southern foothills produce abundant crops of wet rice, but a fair amount of dry rice is grown in the north of the island where rainfall and water supply is sporadic. The Indonesians have three separate words for rice: *padi* while it is in the field (hence our term 'paddy fields'); harvested rice is called *beras*; and cooked rice is *nasi*.

Rice terraces in Bali are usually ploughed by hand, or with ploughs pulled by yoked oxen. Farm machinery is virtually unknown. Wet rice is grown from seed in the corner of the flooded paddy; later the seedlings will be transferred (by men) and planted in neat rows in calf-deep water and mud. The terrace will remain flooded until the rice grain matures, whereupon it will be drained to allow the rice to ripen, then harvested by men and women together, threshed to remove the outer husks, and stored—traditionally in the tall thatched houses called *lumbung padi* which have now proved a popular design for hotel accommodation.

101

Each rice field, or group of fields has its own shrine, and all parts of the cycle of cultivation are marked by ceremony and offerings, normally to the rice goddess, Dewi Sri. She is associated with the doll-like figure—usually of woven palmleaf—called *cili*, an ancient fertility symbol that predates Balinese Hinduism. Throughout the process, rice is addressed as if it were a woman, becoming pregnant and giving birth.

Imagine a river travelling downstream from its mountain source, gathering in size as tributaries feed into it, but in turn being tapped to water fields in the valleys through which it flows, periodically dammed and diverted to feed large-scale irrigation schemes, sometimes via an extensive system of tunnels. In its progress towards the sea, more and more communities become dependent on the management of its water at higher levels: misplaced water diversion at one level, accidental or malicious, can severely affect the crops and livelihood of communities at all lower levels. Since farmers can now harvest three crops a year in Bali, regardless of the season, and paddies have to be flooded at planting, it is essential that everyone using the same water source is not planting at the same time. Suddenly you become aware of the immense complexities of water management that belie the tranquil terraces.

The traditional organization responsible for the water distribution in each rice-growing community is known as the *subak*, or rice council, which operates alongside, but separate from, the *banjar*, and is led by a specially elected *klian subak*. Anyone who has land under rice cultivation within the boundaries of the *subak* will be a member of the organization; the areas encompassed by individual *subak*s vary enormously, but the average is around 100 hectares (247 acres). *Subak*s make sure that water within their zone is properly distributed—it is said that farmers with terraces at the foot of the hill make the best *klian*s! They must also look after the *subak* temples and ensure that the correct devotions are paid to the main temple at the head of the irrigation system—usually the lakeside temples are named after the god of the lake, Dewa Ulun Danu. Each *subak* in turn belongs to a larger co-ordinating body called a *sedehan*.

This structure of organizations depends on the age-old traditions of consultation and deliberation. Priests play a key role in decision-making, consulting their charts to discover favourable times for any critical adjustments to water distribution. A recent project undertaken by the University of Southern California has attempted to record the system on computer in order to preserve the pattern of decision making for posterity. It proved no easy task.

The reason why the University of Southern California undertook this project is unsettling: Bali's rice production has started to show the adverse affects of using 'miracle rice', the banner of the 'Green Revolution', which allows farmers to produce three harvests instead of two.

There is no doubt that 'miracle rice' has gone a long way to solving Asia's food problems. It is a short-stalk, high-yield rice, but unfortunately is not resistant to pests. The result has been an increasing use of pesticides, which provide only a short-term solution: pests become resistant by natural selection—those that can survive are those that reproduce. Furthermore, pesticides will kill the natural predators of harmful pests, and begin to erode a whole ecological stratum. They kill the insects which frogs and eels eat, which in turn are not only a source of protein, but help to maintain the food cycle that keeps the rice-paddies fertile.

By 1987 Indonesian rice farmers were encountering problems with pests that they had never experienced before. The ecological checks and balances that had protected their crops from the extreme ravages of pests had been broken down. Indonesia banned 57 out of 66 listed pesticides and introduced a campaign of 'integrated pest management'—selective spraying aimed at killing only the most damaging pests. This campaign was launched in the face of immense pressure exerted by the multi-national chemical manufacturers who continued to promote the benefits of pesticides for the sake of high yields, regardless of the cost to the environment, or to the health of farmers who use them.

This dilemma continues in Bali, where high yields are useful for export, although Bali has nearly always produced enough rice for its own needs. Any Balinese will state that the best rice comes from Bali, meaning the old Balinese rice, with its two harvests a year, still grown for its high quality. The 'miracle rice' is universally dismissed as inferior.

Caste

All Hindus inherit the caste of their parents. It is a class system ordained by the gods, ancient and unchanging.

There are four castes; the heirarchy owes its origin to the court structure of old. The highest is Brahmana, the priestly caste, from whose ranks come the high priests (the *pedanda*s) to this day; in the past Brahmanas were also the *kerta*s or judges, and the scholars. The next caste is Ksatria, the ruling caste. Third come the Wesias, the warrior caste. These three highest castes are known collectively as the 'Triwangsa'. In Bali members of the Triwangsa are considered to be nobler, wiser and purer, are expected to be better educated and have better manners, and are treated as persons of higher status than the ordinary low-caste people. The Triwangsa represents a mere 10% of the Hindu population of Bali. The remainder are Sudra, the fourth caste (there are no 'Untouchables').

Many customs still observed in Bali underpin the status quo of the caste system. First, there is the stratified Balinese language, which provides a framework for the correct way to address people of superior or inferior caste (see pp.35–36). In general, high is holy, so a Brahmana will sit higher than a member of a lower caste—a practical consideration when much sitting is done on verandahs, or on the edge of them. Low-caste people today still feel uncomfortable sitting higher than a caste superior and rush to sit on the floor. Ordinary people are very polite to the Triwangsa 'aristocracy', and give them a great deal of respect, even when their behaviour little merits it.

The taboos surrounding marriage between the castes still remain fairly powerful. A girl who marries below her caste will henceforth be treated as an inferior even by her parents, and expected to address her mother, for example, only in formal terms from then on. Her mother may not visit her, or treat her in any way as her daughter. This at least is the principal, but of course it is impossible to find out how rigidly in practice these taboos are carried out, and how mother and daughter behave together in private.

The 'aristocracy' have always lived a little to one side of the life of the main village community: there are certain roles in the *banjar* and in ceremonies, for example, which traditional practice forbids them from playing. They receive a show of respect, but have no power; they have grandiose ideas about their importance with little to back them up.

Sometimes caste goes with land and money and social power, and higher castes do tend to get better jobs. But high caste is no guarantee of income and many high-caste people do ordinary, menial jobs just like their low-caste neighbours. In such circumstances the most sensible and adaptable of them get on with the practical business of earning a living without too many illusions of their importance; others are hampered by the feeling that their world owes them something more, and that they should not have to dirty their graceful hands with the lowly details of business.

I am Number One

Bali's system of personal names is at one level extremely simple, and on another immensely complex, and at all levels quite unlike ours.

Most children—that is to say Sudra children, as well as Wesias—are named quite simply according to their position in the family, whether boy or girl: Wayan is the first born, Made the second born, Nyoman the third, and Ketut the fourth. If there are more than four children (a rare occurrence now since family planning is widely practised) the cycle begins again and the fifth child is called Wayan. Ksatria children may be named in the same way but the first born will be called Putu, or sometimes Gede, although low-caste families sometimes adopt this practice nowadays.

The Brahmanas and Ksatrias also have titles that distinguish their caste. Brahmanas tend to be called Ida Bagus (men) and Ida Ayu (women). Upper-crust Ksatrias have a wide range of names, which owe their origin to the complexities of caste within the multiple marriages of the rajas of old. The children of each of the many wives of a raja might have a different title, to indicate the caste and rank of the wife. For example, the highest Ksatria title, Anak Agung, went only to the first-born son of the most senior raja, the inheritor of the kingdom, and the child of the first wife of equal rank to the raja. The children of other high-ranking wives might be called Cokorda, while the children of low-caste wives would only have the title Dewa. Ratu and Ngurah are other Ksatria names.

Most of the Wesia caste come from a division known as the 'Pregustis', in which both men and women have the title Gusti. There are other names which indicate social standing: for example, Jero is someone who lives inside (*jero*) the palace, i.e. a commoner who has risen in social status, usually by marriage.

The prefix 'I', as in 'I Gusti', is just a mild honorific meaning something like 'Mr'. Sudra women are sometimes addressed by the female equivalent, 'Ni'.

Other names are chosen by individuals for themselves when they reach a certain age. Such names may have a religious significance, be an indication of temperament or aspiration, or simply be governed by current fashions: among the Ksatrias, for example, it is currently popular to choose a name for something in the elevated world of the sky, such as Rate (Balinese for moon), Kartika (star) or Suarsana (heaven or 'atmosphere'). Other popular names among the Triwangsa are Raka and Rai, Agung and Alit, meaning the elder and the younger (or smaller) in both cases.

There is no such thing as a family name, and women do not take their husband's name on marriage. Parents are sometimes called by a teknonym, that is to say, they become called 'mother/father of the child'—for example 'Ibu Dewi', mother of Dewi.

Names given by the family in recognition of circumstances of birth or early characteristics often stick into adulthood. We know of a Ketut Jangling, the 'fourth born child who cries when he is put down'; a Keplag, meaning 'bursts or explodes'; a Kari, 'the living one' (the survivor in a family in which many children died); and even a Kutang, the Balinese for bra, who always played with his mother's bra when he was a child. The new-born daughter of a friend of ours is called Sigma Wati, because she came into the world in a Sigma car held up in traffic on the way to the hospital.

If the system seems confusing, bear in mind that it was forged in a bygone eras when everyone was known to the community; no formal system of registration existed until the 1950s. When compulsory schooling was introduced there was no means of telling the age of a child, and parents were often extremely vague about this. (Even today birthdays are known by the Balinese calendar rather than the Western one, and have little significance even if they are known.) Children were sent to school when they were able to reach over their head to touch the lobe of their opposite ear.

The *Dukun*

Once, on arriving late at a village on the eve of a big cremation ceremony, we were unable to find any place to stay. All the *losmens* were packed like a Balinese bat cave, with no inch of space let alone two rooms to rent. Most families were playing host to relatives from other villages. Finally friends intervened to find us accommodation at the house of the local *dukun*, or 'native doctor'. For reasons we did not understand at the time, there were two rooms there miraculously empty.

Early the next morning, just after sunrise, we were woken by howls and moans from the verandah outside. A crowd of more than twenty people had gathered in the courtyard, mostly sitting in a circle around one woman who seemed to be struggling with our *dukun* landlord. We learned that she had been brought to the *dukun* by this crowd of family and relations because she was possessed. The family were required to be present during treatment, as part of the healing process; sometimes some of them joined her in a litany of cries and moans and shrieks. Contrary to appearances, they assured us, the woman was not in any physical pain: it was only the struggle of the bad spirits which possessed her that made her cry out. It transpired that we were occupying the *dukun*'s consulting rooms, not normally let out to guests, and considered spooky by other Balinese.

A *dukun* (or *balian* in Indonesian) practises his art according to ancient wisdom, recorded in *lontar* books and handed down from father to son. The ownership of such treasured old books and their skills in dealing with the bad spirits which cause disease and other human misfortune can give *dukun*s considerable standing in the community.

But there are all kinds of *dukun*s, with different levels of social standing. Some seem little better than soothsayers and peddlers of arcane charms and brews, who appear at times of festivals to spread their wares on the ground and mutter chants. There are women *dukun*s as well as men, but more often you will see women in the role of assistants.

Some *dukun*s acquire a reputation for practising black magic, or dealing with what the Indonesians call *guna-guna*—love magic. They have spells and charms to make people fall in love, to make lovers faithful, and so forth. Those who deal in spells of this kind seem generally to be feared and mistrusted by the rest of the village. When we visited one such *dukun*, he denied any truck with black magic, though all his neighbours insisted he dealt in spells, some of them harmful, which he would sell for a price. However, he was eager to show us his *lontar* books containing details of his love spells and potions and he also produced a book of glowing letters of thanks from grateful Westerners who had apparently benefited from his intervention.

*Dukun*s who practise strictly as doctors, prescribing herbal and animal remedies according to the old books are apparently not as popular as before, although many people will consult them for ailments that fall beyond the pale of clinical medicine. Such *dukun*s use a mixture of practical healing, diet and herbal treatment, religious observance and symbolic gestures. There are remedies for everything, from special diets to promote fertility, or concoctions of fresh bat's blood for asthma sufferers, to the claws of a bird that catches snakes as an antidote to snake bite. A common technique of the *dukun* is to chew herbs, and then spit the masticated pulp on to the patient. We have heard several reports of the efficacy of this treatment. His version of a little black bag will contain holy water, incense (*dupa*), a sacred *kris*, the twigs and leaves of the sacred *dapdap* tree. Mostly their practices are not nearly so obscure or mystifying as the old term 'witchdoctor' suggests. Many Balinese still study, at least for a while, with a *dukun*, to learn a kind of First Aid for physical, emotional and spiritual well-being. Mind and body are not held to be divided and compartmentalized as they are in the Western medical practice. *Dukun* and priest and doctor may all be consulted to find the root of an ailment. An Australian friend of ours was referred by his *dukun* to a specialist doctor. One assumes though that doctors are not so ready to acknowledge the limits of their powers as to refer their patients to a *dukun*.

Leyaks

There is only one way to be sure of seeing a *leyak*: you stand naked in a cemetery at night, bend over and look between your legs. But you might see one by chance in the form of a beautiful girl alone on a remote road at night, or as dancing balls of green light hovering eerily over the rice field; or as a hen in a deserted dwelling after nightfall. Be wary: your life may be in danger.

This, at least is what almost all Balinese believe, for *leyak*s are evil, malevolent spirits and may bring misfortune or illness to their intended victims. Witches and other practitioners of black magic can turn themselves into *leyak*s, and *leyak*s may possess the body of a villager who then becomes their agent. There are many *leyak*s around, always ready to play little tricks when your back is turned, like sending a pan clattering to the floor to remind you of their presence. Ask any Balinese—any but a practitioner of the black arts, who is pledged to deny that *leyak*s exist. It is the Balinese Catch 22: the very denial of *leyak*s is sure proof that an individual practices black magic.

Cemeteries, crossroads, hairpin bends, bridges, the confluences of rivers, deserted beaches, banyan and kepuh trees, houses abandoned because of spiritual disturbances or 'hotness'—all are the traditional haunts of *leyak*s, where drivers and passers-by will utter prayers to request a safe passage. It is possible to strike a bargain with the *leyak*: 'leave me in peace while I complete such and such a project, then you can take my soul'. Gossip will soon pick out the man who consistently delays completing his house, an irrigation channel, marrying.

You may not come across a *leyak*, and they do not crop up in casual conversation. But you may see the image of the Queen of the *leyak*s, the terrifying fanged witch with her wild tresses of hair, pendulous dugs, and huge, rattling fingernails. This is Rangda, the embodiment of evil, who grapples with the Barong, the good dragon, in the famous Barong dances. Even in the performances of this dance staged in the international hotels, she can send a chill through the tropical night.

Making a date in Bali

The Balinese calendar is a mechanism of amazing complexity. The coloured versions (called *tika*), with their neat lines, triangles and diagonals, look something like a flattened Rubik's cube and are just about as boggling. This represents the *pawukon* calendar, which is used to calculate auspicious days.

A year in the *pawukon* calendar is 210 days long and contains 30 seven-day weeks or *wuku*, each with a name: Sinta, Landep, Ukir and so forth. These are divided into cycles of six weeks each called *inkel*, Wong, Sato, Mina, Manuk, Taru and Buku, which have specific devotional connotations.

Each of the days of this seven-day week has a name: Redite is our equivalent of Sunday, followed by Soma, Anggara, Buda, Wrehaspati, Sukra and Sanescara. That is the easy part. Each of these days has at least ten other names, for running concurrently with the seven-day week are weeks of ten days, nine days, eight days and so on, down to a 'week' of one day. To take an example, Tuesday 3 January 1989 was Anggara in the seven-day week, but also Menga in the two-day week, Kajeng in the three-day week, Sri in the four-day week, Umanis in the five-day week, Urukung in the six-day week, Ludra in the eight-day week, Brahma in the nine-day week.

Why do the Balinese do this to themselves? The answer is they don't, really. They leave the calendar to the priests and the *dukun*s whose job is to work out auspicious conjunctions of the weeks. Any event, from temple ceremonies to blessings, from the start of a journey to laying the foundations of a house or opening a business should be undertaken on an auspicious day, and this usually means when a good day from one kind of week coincides with a good day from another. A frequently occurring auspicious day, particularly for offerings to placate the malevolent spirits is Kajeng-Kliwon, when Kliwon in the five-day week falls on Kajeng of the three-day week—thus every 15 days. Another occurs when Kliwon coincides with Anggara of the seven-day week. Yet more auspicious days will be signalled by the conjunction of good days from three different weeks on the same day.

The *odalan* ceremonies which take place in every temple every 210 days are fixed by the same calendar. Thus the *odalan* of Pura Luhur at Batukau is Anggara Kliwon Medangsia, in other words, the day when Anggara (Tuesday) coincides with Kliwon (of the five day week) in the week called Medangsia. Markets take place every three days in Bali, which will seem odd in terms of the seven-day week, but makes perfect sense when you know that they operate according to the three-day week.

But it gets yet more complex. Bali also uses another calendar, called *saka* (or *çaka*) which has ancient origins in Southern India. This is a lunar calendar in that it contains twelve months that begin and end with the new moon (in principle). This calendar is used to calculate the correct timing of a number of religious ceremonies, including the new year, Nyepi, and any that should be held on or around the new moon *tilem*, or the full moon *purnama*. There are 30 days in every month, each with a separate name such as Hari Ikan ('fish day') and Hari Kelapa ('coconut day'); and there are twelve months in the year, Jie Gwee, Sha Gwee, Sie Gwee etc.

The moon, however, is not so compliant: it only takes $29^1/_2$ days to complete its cycle, so in order not to get out of kilter, every 63 days is a double day, into which two lunar days are slotted—in other words, there are 29 days in some months. The proper lunar year is actually about 354 days long. The Western Gregorian calendar of 365 days is a solar one, which has the advantage of coinciding with the changing seasons. Strict lunar calendars will not follow seasons; because they fall a dozen or so days short of the solar year, the months gradually move backwards through the seasons. This is the case with the Muslim calendar. In Bali, however, the lunar calendar is adjusted to keep in step with the seasons, and once every three or four years an extra month is added to put the lunar calendar back in line. Thus Nyepi will always fall in or around our month of March. The Gregorian year 1990 is 1912 in the *saka* calendar.

The Balinese also use the Gregorian calendar for official business. How can anyone keep track of it all? Well, you purchase one of the intricate calendars produced and printed in Bali which show not only the Gregorian Calendar in English, but the *pawukon* and *saka* weeks and days, not to mention Indonesian, Muslim, Chinese and Japanese days, and give lists of all the major celebrations in Bali. Have a look at one and see what you can devise; we have provided the names of the different categories of days, weeks and months not to confuse, but to help you decipher this splendid puzzle.

Tumpek Landep: the Day of the Motorbike

Do not be curt with the owner of your hired car or motorbike when he suddenly insists with mysterious agitation that you return your vehicle for the day. He is not trying to cheat you; he may just be too shy to tell you that on this one day of the Balinese calendar his vehicle must be treated with the care and affection usually lavished on a pet fighting cock. It will be cleaned and polished, inside and out, decorated with offerings and blessed by the local *pemangku* (priest), and then returned to you still adorned with bits of rice and palm leaf and flower petals, and certainly twice as efficient as it was before. It is the Balinese equivalent of a suburban Sunday.

Tumpek Landep is the day on which all things metal are honoured, not just cars and bikes but also *kris*es and knives and metal tools of all kinds. There are numerous such days in the Balinese calendar, each honouring the very existence of the things that surround us, animate and inanimate alike. Tumpek Kandang honours animals; Tumpek Uduh, plants, vegetables and fruits; Tumpek Wayang, the theatre.

Tumpek always falls on a Saturday, for a Tumpek day is when Kliwon of the five-day week coincides with Saniscara (Saturday) of the seven-day week, thus once every 35 days.

Cockfighting

You can feel the atmosphere a mile off: the rest of the village is strangely deserted. Around the cockpit, be it permanent or makeshift, is a great press of men and boys, huddled in tense anticipation. On the peripheries are women selling fruit and snacks.

The roosters are passed from hand to hand, discussed with nods and undertones in a subdued hush. Then the pair for the next fight is chosen, and while long and vicious metal spurs are attached to their rear talons the bidding gets under way, rising to a furious crescendo as promises of money are called out, accepted or rejected. Then suddenly everything goes quiet and the fight begins.

It may be over in seconds, with a deadly flash of spurs to the head, dismissing the loser to the stockpot. Or it may drag on for minutes, increasingly bloody and agonizing, until one cock gets the upper hand. Until the final blow, nothing is decided.

If the contestants last long enough, fights will last five rounds—traditionally timed by a coconut shell with a hole in the bottom which gradually sinks in a container of water. But in many cock fights the rounds last as long as the cocks remain in the ring, and only come to a close if one escapes or is despatched to his maker. If there is no conclusion after five rounds, the contest is declared a draw.

At official cock fights there will be a formal bookie who levies a 10% tax on winnings: most betting, however, will be done on an informal basis, between individuals. It is said that vast sums of money are lost to cockfights—tales of men who have wagered away all their possessions in a single afternoon and ruined themselves and their family. Such excesses may be a thing of the past, but considerable sums do change hands on these occasions. This is the main reason why cockfighting is officially banned throughout Indonesia. But an exception is made in Bali because it is a sacred pursuit; in principle at least, cockfights are permitted if they are attached to a religious ceremony. The spilling of blood is considered a necessary ritual to appease bad spirits. But enthusiasm for cockfights seems to outstrip even the Balinese enthusiasm for ceremonies. The alibis can be tenuous, which explains why cock fights often take place in a distinctly furtive atmosphere.

There is nothing furtive about the ownership of fighting cocks, however. Everywhere you go in Bali, from the airport and Denpasar to a remote village, you will see the large bell-shaped bamboo cages in which cocks are put to pass the time of day and watch the local goings-on. It is not good for them to be bored: they need interest and stimulation. Men, in their idle hours, which can be many, will sit holding a bird tenderly, caressing its feathers and massaging its sinews. And sometimes you may see a man on a motorbike, and slung over his shoulder a tiny rattan basket with just the tail plumage of a fighting cock protruding—on their way to augment the family savings, or to appease the bad spirits.

When there is no cockfight in the offing, there can always be a cricket fight. Men and boys of all ages nurture crickets at home in net-like tubes of plaited bamboo. For the fight two tubes are put together to form a corridor. To win, a cricket must kill its opponent, or force it back to the end of the corridor. Here again, serious money changes hands.

Tourism

The volume of tourists visiting Bali is currently increasing at about 15% or more per annum, giving rise to the projection that 1,000,000 foreign visitors will come to Bali each year by the early 1990s. The average stay is 10.8 days; the longest stayers are Australian and European, the shortest the Japanese, many of whom come for a mere two or three days. Tourists spend on average $75 US per person per day.

Bali is under pressure. Visitors want increasingly high standards of accommodation, service, transport, facilities—and in increasing numbers. Having created this appetite, Bali cannot now turn the clocks back: it has to meet this growing market with yet more hotels, new developments, new roads. Can it survive?

People have been predicting the corruption of Bali for many years now, and those who return here after, say, 20 years can no doubt have their prejudices confirmed. Mainly by dint of tourism, Bali has become if not rich, then at least comfortable. The island is changing rapidly, and is now toying with all the usual benefits and detritus of Western materialism. What place in the world was not more lovely in the soft focus of the past?

Yet the surprising thing about the Balinese is how underwhelmed they are by it all. The greater world outside inspires more curiosity than envy. The wealth from tourism may provide television sets, or even a new car, but equally it can fund a new *gamelan* orchestra, or a new dance troupe, or a yet more lavish cremation. Dancing, painting, woodcarving are now flourishing with renewed vigour under the patronage of tourism.

The development of tourism in Bali is carefully monitored and controlled by a specially created government agency called Diparda, which is keenly aware of the dilemmas that tourism poses. On the one hand, they must provide beds and facilities to satisfy the ever-growing market; on the other, they know that people come to Bali to enjoy the richness of its culture, as well as the easy-going atmosphere created by the personal style of accommodation. Allow this to be swamped by mass tourism, and Bali will lose its individuality and become just another 'Island in the sun'.

A number of new sites have been earmarked for tourist development: Jimbaran, Tanah Lot, Padangbai. To those who know these places now, tranquil, uncluttered havens, the very suggestion inspires gloom. But the intention is to keep these new developments low-key, like Sanur, with traditional Balinese-style accommodation in the mid-price range. The super-de luxe international 'palaces' will, for the time being, remain in Nusa Dua.

The Balinese see tourism as opportunity—lucrative, frustrating, invasive, hilarious—and accept philosophically that there is no good without evil.

Part IV

RELIGION, FESTIVALS, MUSIC AND DANCE

Sanghyang Widi Wasa, the supreme god

Balinese Hinduism

Balinese religious ceremonies must be among the most joyful and beautiful in the world. An ordinary village temple ceremony will greet the eye with massive banks of specially prepared temple offerings—ordered stacks of fruit, coloured rice-cakes and fresh flowers. The air will be full of the heady perfume of incense, frangipani and *cempaka* blossom, of fruit and the smoke of the little stalls outside the temple selling *sate* and other snacks. The villagers will be dressed in their finest clothes—a moving tapestry of pink, gold, green and sky blue. The tinkling and crashing of the *gamelan* orchestra provides a backdrop to the quiet, restrained chatter. Children hover in barely suppressed excitement. Later, as the night draws on, there may be dancing, or a dance-drama, performed to rigorous standards.

For the ordinary Balinese, the key to religion is participation. The world is inhabited by a bewildering number of gods and spirits, some good, some bad, all of whom have their own intentions and aspirations which the layman can only guess at. There are the gods of the elements, fertility, harvest, welfare, knowledge; there are the spirits of the ancestors, the founding fathers of communities; there are the spirits which inhabit certain locations, and which animate all aspects of Nature; there are evil spirits which hover around the communities ready to do harm. Over the centuries ways have been devised to keep the gods and spirits happy. They have to be respected and honoured with

111

offerings and ceremonies lest they be offended and show it by bringing about misfortune. If the correct patterns of behaviour are observed, all should be well.

The Balinese do not question this. There are no protestations of faith, no real theological wrangles: this would be presumption about the world of the gods and spirits about which only the very few have real knowledge. The individual has an obligation to behave in the approved way before the gods and fellow human beings. Doing this satisfactorily can ensure the well-being of the community as a whole; it can also mean that after death, and after a proper cremation to release the soul to heaven, a person will be reincarnated in Bali, ideally as someone better, and within the same ancestral clan. A major slip-up in this life, however, could send you tumbling down the snakes and ladders of the afterworld to end up as a leech, or even a dog.

This system of beliefs clearly owes its origins to the rural communities that pre-date the arrival of Hinduism in this region. Hinduism has been grafted on to ancient practices of animism and ancestor worship, and is now firmly entwined with them, but has never supplanted them. At the apex of the Balinese religious hierarchy are the high priests, *pedanda*s, from the Brahmana caste. Through their rituals they provide the essential connection between Hindu cosmology and Bali's more local practices. Theirs is to a great extent a form of classical Hinduism, relating to Brahma, Vishnu and, in particular, Shiva.

Writers on Bali seem to be greatly concerned about whether the Balinese religion is or is not Hinduism. The Balinese practice of Hinduism certainly differs from that of India. Yet in India itself Hinduism is practised in many different ways; there is no such thing as a Hindu orthodoxy. The Balinese seem quite satisfied that their religion is Hindu: *agama* is the word for religion, and they describe theirs as *agama Hindu*. Some however qualify this as *agama Hindu Bali*.

Priests

High priests, *pedanda*s, are impressive characters who only really make themselves noticed at large ceremonies, particularly cremations. On such occasions, wearing be-jewelled mitres of various shapes and sizes, they sit cross-legged on a raised platform or *bale* and recite their *mantra*s—arcane chants in Sanskrit and old Javanese—ringing a small handbell and periodically distributing libations of holy water. All this will be totally ignored by the Balinese worshippers. They do not know what the *mantra*s mean, and have little inclination to find out. All that is important to them is that the prescribed rituals and chants are performed in the correct way.

Only members of the Brahmana caste can become *pedanda*s, and they are likely to come from families of priests. They undergo a rigorous training in all aspects of theology and ritual before being consecrated. They are usually married, and their wives will take an active role in their priestly duties as assistants, and sometimes as successors. Single women may also become *pedanda*s, but this is rare. Their duties are entirely spiritual, and to this degree they remain somewhat distanced from the rest of the community, living with their Brahmana families in a priest's compound or *griya*.

*Pedanda*s are on a direct line to god. Besides attending ceremonies, and their daily study of the scriptures, the most important role of the *pedanda*s is to provide holy water, which is an essential ingredient of almost any religious occasion. The water may come from a local spring, or special water considered particularly pure and effective may be collected from hallowed sources. But it only becomes holy water (*tirta* or *toya*) with the blessing of a priest. The *pedanda* will rise before dawn every day to begin the ritual of preparing holy water, which involves a long series of *mantras*, and prescribed gestures (*mudras*). During this process, the priest is said to invoke Shiva to the extent that he actually becomes one with Shiva. Some *pedandas* are not Shivaic, but Buddhist, but although their rituals are different the distinction goes virtually unremarked by the layman.

The village priest or *pemangku* is a far less lofty character, more the vicar of his flock, distinguished only by his white clothes and white *destar* (headdress). He is usually a Sudra, but may be of another caste. The primary task of the *pemangku* is to look after his temple, sweeping it and keeping it well maintained through all those idle days that separate the major ceremonies. Failure to look after a temple can invite the wrath of the gods, so it is a task undertaken with diligence.

The *pemangku* partakes in numerous ceremonies and rituals in everyday village life, and generally advises on spiritual matters, on questions about appropriate offerings and so forth. But his life becomes considerably more animated around the time of the *odalan*, the anniversary festival of his temple. He is the main co-ordinator of this event, organizing the disposition of offerings, the progress of events and the entertainment. The *pemangku*—often assisted by his wife—leads the worship, inviting the gods to come down from the mountains to occupy the various seats and shrines that have been prepared for them. He leads the supplications for blessings and showers the worshippers with the holy water collected from the *pedanda* (who does not officiate). If, during the ceremony, one of the worshippers falls into a trance, he will oversee the way that this is handled, calling in if necessary the village seers with known gifts in interpreting trance and guiding it; it is the *pemangku* who will help to bring the person out of the trance by sprinkling him or her with holy water.

There are a number of other priests, or priest-like figures, in the Balinese community who occupy various rungs on the hierarchy. There are *pedanda*-like priests called *sengguhu*, who are however non-Brahmana but, as adepts in Hindu rites, can perform certain functions such as exorcism or reading of the calendar to ascertain auspicious days.

Dalangs, the puppeteers of the *wayang* performances also have a religious role: these are Brahmana men who are entrusted with entertaining the gods with shadow-puppet performances at religious ceremonies. It is thought that the gods have no need for a screen, so the *wayang lemah* (puppet show for the gods) is performed in front of a string suspended between two branches of the holy *dadap* tree.

Lastly the *dukuns* have a kind of unofficial function as priests, widely consulted by the populace not only for medical matters, but also on spiritual questions, particularly to do with the making or breaking of spells.

The Gods

The Balinese only have one god, Tintiya (meaning 'he who cannot be imagined'), or Sanghyang Widi Wasa. This is one and the same as Brahman, the 'all-pervading, self-existent power', the universal principle. All the other gods are manifestations of this god.

This at least is the theological argument which leads to the conclusion that Hinduism is monotheistic—all of which would be academic in Bali were it not for the fact that the Indonesian constitution demands, in the first of the principles of Pancasila, 'Belief in one god', thus Bali can claim to pass muster.

Brahman has three primary manifestations: Brahma, the creator; Shiva, the destroyer (and the principle of regeneration); and Vishnu, the preserver. These three form the Trimurti or Trisakti (Trinity). Each of the Trinity has a variety of other forms, an associated animal or 'vehicle' to carry him about, and a consort. Thus Vishnu appears as Rama and Krishna; his vehicle is the Garuda (half man, half eagle); and his consort is Lakshmi, goddess of prosperity. Shiva rides on a bull; his consort is the beautiful Parvati, who in turn can manifest herself as the terrifying Durga. Shiva and Parvati have two children: one the elephant-headed Ganesha, the ever-popular god of 'right insight' and solver of difficulties; the other Karttikeya, the six-headed, six-armed god of war. Brahma's consort is Saraswati, goddess of learning, who rides a white swan.

The main elements of the Hindu pantheon make their appearance in Bali in some form or other. Ganesha, for example is found at the famous Goa Gajah cave near Peliatan; the phallic *lingam* symbol of Shiva will be found in many of the older temples; worship of the sun is interpreted as worship of Shiva, as Surya; Brahma, as the god of fire, is celebrated in kitchens; Durga is closely associated with the sorceress-figure Rangda; the great Hindu epics, the *Ramayana* and the *Mahabharata* feature prominently in dance, sculpture and painting. But although temples will be associated with these various gods, there are no temples devoted specifically to them: they appear almost incidentally.

A higher profile is given to the lesser gods, signalled by the title Batara, or Dewa (masculine) or Dewi (feminine). A very important goddess in Bali is Dewi Sri, goddess of rice and good fortune; her spouse is Dewa Sedana, god of welfare and prosperity. Dewi Melanting is the goddess of commerce and shopkeeping. Dewi Ratih is the goddess of the moon. Batara Baruna is the awesome god of the sea; Batara Yama is the judge in the kingdom of the dead, whose image is frequently used in the casting of spells. There are many more, including the innumerable deified ancestors, the nameless evil spirits called *buta*s and *kala*s who lurk in certain places, and the more nomadic, less substantial but equally feared *leyak*s, agents of witchcraft.

Temples

For most of the year, a Balinese temple (*pura*) is nothing but an empty stage. There may be a few prettily painted and gilded shrines, some fine carving, and usually a splendid split gate (*candi bentar*). There may be a fine view, or a mass of flowering trees. But generally, in the majority of temples there is little in the way of architecture, and little animation. These are not places of daily worship.

Come the temple festivals, however, they are transformed by a slowly building crescendo of activity into magical theatres. During these occasions the gods are invoked by the priests to come down from high and to occupy the places specially reserved for them. Entertainment is provided for the visiting gods by poetry, music and dancing; and

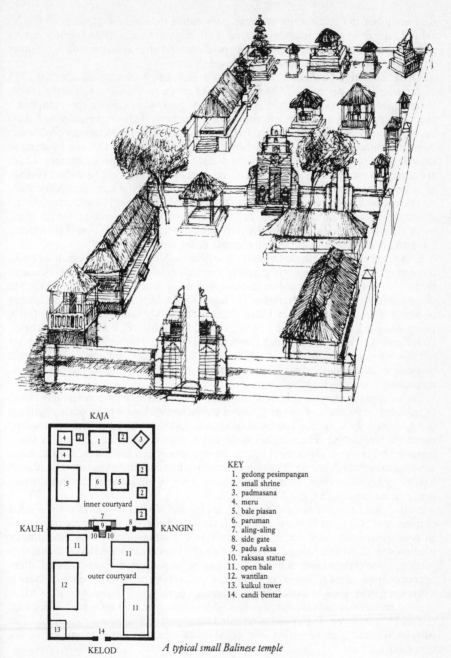

KAJA

KAUH

KANGIN

KELOD

inner courtyard

outer courtyard

KEY
1. gedong pesimpangan
2. small shrine
3. padmasana
4. meru
5. bale piasan
6. paruman
7. aling-aling
8. side gate
9. padu raksa
10. raksasa statue
11. open bale
12. wantilan
13. kulkul tower
14. candi bentar

A typical small Balinese temple

they are given the opportunity to speak their minds through the medium of trance. Within a day or so, the temples are cleared of offerings and decorations, the holy images and relics are returned to their little closed pavilions, and once again the temple becomes an empty theatre awaiting the next scheduled show.

There are said to be about 20,000 temples in Bali, a figure computed after the 1917 earthquake which destroyed 2,431 temples in an area covering one ninth of the island. Each village has at least three temples. There is the *pura puseh* in the *kaja* position; this is the 'temple of origin', devoted to the founding fathers of the community and their ancestral spirits. Near the middle of the village is the *pura desa*, the 'village temple', which may sometimes contain a *bale agung* where village meetings are held. At the *kelod* end of the village is the *pura dalem*, 'temple of the dead', often placed near the cemetery. There are also numerous temples devoted to the interests of, say, the rice farmers (*pura subak*), or to commerce (*pura melanting*). Other temples, especially the large and particularly revered, appear to occupy places that have traditionally been held to be sacred, be it a spring, or site of an historical event, or just a scene of particular beauty. Furthermore, every family compound will have its own shrine containing their own little shrines (*sanggah*), and devoted to the ancestral spirits of the family.

Some major temples are clan temples (*pura kawitan*), to which members of a certain division of a particular caste will gravitate, from all over the island. Mengwi is one of these. Yet others are major public temples, belonging to the whole island. These are sometimes called 'directional temples' (*kayangan jagat*) which are said to protect Bali and of which there are nine: Ulun Danu (Lake Batur) (N); Sambu (Mt Agung) (NE); Lempuyang (E); Goa Lawah (SE); Masceti (S); Ulu Watu (SW); Pura Luhur (Batukau) (W); Candi Kuning (NW); and in the centre is Besakih, the 'Mother Temple'. Selections of these are also called the 'Six World Temples' (*sad kayangan*), but quite which six will be listed will depend on where you are; others, such as Pura Pusering Jagat in Pejeng, may also get into this list of six.

Each temple is unique, although one can point to certain common features. Most temples are in the form of an open, walled compound divided into an outer courtyard (*jaba*), sometimes a middle courtyard (*jabo-jero*), and then the inner and most sacred courtyard (*jero-dalem*). The entrance to the outer courtyard is usually a split gate (*candi bentar*). This is one of Bali's most extraordinary architectural inventions; it looks like a tapering tower which has been split in two and pushed apart by supernatural forces. It has been given all kinds of interpretations, but in a way its want of a practical explanation is part of its power as a symbol.

Nearby, in one corner of the outer courtyard is a *kulkul* tower, an elevated open-sided pavilion containing one or two wooden bells (*kulkuls*) made of hollowed tree trunks and suspended vertically. These were traditionally used to summon villagers to a meeting or to sound the alarm if the village came under attack. They are still used today to summon participants to certain group activities—such as the preparation of temple feasts. Different codes are used for different occasions. For summoning to prayers at the *pura* there is a slow beat, then quick, then slow again, all lasting one minute. For emergencies, such as fire, the *kulkul* rings out with a strange rapid-fire clunking beat for one round of between one and two minutes. The round is repeated for a theft or if someone runs amok. The *kulkul* pitch can also be varied, for example, to signal to different groups of the community.

116

The outer courtyard will contain a number of plain, open pavilions, usually just roofs of *alang-alang* grass suspended over raised brickwork or concrete floors. These will be used for sheltering pilgrims at large festivals, or for preparing offerings. There may also be a *bale gong*, set aside for the *gamelan* orchestra during temple ceremonies. A very large open *bale*, called a *wantilan*, is used for dance and drama performances and cockfights. Often these covered spaces will be used for storing rice or fodder when there is no ceremony in the offing.

The entrance to the inner courtyard is usually a *padu raksa*, a tall ceremonial gateway, not split, with steps leading up to the door. On either side of the steps there are a couple of sneering bouncers with clubs (*raksasa*), whose job it is to ward off evil spirits. This also is the task of Boma, whose enraged face and claw-like hands appear over the doorway. Evil spirits which manage to bypass these and get through the door may be repulsed by an *aling-aling*, a wall around which you have to step to gain access to the inner courtyard. As is well known, evil spirits cannot negotiate right-angle turns, and so rebound into the hands of the *raksasa*s.

The inner courtyard contains the most important elements of the temple. There will be pavilions for offerings (*bale piasan*), a number of small shrines (*gedong*), reserved for certain gods during ceremonies, and which may or may not contain images or relics (many are empty); and there will be a principal shrine, the *gedong pesimpangan*. There will be a number of open *bale*s on which offerings are laid during ceremonies, some of which will have empty seats reserved for the gods.

Many temples will have at least one *meru*, sometimes a large number of them. These are the very distinctive, pagoda-like constructions which have a number of tiered roofs, tapering in size as they reach upwards. The roofs of these *meru*s are usually thatched in black sugar-palm fibre (*ijuk*), which is very durable, and which is only used for sacred buildings. *Meru*s are purely symbolic, said to represent the archetypal mountain of the gods, the Mahameru, and constructed in honour of the gods, and, by association, ancestral spirits and caste. There is always an odd number of roofs—three, five, seven, nine, eleven.

There may be a small stone niche reserved for Taksu, interpreter of the gods, who channels the words of the gods to the mouths of people in trance during ceremonies.

In the *kaja* position, nearest Mt Agung or another mountain peak, is the *padmasana*, the 'lotus throne', reserved for Surya the sun god (Shiva), or sometimes for Vishnu (identified by the presence of Garuda in the decorations) or sometimes for all the Trinity. This is a raised stone seat, upon which the god will be invited to sit during temple ceremonies. At the base of the *padmasana* is the 'World Turtle', Badawang, who is held in the clutches of two serpents (*naga*); on top of these rest representations of the world, with the sea, the earth and the sky, all surmounted by the throne. These characters all play a part in the Balinese creation myth: Badawang was created by the World Serpent, Antaboga, who founded the world through meditation, following which the world as we know it came about, supported on Badawang's back. This accounts for the turbulence of Bali's volcanic geography: the two *naga*s have a hard time keeping Badawang steady and every now and then their grip slips, resulting in an earthquake.

Offerings

No one really knows the origin of Bali's name, but in Indian as well as Balinese Hinduism *bali* means an offering of rice or grain to the gods and spirits. The coincidence is too obvious to ignore, for Bali is, above all, a land of offerings.

Their preparation is the province of women, who will spend a considerable part of their waking hours at this activity. Every day offerings are laid at the family temple, to trees and statues, to the rice fields. These will usually take the form of tiny baskets made of banana or palm leaf, which will contain some petals and a few grains of rice and be accompanied by a stick of incense; these are the *bali* or *wali*. Similar offerings called *segehan*—sometimes also containing meat, or betel nut, or other food—are prepared for the evil spirits and placed strategically on the ground, where the contents are usually snaffled up by the dogs. More substantial offerings of meat, especially chicken, are called *caru*.

Offerings of food for temple ceremonies take on more lavish proportions. The idea is that during the ceremony the gods will devour the essence of the food; after this it can be taken home and eaten by the family. The towering piles of fruit and cakes (*banten*) which the women carry on their heads to the temple are constructed to prescribed patterns. There are Brahmana women who specialize in this art and who lend advice to other women. The basic structure is a kind of scaffold of bamboo with horizontal sticks onto which fruit, cakes and fresh flowers are impaled. Coloured rice dough is used to make up large pictorial tableaux (*sarad*) containing faces, figurines and patterns, reminiscent of South American dough work. Offerings can take almost any form, and may well include skewered pieces of pork fat, smoked duck and other unattractive titbits.

Many offerings are purely decorative, such as the palm-leaf pendants. These will soon fade and eventually rot away—as with all temple offerings, the work that goes into them is for the moment only, not for posterity.

Animal sacrifice is still widely practised in Bali, especially for the New Year festival of Nyepi, and for major ceremonies such as the Eka Dasa Rudra at Besakih. It is considered necessary to spill blood to appease the evil spirits, and ducks, chickens, geese, cows and dogs are recruited for this purpose, as compensation for which they are assured of an improved lot when reincarnated in their next life.

Festivals

If there are 20,000 temples in Bali there will be at least 35,000 major temple festivals in every year of our calendar. Barely a day goes by when there is not something going on somewhere. The majority will be the anniversary festival which each temple holds once every Balinese year, called *odalan* (or *piodalan*), usually lasting three days. These are held primarily as an act of spiritual purification and renewal for the local village community, although the *odalan* of a large public temple, such as Pura Kehen in Bangli, will attract pilgrims from far and wide.

The *odalan* of any reasonably-sized temple is a fascinating and mysterious ceremony which continues well into the night. It is well worth the effort of seeking one out, but remember that nothing happens to a fixed schedule; *jam karet*, 'rubber time', applies.

For the correct way to dress when attending a temple ceremony, see pp. 51–52.

There are other major festivals throughout the year, each with its own distinctive flavour.

Nyepi

This usually occurs in March and is the celebration of the New Year of the *saka* (lunar) calendar. Purification is a key theme to all of Balinese temple ceremonies: Nyepi is the big spring-clean to get rid of evil spirits. Three days of joyous preparations precede it, culminating in Melis. Processions take temple artefacts to the sea or to springs to be purified. There are cockfights and other sacrifices which are then displayed on the ground where evil spirits lurk, such as crossroads. These festivities are designed to rouse the appetites of the evil spirits and tempt them out into the open, whereupon the *pedanda*s will exorcise them with powerful *mantra*s. Then, by flaming torch light, everyone turns out into the street to make a fearful din, clattering anything to hand, to frighten the weakened evil spirits away. Firecrackers explode; kids hurl burning coconut husks at each other. This is the moment when the *ogoh-ogoh* appear—vast monsters made of bamboo, papier-mâché and cloth, dragons, demons and all kinds of weird beasties—that are paraded around by the youth clubs that have constructed them.

The next day is a complete contrast; there is a deathly hush. People stay in their compounds, make as little noise as possible, should not light fires (even cigarettes) or cook, or do any work. This, apparently, will convince the evil spirits that the island has been deserted, that there is no more fun to be had, so they will up sticks and go. Clearly, not all are fooled by this, and will be back again for next year.

Galungan and Kuningan

Galungan is a ten-day festival, celebrating the victory of virtue (*dharma*) over evil (*adharma*), or—in similar vein—the victory of Indra over the evil Mahadanawa (see Tampaksiring, p.219). It is also a time when celebrants offer their thanks to the great god, Sanghyang Widi Wasa. Galungan starts on Buda-Kliwon Wuku Dungalan—the Wednesday in the eleventh week (Dungalan) of the *pawukon* (210-day) calendar.

Preparations begin seven days in advance, and are marked by the raising of long, curving bamboo poles (*penjor*) that line the villages, decorated with fruit and rice, and with palm-leaf ornaments dangling from the tip. On the day before Galungan scores of domestic animals are slaughtered as sacrifices and for the feasts.

Galungan is a time of particularly lavish offerings and celebrations at all temples and at family temples, during which the the deities and ancestral spirits descend to earth to be honoured. The eleventh day is Kuningan, the morning of which is devoted to honouring the ancestral spirits with food (particularly yellow rice) before giving them a good send-off, completing this run of ceremonies by dusk.

Other festivals

Saraswati is a day put aside each year to do honour to the goddess of that name, the goddess of knowledge and learning, and the creative arts. This is Saniscara Umanis

Watugunung—the Saturday in the 30th week (Watugunung) of the *pawukon* (210-day) calendar. Before dawn, *lontar* books as well as books of all kinds are taken out and dusted, and then gathered together in a place where rituals are performed by priests and *dukun*s in their honour. Schools and libraries, and many public offices are closed on that day.

Pagerwesi is a joyful celebration in honour of Batara Guru, one of the key Hindu gods in the creation myth, responsible for creating human beings in an acrimonious contest with Brahma. The name means 'iron fence' (against greed) and the celebration, particularly popular in the north of the island, is a kind of mental preparation held some nine weeks before Galungan.

There is one major non-religious festival in Bali: Independence Day, 17 August, which is a national holiday, marked by various civic parades, and only a little bit of religion.

Tooth-filing and cremation

Each stage of a Balinese person's life is marked by ritual: at various points of childhood, at puberty, marriage and death. Two rituals in particular arouse the fascination of the visitor: tooth-filing and cremation. Both of these are the focus of lavish preparation, and are used by the participating families to give clear signals of their status.

Tooth-filing

Tooth-filing is an important ritual in the lives of all Balinese. There is no fixed age for it, usually late adolescence: it depends when the money can be gathered together to mount a suitably impressive celebration to which family and clan will flock from far and wide. Because this can involve major expense, huge numbers of boys and girls from an extended family may be filed at a single ceremony.

Strictly, all Balinese people, men and women, should have their teeth filed before entering adult life and marriage. Those to be filed will undergo special preparation in the days before the event. Temporary *bale*s are built in the family compound for offerings, and there will be *gamelan* music and puppet shows throughout the preceding night.

The tooth-filing takes place around midday. Those to be filed, dressed in their finest clothes and wearing make-up (boys and girls), are borne aloft to the *bale gede*, where they lie on a cushioned bed. Surrounded by women singing wavering chants to the accompaniment of a small *gamelan* orchestra (the same that accompanies the *wayang* puppet shows), their teeth are filed with fairly crude metal rasps by men of the Brahmana caste, and polished with pumice and ointment. The extent of the dentistry depends upon the individual: it can be fairly lengthy and drastic, removing the points of the canine teeth and rendering the line of the upper teeth more or less straight. Others opt for a symbolic scrape of the file. From time to time the filee will peer into a little mirror to check progress. The filings are spat out into a coconut husk to be ritually disposed of.

It is said that tooth-filing, by flattening the six upper front teeth, symbolically prepares an individual for adulthood by removing six vices, the *sad ripu*: lust, greed, anger, confusion, jealousy and drunkenness. More literally, canine teeth are associated with demons and dogs, which might cause problems when an individual tries to pass through the gates of heaven. For this reason if anyone dies with his or her teeth yet unfiled, this will be done prior to burial or cremation.

You may well be invited to a tooth-filing ceremony, but remember that these are still private, family events and not tourist shows.

Cremation

Cremations are the most spectacular of all Balinese ceremonies. They usually involve massive preparations costing considerable fortunes, as a result of which very large ones are now comparatively rare. These days, when a great Balinese dignitary dies and a cremation is announced, telephone wires buzz across the oceans with the news, bringing tourists flocking with their cameras, making the event into something of an international media circus. Such cremations are open to all comers; they take place in the heat of the day and involve vigorous commotion—you need a certain amount of stamina to attend.

Cremation is a vital step in the Balinese and Hindu cycle of reincarnation. We are born into this world with a soul, *atman* which is a part of Brahman, the universal principle, and which is eternal. Thus when one dies, the *atman* continues to exist and will be born again as another being. The cycle of life and death (*samsara*) can only be broken by achieving *moksa*, the state of release, at which the *atman* is finally reunited with Brahman in a state of blissful enlightenment (*nirvana*). This is accomplished by a series of rebirths of progressive ascent, each stage of which is governed by *karma*, the principle of one's disposition that causes either progression in the cycle or regression.

Atman cannot be released from the human body except by the correct performance of cremation. Failure to do this means that the soul will be stuck on earth and frustrated, and will show this by bothering living relatives. In principle, therefore, all Balinese should be cremated. But because it is such an enormously expensive ceremony—if it is to be done properly, as it must be—only the most elevated in society, including all Brahmanas, are cremated immediately after death. The others are buried in a cemetery with modest ceremony, to wait until the family can afford a cremation, which may be up to ten or so years later, if at all. Every ten years there is a large ceremony at Besakih called Panca Wali Krama—and every 100 years an even greater one called Eka Desa Rudra—for which the whole island should be purified. This means emptying the cemeteries, and prior to these festivals there are widespread mass cremations for which families can club together to burn the bones of the dead in a comparatively modest way.

Because cremation is actually advancing the fortunes of the dead, the ceremony is accompanied by very little of the tearful distress of Western funerals; by contrast it is flamboyant and festive, although it would be wrong to suggest that members of the family are not upset by the death of the departed and the gap that will be left in their lives. Cremation is seen not only as a duty, but as the way in which children can repay their parents for all they have done for them.

Preparation for a cremation is an affair that calls upon the skills of the entire community, who will build the effigies and cremation tower out of bamboo, wood, paper and cloth over a period of 20 days, offering their services free. One of the family's most onerous and expensive duties, however, is to keep this task force fed during this period. A glittering effigy will be constructed to house the body. For Triwangsa cremations there will also be a tall, bamboo cremation tower, called a *wadah* or *bade*; as with *meru*s, the number of tiers will indicate the caste of the dead. Traditionally each caste has its own effigy: a black bull or a red lion for the Ksatrias; a white bull for Brahmanas and so forth. However, local practice varies enormously in all matters to do with cremations.

Accompanied by prescribed rituals, the body is wrapped in a shroud along with amulets and strings of *kepeng*s and placed in the *wadah*, which will by now be glamorously decorated and attached to a huge length of white cloth (to guide the soul). Both the *wadah* and the effigy are mounted onto large bamboo stretchers. These are picked up by teams of young men, and carried off to the cremation ground, at some distance in the *kelod* direction from the village. This is no mean task: priests and members of the family will be sitting at the top of the *wadah*, and there may even be a small *gamelan* orchestra and a puppeteer on the lower storeys. Added to this, it is necessary to confuse any evil spirits which might be following the procession, so the teams of bearers will charge this way and that, roaring and swirling about. The momentum of these great constructions can be awesome: bystanders should be very careful to keep out of their way.

At the cremation ground the body will be transferred to the effigy. A *pedanda* (or several *pedanda*s), in a specially built *bale* will be there to recite the necessary cremation *mantra*s and to sprinkle the holy water which is so vital to the purification of the dead. *Pemangku*s assist with the cremation itself. They will set fire to both the effigy and the *wadah* (often with the assistance of kerosene, or even flame-throwers), and both of these splendid constructions will be quickly consumed by a dramatic conflagration.

This actually reduces the human body to ashes: the body contains enough fat to cause it to burn intensely, like a candle. Bones will become brittle and powdery. Any remains are collected up carefully by the family, crushed in mortars, and then wrapped in cloth to look like small, doll-like effigies.

These remains are the focus of a subsequent ceremony, *nyekah*, held 12 or more days later. Now the family and the rest of community gather with their offerings to honour the dead and receive blessings; during this ceremony *mantra*s are recited by the *pedanda* to free the souls of the dead from their mortal coil. This can be a joyous celebration, with dancing, poetry, shadow puppets—and foodstalls, even small-scale gambling beyond the perimeter. After this the family must wait to see if there are signs that something was amiss at the cremation. If all is well, in another ceremony called *melasti*, the ashes will be taken to the sea or to a river where they will be scattered.

Music

How can the music of the Balinese *gamelan* orchestra be described in words? Its voices are so varied, from a rippling gaiety to a stately melancholy, from a soporific repetitiveness to vibrant electricity.

Gamelan (or *gambelan*) music is a complex tapestry of sound and rhythm, virtually without tunes as we would know them and yet with such a discipline of phrasing that the whole orchestra can stop and start with amazing synchronization. Some Western visitors never become attuned to it; most hear it as something alien, exotic and incomprehensible at first, but as it begins to form an integral part of the landscape of Bali it eases itself into their sub-conscious, gradually unfolding its beauty, beckoning.

The *gamelan* orchestra is composed primarily of instruments resembling a xylophone.

The keys are usually made of bronze, placed over bamboo resonators in an ordered scale on carved and decorated wooden mounts. Musicians sit cross-legged on the floor behind their instruments and strike the keys with a hammer held in the right hand, damping the sound with a touch of the left hand.

All *gamelan* orchestras are different, made as single units with their own unique sound. There are said to be 28 different kinds, but the most common form of metallophone *gamelan*, known as a *gong kebyar*, usually contains the following instruments. The *gansa*, which stands about knee height, has five thick keys giving a deep booming sound. The *gender*, a larger version of this, with 12 keys of a higher pitch, is the instrument that creates the basic melody. The distinctive *trompong*, very long and low, about the length of one and a half piano keyboards, consists of 10 large bell-shaped kettles that make a hollow, ringing sound, but which can also create a rushing, rippling sensation; because of its width it is often played by two people. There is a similar instrument with 12 kettles called a *reong*. There will usually be only one *trompong* and one *reong* in an orchestra, but there will be four or more *gender*s and *gangsa*s.

In addition to these, there will be the large *gong*, the origin of our word, plus one or two smaller ones. (The word *gong* is also used to refer to the whole of the *gamelan* orchestra.) There will be a couple of single bells, like those on the *trompong*, the larger one called a *kaja*, the smaller a *kienang*. There is also an instrument made up of a group of small, castanet-like bells, often mounted on an animal-shaped base; this gives off a scratchy, rattling sound, and is called, imitatively, *rincik* or *cengceng*.

Accompanying these metallophones are the all-important drums, the *kendang lanang* (the larger 'male' drum) and the *kendang wadon* (smaller, 'female'); these are long and thin, and played on their sides with a stick, the palm of the hand and fingers. The drummers are in effect the conductors, leading the rhythm. Certain performances also require a flute called a *suling*, which may have four, five or six holes, and which produces a high-pitched whining kind of melody. You may also see a *gamelan* accompanied by the simple string instrument called a *rebab*, which is played with a bow.

A similar kind of *gamelan* is called the *gong semar penulingan*, now something of a rarity,

A gangsa, one of the main instruments in the gamelan orchestra

123

and once associated with court love music. The *gong selunding* is composed of instruments with iron keys, which make a distinctive sound. A kind of xylophone with long keys of hollowed bamboo is called a *tengkleg*, and an orchestra of such instruments is called an *angklung kocok*. There are numerous local variations.

Gamelan music is serious business in Bali. There are many orchestras in the island; most *banjar*s will have their own and their regular practice sessions make this one of the most familiar sounds of the evening. Players start at a very young age; it is not unusual to see a child as young as four playing quite adeptly. The musicians are never professional; any income derived from playing to tourists in the hotels, for instance, is channelled back into their club funds. Almost all *gamelan* musicians are male, but there is a notable exception—an accomplished all-female orchestra in Ubud.

There is no written music; all the pieces are learnt by ear. Western musicians studying in Bali are always amazed at the musicians' ability to pick up new pieces and memorize them. The basic scale of *gamelan* music consists of five or seven notes spread over an octave, thus producing a series of notes that we cannot easily imitate on Western keyed instruments; nonetheless, *gamelan* music has had a profound effect on Western music since its first encounter, from Mahler to Philip Glass and Steve Reich. Generally Balinese musicians are not very interested in Western music. They seem to find the melody simplistic, and the rhythm, even of jazz, laughably primitive.

Dance and dance-drama

Balinese of all ages are quite exceptionally lithe and supple. There is no greater expression of this than their dancing. The traditions of Balinese dance derive directly from Hindu Java, and ultimately from India, a combination of temple and court dancing, rich in symbolic gesture. Bali's dance has developed its own particular style, criticized by the dance schools of southern Java as lacking refinement and composure—qualities that the Balinese seem glad to exchange for zest and joyousness.

Dancers begin their training at an early age, learning the exacting routines of the classic dances from attentive, tender but disciplinarian masters. The greatest of the Balinese dances is the *legong kraton* performed by girl dancers who should be no more than about 12 years old. After this, their bodies change and the magic is gone. Thus a girl's dancing career may well peak at this very young age; although there are many dances for older women, less glamour and status is attached to them. Male dancers also start young, but their career can last well into their twenties.

The real purpose of dance is to please the gods at temple ceremonies, and dancers at such performances will be under considerable pressure from their highly critical audience to perform well, for upon this may rest the welfare of the community. Certain dances also incorporate trance, a dramatic and chilling occurrence which can be seen as an important pressure valve in such a regulated society.

Dancing always has spiritual overtones, and is accompanied by ritual, even when the audience is entirely composed of pool-side diners. The dress is ornate, usually of gold-printed cloth; the flowers in the gold-painted leather crowns will be fresh. This does not mean that dance is always solemn. The Balinese love nothing so much as mimicry and pantomime, and there are a whole range of dance-dramas, including the famous Barong dance, parts of which will have the audience helpless with laughter, even in a temple ceremony.

There are many different kinds of dances in Bali, only a small percentage of which are presented in tourist performances, usually in specially adapted, abbreviated forms. We describe the most common of these below. With the patronage of tourism, dance is undergoing something of a renaissance and the two influential performing arts schools, KOKAR (high school level) and ASTI (academy level) in Batubulan, are constantly working on new ideas, some of which are every bit as delightful as the classic dances. Some years ago, there may have been justified fears that standards of dance were lapsing in the face of indifferent and uninformed tourist audiences: costumes became garish, the *gamelan* orchestras accompanying the dance became lacklustre, the dancing sloppy. There is some evidence that the tide has turned, and standards at many hotel performances can be very high indeed.

Legong Kraton

This, the most treasured dance of Bali, relates an episode from a tale said to date back to historical events of the 12th or 13th century, although the dance itself seems to have developed in the 19th century. First on stage is a court lady, the *condong*, who is soon joined by Princess Rangkesari and Prince Lasem, the two *legong*s, dressed almost identically in gold-printed cloth, their torsos tightly bound, and with crowns decorated with a mass of fresh frangipani flowers. The Princess has been abducted by the prince, whose efforts to seduce her are tenderly rejected. They play out this gentle and touching struggle after the *condong* has handed them a fan each and left the stage. Soon they learn that the princess's intended husband is coming to rescue her, and Prince Lasem prepares to go out to fight him, despite the princess's impassioned pleading that the quest is hopeless and he should simply release her. Hitting him with her fan as a final gesture of rebuff, the princess leaves, and Prince Lasem goes out to meet his enemy. On his way he encounters a raven (usually played by the *condong*), which is an omen that he will die in battle. The episode ends on this curious open-ended note as the prince tries to chase the raven away.

The *legong kraton* is played by three young girls; this can be a dance of mesmeric beauty, and good *legong*s achieve a status as near to stardom as Bali will ever concede.

There are other forms of *legong* dance, telling different tales from Hindu mythology and Balinese folklore. *Leko*, danced to a bamboo *gamelan*, is similar to *legong kraton*, but ends with the dancers inviting members of the audience on stage.

Pendet

This is a temple dance which, in its proper place, is danced by male and female *pemangku*s and other women and girls to welcome the gods to a ceremony, visiting each of the shrines and showering them with petals. It is now a popular opener for dance perfomances, performed by six or more girls. They hold little metal trays containing the petals which they will cast over the stage towards the end of the dance.

Baris

There are a number of forms of this 'warrior dance'; *baris* means literally rank or file. A popular version is a demanding solo for boy dancers. The warrior is dressed in his formal, rather stiff warrior's outfit, usually with a *kris* strapped to his back, and a triangular headdress. During the performance he has to show a whole range of emotions equated with the ideals of soldiery: fierceness, dignity, pride, strength, disdain, tenderness and mercy. This is achieved by a sequence of stylized gestures, and a mask-like, rather bloated facial expression animated only by exaggerated eye movements. It can provide the platform for a stunning *tour de force* by young male dancers.

Kebyar Trompong

A group of dances called *kebyar* were developed by the famous choreographer Mario of Tabanan in the first two decades of the century. One is the *kebyar duduk*, in which the dancer will perform in a seated position (*duduk* means to sit). *Kebyar trompong* is a development of this. A single male dancer enters the stage and will seat himself behind a *trompong*, the long, low *gamelan* instrument with a series of bell-like kettles, which is specially placed for him at the front of the stage. With a showy twirling of the drumsticks, he will play the *trompong* intermittently, and in sychronization with the orchestra. Performed by a good dancer, the effect is entrancing: restricted though he is to gestures of his upper body, he can somehow persuade you that he embodies the very spirit of the instrument.

Oleg Tambulilingan

This is another dance created by Mario, in this case in the 1950s. *Tambulilingan* means bumblebee, and *oleg* to sway. The two dancers—in shimmering golden headdresses and long scarves trailing from each hip—represent male and female bumblebees searching out nectar in a garden. The male pesters the female with his attentions, and there follows a delightful exchange of discreet flirtation. The success of the dance depends on the degree to which the dancers can combine coquettish grace with convincing characterization. This dance is often performed by two girls.

Topeng

The name simply means 'mask', and there are numerous forms of masked dances. Their intrigue derives from the fact that the dancers are completely deprived of facial expression: they must use their body gestures alone to express the character represented by the mask. The Balinese have their own view of this process: dancers do not just put on a mask, they are possessed by its spirit. Hence masks are treated with great reverence.

A famous one is *topeng tua*, the old man; another represents an old, retired warrior trying to rediscover the lost vigour of his youth, a scene both humorous and touching. Other masks represent an enormous range of characters, from courtly figures to clowns.

Jauk is a masked dance representing the antics of a male demon playing in the forest; the dancer is distinguished by his moustached mask and leather crown, similar to that worn by a *baris*. *Telek* involves a number of masked dancers, white-faced beauties and devils.

Kecak

The unworldly rattle of voices in the *kecak* dance creates one of Bali's most haunting and memorable impressions. A large group of men, up to 150 or so, with bare torsos and chequered sarongs sit in a deep circle, creating a small arena. They then begin to intone a series of rapid, syncopated chants ('chicka-chacka chicka-chacka') whilst a dance is performed in their midst. The dance itself is usually an episode from the *Ramayana*, often that concerning Hanuman, the monkey general, which is why *kecak* is dubbed the 'Monkey Dance'. This dance was created by Walter Spies and Katherine Mershon in the 1930s out of existing traditions.

Janger

Janger literally means 'infatuation'. It is performed by an unusually large mixed cast of 12 male and 12 female dancers. It was all the rage in the middle decades of this century but has since slipped from popularity. The girls enter first and take up a kneeling position, swaying to the rhythm of the music; the male dancers then come in, swaggering under their painted moustaches. They then break into a feverish dance which is suddenly brought to an abrupt end. The dance is accompanied by a flute and two girl singers, reminiscent of Malay opera to which this dance apparently owes its origins.

Joged bumbung and jegog

Dances performed to the music of bamboo orchestras, known as *joged bumbung*, are popular in Jembrana, where they probably originated. One dance, *jegog*, called after the huge bamboo instrument of that name, is now common in tourist resorts: it's the one where a graceful Balinese dancer flirtatiously picks out a member of the audience to dance with her. Where Westerners are involved it can be very funny, and it can also be painful: even lithe young volunteers who fancy their skill on a dance floor become galumphing muppets in the shadow of a Balinese dancer, to their mortification and the delight of the audience. In small village communities, though, it's the occasion for real hilarity, as the chosen partners are all well known to the audience. Out come old men to show off their ageing talents and tease the dancing girl unmercifully; out come the bashful youths to roars from their mates.

Gambuh and Arja

Gambuh is a stately form of traditional dance-drama performed by a troupe of 25 to 50 players, a mixture of everything from ballet to pantomime. The words are in the ancient kawi language characteristically sung in a kind of high-pitched chant accompanied by wailing flutes and *gamelan*. The plot is usually based on *Panji* tales of courtly love intrigues from the Majapahit era, portraying at once the pride and dignity of the rajas and their household, and the knock-about comedy of their minions. *Arja* is a popularized

127

version of this in Balinese, developed over the last century. The Balinese adore *arja*, which is often spiced with updated quips and local references, usually in the mouths of the clowns, who provide interpolations of the main action.

Trance dances

Trance is one of Bali's unexplained mysteries that have puzzled observers for decades. *Sanghyang dedari* is an impressive trance dance performed by two young girls; it has a serious function as a tool of exorcism. Dressed in outfits similar to those of the *legong* dancers, the girls fall into a trance and are supported on the shoulders of two men. Apparently quite unaware of each other, they perform a perfectly synchronized dance, displaying exceptional feats of balance. During this dance they are said to be possessed by heavenly spirits (*dedari*). The performance is accompanied only by the chanting of women.

Another kind of trance dance is the 'fire dance'. *Sanghyang jaran* (*jaran* means horse) is performed by men who walk through glowing embers on hobbyhorses, representing the horse on which the ancestral spirits come to earth.

These dances really belong in temple ceremonies, but now form part of some regular tourist shows, where the authenticity of the trance is open to question.

Barong and Rangda

The dance-drama depicting the epic battle between the good dragon-like figure Barong (operated by two skilled dancers) and the evil witch Rangda is one of the great spectacles of Bali. It is performed daily for tourists at Batubulan, but it is nonetheless an important temple performance. Both Barong and Rangda are treated with great respect and the masks themselves are believed to have spiritual power. This is the story.

The child of a villager has been killed by a tiger. Soon after, this villager is out in the forest making palm wine with two friends. The Barong enters, with the familiar clacking of his jaws. The villagers are terrified, and mistaking the Barong for the tiger, try to kill it. The Barong is rescued from this onslaught by a monkey.

Now two female servants of the evil witch Rangda appear. They are on the lookout for the servants of Dewi Kunti, who has offered to sacrifice her son, Sadewa, to Rangda. Rangda's servants turn into witches and possess Dewi Kunti's servants and Dewi Kunti herself, as well as the Patih (Prime Minister) to whom they had hoped to appeal. Sadewa is summoned, but little do the others know that Shiva has granted immortality to Sadewa. When Rangda attempts to devour Sadewa, she is repulsed; Rangda recants, and begs Sadewa to purge her of evil and kill her. This he does.

One of Rangda's servants, Kalika, pleads with Sadewa to do the same to her, but he refuses. She becomes furious, and transforms herself into a wild boar to attack Sadewa. As Sadewa defeats the boar, it transforms into a bird; as he defeats the bird, it transforms into a newly created form of Rangda. Sadewa has now met his match and, unable to conclude this battle, he turns himself into Barong. The fight is inconclusive, and as it rages, a team of followers of the Barong enter—men naked to the waist, wearing chequered sarongs and each carrying a *kris*. Entranced, under the spell of Rangda, they turn the *krises* on themselves. Suddenly the stage is filled with these frenzied men uttering blood-curdling cries as they attempt to push their knives into their breasts with savage circular motions. Only the intervention of Barong prevents them from piercing their flesh, and eventually they collapse to the ground, to be revived by a *pemangku* sprinkling them with holy water.

The Barong and Rangda spectacle has everything: music and dance, knock-about comedy and drama. The Rangda figure is genuinely chilling, and the explosive conclusion is still a dramatic shock, even in daily performance.

The Barong you normally see in this dance-drama is the *barong ket*, symbol of white magic. His beard, made of human hair, is believed to have especially powerful properties. No one seems to know quite where the *barong ket* comes from, but its similarity to the Chinese dragon is striking. There are numerous other kinds of Barong, taking the form of pigs or bulls or other unrecognizable beasts; there is even the monstrous giant figure, Barong Landung (Jero Gede Macaling, see pp.251–52).

Another dance-drama called *calonarang* relates the story of the origin of the Rangda figure and the battle with the priest Empu Bharada (see pp.229–30).

The *Ramayana* ballet

The *Ramayana*, the great Hindu epic, has formed the basis of shadow puppet plays and various forms of dance-drama for centuries; it has recently been freshly choreographed in an abbreviated form by KOKAR, and this is now frequently performed on the hotel circuit. The *Ramayana* is the story of Rama, and incarnation of Vishnu.

In the Kingdom of Kosala (or Ayodya) there is a succession crisis. The king has allowed one of his wives to promote her son Barata, unfairly prejudicing the claims of Rama, the true heir. Rama goes into exile in the forest of Danata with his wife Sita and his brother Laksmana. When the king dies, Barata refuses the crown, but takes the throne on his brother's behalf. Meanwhile, in the forest the demon king Rawana has taken a fancy to Sita. In order to have his evil way he gets his minister to lure Rama and Laksmana away from her; the minister disguises himself as a golden hind, and Rama, armed with his magical bow, shoots him. While the brothers are away sorting out this turn of events, Rawana calls on Sita claiming to be a begging Brahmana. As she opens the door he grabs her and takes her off to his home in Lanka. Rama hears what has happened from a bird, Jataya, which has attempted to save her, only to be mortally wounded.

Rama and Laksmana now set about rescuing Sita, recruiting the monkey general Hanuman and his monkey army to their cause by first of all reinstating Hanuman's king, Sugriwa, to the throne from which he was usurped by his brother Subali (this episode is told in the *legong jogog*, a separate dance). Hanuman pays a secret visit to Sita in Lanka, giving her Rama's ring in exchange for a hairpin. There then follows a great battle in which Rawana is killed by Rama using his magical bow, and Sita and Rama are reunited.

The *Rajapala*

This is the story of the hunter Rajapala, who stumbles across a group of heavenly nymphs bathing in a pool in the forest and is filled with desire. He steals one of the discarded robes on the bank, the owner of which, Sulasih, has thus lost her power to return to heaven. Holding the poor girl to ransom, he forces her to agree to marry him, on the understanding that he will return the shawl after the birth of their first child. Sulasih gives birth to Durma, and is then allowed to return to heaven.

Modern dances

It is easy to forget that many dances which are now an established feature of popular repertoires are in fact fairly recent. A number of new dances are produced and choreographed every year, and some of these look like having lasting appeal.

Kidjang kencana ('the deer dance') is one of these. The dance is performed by three or more young girls. Their yellow and gold costumes help to set this dance apart: they wear ample blouses and short sarongs hitched up on one side to reveal yellow anklets with bells, which jangle throughout this vigorous performance. In their golden crowns are tiny sets of antlers. This is a graceful, light, tripping dance, full of charm.

Other modern dances include *manuk rawa* ('swamp birds'), and *merak* ('peacock'). The 'frog dance', developed in Batuan in the 1970s and danced to the accompaniment of Jew's harps, is a great favourite on the hotel circuit.

Shadow puppets

Even surrounded by its customary throngs of wide-eyed children and enthralled adults, there is something strangely private and intimate about the shadow puppet theatre. This is an extraordinary virtuoso one-man show: the puppeteer, or *dalang*, will set up his screen at the chosen site and, to the accompaniment of a four-piece *gamelan* undertake to enact events on an epic scale. Sitting cross-legged behind the screen, and lit from behind by the naked flame of an ancient oil lamp, he will reproduce a whole panoply of voices, operating two puppets at a time, and with as many as twenty puppets or so on stage at any given moment. There you will be tender love scenes and raucous clowning; there will be frenzied battles, with arrows and lances shooting across the screen, all punctuated by the characteristic rapping sound produced by a piece of horn held between the toes of the *dalang*'s right foot. His left foot is his only idle limb.

You are free to walk behind the screen, into the wings as it were, to watch the *dalang* at work. There you will see not the frenzied activity that you might expect by the tumult on the screen, but a man unruffled and undaunted by his task, in complete command of his own world of make-believe. An assistant heaps the puppets in an ordered sequence to the *dalang*'s right, and replaces them tenderly in their wooden box when their work is done.

The Indonesian term for shadow puppets is *wayang kulit*, literally 'leather puppet'; for the puppets are made of flat sheets of cowhide, shaped and pierced, painted, and attached to firm sticks of bamboo. The paint, of course, is not seen by the viewers, only the delicate tracery of the silhouettes. An arm or a jaw, maybe both, will be attached to lighter sticks, so that they can be manipulated by the *dalang*. The puppet sticks are inserted into holes in a log at the foot of the screen awaiting use. In addition to the cast of characters from the epic tales, there are animals, and trees, arrows and lances. A large leaf-shaped 'puppet', representing the tree of life is placed against the screen at the beginning and end of every performance.

*Dalang*s are highly respected members of the community; they have a status akin to priests and perform puppet shows for the gods at temple ceremonies. All shows will be accompanied by elaborate ritual, before and after the performance.

The language of the shows is old Javanese or Kawi, and a *dalang* is held to be something of a scholar. Through the clowns, however, he is able to interpolate the action in ordinary Balinese, as in the *gambuh* dance-drama. This does not help the tourist much, of course, although some *dalang*s make the clowns speak some of their lines in English or Japanese if the audience warrants it. In 18th and 19th century Java *wayang kulit* became a tool of subversion against the Dutch by this very means; comments and criticisms could be put into the mouths of the clowns, whilst the noble characters could uphold the ideals of correct *adat* behaviour.

The *Ramayana* and the *Mahabharata* (see below) are favourite themes; another popular story is that of Cupak, the obese, greedy and treacherous Balinese prince who tries to cheat his handsome brother of the hand of a beautiful princess.

The *Mahabharata*

The Sanskrit story of the *Mahabharata* is the longest poem in world literature, and is believed to be about 2,000 years old. It concerns two warring families, the Pandawas (five sons of King Pandu) and the Korawas. The Pandawas provide all the heroes, especially the romantic, charismatic and comfortingly flawed Arjuna, always a popular figure. The others are Yudhistira, Bhima, Nakula and Sahadewa. The Korawas, by contrast do not have a virtue to share between them.

At the death of Pandu, the oldest of the Pandawas, Yudhistira, becomes king, much to the disgust of the rival Korawas, who attack the Pandawa brothers and succeed in forcing them to divide the kingdom. Through a dishonest dice game, the Korawas manage to wrest the Pandawas' kingdom from Yudhistira, forcing the five brothers into exile for twelve years, during which time they do menial jobs in the household of another king. At the end of their term of exile, the Pandawas return to claim their kingdom back from the Korawas, who refuse. A tragic battle ensues, during which Arjuna and Bhima lose their sons. Before the battle Arjuna and Krishna (his brother-in-law) engage in a long dialogue about ways of achieving union with god, and this forms the Hindu classic the *Bhagavad-gita*. After the heroic struggles, especially by Arjuna, the Pandawas are victorious; but it is a victory tinged with great sadness.

131

Part V
BADUNG REGENCY

Cinema poster

'We sat in two bamboo chairs, looking toward the beach, where we could hear the breakers gently pounding the white sweep of Kuta Bay. Between our grass-thatched hut and the sea lay only a shallow strip of coconut palms, beneath which the grey, sandy soil baked in the afternoon sun. The breezes blowing in steadily off the Indian Ocean made us want to sleep twelve hours a day. We had only been living in Bali for two weeks, but already we wanted to stay there indefinitely. Kuta was a fishing village . . .'

So begins John Coast's book *Dancing out of Bali*, describing events in 1952. In the forty years or so since those days, **Kuta** has changed beyond recognition, transformed by the hundreds of thousands of tourists who have tramped along that beach.

Badung Regency has been at the forefront of Bali's mushrooming tourist industry, and now its long white-sand beaches, fringed with coconut palms, boast top-class hotels, restaurants serving every kind of food, supermarkets, Suzuki jeeps for hire and water sports, and a neon-lit nightlife. Of the million or so tourists who now come to Bali each year virtually all pass through Badung, and stay in accommodation there, while the regency's total population is less than half that figure.

So much of Badung's territory is devoted to tourism that it can seem like another country, separate from the rest of Bali. But appearances are deceptive. Beneath the city-bustle of **Denpasar** or the Aussie fun-loving veneer of Kuta and **Legian**, and in the shadow of the luxurious international hotels of **Sanur** and **Jimbaran**, the structure of *banjar*-based community life remains oddly intact. Only in the new, purpose-built tourist enclave of **Nusa Dua** is village life absent.

Balinese cultural life continues even here in Badung, but the tourist who stays exclusively in this regency can be forgiven for thinking that it has been totally corrupted

132

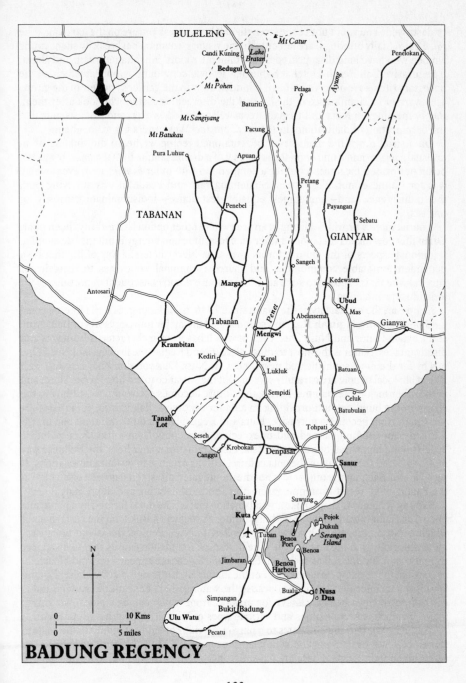

BULELENG

Mt Catur

Penelokan

Candi Kuning
Lake
Bratan

Bedugul

Pelaga

Ayung

Mt Pohen

Baturiti

Mt Sangiyang

Pacung

Petang

Mt Batukau

Apuan

Payangan

Sebatu

Pura Luhur

Petang

GIANYAR

TABANAN

Penebel

Sangeh

Kedewatan

Marga

Ubud
Mas

Antosari

Abeansemal

Gianyar

Tabanan

Pened

Mengwi

Krambitan

Kediri

Kapal

Batuan

Lukluk

Celuk

Sempidi

Batubulan

**Tanah
Lot**

Ubung

Tohpati

Seseh

Krobokan

Denpasar

Canggu

Sanur

Legian

Suwung

Kuta

Pojok
Dukuh

Tuban

Benoa
Port

*Serangan
Island*

Jimbaran

Benoa

Benoa
Harbour

Bualu

**Nusa
Dua**

Simpangan

Bukit Badung

N

0   10 Kms

Ulu Watu

0   5 miles

Pecatu

BADUNG REGENCY

133

or destroyed. You won't notice the strength of it here unless you are on the look-out. The *sajen-sajen* (daily offerings) are left outside the visitors' rooms at daybreak by silent young women who have long disappeared by the time the rooms' inhabitants are up and about. The massive Bali Beach Hotel at Sanur has its own compound temple at which all the necessary rituals are observed—but it is hidden away in the gardens and few of the guests are aware of its significance in the lives of the discreet hotel staff who look after them. *Banjar* meetings in Kuta and Legian are as well attended as ever, and just as seminal to the organization of daily affairs in the area, but few Westerners get to see them.

On a stroll down the main street of Kuta one evening we heard the tinkling of an unusual *gamelan* and came upon the rehearsal of a drama unique to that *banjar*. It was not being performed for tourists but for a competition with other *banjar*s at an event which was for Balinese, not Westerners. Something rare and beautiful was surviving both the indifference and—sometimes equally destructive—indiscriminate curiosity of tourists.

Tourist money provides a living in an area where other options have always been poor. Often this now means that more, rather than less, time and energy is put into developing traditional aspects of the culture for its own sake. Nevertheless, a way of life that is so dependent on stable communities and shared communal values has to struggle for survival when it is exposed to such an influx of tourists and consequent opportunities for individual profiteering.

Denpasar, the capital city of the island since 1946, is in Badung, as is the international (and only) airport, **Ngurah Rai**; and so too are all the major tourist resorts of Bali: Kuta and Legian, Sanur and Nusa Dua, each of which has its own character, advantages and disadvantages. Sanur is the most traditional, Kuta and Legian the liveliest and Nusa Dua has by far the most sophisticated new hotels. At Nusa Dua you don't have to deal with Bali at all: local people are carefully screened at the entrance to the hotel zone. Here, and in the other major international hotels, the culture becomes a flavour only, adding to the charm of the buildings and providing an alibi for decorative floorshows, but is carefully prevented from becoming obtrusive. Kuta and Legian have a quite different tale to tell: tourism happened unplanned and unexpected, developing from a travellers' paradise beach on the hippy trail of Southeast Asia. Here, more than anywhere, the Balinese way of life suffered the assault of the cola culture, with its promise of instant gratifications. It says a lot for Bali that the outcome is not the unmitigated disaster it has been elsewhere in the Pacific. The result is unique, fascinating, both exhilarating and depressing.

Badung Regency is shaped like an exclamation mark. The dot is formed by a peninsula known as Bukit (meaning 'hill') Badung, or more usually just Bukit, on the eastern tip of which is Nusa Dua. Bukit has a similar geology to Nusa Penida, the island to its east, quite different from the rest of Bali. The limestone foundation causes rain to disappear from the thin surface soil as soon as it falls, so the landscape appears arid and bleached, in contrast to the damp, green fertility of the mainland. Little rice is grown here. But the land is not as infertile as it seems because the water gathers beneath the surface and is easily tapped. Soya beans, cassava (or manioc, from which comes tapioca), sorghum, maize, peanuts, sweet potatoes and various types of bean are all cultivated on Bukit.

To the north, Badung elongates to a narrow corridor of land extending to the eastern shores of Lake Bratan and the southern slopes of Mt Catur (2,096 m, 6875 ft) in the central mountain range. These are the lands once ruled by the old Rajadom of Mengwi, split between Badung and Tabanan in 1885, which accounts for the peculiar shape of Badung, and for the inclusion of the old royal complex of Mengwi, with its exceptionally beautiful temple.

Most visitors do not venture further than the monkey forest at **Sangeh**, a rather tacky and overvisited attraction. Beyond Sangeh, in the northern part, Badung is much like its neighbours, Tabanan and Gianyar, an area of small agricultural villages dependent on rice cultivation, where life carries on much as it has done for hundreds of years.

Historical Notes

Arrivals and Departures
Point of exit and point of entry, Badung has always played a key role in Bali's fortunes. The narrow isthmus which tethers Bukit to the mainland provides one of the few places in southern Bali where traders could anchor and unload; part of the year the winds favour Kuta, and part of year they favour Sanur, but the neck of land is narrow enough to profit from both. Since the northern port of Singaraja was separated from the south by the central mountains, almost all the dealings of the wealthy rice-growing south with the outside world were through the port of Kuta.

When the Dutch captain Cornelis de Houtman and his motley crew pitched up here in 1597, their arrival coincided with the movement of 20,000 Balinese troops on their way to defend the province of Blambangan, eastern Java, from the encroaching Muslim Mataram empire. Kuta was also a slave port, the place from which up to 2,000 Balinese a year were being exported by the late 18th century, to find owners throughout Dutch Indonesia, who would cherish them for their diligent work and craftsmanship, their grace and their application. Traders of any flag or none would call in here, Europeans, Chinese and Bugis from Sulawesi, stopping for fresh provisions, exchanging manufactured nick-nacks, textiles, gems, opium and Chinese coins for rice, vegetables, fruit, livestock and slaves. In the 1830s the Danish adventurer, Mads Lange, set up a thriving trading post in Kuta, shaming the Dutch by his brilliant successes, both in trade and in his dealings with the local rajas.

There have been ruder incursions. The Majapahit armies under Gajah Mada landed at Kuta in 1343. The Dutch used Sanur in 1906, unloading their artillery and horses across the reef before their march on Denpasar (see pp.88–89). In 1942, the Japanese followed their example, landing a small force on that same beach and marching inland unopposed to set up headquarters in Denpasar and Singaraja. In the post-war era a new invasion has taken place across the very same ground: tourism.

Mads Lange
Badung Regency was forged in the late 18th century by Gusti Ngurah Made Pemecutan, who is said to have had 500 wives and to have fathered 800 sons, and still managed to find time to push back the frontiers of neighbouring Mengwi, and to conquer Jembrana, aided by a magical *kris*. He ruled until 1810, to be succeeded by two other rajas, of whom the demise of both seems to have been engineered by their cunning successor, and presumably brother, Raja Kesiman, who ruled through the crucial years of the 19th century, from 1829 to 1863. Kesiman showed himself to be rather more predisposed to

the world beyond Bali than most of his fellow rajas, giving cause for hope to the Dutch who toiled from one *puri* to the next during the 1820s and 1830s with their ill-fated treaties. The Dutch, looking for troops to help them against the remnants of the Mataram empire, were allowed to set up a recruiting station at Kuta in 1826, in return for a handsome bounty paid to the raja; but both parties were to be disappointed by the response. For some reason the Dutch failed to find their way to the rajas' hearts. Only one person, it would seem, did: the Danish trader Mads Johansen Lange, and what he offered was probably nothing more than the diplomatic gifts of a charmed adventurer and out-and-out commercialism, from which Raja Kesiman could take an attractive cut.

Mads Lange was born in 1806 and at eighteen went to sea with his three brothers, serving under the Scottish captain John Burd. In the port of Ampenan, on the island of Lombok, Lange established a powerful trading empire, alongside and in rivalry with a similarly swashbuckling Englishman, George King. These were the kind of independent traders who earned themselves such titles as 'White Rajas', running their own virtually autonomous patches by dint of clever empire building, playing off local rulers and jealous colonists by barter, graft and the exchange of favours. They lived in great comfort, unrestrained by Western social convention, astride both cultures. With such self-confidence and swagger, how could such people fail to be unbearable? Yet the fact is, everyone speaks highly of Mads Lange, and the Balinese remember him fondly.

Mads Lange and George King each had their own patrons among the ruling families of Lombok, and when the rivalry between these factions turned to bloodshed, Lange found himself on the losing side. He was lucky enough to escape with his life, fleeing Lombok in 1839 with his last remaining ship, the *Venus*, to Kuta, where he had had the good sense to found a trading post three years earlier. Here he quickly set about restoring his fortunes, establishing good relations with Raja Kesiman, as well as the Raja of Tabanan and the Dewa Agung, and somehow managing to make peace with Kesiman's widely detested tearaway nephew, Gusti Ngurah Ketut, who, with a band of thugs, terrorized the people of Kuta. Within a couple of years Lange had created a new empire, acquiring a fleet of a dozen or so ships and running a vastly prosperous 'factory' (trading station) built at the navigable mouth of the Mati river, which flows through Kuta into the bay of Benoa Harbour. A Dutch trading station nearby could only look on in despondent envy, and when it closed down in 1844 the Dutch appointed Lange as their agent in acknowledgement of his superior diplomatic and trading skills.

Lange's success and life style are well documented. A Chinese artist painted pictures of his stylish residence, an ample walled compound containing separate buildings in the Balinese manner, but finished with that touch of whitewashed classical arrogance that sets colonial architecture apart. He lived here with his two wives, one Balinese, the other Chinese, and his brothers and their families, plus a whole team of assistants and servants. He was visited by Balinese nobility, and the numerous traders who passed this way, including the 57 survivors of the wreck of the Dutch ship, the *Overijssel*, which in 1841 foundered off Serangan island. A host who could offer champagne, a groaning table of food cooked to Chinese, European and Balinese taste, evenings of classical music beneath the frangipani trees (he played the violin with distinction), billiards for the gentlemen after dinner—Lange, still in his mid-thirties, cut a dashing figure.

But there was hard work, shrewdness and a driving energy behind this fortune, as well as impetuousness which may well have been his eventual downfall. Ludvig Helms, a

136

fellow Dane, spent a year with Lange when roving the Orient, eventually writing an account of his adventures which was published in English in 1882 as *Pioneering in the Far East*. 'There was more of the bold Viking than the prudent trader in his nature,' he wrote of Lange. 'He knew every rope and spar in his considerable fleet, and no laggard captain could return home from a needlessly protracted voyage with impunity.'

Lange increasingly found himself in the role of mediator between the Dutch and the Balinese. He brought about a peaceful, if not lasting, settlement to the First Dutch Military Expedition launched against Jagaraga in 1846; but he really showed his mettle in 1850, when a Dutch military mission stood face to face with a force of 33,000 warriors drawn up by the Dewa Agung in Klungkung. Lange's livelihood was clearly on the line, for it depended largely on the profitable exchange of goods between these two warring parties. Backed by additional troops raised by his friend, the Raja of Tabanan, Lange went to Klungkung, then rode out to meet the oncoming Dutch forces. The festivities to celebrate the resulting treaty took place in and around Lange's base in Kuta: Lange played host and footed the bill, and apparently did not stint, even though the party was said to have been attended by some 40,000 troops.

Lange had peaked. The 1850s saw a general decline in trade, which coincided with a series of disastrous rice harvests. The rajas had no money to spend, and Lange had little to sell. In 1856, Lange, ill and tired, decided to head back to Denmark for the first time in 17 years—for rest or retirement, it is not clear which. He died suddenly, before his ship left port (some suggest he might have been poisoned by an enemy), and is buried near the site of his factory, along with his brother Hans. A dreary monument to Lange, erected by the Dutch in 1927 and inscribed with a metal plaque—in English, oddly—now marks this place, near Kuta's night market. This, and a nearby lane called Gang Langa, are the only physical reminders in Bali of his extraordinary life.

The First Balinese-style Hotel

In the 1930s, as tourists began coming to Bali at the rate of about 100 per month, there was only one hotel in southern Bali, the Bali Hotel in Denpasar; built in 1927, it was grand, sedate and quite sufficient. That, at least, was the view of the Dutch authorities. When, therefore, a couple of Americans decided to create alternative, informal accommodation beside Kuta beach, the idea was treated as some kind of subversion.

In this strained atmosphere, the Kuta Beach Hotel came into existence in 1936, the brainchild of an American photographer Robert Koke and his wife Louise, an artist. Despite Dutch discouragement, they created a series of bungalows amongst the palms on an empty shorefront, in simple Balinese style, which came to be warmly admired by a faithful and charmed clientele. 'Dirty native-style huts', was how visiting Dutch tour agents described it; how poor was their vision of the future of tourism in Bali! But then to have seen that would have been to see beyond the war which was to come—and they failed to foresee that as well.

The Dutch built an airstrip on Bukit in the early 1930s, and then another safer and more permanent runway at Tuban south of Kuta, where the modern international airport now lies. A visitor to the Kuta Beach Hotel in those days was a young officer of the Dutch colonial army stationed at the airport. His name was Ngurah Rai, who in 1946 was to die at Marga in a heroic fight against the Dutch during the struggle for independence; the airport now bears his name.

137

The proximity of the airport brought customers from all over the Far East, the USA and Australia to the Kokes' hotel. But in 1942 the airport's strategic importance provided good reason for the Japanese to take Bali from the south. The Kokes had fled in 1941; the Japanese ransacked the hotel and it fell into ruins. It was never to recover, but its spirit seeded another generation of hotels some twenty, thirty years later, converting these lonely and idyllic Kuta shores into a forcing bed of modern Balinese tourism—but not entirely devoid of the charm of the original Kuta Beach Hotel.

In 1942 Louise Koke wrote an account of her experiences in Bali, which Hugh Mabbett came across when he was researching his book *In Praise of Kuta* (1987). This has now been published under the title *Our Hotel in Bali* (1988), accompanied by drawings by the author, and photographs by her husband. It is idiosyncratic, and creates a resonant picture of Bali's not-so-distant past.

DENPASAR

Noisy, dirty, smelly, squalid and unpleasantly humid as it is, most people visit the capital of the island because they need its facilities. The biggest shops are here, together with the main market, the island's two universities (Udayana and Warmadewa), banks, airline offices, some tour agencies, the main tourist information office, central post office and telecommunications office. These days, however, an increasing number of tour agencies operate from the resorts, and Garuda airline offices are to be found in both Kuta and Sanur.

The **Bali Museum** is definitely worth a visit. It is conveniently close to the **Badung Tourist Office**, the place to go for up-to-date information on current events, local ceremonies, permits, maps and so on. The **Arts Centre**, out towards Sanur, is also interesting. If the annual Arts Festival is on (June/July), it is a must—here you will see the best of traditional dances and dramas, hear the best *gamelan* and probably see some good temporary exhibitions.

The new government buildings, including those concerned with tourism, are on the edge of town in a suburb known as **Renon**. The architecture of these new buildings is quite remarkable, grandiose and imaginative extrapolations of the traditional Balinese style, successfully combining functional needs and modern technology with visual pleasure. A great deal of money has been spent on them, a mark of Bali's prosperity as well as its confidence in its own traditions. The part of Renon where many of them are situated is called **Niti Mandala**; the immigration office and central post office are in this area.

The average holiday-maker is more likely to visit **Jl. Gajah Mada**, where the main market, tourist shops and banks are to be found. Travellers using the *bemo*s and buses will become well acquainted with the noisy chaos of **Kereneng**, the busiest of Denpasar's **bus stations**, serving Ubud and all points east. Other stations are **Ubung**, on the northwest road out of town, which serves the west and northwest of Bali, and the **Tegal** terminus on **Jl. Imam Bonjol**, which serves Kuta, the airport and Nusa Dua.

The centre of town is not unattractive. The wide river crossed by Jl. Gajah Mada is muddy and littered. It is disconcerting to see local people bathing and doing their

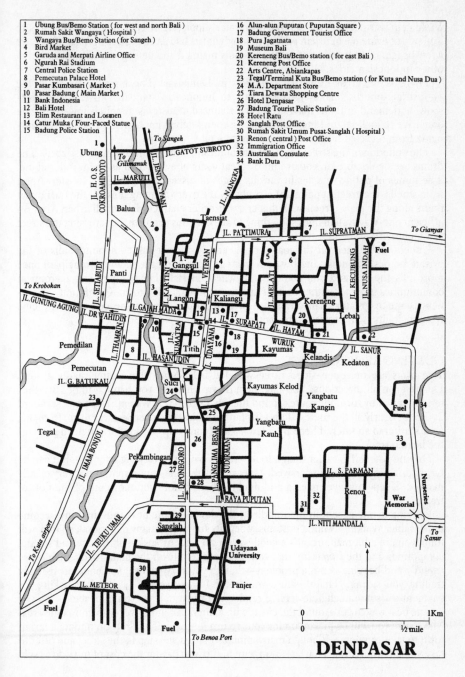

1 Ubung Bus/Bemo Station (for west and north Bali)
2 Rumah Sakit Wangaya (Hospital)
3 Wangaya Bus/Bemo Station (for Sangeh)
4 Bird Market
5 Garuda and Merpati Airline Office
6 Ngurah Rai Stadium
7 Central Police Station
8 Pemecutan Palace Hotel
9 Pasar Kumbasari (Market)
10 Pasar Badung (Main Market)
11 Bank Indonesia
12 Bali Hotel
13 Elim Restaurant and Losmen
14 Catur Muka (Four-Faced Statue)
15 Badung Police Station
16 Alun-alun Puputan (Puputan Square)
17 Badung Government Tourist Office
18 Pura Jagatnata
19 Museum Bali
20 Kereneng Bus/Bemo station (for east Bali)
21 Kereneng Post Office
22 Arts Centre, Abiankapas
23 Tegal/Terminal Kuta Bus/Bemo station (for Kuta and Nusa Dua)
24 M.A. Department Store
25 Tiara Dewata Shopping Centre
26 Hotel Denpasar
27 Badung Tourist Police Station
28 Hotel Ratu
29 Sanglah Post Office
30 Rumah Sakit Umum Pusat-Sanglah (Hospital)
31 Renon (central) Post Office
32 Immigration Office
33 Australian Consulate
34 Bank Duta

DENPASAR

139

washing in it as if it were a treasured holy water supply, fresh from the mountains. There is plenty of evidence of urban poverty, though not as bad as elsewhere in Asia. There are a few beggars, but you do not see the horribly maimed and damaged humanity found in other Indonesian cities.

There is no great industrial pollution in Denpasar. The biggest factory in the 'industrial suburbs' makes Japanese cars to Indonesian standards to feed the ever-growing demand in Bali. Apart from cars, Balinese industry is definitely low-tech. You only have to look around the marketplaces: even kitchen implements are largely hand-made from recycled bits of hammered-out metal.

The pollution of the streets comes from domestic rather than commercial debris. The drains are deplorable, so you are hit by great wafts of evil stench as you wander along. The fumes of public vehicles in various stages of disrepair are another disaster. Apart from smells, the greatest pollutant is probably the overwhelming noise of the traffic as it pours along the main streets with that crazy disorder characteristic of all urban Asia. An efficient one-way system does something to alleviate this problem, but crossing the street is a nightmare.

Unbelievably, once off the main streets and inside the tall compound walls of the private homes, the noise and bustle retreats to a far hum, the scent of frangipani once more fills the air, and you could be anywhere in Bali. Denpasar is just a group of communities grown together to melt into the semblance of a town. Community aware-ness is much greater than any sense of civic pride, even in the centre of the city. Responsibility is still towards the *banjar*.

GETTING AROUND

*Tiga roda*s are the open-sided three-wheeled baby *bemo*s that clatter madly around Denpasar in all directions. You flag them down wherever you happen to be. But they tend to travel by tortuous routes round the town's one-way system. You pay a standard 200rp for nearly all the routes. This is by far the easiest and cheapest way to get from one *bemo* station to another. There are a few *dokar*s (pony traps) around if you need to go off the beaten track.

Driving yourself is easier than it looks—the town is not very big after all—but can be bewildering if you have just arrived, especially as the one-way system is not very clearly marked. Keep your eyes peeled and double-check before you move out of the flow of traffic.

Walking is fine except in the middle of the day when the heat and humidity become unbearable. Walking is not a customary activity for Indonesians in general, so they will think you are a bit mad, but it's a good way to get under the skin of the city and see the compounds and the *banjar* life that continues peacefully off the main roads. People are friendly and begging is not a problem—though you may well get someone persistently trailing you saying, 'Hello, where you from? I show you . . .', and then asking for payment for some negligible service rendered, or just to leave you in peace.

The best way to get around the city is with a hired car and driver who knows the area. Make sure you will be picked up for your return journey; do not rely on finding a taxi in town to take you home. Though many minibus drivers will stop in the street and offer to take you anywhere by a 'charter' arrangement (i.e. you pay for the cost of the ride as sole passenger), they can be unscrupulous; besides, they are seldom around when you need them.

Kereneng bus *bemo* station is on the east side of town. Use it to go east, to Gianyar/Klungkung/Candi Dasa/Amlapura and beyond; to Ubud and Tampaksiring and Bangli; north to Kintamani; and southeast to Sanur. Ubung is the station for the west and north via Bedugul; you also come here to catch the long-distance buses to Java. There is another terminal for Kuta, the airport and Nusa Dua called Tegal. For trips to Sangeh Monkey Forest you need to ask for Jl. Kartini, which is a street off Jl. Gajah Mada, near the river on the north side; the bus station here is called **Wangaya**. Other *bemo* terminals are **Suci** (for Kerobokan, west of Denpasar) and **Sanglah** in south Denpasar (for Benoa Port).

From the airport there is a direct taxi service into Denpasar. The set fare is 6,800rp.

Remember that Denpasar used to be called Badung, and is sometimes still referred to by that name.

TOURIST INFORMATION

The most useful tourist information office in Denpasar, and indeed in the whole of Bali, is the **Badung Government Tourist Office**, tel (0361) 23602, on **Jl. Surapati**, which is an extension of Jl. Gajah Mada just beyond the 'Catur Muka' statue. They have maps, information about local events, and a printed diary of temple festivals throughout the year. Here they can advise you about guides; 'Puri Nights' at Kerambitan; the bull-races at Negara or Buleleng; whom to contact for specialist sports such as hang-gliding, helicopter rides or kite-flying; permits to enter the West Bali National Park or the forest on the side of Mt Abang, and so forth.

The people here are friendly and well informed, and those in charge are important and well-respected figures in the tourist-development bureaucracy, so if you have any kind of serious problem this is the best place to start looking for advice.

It is open Mon–Thur 8–2, Fri 8–11, Sat 8–12.30, closed Sun.

There is another tourist office out in Renon, the Bali Government Tourist Office or Diparda Bali, but this is really the centre for the administration of tourism and is not geared to giving travel information to tourists—despite what you may be told.

TELEPHONE AND POST OFFICES

The Denpasar international telephone office is now in **Jl. Teuku Umar** 6, tel (0361) 28011 ext. 292. It has every one of the problems which one quickly comes to associate with telephoning out of Bali (see pp.41–2). Much better is the international telephone office at the airport which now has direct dialling. You can be through to your number in a matter of minutes if you are paying on the spot.

The Denpasar office has fax and telex to which letters and messages can be sent: fax (0361) 26021; telex 35105 TELTEX. If they are properly addressed to you, they will be delivered.

Note that the local telephone code for Denpasar and region is 0361.

The so-called Central Post Office is out at Renon now, on **Jl. Raya Puputan**. It is open Mon–Thurs 8–2, Fri 8–12, and Sat 8–1. There is a poste restante service for visitors here. Other major post offices are at Kereneng, conveniently close to the bus/*bemo* station, and at Sanglah, on Jl. Diponegoro, the road out to Benoa, near the Udayana University campus. The Sanglah office deals with all incoming packages.

BANKS
Money and travellers' cheques can be changed at any of the main banks on or around Jl. Gajah Mada. All the major banks have branches in or around Denpasar, and most are as efficient as any in Indonesia. The cash desks are usually open Mon–Thur 8–2, Fri and Sat 8–11. For those banks and agencies handling Access/Mastercard, Barclaycard/Visa and American Express, see p.8.

OTHER OFFICES
Full details of other important offices in Denpasar are given in Part I. For consulates, see pp.42–43; Immigration Office, see pp.41–42; airline offices, see p.42; Directorate of Nature Conservation and Wildlife Management (PPHA) (for permits to visit the wildlife parks), see p.41.

Museum Bali
Originally founded by the Dutch in 1932, this small museum does its best to present something of the nature of a living culture which is totally alien to the formality of a museum. Remember that to the Balinese the spirit is everything, the outward trappings unimportant. Given that the very idea is at odds with the contents, the museum does rather well.

The museum is nicely laid out in a series of grassed courtyards containing examples of various facets of Balinese architecture, such as the *candi bentar* (split gate), *kulkul* tower, and the *aling-aling* (the wall behind an entrance which prevents the passage of evil spirits). Grouped into loose categories in four pavilions—three of them in traditional style, but now rather decrepit—are examples of paintings and sculpture, other arts and crafts, ritual objects connected with the various ceremonies, dance masks, puppets and *gamelan* instruments, agricultural tools, domestic furniture and utensils.

It is very short on information and the exhibits are erratically labelled but, despite such frustrations, this collection will give an insight into the breadth of Balinese culture, much of which is missed by the average tourist. In the furthest pavilion from the ticket office, for example, you will see barong masks which represent not the usual Chinese-like dragon, but a pig, or a bull or a tiger; you will see how the hilt of a *kris* can be shaped into a demon figure, but might also be a flower or an animal (including a splendid long-horn beetle). In the most modern pavilion, nearest the ticket office, are some excellent examples of the older Batuan paintings, and the tiny rattan cages used to stage cricket fights. Also you can admire the collection of household tools embellished by a splendidly earthy wit. First prize goes to a spinning wheel in the form of a naked woman lying on her back with the wheel supported between her legs: the wheel is carved in relief with the figure of an energetic little man, and the woman has a blissful smile on her face.

The museum is in **Jl. May Wisnu**, just to the south of the Badung Tourist Office, on **Puputan Square**. It is open Tues–Thur 8–2, Fri 8–11, Sat 8–12.30, Sun 8–2. Entrance is 200rp for adults and 100rp for children. The ticket office also has a fair selection of books about Bali and things Balinese.

Pura Jagatnata
The temple is next door to the Museum Bali. Built in 1953, this is Bali's new state temple, dedicated to Sanghyang Widi Wasa, the Supreme God (here interpreted as

Jagatnata, 'Lord of the World'), and a declaration of Bali's official monotheism. It is unusual because the central feature is a vast *padmasana*, the 'lotus throne' upon which the god will sit when invoked during a ceremony. On the back of the throne, high above you, is the gilded figure of Sanghyang Widi in his familiar and distinctive pose (see p.111). The *padmasana* rests on the back of the World Turtle, clenched by the *naga*s, and mounted on a series of plinths surrounded by a lotus pond. The outer walls of the plinths have been lavishly decorated by relief carvings of scenes from the *Ramayana* and *Mahabharata*, impressive work by sculptors from Batubulan.

Puputan Square

Puputan Square (*alun-alun* Puputan) is a dreary, open space on the site where the last Raja of Badung and his court met their deaths in the *puputan* of 1906 (see pp.88–89). There is a monument in memory of the *puputan* overlooking Jl. Surapati—large but unimpressive, an example of civic pride rather than an object of beauty. Note the woman holding a knife in one hand and jewels in another. Dutch witnesses to the slaughter reported how the women had mockingly thrown their jewellery at them as they goaded them into firing upon them.

To the west of the statue is the crossroads formed by the Jl. Gajah Mada/Jl. Surapati and Jl. Udayana/Jl. Veteran, at the centre of which is the large and curious statue called **'Catur Muka'** (literally 'four faces'), representing Batara Guru, Guardian of the Four Directions (a key god in Balinese creation mythology), erected in 1972.

The *alun-alun* is used as a promenade by the families of Denpasar in the late afternoon. People sit and chat or walk about, or patronize the sellers of novelties who gather here at this time. The large modern building overlooking the *alun-alun* from the other side of the Jl. Udayana is the military headquarters.

Arts Centre (Taman Budaya), Abiankapas

Established in 1973, this is a centre for permanent exhibitions of painting and wood-carving, as well as temporary exhibitions, some small handicraft shops (reasonable fixed prices) and a large performance centre for traditional-style dances and dramas, all set in and around a gracious open pavilion with lovely gardens. It is a good idea to check what is going on here while you are in Bali. Some of the best performances are held here, particularly in the summer festival (mid-June and July). It is used as a showcase for the latest dances and dramas choreographed at KOKAR (high-school institute of the performing arts) and ASTI (Academy of Indonesian Dance—more advanced level), which have moved out of Denpasar. The *kecak* 'monkey dance' is performed here every evening at 6.30 pm for the benefit of tourists.

Special exhibitions for the summer arts festival often focus on the dynamic way in which Balinese traditional crafts are responding to ideas from outside. Some of the most interesting shown recently include modern Balinese architecture, new directions in weaving and ceramics, and toy-making.

The **Gedung Kriya** at the back of the grounds, behind the main pavilion, is where temporary exhibitions of contemporary Balinese painters are held, and beside this is the permanent exhibition hall. There are some excellent paintings here by both Balinese painters and other Indonesians connected with Bali. Woodcarvings, including masks, are also represented.

The Arts Centre is in Jl. **Nusa Indah,** which you can reach by going along Jl. Hayam Wuruk in the direction of Sanur. It is only a 15-minute walk east from Kereneng *bemo* station. If you are coming into Denpasar from the east (along Jl. Supratman), take the turning signposted south to Sanur at traffic lights; this is Jl. Nusa Indah and the Arts Centre is 100 m (100 yards) from the southern end. There is a large car park. Admission 200rp; open Tues–Sun 8–5 pm, closed Mon.

SHOPPING

Badung market

Pasar Badung, the largest market of Denpasar, and the oldest established in the city, is good value both for shopping and for a review of what is available in Bali in the way of local handicrafts, imported clothes and textiles and all kinds of natural produce. The top two floors are for handicrafts, textiles and clothes, and a refreshment area. Downstairs are fruit and vegetables, an exotic array of herbs and spices, and, on the very lowest floor for those with strong stomachs only, a meat market. Pig-slaughtering takes place at 5 am!

Prices are reasonable here, once you know how to bargain. Have a look at the range of textiles, including Javanese batik and Balinese ikat, and the huge variety of things made from woven palm leaves, such as sunhats, purses, household goods, not so often seen elsewhere on the island.

The market is alongside the river on the south side of Jl. Gajah Mada, set back a little from the road. The large concrete parking area in front of it turns into a lively market once darkness falls.

On the other side of the river is **Pasar Kumbasari,** an array of small shops selling all kinds of handicrafts. It is not recommended for paintings and woodcarvings—there are better quality goods available at better prices elsewhere—but the textiles, especially the thick cotton bedcovers and bags, are good value.

Sanggraha Kriya Asta

The publicity says this is a government-controlled handicraft shop for tourists, but, although the range is good, prices are in some cases outrageously high for goods of indifferent quality.

Sanggraha Kriya Asta is in **Tohpati,** just outside Denpasar on the road to Batubulan, past the Sanur bypass turning. It is easily accessible by *bemo* from Denpasar going towards Ubud. It is open Mon–Sat 9–5. It also offers a free transport service from your hotel in Kuta, Sanur or Denpasar, which compensates for the disadvantages, tel (0361) 22942. Buy here if you haven't the opportunity to look around elsewhere; the handicraft market at **Sukawati** would provide a useful comparison.

OTHER ART SHOPS

Try **Surya Indah** on Jl. Gajah Mada for traditional *ikat* from Sumba and other islands—good fixed prices, and a good selection. They have some other interesting textiles too, including the blue/red/white 'batik Tuban' scarves, handwoven and batik-dyed from one particular village in Java. This beautiful fabric nearly went out of production two years ago, but was rescued through the determination of some discriminating Western visitors. The rough woven cloth and the glow of the natural dyes make these attractive presents at 8,500rp upwards.

There are a number of artshops in Denpasar selling traditional crafts from Bali and from the other islands: **Besakih Artshop**, Jl. Surapati 20; **Garuda Artshop**, Jl. Setiabudi 36; **Handayani House of Art**, Jl. Gianyar; **Kekasihku Artshop**, Jl. Raya Sesetan 145; **Joger Art & Batik Shop**, Jl. Sulawesi 37; **Pelangi Artshop**, Jl. Gajah Mada 54; **Mega Gallery of Arts**, Jl. Raya Gianyar, Tohpati.

SUPERMARKETS

These are a completely new development in Bali, and the delight of Denpasar's citizenry. Spacious, clean, air-conditioned and thoroughly Western, with all goods well-displayed and at fixed prices, it is easy to understand the appeal of their contrast to a traditional Balinese market. **Tiara Dewata** in Jl. May Jen Sutoyo, comes complete with restaurant and bakery, parking space, play areas for the children and swimming pool and games facilities for the adults. You can buy food and drink, goods for the home, stationery, clothes including a wide range of children's clothes, accessories and cosmetics. It is open seven days a week, 9 am–9.30 pm, except on Saturdays when it is open until 10 pm.

M.A. (supposed to stand for 'Master of Arts'!) **Department Store** in Jl. Diponegoro has three floors of up-market, reasonably priced clothes and fashion accessories. It is the delight of the urbanized young Balinese, the height of their fashion aspirations.

WHERE TO STAY

Most visitors to Denpasar's hotels are Indonesians and businessmen. Denpasar is not a tourist centre and the resorts of Kuta and Sanur are close by. There are, however, a few hotels which cater for tourists.

The **Bali Hotel** (Natour Bali Hotel) (Jl. Veteran 3, P.O.Box 3, Denpasar 80001, tel (0361) 25681, 25685; cable BALIHOTEL; telex 35166 BALIHOTEL) is centrally located and the best place if you want to stay in the town, for its historical interest as well as for its facilities. The Dutch built the Bali Hotel in 1927 for official visitors and the few independent travellers who found their way here over the hills from Singaraja. By the 1930s it had become well known because of the illustrious guests who were attracted by tales of the magic of the little island east of Java. The place still has a definite colonial feel from the heavy black fans, dark wood panelling, tiled floor and art-deco lights—in fact it is like stepping into a time warp. Some of the older rooms are tacky, with formica-topped tables and plastic upholstery and threadbare carpets; newer rooms are better value, although some of these are sited in a separate annexe over the road. There is plenty of garden space and a small swimming-pool, conference facilities, a gift shop and a laundry. The **Puri Agung Restaurant** beyond the lobby is cool and formal with crisp white linen adding to the gracious effect. Fan-cooled rooms are $22 US single or $26 US double, air-conditioned rooms are $32 US single or $36 US double. Extra beds are available for an additional fee. Rates include breakfast, tax and service charges.

Pemecutan Palace Hotel (Puri Pemecutan) (Jl. Thamrin, Denpasar, tel (0361) 23491), is interesting for being on the site of the old Puri, largely destroyed in the 1906 *puputan* which wiped out the royal family living here. There are remains of the palace, including an ancient cannon, possibly the one brought to the Raja of Badung as a gift from the Dutch in 1840. It is a nice setting but the standard of accommodation is nothing to get excited about. With TV, phone, air conditioning and hot water, rooms are 30,000rp single or 35,000rp double; with a fan and hot water they are 22,000rp single or 27,000rp double; with no fan, 7,575rp single or 8,775 rp double. Prices include tax and service but not breakfast, which is available in the restaurant. Jl. Thamrin is in the west of the city on the road to Kuta and the airport.

Hotel Denpasar (Jl. Diponegoro 103, P.O. Box 111, Denpasar 80113, tel (0361) 28336; cable DENPASARHOTEL) has some pleasant accommodation in a traditional Balinese style 'cottage' (25,000rp single or 32,500rp double, with air conditioning and hot water). Half of the other rooms have air conditioning, and all have private bathrooms. With air conditioning and hot water they are 20,000rp single or 27,500rp double; with fan (no hot water) 11,000rp single or 15,000rp double; no fan and no hot water, 7,500rp single or 11,500rp double. These rates include breakfast. The hotel is in the south of the city on the road to Benoa.

Elim Restaurant and Losmen (Jl. Kaliasem 3, Denpasar, tel (0361) 22165) is centrally located close to Puputan Square and near the tourist office, but on a quiet back street. Its position is convenient and the rooms are pleasant and clean. You pay 20,000rp for a double with air conditioning, or 12,500rp for a double with a fan. Note that there is no hot water here, and breakfast is not included, though unlimited quantities of hot tea are provided. The restaurant is really a *rumah makan*, with the standard Indonesian menu.

Hotel Ratu (ex-Queen Hotel) (Jl. Yos Sudarso 4, Sanglah, Denpasar, tel (0361) 26922) is quiet and central, acceptable but no frills—it is aimed principally at Indonesian businessmen. There is no hot water, but all rooms have a private shower. A room with air conditioning is 12,000rp single or 15,000rp double; with a fan, 10,000rp single, 12,000rp double. Breakfast is not included but hot drinks, tax and service are.

Losmen Marhaen (Gang VII/4, Jl. Diponegoro, tel (0361) 23781) presents good value budget accommodation, quiet and clean, though rooms are small. The 12 rooms have private *mandi*s and cost 6,000rp single or 7,000rp double, without breakfast.

WHERE TO EAT

Like the hotels, the restaurants of Denpasar are geared more towards Indonesian than Western tastes. There are plenty of *rumah makan*s and *warung*s of all types, serving *babi guling*, *ayam goreng* and so forth, and Chinese food. The Bali Hotel has its own **Puri Agung Restaurant**, with fixed price meals at $6 US for lunch and $7.50 US for dinner, as well as à la carte. It also has an outdoor café where you can buy durian icecream—not to everyone's taste.

There are other possibilities. **Café Amsterdam**, Jl. Diponegoro, with its delicious-smelling bakery, specializes in steaks and ice creams. **Bali Garden**, Jl. Diponegoro, next to the cinema, has a mixture of Indonesian and Chinese food, and as a speciality, a pool of Gurani fish—pick your own to have cooked fresh with your chosen sauce.

Restaurant Melati (*melati* means 'jasmine'), on Jl. Diponegoro, next to the M.A. Department Store, is renowned for its *nasi rames* (a Javanese version of *nasi campur*) and range of juices, including *salak* juice for 700rp. One curiosity on the menu is 'chicken and cola'. The *sayur lodeh* (vegetables in coconut sauce), 800rp, is excellent.

Warung Java, a very basic *rumah makan* on Jl. Veteran opposite the Bali Hotel, has up-to-standard Indonesian food, and next door there is a *warung* specializing in the spicy *makan Padang* from Sumatra. With cold drinks and tea or coffee, it will come to around 5,000rp for two.

The *rumah makan* by the telephone office near the bird market is also above average for this kind of meal.

But we found the most interesting places to eat in Denpasar lining just one street, Jl. **Teuku Umar** (which joins the Kuta road from Jl. Diponegoro), where there are upwards of 30 *rumah makans* of all standards, catering to city-dwellers rather than tourists. Here you can find authentic Balinese eating places, with the weird and wonderful bits and pieces that you find served in *warungs* throughout Bali, but in more palatable form. Better still, you can discover from the English/Indonesian menus what it is you are eating. The adventurous will go for heart and intestines and frogs' legs, others will settle for the ubiquitous chicken or shrimps. At **Simpang Enam** (Jl. Teuku Umar 65, tel (0361) 26646), for example, you get Balinese, Indonesian, Chinese and token Western dishes. We recommend *ayam betutu* (1,750rp), *sate lilit* (five sticks for 850rp), *lawar Bali* (500rp), *sayur pelecing* (also known as *gonde à la Tabanan*) (500rp), frogs' legs (2,000rp), and the vegetables *lalap-lalapan 'à la Bedugul'*. **Kak Man** is an up-market Balinese-speciality restaurant, slightly more expensive but definitely worth a visit. **Pondok Baru** (opposite Simpang Enam) and **Kalasan Baru II** (Jl. Tenku Uman 129, tel (0361) 24387) specialize in Javanese food. Pondok Baru has some private tables in little thatched *pondoks* (shelters found in the ricefields). Kalasan Baru II is the sister of a restaurant on the road into Denpasar from Gianyar. Its speciality is roast chicken. The decoration lacks romance but the food is excellent. You might choose to avoid *parsi kotok kepala ikan* (fish head fried with *gado-gado* sauce), *sambel* (cow's foot), or *kikil ayam* (chicken claws), however. A meal here comes to about 2,500rp a head for a couple of dishes, rice and a drink.

Kuta and Legian

Once there was a poor fishing community with a history as a slave port and a colony for exiles, including lepers, plus an unpleasant reputation for black magic. Then came the Westerners, a trickle at first in the late 1960s, swelling to a flood in the 1970s. They came in search not of trade, as Mads Lange once had done, nor of culture, but of the sybaritic pleasures of empty beaches, sun, unlicensed freedom to pursue their own lifestyle, cheap food and accommodation. Kuta became a key point on the route from India through Southeast Asia to Australia. Hugh Mabbett, in his book *In Praise of Kuta* (1987) has some nice quotes from local inhabitants on their initial reactions to the long-nosed foreigners ('Our mothers used to tell us that if we didn't behave the tourists would get us'). It was not long, however, before the people of Kuta lost their wonderment and began to provide what the visitors wanted. Soon nearly every family had a couple of rooms to let, or a food stall. Kuta was not planned. Like Topsy, it just grew. And grew, and grew. Today, it is an exciting, vibrant, noisy, infuriating mixture of Asian and Western cultures. Think what you like, a visit to Bali is not complete without the Kuta experience.

The hotels and restaurants are ever more sophisticated, catering for increasingly discriminating demands, while the shops are amazing in their variety and, in some cases,

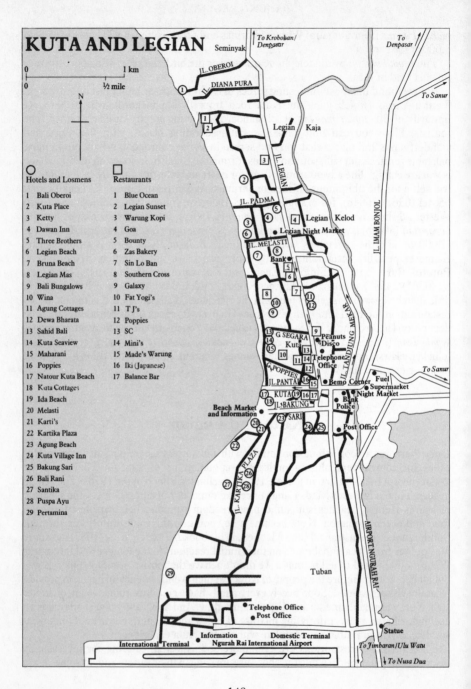

KUTA AND LEGIAN

Seminyak

To Krobokan/ Denpasar

To Denpasar

To Sanur

JL. OBEROI

JL. DIANA PURA

JL. LEGIAN

Legian Kaja

0 ____ 1 km
0 ____ ½ mile

N

JL. IMAM BONJOL

○ Hotels and Losmens

□ Restaurants

Hotels and Losmens	Restaurants
1 Bali Oberoi	1 Blue Ocean
2 Kuta Place	2 Legian Sunset
3 Ketty	3 Warung Kopi
4 Dawan Inn	4 Goa
5 Three Brothers	5 Bounty
6 Legian Beach	6 Zas Bakery
7 Bruna Beach	7 Sin Lo Ban
8 Legian Mas	8 Southern Cross
9 Bali Bungalows	9 Galaxy
10 Wina	10 Fat Yogi's
11 Agung Cottages	11 T J's
12 Dewa Bharata	12 Poppies
13 Sahid Bali	13 SC
14 Kuta Seaview	14 Mini's
15 Maharani	15 Made's Warung
16 Poppies	16 Iki (Japanese)
17 Natour Kuta Beach	17 Balance Bar
18 Kuta Cottages	
19 Ida Beach	
20 Melasti	
21 Karti's	
22 Kartika Plaza	
23 Agung Beach	
24 Kuta Village Inn	
25 Bakung Sari	
26 Bali Rani	
27 Santika	
28 Puspa Ayu	
29 Pertamina	

JL. PADMA

Legian Kelod

Legian Night Market

JL. MELASTI

Bank

JL. TANDUNG MEKAR

Peanuts Disco

Kuta

G SEGARA

Telephone Office

POPPIES

JL. PANTAI

Bemo Corner

Fuel

Supermarket

Night Market

KUTA

JL. BAKUNG

Bank

Police

To Sanur

Beach Market and Information

SARI

Post Office

JL. KARTIKA PLAZA

Tuban

AIRPORT NGURAH RAI

Telephone Office

Post Office

Statue

Information
Ngurah Rai International Airport

Domestic Terminal

International Terminal

To Jimbaran/Ulu Watu

To Nusa Dua

value for money. Kuta has a flourishing export industry of leisure clothes and accessories, and the shops are full of the latest ideas that feed this market—hand-painted ceramics and Balinese 'cabbage patch' rag dolls are recent additions. Some of these are very fine indeed; others, a lot of rubbish.

The exuberance of the place owes a lot to the lack of any central planning body or large-scale outside investment. Development happened spontaneously in response to demand, and businesses have remained largely in the hands of the local people. It makes the place more interesting than the rather soulless developments on the Bukit, or the more traditional Sanur. But this saving grace could become its downfall unless the *banjar*s are encouraged to take part in planning, sorting out the traffic and drainage problems, and cleaning up the beach and streets. The matter is a delicate one. No one wants to see the atmosphere of the place destroyed by unimaginative, heavy-handed planning.

Kuta has managed to rid itself of the worst of the thieving and drug abuse that threatened its life as a tourist resort in the late 1970s. This was achieved largely by the local *banjar*s, acting in consort to seek out, punish and evict the troublemakers. The availability of soft drugs has decreased too, so that the famous magic mushroom omelettes which enhanced the beauty of the sunsets for earlier visitors are now more talked about than consumed. Despite the clean-up, however, Kuta has its thieves, drug pushers and prostitutes, male and female. The Balinese are quick to point out that these 'undesirables' are invariably Javanese and Madurese.

The name Kuta can refer to the original village of Kuta, or to the larger Kuta district (*kecamatan*), which includes the villages of **Tuban**, **Legian** and **Seminyak**, now very much part of the Kuta scene. It has developed along two parallel roads running down to the beach, Jl. Bakung Sari and Jl. Pantai Kuta (*pantai* means beach), and a third long road north through Legian, Jl. Legian.

GETTING AROUND

The narrow lanes and *gang*s (alleys) of the original fishing villages of Kuta and Legian have not been much widened, while the traffic on them seems to increase daily. Despite an elaborate one-way system, the roads get packed, especially in the early evening when everyone comes out to play. It is a headache. With Western lifestyle come Western stress and bad manners—you can get sworn at in full Aussie style by gentle-looking Balinese here.

There is no public transport system worth speaking of, though when you can find them public *bemo*s do run along Jl. Legian to Denpasar and back. Note that the one-way system (south only) on the lower part of Jl. Legian means you must walk to **Bemo Corner** to find the *bemo*s going north. The ruthless drivers pester newcomers with cries of 'Transport? Charter? Where you want to go?' every five steps, charging outrageous sums just to get around town. Our advice is to use the taxis recommended by your hotel/*losmen* or walk, at least until you know what prices should be.

Walking can have its own hazards, by the way, apart from persistent taxi drivers. When it is wet the narrow side paths turn into a sea of mud, and there always seems to be repair work going on at the edge of the road. Major work is underway to make concrete pavements, but they are patchy. Expect to ruin all footwear except for rubber flip-flops or stout shoes.

Taxis

The taxi fare from the airport is 3,200–4,500rp to Kuta or 5,000–6,500rp to Legian. You pay in advance at the airport desk. Air-conditioned taxis are more expensive. If you turn to the right coming out of the terminal and go to the airport exit, there are *bemo*s to do the five-minute journey into Kuta for 300rp per person. The larger hotels will arrange free transport from the airport. Motorcyclists hang around to meet flights, and will whisk you off to their family *losmen* for between 1,000 and 2,000rp.

From Kuta/Legian to Ubud by taxi expect to pay around 20,000rp these days, unless you are very lucky or fond of bargaining.

Car Hire

Cars (mostly Suzuki jeeps) and motorbikes for hire are easy to come by. Try **Kader Silver Car Rent**, Jl. Legian, tel (0361) 51528, which is more professional than most agencies, and has a good choice of vehicles; or **Semadi & Co.** out on the bypass to the airport, tel (0361) 8607. Also on the airport road is **Bali Happy Rent-A-Car**, and on Jl. Imam Bonjol, towards Denpasar, opposite the Kentucky Ayam Goreng (yes indeed), is **C.V. Bali Wisata Motor Co.** These places include insurance in the price (check the excess amount, it is usually $100 US) and refund your money if there are problems. The battered heaps you can get from small businesses, while cheaper, can be expensive on petrol.

TOURIST INFORMATION

There is a government Tourist Information Office in the airport, and another in Kuta itself, buried in the Art Market at the beach end of Jl. Bakung Sari, open Mon–Thurs and Sat 8–2, Fri 8–11. It's fairly unprepossessing, but you will find maps, brochures about hotels, lists of events, and general information.

POST OFFICE

The main post office is hidden away off Jl. Raya Kuta, next to the cinema. A 'Kantor Pos dan Giro' sign will guide you from the main road. It is small but efficient. There's a poste restante service which costs 50rp for each letter collected. Opening hours are Mon–Thurs 8–2, Fri 8–11, Sat 8–12.30.

The postal agent on Jl. Legian, at the Kuta end, will also keep poste restante mail for you, but it must specify Poste Restante Jl. Legian on the envelope.

Many other places offer 'postal service' where you can buy stamps and send letters and postcards.

TELEPHONE

There is a 24-hour international telephone office at the airport, some distance from the terminal itself, near the car park exit. It now has direct-dialling facilities. Wake up the staff behind the counter if you go at night, and be prepared for displays of surliness.

There is also a small international telephone office on Jl. Legian, in a shopping complex by Peanuts Discotheque, 300 m (300 yards) from Bemo Corner. You get as good a line here as anywhere in Bali, but you may have a long wait—there are only two lines at present. It also has telegram, telex and fax facilities. Opening hours are Mon–Sat 8–6.

There are several public phone booths around Kuta and Legian for local calls (including Denpasar), but it can be difficult to hear above the traffic noise. Calls cost 50rp for three minutes.

MONEYCHANGERS AND SAFE-DEPOSIT BOXES

An increasing number of banks have opened branches in Kuta. There are also hordes of moneychangers. Rates are often rather better in Kuta than elsewhere on the island (but not always); they will vary a bit between the various banks and moneychangers, but seldom by more than 1%. It is advisable to count your money carefully. **C.V. Masaja**, Jl. Airport Tubau 30, near the post office, has a proven track record as Kuta's best moneychanger. There are occasional problems in changing American Express travellers' cheques in Kuta, owing to the thriving black market in stolen ones.

Several banks and moneychangers have safe-deposit boxes where you can store those valuables you will not need regularly. Remember that you will need your passport for checking in at hotels and arranging car hire, as well as for changing money.

POLICE AND SECURITY

Do be conscious of security in the Kuta area. It attracts thieves and pickpockets from all over Indonesia, and, however hard the Balinese try to stamp on the problem, incidents still happen.

The police station is in Jl. Raya Kuta, opposite the top of Jl. Bakung Sari, tel (0361) 51598. Remember to change out of singlet and shorts into something rather smarter if you need to make a report here (see p.40).

PROSTITUTES

In Indonesia they are known as *gadis jalanan*s (street girls) or *kupu-kupu malam*s (night butterflies). Usually they come from Java. While they are trying to convince you to invest in their charms, with hands in compromising positions, keep a free hand on your wallet or other valuables. Theft is commonplace. Girls who strongly deny they want money will sometimes take everything they can as they leave, including the belongings of other guests in your *losmen* or hotel—even to the extent of removing tablecloths and towels hung out to dry.

DRUGS

Do not accept them. It is just not worth it. Jail sentences for possession could extend your stay in Kuta for 10 years or more.

The Kuta scene

Kuta is large enough to have developed certain definite 'scenes', sets of visitors with a common aim, and the facilities which cater for them. There are, for example, the surfers, largely Australian, with any number of surfing equipment hire-shops; the Aussie beer drinkers, the equivalent of British hooligans set loose in Spain, who have come to Bali because this is the cheapest option for a holiday abroad, and certain restaurants and bars that cater exclusively for them; and the fashionable 'glitterati', usually involved in the rag trade or the jewellery business, who also have their own favourite haunts. A lot of the fun in Kuta is generated by the variety and colour which the different visitors bring with them. You also find Indonesians from other islands, usually involved in business here, some of it dubious, much of it resented by the Balinese.

The chief occupation in Kuta is just 'hanging around'—a walk to the beach; a massage; a bit of browsing among the huge variety of shops selling clothes, jewellery, handicrafts and 'antiques'; an extended lunch in the heat of the day; a swim in the hotel pool; and then out onto the streets to pick up the excitement of the evening, when everyone seems to emerge in search of congenial bars, restaurants and good company. Note that everything happens earlier than you would expect in the West, although that too is steadily changing.

The beach
The long sweep of white sand round Kuta's picturesque bay was the main attraction for the early visitors, the inspiration behind Bali's first cottage-style beach hotel built by the Kokes in 1936 (see pp.137–38), which set the pattern for the numerous 'beach bunga-low' hotels now available.

Come here for the famous Kuta sunsets, and enjoy the tranquil, balmy atmosphere that swathes the coastline at the end of the day. There are mountain views from the beach on a clear day, especially early in the morning.

The beach, however, is not what it was. Efforts are being made to clean up the rubbish and keep the number of sellers under control, but so far without much success. The sea is cloudy, the beach grubby.

Bathing is quite possible inside the reef, but swimming areas are restricted because of the strong currents. The water does not get really deep here, but the waves are too big for serious swimming. It's fun to splash about in the surf though. The Australian-trained life-saving club regulates the areas safe for bathing by flag signals on the beach. If you see people waving or hear them whistling, it may mean you have strayed out of the safe area and should move. The currents are not to be trifled with.

Note that several hotels will let the public use their swimming pools for a fee, usually 2–3,000rp. Southern Cross, for example, on the beach road, has a public pool and changing rooms.

SURFING
Hunky surfers zooming through the streets on their motorbikes, boards casually slung over their shoulders, are very much a part of the Kuta scene. Surfing is the main water sport here. It was apparently introduced in the 1930s by Robert Koke, founder of Kuta's first hotel. He had surfed in Waikiki, and encouraged hotel guests and Balinese to take advantage of the spectacular surf that pounds onto Kuta beach. It was taken up in a big way by the Australians in the 1970s. There is now a well-organized surfing sub-culture, buzzing with information about the best surfing spots from one day to the next and supplied by numerous surf shops. Boards can be hired from around 5,000rp a day. See pp.44–46 for details of the surfing beaches.

SHOPPING
Shopping is an exciting pastime in Kuta. Both Kuta and Legian are packed with little retail and wholesale businesses, independently run by local entrepreneurs, sometimes in association with foreigners. Prices and quality vary wildly. The best buys are undoubt-

edly clothes, which you will not find to this standard anywhere else on Bali. The input of foreign and Indonesian designers combined with the knowledge of traditional textile dyeing techniques make for some rich pickings. Note, however, that at the cheaper end of the scale many of the clothes may be seconds, a by-product of the clothing-export business, so keep an eye out.

Traditional handicrafts
The quality of woodcarvings, bone carvings and paintings is usually not as good here as, say, in Ubud. The **Art Market** (Pasar Seni) at the beach end of Jl. Bakung Sari is a good place to check prices and buy woodcarvings if you intend to go no further than Kuta.

There are some good 'antique' shops, with goods from all over the archipelago. Look for the sombre colours of traditional *ikat* cloth from Sumba, Flores and Lombok, for interesting ethnic woodcarvings, ceramic pots from Lombok, bronze pieces and masks. As to prices, take your time and look in several shops, just as any canny shopper anywhere would do.

Fashion and accessories
You will find all kinds of **jewellery** in Kuta, from antique work to brightly painted wooden earrings with pendant parrots, tigers and fish. There are exciting designs in silver, many of them ornate, incorporating semi-precious stones. These are generally good buys. The silver is imported and worked in local studios; it is usually sterling, of good quality, and the handiwork is excellent for the price.

Recently **leather** has been the big fashion story, especially in the boutiques at the north end of Jl. Legian. There are wild multicolour belts and jackets—not particularly cheap, but exciting buys. Expect to pay 25–30,000rp for a really unusual leather belt; 120,000rp for a good leather jacket.

The **high-fashion boutiques** are good for browsing. You do have to watch that the quality of production matches the more ambitious designs. Try some of the better established places such as **Hey** or **Indigo**. Many of the boutiques have fixed prices and resent attempts to bargain.

The very best buys are probably the cheap **beachwear** in lightweight cotton or cotton-jersey that you see everywhere. Bikinis, bathers, boxer shorts and Bermudas, singlets, leggings, T-shirts and beach bags in tie-dye, printed or batiked in brilliant colours are all excellent value.

Audio cassettes
Until 1988 shops selling unauthorized cassettes were big business in all the tourist resorts in Bali. Copyright law was not enforced by Jakarta, so you could find recordings of all kinds of well-known and popular music at 3,000rp for a C90 cassette. Then some big names in the Western music world saw what was going on and put pressure on the central government to do something about it. In the summer of 1988 all cassette shops in Kuta, Sanur and Ubud were obliged to close while the recordings in question were returned to source (they did get some compensation), and many did not re-open. You can still get recordings of Western musicians in Bali, where copyright has been observed; but the prices are no longer quite as keen and the halcyon days are over.

Peddlers of pirated goods have now turned their attention from cassettes to sunglasses and watches ('want a Rolex for 30,000rp?'). They also go in for bottles of cheap perfume with expensive labels; the appearance of these is a triumph of forgery, but the scent is not.

Books
Books are generally hard to come by in Bali, so it was good news when a couple of reasonably good bookshops opened in Kuta/Legian recently. **Krishna Books**, 600 m (600 yards) along Jl. Legian from Bemo Corner on the beach side, has plenty of travel books, some on Bali, novels, and a selection of magazines including *Newsweek* and *Time*. It is also air-conditioned. **Kerta Books**, a little closer to Bemo Corner on the other side of the road, has a good selection of second-hand books in all the major languages, including some interesting old travel books and journals.

Supermarkets
As in Denpasar, supermarkets are the latest craze, here aimed noticeably at the tourist market. There is a large **Gelael Dewata** supermarket at the entrance to Kuta on the road to Sanur, by the Kentucky Ayam Goreng. This can prove quite a blessing for long-term visitors since you can find here under one roof what might take an age to collect from various shops elsewhere. There is wide range of goods, including drinks, groceries, cheap clothing, suntan lotion, toothpaste, disposable nappies/diapers and so forth. The lily is gilded by the accompanying Western-style bakery and ice-cream parlour. There is another, older supermarket on Jl. Bakung Sari; and Loji II in Jl. Legian, near Jl. Melasti, is well stocked with food and drink.

Photo developing
This is done quickly, cheaply and quite reliably at several centres, though you will get better quality if you wait till you get home. The best is probably the **Bali Foto Centre** on Jl. Pantai Kuta, where the road turns towards Denpasar. They have a half-day service. Film bought at these rapid turnover centres is fine.

NIGHTLIFE
Kuta has a noisily vibrant nightlife. You could not call it sophisticated, so leave the little black dress in the suitcase, and forget the party shoes or they will be ruined by dust/mud and beer. Australians come here to get wild and it's not a pretty sight, so avoid places that have Vegemite on the menu or call themselves 'an Aussie kind of pub'. **'Bali Billabong'**, **'Norm's Bar'** and the like feature on the Aussie pub-crawl, where busloads of Australians descend to get totally pissed and yell their heads off.

There are several **discos** of varying quality. **Peanuts** and **The Spotlight** on Jl. Legian seem to be full seven nights a week all year round; **Gado Gado**, near the beach at the Seminyak end, has aficionados who consider it a cut above the others (more romantic). Also on Jl. Legian, just south of Jl. Melasti and near Gado Gado, **Il Pirata Restaurant** stays open 24 hours, serving pizzas and beer. The first disco in Kuta was the Rum Jungle, where Aussies went 'tropo'; it even had the street named after it, but it closed and the street has been renamed Jl. Pura Bagus Teruna.

Two nights a week there is live music—sometimes reggae—down by the beach at the restaurant attached to **Bruna Beach Inn** (the hotel caters largely for Australian package tours). There is a good lively atmosphere.

A taste of culture is on offer at **Wanalita Restaurant** two nights a week, when they put on a show which includes bits of *legong*, barong and frog dances. The show is free if you book a table. The food is pretty good, including fish, steaks, pizzas and spaghetti; 'real' wines 5–8,000rp for a half carafe, and the little boys sell their frog masks cheap afterwards (3–5,000rp for a mask). It is all very pleasant, set in a nice garden.

For late-night camaraderie wander down to **Gang Chandrawasih, Warung Santai**, in between Poppies Lane and Jl. Pantai Kuta, where *tuak*, Balinese palm wine from which *arak* is brewed, is on sale in bamboo flasks. A small one is 150rp, a big one 300rp. Sometimes someone plays a guitar, competing with the motorbikes.

WHERE TO STAY

Looking for a palace? Try **Bali Oberoi**, at the Seminyak end of the beach. Or just the cheapest possible place to rest your head after a punishing tour of Kuta's bars? Walk down any of the *gang*s, the little lanes connecting the main streets and the beach. Whatever you want, you are bound to find it in Kuta. There are literally hundreds of 'accommodations', from $2 US to $200 US a night. Competition is fierce and prices are keen. An increasing number of places in the middle range now have swimming pools, as well as a number of new hotels aimed at the package-holiday market. Efforts to up-grade Kuta are being spearheaded by the four-star **Bintang Bali Indah** with 330 rooms, which is being constructed near the Kartika Plaza and due to open in December 1990.

Meanwhile, for those who are looking to enjoy Kuta in its own image, there are still plenty of rooms in small family-run *losmen*s, with private shower (no hot water), a basic room, verandah with bamboo table and chairs, pretty gardens and breakfast included. The **Kuta Hotel Directory** published by the Badung Tourist Promotion Board (Jl. Surapati 7, Denpasar) lists 177 homestays and other hotels, but there are many more.

Here are some useful tips to bear in mind if you are an independent traveller:

- It is smellier, noisier and dirtier in the central part of Kuta and close to the Legian road. Just 5 or 10 minutes' walk off the beaten track there is plenty of accommodation in a more peaceful setting.
- Some *losmen*s will take care of your valuables for you; otherwise consider putting your valuables in a bank safe deposit (see p.151). There are more thefts in central places.
- Balinese school, first sitting, starts at 6.30am, six days a week. Some *losmen*s/hotels are right next-door to schools. School children are noisy anywhere in the world.
- Others are near late-night bars or discos.
- Check what you will get for breakfast. The Balinese *losmen* breakfast (fruit salad, egg, toast, coffee) is still served in many of the family-run places, but is sometimes skimped in the larger versions.
- *Losmen*s do not usually charge extra for government tax and service (15.5% altogether). Check whether your hotel includes them or not.

Top of the range

The **Bali Oberoi** in Seminyak (Jl. Kayu Aya, P.O. Box 351, Denpasar 80001, tel (0361) 51061, 53044; telex 35125, 35352 OBHOTL; cable BALI OBEROI; fax (0361) 72791) is the last word in luxury Balinese-style, according to its brochure. Originally built as a private retreat for an American businessman, it fell into disuse and was home to a hippy colony until 1978, when it was bought by an enterprising Balinese who struck a deal with India's up-market Oberoi chain. The little coral cottages and bigger private villas are built by the hotel's secluded beach, set among rice-fields and away from the hoi polloi of Kuta. There is a shopping arcade, a restaurant, café and beachside bar, and an 'amphitheatre restaurant' set beside a stage for dance and drama performances. There is also a health club, with sauna and massage, and a beauty salon, pool, and tennis courts. There is international direct dialling from the room phones (a rarity in Bali), so you can stay in touch with business at home, even if you are a bit cut off from Bali. You can arrange car or bike hire here, or use the hotel's free transport into Kuta. The cottages are $120–170 US single or double; villas are $250–400 US, or $650 US for the Presidential villas, which have their own pools set in garden courtyards. Extra beds (for children) cost $20 US. An additional $25 US per room is charged during the high season (August and around Christmas). Prices are exclusive of 15.5% tax and service charge.

Pertamina Cottages, Kuta Beach (P.O. Box 121, Denpasar, tel (0361) 51161, 52810; telex 35131; cable PERCOT BALI; fax (0361) 52030) was built by Pertamina, the government-owned Indonesian oil company, for executives of the industry working in Indonesia, and is the favourite haunt of Indonesian businessmen. It is suitably luxurious, with 255 rooms spread over 10 hectares (25 acres) along the narrow beach near the airport. There is a golf course (three-hole!), tennis courts, children's playground, facilities for water sports; a shopping arcade with a bank, beauty salon and massage parlour; an open-air stage for cultural performances. There are several bars and restaurants, one of which is Japanese. All rooms are air-conditioned and have fridges, phones and private living rooms. They cost $80–85 US single, $85–90 US double, or $90–110 US for a cottage. There is also an 'executive suite' for $800 US a night. All prices are subject to 15.5% tax and service charge.

Santika Beach Hotel (Jl. Kartika, P.O. Box 1008, Tuban, Denpasar, tel (0361) 51260/7/8/9; telex 35277; cable SANTIKA BEACH BALI) is an international hotel with all appropriate facilities, Bali-style. It is on the beach, giving the benefit of the romantic sunsets, and Balinese woodcarvings and paintings decorate the rooms. Some rooms are in two-storey buildings. All are air-conditioned, with hot water, phone, colour TV with a taped video programme, radio and fridge. There is 24-hour room service, a restaurant and bar, and a café beside the beach, three swimming pools, tennis courts, playground and games room, laundry service, safe deposit boxes, tour service etc. Rates are $50 US (standard), $60 US (superior), and $70 US (de luxe). There is no difference in the price whether the room is for one person or two. There are suites at $80 US and $150 US. Breakfast costs $3.50–5 US. No charge is made for children up to 12 sharing a room with their parents. All prices are exclusive of 15.5% tax and service charge.

Natour Kuta Beach Hotel (Jl. Pantai Kuta 1, P.O. Box 393, Denpasar; tel (0361) 51361/2; telex 35166) is run by the same Natour group as the Bali Hotel in Denpasar. The position is excellent, right on the beach in full view of the amazing Kuta sunset, and central to everything going on in Kuta. It is built near the site of the Kokes' original Kuta Hotel (see pp.137–38). Rooms are in the 'bungalow' style pioneered by that first hotel, set in lush green gardens. All air-conditioned, with hot water, they have phones, colour TVs with a video programme, radios, and fridges. The bathrooms are of the open-air garden kind. There is a swimming pool, restaurant and bar, laundry, dry cleaning and postal services; and a babysitter is available. Garuda Airlines has an office in the hotel. Bungalows are $40US single and $45US double; suites are $60US, $80US and $125US. The 15.5% tax and service charge are not included, but breakfast is.

Kuta Palace Hotel (Jl. Pura Bagus Teruna, P.O. Box 244, Denpasar, tel (0361) 51434/5/6; telex 35234 KPH DPR) is further north than most of the best Kuta hotels (except the Bali Oberoi) in Legian. This an interesting area to stay in, quieter than the centre of Kuta. There is a good-sized pool, with children's pool attached, tennis court and table tennis, restaurant and bar. The open-air theatre has local Balinese performances. Rooms are air-conditioned, with hot water, fridge, and piped music. Free transport into Kuta is available. Single rooms are $40–50US and double rooms are $45–55US, according to standard. There are suites for $75US and $85US. Prices are exclusive of the 15.5% tax and service charge.

The Kartika Plaza (Jl. Kartika, P.O. Box 84, Denpasar, tel 51067/8/9; telex 35142 KAZADP; cable KAZABALI) is next to the Santika. It is somewhat less luxurious, and cheaper, but has the advantage of an Olympic-size swimming-pool. Otherwise its facilities are much the same as the others in this class. Watch out for the situation of the rooms—some are too close to Godfrey's Restaurant next door, which has ear-blasting music at night. Rooms cost $34US single or $40US double for a garden view, $36US single or $44US double for a sea view. Suites are $55US, $60US, and $70US. Breakfast is $3–4US. Children under 12 sharing with their parents are free; there is a babysitting service. Prices are exclusive of the 15.5% tax and service charge.

Poppies, in Poppies Lane, off Jl. Legian (P.O. Box 378, Denpasar 80001, tel (0361) 51059; telex 35516 POPCOT; cable POPPIES KUTA BALI; fax (0361) 52364) is in a class of its own, having risen from very humble beginnings catering for the early travellers, and now competing with the new, corporate hotels without losing any of its charm. 'Cenik', the owner, built up this business from a simple *warung* on the beach. There are 20 cottages set in a compact compound featuring a lovely rock-edged pool and gardens which are special even for Bali. The presentation is to a very high standard, fresh, intimate and well cared for. The rooms have hot water, 'garden bathrooms', fridges and room service, both air conditioning and big ceiling fans. Rooms are $37US single or $38US double. An extra bed costs $8US; you can also have your own cooking facilities if you wish, for an extra $8US per night. Poppies' famous restaurant is on the opposite side of the *gang*. Tours are arranged with the hotel's own minibus and guide. All prices are subject to the standard 15.5% tax and service charge.

Poppies also has some cheaper cottages nearby without a pool for $21US for a single and $22US for doubles.

Sahid Bali Seaside Cottages (Jl. Pantai Kuta, Kuta, tel (0361) 51278, 71190; telex 35103; cable SABCO) is one of a chain of Sahid Hotels, a group based in Singapore. It is on the main Kuta beach road and the architecture is traditional Balinese 'cottages'—if somewhat bare of charm—in landscaped gardens, air-conditioned, with phones in the rooms, colour TVs with nightly video film service, radios, mini bars and fridges, and 24-hour room service. There are standard cottages ($40US single and $50US double); de luxe cottages ($45US single and $51US double); and family cottages which go up to $130US. There is no charge for up to two children sharing a room with their parents. Government tax and service are charged on top of these prices, as is breakfast

($4–5 US). There is a bar and restaurant on the premises, and laundry, dry cleaning and car hire services.

There are several other hotels in this class with similar facilities and prices. Some of them suffer from organizational overkill and end up being soulless. **Bali Rani** in Jl. Kartika (P.O. Box 1034, Tuban, tel (0361) 51369; telex 35279 BRANI DPR) is nicely furnished and smaller than some of the others; a five-minute walk south of the Art Market in a good quiet position. Similar accommodation is offered by **Bali Bungalows** in Jl. Pantai Kuta (P.O. Box 371, Kuta, tel: (0361) 51799, 51899; telex 35285 BBKUTA).

Middle of the range

Melasti Beach Bungalows in Jl. Kartika (P.O. Box 295, Denpasar 80001, tel (0361) 51860; telex 35322 MELAST) is on the same road as the Santika and Kartika Plaza but is smaller, with 50 rooms in thatched bungalows (some fan-cooled and some air-conditioned, all with hot water), a small swimming pool with pleasant shade from overhanging greenery, video movies, a bar and restaurant. Rooms are $20–30 US single, $23–35 US double. The price includes a light breakfast but not the 15.5% tax and service charges.

Agung Beach Bungalows in Jl. Bakung Sari (P.O. Box 353, Denpasar, tel (0361) 51263/4; telex 35399 ABBDPR) has 70 rooms, some air-conditioned, some fan-cooled, room service, a sizeable swimming pool set amidst palm trees, restaurant and bar, laundry and postal service, safe deposit boxes, and tour service. Jl. Bakung Sari runs down to the beach parallel to Jl. Pantai Kuta, and close to shops and restaurants. Choose a room away from the street to be sure of peace. The rooms are in two-storey buildings, in Balinese traditional architectural style. Decent-sized air-conditioned rooms are $20 US single and $25 US double; with fans only they are $17.50 US single and $20 US double. These rates include a light breakfast, service and tax.

Hotel Kuta Cottages in Jl. Bakung Sari (P.O. Box 300, Denpasar, tel (0361) 51101, 51406) has Balinese-style cottages, air-conditioned, with hot water. There is a swimming pool, bar and restaurant, laundry service, safe deposit boxes, car rental service, and tour service. Rooms cost $20–28 US single and $25–34 US double, according to standard, inclusive of service and government tax, and a light breakfast. It is well run and central.

Kuta Village Inn (P.O. Box 186, Kuta, tel (0361) 51095, 51724; telex 31502 (attn Kuta Village Inn)) is also in Jl. Bakung Sari. It has a pool, bar and restaurant, nice gardens, either air conditioning or ceiling fans in the rooms, transport for hire. Friendly people here, too. Rooms with hot water are $14 US single with fan, $18 US double, or $21 US single with air conditioning, $28 US double. There are some rooms with cold water only, which are a little cheaper. Prices include full breakfast; the 15.5% tax and service charge are extra.

Wina Cottages (Br Pengabetan, Kuta, tel (0361) 51867, 51569; telex 35196 WICOT) is one of a rash of new hotels springing up along the beach road between Jl. Pantai Kuta and Jl. Legian. It is about a hundred yards from the beach, and good value. The pool is fine; there is a bar and restaurant, games room and videos on TV. Transport is available for hire. Rooms are $16–30 US single and $18.50–36 US double, according to standard. The cheaper ones are fan-cooled. All have hot water, radio and room service

158

phone. There is no extra charge for children under 12 years old if they share with parents. Prices are exclusive of the 15.5% tax and service charge, but include a full breakfast. The kind of extra touch that wins loyalty is the fresh fruit served with hot tea, which is brought to the rooms in the afternoons.

Ketty Beach Inn in Gang Dawan (formerly Gang Tanjung), Jl. Padma (P.O. Box 354, Legian, tel (0361) 51134) is further north in Legian, where the beach is a little quieter. It is only a minute from the beach—not as pretty as some of the others as there is no garden to speak of, but it has a pool and bar; some rooms are air-conditioned, all have hot water. Prices are $15–23 US single, $17–25 US double, according to standard, and include tax and service. All major credit cards are accepted.

Economy

Bakungsari Cottages (P.O. Box 1044, Kuta, tel (0361) 51868, 51704; telex 35218 PRWADPR (attn Bakungsari Cottages)) is just off Jl. Bakung Sari. It has a pool, restaurant, fan-cooled rooms, and laundry service. There is no hot water, though. The gardens are pleasant. The rooms are beginning to show their age, but this is still good value. Prices are $15 US single and $18 US double. (There is a $3 US reduction outside the high-season months of July/August, December/January.)

Ida Beach Bungalows (P.O. Box 270, Kuta, tel (0361) 51205, 51934; telex 35199 IDAKUTA) is right on Jl. Pantai Kuta, but it is not noisy. There is a pool, a restaurant and bar; transport and tours can be arranged. The rooms are nicely designed, with bamboo walls, but are vaguely oppressive and show their age. They cost $17 US single, $20 US double with air conditioning, $5 US cheaper for fan only. Prices include service and government tax, but not breakfast, which costs $1.50–2 US in the hotel's own restaurant by the pool.

Agung Cottages is down Jl. Legian, where many of the more interesting shops and restaurants are. It has a small, attractive pool surrounded by loungers which have seen better days. The 'bungalows' are fine, spacious with open-air bathrooms, $23 US single or $28 US double with air conditioning, $15 US single or $17 US double with fan, but there is no hot water. The 'cottages' are rooms in two-storey buildings, and of variable standards (some are very tatty indeed; check the plumbing); they cost $13 US or $10 US single, $15 US or $12 US double. The prices include tax, service and a nominal breakfast.

Bruna Beach Inn (P.O. Box 116, Legian, tel (0361) 51564/5), on the beach road between Kuta and Legian, is a modest hotel but better run than many. Rooms have fans; there is a laundry and dry cleaning service, a beachside restaurant and bar, a television room, and table tennis. It also offers transport and surfboards for hire. The bungalows are $12 US single and $15 US double; other rooms are $9 US single, $12 US double, plus the 15.5% tax and service charge. Breakfast in the restaurant costs $1–1.50 US. The hotel is much patronized by German package tours.

Dewa Bharata (Jl. Legian, Kuta, tel (0361) 51764) is probably the cheapest place in town with a swimming pool, and a decent-sized pool as well. It is also a very friendly *losmen*. The rooms have fans but are rather on the tatty side. There is a snack bar and small shop. Bungalows are $7 US single or $10 US double, or $10 US single and $12 US double for the newer ones by the pool. Dewa Bharata is tucked away behind Agung Cottages, just off Jl. Legian, convenient for Legian's shops and restaurants.

Sari Beach Inn (Legian Tengah, Kuta, tel (0361) 51635) is off Jl. Legian, where there are are masses of small homestays. This is one of the better ones. Pleasant clean rooms have fans and Western bathrooms (but no hot water), and it is is close to the beach. Rooms are $8 US single, $10 US double.

The Three Brothers Inn (Jl. Legian, Kuta, tel (0361) 51566) is another good choice if you want somewhere down Legian way. The owner, Ngurah Alit, comes from the noble family of the Puri Pemecutan in Denpasar. Its big gardens are lovely, and there are plenty of pushbikes to rent. It is 200 m (200 yards) from the beach. Rooms are 9,000rp for a single, 25,000rp for doubles.

Finally, there is plenty of really cheap, basic accommodation in the small *gang*s between the main streets. Just ask around, or take a wander. Many are well off the beaten track, but some are tucked away off the main roads in central locations. Here are some examples:

Puspa Ayu (Jl. Kartika Plaza) offers 10 bungalows in a quiet spot, lovely people, great restaurant. Rooms cost 10,000rp double or single.

Dewa Berata Pension (Jl. Legian) is a real *losmen*, with 10 small, quiet, basic rooms for 8000rp single or 10,000rp double.

Sayang Beach Lodgings (Jl. Melasti) has 16 rooms set in lovely, spacious gardens, away from roads, run by a friendly family. Some rooms have fans. They cost 4–8,000rp single and 8–12,000rp double. A token breakfast is included.

Legian Mas (Jl. Melasti) has six rooms in quiet, pretty gardens, for 4,000rp single and 7,000rp double.

Karti's Beach Inn (Jl. Melasti) costs 5,000rp single, 7,000rp double; **Dawan Beach Inn**, also on Jl. Melasti, costs 5,000rp single, 8,000rp double. Both have rooms in small compounds, with private bathrooms with showers.

There are also houses available if you want a longer term let. For these, explore the roads that run from Jl. Legian at the north end down to the sea.

WHERE TO EAT

There are hundreds of restaurants in the Kuta area including many attached to hotels, so we have just picked out some of our favourites. We have excluded all those that feature the weekly Aussie pub crawl, partly because without exception the food they offer is dreadful, and partly because unless you really want to join this beer-swilling tribe and understand their lingo, you will feel out of things.

Made's Warung on Jl. Pantai Kuta, near Bemo Corner, was started by Made Masih, who used to help her mother run a little *warung* stall, gradually catering more and more for tourists and adapting the cooking to suit their tastes. Nowadays this is the place to go to watch and be watched; it is still the favourite haunt of the rag trade and jewellery buyers/designers who spend long periods in Kuta and like to outdress each other. If you do not mind the self-conscious atmosphere, it is a great place to eat and watch the world go by. Food is interesting here, and good value.

Zas Bakery/Deli, Jl. Legian, past the turning for Jl. Tanjung Mekar (the one-way route from the Denpasar direction) is unbeatable for breakfast; excellent for a snack anytime of day. This place has the best bread (milk rolls, French bread, wholemeal bread, croissants) in Bali. Coffee (best of Balinese) is served in a ceramic pot. The fruit juices, pastries, pancakes and cakes are excellent too. Croissants are 400rp with butter and home-made jams (delicious), cakes 700rp, pot of *kopi Bali* 500rp, pancakes 1,200–1,500rp.

Galaxy Bakery, Jl. Legian, offers more pastries, snacks, and burgers at 1,500–2,000rp.

We also recommend the '**New Bakery**' down Poppies Lane, near the beach. It is only open in the daytime. They sell excellent fresh bread (500rp for a brown loaf); banana cake and 'English cake' with nuts and raisins; and good pizzas too.

Japanese food is the latest food fad in Kuta. Our preference is for the **Iki Restaurant** in a small *gang* off Jl. Buni Sari. An interesting atmosphere here behind the bland entrance wall—at one end, marble-top tables are sunk below floor level, Japanese-style. It is often open to the small hours, when Japanese drink beer (at 3,000rp for a large bottle) and do their traditional sing-along to the music machine with video screen attached. Waitresses are demure in beautiful kimonos. We enjoyed our set meal here for 7,000rp, including fresh fruit dessert. The other Japanese restaurants in Kuta lack conviction. **Serima**, upstairs, half-way along Jl. Buni Sari is more expensive and nowhere near as stylish, while **Daruma** on Jl. Pantai Kuta just by Bemo Corner costs only 3,600–5,000rp for a set meal with fruit and dessert, but is only nominally Japanese.

Go Sha Restaurant on Jl. Melasti is one of the more up-market and formal of Kuta's restaurants. There are 150 seats in a magnificent bamboo structure, most of which are usually occupied. The food is excellent with a mind-boggling choice; and so is the service, by waiters handsomely kitted out in white shirts and sarongs. Seafood is a speciality.

SC (Sari's Club) Restaurant, Jl. Legian, opposite Peanuts, is another up-market place, though bland in atmosphere. The kitchen is in full view of passers-by: good seafood and matching service. Lobsters are 8,000rp per kilo; choose your own from the pool.

Warung Kopi (Jl. Legian, near the Jl. Padma turning) is an old-timer that has kept its food-for-travellers image, serving vegetarian Indian and Lebanese food as well as some more usual fare, with a peaceful courtyard-style setting at the back. The food is very good, and excellent value. Lebanese green beans, yoghurt, tahini salad and chapati is 3,000rp, as are the Indian 'plates' of curry, rice and vegetables. They often have good cakes too.

Nearby is another old-timer that has kept its appeal. Owned by the man behind Gringsing Jewellery across the road, **Goa Restaurant** is a great favourite, especially late at night, when you can hear good music. It specializes in Indian food: the chicken samosas (1,000rp), curries (1,750–2,000rp), chicken mogli and chicken masala (4,000rp) are all excellent. Get there early for these though: the chicken is often finished by 8 pm.

Bounty, on Jl. Legian, opposite Peanuts Discotheque, is relatively new and unmis-takable— built like a ship, bearing down on the small craft that race up and down Jl. Legian. Its upper deck is a restaurant, where you can get good but relatively expensive food, e.g. steak and kidney pie at 6,000rp. With that kind of menu it is no surprise that it is run by a young Scotsman, married to an Indonesian. The major attraction of the Bounty is the free show of three films every night, at 9 pm, 11 pm and 1 am. If you are still awake by the end, you can enjoy their special breakfast! The screen production is excellent, but if you do not want to watch the movies there is a separate Captain's Bar.

Legian Sunset Beach and **Blue Ocean Restaurants** are next to one another on Legian Beach and offer similar fare at similar prices. Of the two we think Blue Ocean has the edge for its seafood delights. Sit outside in this peaceful spot and enjoy the legendary sunset. Crab and corn soup is 1,500rp (delicious); main dishes include big portions of fresh tuna, 3–4,000rp and *nasi campur* at 2,000rp. Blue Ocean also does a good set breakfast for 1,750rp. To get to these restaurants follow the path beside the Kuta Palace Hotel off Jl. Pura Bagus Teruna (the old Jl. Rumjungle), then turn left along the path to the beach. Walking or bikes only, there is no room for cars.

Right up the north end of Jl. Legian into Seminyak is another of our favourites, the **Taman Sari** 'Coffee House', owned by a German–Balinese couple. There is good solid German food here, as well as salads and some imaginative vegetarian dishes. Main meals are 1,650–4,500rp. Breakfasts with home-made brown bread are from 1,750–3,500rp, the choice including smoked ham, cheese, egg, fruit, toast and jam, tea or coffee.

Poppies Restaurant in Poppies Lane is a long-standing favourite. See Poppies Cottages (p.157) for the story. Poppies offers good food, both Western and Indonesian, at reasonable prices, in a romantic setting under a pergola, with a well-stocked bar as a bonus. Telephone (0361) 51059, 51149 for an evening reservation.

TJs, also in Poppies Lane, offers the same widely ranging fare and up-tempo atmosphere as its branch in Candi Dasa: tasty, comparatively pricey. TJs has three owners, a Balinese, an American and a Londoner with a Mexican restaurant on the Fulham Road. There are Mexican touches to this menu too, e.g. chicken mole (10,000rp for two), plus an imaginative range of whole food, salads, seafood as well as hamburgers and chips. The hot dips on the bar are free with drinks, and the setting is lovely, with a garden and pond.

Also in Poppies Lane is **Fat Yogi's**, where you will find probably the best Italian food in Kuta, although that's not saying much: like French food, it is hard to get an authentic taste with local ingredients.

It is surprisingly difficult to find good Chinese food in Kuta; our choice is **Sin Lo Ban**, on Jl. Legian, between Bounty and Gang Segara.

Mini's Restaurant, also on Jl. Legian, is one of those with the kitchen out at the front for all to see, where you can choose your own seafood before it is cooked. It is very good value. **Indah Sari**, just opposite, is a more upmarket version of Mini's. The bamboo interior is beautiful, with old-style ceiling fans, open sides and coral walls, but prices are correspondingly higher.

Dayu I and II in Jl. Buni Sari is good value for steaks served sizzling hot on black steel bull-shaped dishes. The nearby **Balance Bar**, also on Jl. Bani Sari, has a restaurant upstairs with a wrought-iron verandah screen, lots of plants, but uncomfortable bamboo seats and low tables. Snack and cocktails are good here: tasty samosas for 2,000rp for three plus coleslaw and chutney. The excellent pasta comes served in a banana leaf and basket (3,500rp for spaghetti bolognese).

The real bargain places are **Wina's Warung**, down Gang Segara towards the Bali Indah *losmen*, and the **Warung Indonesia** in Legian Night Market, Jl. Melasti. Wina's Warung is run by Made—another Made—it is friendly and has Indonesian food, steaks for 3,000rp, chicken 'Gordon Blue', tasty spaghetti, garlic bread and cheap beer. Warung Indonesia has an Indian owner. You get good, cheap, filling food here— vegetable curry and *parathas* for 2,500rp.

The cheapest beer in town is at the **Blue Pub** in Jl. Legian—1,700rp—and they also have cheap *arak*, excellent juices and 'paper steak' (pepper steak) for 1,750rp.

The Night Market apart (see below), good Indonesian cooking is hard to find in Kuta, but we suggest two *warung*s for the spicy Padang food—one on Jl. Bakung Sari, just past the Jl. Buni Sari junction if you are coming from the beach, and the other on Jl. Raya Kuta near the police station. There is a *warung* specialising in *babi guling* opposite the road leading to Kuta's main post office. Expect to pay 1,500–2,000rp for rice and a selection of roast pig delicacies. Finally, the very best *nasi campur* we know is at the modest **Warung Nasi Campur** on Jl. Raya Kuta, near to the airport junction. It is just past Balindo Cottages, on the right. 1,000rp will buy you a tasty and filling plateful.

NIGHT MARKET

The Night Market (*pasar malam*) is on a small turning off the airport road, opposite Jl. Bakung Sari; walk 100 m (100 yards) along here and it is on your right. You can park a motorbike in the middle for 50rp.

There is a wonderful atmosphere here: it is truly Indonesian, which the restaurants listed above so clearly are not. The smell of cooking from the many *warung*s and open-fronted *rumah makan*s, the sizzle of *sate* grilling, the chatter, the roar of motorbikes . . . it is all magic after an overdose of bland tourist life.

Follow your noses to the *warung* of your choice, or look for the busiest and you won't go wrong. Special mention goes to **Depot Kuta**, in the far left corner as you enter, a favourite with the fish-loving Japanese. Choose your fish from the ice-bucket out front with the aid of the testy Chinese owner. The smallest are 2,000rp, 3,000rp buys plenty for two, an entire family can feed on a 7,000rp-size fish. With rice and your choice of sauces this is a rare feast. The menu also includes chips and tomato ketchup if you have come all this way for that sort of thing; the beer and soft drinks are cheap too.

Sanur

Sanur has an entirely different character to both of its neighbouring resorts, Kuta and Nusa Dua. You could say it fills the middle ground. It is not really a town at all, more a string of hotels, the best of which front onto the sea; but unlike Nusa Dua which had no life before tourism, Sanur is a community with a sense of cohesion. Village life continues after a fashion—until recently the Sanur *gamelan* won all the prizes, and its tradition of skill in dance performances and painting is not lost, though it has become more tourist orientated. Its *dukun*s (native doctors) are famed throughout the island.

Sanur is much smaller, more restrained, and prettier, than Kuta. But you could hardly say it was a picture: the main road through the resort, the Jl. Tanjung Sari, is the usual haphazard mixture of shops, hotels and restaurants with their gaudy signboards on either side of a potholed road flanked by a broken pavement and storm drains. The beauty of Sanur lies in the leafy garden compounds of the hotels themselves, and the white-sand beach with views over a coral lagoon to Mt Agung across the bay. Kuta is where you see the sun set in all its glory: Sanur offers spectacular sunrises.

The lagoon is formed by a coral reef some 100 m (100 yards) out from the shore, offering safe swimming at high tide (but beware of sea urchins) in contrast to the thrill of

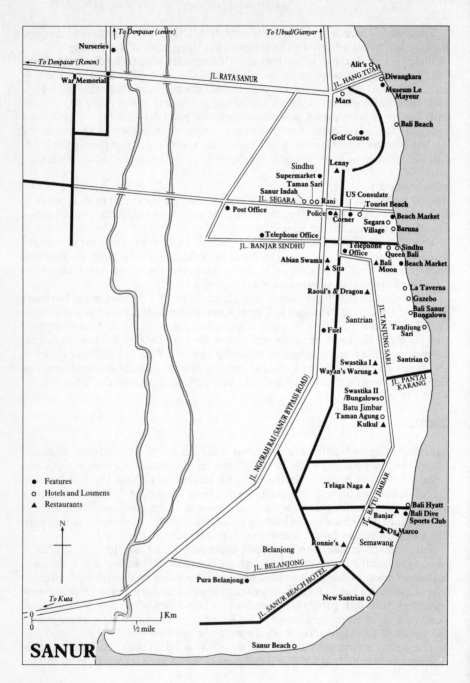

To Denpasar (centre)

To Ubud/Gianyar

Nurseries

To Denpasar (Renon)

JL. HANG TUAH

Alit's

Diwangkara

War Memorial

JL. RAYA SANUR

Museum Le Mayeur

Mars

Bali Beach

Golf Course

Lenny

Sindhu
Supermarket
Taman Sari
Sanur Indah

US Consulate
Tourist Beach

Rani

Beach Market

JL. SEGARA

Post Office

Police

Corner

Segara
Village

Baruna

Telephone Office

JL. BANJAR SINDHU

Telephone
Office

Sindhu
Queen Bali

Abian Swama

Sita

Bali
Moon

Beach Market

La Taverna

Raoul's & Dragon

Gazebo

Bali Sanur
Bungalows

Santrian

Tandjung
Sari

JL. TANJUNG SARI

Fuel

Santrian

Swastika I
Wayan's Warung

JL. PANTAI
KARANG

Swastika II
/Bungalows
Batu Jimbar
Taman Agung
Kulkul

JL. NGURAH RAI (SANUR BYPASS ROAD)

• Features
○ Hotels and Losmens
▲ Restaurants

N

Telaga Naga

JL. BATU JIMBAR

Bali Hyatt
Bali Dive
Sports Club

Banjar

Da Marco

Ronnie's

Semawang

Belanjong

0

1 Km

0

½ mile

JL. BELANJONG

Pura Belanjong

To Kuta

JL. SANUR BEACH HOTEL

New Santrian

SANUR

Sanur Beach

164

Kuta's surf. It is impossible to swim at low tide when the retreating sea draws back to reveal a muddy expanse of pools and rocks; for the locals, who really don't like to swim, this is the time to come to the shore and wallow in idle pools. Fishermen wade out to the reef with rod and line in pursuit of tiny, bony fish trapped by the tide. There are charms in such scenes, but tourists coming to Sanur for its beach (lured by photographs taken at high tide), are often disappointed. This is why most of the hotels have swimming pools, and visitors use the beach only to soak up the sun and salt-laden air beneath the rustling palms. Here, however, they will encounter another part of Sanur beach-life: interminable vendors of every age offering postcards, pirated watches, kites, masks, sculptures and massage. A determined but polite *'tidak mau'* ['don't want'] will usually buy temporary remission.

So why Sanur? Because Sanur is a splendid place to relax in: it has some of the best hotels on the island, combining a sense of what Bali's all about with the kind of comfort and facilities international tourists expect; it is far enough removed from the razzmatazz of Kuta not to be infected by it, and provides a good base from which to set out and enjoy the rest of the island. Sanur is linked by a bypass road (the best road in Bali) to the areas of interest inland. The regencies of Gianyar, Klungkung, Bangli and Tabanan are all easily accessible.

Sanur does not have to be expensive. There are reasonable prices at some of the middle-range hotels, and some equally reasonable meals to be found. For Australians a package holiday to a hotel in Sanur is unbelievably good value, and can be cheaper than an equivalent holiday in Queensland. Package-holiday tourism rescued Sanur from a decline during the mid-1970s, when Kuta led the tune. This accounts for something of the character of Sanur: hotel life dominates to the extent that there are no really good restaurants outside the hotels, nor indeed even a tourist office.

GETTING AROUND
From the airport, taxis take 20 minutes and cost around 8,700–12,000rp. You can only get to Sanur from the airport by *bemo* if you go right into Denpasar—not advisable for the newly arrived. It is also impossible to get to Sanur from Kuta along the bypass by *bemo* or bus. *Bemo*s to Sanur run from Kereneng bus station in the east of Denpasar. It is a quick trip and costs 300rp. *Bemo*s cover all the roads of Sanur except the bypass.

Car and bike hire is usually arranged by the Sanur hotels, and prices are fairly competitive. The large independent car-hire firms out on the bypass have plenty of choice and are generally reliable, but they tend to be expensive. The cheapest place in Sanur is **Norman's Bar** in the south, which has a jeep for 35,000rp a day and a VW Safari for 25,000rp. Otherwise try **Holidays Company**, Jl. Sanur Beach, tel (0361) 88328; **Samudra Car Rental**, Jl. Sanur Beach, tel (0361) 88471; or **Bali Setia Motor**, Jl. Tanjung Sari 50, tel (0361) 88698.

TOURIST INFORMATION
There is no tourist office in Sanur. The nearest place for independent information is the Badung Government Tourist Office in Denpasar. Otherwise you are dependent on the hotels and tour agents.

POST OFFICE AND TELEPHONES
The main post office of Sanur is not handy for tourists. It is out on the other side of the

bypass opposite the Rani Hotel. There are plenty of postal agents in and around Sanur who sell stamps and take your letters and postcards, and most hotels have their own service.

There are two telephone offices in Sanur: one behind the main post office, on Jl. Banjar Sindhu, the other on Jl. Tanjung Sari, just after the double bend following the Bali Moon Restaurant, coming from the south. It is more convenient to use the hotel telephones.

MONEYCHANGERS

There are no banks in Sanur: if you have major transactions to carry out, you will have to go to Denpasar. But you can change money at your hotel (often at a better rate). There is also a moneychanger at Jl. Tanjung Sari 64 (opposite La Taverna Hotel) called **C.V. Dirgahaya**, open every day 8–7, which offers good rates and will change most travellers' cheques.

Museum Le Mayeur

Approaching the Museum Le Mayeur from the northern end of Sanur beach, you see a low wall, marking the edge of a shaded garden of hibiscus and bougainvillea, and the suggestion of something remarkable behind in the glimpses of faded gilding on carved eaves.

This was where A.J. Le Mayeur de Merprès, a Belgian painter, chose to build a home in the 1930s. He had come to Bali in 1932 at the age of 52 and, like so many artists, writers, musicians and others, became totally enamoured. He met a beautiful and celebrated *legong* dancer called Ni Pollok and began to paint portraits of her. In 1935 they married; she cannot have been much older than 15. He leased a plot of land in an isolated spot on the beach in Sanur and began building a house, Balinese-style. His paintings, especially of the beautiful Ni Pollok baring her breasts in traditional Balinese manner, found an eager market abroad and established Le Mayeur's reputation. As time went by he collected pieces of antique architectural carving, in stone and wood, from all over the island, restoring them and subsequently incorporating them in the construction of this house. Le Mayeur and Ni Pollok lived here until 1958, when they went back to Belgium so that he could be treated for cancer; he died that same year.

Sadly, the marriage produced no children, so Le Mayeur made over the house to the Indonesian Government, which holds it in trust to be maintained in perpetuity as a museum. For many years Ni Pollok, remarried to an Italian doctor, ran the museum herself. She died in 1985, aged 65.

The museum is a series of airy rooms on a modest scale, opening directly on to the garden and the sea over balustrades or through carved wooden shutters. The walls are lined with Le Mayeur's paintings—images of Paris, Vienna, rural France, as well as of Bali, executed in broad variations of a deft, post-Impressionist style, sometimes on the rugged canvases made of woven palm leaves which he was forced to use during the Japanese occupation. Gauguin, of course, springs to mind. The canvases are yellowing with age, crumbling slowly in the salt air. There are also black-and-white photographs of Ni Pollok, and personal items of furniture—evocative touches to remind one that this was once a home. There are also examples of quite superb Balinese carving.

The Museum Le Mayeur is situated beside the beach slightly to the north of the Bali

Beach Hotel. You can reach it by walking along the beach—a pleasant early-morning stroll—or by going past the main entrance of the Bali Beach Hotel on the road that leads to the sea (there is a small charge for parking here) and then turning right along the path that leads in front of a row of rather forlorn beachside shops and *warung*s. (This area, incidentally, comes to life on Sundays, when the Balinese gather to enjoy the seaside.) Ask for Museum Ni Pollok if in doubt; this is the alternative name.

It costs 200rp to enter. The visitors' book reveals an average daily attendance of about 10 people. It is open Tues–Sat 8–2, closed Sun and Mon.

The shop next door still bears Ni Pollok's name and is run by her family.

Pura Belanjong

Sanur is the site of one of the major archaeological treasures of Bali: a stone pillar believed to date from AD 913, which commemorates a victory by Sri Kesari, a king of the Warmadewa dynasty. Its importance lies in the inscriptions in both old Balinese and Sanskrit, evidence that Hinduization was then already in an advanced state.

This pillar now rests in a grey stone bunker, built by the archaeological service in 1961. It is about 2 m (6 ft 6 in) tall and 75 cm (2 ft 6 in) in diameter, with a carved crown. Most of the inscription has been worn away, except at the top.

The pillar is actually behind the Pura Belanjong, which lies in an isolated spot 1 km (0.6 miles) in the direction of Kuta from the crossroads near the entrance to the Sanur Beach Hotel. Not many people seek it out, but there is pleasure in making a pilgrimage to this vestige of the remote past.

SHOPPING

There are some good shops in Sanur. As you would expect, you pay rather more than elsewhere for the equivalent goods, but some things here are of better quality. The **Nogo Bali Ikat Centre**, Jl. Tanjung Sari 173 (near the Swastika restaurants) has some beautiful clothes, especially jackets, made from Bali's home woven modern *ikat* fabric in luscious colours.

There are also numerous shops selling crafts such as carvings, seashells, kites, bags made of *ikat* and patchwork, batik table cloths, and beach clothing. Bargain like mad: these shops are used to people who have just stepped off the plane and haven't the first idea of the value of anything.

There is a kind of tourist market which runs along a wide track away from the beach just to the north of La Taverna hotel, and another further north still, just beyond the Segara Village hotel. You will be hounded by a whining chorus of 'You come see my sharp?'; and if you walk out empty-handed you will be treated as though you have just walked out of a marriage. But there are some good bargains to be had if you work at it. Buy your holiday clothes here: brightly coloured cotton shirts and shorts for under 5,000rp.

There is a large sign saying **'Sanur Art Market'** on the second corner of the double bend as you head north on the Jl. Tanjung Sari, near the Bali Moon Restaurant. It is nothing of the sort, but a local daily market selling fruit and vegetables, dried fish and weird culinary concoctions, clothes and household goods. With its rich smells, colour and scavenging dogs, this is a refreshing slice of real Bali, away from the suntan oil and pizza.

167

There is another branch of the **Galael Dewata** supermarket chain (plus bakery, icecream parlour, and Kentucky Ayam Goreng) on the Sanur bypass, just to the north of the crossroads that leads to the Segara Village hotel.

WATER SPORTS
Sail out over the reef in a traditional-styled outrigger or *prahu*, go parasailing, waterskiing, snorkelling, scuba-diving or windsurfing: Sanur offers all these things. None could claim to be the best in the world, but for this reason the atmosphere is relaxed, friendly and pleasurable. Many of the large hotels provide water-sports facilities of one kind or another. Alternatively, go to one of the reputable 'clubs'. **The Bali Dive Sports Club** offers a range of activities from its base on the beach just to the south of the Bali Hyatt (Jl. Duyung, the road to the beach next to the Hyatt; tel (0361) 88582). Windsurfing, $5 US per hour; snorkelling equipment, $3 US per half day; parasailing, $10 US per round; waterskiing, $10 US for 15 minutes; water scooter, $10 US per 15 minutes, and so forth. They also run scuba-diving excursions (see pp.46–47).

For a gentle trip in a *prahu* catch one of the 'captains' who come to the beach to offer trips for around 8,000rp per hour. They will also also take you to good snorkelling sites, or for a trip to Serangan Island.

GOLF
Bali Beach Hotel has a 9-hole golf course which is open to non-residents. It is flat and somewhat uneventful, but quite good enough for a casual seaside round. The green fee is $25 US (25% less for Bali Beach residents); you can rent a half-set of clubs for $7 US and golf shoes for $2.50 US.

DANCE AND DRAMA
Many hotels have their own cultural shows, usually also open to non-residents. Your hotel will have details of what is available. Otherwise you can usually follow your ears: almost every night there will be the tinkle of the *gamelan* somewhere along the shorefront.

You can watch dancing as you dine at two of the large tourist restaurants on the Sanur bypass, **Abian Swama** and **Sita Restaurant**. The dancing is performed by pupils of the ASTI dance school in Denpasar and so is produced with some integrity, but such places are really not sympathetic environments for Balinese dance. Of the two, Sita Restaurant is the superior, with well-cooked food, at a price.

We specially recommend the *wayang kulit* (shadow puppet) show at the **Mars Hotel** near the west gate of Bali Beach Hotel tel (0361) 88236, for a chance to hear a first-class *dalang* (I Wayan Pater); he does part of the show in English as well as Kawi, Balinese, Indonesian and Japanese, depending on the composition of the audience (Sun, Tues and Thurs, at 6–7 pm, admission 2,500rp).

On Saturday evenings (7 pm) the **Tandjung Sari Hotel** (Jl. Tanjung Sari, tel (0361) 88441) produces a spectacular and quite delicious Balinese *rijsttafel*, which is preceded by traditional dancing by their own troupe composed of children of the staff. Everything the Tandjung Sari does is near enough perfection, and this evening is no exception: the dancing is exquisite. You will see *pendet*, *legong*, *baris* and *topeng* performed to very high standards by very young dancers, accompanied by an excellent *gamelan*. At $25 US per head it may have to be a special treat, but a special treat it is.

NIGHTLIFE
Such as it is, the nightlife here revolves round the discos, mostly in the big hotels. The largest disco in Bali is run independently, with supposedly the best DJ in Southeast Asia. It is **'Subec'**, next to Bali Moon Restaurant. Dress is informal. **'No. 1'** is the other big one, with a reputation for being the 'cleanest', i.e. no prostitutes and a strict dress code. Like discos the world over, prices for drinks are high, the music is loud, and the lights flashy. There are special events such as Ladies' Nights and Fancy Dress Nights. Recently opening hours for discos have been restricted and they now have to close at 2 am.

The **Matahari** disco in the Bali Hyatt is well attended. Entrance is 5,000rp; no shorts, jeans, or sandals. It opens at 8.30 pm and closes 1 am weekdays and 2 am weekends.

Generally speaking the discos in Sanur are more subdued than those in Kuta. In any case, most people are in bed by 10 pm.

WHERE TO STAY
The best hotels adjoin the beach, on the sea side of Jl. Tanjung Sari and Jl. Batu Jimbar.

Top of the range
The **Bali Hyatt** on Jl. Tanjung Sari (P.O. Box 392, Sanur, tel (0361) 88271,88361; telex 35127,35527 HYTDPR; fax (0361) 87693) is a large international hotel (387 rooms) with everything you could expect, and more. The public spaces really are quite wonderful: the main buildings are set in a beautiful tropical water garden, recently graced by a pair of pink flamingos. There are plenty of bars and restaurants, two lovely pools offering the largest swimming area on the island, tennis courts, a (three-hole!) golf course, two pleasure cruisers, sauna, videos, IDD telephones, and so on. It has convention and business facilities. There is everything here for the water-sports enthusiast:

Accommodation at the PanSea Puri Bali, Jimbaran

windsurfing, waterskiing, scuba-diving, snorkelling, and deep-sea fishing. And a discotheque for those with excessive energy. Room prices range from $105–495 US a night single or double plus the 15.5% tax and service charge. A high-season supplement adds about 20% to these prices. They are the same price double or single.

Hotel Bali Beach (Jl. Raya, Sanur, Box 275, Denpasar 80001, tel (0361) 88511; telex 35133 HBBDPR; cable HBB BALI; fax (0361) 88406) is a monster, but, fortunately, the exception that proves the rule. When it was built in 1966 as a sign that big business tourism had come to Bali, it so shocked the Balinese that a law was passed limiting the height of any new building to that of a palm tree. Thereafter, most hotels have been designed with some sympathy for the environment. The Bali Beach Hotel is faceless, adorned by lime green and white perforated brick; the interior is soullessly international, like an airport. In the early days the hotel suffered from a plague of bad spirits: apparitions of people and animals haunted the shiny new rooms. It seemed that the gods were showing their anger because the new hotel had been built on the site of an old burial ground, and without the necessary religious rituals. The problem was resolved by building a temple in the hotel grounds. There are 600 rooms in the high-rise block and in cottages and two-storey buildings in the extensive grounds, and conference rooms with a capacity for 1,000. It is used for conventions, and also for block bookings for package tours. The facilities are all that you would expect: lots of restaurants and bars, three pools, a nine-hole golf course, bowling alley, tennis courts, motor boat for water sports, steam room, children's playground, etc. In the shopping arcade there is a bank, travel agent, drugstore, post office, souvenir shop, boutique, beauty salon and barber, plus all the airline offices. To be fair, the Bali Beach Hotel is extremely useful for the services it can offer all of Sanur, saving tiresome journeys into Denpasar. Rooms are $60–68 US single or $70–80 US double. There are suites from $95–245 US. Prices are subject to the 15.5% tax and service charge. There is no extra charge for children under 12 occupying the same room as their parents.

Hotel Sanur Beach (P.O. Box 279, Denpasar 80001 tel (0361) 88011; telex 35135 SITA; fax (0361) 71566; cable AEROPACIFIC) is another top class international hotel, owned by Aerowisata, the Garuda airline hotel chain. As you enter the place it has the atmosphere of a classy suburban apartment block. The foyer is all marble and fountains; doormen hover. This is a hotel catering for package holidays, so be prepared to eat your poolside dinner to the accompaniment of electric *gamelan* music and the strains of Frank Sinatra. Service, however, is not this hotel's strong suit. Most rooms and suites are in the main block, but there are also 26 bungalows in the grounds, and a 'de luxe bungalow' with private servant and pool. There is a pool, mini golf, tennis, volleyball and badminton, various restaurants and bars, as well as a shopping area, with bank, travel agency, drugstore, bookshop and beauty salon. Conference and telex services are available. Rooms are $75–80 US single, $85–90 US double. Suites are from $125–750 US, the latter for two rooms in the de luxe beachside bungalow. Rates are subject to 15.5% tax and service charge.

The **Tandjung Sari** on Jl. Tanjung Sari (P.O. Box 25, Denpasar 80001, tel (0361) 88441; telex 35157 TANSRI ; cable TANDJUNG SARI, DENPASAR; fax (0361) 87930) is quite another matter. This is the kind of small, family-run hotel with exacting standards that commands great loyalty, and which means its books are filled from one season to the next. It makes up in style what it lacks in terms of facilities such as banks and golf courses. The individual bungalows (only 24) are all made with traditional materials elaborately carved and decorated; 12 are two-storey, with the bedroom upstairs, so you look out in the morning onto the birds, flowers and greenery of the lush garden immediately outside. Real Indonesian food is served in a peaceful Balinese setting, by women in sarongs and *kebayas*, to the accompaniment of soft *gamelan* music. Even the ancient bus (still occasionally wheeled out to make the airport run) has been painted by the artists of Ubud. The service is graceful and friendly. It is the best introduction to Bali you could have. There is a pool (recently enlarged), sailing, windsurfing and snorkelling facilities, badminton and table tennis. The rooms have fridges and (unusually) IDD telephones. The two-storey bungalows cost $96 US single or $108 US double (proper double beds here), except for Nos 7 and 8 which front directly onto the sea and cost $110 US single and $120 US double. The splendid 'garden suite' costs $160 US single and $175 US double. The single-storey bungalows in an enclave away from the sea cost $80 US single and $108 US double. An extra bed for a third person costs $15–20 US. The high season supplement adds a further $20 US at Easter, Christmas and from the beginning of July to the end of August. These prices do not include breakfast or the 15.5% tax and service charge. If nothing else, visit their splendid bar by the sea and sample an '*arak* special' before dinner: the barman's blend is unrivalled—and potent.

La Taverna is also in Jl. Tanjung Sari (P.O. Box 40, Denpasar, tel (0361) 88497, 88387; telex 35163 LTVN; cable LATAVERNA BALI). This is another hotel that rates highly for its friendly atmosphere, and its pleasantly village-like layout in a garden filled with flowering trees and a pond. The rooms are all in thatched houses, with their own little terraces, decorated in traditional style. Some of them definitely could do with updating, but these tend also to be the largest. There is a pool with a sunken bar, and a restaurant with excellent food, including pizzas from a proper pizza oven and other Italian dishes, reflecting the hotel's Italian origins. All the rooms have fridges; there is a video TV, table tennis, car hire facilities and so forth. The rooms are reasonably priced at $70–80 US, single or double, rising to $160 US for a 'garden duplex' Prices are subject to the 15.5% tax and service charge, and there is a high season supplement of $15 US at Christmas and from 15 July to the end of August.

Middle of the range
Santrian Beach Cottages on Jl. Tanjung Sari (P.O. Box 55, Denpasar, tel (0361) 88181–5; telex 35169) offers spacious, well-appointed, attractive rooms, in rice-barn style buildings in luxuriant gardens. Rooms have telephones, there is a decent-sized pool, a bar and two restaurants, one of them beside the beach. Food served in the rooms costs an additional 10%. Prices are $40 US single and $45 US double with a garden view, and $45 US single, $50 US double with a sea view. This hotel prides itself on its regular cultural evenings of dance and drama. There is also a **New Santrian Beach Cottages** (same booking address) with similar facilities further south, on the Jl. Batu Jimbar. Room rates here are slightly higher: $55 US single and $60 US double.

Segara Village hotel on Jl. Tanjung Sari (P.O. Box 91, Denpasar, tel (0361) 88407, 88408, 88231; telex 35143 SEGARA DPR) is good value. There are two pools, a tennis court, three bars and two restaurants, a library, drugstore and boutique and a

171

children's playground. Cultural activities are organized through a 'Culture Club', where you can learn Balinese dancing, music, batik dyeing, painting or woodcarving. Rooms are from $36–80 US single, $42–100 US double. The latter price is for a family suite. All prices are subject to the 15.5% tax and service charge.

Bali Sanur Bungalows on Jl. Tanjung Sari (P.O. Box 306, Denpasar, tel (0361) 88421/2; telex 35178 GHCBSB; cable BALI BUNGALOWS) are bungalows arranged in separate groups, with shared facilities. There are several pools, bars and restaurants, phones and fridges in the rooms, laundry, car hire, photo-processing, telex and money-changing facilities, and water sports. It is very comfortable, and its customers return year after year, but the rooms are actually not special. Prices go from $32–37 US single and $37–42 US double, plus the 15.5% tax and service charge.

Sindhu Beach Hotel on Jl. Tanjung Sari (P.O. Box 181, Denpasar, tel (0361) 88351/2; telex 35166 BALIHOT; cable SINDUHOT DENPASAR) is a bit older than some, as the rooms show, but the facilities are good for this range: the air-conditioned rooms have phones, fridges and colour TVs with video service. There is a restaurant beside the pleasant pool area (it closes at 11 pm, though the sign declares it is open 24 hours) and a beachside bar. There is also a shopping arcade with money-changer and tour services. Rooms are $35–50 US single and $40–60 US double. The latter prices are for a suite. The rates include breakfast, service and tax.

Alit's Beach Bungalows (Jl. Hang Tuah, P.O. Box 102, Sanur, tel (0361) 88560/6/7; telex 35165 ALIT) are rather impersonal rooms arranged in a splendid garden of tall trees, with all the usual facilities in this bracket: pool, tennis court, bar and restaurant, mini-golf, air conditioning and hot water in the rooms, tour facilities on request. Conference facilities are available. Rooms cost $35 US single or $37 US double.

Diwangkara Beach Hotel & Bungalows (Jl. Hang Tuah, P.O. Box 120, Sanur, tel (0361) 88577; telex 35154 BPU (attn Mr Diwangkara)) offers much the same facilities as above. The 36 rooms are in a central unit or in bungalows in the gardens. There are plenty of Balinese touches in the tropical gardens and room decoration. Rooms cost $23–30 US single or $28–35 US double. The rates are inclusive of breakfast, tax and service. Good value.

Gazebo Cottages Beach Hotel (Jl. Tanjung Sari, P.O. Box 134, Denpasar, tel (0361) 88300,88212; telex 35178 GRIYA BSB (attn GAZEBO); cable GAZCOT BALI). A pink plaque in the car park announces 'The Gazebo Cottage Beach Hotel has been built by S. Yahya not only with bricks and mortar but with his mind, imagination and heart'. The Gazebo does, in fact, have a pleasant Balinese feel to it, though the rooms are beginning to show their age and the swimming pool is too small for the 60 rooms. It costs $25.30–40.25 US single and $34.50–51.75 US double, depending on whether you have a standard room or a cottage and on the time of year. There is a beach bar and a restaurant.

Swastika Bungalows (Jl. Batu Jimbar, Sanur, tel (0361) 88693,88573), is good value. It has the basics necessary in this class of hotel—air-conditioned or fan-cooled rooms, hot water, a decent-sized pool, room service (till 11 pm). The rooms are pleasantly spacious too, with some lovely garden-style bathrooms. There are two adjacent restaurants, Swastika I and Swastika II, which have some of the most reasonable food in Sanur, and a Swastika Drugstore (the swastika is a Hindu good-luck symbol, by the way). The hotel is a bit inland, on the west side of Jl. Tanjung Sari. Rooms cost $20 US single and $25 US double, fan-cooled; $30 US single and $35 US double with air conditioning. These prices include tax and service and a light breakfast.

Baruna Beach Inn (Jl. Pantai Sindhu 17, Banjar Sindhu Kaja, Sanur, 80228, tel (0361) 88546) has good accommodation without a pool. It is included in this section for its air-conditioned units with attached private kitchens, which are let on a monthly basis. This is an unusual option for Sanur. The units have hot water and fridges.

Economy

The cheapest accommodation in Sanur is to be found in Jl. Segara, up by the small post office, about 10 minutes walk from the beach. The hotels **Sanur Indah, Taman** and **Rani** all have basic rooms with private bathrooms for 10,000rp double or single, excluding breakfast. We thought the Hotel Rani marginally the best of the three.

Near the beach, the **Tourist Beach Inn** in Jl. Segara Ayu has older rooms for 15,000rp and newer ones for 18,000rp, including breakfast. Clean, friendly, and good value.

Abian Srama is accessible from the bypass or from Jl. Tanjung Sari. It has a lot of rooms in two blocks facing each other across a narrow but attractive central garden. Downstairs with fans, the rooms are $14 US; upstairs with air conditioning, they are $20 US. Prices are inclusive of tax and service, no breakfast is included.

Hotel Taman Agung Beach Inn is on the west side of the Jl. Batu Jimbar, near the Bali Hyatt, tel (0361) 88549. There are rooms with fan and no hot water for $11 US single, $14 US double. With hot water, rooms cost $16 US single and $17 US double. There is also a 'VIP bungalow' with air conditioning, hot water and a private lounge for $26.50 US double. There are no additional charges, but breakfast is not included.

Semawang Beach Inn has some fan-cooled rooms for $20 US single and $25 US double, with hot water. Gleamingly white and well cared for, its only disadvantage is that there is no pool.

At the entrance to Santrian Beach Cottages is a small place called **Shanti Village** (P.O. Box 460, Denpasar, tel (0361) 88060) which has just eight rooms, 50 metres (50 yards) from the beach. The rooms cost $25 US single and $30 US double, with air conditioning, and hot water. Prices include a light breakfast. Guests can use the pool at the Santrian.

Queen Bali on Jl. Sindhu (P.O. Box 119, Sanur, tel (0361) 88054; telex 35203) is another hotel which would be in the middle range but for its lack of a pool. Prices are $32 US single and $35 US double, which includes colour TV in the rooms.

WHERE TO EAT

The hotels at Sanur provide fairly good cooking, sufficient it seems to keep their clients in, and there is little call for independent eating places. Thus, unlike Kuta, Sanur does not have much choice of restaurants. This can be a disappointment to those for whom an important part of travel is eating.

Non-residents are welcome in the restaurants of the major hotels, of course. The larger hotels tend to have rather impersonal restaurants to match their scale. The **Tandjung Sari** (Jl. Tanjung Sari, tel (0361) 88441), on the other hand, has an excellent and intimate restaurant with tables set around a spacious courtyard. There is a set menu, and prices are not cheap, but the standard of cooking is higher than most other restaurants in Bali. Try the *sate*, served on hot coals in an earthenware dish, or their *ikan pepes*; and follow this with their quite excellent black-rice pudding. For the special *rijsttafel* nights on Saturdays, with dancing, see p.168.

Next door, La Taverna, tel (0361) 88497,88387, has an attractive restaurant serving Italian and Indonesian food, well prepared and at reasonable prices for Sanur.

Opposite the Bali Hyatt is the Chinese (Szechuan and Cantonese) Restaurant, **Telaga Naga**, open evenings only 8.30–11, tel: (0361) 88271,88361. The setting, on wooden decks over a series of carp-filled lily ponds, is spectacular. This is a lively spot, since it is one of the few good restaurants that is not attached to a hotel, and certainly matches Western standards. Whether the cooking is as good as the surroundings is a matter of debate. Prices are mid to high.

The **Bali Moon**, on the Jl. Tanjung Sari, near La Taverna hotel, tel (0361) 88486 is another independent restaurant. There are seats in a garden and in a two-storey round building with a circular central bar that serves a whole range of exotic cocktails. Bookings are usually necessary for the evening, but until 4pm there are special offers and no tax is charged. Pizzas are 4,500–5,800rp, spaghetti bolognese 4,500rp, Chicken 'Gordon Blue' 4,800rp. Lobster Thermidor is 15,800rp. (All these are subject to 15.5% tax and service charge after 4pm.)

The **Seahorse Restaurant** at the Sanur Beach Hotel, tel (0361) 88011, is set right by the sea, where you can sink into over-stuffed armchairs and drink cocktails with names like 'Batur Eruption'. Seafood is the speciality, and is copious. Choose modestly: for around 20,000rp a seafood basket will provide you with as much seafood as you want. Sadly, something in the cooking renders all this marine life rather bland.

In the middle of the range, **Swastika II** on Jl. Tanjung Sari is a good choice for the speciality, *rijsttafel*, at 5,740rp (plus 10% service); while the nearby **Ratu's Pizzeria and Bar** has pizzas at 3,000–4,500rp, *ayam betutu* at 3,500rp, *ikan pepes* at 3,500rp and *ayam goreng bumbu manis* (fried chicken with a sweet sauce) at 3,500rp. All these include rice and trimmings and are recommended. Also reasonable is **Sari's Cafe**, which serves Indonesian and Chinese food, and seafood at mid to low prices (main dishes around 3,000rp).

The **Corner Restaurant**, on the corner between Jl. Tanjung Sari and the road leading to Segara Village Hotel, offers good seafood as well as Chinese, Italian and Indonesian food at standard prices (4–6,000rp for a main meal) in a pleasant, if modest, setting. (Ring (0361) 88462 to take advantage of their free pick-up service to and from hotels in Sanur.)

Raouls & Dragon, also on the Jl. Tanjung Sari, is more up-market and more expensive, with a wide choice of food served by Balinese women in traditional dress.

For lunch by the sea, or indeed dinner, you might like the pleasant but modest **Banjar Restaurant**, in Jl. Duyung (on the south side of the Bali Hyatt), next to the Bali Dive Sports Club. Open 8am–10pm, it serves pasta, steaks, squid and lobster, standard Indonesian rice dishes, sandwiches, 'jaffles' and so forth at very reasonable prices (2–4,000rp for a main course).

Trattoria da Marco, in Semawang in the south of Sanur, on the road to the beach, is still the best place for pasta. In its old site on the bypass it had a loyal following and served much-prized steaks, but now, newly relocated to a spacious but rather impersonal setting, the soul also seems to have left the cooking. 'Uncle Ronnie', as the owner Renaldo is called, comes round the tables personally to check that everything is O.K. He is the Italian consul and has a Javanese wife.

Other restaurants where you can expect a reasonable meal at reasonable prices include: **Lenny Bar and Restaurant**, on Hotel Bali Beach Road, tel (0361) 88585,88572—they run a pick-up service to and from hotels—which specializes in seafood and Chinese food; **Kulkul Restaurant** on the Jl. Tanjung Sari, and **Ronnie's**, in Semawang, between the Hyatt and the Sanur Beach Hotel. Ronnie's is the sort of Western-style restaurant that is good for cushioning culture shock on first arrival.

In Semawang, south of the Bali Hyatt, there are a number of modest *warung*s where you can eat well and cheaply. But, out of defiant perversity, in the face of the lack of good restaurants in Sanur, we nominate **Wayan's Warung**, on Jl. Tanjung Sari, opposite the entrance to the Jl. Pantai Karang, which leads down the beach, as the best restaurant in Sanur. This tiny *warung* which opens directly on to the road has just five tables, and is totally unassuming. Yet for 5,000rp per head you will eat here as well as anywhere in Sanur—excellent seafood, curry and soups.

Serangan Island

Pulau Serangan, Serangan Island (also known as Turtle Island) is a scruffy, low-lying slither of land, about 3 km (1.8 miles) long, which has accumulated on the sandbar that runs across the entrance of Benoa Harbour. From the village of Benoa on the Bukit, Serangan's southern beach, lined with a row of tall palms silhouetted against the sky, is a memorable sight. If you never get any nearer to it, you have not missed much.

Serangan is on the tourist circuit, but it is hard to imagine that it arouses more than disappointment in the large numbers of people who are taken across the sound to see it. On the northern tip of the island there are two villages, **Pojok** and **Dukuh**, separated by a bridged inlet. These are fetching from a distance—clusters of red-tiled roofs and walls of coral—less so close up, as you will discover if you go to Serangan's main attraction: a muddy pond inhabited by 27 Greenback turtles (donation requested). This is surrounded by little shops selling geegaws made of seashells and turtle shell. The Greenback turtles are apparently 'protected'; those that provide the raw material for turtle shell jewellery clearly are not. Remember that it is illegal to import turtle shell into Great Britain, the USA and Australia. You can tell the insistent vendors this, too, but it won't help much: 'Just one thing . . . no business today . . . for good luck', they plead.

A stone's throw away Balinese life continues unscathed. In the quiet precincts of the **Pura Dalem Segara** of Pojok, behind the turtle pond, there is an unusual and ancient *candi* with a lopsided stone crown, set beneath a huge *kepuh* tree.

Serangan is also the site of an important temple, **Pura Sakenan**, said to have been founded by the great 16th-century priest Nirartha (see p.78). To reach it, walk south along the dusty streets of Dukuh. No traffic here, just villagers going about their daily lives, women carrying bowls of fresh tuna on their heads. A five-minute walk takes you to the *banjar* of Dukuh–Sakenan, reached by crossing a causeway over a shallow inlet where fishermen, calf-deep, trawl for tiny fish. There is a snow-white mosque across the lagoon, serving a community of about 100 Muslims from Sulawesi.

Banjar Dukuh–Sakenan, a quiet little hamlet, lies at the head of a path which leads through a coconut grove back to the coast and to Pura Sakenan. There are two parts to the temple. Near the shore is a small *pura dalem*, built of grey volcanic stone and elaborately carved, and including some lovely statues of Ganesha and pigs, among others. Close at hand is Pura Sakenan itself, and a total contrast. This is nothing but a large, grassed compound, empty but for a selection of broad, squat *merus*, four with three roofs and one with five. It is a classic example of the temple as an empty stage; this compound contains nothing of great architectural interest, but it is a sacred spot to which thousands will come to celebrate *odalan* (which coincides with Galungan), crossing from the mainland by boat or wading in the mud at low tide, bearing their offerings. This quiet, tranquil and beautiful spot becomes a seething throng, requiring police to maintain the flow of pilgrims through the temple compound.

GETTING THERE
The usual way to get to Serangan Island is by boat from a *banjar* called **Suwung** 1 km (0.6 miles) south of Sanur. The boats (motorized *jukungs*) leave from the head of a muddy inlet. To reach this point take a small road off the main Sanur–Kuta road; a large sign indicates Serangan Island. The road leads through the grim landscape created by the people who extract salt from the black sand, dotted with their scruffy thatched houses. The *jukung* will take you down the winding creek, lined with mangroves, where fiddler crabs scrabble about in the mud and fishermen wade about with scoop-nets. The pipes and pumps to one side of the creek are evidence of the new industry of the area, shrimp-farming, which is gradually taking over the territory once occupied only by salt workers. The creek emerges into a stretch of open water, with Serangan in front of you. The journey takes 15 minutes, and will cost about 12,000rp there and back; it is exorbitant, but the boats take up to a dozen or so people and so the more there are in your party the softer the blow.

One thing, though, you must know. These boats cannot get in and out of the creek at low tide. So before you plan a trip to Sakenan, watch the tides, and time your trip to go when the tide is rising.

You can also reach the island from Benoa village on the Bukit where the water-sports 'clubs' offer excursions costing around 2,000rp per head.

Nusa Dua

Nusa Dua tourist resort has a style all of its own; stuck out on the eastern tip of Bali's southernmost peninsula, it is a kind of five-star park, like a beautiful ghetto of romantic palm trees, swimming pools, and endless hotel corridors; a never-never land where no one really lives, cocks don't crow and traffic doesn't screech and emit fumes, and no one is allowed to hassle you to buy something you do not want. It is not, in other words, the slightest bit like the rest of Bali. If this is what you are after, it's perfect. You have all of Bali's advantages of wonderful climate, long white-sand beaches, luxury hotels, water sports, and luxuriant tropical vegetation, and none of the awkward problems that staying in such a different culture can pose. It is also conveniently near the airport.

On the other hand, Bali's greatest asset is the people, their way of life, their humour and their culture. If you spend all your time here you will get an unbalanced picture of the

Balinese, because you will only meet the Balinese who are there to cater for your needs, and such culture as is allowed through the gates is carefully controlled. When you set out in your tour bus you are like an illuminated dollar sign in a still poor country, and you will visit specially appointed tourist sites where people hang around all day waiting to sell you the kind of tourist 'tat' they think you want. So be warned: this is not the real Bali.

The road to Nusa Dua passes through the flatter coastal parts of 'the Bukit', the lemon-shaped peninsula at the southern tip of lemon-shaped Bali. The Bukit is unlike the rest of the island, but resembles Nusa Penida, one of the small islands off the southeast coast. The landscape is desolate, sparsely inhabited marshy scrub, with untidy banana groves and, in the languid estuaries, mangroves planted in neat rows to stabilize the boggy ground. Note the large Catholic cemetery (**Kuburan Katolik**) near the village of **Bualu**—the Christian dead banished to this remote spot where they might cause the least offence.

As you come close to the Nusa Dua area there are more signs of life. At 1.5 km (1 mile) outside, a large new shopping precinct has been built, some of its lock-up units still empty. Nearer Nusa Dua some *warung*s appear, and people selling fruit. To the left, a road leads to Benoa, to the right is a turning for **Jimbaran**. Straight ahead is a splendid *candi bentar*, a traditional split gateway announcing the entrance to the Nusa Dua precinct. Inside is the antithesis of Kuta's sprawling chaos, noise and dirt: calm expanses of manicured lawn shaded by massive palms, with drifts of flowering shrubs. Set along the shoreline are the five major hotels of the complex, each in its gloriously landscaped, spacious setting. The hotels look out upon two little knobs of land, barely attached to the shore. These are the two 'islands' that give the place its name: *nusa* (island), *dua* (two).

Nusa Dua is something of a triumph of planning. The travel industry demanded a big increase in first-class accommodation to meet demand, and rather than overload the already stretched facilities of Kuta and Sanur, this luxurious parkland was created in a spot that would cause the minimum of disturbance. The project came under the United Nations development programme and the International Bank for Reconstruction and Development; the master plan was produced by a team of Japanese consultants as early as 1973. In contracting with the major hotel international companies, the Indonesian government were able to insist on a major shareholding, on Garuda being the primary carrier, on the use of local produce in the restaurants, on the terms and conditions of the staff, on the sale and promotion of local crafts, and so forth. Needless to say, the story is not one of unalloyed enlightenment, but considerable care was taken to ensure that Bali and Indonesia would share in the benefits of this expansion.

As for the future, further expansion is planned. Phase 2 of the development envisages two more major hotels by 1991, a Bali Hilton, with 350 rooms (on a site next to the Bali Sol), and a Hyatt Regency with 750 rooms (next to the Putri Bali). By that time Nusa Dua will be capable of offering four- or five-star accommodation to over 200,000 guests a year.

GETTING AROUND

Nusa Dua is 11 km (6.8 miles) south of the airport. Taxis will take you there for about 9,200–12,000rp, but if you have pre-booked your hotel you should get free hotel transport. Public transport to Nusa Dua is sketchy, but there are services running between Denpasar (Terminal Kuta/Tegal) and Nusa Dua on their way to Benoa; a *bemo* ride will cost about 700rp. Otherwise you have to use your own transport.

TOURIST INFORMATION
'The hotels will be able to provide most of the information you need, as well as postal and transport services, international direct dialling phones, telex and fax, religious services, medical facilities, laundry and (limited) shopping. This information is likely to be tourist-oriented; if you have more penetrating questions about what is going on where (ceremonies etc.), take a trip to the Badung Government Tourist Office in Denpasar.

Sun and sea
Well, there's precious little else at Nusa Dua. The hotels will be able to provide everything in the way of water-sports facilities, swimming pools, golf, tennis, food, cultural shows, fashion shows and discotheques.

If you just come for the day, it will be for the beaches, which rank among the best of the island (beware of the currents, though, which can be fearsome, especially towards the south of the zone).

Just settle in your chosen spot and enjoy the peace. The views up towards the volcanoes on the main part of the island are quite wonderful. Or take a gentle wander around the park; you can also walk out to the two little islands from which Nusa Dua gets its name.

WHERE TO STAY
There are five international-class hotels in Nusa Dua. The Nusa Dua Beach Hotel is exceptionally palatial; the Bali Sol is probably the most attractive; the Putri Bali is attractive enough in a business-like way; the Club Mediterranée has its own unique style which will appeal to its aficionados; Hotel Club Bualu is the smallest and most modest, and retains a rather special, tranquil dignity. All have the facilities you expect from this type of hotel, and all but the Bualu front the same long sweep of coastline.

Nusa Dua Beach Hotel (P.O. Box 1028, Denpasar, tel (0361) 71210, 71220; telex 35206 NDBH DPR; fax (0361) 71229) is owned, like the Hotel Sanur Beach, by Aerowisata Hotels. This is incredibly big; its four-storey buildings zigzag over 8.5 hectares (21 acres) of gardens, running alongside the beach. It is all marble and fountains, the various levels connected by hushing lifts; gilt, carved stone and polished wood. Arrive here at night to enjoy the drama of its monumental entrance in Balinese-style architecture. You need to be fit just to get around the hotel, never mind the exercise on offer at the health centre, gym, squash courts, tennis courts and swimming pool. There is a great array of restaurants and bars, and a disco. It is geared very much towards conferences and 'incentive' holidays, with an impressive range of business services and audio-visual equipment. Note that the regular programme of events includes a *janger* dance, very popular with the young Balinese in the 1930s, but now hard to find anywhere on the island. Rooms are $80–110US single and $90–120US double. Suites range from $140US to $1,200US. All prices are subject to the 15.5% tax and service charge.

Meliá Bali Sol (P.O. Box 1048, Tuban, tel (0361) 71510/11/12; telex 35237 SOLDPR; fax (0361) 71360) is owned by Spain's leading hotel chain. It is set in exceptionally luxuriant and graceful tropical gardens. The interior of the hotel is beautiful too. It includes a health centre with sauna, massage and gym. The rooms are decorated to a high international-standard, have IDD telephones and mini bars, but no TV (though there is a TV lounge). There are plenty of bars and restaurants, shops, tennis and squash courts, swimming pool and water-sports facilities, children's playground, and discotheque, and a wonderful outdoor theatre for cultural shows, besides the huge swimming pool. There are full conference facilities. Bali Sol has 390 rooms and suites. Rooms cost $86 US single and $92 US double. There are suites for $142 US and $605 US. All rates are subject to the 15.5% tax and service charge.

Putri Bali (P.O. Box 1, Denpasar 80363, tel (0361) 71020, 71420; telex 35247 HPBDPR; cable NUSA BALI; fax (0361) 71139) is another massive hotel, with 425 rooms and suites and extensive conference and business facilities. It opened in 1985 and is owned by the Indonesian government. There is all you can think of in the way of sports and entertainment facilities, plenty of bars and restaurants, a disco, swimming pool and so on. The exterior, looking down over the beach and blue sea, is very romantic, but the rooms and corridors are impersonal. Rooms have telephone, mini bar and TV with video programmes. They cost $70–78 US single, $80–88 US double. Suites and cottages are $100–500 US. All prices are subject to the 15.5% tax and service charge.

Club Méditerranée (P.O. Box 7, Nusa Dua, tel (0361) 71520/2; telex 35216 BHVCM; bookings through Club offices around the world) is, of course, similar in organization to other Club Meds. Seasoned guests (or '*gentils membres*', GMs) wouldn't have it any other way. The concept of Club Med is that the GMs should be supplied with everything they need on site for an all-inclusive price, and that there should be a constant flow of organized activities to keep them amused. In all Club Meds the food is excellent, as are the sports facilities, but the accommodation can be rudimentary; single GMs may have to share a room. Club Med is French, but the majority of visitors here are Japanese (especially honeymooners) and Australian. It has all the style, elegance and 'pazzazz' associated with the Club's highly successful formula, but you have to like this kind of organized fun to make the most of it. Club Med Nusa Dua offers its 700 GMs sailing, windsurfing, snorkelling, tennis, squash, archery, aerobics, yoga, basketball, volleyball, badminton and golf, and a large swimming pool (no scuba-diving, though). The keep fit centre includes sauna and steam room, jacuzzi and massage. This is a 'family club' (unlike the riotous singles club for which Club Med was once renowned) and there are plenty of supervised activities for children. Workshops for local craft skills are available, such as batik and woodcarving. Holidays here are usually organized as a package with all-inclusive prices, but you can also book in on a nightly basis. The tariff per 24 hours is $100 US per person on Fri, Sat and Sun; $85 US weekdays.

Hotel Club Bualu (P.O. Box 6, Nusa Dusa, Denpasar, tel (0361) 71310/1; telex 35231 BUALU ND) is the smallest of the Nusa Dua hotels, with 50 rooms in modern two-storey blocks set in pleasant gardens. The beach is 500 m (500 yards) from the hotel, but there are quaint horse-drawn carriages to take you there for free. The same carriages take guests on tours of the Nusa Dua park area. There are good water-sports facilities, plus tennis, archery, and jogging tracks. An extra attraction is the availability of horses for riding, perfect on Bali's broad beaches (see p.50). Another speciality is scuba-diving, for which the hotel is the best equipped on the island (this is the only P.A.D.I. diving centre in Indonesia). A six-day instruction programme leading to a basic P.A.D.I. certificate costs $150 US, including the cost of equipment. Although there are full conference facilities here as at the other Nusa Dua hotels, they are smaller in scale.

Despite being government-run, the Bualu has an intimate, friendly feeling to it, and the arrangements for children are good. There is the usual array of bars and restaurants, but no disco. The place serves as a training ground for the students of the next-door government-run school for hotel and restaurant staff (BPLP). The Benoa Harbour Restaurant, the best of its kind in Bali, is but a stone's throw away, and effectively part of the hotel's facilities. Room rates are $55 US single and $60 US double. There are suites for $90 US. An additional $10 US per night is payable in the high season at Christmas and during July and August. All rates are subject to the 15.5% tax and service charge.

WHERE TO EAT

All the restaurants are attached to hotels, and since they are specifically designed to keep you in, you may find there is no cause to venture out.

The **Benoa Harbour Restaurant** next to the Hotel Club Bualu, however, deserves special commendation. You are impeccably served by students from the next-door hotel training school, and the food, especially seafood, is fresh and delicious, at very reasonable prices. Try the lobster, crab and prawn in papaya for a starter, 6,500rp. Main courses are between 5,000 and 8,000rp. Bali really does not have first-class independent restaurants which stand on the reputation of their cuisine, as in the West. But the Benoa Harbour Restaurant, in its tranquil garden setting, gets pretty near the mark. It is open 7 am–11 pm; tel (0361) 71310 (Hotel Bualu) for reservations.

Nusa Dua residents who wish to stray beyond the barricades to sample some ordinary Indonesian food could try the **Sumarta Restaurant**, next to the main entrance to the hotel zone, where prices for the usual fare are reasonable.

Benoa

Just outside the Nusa Dua complex, a turning north (no sign) takes you onto the narrow peninsula of land which terminates in the small village of Benoa. (For **Benoa Port**, see below.) Just travelling this short distance from Nusa Dua is a culture shock. The village itself has the open, salty charm of any active, undeveloped fishing village, and the aroma to go with it. There are few concessions to tourists here. From the concrete pierhead you can see over to Serangan Island, lying long and low in the water. Scruffy children gather here, along with Bugis seamen from the traditional schooners moored in the harbour.

The patch of sea enclosed by this narrow stretch of land and the long breakwater of Benoa Port across the water makes the best natural harbour of the island. Deep-water ships can moor here, including cruise ships.

Some of the ships in Benoa import live turtles from Sulawesi, some with shells over 1.5 m (5 ft) in length, which take four men to carry. It is a heartbreaking sight. Their front flippers are stitched together to immobilize them for the voyage. The Greenback turtles of Serangan Island are much smaller, between 45 cm (18 in) and 1 m (3 ft). On some parts of the beach around Benoa you see bamboo cages several yards out into the water, where turtles are kept for fattening up. Denpasar is a centre for the sale of turtles, for Bali and for other islands. In Bali they are part of certain age-old ceremonies and religious offerings. They are also considered a great delicacy, as soup and as *sate*.

You do not see many Chinese in the village, but there is a large and garish Chinese temple on the northeastern corner of the village, guarded by strange painted mythological creatures. There is also a big Chinese cemetery beside the road to the south of the village. It seems likely that the Chinese population was decimated during the anti-Communist killings of 1965. The Balinese temple as you enter the village has a Chinese influence apparent in the painted *raksasa* guarding it.

People come to Benoa to enjoy the wide range of water sports offered at competitive prices by the 'clubs' along the beach to the south. It is not a particularly lovely spot, but you do feel as though you are getting away from it all, and Benoa certainly has the tang of authenticity.

GETTING THERE
*Bemo*s come here from Denpasar's Tegal/Terminal Kuta station, via Kuta (700rp). If you have your own transport, turn left before the entrance to the Nusa Dua complex. Benoa is about 4km (2.5miles) from this point.

WATER SPORTS
Along the approach road to Benoa several water-sports centres have sprung up, catering for parties who come out from Kuta, Sanur and Nusa Dua for diving, windsurfing and the like. Note that swimming from the beach is forbidden, and low tide reveals an unattractive spread of rocks, mud and seaweed.

At **Rai Restaurant**, for example, you can book a snorkelling expedition to Serangan Island for 5,000rp per person, for a three-hour trip. It also offers scuba-diving, wind-surfing, parasailing, fishing, waterskiing and power boats. The **Mekau Sari Club** has facilities for snorkelling, scuba-diving, fishing, sailing and water bikes. 'Tonny Rude' invites you to go paraflying, 'The New Wave Flying Sport'. The **Samudra Water-Sports Club**, tel (0361) 88776, will arrange scuba-diving and snorkelling trips all over the island.

WHERE TO STAY AND EAT
There are a few *losmen* near the water-sports clubs on the southern approach to Benoa, beside the road and facing the sea.

Agung Losmen is new, spacious and attractive, decked with bougainvillea and with lots of space to sit outside. At present there are only four rooms, costing 20,000rp single or double, not including breakfast.

Rai Seafood Restaurant is open daily from 7am–10pm. Its prices reflect its proximity to Nusa Dua—lobster is 17,000rp and prawns 4,000rp. They entice their clients with special attractions such as cockfighting and *legong* dancing. For these you must book, tel (0361) 71633, and free transport can be provided from your hotel.

Dalang Restaurant is next door to Agung Losmen, and handy for breakfast. Again, seafood is the speciality, and prices are slightly keener than at Rai.

Benoa Port
Confusion arises here because a small port at the end of a jetty on the opposite side of the bay to Benoa village is called Benoa Port; the natural harbour formed in this bay is Labuhan Benoa, or Benoa Harbour.

Benoa Port is reached from the bypass between Kuta and Sanur. There is nothing much here, just a small group of warehouses, fuel tanks, a lighthouse and a quay where cargo-ships dock. Out in the bay is an anchorage for ocean-going yachts. The Bali International Yacht Club has a base here, and there are a couple of fly-blown bars. There is small charge for entering the harbour area.

Jimbaran

The quiet village of Jimbaran is on the western side of the neck of land connecting the Bukit with the mainland, just south of the airport. The village itself is of no great interest, the last of a string of three villages that line a dusty, pot-holed road across the Bukit to Ulu Watu. Jimbaran is still an active fishing village. At dawn, the beach fills with fishing folk unloading baskets of shiny tuna from the boats. They use keeled fishing boats (not outriggers) which are anchored off-shore, travelling over to the Javanese coast to find their catch, a hard life which makes them a surly breed. They don't care a fig for tourists.

The beach is lovely, one of the best in Bali, a broad sweep of white sand, peaceful and clean (except for the occasional dead fish washed up from the fishing boats), with a sea quiet enough to make it ideal for swimming. This is one of the zones which has been earmarked for tourist development in the next few years. To date there are but two hotels, both of a high standard. Enjoy it now: this is the perfect spot to find repose after a long flight.

WHERE TO STAY AND EAT

PanSea Puri Bali (reservations to Golden Kris, Jl. Sanur 58A, Kedaton, P.O. Box 108, Denpasar 80001, tel (0361) 25850; telex 35187 GKRIS (attn. Pansea Bali); fax (0361) 27769) is owned by a French group which specializes in small-scale hotels in exceptional locations; this connection no doubt also explains its extremely good food. The 41 rooms (33 bungalows and eight two-storey family rooms) are built in traditional Balinese style, with garden bathrooms, and are pretty and comfortable. There is plenty of space here: Sanur and Kuta seem comparatively cramped. There is a large swimming pool, tennis court, badminton, volleyball, table tennis, windsurfing, and boats can be hired for fishing. The beach restaurant is uninteresting, but the buffet-style food for breakfast and dinner is very good indeed. Seafood nights, accompanied by some excellent dancing, are quite delicious; non-residents are welcome for the fixed price of 15,000rp. We recommend staying on a half-board basis, which includes breakfast and dinner. However, the buffet-style catering entails rather inflexible eating hours, which may not be ideal for families with young children. Full board is $66–82 US single, $82–102 US double. Half-board is $58–74 US single and $66–86 US double. These prices include 15.5% tax and service charge, which makes the Puri Bali excellent value in this range. Note, however, that the PanSea takes a block booking from Asia Holidays during the peak periods (Christmas and July/August) so cannot take other bookings during these times.

Jimbaran Beach Club (P.O. Box 21, Nusa Dua 80363, tel (0361) 51505) is built above the beach beside a dramatic moonscape of limestone quarries, which gives it a lonesome, other-worldly atmosphere. It is Japanese-owned and largely patronized by Japanese. There are 30 rooms in well-designed, if stark, two-storey buildings, all air-conditioned, with hot water, telephones and fridges. The facilities include water-sports equipment and a large but unattractive swimming pool. Rooms are $45 US single and $50 US double, which does not include breakfast and the 15.5% tax and service charge.

Budget travellers will be able to find rooms in family compounds in Jimbaran for 7,000rp or so. Just ask around. However, these are unlikely to have direct access to the sea.

Ulu Watu

At the most western tip of the Bukit, Pura Luhur Ula Watu is one of Bali's most important temples—one of the *kayangan jagat*, the nine 'directional temples' of Bali (see p.116). Its location is dramatic, perched on the edge of a high cliff. Try to see it at sunset. Some say it was first used as a place of worship in the early 11th century at the time of Kuturan, who came to Bali from Java to teach the Hindu religion. But the temple also honours the doctrine of the holy man Nirartha, who came at a later date, around 1550. It is said that Nirartha spent his last days here, where he achieved *moksa*, the moment of enlightenment and the release of the soul. The title 'Luhur' comes from the Balinese word for *moksa*, *ngeluhur*. Unusually the temple faces west; there is no *padmasana* facing Mt Agung.

It is really its location that makes it so special. The views up and down the rocky coast are spectacular, with the distant heave of the sea far below and the scent of the frangipani blossom mixed with the warm salt air. This is also home to a small band of friendly monkeys.

The temple is made of grey volcanic stone, all well restored, and there are some fine carvings. The unusual arched gateway to the inner temple is flanked by a pair of splendid Ganeshas. To the left of the main entrance, at the top of the long flight of steps, is a small courtyard which is the site of Nirartha's *moksa*. In the stone shrine at the back of this is a weather-beaten stone statue of Nirartha.

GETTING THERE

Ulu Watu is about 27 km (18 miles) from Denpasar, at the end of the road which runs southwest across the Bukit. *Bemo*s from Tegal/Terminal Kuta in Denpasar cost 800rp and take up to an hour.

There are spectacular views northwards at the point where this road rises into the Bukit beyond Jimbaran; you can see both sides of the isthmus, with the airport to the west and Benoa Harbour to the east. The enterprising **Warung Indah** has been built here to exploit the view. The road continues through dry scrubland, dotted with eucalyptus and kapok trees and coconut palms. Cattle browse in small pastures, hedged in by lines of entwined cactus. The earth is a deep red, punctuated by the brilliant white of small limestone quarries where the soft stone is eked out into neatly squared blocks. Some carpenters along this route specialize in building wooden shrines for family temples. You pass through only two villages: Simpangan and Pecatu.

You can park a short walk from the temple. The car park has the usual throng of vendors, but the calm of Ulu Watu is strong enough to affect even them.

SURFING AT ULU WATU

Pantai Suluban
About 500 m (500 yards) short of Ulu Watu a path leads to the most celebrated surfing beach on Bali (see Surfing, pp.44–46).

To reach the beach (clearly signposted) you have to walk 3 km (1.85 miles), or bump for 10 minutes down a very bad, narrow track on a motorbike, to a parking place (200rp) where there are shelters for bikes. Beyond this, steps lead down to a place above the shoreline where there are *warung*s, and shops offering surfboards for hire (10,000rp per hour) and massages. The view over the sea is beautiful; there is a friendly, relaxed atmosphere here. High tide is the time to surf; low tide exposes a large expanse of beach.

North of Denpasar

Out of Denpasar a busy road goes through the villages of **Sempidi**, **Lukluk** and **Kapal** (now run together to make an almost continuous built-up area) and on to Tabanan. You can also go north by the Seminyak road from Legian, avoiding Denpasar. Follow the signs to **Canggu** and **Canggu Beach** (noted for its pleasantly gentle surf, and an area that has caught the attention of developers). It is a pretty road with a very bad surface. You join the Denpasar road at Sempidi. Sempidi, Lukluk and Kapal all have lively, imaginative stone carvings on their temples. Ask for the three village (*desa*) temples in Sempidi; and the **Pura Dalem** in Lukluk, which is some way out of the town, set in coconut groves. Kapal specializes in stone carving and decorative ceramics, which are sold to *banjar*s all over Bali for their gardens and temples. Some are garishly painted; suburban garden gnomes have nothing on these. They delight by their outrageousness.

A right turn just before **Kapal** takes you north to the monkey forest of Sangeh.

Pura Sadha, Kapal

The decorative carvings here are famous for their intricacy and ingenuity. The temple honours Ratu Sakti Jayengrat, a noble who was said to have sailed from the Majapahit empire in Java, and to have been stranded on a coral reef at Kapal (*kapal* means 'boat'), in the days when the sea came this far inland. It seems rather far-fetched; *puras* means low tide, so it may just be a play on words. When the area was under the rule of the Mengwi rajadom, the temple was rebuilt as a state shrine. It was destroyed by an earthquake in 1917 and not rebuilt again until 1950.

There are 64 stone seats in the temple, which may be representations of megalithic stone seats for the spirits of ancestors. On the top of a modern brick *candi* are statues of the nine lords of directions (the ninth is the lord of the centre).

The temple is set back from the main road, down a bumpy old track to the left as you come from the south, and signalled by a massive banyan tree in its outer courtyard.

GETTING THERE
Kapal is 16 km (10 miles) north of Denpasar on the main road to Tabanan and points west, so is well served by public transport, which leaves from Ubung station. A *bemo* will cost 350rp.

Pura Taman Ayun, Mengwi

This is high on the stakes for Bali's most beautiful temple. It was once the temple of the royal family of Mengwi, the old rajadom which was eradicated and split in two by Badung and Tabanan in 1885. Descendents of the royal family still maintain the temple—making it an important 'clan temple' (*pura kawitan*, see pp.116–17) for the Ksatria caste associated with Mengwi.

Mengwi became a rajadom in 1627, and the temple was built in 1634. A moat surrounds the large, grassy terraces of the outer temple; on its banks are perfumed flowering trees such as frangipani and *cempaka*, as well as fruit trees bearing mangosteen, durian, mango and rambutan. The peaceful waters of a second moat surround the inner courtyard of the temple. There is an atmosphere of meditative calm.

Entrance to the middle courtyard is through a split gate, *candi bentar*. The inner courtyard contains the important shrines of the temple, lined along the right-hand wall. The impressive thicket of tall, many-tiered towers stands up above the greenery surrounding the temple grounds, mysterious and exotic. There are some 50 buildings and shrines within the temple complex. The *gedong Paibon* (third from the end on the right) is dedicated to Ibu Paibon, the ancestral soul of the royal family. The other shrines represent the major temples of Bali, so that the people of Mengwi could celebrate the main ceremonies of those temples here, and share in the benefits from them. Pura Ulu Watu, for instance, is represented by the eleven-tiered *meru* in the far right-hand corner, and Pura Sakenan by the *meru* to the right of this. The tallest of the *meru*s represents Besakih. Unusually, the line of the temple is directed not towards Agung, but towards Mt Batukau, and the eleven-tiered *meru* to Pura Luhur on Batukau stands at the far end. The *trimurti padmasana*, dedicated to the Hindu trinity, faces the *kaja* position (towards Mt Agung) on the right-hand side as you enter the courtyard.

There is a revealing story attached to the two-tiered shrine immediately on the right as you enter the courtyard. This is dedicated to Pasek Badak, an enemy of the King of Mengwi. At the moment of Badak's death in defeat, Badak pleaded that he should be allowed a shrine in the Mengwi temple; the concession was granted, so within the royal Mengwi complex is a shrine to an enemy.

Outside the moat, a complex which caters for tourists has been built (open during daylight hours, closed Sun), including a large shop selling local handicrafts, a painting workshop, a restaurant and a museum. You can reach it from the temple on a little raft which is pulled across the moat on ropes, free of charge. It's all very pleasant, unless your arrival coincides with that of a large tour bus. The shop has some good quality handicrafts: woodcarvings, baskets, textiles and some clothes, and the prices are reasonable. Vendors are under strict instructions not to pester. The museum is boldly entitled 'Musium of Complete Cremation' but has a rather pathetic atmosphere of incompletion; funds ran out before it was finished. The collection consists of the many different kinds of palm-woven offerings made for the various ceremonies—temple ceremonies and life-cycle ceremonies such as childbirth, tooth-filing, marriage and cremation and so forth.

The restaurant serves good Indonesian and Chinese food at fairly high prices, and has the blessing of a beautiful setting overlooking the moat and the temple beyond. There are no other restaurants here, nor places to stay.

GETTING THERE

*Bemo*s run north from Ubung bus station in Denpasar to Mengwi and beyond to Bedugul. To Mengwi takes an hour and costs 400rp. It is virtually impossible to get across to Mengwi from Ubud by public transport. By motorbike or car it is straight forward from Denpasar—take the right turn just after Kapal, it is signposted—but slightly complicated if you're cutting across from Ubud. You need to turn right off the Sayan road to Denpasar, through Semana, Aseman and Cemengan. The surface on these back roads is full of potholes but still negotiable.

Sangeh monkey forest

There is a lovely mossy temple here, hidden among tall, gracious trees, but you hardly notice it for the swarms of monkeys and their tourist prey. Do not take any food for the monkeys or encourage them in any way, unless you think it's funny to lose your keys, your sunglasses or your camera . . . Locals will offer you sticks to fend them off.

Sangeh, or Bukit Sari, is a sacred forest, where no one may chop wood. The story goes that Hanuman, the monkey general in the *Ramayana* stories, tried to kill the evil demon Rawana by squashing him between two halves of the sacred Mahameru mountain. In the process part of the mountain fell to earth with a group of Hanuman's monkey army. This created the Bukit (*bukit* means 'hill'), and the monkeys live there to this day.

The temple, Pura Bukit Sari, is not as old as it looks. It was probably built in the 17th century, but was restored as recently as 1973. The Garuda statue may predate the temple. The soaring trees are nutmeg trees, not seen elsewhere in Bali, and assumed to have been cultivated long ago.

GETTING THERE
Sangeh is very much on the tourist route, and you can steam up here in a tour bus from virtually any resort you care to mention. It lies 21 km (13 miles) north of Denpasar, on its own road that leads on up the slopes of Mt Catur, through the villages of Petang and Pelaga. You can come here by *bemo*, leaving Denpasar's Wangaya bus station, which serves mainly this route. It will cost about 400rp.

Part VI

GIANYAR REGENCY

The candis at Gunung Kawi

If you leave the southern tourist spots your route will probably take you to Gianyar regency. Gianyar is the heartland of Bali's arts and crafts, with Ubud and its neighbouring villages as the central focus. The regency encompasses a broad swathe of fertile hills that rise quickly from the sea towards Mt Batur. Most of the hills have been sculpted into rice terraces, fed by rivers and streams. Its very fertility has given the region a long history of wealth and culture: here are the royal temples and archaeological remains of the kingdom that centred upon Pejeng in the earliest phase of Bali's recorded past. The whole landscape speaks of centuries of unfolding history based upon the diligent management of the rivers and the soil.

Today Gianyar is still primarily rural—a mass of small communities working their adjoining fields. Many of these have long-standing traditions of producing their own specialist crafts, handed down from generation to generation. Since the 1930s when crafts first started to become an economic pursuit, not just a religious one, these activities have burgeoned, so that nowadays throughout the region people sculpt, paint, weave, sew, dance and play *gamelan* music, either full-time or in the free hours afforded by the routine of rice cultivation.

It is the creative arts and the richness of traditions that attract tourists to the region now. Accommodation—which is almost exclusively located in the Ubud area—is mostly family based: relaxed and informal, friendly and inexpensive. The foothills in the centre of the regency have the further advantage of a relatively cool, fresh climate, a relief after the sweltering heat of the coastal resorts—excellent for walking or cycling to the outlying villages and seeing Bali at its most beguiling. The coastline, with its wide sweeps of

187

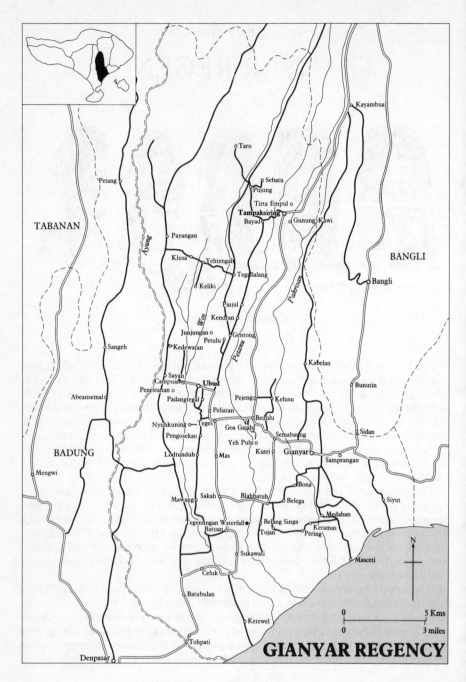

GIANYAR REGENCY

TABANAN

BADUNG

BANGLI

Kayambua

Taro

Petang

Sebatu
Pujung
Tirta Empul
Tampaksiring
Bayad
Gunung Kawi

Payangan

Klusa
Yehtengah
Tegallalang
Bangli

Keliki

Pinjul
Kendran
Gentong
Junjungan
Petulu
Sangeh
Kedewatan

Kabelan

Bunutin

Sayan
Campuan
Ubud
Penestanan
Padangtegal
Pejeng
Kelusu
Abeansemal
Peliatan
Bedulu
Sidan
Nyuhkuning
Teges
Goa Gajah
Semabaung
Pengosekan
Yeh Pulu
Mengwi
Lodtunduh
Mas
Kutri
Gianyar
Samprangan

Bona
Mawang
Sakah
Blahbatuh
Belega
Siyut
Medahan
Tegenungan Waterfall
Belang Singa
Keramas
Batuan
Tojan
Pering
Sukawati
Masceti
Celuk

Batubulan

Ketewel

Tohpati

Denpasar

Ayung

Wos

Petanu

Pakrisan

N

0   5 Kms
0   3 miles

volcanic sand on to which beats a turbulent sea, is refreshingly beautiful, and quite undeveloped.

Historical notes

From Pejeng dynasty to the Dewa Manggis

Gianyar has been the stamping ground of Bali's earliest dynasties in recorded history. It is here that the first great lines of Hinduized kings established themselves around a place which has given the kingdom its historic name: Pejeng.

Pejeng was the centre of power until the early 14th century, ruled by a series of kings of the Warmadewa line with varying degrees of autonomy, the last of whom was defeated in 1343 by the Majapahit empire of eastern Java under Gajah Mada. During the Pejeng period a series of royal temples, meditation cells, baths and other monuments were built along the banks of the sacred Pakrisan river from Bitra to Tirtha Empul. The whole of the central region of the regency is now dotted with ancient remains.

It was not, however, until the late 17th century that the territory began to emerge as a separate identity as the power of the Dewa Agung, the chief raja of Bali, waned and other rajadoms established themselves with differing degrees of independence. Gianyar was founded in 1667 by a son of the fourth Dewa Agung, later taking the title of Dewa Manggis Kuning. Manggis, meaning literally mangosteen, is the family name and is believed to relate to the village of Manggis in Klungkung. Kuning means yellow, the peculiar colour of the man's skin. Dewa Manggis Kuning is not flattered by history: he is said to have been so despicable that he turned into a snake after death. A famous story is told of an escapade in his youth. As a young man, he was sent by his father, the Dewa Agung, as ambassador to the court of the Raja of Badung. Here he had a passionate affair with the raja's most beautiful wife, an offence punishable by death. When the truth came out, however, Dewa Manggis effected his escape by having himself rolled up in a mat and carried out of the *puri* on the head of an old woman. This tale does rather more credit to the strength of Balinese women than it does to its hero.

All of Gianyar's history until the turn of the 20th century, was coloured by continuing squabbles over boundaries and water rights with the neighbouring rajadoms, but by the 1870s Gianyar was prospering and set to become the most powerful rajadom under the charismatic leadership of Dewa Manggis VII. However, on a reconciliatory mission to Klungkung he and his four sons were imprisoned by the Dewa Agung, who then set about dividing up Gianyar between himself and the Raja of Bangli. Two of the sons escaped and one of them, Dewa Gede Raka, went to Ubud, whose powerful *punggawa*, Cokorda Sukawati, helped him to raise an army, and by 1892 Dewa Gede Raka was able to assume his father's seat in Gianyar. To consolidate his position, Dewa Gede Raka decided to solicit the support of the Dutch, with the ultimate result that in 1900 Gianyar slipped voluntarily into the ambit of Dutch colonial rule. Dewa Gede Raka was formally made Dewa Manggis VIII in 1908, the last in the line to hold this title.

His two successors are representative of the changes that have taken place in Bali in the 20th century. Agung Ngurah Agung, born in 1892, ruled from 1912 to 1943 when conditions under the Japanese occupation forced him out of office and into exile in Lombok. He died in 1960. He was one of the last great Balinese rajas—if greatness is measured by autocratic flamboyance. He had 24 wives (but only nine children), and was driven about in a grand Fiat Phaeton, so weighed down with ornament, including the golden Garuda on the bonnet, that it had to be pushed whenever it encountered a hill. He played host to numerous Western dignitaries, including Charlie Chaplin, and was celebrated for his lavish hospitality. Ide Anak Agung Ngurah Agung was accomplished in all things relating to Balinese culture. His son, Anak Agung, by contrast, went to Western-style schools and was a child of the larger world.

Anak Agung 'Belga', fluent in Dutch, German, French and English as well as the three Balinese languages and Indonesian, succeeded his father in 1943. He played a leading role at the Round Table Conference in the Hague, during which the integrated state of the Republic of Indonesia was forged, and became Minister of the Interior for the central Indonesian government. He was later appointed ambassador to Belgium (hence his title 'Belga'), then France, before being imprisoned in Indonesia in 1962 for his alleged associations with parties critical of Sukarno. He spent four years in jail, was released in 1966 and from 1970–74, was ambassador to Austria. Meanwhile the palace at Gianyar remained a family home in the traditional style of the rajas of old, albeit informed by experience of the world outside.

Renaissance in Ubud: Spies and Bonnet
During the 1930s certain Western visitors began to have a more profound influence on Balinese culture than the small but steady influx of tourists. Ubud had long been established as a centre of painting, music and dancing, and during the 1930s it was to this area that visitors interested in Balinese culture came to live and study. Some of them worked with the Balinese, influencing and being influenced by Bali's creative life. Among them were the painters Walter Spies and Rudolf Bonnet; Colin McPhee, who came to study *gamelan* music and later wrote *A House in Bali* (1944), and his anthropologist wife, Jane Belo; and whole string of other writers, painters, film makers, photographers and intellectuals.

An important figure in this development was the 'Prince' of Ubud, the Cokorda Gede Agung Sukawati, who held court in his *puri*, receiving visits from numerous Westerners and who was a founding father of the Pitha Maha painters' co-operative in 1935, along with Spies and Bonnet. (For the significance of these Western artists in Balinese art, see pp.62–3.)

Walter Spies was a German, born in Moscow in 1895. He was already a painter of some renown when in 1925 he landed the job of director of music of the European orchestra of the Sultan of Jogyakarta, but by 1927 he had moved to Bali, where he became something of an institution to visiting Westerners. He painted very little—but those paintings he did produce have a unique and luminous quality that proved highly influential. In 1938, Spies, a homosexual, was arrested by the Dutch authorities for fear that his moral behaviour was tarnishing the colonists' reputation. He remained imprisoned in Denpasar, then in Java, then in Sumatra until the outbreak of war in Europe, whereupon, as a German, he became doubly suspect. In 1942, on the eve of the Japanese invasion, he found himself with 15,000 other German internees, who were put aboard three ships bound for India and Ceylon. Two days out of Padang, Sumatra, Spies's ship was attacked from the air by the Japanese and sunk.

Interned by the Japanese during the Second World War, Rudolf Bonnet lived on until

190

1978, returning to Bali after the war to help create the Museum Puri Lukisan in Ubud. When he died, his ashes were brought back to Bali and were scattered in the sea at the cremation of his friend, Cokorda Gede Agung Sukawati in 1979.

Spies, it seems, was not happy about the way Balinese painters copied and adapted Western styles of art. But this is history: the marriage had been made.

Gianyar

Gianyar is a busy market town, a staging post between the various regions fed by the roads east, north and west. It is also the centre of administration for a regency that is the fastest developing area of Bali outside of Badung.

Gianyar is no real tourist attraction. The main part of town is a dusty place, stretching along the heavily used main road, lined with parked vehicles and three-storey buildings, most of which seem to be occupied by sprawling, oily motor repair workshops going about their business beneath a net of telegraph wires. It centres around the old palace (*puri*) of the rajas, and the huge open space, the *alun-alun*, opposite it. The *puri* has played a venerable part in Gianyar's history, but it is still a private residence and not open to the public without prior permission. The big tour buses stop at the weaving workshops on the outskirts on the Ubud road, then pass straight through on their way east or north.

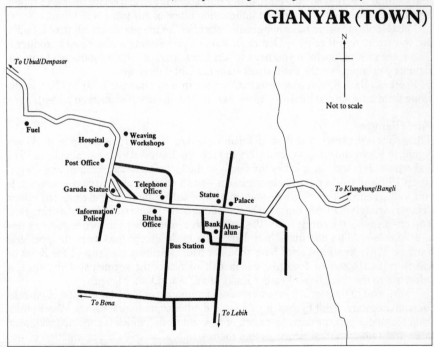

Gianyar Town

191

Where the road sweeps in from Ubud on a short stretch of dual-carriageway, there is a splendidly vigorous modern statue of Garuda, with Vishnu—the preserver of universal order—on his shoulders. Garuda has a human form, except for his bird-like head, with its fearsomely toothed beak.

From time to time popular fairs are held in the open ground opposite the *puri* where the unmarried young Balinese can meet in an atmosphere reminiscent of traditional English fairs. The Balinese children we took gazed open-mouthed at the tawdry delights of a tatty roundabout and near-derelict house of horrors, but were much too terrified to try them. These events are always packed and very noisy.

GETTING AROUND

You pass through Gianyar if you are heading east to Klungkung and beyond, but you don't usually have to change *bemo* or bus. If you are going north you need to change here for Bangli. The *bemo* station is outside the market on the main road. Transport is regular—it's a busy region. From Ubud the 12 km (7.5 mile) journey to Gianyar by *bemo* costs 450rp.

TOURIST INFORMATION

The so-called 'Information' office next to the road by the military building on the way into Gianyar seems to be little more than a bureaucratic quirk: it seems unable to supply any information at all. The nearest information office of any value is in Ubud.

The **telephone** office has a marginally better line for international calls than Ubud's, but you are better off going to Denpasar, where direct dialling is now being introduced. The Elteha office, useful if you need to send large parcels within Indonesia, is on the right as you come into the main street from the Ubud direction.

There is a Bank Rakyat Indonesia ('authorized **money changer**') 200 m (200 yards) along from a turning to the right by the *puri* (follow the signpost marked Lebih).

Puri Gianyar

The palace is the seat of the Rajas of Gianyar, first built in 1771, destroyed by the Dewa Agung of Klungkung in or around 1885 and rebuilt, destroyed by an earthquake in 1917 and rebuilt. It is still occupied by the family of the incumbent raja, Anak Agung 'Belga' (see p.190) and you need special permission—and a good reason—to gain admission. If you walk along by the high wall that lines the road to the main gate, marked rather democratically No.99, you can glimpse something of the gilded splendour of a living *puri*. You can also visit the courtyard on the western side, where there are two imposing gates and four *bale*s. The guardians here have little to do except turn away disappointed tourists. Their smart uniforms have shoulder badges bearing the crest of the Rajas of Gianyar: a mangosteen (*manggis*) cut in half to reveal the segments of the fruit, a reference to the title given to earlier Rajas of Gianyar, Dewa Manggis.

To the west of the *puri* is a curious modern monument of black lava, a kind of languid fountain decorated with figures of *raksasas* and other supernatural beings. Water pours from the upper part through the mouth of a 'world turtle', which is entwined with four large and rather startled *nagas*. Before them stands a horse—a representation of the famous white charger of Kapakisan, the first Majapahit ruler of Bali, whose palace was down the road at Samprangan.

Ikat weaving

Most tours going east from Sanur and Kuta stop at the factory workshops outside Gianyar to see the local weaving. These are geared to expect tourists, so someone usually speaks English and they have stocks of fabric for sale, so it's not a bad idea to stop here. Good quality *ikat* from these workshops costs around 15,000rp per metre/yard. If you ever have your clothes tailored, or make them yourself, this fabric is worth serious consideration. See pp.65–66 for a description of the process of production.

East of Gianyar

The town of Gianyar peters out quickly to the east, where a bridge spans a tributary of the Sangsang river. A pretty stretch of road through ricefields lies between this bridge and the next, over the Sangsang itself, and on to **Samprangan** and the turning north to Bangli at Pegesangan, near the border with Klungkung regency. Just to the north of this lies **Sidan** with its remarkable *pura dalem*.

Samprangan

When the general Gajah Mada defeated the Balinese Pejeng dynasty in 1343, he set up Kapakisan, a Javanese nobleman, as the new raja to rule the kingdom in the name of the Majapahit empire. The new palace was at Samprangan (also spelled Samplangan), 2 km (1.25 miles) to the east of Gianyar.

Nothing remains of the palace itself. The *pura dalem*, set back to the north of the road in the middle of the village, behind the large village *wantilan*, is said to have formed part of it. It is certainly very old, particularly the main shrine (the *gedong pesimpangan*). Note the series of empty cavities in the walls of this building, where once Chinese porcelain plates were set, dislodged by an earth tremor (*gejor*) of unknown date. The unusual tall megalith to the right is a kind of safe: here religious treasures are stored way above ground behind the pair of closed doors, beyond the reach of thieving hands.

There are a number of sugar-palm thatched god-houses to the right of this, in the *kangin* direction. Note the one with the wooden image of the deer, with horns. This is called the *menjangan luang*, associated with the Golden deer of the Ramayana epic, but also symbolic of Majapahit ancestry.

There is a round bowl on a stand to the left of the main god-house. This is reputed to be the drinking bowl used by Kapakisan's white charger. Some villagers claim they see the soul of the horse drinking here from time to time.

Sidan

The Pura Dalem of Sidan is worth a visit for its stone carvings of demons on the outer walls. The vitality of the stone friezes make it an unnerving place at dusk, though the lively representations of Boma, Durga and Rangda over the gates are supposed to keep out malevolent spirits. The temple is on the main Bangli–Gianyar road, and is clearly marked.

, TO STAY AND EAT

; nowhere to stay in Gianyar that we can recommend. Ubud is only 10 km (6.25 miles) away, and has all the facilities you could wish for.

Much the same applies to eating, although Gianyar does have a celebrated speciality: *babi guling* (roast piglet). The best place to buy this is the *warung*s in the Bioskop (cinema) building, but get there early; it's all gone by 11 am, Balinese lunch time.

UBUD

Although Gianyar is technically the main town of the regency, the heart of its interest for tourists is Ubud, 10 km (6.25 miles) to the northwest, ideally placed to use as a base to explore Gianyar and the rest of the island.

Ubud has grown on the fertile land between rivers that carry life-giving water from the great central ridge of mountains. In Ubud the air is fresher and less humid than in the coastal resorts, so that you often need a jacket in the evening and a blanket at night. In the dry season the climate resembles the best of a European summer, only hotter and more luxuriant. All around is the kind of scenery that makes you want to explore: full of pattern and variety, mysterious ravines with rushing rivers, deep pools hidden among black rocks; waving palm trees, clumps of bamboo, and, everywhere, the ricefields and terraces to which the region owed its initial prosperity.

Ubud is in the throes of rapid expansion, gradually obscuring the boundaries with the neighbouring villages of Campuan, Penestanan, Padangtegal, Pengosekan and Peliatan. Despite all the efforts of its more aware residents to keep it traditional, quiet, a place to absorb local culture rather than ride rough-shod over it, big time tourism is sweeping in.

In the meantime, behind the dusty Wild West frontier-like main street, village life continues its age-old patterns of ritual and community obligations. Here you can meet some of the most sophisticated Balinese, conscious of the value of their culture and social organization, knowledgeable about Western ways—in particular the ways of tourists— and thinking hard about how to manage the conjunction of the two. People in Ubud have watched and learned from developments in Kuta, and vowed that their village of painters, dancers and craftsmen should not go the same way. No building is higher than the palm trees, hotels are small and traditional in design. Visitors here are still travellers rather than tourists, eager to take a bit of time to make contact with the Balinese and try to understand the complexities of their way of life. A significant number of Europeans, Americans, Australians, Japanese and Indonesians from outside Bali have made Ubud their headquarters. Many of the outsiders are married to Balinese, others are studying some aspect of Balinese life, are artists, writers, or involved in some business venture. This too makes a difference in the atmosphere of Ubud, continuing a tradition of interaction (sometimes fraught with disaster) between local people and foreign visitors.

GETTING AROUND

Ubud is laid out on a simple grid, stretching out from a T-shape formed by the two main roads of the town. One of these is the main road from Denpasar, which enters the town at a right-angled turn in Peliatan and passes right through to Campuan on the western side

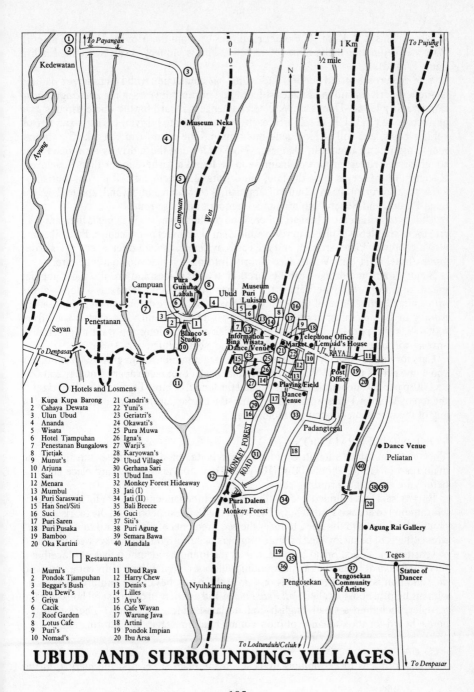

Hotels and Losmens

1	Kupa Kupa Barong	21	Candri's
2	Cahaya Dewata	22	Yuni's
3	Ulun Ubud	23	Geriatri's
4	Ananda	24	Okawati's
5	Wisata	25	Pura Muwa
6	Hotel Tjampuhan	26	Igna's
7	Penestanan Bungalows	27	Warji's
8	Tjetjak	28	Karyowan's
9	Munut's	29	Ubud Village
10	Arjuna	30	Gerhana Sari
11	Sari	31	Ubud Inn
12	Menara	32	Monkey Forest Hideaway
13	Mumbul	33	Jati (I)
14	Puri Saraswati	34	Jati (II)
15	Han Snel/Siti	35	Bali Breeze
16	Suci	36	Guci
17	Puri Saren	37	Siti's
18	Puri Pusaka	38	Puri Agung
19	Bamboo	39	Semara Bawa
20	Oka Kartini	40	Mandala

Restaurants

1	Murni's	11	Ubud Raya
2	Pondok Tjampuhan	12	Harry Chew
3	Beggar's Bush	13	Denis's
4	Ibu Dewi's	14	Lilles
5	Griya	15	Ayu's
6	Cacik	16	Cafe Wayan
7	Roof Garden	17	Warung Java
8	Lotus Cafe	18	Artini
9	Puri's	19	Pondok Impian
10	Nomad's	20	Ibu Arsa

UBUD AND SURROUNDING VILLAGES

of Ubud. This is Jl. Raya. The other road runs up from the Monkey Forest to meet Jl. Raya at a T-junction in the centre of the town. This is Monkey Forest Road (the English name is used).

The main route in and out of Ubud is the *bemo* connection with Denpasar, or Badung as the *bemo* drivers and their mates still call it. This ran for years at the amazingly cheap fare of 350rp Ubud–Denpasar. With ten passengers aboard for the whole trip this gave an income of £1.35 UK ($2.25 US) each way, to cover the driver, his assistant, petrol, vehicle costs, and toll at Kereneng bus station. The round trip can take 3–4 hours, including waiting around in Denpasar. No wonder that these drivers form one of the roughest and rudest groups of Balinese to be found anywhere lower than Penelokan. Recently 400rp seems to be the fare, but drivers often demand 500rp from tourists.

*Bemo*s also run on from Ubud to Campuan, Kedewatan and beyond, and to Tegalla-lang, Pujung and Sebatu, but are not so frequent on these routes.

Otherwise within the Ubud area there is no public transport. Walking is pleasant here and there are plenty of places to visit within 2 km (1.25 mile) of the centre. Pushbikes are also a good way to get around, and are easily available, though often aged. Ask at your *losmen*/hotel or at Bina Wisata (see Tourist Information below) about bike hire.

Scooters and motorbikes can be hired in several places and are the most popular means of transport for the Balinese. For reliability, try Ketut Bengkur—'Ben'—at the office outside the Mumbul Inn, opposite Bina Wisata; or ask for Asman at Ibu Dewi's *warung* in Campuan; or try Oka's place opposite Ubud Inn. The price varies from 6,000–9,000rp per day, depending on the bike and how long you want it for. Almost anyone will hire you their own bike in the quiet season (October–April).

Cars for hire are usually Suzuki jeeps or the larger minibuses for groups. Occasionally you come across the old VW convertibles that haven't yet fallen apart. You pay 25,000–35,000rp per day, depending on the car and the length of hire. Try **Gusti's Shop** right at the top of Monkey Forest road backing on to the market, or the travel office opposite, or any of the places mentioned for motorbikes.

TOURIST INFORMATION

The source of information in Ubud is **Bina Wisata**, an office on the south side of the main road of Ubud, about 100 m (100 yards) beyond the *bemo* parking place and just before the large, modern drug store.

Bina Wisata was founded and is still run by an independent group of local volunteers who attempt to act as a kind of buffer between the Balinese people and the tourists. It is a practical response to the need to meet the requirements of visitors, and to mitigate the worst effects of being invaded by large numbers of curious but not always well-informed or sensitive outsiders. Silvio Santosa, one of the founding members, has put together a very good map of Ubud and its surrounding villages, complete with pithy comments and do's and don'ts for the visitor. It is on sale at the booth beside the enquiry desk, along with his helpful booklet called *Bali Path Finder*, and a variety of other useful books for the traveller, including a small English–Indonesian–Balinese dictionary. There is also a notice board for the exchange of (non-commercial) messages and information.

POST OFFICE

The post office is three minutes' walk down the main street past the market, in the direction of Denpasar; it is set back from the road, on the southern side. There is a poste restante service here. The address is Poste Restante, Kantor Pos, Ubud, Bali; 50rp is charged per letter on collection. There are some other places to buy stamps and send letters and parcels: one is back towards the town centre on the other side of the road from the post office, and one is on Monkey Forest Road; both are clearly indicated by the 'postal service' sign.

TELEPHONE

The Perumtel telephone office is opposite the new market, above a shop, on the main road and next to the Puri Pusaka hotel and restaurant. It claims to be open every day except Sunday, 8–7, but these times are unreliable; it is most likely to be open from 9–12 in the morning and from 5–7 in the evening. It is sometimes open on Sunday mornings. From here you can call anywhere in Indonesia with a reasonably good line, though you may have to wait an eternity to get through: there is only one phone. For international calls the line is not good and you would be better off going into Denpasar. No collect charge calls can be made from here and no calls can be received. There are only one or two places in Ubud that have their own phones: Hotel Tjampuhan is one, Han Snel Cottages another. A proper telephone system has been promised every year for the past four years.

From the telephone office you can also send and receive telegrams and telexes. The telex number is 35428 UBUD IA. If incoming telexes and telegrams are addressed fully, they will, apparently, be delivered to you at your hotel.

MONEY

There are plenty of places to change money in Ubud. It's worth checking their boards because the rates vary. Usually you get a rate comparable with Denpasar but not so good as Kuta. Most known travellers' cheques are accepted.

Museum Puri Lukisan

Founded in 1954 by members of the Pitha Maha group (see p.190), this art gallery opened two years later as a showcase for the best in Bali's art since the great renaissance of the 1930s (admission 200rp, open 8–4). The Puri Lukisan has a beautiful setting in a spacious tropical garden near the centre of Ubud. At the top of the hill is the old pavilion, now showing its age somewhat and prey to a variety of wood-boring insects. The museum's permanent collection is displayed here in a series of six rooms. There are some superb paintings and drawings and a few memorable sculptures. Many of these were donated by Rudolf Bonnet, who returned to Bali in 1973 to help organize this permanent collection. The works by the older generation of artists often show an originality of vision and a discretion not so evident in post-war work. Look out for the following:

In the first room to the left of the entrance: pictures by the great Ubud artist I Gusti Nyoman Lempad (1875?–1978), showing his simple, restrained style, often in spite of the subject matter: the left-hand work illustrates a *buta* (demon) helping parents who have aborted a child across a rickety bridge, with the discarded foetus below.

In the next room to the left: sculpture No. 18 in the right-hand cabinet is of a man assisting his wife in childbirth; the wife is in the traditional crouching position. Painting No. 19 by Anak Agung Sobrat (b.1917) is a *rangda*-like portrait entitled 'Liyak' (*leyak*).

In the first room to the right of the entrance: the portrait entitled 'Dewa Rambut Sedana' by I Nyoman Meja shows the god of prosperity decorated with *kepeng*s, the old Chinese coins used in trade and now an essential feature in many rituals.

In the fourth (last) room to the right: sculpture No. 35 on the middle shelf of the right-hand cabinet is by the great sculptor of Mas, Ida Bagus Nyana (1912–85)—a wonderful slab of wood turned into 'Woman in Slumber', demonstrating his skill in exploiting the natural shape of pieces of wood.

A pavilion downhill and a little to the west houses further works of the permanent collection—in a similar state of deterioration. Further to the west, along a small path beside a patch of cultivated land is another even larger pavilion where a large selection of works for sale is on display. This is a useful service: here you can see the range of work that local artists are currently producing and get an idea of prices (not unreasonable here). This exhibition is due to move into the large new pavilion being built to the east of the old pavilion.

Museum Neka

This important art gallery (admission 200rp, open daily 8.30–5) is actually 2 km (1.25 miles) outside Ubud, past the adjoining village of Campuan. It was started in 1982 by a local art collector and teacher, Suteja Neka, whose father was a well-known woodcarver. There are some outstanding paintings among the permanent collection of 150 or so works.

The museum is organized around four galleries: one for well-known traditional Balinese artists, including Lempad, Sobrat, Kebot and Ida Bagus Made; the second contains work by Balinese and other Indonesian artists with an academic-art background, such as Affandi, Abbas Dullah and Abdul Aziz; a third is devoted to Walter Spies, Rudolf Bonnet and Ari Smidt; and the fourth shows the paintings of other foreign artists including Theo Meier, Willem Hoffker, Miguel Covarrubias (author of the famous *Island of Bali*, 1937), Donald Friend, Han Snel and Antonio Blanco, all of whom have been influenced by Bali, and the latter two of whom are now living in the Ubud area with galleries of their own. There is a small bookshop which also sells cards of some of the best-known paintings.

The gallery has a fine setting: it looks out over the valley of the river that flows down past Hotel Tjampuhan to pass under the Campuan bridge.

Antonio Blanco's studio

Immediately after the Campuan bridge, up a steep driveway to the left, the Catalan artist Antonio Blanco lives, works and entertains visitors in fine style. Make what you will of the somewhat eccentric works of art exhibited in his studio (admission 500rp, open most days 9–5), it would be a shame to miss them, especially when the artist himself is on hand to provoke, outrage or delight you. Some paintings are witty or bawdy, some are beautiful portraits of Balinese, including his Balinese wife and daughters. If you can, take a look at Blanco's English garden.

Han Snel's gallery

Up the narrow road to the north in the centre of Ubud, opposite Bina Wisata, the Dutch artist Han Snel has established his home, gallery, restaurant and bungalows (called Siti

Bungalows). The way is marked by paving stones engraved with the names of past visitors to Ubud. Like Antonio Blanco, Han Snel is married to a Balinese woman (Siti) and lives here with his family. The gallery is small, the paintings abstract, the use of colour brilliant. The hotel and restaurant were opened in 1978, apparently at the behest of numerous visitors who delighted in the hospitality and cooking of the Snel household.

Lempad's House

I Gusti Nyoman Lempad became the most famous of Balinese painters, living to the grand old age of somewhere between 103 and 116 (no one seems quite sure)—a lifetime that saw Bali through the last days of the independent rajas, colonial times (he was at least 30 when the Dutch took Badung in 1906), the coming of the European artists, Japanese invasion and independence. He was closely involved with the Europeans Walter Spies and Rudolf Bonnet, and with them was active in helping younger painters, founding the Pitha Maha school and creating the Museum Puri Lukisan.

When Lempad died in 1978 a magnificent cremation was prepared for him, the subject of a documentary film by John Darling and Lorne Blair called 'Lempad of Bali'—worth seeing if you get the chance (some of the larger hotels in the south have copies). You are welcome to visit his house, on the north side of the road in the centre of Ubud, near the new market. It is still lived in by his family, and is more a private home than public gallery and should be treated as such. For this reason it is a fascinating insight into a traditional home of a well-to-do family, and is kept in much the same way as you see it in scenes in the film where the very aged and frail Lempad sits on the *bale gede* with his long fingernails (a symbol that he was not engaged in manual labour). The family run a gallery of modern paintings, mainly rather pretty small-scale work; none of Lempad's paintings are on view here, but a number of his statues, with their elongated forms similar to the figures in his painting, can be seen in the courtyard. Lempad's second wife, who must now be well into her nineties, sits in the courtyard preparing temple offerings; his granddaughter runs the gallery. And one of his great-grandsons, the dashing Sar, is sometimes to be seen in Ubud's streets, colourfully dressed as pirate or punk or 18th-century courtier.

Agung Raka and Agung Rai: the big galleries

These two brothers started selling paintings at an early age. Their galleries have expanded and flourished into an international art-dealing business. They present some of the finest of local paintings, at prices which reflect the interest of well-established markets in Jakarta, Japan, Europe, America and Australia.

Agung Rai's place is on the main road out of Ubud at Peliatan, midway into the village on the left-hand side as you come from Ubud; Agung Raka's is further along, at the entrance to Mas as you come from Ubud. They have European and Indonesian, as well as Balinese paintings.

Pura Gunung Labah

From the Campuan bridge look to your north across the wooded ravine. All but hidden in the greenery is one of Bali's most ancient temples, thought to have been founded by the Javanese Shivaite priest Danghyang Markandeya in the 8th century—a place with the tranquillity of old stone and extreme age, a wonderfully cool refuge on a hot day.

The temple has been strategically positioned to overlook the **Goa Raksasa**, a cave said to have been the home of a demonic giant (*raksasa*), who terrorized the villagers, killing and eating his victims.

When there is a festival, the whole area below the bridge is flooded with colour and activity. Periodically *barong*s from other villages are paraded through the streets of Ubud to come and visit this temple.

The Monkey Forest (Wanara Wana)

The straggling remains of what was once a large forested area lies at the end of a ten-minute walk down Monkey Forest Road and is still home to a small tribe of grey monkeys. Caught unawares beside the road, peacefully pursuing their monkey lives, these monkeys are charming. As the objects of tourist interest on the other hand, they are far from ideal. Over the years they have become much too bold for comfort, grabbing the peanuts or banana from your hand, sometimes going for your camera, occasionally biting; they have been known to disappear up trees clasping car keys. The secret is not to buy any peanuts, despite the pleadings of the vendors, and to give absolutely no suggestion that you have anything about you that the monkeys can eat. Don't delve into your bag, and don't get too close to the babies or you will incur the wrath of Big Daddy, a terrifying experience. Should you get bitten seek medical attention without delay; for on-the-spot treatment the Balinese have their own ointment.

Admission to the forest is by 'donation' at the small stand at the entrance on the Ubud side; 500rp is plenty. If you are just passing through, turn up the little bypass road to your left as you reach the forest from Ubud.

The monkeys apart, this is a lovely forest, filled with deep green, mature trees that tower over the path and clutter the ravine below, a favourite place for bathing. There is a wonderful echoing stillness here, broken only by the occasional fall of twigs, the padding of the odd stray mongrel, and the squawking of tourists receiving their initiation from the monkeys.

There is also an interesting temple on the west side of the Monkey Forest, mossy and hidden by creepers. This is the **Pura Dalem** for Padangtegal *banjar*, which lies through the Monkey Forest to the east. It is the site of some exuberant stone *rangda* figures, which line the entrance to the inner temple; one has been caught in the act of devouring a child, while others drool with their huge tongues between their pendulous breasts in eager anticipation. They cluster around a magnificent 'world turtle', whose accompanying *naga*s ingeniously lend their snaking forms to the balusters lining the steps that are set on the turtle's back.

WALKS AND SHORT TOURS

Campuan–Penestanan–Sayan–Kedewatan–Payangan

This area, to the west of Ubud, is full of interesting walks of any distance that suits you. Campuan, Penestanan, Sayan and Kedewatan are all within fairly comfortable walking distance. Payangan is 11 km (6.8 miles) from Ubud, so you may need the help of a *bemo* (they pass fairly regularly on this route), or other transport, one way or both.

Campuan

From the centre of Ubud, walk west, past Bina Wisata and Museum Puri Lukisan. The road soon goes steeply downhill. Pass Ibu Dewi's *warung* on your right. At the bottom is the Campuan river in a green gorge spanned by an old suspension bridge (picturesque) and a new paved bridge (functional). On your right is the Pura Gunung Labah (see above).

By the temple is the start of a walk that takes you to Keliki and Yehtengah. Before the bridge, on the left, is Murni's restaurant and shop. Across the bridge is the Pondok Tjampuhan restaurant and the driveway to Antonio Blanco's studio on the left and the Beggar's Bush 'pub', run by Englishman Victor Mason, on your right. Further up the hill on your right is the Hotel Tjampuhan (the old spelling of Campuan), the first of its kind in Ubud. This was once the home of the German painter Walter Spies (see pp.190–91). It has a wonderful position, overlooking the river. Come here to swim in the hotel pool on a hot and lazy afternoon.

Further up the hill, climb the steep old steps that lead off to the left. A short walk from here takes you out to some of the loveliest ricefields around Ubud, with a peaceful, open view way over to the west. Towards harvest time you will see the human scarecrows standing in these fields, making their unearthly calls every few minutes to scare off scavengers.

Penestanan

Continue along the track to Penestanan, the village noted for the 'School of Young Artists' who, under the guidance of the Dutch painter Ari Smidt in the 1950s, began to paint natural scenes rather than the ritualized mythological themes characteristic of the traditional Kamasan style of Balinese painting (see p.63). The Young Artists are no longer young, but numerous examples of the naturalistic style developed at that time can be seen in the small studios along the way.

From Penestanan you can take a path across the fields to the north, which will bring you back onto the Campuan road just above Museum Neka (see p.198). Turn back towards Ubud to visit the Museum and be back at Murni's for tea with iced banana cheesecake. The round trip will have been around 4 km (2.5 miles) of easy walking.

You can continue west from Penestanan to Sayan, or take the path south to bring you back to Nyuhkuning by the Monkey Forest.

Sayan

Sayan is the village where the American musicologist Colin McPhee built his home in the 1930s, and its various quirks are humorously described in his book *A House in Bali* (1944). Other Westerners have followed his example and rented property here: David Bowie and Mick Jagger are among the best known.

To the west, parallel to the road, but not visible from it, runs the deep valley of the fast-flowing Ayung river (Sungai Ayung or Yeh Ayung). Follow one of the paths through the trees on the west side of the road to come out onto the edge of the valley. Looking down you can see the tiny figures of farmers cultivating their rice terraces way below. The terraces are carved out of the sides of the ravine almost to the river's edge. Westerners' houses now decorate (or defile) the side of the gorge. It is easier than it looks to find your way down along the edge of rice terraces, which act as giant steps. There is no better way of passing time on a baking hot day than immersed in a natural jacuzzi of rushing, foaming mountain water or sunbathing on the smooth black rocks alongside the river. Above, the blue sky, on each side ricefield rising upon ricefield, here and there little processions of women winding their way down to do the laundry, upstream the sound of children splashing and laughing at the water's edge.

Kedewatan

About 2 km (1.25 miles) on the road leading north through Sayan there is a road to the right forming a T-junction. This road leads back to Ubud past the Museum Neka. The area around this T-junction comprises the village of Kedewatan. Continuing north, pass—or stop at—the *babi guling* stand, one of the best of its kind. Turn down the path just north of here, signposted 'Gang Wisnu' and 'magical cave'—a half-immersed, bat-filled cave at the water's edge, at the end of a precipitous path. The path leads past the best position on the edge of the ravine for further views of the Ayung river gorge.

There are two new, expensive, idyllically situated places to stay along this stretch of road, one called Cahaya Dewata, the other Kupu Kupu Barong (see pp.208–9). Kupu Kupu Barong has a spectacular restaurant, perched on the edge of a cliff—a fine place to sit and have a drink and watch the valley change colours as the sun sets over the opposite ridge.

Payangan

The air gets cooler as the road begins to climb towards the central mountains. Eventually this road goes into the Bangli regency, and joins the Batur–Kintamani road. Payangan is the only place in Bali where lychees are cultivated. Durians and pineapples are also grown here. There is a market every three days.

Just before the village, which lies 7 km (4.3 miles) north of Kedewatan and 11 km (6.8 miles) north of Ubud, a sign on the east side of the road points to Desa Melinggih. You can take a *bemo* for 200rp from Ubud to this point for a 7 km (4.3 mile) walk through ricefields and a steep river valley to join the path that leads back down to Campuan.

Alternatively continue into the marketplace at Payangan, turn right and walk for 2 km (1.25 miles) through Klusa to Keliki and Yehtengah, which lies between two rivers. If you continue east along this track you cross another valley to join the Ubud–Pujung road just north of Tegalallang. You can also turn right at Keliki to come back to Campuan. This is a pleasantly grassy walk, though rather exposed on a very hot day. Carry a water bottle and a compass. From Keliki to Ubud takes 3 hours.

Nyuhkuning

The village of Nyuhkuning lies 2 km (1.25 miles) to the south of Ubud and offers a pleasant walk and a chance to wander the paths that lead to, and along, the Campuan river. Follow the path through the Monkey Forest, forking right in the forest to pass beneath the Pura Dalem before emerging into open countryside and dropping between ricefields to Nyuhkuning below. The village is laid out on a grid of grassy streets, barely bruised by motor traffic. It is noted for its contemporary woodcarvings, the production of which is the chief occupation of many of the villagers. The river lies to the west; follow any path on the downhill gradient. There is a swimming place here, beneath a spot where the moss-covered rocks in the valley wall have been carved with strange animal reliefs. If you cross the river, you can follow a path that leads round to Penestanan.

Padangtegal–Pengosekan–Peliatan

This is another short excursion, this time to villages to the south and east of Ubud, through woodland and ricefields. It is an undemanding amble of 4 km (2.5 miles) in all.

Padangtegal

A large, faded white sign on the main road out of Ubud towards Peliatan, before it slopes down towards the post office, indicates the road to south Padangtegal, which is more or less a suburb of Ubud. Some of the cheaper *losmen*s of Ubud are to be found between here and Monkey Forest Road.

At about 200 m (200 yards) down this road, on the right, near the large Hanuman statue, is the *bale banjar* where the Padangtegal *kecak* group do a weekly performance. Just before this a turning to the right leads down a dark, dank lane to Monkey Forest Road. Further along the Padangtegal road is a *warung kopi*, set above the road, which is good for thick, strong Balinese coffee; beyond this, Artini's little restaurant serves good, tasty, cheap lunches.

Notice the black-painted plates on the gateposts of the family compounds—common to many villages throughout Bali. They give the name of the head of the family living within, the number of males (*laki-laki*), females (*perempuan*), and the total number of residents (*jumlah*). These plates are supposed to be updated every year or so by the authorities.

The trees clear as you emerge above the Monkey Forest to views of open ricefields and waving palm trees. You may pass the gentle, doe-like cows, pegged out to graze, or ducks scuttling along the edges of the flooded rice paddies, or children with the long wands they use to entrap dragonflies for their dinner. This pretty stretch of road is becoming built-up at an alarming rate as you reach the Pengosekan end.

Pengosekan

At the next junction Pengosekan is straight ahead, Peliatan to your left. Continuing into Pengosekan, pass the Pondok Impian, Bali Breeze and Guci Inn on your right. This is a village of painters, basket-makers and woodcarvers. Queen Elizabeth II came here in 1974 on a visit to Bali, hence the road was paved long before that of neighbouring villages, so the Balinese tell you. Apparently she liked the paintings, and bought several.

The work of the village goes on largely behind the high walls of the compounds, though you are likely to be invited in to see paintings in progress. There is a big new gallery for Pengosekan paintings on the left as you enter the village. These are in a naturalistic style ranging from a Rousseauesque explosion of colour, in parrots and vivid jungle flowers and rich green creepers, to the quieter, softer colours of herons at the waterside, or small birds and butterflies in subdued light. You can sometimes find marvellous painted screens here too, though the prices are not cheap. Most work is commissioned. Try the family compounds to the right, opposite the gallery, and to the left, behind it. You will also find paintings by these artists in the big galleries in Peliatan and in Sanur.

The road through Pengosekan continues on through Lodtunduh and Mawang to join the Denpasar road at Celuk. This is becoming an increasingly popular route for traffic avoiding the more heavily-laden main road from Gianyar.

Retracing your steps, turn off to Peliatan at the Alpha Sigma Packing & Shipping sign.

At the top of the road, near the junction, is the large workshop and showroom of the **Pengosekan Community of Artists**. Dewa Batuan and his son Putu look after their growing business which produces woodcarvings for home decoration: mirrors, screens, boxes, tables, bathroom cabinets, all covered with a rich profusion of carved and painted flowers and birds.

Peliatan

Peliatan is a long village, stretching about a full kilometre (0.6 mile) from one bend in the road (by Teges) to the next (at the entrance to Ubud). The peaceful atmosphere is somewhat eroded by the frequency of traffic, but the village has its charms and some travellers prefer to stay here at arm's length from the more intense bustle of Ubud.

Do your shopping in Peliatan—woodcarving, toys, patchwork bedcovers, paintings—or stop for a meal at Ibu Arsa's traditional Balinese restaurant under the big banyan tree near the centre of the village. Peliatan has a long tradition of having exceptionally gifted *gamelan* musicians and *legong* dancers who perform regularly here in the village and in Ubud (see 'Music and Dance', p.205).

Continue on the road northwards to the right-angle bend that takes you back into Ubud.

Petulu–Junjungan

There are some beautiful walks to the north of Ubud, in particular to the 'heron village' of Petulu. The furthest point north in this walk is Junjungan, 5 km (3.1 miles) from Ubud.

Petulu

Petulu is famous for its large flock of herons—variously estimated as numbering between 5,000 and 15,000—which nest in the tall trees lining the road into the village. It is an unforgettable sight to see them flying home in formation to roost in the late afternoon; time your walk to be there at 4 pm.

To get to Petulu, walk north along the Peliatan–Tegalallang–Pujung road for about 1.5 km (1 mile). Turn left at the umbrella maker's shop.

Junjungan

Beyond Petulu is an area of rivers and rocks, little rough grass hillocks and bamboo clumps, a wonderful landscape for picnics and walks. The track is manageable by motorbike. Eventually the path turns round on itself to take you through the village of Junjungan. Time has stood still for Junjungan. Cars do not come through here, and the bamboo has not all been cut down for new buildings. This is how all the little villages around Ubud would have looked fifty years ago.

From Junjungan you can return south to Ubud along a beautiful path through ricefields, scented by white-flowered *cempaka* trees. Or you can make your way west to Bentuyung, across a small river, and south to Sambahan and Sakti, where you can join the road that comes out at Ubud's *bemo* station. The latter route is about 7 km (4.3 miles).

MUSIC AND DANCE

To see a representative slice of traditional dances, dramas, and *wayang kulit* there is no better place to stay than Ubud. Many of the best *gamelan* orchestras and dancers come from this area, supported by tourist money but fed by a tradition and local enthusiasm that goes back a thousand years. On the one hand there are events put on regularly for tourists; on the other there are the temple *odalan*s and other ceremonies where the real dancing takes place. These may be no more beautiful here in Ubud than in thousands of tiny villages scattered throughout Bali, but they are certainly more accessible.

Scheduled performances of dance in or near Ubud include Barong and Randa at Batubulan at 9.30 am every morning; *kecak* and trance dance, which includes the Fire Dance, at Bona one or two evenings a week; *kecak* at Padangtegal (now more or less part of Ubud) once a week; *legong* at two different venues in Peliatan every week; *legong* at Pengosekan once a week; dance-dramas at the *bale banjar* on Monkey Forest Road one evening a week, at the Puri opposite the market once a week and at the Menara Hotel on the left near Bina Wisata once a week. You can see a regular weekly performance of *wayang kulit* (shadow puppets) by the talented *dalang* (puppeteer) Ida Bagus Belawa at Oka Kartini's, on the right hand side of the road leading eastwards out of Ubud, before the corner to Peliatan.

Bina Wisata will arrange transport to dances in the outlying villages for an all-in price (around 3,000rp). Local events cost 2,000rp or 2,500rp.

Check times and days with Bina Wisata or with the official ticket sellers in the streets, who will make themselves unavoidably known to you.

If you feel spoilt for choice, we can recommend in particular the **Peliatan troupes**. There are three: the **Gunung Sari**, which tends to perform at the *wantilan* hall at the corner between Ubud and Peliatan; the **Tirta Sari** group which performs at the small open-flanked community hall in the middle of Peliatan; and the unusual **Mekar Sari** group, unusual because the *gamelan* is played entirely by women. These troupes include some greatly celebrated dancers. Since *legong*s are at their best at about 12 years of age, the composition of the troupes changes continually. Try to see them all, and you will be rewarded by at least one electrifying performance.

SWIMMING

Most of the larger new hotels have pools, and some will let non-residents use them for a fee. Perhaps the nicest is also the oldest: **Hotel Tjampuhan** has a beautifully situated pool at the bottom of a rockface on the hillside overlooking the river. It is set in a long-established garden, with shady patches under the trees, and a place to change. Though the pool is not large, the water is clear and fresh. It now costs 2,000rp to swim here.

Ubud Inn, and the new **Ubud Village Hotel** down Monkey Forest Road, both have pools. Ubud Inn charges 3,000rp to the public. Ubud Village Hotel has a large pool with a sunken bar and poolside restaurant; it costs 2,600rp to swim here.

Local people use the many fast-flowing rivers to bathe in—a pleasantly refreshing experience so long as you don't think about the use to which the river may have been put upstream. Follow the path beside the Monkey Forest Hideaway (at the bottom of Monkey Forest Road) to clamber over rocks which surround a lovely secluded bathing pool, just large enough for swimming, with deep, cool water, almost green in the shade.

There are many other popular spots for bathing on the Campuan river, but these aren't really places where you can swim.

SHOPPING
Ubud is packed with craft shops of one kind or another. It is more interesting to visit the various villages which specialize in each craft if you have the time, but often prices are just as good in Ubud.

Paintings
Painting is, of course, Ubud's claim to fame: there are numerous local artists, hundreds of them, and you can call by on their studios and watch them at work, without obligation. (See pp.62–3 for an introduction to Balinese painting.)

The best advice is to visit a number of galleries to get a feel for what is available; the Museum Puri Lukisan is useful for this purpose. Choose what you like and decide what you are prepared to pay for it, then bargain till you reach a satisfactory price.

A small traditional painting with a lot of fine detail can cost 30,000–40,000rp; an ink drawing on stiffened cloth might be around 5,000rp; a canvas of poor quality 60 × 40 cm (24 × 15 inches) might cost 15,000rp, while a good one of the same size could go up to 200,000rp from the best painters (and even more from a gallery). **Pengosekan paintings** are highly prized. The best place for them in Ubud is **Dewa Santana's** tiny studio down Monkey Forest Road opposite Karyowan's.

Fabrics, clothes and soft furnishings
Clothes, bags, quilted bedcovers, cushion covers, tablecloths and the like are made here in Ubud, or close by, in a multitude of small workshops. They represent excellent value. Fabrics used for clothes may be printed batik-style cotton; real old Javanese batik which has been worn and washed to give it the softness suitable for draping; or the hand-dyed Balinese 'batik', which is handpainted on to white cotton. Some bags and little jackets are made from a rough cotton woven in Gianyar in clear strong colours, which wears very well indeed. There is traditional *ikat* from Sumba and other islands, predominantly red and black with some white threads; and also *ikat* or *endek* cloth, of the kind you can see being woven outside Gianyar—this is more expensive but can be exceptionally lovely.

Examples of prices could be: a sleeveless printed batik-style cotton dress 8,000rp; a shirt from real old batik in the traditional colours of brown (soga dye) and blue (indigo) 10,000rp (watch for the quality of the fabric—some may be too old and tear quickly); a traditional *ikat* jacket 40,000rp; a handpainted cushion cover, quilted, 5,000rp; a patchwork double-size bedcover 25,000rp; a Gianyar-woven, brightly coloured shoulder bag 7,000rp; a mercerized *endek* sarong 15,000–35,000rp.

Ubud abounds with skilled **tailors and seamstresses,** so you can buy fabric and then have it made up in your own design. They don't have to work from a pattern; just give them a sample or draw what you want. For reliable results we can recommend **Astiti,** who has his tiny workshop opposite the market on the main street of Ubud. For all kinds of soft furnishings, including fine quilting, go to **Made Sukerti,** who has a shop and workshop in Padangtegal on the way to Pengosekan.

There is a wonderful collection of fine **fabrics** at the shop owned by beautiful **Gusti,** wife of Karyowan who owns the *losmen* bearing his name in Monkey Forest Road (past the playing field and opposite Dian's Restaurant). Gusti will also make clothes for you. Further down the road, on the left, the shop attached to *losmen* Gerhana Sari has a good collection of traditional Sumbanese *ikat*.

Back on the main road, turn left and walk towards Campuan to find good places for **woven bags**. Go as far as Cacik Restaurant to find **Warji's shop**, where **children's clothes** are a speciality. Note that the popular 'Jakpac' clothes in bright colours, made near Gianyar, can be bought here in Ubud, but watch out for imitations which lose their colour when washed.

Beautiful goods of all kinds can be found at **Murni's shop** next to her restaurant by the bridge in Campuan.

The best places for handpainted fabric are in the other direction towards the post office. Down here you can also find bright cotton clothes in printed fabric which resembles *endek*. **'Bamboo'**, just to the east of the post office, has an impressive collection of **designer-style clothing**—exotic evening jackets and shirts which call out for the bright lights of city night life a thousand miles from Bali.

Antiques

There are plenty of little shops at the top of Monkey Forest Road, to the left on the way to Bina Wisata, and on your left as you go down past the market towards the post office. All kinds of interesting woodcarvings and pieces in bronze can be found here. For the most part these are ingeniously 'antiqued', not genuinely old, but attractive nonetheless. You might pay 40,000rp for a pair of carved wooden elephants, 6,000rp for a small antique style mask, 50,000rp for a splendid hairy Rangda. Prices depend on the kind of wood used as well as the quality of the carving, which can vary enormously.

Modern woodcarvings

This is one of the most exciting areas of development; there are always new, colourful and often witty designs emerging as a spin off from the export market. Good places to look are **Wayan Ludra's** shop down Monkey Forest Road, past the playing field and **Dian's Restaurant**, on your left; Batuan's **Community of Artists** in Pengosekan, just near the Peliatan corner; **Made Geriya**, the toymaker, on your left as you go through Peliatan towards Denpasar; and the many small shops springing up on Monkey Forest Road, in Peliatan and in Mas. Prices range from 2,000rp for a painted owl to 25,000rp for a 60 cm (24 inch) high mirror frame. Once again prices vary enormously with quality and the size of shop.

'Parasite' carvings are a recent fashion, made in all sorts of weird and wonderful forms inspired by the wood itself. This comes from the roots of certain trees which have been gnarled by a parasitic growth, creating a mushroom-like protrusion across the grain. The wood is harder to carve than some of the soft woods used for the painted carvings, so prices can be a bit higher. The carvings can vary from the crass to the exceptionally beautiful, so we hesitate to give prices. Say 12,000rp for a medium quality bird 25 cms (9 inches) high.

The market

Every third day Ubud's main street is packed out as far as the main crossroads. Cars, people, pigs and chickens create havoc, and the area surrounding the big, modern market building comes to life. Drivers should find out about the market days in advance—the road is closed for incoming traffic, which has to wind its way round from the Padangtegal road to get into the centre of town.

This market is entirely local, and a fascinating concoction of strange sights and smells. There are dried roots, leaves and pods that may be herbs and spices, or the ingredients of the *dukun*'s special potions. There are clothes, dirt-cheap rubber sandals, numerous household goods, fruits of all kinds, powerfully scented dried fish, and many kinds of rice, including black rice.

The market starts just before dawn, and it is well worth the effort of getting up this early to witness the traders gathering in the half light and assembling their wares.

Books
Reading is an essential part of Ubud life, so the library/bookshop on Monkey Forest Road was a welcome arrival. It has a system whereby you can exchange books as well as buy second-hand ones.

Murni also has a good selection in her restaurant, or try the shop at Museum Neka.

NIGHT-LIFE
The temple ceremonies are the big crowd pullers. Compared to this, anything else on offer is tame. Restaurants stay open a little later these days, particularly June–September which is Ubud's busiest season, but many will stop serving food at 8.30pm. Late-night gathering places are **Beggars' Bush** (the 'English pub') at Campuan, **Puri's** on the main road opposite the market place, and **Ayu's Kitchen** just round the corner on Monkey Forest Road—or anywhere you can persuade the proprietor to keep serving you beer, *brem*, *arak* or coffee.

The youth group of each *banjar* periodically arranges a 'bar' or evening's dancing and food to raise money for its various projects. This can be a good way to meet the younger members of the *banjar* on their home ground, and see another side of Bali which is not usually shown to tourists.

WHERE TO STAY
There are literally hundreds of places to stay in the Ubud area, many of them very attractive indeed, at a great range of prices—from $130US to 4,000rp for a night, including breakfast. We cannot possibly list them all. We have picked out a few that we like, across the price range. For a note about booking, see pp.16–17.

Top of the range
Kupu Kupu Barong in Kedewatan, opened in December 1987 under Australian and Balinese management, trades on its stunning position in a large and tranquil garden perched on the edge of the Ayung river valley. Six houses (soon to be 12), built in the traditional rice-barn style and finished to very high standards, line the ridge, with magnificent views down the river from their balconies and bedrooms. You have exclusive use of your house, which has a beautifully furnished living room (complete with fridge), sunken bath with hot water (some houses have jacuzzis) and two bedrooms. A small swimming pool is set among the trees, stepped like the rice terraces in the valley below. The hotel has been carefully laid out in a luxuriant garden and is designed to be

exclusive: 'children under 12 are not catered for', management states firmly. Further-more, the prices will help to maintain its exclusivity: $115 US per night, inclusive of tax, service and breakfast, single or doubles, extra person (i.e. in the second bedroom) $20 US. The rooms with jacuzzi (or 'spa') cost $130 US. This is a superb spot for those who wish to afford it—honeymoon couples should consider it carefully. The restaurant also has a magnificent position overlooking the valley. It is expensive by local standards, reasonable by those of Kuta and Sanur. Booking office: Jl. Kecubung 72, Denpasar, Bali, tel 23172, fax (62) 361 23172. International high-fliers might take note that there are no telephones at Kupu Kupu Barong yet.

Cahaya Dewata is also perched on the side of the Ayung river gorge, with an outstanding view. The 20 rooms are in pairs in bungalows built on different levels of the steep hillside. The rooms are simply but beautifully decorated with furniture made by local craftsmen. There are two swimming pools on different levels, and a restaurant with the same wonderful views over the terraced valley and the river. The rooms cost $45 US double and $35 US single, including breakfast, hot water, tax and service. Extra beds are $8 US. At the moment there is no telephone at Cahaya Dewata. To book, send a telegram (or letter) to Wayan Candri, Cahaya Dewata, Kedewatan, Ubud, Bali. Wayan is the wife of Munut, who has more accommodation to rent in Campuan. She looks after her guests well, and can tell you about places to visit and local events.

Ulun Ubud Cottages is closer to Ubud, on the road out from Campuan, and near to Neka Gallery. It has the sort of facilities you would expect in a resort hotel: spacious accommodation, modern Western-style bathrooms with hot water, room service, restau-rant and bar, good-sized swimming pool. What you don't anticipate is the beauty of the setting, surrounded by palm trees and jungle undergrowth, on a hillside overlooking a river valley, and the traditional grace of the design of the 'cottages', built and decorated with local materials and handicrafts. It's really special in this respect. There are 16 rooms, for $35 US single and $50 US double. Family rooms are $80 US for a triple, or $100 US for two doubles. The price includes tax, service and breakfast. You can contact the hotel direct by writing to Ulun Ubud Cottages, P.O.Box 333, Denpasar 80001, Bali, or telex 35190 SUNDT IA.

Ananda Cottages, past Campuan on the left, one of the older hotels in Ubud—it has been there nine years—offers good, big rooms with hot water, a swimming pool and fridges. The new rooms are especially attractive because of their size and views: they have enormous open windows so it's almost like sleeping on a terrace. The rooms are usually $25 US single and $35 US double, including breakfast, but the downstairs rooms may cost less, depending on the season. Extra beds are available for $7 US extra. These prices do not include the 15.5% government tax and service charge. Ananda Cottages has a restaurant, with main meals at 2,000–4,000rp. The telex number is 35105 UBUD IA (attn. Ananda Cottages), or write to W. Pageh (manager), Ananda Cottages, P.O.Box 205, Denpasar 80001, Bali.

Hotel Tjampuhan occupies the site of Walter Spies's home, built by the artist in the 1930s. It has been here a long time and is more noticeably Balinese in style than the newer places—which has advantages and disadvantages. In this case the disadvantage is that the individual houses, built on the side of a small river gorge, are not always very well maintained. Guests complain of insufficient hot water, not enough blankets (it's quite high here, and the nights can be cool), and a general air of decay. The advantage is the setting of the houses, in beautiful gardens. The swimming pool is a major plus, since it has been there long enough to be surrounded by shady vegetation. Its clear mountain water is delicious, as is the view over the river below. There is a tennis court, floodlit at night, but there is not always sufficient equipment for hire. The room rates vary from $24 US for standard single room with breakfast, $32 US for the same with full board, to $85 US for the 'Raja' room with full board, double, with extra bed $18 US (full board). There is no charge for children under five years old. The 15.5% tax and service charge is not included in the price. There is a telephone at the hotel, tel (0361) 28871, or write to P.O. Box 15, Denpasar 80001, Bali.

Ubud Village Hotel, opened in June 1989, is on the other side of Ubud, down the Monkey Forest Road. The design of the hotel is curious—rooms are smallish, in two neat rows, each enclosed in its own private garden. The pool is excellent, with a view over the ricefields. The price of $20 US for a single or $25 US for doubles (exclusive of the 15.5% tax and service charge) buys you such comforts as hot water, a fan, and room service. The food in the large open *bale*-type restaurant is pretty good too. The hotel is owned by Suteja Neka of the Neka Museum. Bookings to Ubud Village Hotel, P.O. Box 271, Denpasar, Bali.

Ubud Inn also has a small swimming pool. There are 13 rooms, at 45,000rp double or 35,000rp single, including hot water, breakfast, tax and service. The Ubud Restaurant next door has some excellent traditional Balinese dishes. Car and bike hire can be arranged through the manager, Oka, who has a transport office opposite the hotel. To book, write to 1 Gusti N. Berata, Ubud Inn, Monkey Forest Road, Ubud.

In the centre of town, Han Snel runs his **Siti Bungalows** in beautiful gardens conveniently close to Ubud's main road, near the Lotus Café. The layout is excellent, with the houses on different levels of the garden, designed so there is a real sense of privacy, very well furnished, and with lovely bathrooms and spacious verandahs. There are six rooms at prices between $30 and $40 US, double and single. Prices include hot water, breakfast, tax and service. There is a good restaurant in the grounds, and a gallery with Han Snel's own paintings. There is also a beauty salon and hairdresser's available for guests and public, run by Han Snel's daughter. Book by writing to Han Snel, Siti Bungalows, P.O. Box 227, Denpasar 80001, Bali; or tel (0361) 28690.

Also central, **Hotel Puri Saren** lies within the palace of the old Raja of Ubud, and is run by his family. It's unusual in that you really are in the home of the family, surrounded by beautiful antiques and carved wooden doors. The rooms are old, but have Western-style bathrooms, hot water and fans: they cost $23 US single and $29 US double, unless long-term arrangements are made.

The **Puri Saraswati** is another hotel which is part of the palace complex, the home of the old raja's sister's family. The old rooms have a strangely Miss Haversham-style air of decayed splendour, stuck in time, though the bathrooms are Western-style. It's quite an extraordinary place: huge beds draped with white mosquito nets, carved and gilded doors, spacious bathrooms. The newer rooms are in better condition and have hot water. Older rooms are $20 US double and $15 US single, newer ones $35 US double and $30 US single, with breakfast and taxes included. Puri Saraswati now has its own (small) swimming pool which on completion will push prices up 25–30%.

Hotel Puri Pusaka is the newest addition to the accommodation on offer within the old palace complex. There are ten rooms at $15 US single and $20 US double, $25 US for a family suite; taxes, hot water and an English breakfast with ham and eggs are included. Again the attraction is that you are staying in the old palace, surrounded by carved furniture and antiques, the guests of the Ubud royal family. The arrangement of rooms around the restaurant might, however, be rather too public for some.

Okawati's Sunset Cottages have a good situation, the upper rooms overlooking the ricefields and the sunset, but still close to the centre of things. You will find them tucked away off Monkey Forest Road behind Igna's Accommodation, near the bookshop and opposite the Padangtegal turning. The eight rooms are well furnished and well maintained, and the service is unusually good. Two of the rooms (downstairs) have hot water, and cost 26,000rp single or double; six of them are upstairs with excellent views and cost 20,000rp single, 23,000rp double. All prices include good breakfasts and taxes. Okawati's wonderful restaurant is just opposite the rooms. Okawati was one of the first in the business of catering for visitors to Ubud, and she is a mine of information about all aspects of Balinese culture.

Several families in central Ubud have individual houses, beautifully furnished, with hot water, available for overnight or longer-term stays. For the best in comfort and good design, speak to **Murni** at her restaurant by the Campuan bridge; also try **Oka Kartini's**, down the main road past the post office, where the *wayang kulit* (shadow puppet) performances are held; and **Wayan's Café**, about 100 m (100 yards) down Monkey Forest Road, on the right. There are also rooms to rent attached to the **Pondok Tjampuhan** restaurant, opposite Murni's.

Finally, the **Bamboo Gallery**, near the post office, has a beautiful cottage called 'Pelangi' set in a Douanier Rousseau ravine, complete with parrots and other exotic birds, tropical fish and turtles. It costs $40 US per night (there are three beds) inclusive of breakfast, is very tastefully decorated and has a good modern bathroom. The price is high, but worth it for its special location and the friendliness of its owners, Anak Agung Alit Wartika and his family.

Middle to basic

CAMPUAN AREA

We recommend **Munut's Bungalows**, up a steep track just beyond Antonio Blanco's studio, with seven rooms at 10,000rp double or single, including breakfast, or larger rooms at 20,000 and 25,000rp which include the use of a kitchen and fridge. Breakfast and taxes are included but there is no hot water. Munut's has a lovely garden and is well run.

A little cheaper, directly opposite Munut's, is **Arjuna Inn**, owned by Antonio Blanco, whose studio backs on to the *losmen*. This is one of the best of its kind, with good service from friendly people, delicious breakfasts, pleasant rooms with small but attractive garden-style bathrooms, and good spring water from the taps. The rooms have table lamps too, a definite advantage over the single, bare, overhead bulbs sometimes found in this price range. There are rooms for 4,000 and 5,000rp single, or 6,000 and 7,000rp double. Excellent value.

There are many really beautiful places to stay beyond Munut's and Arjuna, overlooking the ricefields which lie along the way to Penestanan. They are more appropriate for longer stays, being a little off the beaten track. Some are just individual rooms; some, like **Homestay Sari**, which overlooks a river valley, and **Penestanan Bungalows**, which has a spectacular view of the ricefields, are bigger operations with better facilities. Just wander along and ask when you find something that suits. There are also small individual houses with their own cooking facilities up at the top of the Penestanan steps.

Other possibilities in this area are **Wisata Cottages**, beyond Hotel Tjampuhan, hot water and good views but shabby rooms, a bit overpriced at 20,000rp single and 25,000rp double; and **Tjetjak Inn**, down by the Pura Gunung Lebah, again with a lovely situation but unexciting rooms at 10,000rp single, 25,000rp double.

CENTRAL UBUD

Mumbul Inn is set back from the main road opposite Bina Wisata. It's central without being noisy. The rooms are attractive, some have a great view over the adjoining jungle-filled gorge, and service here is good. Prices are 10,000rp double, 6,000rp single downstairs; and 12,000rp double, 7,000rp single upstairs. The upstairs rooms are better value. There is a good restaurant, and also a transport office right outside the entrance.

Further down towards Campuan, climb the steps on the left opposite Cacik Restaurant for some places to stay which look right over peaceful ricefields towards Mt Agung. There is a good range of places to stay up here, at a variety of prices.

For the cheapest accommodation in Ubud, look in the area between the market and the post office, along small back roads that go down towards Padangtegal. There is a wide range here, but most are inexpensive, around 4,000rp including breakfast, and often have attractive gardens.

You could also ask at Bina Wisata—many families have rooms to let in their compounds for around 7,000rp or less, and it can be a rewarding and delightful experience to stay at close quarters to a Balinese family in this way.

MONKEY FOREST ROAD

The top part of Monkey Forest Road has some of the longest established accommodation in Ubud—**Candri's, Pura Muwa, Geriatri's, Igna's, Warsi's**. Often these have aged and not been repaired or renewed. Further south, look along the track by Okawati's Sunset Cottages for some small *losmen* with attractive and comfortable rooms. **Warji's House** might be the best here; the garden is unusually beautiful—Warji's husband teaches horticulture at the local school. The rooms are well-cared for, have fans and bedside lamps, and the upper rooms have views over the river gorge at the back and to the ricefields beyond. No hot water here though. Upstairs rooms are 14,000rp double, 10,000rp single, downstairs are 12,000rp double and 8,000rp single.

Further down, we recommend **Karyowan's** place for its setting in a delightful garden, a miniature botanical park. He also has a room right out in the ricefields beyond, picturesque and peaceful, perfect for a honeymooning couple on a budget. Prices are around 8,000–12,000rp single or double, depending on the size of the room, and include a good breakfast.

Just beyond, on the left, is **Gerhana Sari**, small but one of the best in all Bali in its bracket. The rooms are well cared for, the garden is lovely, the position is convenient for walks, shops, restaurants and local transport, service is good. Prices range from 6,000rp single and 8,000rp double for a standard room, to 15,000rp single and 20,000rp double for a spacious room with hot water.

At the bottom of the road, just beside the Monkey Forest, **Monkey Forest Hideaway** is tucked away in richly green jungle. This place is unusually well designed, with lots of choice of different kinds of rooms, all with good bathrooms. New rooms are being added. Prices are $10 US double and $8 US single downstairs, $20 US double and $15 US single for the bigger upstairs rooms. There is a restaurant here, too.

PENGOSEKAN

Jati's Homestay is a popular choice on the road into Pengosekan. The rooms down-stairs, with attractive garden-style bathrooms, are 12,000rp double and 10,000rp single; upstairs, with views south over the ricefields, they are 15,000rp double and 12,000rp single. Some of the bigger rooms have four-poster beds. There's a good new restaurant here.

Bali Breeze is opposite the turning to Peliatan. The two-storey buildings are thatched like a traditional rice barn, and the upper rooms look over wonderful views towards Penestanan. Long-term stayers often come here: prices by negotiation.

Guci Inn, the newest addition to accommodation in Pengosekan, is strongly rec-ommended for the care taken in the design and upkeep of the bungalows and the gardens, and for the breakfasts. Run by a Balinese and German couple, Nyoman and Uli, it fills the gap between the expensive new hotels and the rather haphazardly-run older *losmen*s. The rooms mostly face the pretty garden with its fishponds, though three look out over ricefields to the mountains in the distance. Nyoman and Uli prepare breakfasts themselves, with plenty of variety, including seasonal fruits and Balinese cakes. At present there is no electricity in Pengosekan, but the cables have now been laid, and it should reach individual homes in late 1989. Prices are 10,000rp single and 13,000rp double. Guci Inn tends to fill up quickly, so it is a good idea to write in advance to Uli and Nyoman, Guci Inn, Pengosekan, Ubud, Bali.

For accommodation in the heart of a traditional Balinese village family, try **Oka's Homestay**, down a left turn in the village. It has a nice open situation, and you really are part of the family. Oka's wife, Gusti, will cook your meals by arrangement, look after your laundry and so forth. Prices by arrangement.

PELIATAN

Puri Agung and **Semara Bawa Homestay** are perhaps the most interesting places to stay in Peliatan. Two brothers, Cokordas (heads of the former ruling families of the *ksatria* caste), have *losmen*s within their old *puri* complex. Here you stay within the family compound, effectively as guests of the royal family of Peliatan. For those seriously interested in traditional dance, music and drama, or in the Balinese religion and traditions, this is an excellent choice. Anom, who runs Puri Agung, was a leading *legong* dancer, and was taken on a world tour with the Peliatan troupe in 1952—the subject of John Coast's absorbing book *Dancing out of Bali* (1954). Anom gives lessons to pupils on the large stage-like *bale* to one side of the *losmen*. Prices at both Puri Agung and Semara Bawa are around 15,000rp to 20,000rp, depending on the room and your length of stay. You can write to Cokorda Gde Parta of Semara Bawa Homestay at Jl. Dahlia No. 4B, Denpasar, Bali.

Ibu Arsa has rooms behind her restaurant for 10,000–15,000rp, and **Mandala Cottages** on the opposite side of the road is in the same price range.

At the junction of the Pengosekan road with the main road, behind the large public building which is used as a cinema, a path leads to pretty, open country beside a small river. There is a small homestay here, called **Siti's Bungalows**, which is good value, especially if you are planning to stay for some time. Rooms are 3,000rp single, 4,000rp double. They are basic but clean. Siti runs a small shop where you can buy cold drinks.

PETULU

The road to Petulu, known as Jalan Andong, has recently blossomed with several homestays amid the ricefields.

Petulu Inn has the interesting but unfortunate reputation as being the best place for an afternoon, night or weekend tryst between young Balinese and their Western boy/girlfriends who don't wish to tarnish their reputations by being seen together in Ubud. A room for the night with breakfast—or an afternoon—costs 6,000rp double. The setting is suitably romantic and discreet.

Doctor Siada, from Ubud, and his wife, have recently opened **Andong Inn** with six double and one single room. Prices for the double rooms are $25 US downstairs, with hot water, or $20 US upstairs with views but no hot water. The single bungalow is $20 US single with hot water. Two new, smaller rooms are $15 US double with no hot water. Prices include breakfast. The rooms have fans, and some have Western-style baths.

WHERE TO EAT

Restaurants, like *losmen*s, are springing up overnight all round Ubud, and most have their own dedicated supporters. Because of the general lack of refrigeration, food has to be bought fresh in the market and prepared quickly, so it is generally wholesome and lacking in unpleasant additives, though sophistication and variety are limited and you should be cautious with uncooked food. The complications of preparing your own food here are such that even long-term visitors tend to eat out every day, and the Balinese themselves often live off bought food prepared at the little *warung*s which cater for their tastes, or from the *bakmi* man with his food trolley.

We have included some of our favourite restaurants here from across the price range, as well as the more famous names.

Murni's Warung down by the Campuan bridge is one of just a few places—including Oka Kartini's and Okawati's—which have been catering for travellers since they began to come to Ubud in the 1960s. This *warung* is actually a restaurant with an excellent menu of traditional and Western-style food, including mouth-watering delicacies such as frozen banana cheesecake for 3,000rp.

On the main road a short hop west of the *bemo* station, **Lotus Café** is set in the corner of a lotus garden—a large, square, lily-filled pool surrounded by frangipani trees—with well-designed tables, chairs, place settings, menus and food. Prices are steep for Ubud, at 2,000rp upwards for soup and 5,000–7,000rp for main dishes, but the standard of cooking is much better than at most of Ubud's restaurants, and it scores highly for originality. Incidentally, Lotus Café is the only restaurant in Ubud where you can get portions of the Balinese speciality *betutu bebek* (smoked duck) without ordering a day in advance.

Pondok Tjampuhan opened late 1988 across the bridge from Murni's, just below Antonio Blanco's house. It's well-designed, well-lit, and the food is imaginative and well-prepared. It includes seafood salad (2,500rp), papaya with ham (2,000rp), good spaghetti (3,500rp), steaks (5,000rp), and fish *sate* (5,000rp). The bar has a good selection, cocktails are 3,000rp. It is owned by Cokorda Sukawati, the grandson of the old raja of Ubud.

Café Wayan is our favourite restaurant in Ubud; it is down Monkey Forest Road, about 50 m (50 yards) past the playing fields, on the right-hand side. The open *bale* at the back has a good garden setting. It earns this affection for its good, fresh, tasty food, which includes by far and away the best salads in Ubud, for bread and cakes prepared with loving care, and for the best in Balinese friendliness and good humour from host and hostess. Prices are very reasonable: 3,000–5,000rp for main dishes such as saffron chicken, *nasi campur* or pizza, 1,700rp for melt-in-the-mouth cakes.

Nomad's has also been around a long time, though it has moved sites and is now on the main street to the east of the new market. It is the best place in Ubud for steak, which is tender and cooked by flash frying rather than the awful deep-frying to which most meat is subjected elsewhere. Pepper steak with chips and a tasty, unusual salad is 4,500rp. The Saziki kebab is also excellent. Nomad's has a pleasant, leafy, low-lit atmosphere for an evening meal.

Okawati's Restaurant also has a romantic setting for dinner, just off Monkey Forest Road, opposite her accommodation. Most dishes are good here, ranging in price from 3,000 to 5,000rp, but the speciality is traditional Balinese food such as *betutu bebek*, which must be ordered a day in advance.

Another wonderful setting is to be found at the **Roof Garden Restaurant**, perched up on the rock beside the main road as you go down towards Campuan. Excellent original food here. This is the only place in Ubud which serves the traditional Indonesian spicy-hot beef dish, *rendang*.

On the same road, further down towards Campuan, **Griya Bar-B-Que** does tuna steak, chicken and beef grilled over charcoal, with salad and chips at 3,500rp. Pancakes are often good here too.

Try Japanese food at **Ubud Raya**, down the main road, past the post office, on the opposite side of the road. Again, main courses are 3,000–5,000rp.

The best Chinese food is to be found at **Denis's** on Monkey Forest Road. The crab is very good. Just next door, **Lilies Restaurant** has not quite lived up to its early promise—the menu suggests something better than the reality, but the pumpkin soup is a winner. **Bendi's** is popular for its pleasantly open setting and the cheap price of its beers.

Go to **Ubud Restaurant** further down the Monkey Forest Road for delicious Balinese pork and coconut *sate*, made from meat finely ground and blended with spices and grilled in the usual way. This is the best place for Balinese food, where it has been subtly adapted to suit Western palates.

For local colour try the small *warung*s with more traditional menus. **Ibu Dewi's**, down the hill to Campuan, on the right, just before the bridge, has brilliant food, very cheap, very tasty. She is much frequented by the Campuan 'set' of long-term stayers—those involved in some kind of business, studying the culture, or just enjoying Balinese life. *Nasi campur* for 1,500rp is unbeatable value, as is her black-rice pudding with fruit salad, 500rp. Fried chicken, when she has it, is delicious. Dewi, Ibu's daughter, is a dancer of prima donna temperament and beauty.

At the top of Monkey Forest Road, **Ayu's Kitchen** is always deservedly popular. This is a friendly place where you'll always find someone to chat to, including Ayu herself. The food is fine, prices are from 1,500–3,000rp for a main meal. It is a good place to while away a rainy afternoon—the restaurant will supply you with backgammon, chess and draughts.

Further down Monkey Forest Road, **Dian's Restaurant**, just past the playing field on the left has more good, cheap food, this time with a Javanese flavour. This is also a good place to hang around for beers and coffee in the evenings.

The only restaurant much favoured by the Balinese is **Cacik**, down the main road towards Campuan on the right. They say the flavour is more authentic here. It is good value. But for eating in the real Balinese way you have to go to the *sate warung* which sets up at night just past the market. Here you get a set meal of soup, rice and *sate*, with a rich peanut sauce and *sambal*, and tea, for 2,000rp. The *sate* is usually made from goat meat. The speciality is goat testicles, said to be the tastiest part, and naturally, believed to be good for virility. The meal is eaten al fresco, on benches set up for the purpose. There is always much gossip, good humour and ribaldry around the table.

Wayan at **Suci Inn** to the north of the *bemo* station arranges feasts of real Balinese dishes at his home from time to time. You are served by the women of his family. He explains some Balinese customs and ways of preparing food, and the layout of a traditional Balinese house. It is interesting and the food is delicious: well worth 6,500rp.

KEDEWATAN

Kupu Kupu Barong Restaurant is recommended as a place to go for a drink to watch the sun setting. The menu includes Japanese, European and Indonesian food, all well prepared, but prices are rather higher than elsewhere.

The *warung* at the T-junction with the road to Campuan serves the local speciality, *babi guling*, roast piglet, but get there before 11 am.

PADANGTEGAL

Artini has a small restaurant down the Padangtegal road. Food is standard, prices are good, and it's convenient if you are staying out this way.

PENGOSEKAN

Jati now has a restaurant along the road to Pengosekan. Good food here; the quality, and the prices, are slightly higher than average.

Pondok Impian ('Primitive Bar and Restaurant') opened its doors in June 1989. Go to see genuine antiques from all over Indonesia in little huts (*pondoks*) dotted through the gardens. Prices are very reasonable here for well above average food. We recommend the 'pork soya sauce' cooked with tasty fresh red peppers (capsicums), 3,000rp.

PELIATAN

Ibu Arsa's restaurant is strongly recommended for good, cheap well-flavoured traditional food. *Babi kecap* (pork with sweet soy sauce) and, less traditional, guacamole are excellent. Ibu Arsa knows all about what's going on in Peliatan, so come here with your questions and enjoy the good home cooking, Bali-style.

Roads north of Ubud: Pujung, Taro and Sebatu

The road north of Ubud, via Tegallalang, leads to a series of quiet, rural villages set amongst some of the loveliest landscape in Bali. From Sebatu, which discreetly preserves its beautiful temple and public baths from the covetous eye of mass tourism, you can continue to the famous temples of the Pejeng dynasty at Tampaksiring (see below) to make a comfortable round trip in a day's outing.

Between Tegallalang and Pujung the narrow road winds along the edge of an incline overlooking an impressively terraced valley. Pujung, divided into two *banjar*s, Pujung-kelod and Pujungkaja, is stretched out along the road some 16 km (10 miles) north of Ubud.

There is a mass of small woodcarving shops dotted around the landscape from Tegalallang to Pujung and to Sebatu. In Pujung and Sebatu the majority of carvers work to order, but you can find some real bargains if you take your time. This is the home of the painted wooden banana tree, now familiar throughout the world. Tegallalang specializes in carved Garuda statues.

Beyond Pujung the road climbs until it reaches the Batur–Kintamani road in Bangli regency. In these higher villages the faces of the people begin to change. They are a little less expressive, less quick to smile; in them you can detect the hardness of their lives.

Taro

Between Pujungkelod and Pujungkaja, a small turning to the left marks the start of a rough road—suitable for motorbikes or walking—that leads the 6 km (3.75 miles) to the village of Taro. Taro is held to mark the centre point of Bali. It has the island's longest *bale banjar*, the equivalent of a community hall. This is a wonderfully sleepy village, not yet shaken up to the pace of life in Ubud some 18 km (11 miles) to the south. Taro's so-called 'white' cattle, the only ones in Bali, are considered to be holy.

It was here that the priest Danghyang Markandeya is said to have come, with his followers, from a hermitage on Mt Raung in Java, in the 8th century. In a place they called 'Sarwada', on the site of Taro village, they built the Pura Gunung Raung temple and founded the herd of white cattle, before going on to found the Gunung Lebah temple in Campuan and, according to some, Pura Besakih on Mt Agung.

Sebatu

Lying 2 km (1.25 miles) down a road to the right in Pujung (opposite the Taro turning), is the village of Sebatu. Set back from the road, on the left-hand side and opposite a row of small *warung*s and 'antique' shops, are **Pura Gunung Kawi** (not to be confused with Gunung Kawi near Tampaksiring) and **Pura Panti Pasek Gelgel**, and a bathing place where *air suci*, pure mountain water which the Balinese believe to be holy, springs out of the rockface through rows of carved spouts into rectangular pools, one for men, one for women. This is an exceptionally beautiful spot, with carved stone *naga*s, mossy temple walls and beautifully painted and gilded shrines set against the rich green foliage and creeper-decked hillside. The temple carp pond is especially picturesque, with its tiny rocky island surmounted by another little painted shrine. At dusk the men's and women's bathing places are busy as the villagers come for their evening *mandi*, and the air is thick with bats.

On the patch of land outside the temples the Sebatu market is held every third day.

Two roads go east to Tampaksiring from Pujung. They are both lovely, but the best views are from the smaller one that bears off the main road as it veers left down to the market place and temple.

Tampaksiring

The village of Tampaksiring is known for producing the best quality painted wood jewellery and for its fine bone carvings. It is also the site of **Tirta Empul** and **Gunung Kawi**, two of Bali's most impressive ancient monuments, dating back to the time of King Udayana in the late 10th and early 11th centuries.

GETTING THERE

Tampaksiring lies 14 km (8.7 miles) from Ubud, 37 km (23 miles) from Denpasar. *Bemos* travel the routes up here, but since these are not major roads the service is irregular and may require a number of changes. *Bemos* turn towards Tampaksiring at Semabaung, just north of Kutri, on the main Denpasar–Gianyar road (300rp). Or you can join one of the many tour buses which travel this way, which will save the bother of getting from one site to another.

There are a number of beautiful roads leading up to Tampaksiring. If you have your own robust transport (a motorbike or jeep), try this one from Ubud. On the Denpasar road out of Ubud turn left at the T-junction before Peliatan and turn northwards towards Petulu. Follow this road as far as Gentong. In this village you take a small right-hand turn towards Kendran. Between Kendran and Pinjul there is a section of quite appalling unmade road, but after Pinjul it improves and takes you through a variety of rice-growing landscapes all the way to the village of Bayad, where you turn right for Tampaksiring.

The approaches to Tampaksiring are well enough signposted until the very last moment; when you arrive you wonder if you are really there—there's no village to speak of, just a huge car park with a row of tatty modern shops. **Tirta Empul** is a five-minute walk from here. **Pura Mengening** is a little further to the west (follow the road round the hill; the entrance is well marked).

Gunung Kawi is really a drive away from Tampaksiring, in the same direction as Pura Mengening—unless you wish to walk the 3 km (1.8 miles) or so, and then down the 230 steps.

Tirta Empul

This temple, with its lily-filled ponds, fed by a spring of mountain water, has an exceptionally beautiful, mossy and mysterious setting against its backdrop of the surviving patches of forest. This can come as some surprise after the approach, devastated by the effects of a mass assault by commercial tourism. All around the car park and lining the pathway to the temple are tiny booths selling tacky souvenirs. The vendors call out to you as you go past, asking the most exorbitant prices. Go in the early morning, when the vendors are still sleepy and the bus loads of tourists are still thundering up from the coasts. The light at this time of day can be especially beautiful. You need to come equipped with scarf and sarong, or pay 1,000rp to hire a scarf at the entrance. Admission costs 200rp, plus a donation of 500rp or so.

There is a myth concerning the origin of Tirta Empul which is related in the ancient chronicle, the *Usana Bali*. The demon King of Bedulu, Mahadanawa, having provoked the gods by his attempts to disrupt the ceremonies of dedication of the temple at Besakih, was pursued by Indra and his heavenly army the length and breadth of the island. Mahadanawa, after putting up fierce resistance, was eventually sent packing, but as he fled he used his magical powers to create a river of poisoned water which killed a large number of Indra's men. Indra in his turn created Tirta Empul, a spring of sacred, healing water which revived his ailing troops. Mahadanawa then changed himself into a cock, then into some rice, and lastly into a rock in order to evade his pursuers. Indra, however, managed to finish him off by firing an arrow into the rock, but as the evil king died his poisoned blood had seeped forth, creating the Petanu river—a river which long remained the object of deep suspicion for the Balinese for this reason.

The cold-water spring created by Indra bubbles up through black volcanic sand in the floor of a large rectangular pool (the 'Taman Suci') of the *kagin* side of the temple complex—a tranquil spot and home to a number of fish and an enormous eel. The sacred water also feeds into two further rectangular tanks where the public come to bathe. The water has spiritual healing powers, and bathing in it is part of ritual purification ceremonies.

The complex contains numerous *bale*s and a number of highly decorated shrines, all thatched in sugar-palm fibre. In the *kaja* position there is an unusual *padmasana* flanked by two huge *naga*s. The series of plinths looks more Chinese than Balinese. Note in particular the four small shrines to the right of the *padmasana*, with relief work that has been beautifully painted and gilded.

A stone inscription found nearby states that Tirta Empul bathing place was built by King Chandrabhayasingha (a ruler of the kingdom based in Pejeng) in AD 962. The massive tree, the roots of which drape themselves in extraordinary rectangular shapes over the stonework just below the public pools, is said to be 400 years old. The temple was heavily restored in 1969.

What is not so old is the government resthouse which hovers incongruously on the two hills above the temple. This was built by the Dutch, much to the resentment of local people. An official Dutch tourist guide of the 1930s reads: 'In front of the temple a swimming pool has been made for Europeans. A special pipe leads the water from the spring directly to this pool. There are a few dressing rooms provided here and a diving board.'

The resthouse was renovated and extended by the late President Sukarno to create a palace. A telescope was placed on the balcony overlooking Tirta Empul, and it was said that the president trained it on the women bathing below. Scandalous rumours of licentious parties at the palace circulated and this palace became a potent symbol for the increasing disenchantment during the Sukarno era. These days it is still used as a government resthouse, but its role has become rather more discreet.

Pura Mengening

You will see this old temple set back from the road near the junction that leads to Tirta Empul. A sign written in Balinese script tells you that this is a historical site; the temple is

219

said to be associated with King Udayana. Pura Mengening has another spring and a *candi* similar to those of Gunung Kawi.

Gunung Kawi

The temple of Gunung Kawi consists of a series of ten *candi*s carved into the rock walls that line the banks of the Pakrisan river. This is a beautiful site, not just for the impressive *candi*s, but also for their setting in this lush and intimate valley, reached only by a rather exhausting walk down 230 steps from the car park. Go here in the cool of the morning, unless you want to lose weight: this is not a site to visit if you are feeling frail.

The path is heralded by a series of little shops selling clothes, earrings and so forth. The vendors seem desperate for trade. Below this, a view north across a heavily wooded valley reveals the tip of Pura Mengening. Further down is a hut where you pay your donation and rent a temple sash if you have forgotten to bring your own.

You can take a short detour just beyond this hut by negotiating a narrow and rather tricky little footpath to the right. Some 300 m (300 yards) as the crow flies from this point, out on its own and set near the river is an isolated *candi* with accompanying cells. You can persist all the way along the path if you like, but a short walk along here leads you to a point overlooking the *candi*, giving you a good view of it and its setting. And what a setting! The rice terraces cling to the contours of the steep valley walls, a quilt of fields and banks, undisturbed but for the purr of trickling and gushing water. Notice how incredibly small some of these terraces are—some no bigger than a sarong laid out to dry.

Back on the main path to the temple complex you continue down the steps, which drop through a natural passageway until you reach a point where the temple appears before you, framed by the walls of this gateway cut through the soft rock.

The temple itself is a pretty complex of *bale*s roofed with *alang-alang* grass and sugar-palm fibre. In the eastern wall of the temple there is an entrance to a small courtyard hewn out of the rock, with a number of ruggedly excavated cells surrounding an impressive sarcophagus-like roofed cell, said to be the place where the king meditated.

A little further to the east stand five identical *candi*s, 7 m (23 ft) tall, set in their own niches cut out of the valley wall. Four water spouts beneath these feed holy water into a rectangular pool below. This is sculpture on an impressive scale, unusual for Bali where delicacy and decoration are generally preferred to bulk, and underlining the fact that these monuments show an influence from elsewhere, from the Hindu and Buddhist monuments of Java and beyond. The massive stone staircase in front of these *candi*s indicates the depth to which the rock has been carved.

On the other side of the river lie four more identical *candi*s, scraped out of an even deeper mass of rock, but here more heavily eroded.

So what is this complex? Oral tradition says that these monuments represent the kings and queens of the Udayana dynasty dating back to the 11th century: Udayana; his queen Mahendradatta; their son, the illustrious Erlangga, who ruled Eastern Java; and his brothers Anak Wangsa (who ruled Bali after his father's death) and Marakata. Some say that the *candi*s are tombs, but they have no interiors. They are, rather, simply religious monuments which provide the focus of meditation and devotion, perhaps in honour of the royal family. A date of 1080 is given for the complex, and it is thought that Anak

Wangsa was responsible for its construction. Legend however tells how the monstrous Kebo Iwa carved out the monuments with his fingernails in a single night. Kebo Iwa is a giant of huge strength and supernatural powers. He is thought to be a semi-historical figure, a minister to the last king of the Pejeng dynasty, Sri Aji Asura Bumibanten; he was apparently enticed treacherously to Java by Gajah Mada, who promised him marriage with a princess, only to meet his death.

WHERE TO STAY AND EAT
For accommodation, your best bet is to return to Ubud 14 km (8.7 miles) to the south; there is nothing in the surrounds of Tampaksiring that we can recommend.

Eating is similarly unpromising; there are a number of expensive local *warung*s, and also a tourist restaurant at Tampaksiring, overlooking a jungly hillside. The food (mainly Chinese) is reasonably priced and more interesting than usual for this kind of place: bamboo shoot chicken, 3,200rp, shrimp fried rice, 2,700rp, and so forth. But its main attraction is simple convenience.

East of Ubud: Goa Gajah–Bedulu–Pejeng

This is another cluster of historic sites, lying in a compact zone about 5 km (3.1 miles) east of Ubud. Some of these sites are worn thin by bus loads of tourists, some are hidden away, unmarked and unvisited.

GETTING THERE
Once in this zone, you could walk from one site to the next, although they are somewhat scattered. An occasional *bemo* passes this way from Ubud on its way to Tampaksiring (200rp or so); from Denpasar take a *bemo* to Semabaung and change to another heading north on the route to Tampaksiring. Alternatively, use your own transport, or join one of the numerous tours that visit these sites.

There is a fine walk to Pejeng from Peliatan, through romantic river gorges and ricefields. Turn off the main road to Denpasar just beside the *banjar* building next to the pharmacy.

Goa Gajah (Elephant Cave)

This lies 3 km (1.8 miles) to the east of Teges, the village at the foot of Peliatan with the modern statue of a *legong* dancer in the middle of the central T-junction. You can't miss Goa Gajah because to your left is a large parking area surrounded by tacky little tourist shops. The entrance to Goa Gajah is on the opposite side of the road (200rp).

Going down the steps you leave behind you the razzmatazz and hustling. Below you, the steep side of the valley falls away to the Petanu river. Out of the hillside a cave has been carved, guarded by the monstrous face of Boma, through whose mouth you enter. Nearby, female statues form the watering spouts of a sacred bathing pool—a deep tank of dressed stone. The cave was unearthed in 1923, the bathing place was discovered in 1954. More recent investigations have revealed signs of other remains further down the hillside. Because of its proximity to Bedulu and Pejeng it is thought that this was the

221

hermitage for the priests who advised the ruler of the ancient kingdom of Pejeng. Signs of Buddhist as well as Hindu influence suggest that it was founded as early as the 9th century. It is said that the rooms of the hermitage lie buried at the focal point of Boma's eyes, which look away from the bathing pool.

Inside the dark and musty T-shaped cave the local holy man will show you, with the aid of a series of matches, or a flickering cigarette lighter, the niches in the rock wall containing a fragment of what might have been a large stone Buddha, three *lingam*s with their corresponding *yoni* (the male and female principles relating to the cult of Shiva), and a statue of Ganesha, the elephant-headed god from whom the cave gets its name. Ganesha is the son of Shiva and Parvati. He is a much loved Hindu god; he helps people over their difficulties and represents prosperity and happy living.

The remainder of the temple, set in a dusty wood, has an ancient if tatty air about it. You are free to wander and explore the ravine below the cave if you wish.

Yeh Pulu

About 500 m (500 yards) further east along the road a sign by a small turning announces the stone relief of Yeh Pulu. In the wet season you are better off approaching by a side road: continue to the junction at Bedulu, turn right and then take the first small turning off to the right again. Park and follow the path along the edges of the ricefields and across a small stream. Unlike at Goa Gajah, you have the exhilarating feeling of discovery at Yeh Pulu—out in the open ricefields, with sun and sky, the crickets and the old priest-caretaker as your witnesses.

Yeh Pulu is a spring by a stone relief carved on the exposed natural rockface. The style of the carving is quite different to the usual formalized and symbolic Balinese religious carvings: it is realistic and vigorous, and, apart from the Ganesha figure, it is also non-religious in theme. There are some familiar sights: the two men carrying pigs tied upside down between them, the blacksmiths at work. There is also a sequence of scenes which appear to tell a story.

The story is thought to be that of the daughter of a hermit, who married a prince informally, without a proper ceremony (as is still common in Balinese custom); the next scene is of the prince hunting wild boar; then the woman is holding on to the horse, apparently begging her prince not to leave her.

The caves beyond the relief are not dissimilar to those at Gunung Kawi. Yeh Pulu dates from around the same period as both Gunung Kawi and Goa Gajah—somewhere around the 10th and 11th centuries.

A temple has now been built around the spot, and a *pemangku* lives here to care for it. The caves are used by the *gamelan* orchestra at times of temple ceremonies, when the whole area becomes a sea of people. Notice the spring in the temple, where the water seems to be flowing out of an earthenware pot. A pot holding 'Amerta', the holy water of immortality, is an image repeated again and again in this region, where the Hindu concept has been grafted on to the animistic worship of spirits of the mountains, the plains, the coast, which takes water as a central theme.

Pura Samuan Tiga (Temple of the Meeting of the Three)
At the Bedulu crossroads look for a signpost to the government resthouse, and follow this down a stony track for about 100 m (100 yards).

Samuan Tiga is an important temple for the Balinese, thought to have been founded by Kuturan in the 11th century. Unlike that of other temples, the *odalan* of Samuan Tiga is fixed by the lunar calendar and happens only once every lunar year, on the full moon of the 10th month. The site is also connected with the legend of the demon king Mahadanawa (see Tirta Empul, pp.218–19). Three of Indra's holy warriors are said to have met here after the death of the demon.

The temple site is huge, with an outer courtyard big enough to hold the dense crowds who gather here from all over the island to celebrate the *odalan*.

Bedulu

This village is associated with the last king of the Pejeng dynasty, Sri Aji Asura Bumibanten, known in legend as King Beda Ulu.

A pair of girl and boy twins are said to have been conjured up out of the body of Mahadanawa, the evil king killed by Indra at Tampaksiring (see pp.218–19). These twins married and became the founders of the Pejeng dynasty, in turn producing girl and boy twins to succeed them. Seven generations of girl and boy twins then succeeded, one after the other, until the birth of the final king.

Now, this king had supernatural powers. One of the magical tricks by which he demonstrated his power was to have his servant cut off his head with a *kris*; he would then put it back on again as though nothing had happened. Unfortunately the king was so boastful he offended the gods. So one day, when the king was showing off this trick, the gods caused his head to roll off into a river, where it was carried away by the current. In desperation the servant cut off the head of a pig to replace it. So the king became known as 'Beda Ulu', 'he who changed heads'. To hide his shame he ordered that his subjects should never look up at his head, and always sat on a high throne. Around this time the rulers of the Majapahit empire in Java sent the great general, Gajah Mada, to reconquer Bali. Gajah Mada went to see King Beda Ulu, where he observed the practice of keeping his eyes averted. However, during the audience Gajah Mada asked for an urn of water, and, because he had to tip his head back in order to drink from the tall pot, he sneaked a look at the king's head. This so inflamed the wounded pride of King Beda Ulu that he was consumed by spontaneous combustion.

There is a more prosaic explanation: Bedulu may come from 'Badaulu', which means 'upstream'.

What is certain is that somewhere in this region was the ruling court for the ancient kingdom. The exact spot has never been located, though a mass of statuary has been brought into the local temples from the surrounding ricefields.

Arca Gedong or Museum Purbakala (Archaeological Museum)
The building is up the road towards Pejeng, on the right. It contains relics from the area, many of them from the time of the Warmadewa dynasty, and the books of Dutch archaeologists and historians who have worked here. This is, if anything, more of a study centre than a museum (open 8–2 Monday and Thursday, 8–1 other days, closed Sunday; admission by donation). The exhibits are not well displayed or labelled; unless you are a serious student of Balinese archaeology, it will be disappointing.

Note how the stone sarcophagi arranged around the modern courtyard show the way the dead in pre-Hindu Bali were buried in a foetal position: leaving life in the same position as that in which they came to it. These are said to date from around 400 BC.

Pejeng

Once the seat of the kingdom of that name before its fall to the Majapahit invaders in 1343, this village is famous for its three temples.

Pura Penataran Sasih: the Moon Drum of Pejeng

The most famous temple in Pejeng is on your right as you go north, after the Arca Gedong. Huge stone sculptures of wild pigs and a couple of stone *naga*s distinguish the gateway, and there are several very old carvings inside, including a battered Ganesha, which have been brought in from the Pakrisan river valley area. The chief attraction of the temple, however, is the large bronze gong, known as the Moon Drum.

Once upon a time, the story goes, God created seven moons to illuminate the world. One day one of them fell to earth, where it landed in a tree and lit up the whole area, night and day. This didn't suit everyone: it disturbed the plans of a gang of thieves, who gathered together to decide how to get rid of the light so that they could get on with their work. One of them urinated on the moon to extinguish it. The moon cracked, the sacrilegious thief was killed, the light went out, and what remained was the drum you see today. It is now housed on a high platform in a shrine at the back left-hand side of the temple.

The drum is solid bronze, about 3 m (10 ft) long and 1.60 m (5 ft 3 in) diameter, shaped like an hourglass, and carved on the surface in the style characteristic of the bronze age Dong Son dynasty of Vietnam (around 300 BC), which was known to have influence throughout the region. This bronze drum is believed to be the biggest to be cast in a single piece in the world.

Pura Kebo Edan (Crazy Buffalo Temple)

A special attraction at this temple is the huge carving of the monster Bima, decorated with skulls and possessor of six penises, trampling on a man and woman having sex. According to the temple guide, Bima was supposed to have desired the woman, but his penis was too big for her. When he found her lying with an ordinary mortal, he crushed the man beneath his feet. In this manifestation he is Ratu Sakti Ratu Edan, who drinks blood mixed with *arak* from human skulls. This statue is of special significance to *dukun*s, and they gather here at certain phases of the moon.

There are other statues out in the ricefields behind the temple, as well as a collection of very worn relics inside the temple *bale*s.

Pura Pusering Jagat (Temple of the Navel of the World)

This temple is worth investigating for the carved stone vase known as the '**Mandala Giri**', housed in a shrine behind the main courtyard. It is a very old temple site, connected with the earliest Hindu-influenced Balinese religious system (see Pura Tegeh Koripan pp.271–72). The vase is sacred because it is said to have contained 'Amerta', the water of immortality. The carvings on the urn tell the story of the nine gods, each corresponding to a different direction; these gods had their own temples to honour them in Bali, and took holy water from the urn by carrying it in the small leaves of the banyan tree. A demon god became greedy, and used the big leaves known as '*daun lawar-lawar*' to steal more than his fair share of the immortalizing water, whereupon he was shot in the neck by Vishnu. Unfortunately the demon had already drunk enough to make his head immortal. Vishnu cut off his head, but it remained alive. At the time of full moon in the ninth month of each lunar year there is an eclipse, which is when the living head of the monster devours the moon as an act of revenge against Vishnu.

The temple is said to be at the centre of the old Pejeng kingdom (*puset* means navel or centre). This is a special place of pilgrimage for *dukun*s at time of full moon. Couples who want to have a baby come and pray at the stone *lingam* and *yoni* (symbols of the male and female principles) in the inner courtyard.

Pura Pengukur Ukuran and Goa Garba

Hidden away in the Pakrisan river valley, between the villages of Kelusu and Sawa-gunung, these sites are ignored by tourists but are described in archaeological reports on the area written by the Dutch. Finding them is an adventure in itself, well worth it for the feel you get of an ancient kingdom, undisturbed by would-be guides and sellers. It's also a lovely place for a picnic and for bathing in the river.

To get there, turn to the east at a small crossroads by a marketplace just to the north of the Pura Penataran Sasih in Pejeng. An ageing, neglected sign points to Goa Garba. More visible is the sign beside it for Pura Pengukur Ukuran. Pass through villages where the daily business of life, drying corn, weaving, eating and gossiping, is carried out right in the centre of the road. Follow the road round a bend to the right, then turn left, continue for 1 km (0.6 mile). Turn left at the next T-junction. In dense green forest, just beyond the Pejeng Junior School on your right, is Pura Pengukur Ukuran. Beyond it and below it is Goa Garba.

Pura Pengukur Ukuran means the temple from where all things are measured. It is said to have been founded by King Jayaprangus, who succeeded to the throne after the demise of the sons of Udayana at the close of the 11th century.

The outer courtyard is wonderfully scented by a white-blossomed *cempaka* tree. The inner courtyard is crowded with *bale*s containing a number of ancient relics, including a small megalithic stone from a pre-Hindu culture (in a small *bale* to the right). Such megaliths are said to have been superseded by the Hindu *padmasana* (the lotus throne) and there is a fine example of a Vishnu *padmasana* here, with a Garuda in relief on the *kaja* side. The large, principal shrine (the *gedong pesimpangan*) is highly ornate and boasts three *lingam*s on the steps.

Walk out of the side entrance through an incongruous wire-netting gate, past an old cockfighting arena, and climb down massive stone steps, set in the steep side of the valley. Here is the Pakrisan river, flowing down from Tampaksiring and Gunung Kawi. An indentation on the boulder steps is said to be the footstep of the monster who made the stairway, Kebo Iwa, of Gunung Kawi fame. One can believe it: the scale of these steps is not human. There is a formal carved stone gateway, built out of dressed stone blocks, then a drop down to the grassy floor of the valley. To the left are ancient, disused bathing places, said to have been used by Jayaprangus (the bath on the left) and his queen (the double bath). The latter now has a massive *pule* tree growing above it; *pule* trees are valued for their medicinal use, and provide the wood to make *rangda* masks. Below the baths are two meditation cells carved out of the rockface. The strange shapes of old carvings decorate the rock above the caves; an elephant is visible on the left, one cave has a face carved above it, another an unusual circular motif, a symbol from the Javanese Kediri script. Holy water drips down the rocks and is still collected by priests for ceremonial use. An inscribed stone on the floor of one of the cells shows the symbol of the vessel containing 'Amerta', the water of immortality.

This is a cool, richly green spot with a silence that feels as if it has been undisturbed for a thousand years. If you don't fancy the climb down Kebo Iwa's giant steps, there is a track that leads round the hill to the south.

South of Ubud: the craftshop trail

The road to Denpasar passes through villages which have grown wealthy by developing their local craft skills to cater for tourists and the export trade. Since you are most likely to meet this road by coming up from the south, we will tackle it in that order. 'Tackle' is the word: this is the baptism by fire for the car-renter, a very busy, dusty road and built up almost continuously from Denpasar through to Mas, just to the south of Ubud. Bicycles, *bakmi* carts, *bemo*s, buses, *orang putih* at the wheel of their hired jeeps, motorbikes, schoolchildren and dogs lay claim to the surface from ditch to ditch, whilst the borders are lined with innumerable 'art' shops, some tiny, some grandiose. Only after the turning at Sakah do you get a breath of countryside.

GETTING AROUND
All these places, with the exception of Mas, are on the main Denpasar–Sakah–Ubud road, and easily accessible by a regular traffic of *bemo*s (300–500rp) from Denpasar, or in the opposite direction from Ubud.

Batubulan

You will recognize this village straight away when you're passing through because the road is lined with shops selling the wonderfully lively stonecarvings that you see everywhere in Bali, in temples, private homes and restaurants. Batubulan is also a good place to find all kinds of 'antique' woodcarvings—flying creatures, antique mirror frames, *kulkul*s, and carved wooden friezes.

You will see the places where the Barong dance is held; they operate in rotation, with a performance somewhere here every morning of the week at 9.30 am. Entrance is 2,000rp and transport can be arranged from any of the tourist centres. These performances are touched by a certain degenerate languor, born of playing day after day to tourists who haven't the first clue what they are looking at. Nonetheless, these performances do have some of the sparkle of pantomime and some good clowning; Rangda, the witch, is genuinely fearsome in her best tradition, and the *kris* dance at the end is still a shock, even if you know it is coming. Since you may well not have the opportunity to see the Barong dance elsewhere, and as its imagery is so central to Balinese mythology, we recommend that you join the crowds and enjoy it as a good piece of popular theatre.

Celuk

Celuk is the silver and goldsmiths' village. There are some big gallery-type shops here, very well-established and visited regularly by the tour buses. Note the opulent and rather splendid new houses built to the back of these on the proceeds. There are also plenty of smaller workshops still on the way up. Most of the silver is in traditional styles, ornate, with gold worked into the designs, but some derive from designs introduced by exporters to suit European or American tastes. You can watch the craftsmen at work.

Just before it is a turning to the south. This goes down to the coast along a little known road, to the villages of **Ketewel** and **Gumicik** on the coast—a pleasant detour.

Sukawati

The lively market here brings in villagers from miles around. There is no better place to immerse yourself in the sights, sounds and smells of Bali. Sukawati is an old centre of power in Gianyar, and there is a school of thought that maintains its leading family are the true princes of the regency, not the Gianyar family.

Nowadays a big new art market building makes it an attraction for tourists. You can find a wide range of crafts for sale here, from woodcarvings to *kris*es to fabric goods, at reasonable prices. Do bargain here though.

A specially good buy in Sukawati are baskets, made from the *lontar* palm leaf, and dyed with natural dyes, usually with black and brown and white patterns. These still perform their traditional task as containers which the market women carry on their heads. Sukawati is also a good place to buy decorative umbrellas, fans, parasols and so forth.

Just before the market, near the police station, a small path takes you to the village of **Puaya**, 1 km (0.6 mile) from the main road. You can see the leather puppets used in shadow puppet shows (*wayang kulit*) being made here. You pay around 10,000rp for an intricately cut and painted puppet.

Watermelon seller

227

Batuan

This is a village with a long tradition of dancing and painting. The art of Batuan was influenced by the Pitha Maha group, who were based here for a while. The distinctive Batuan style presents minutely detailed images of landscapes dotted with figures, often with humorous touches, such as a camera-wielding tourist in Bermuda shorts. The painter I Made Budi (b.1932) is particularly noted for this kind of work. The early Batuan paintings had more muted and controlled colour—black ink drawings highlighted in white and yellow—and have a power and dignity that many more exuberant but derivative modern works lack. The big galleries today tend to favour safe reproductions of old favourites rather than anything exciting and genuinely creative.

Mas

To get to Mas, you leave the Denpasar–Gianyar road as it sweeps sharply to the right at a place called **Sakah**, continuing straight on to Ubud and the north.

Mas is now a great string of houses along the road stretching almost from Sakah to Teges, 5 km (3.1 miles) to the north, although the original centre of the village is at the mid-point. A village of high-caste Brahmana families, Mas has a place of some importance in the history of the region. The 16th-century Hindu priest from Java, Nirartha (or Bau Rauh), was said to have made a home here, and **Pura Taman Pule** is a particularly venerated temple which is believed to have been built on the site of his home. Nowadays Mas is more famous for its woodcarvers and maskmakers.

There are numerous galleries for **woodcarvings** in traditional and modern styles here. The older, well-established places are often like palaces in their own right, with homes that are full of beautiful carvings, carved doors and pillars, and traditional paintings. Where a gallery is a port of call for the tour buses, it tends to stock the traditional style of carving in polished hardwoods. It can, however, be depressing to see shelf upon shelf of reproduction Shivas or prancing horses. To appreciate a piece you need to see it on its own. Some of the best buys in Mas are the **masks**, in particular the masks used for *topeng* dances.

It may be unfair to select just one of the galleries, but that of **Ida Bagus Tilem**, on the left near the centre of Mas, is an outstanding example and well worth a visit (open 9.30–5.30 daily), not only for the exquisite quality of some of the carving, but also for the beauty of the setting. Much of the considerable wealth amassed by the family of this artist has gone into beautifying the traditional family compound.

Ida Bagus Tilem was born in 1936, the son of Ida Bagus Njana (1912–85), a celebrated sculptor. What has set this family of craftsmen apart is their highly imaginative and sensitive use of natural wood shapes, turning them into running horses or pregnant women, or whatever, depending on the form of the wood—and often with a touch of humour. Brought up in traditional style and living in modest circumstances, Tilem was trained by his father; he is now a sculptor of international repute and only works when the inspiration takes him. In his compound you can see apprentice sculptors sitting on the floor, working solemnly at their pieces under the eye of a master carver, and in the modern gallery you can admire the work of Njana and Tilem, as well as numerous rather less distinguished works by other sculptors of the studio.

WHERE TO STAY AND EAT

There are a number of small eating places and *losmen*s dotted throughout these villages, but none that commend themselves particularly. It is better either to stay near the coast in Badung (Sanur, Kuta, Jimbaran), or head on a little further to Peliatan and Ubud (see pp.208–16), to the established accommodation and eating places there.

Blahbatuh and Kutri

These two villages lie close to each other on the main Denpasar–Gianyar road, to the east of the Sakah turning leading north to Ubud. Kutri has a temple with a rather special association, and a hill with a magnificent view.

Blahbatuh

Blahbatuh occupies a right-angled corner on the main Denpasar–Gianyar road, 4km (2.5 miles) beyond the Sakah turning to Ubud. It has a famous temple called **Pura Gadun**, situated on the left of the road before the corner; this has an impressive entrance up steps overhung by tall trees. Pura Gadun is associated with Kebo Iwa, the minister turned monster who is said to have carved out Gunung Kawi with his fingernails (see pp.220–1). A large stone head in the temple is supposed to be a portrait of him.

At the corner there are two flourishing orchid nurseries; one, the Puspa Sari; the other, the Mantari Budaya, occupying the old palace of a minor prince.

By taking a right-hand turn along a dusty road beyond the corner you can visit the foundries where *gamelan* instruments are made. (But see also Tihingan, p.242)

Tegenungan Waterfall

About 1km (0.6 mile) before the left-hand right-angle bend in Blahbutah a track on the right side of the road leads to a waterfall on the Petanu river. Watch for the sign marked 'Air Tejun Tegenungan Waterfall 2,500m' in the village of Kemenuh. The path makes a good walk, through ricefields and the small village of Belang Singa. The waterfall is also known as **'Srog Srogan'**. It has the reputation of being a place of healing. Nearby, an open *bale* has been built beside four fountains where priests come to bathe, for spiritual and physical cleansing. Specially holy times here and at the temple of **Merta Jiwa** (from 'Amerta', water of immortality) above the water, are full moon and the night before the new moon.

Kutri and Bukit Dharma

Kutri lies at the top end of the good stretch of road that runs for 5km (3.1 miles) north of Blahbatuh. There is no village to speak of here, just an interesting temple, **Pura Kedarman**, the *pura puseh* of Kutri, lying at the foot of a hill called the Bukit Dharma, which offers views right across the southern coast.

The temple is thought to have been built in honour of—some say as the burial place of—Mahendradatta, the wife of King Udayana, King of Bali in the late 10th and early 11th century. Mahendradatta is said to be the origin of the Rangda figure, who is in turn associated with the Hindu deity Durga.

Durga is a composite female goddess, who was created out of the divine wrath of the gods. The story of Durga is that the gods created her in order to destroy an evil demon in the form of a water buffalo. The gods armed her with a selection of powerful weapons, with which she destroyed the demon. However, ambition drove her forward, and she managed to incorporate a part of herself in the consorts of the gods, hence her association with Parvati, consort of Shiva. Durga's beauty disguises her destructive and bloodthirsty nature; but she also has a more beneficent side as the solver of difficulties, albeit at the cost of purging.

Rangda is a Balinese phenomenon. The name means 'widow', and the widow in question was Mahendradatta. The story goes that King Udayana discovered that she was involved in black magic, and so banished her to the forests. When King Udayana died and control passed to their son, Prince Erlangga of Kediri, Mahendradatta aimed her black magic upon Erlangga's kingdom, causing the *leyak*s, the evil spirits, to spread disease through the land. Her motive was vengeance: first, against Erlangga because he had not made efforts to intervene when his father contemplated a second marriage; secondly, against society in general because no man of the correct caste and status would come forward to marry her beautiful daughter, Ratna Menggali. They were no doubt put off by thoughts of the mother-in-law.

Eventually Erlangga managed to assuage the plague with the help of a powerful high priest named Empu Bharada, who arranged a brave suitor for Ratna Menggali. After their marriage, Ratna Menggali's husband succeeded in discovering the secrets of Mahendradatta's power, which he relayed to Empu Bharada. The priest then used this information to conduct an epic battle against Mahendradatta, which, in legend at least, he eventually won, finally finishing her off in human form, repentant and purged of evil. In Bali today, however, Rangda lives on, in the terrifying form that Mahendradatta assumed during the battle with Empu Bharada. She is queen of the *leyak*s, mistress of black magic—a wild, hairy figure with sagging boobs and huge, rattling fingernails, awesome even in her stage manifestation in performances of the Barong dance.

In the inner temple of Kutri you can see two figures of Durga in the small, white-painted god-house to the right. Note that to the left, in the *bale barong* is the body of a *barong*, master of white magic. The head, a sacred object, is kept in one of the *meru*s to the right of this.

Climb the steep stone steps to the right of the inner temple, leading up past great volcanic boulders clasped by the roots of a large banyan tree, to a kind of balcony built on the summit of Bukit Dharma. This is said to be the spot where Mahendradatta meditated, and is now the site of an 11th-century stone relief of Durga, armed with a lance, a *chakra* (a sharp-edged iron disk), a bow, shield and a flask containing Amerta, the water of immortality. Durga conveniently has eight arms (although one is missing here). She is standing on the demon in the form of a water buffalo.

Despite the connotations, this is a peaceful spot with magnificent views; below lie the ricefields and palms of the coastal plains, and you can see as far as the white shoreline of Nusa Lembongan to the southeast.

Belega and Bona

At Blahbatuh the main Denpasar–Gianyar road veers left. A smaller road goes straight ahead leading to the villages of Belega and Bona. Belega, half hidden among the trees, is noted for its **bamboo furniture**, using natural 'black' bamboo as well as the standard variety. Bona, a dusty but pleasantly spacious village, is known for its woven palm-leaf baskets, hats, masks, dolls and whatever else can possibly be made out of *lontar* palm fronds. There are several workshop/stores in Bona where all sorts of palm leaf goodies can be found—notably the Ayuning Art Shop. Little *wayang* puppets on sticks cost 100rp each; an enormous palm leaf hat is 2,000rp.

Bona is also the home of the *kecak* dance to which visitors flock weekly. It is an extraordinary performance, involving a trance dance with two little girls, fire-walking, and the *kecak* chorus of male singers who accompany the dancers without music (see p.127).

Masceti and the Coast

A pleasant excursion of some 10 km (6.25 miles) will take you through a number of lowland villages to the coastal temple of Masceti. Several roads lead to the village of **Medahan**: you could take the one that begins at the right-hand turn shortly after the turning towards Belega and Bona in Blahbatuh. This will take you through Tojan, Pering and Keramas. From Medahan a signpost points the way to Masceti, on a road that descends to the sea between rice terraces.

Pura Masceti is one of the nine protective, directional temples of Bali (see p.116). The walls of the main temple, the *candi bentar* and the impressive gate to the inner temple are all built of hard, stone-like blocks of ancient coral, presenting a striking image of white against the broad, black-sand beach behind and the blue sea beyond.

The interior of the temple is not exceptional, although the inner temple has some elaborate carving and two of the *meru*s here have painted wooded sides in a state of sea-blown deterioration. To the east, a large rectangular pool of modern construction forms a pretty lily pond.

This fetching scene is marred by a hideous carbuncle on the shoreline nearby. A giant concrete swan, painted in vivid colour, houses two swimming pools, adorned by painted concrete pigs, complete with dripping fangs, and other bizarre statuary. The swan faces the beach, its flanks protected by two huge peasant soldiers brandishing swords. Due to open in 1990, this Dali-esque wonder is apparently the result of a cooperative effort by local villagers to attract visitors to the coast here. A stage above one of the pools is to be used for *legong* perfomances. It will probably be enormously successful and spawn imitations all over the island. If you want to stay here, you will, apparently, be able to rent one of the six pokey and dark rooms which have been ingeniously fitted into the rear end of the bird.

Roads in various states of repair run between the main Denpasar–Gianyar–Klungkung road and the sea, to a number of small villages beside black-sand beaches. The best known beach is at **Lebih**. Here, as at other coastal villages in Gianyar, processions of villagers from all over the regency bring the ashes of the dead to the sea in a ceremony known as *melasti*. In another important ritual, temple shrines and artefacts are brought down to the sea for purification.

The fishing villages themselves are not especially remarkable. The most attractive beach is near the village of **Siyut**, 10 km (6.25 miles) south of the main road from the point where the Bangli road goes north. Follow the road that leads south from Tulikup.

Part VII
KLUNGKUNG REGENCY

The Bale Kambung in the Taman Gili, Klungkung

Klungkung regency lies to the east of Gianyar. The smallest regency in Bali, it covers an area of about 315 sq km (121 sq miles), including the three islands of **Nusa Penida**, **Nusa Lembongan** and **Nusa Ceningan**, which fall under its jurisdiction. Despite its size, its influence on Balinese culture has been powerful. Here, in the shadow of the holy Mt Agung, princes and priests of the Majapahit empire gathered in exile in the early 16th century as their kingdom in Java crumbled. In the palace of **Gelgel**, a few kilometres south of the present-day town of **Klungkung**, they established a brilliant and richly artistic court life which flourished for nearly a century. As a result of this dominance during the critical period for the development of Balinese culture and religion, most of the island's royal families are descended from the old Klungkung dynasty and the Raja of Klungkung, the Dewa Agung, has always been held in special respect, even after his political ascendancy had waned.

The largest town, and capital of the regency, is Klungkung itself; the surrounding land is divided into the peaceful terraced rice paddies of the higher ground, and the verdant coconut and banana groves of the coastal strip. Here, as elsewhere in Bali, life centres on the small villages that dot the area. Nusa Penida, Nusa Lembongan and Nusa Ceningan, which lie 10 km (6.25 miles) off the southeast coast, are by comparison impoverished and sparsely populated.

Life in Klungkung regency is still affected by the eruption of Mt Agung in 1963. The brunt of this tragedy was borne by neighbouring Karangasem regency, but lava flowed through the Klungkung area too. Crops were destroyed, the agricultural life of southeastern Bali was shattered, thousands were left homeless. This was a difficult time for Bali because of political disputes in Jakarta: few resources were available to deal with the

232

problems of this tiny area in Indonesia's vast and far-flung territories. When the tourist influx arrived in the 1970s Klungkung was still trying to recover. Although prosperous once more, it has largely been neglected as a tourist region. The centres of interest are harder to find and less well-developed than their counterparts in the south, but places to visit are the **Taman Gili** complex in Klungkung, which includes the **Kerta Gosa**, the old Court of Justice, with its famous painted ceiling; **Pura Taman Sari**, also in Klungkung; and a cluster of villages close by the town which are famous for their handicrafts but also provide a glimpse of traditional Balinese village life. To the south is the old fishing village of **Kusamba**, and neighbouring **Goa Lawah**, the 'bat cave'.

A one-and-a-half-hour boat trip from Kusamba takes you to Nusa Penida, an island poor in agriculture but rich in mythology, and its neighbour Nusa Lembongan, the latest discovery for those in search of a white-sand, surf and palm tree paradise.

Historical Notes

Seat of the Dewa Agung
When Bali was finally subdued by the army of Gajah Mada on behalf of the Majapahit Empire in 1343, a *kraton* (the court, and religious and administrative centre) was set up in Samprangan (in what is now Gianyar regency), but within a couple of generations it had moved to Gelgel, south of modern Klungkung.

During the 16th century the Gelgel court reached its apogee. Following the final collapse, in around 1515, of the Majapahit empire in Java in the face of the growing strength of the Muslim Mataram empire, the ranks of the Javanese rulers in Bali were swelled by a big influx of princes and nobles and their retinues who hoped to preserve their Javanese-Hindu culture in exile.

The gods smiled on Gelgel. Within a generation the Dewa Agung, Batu Renggong, had marked up impressive political and cultural achievements that were to earn his era the title of the 'Golden Age' of Bali. He conquered the eastern province of Java (Blambangan) and brought the neighbouring islands of Lombok and Sumbawa under his control. It was a time of unprecedented prosperity, much of which was channelled into artistic, literary and cultural endeavour which has had lasting influence.

This period coincides with the first contact with Europeans, when three Dutch ships put in at Bali in 1597 after a gruelling voyage. Some of the crew—entertained at Gelgel by Batu Renggong's son Raja Bekung—returned to Europe with dazzling accounts of the court; and two members opted to stay in Bali when the ships set sail for Holland (see pp.78–79).

In 1710 the palace was moved from Gelgel to a new site in the town of Klungkung, where it maintained much of its old prestige; it was still a respected centre of power, and of religious and cultural authority. The Raja of Klungkung continued to be called the Dewa Agung, and was still considered to be the titular leader of all Bali, although by then much of his earlier influence had passed to the rajadoms of other regions.

The Last Piece in the Jigsaw
The Dutch recognized that Klungkung was the key to control over the island; and as soon as they finally overcame Buleleng in 1849, they set about invading the south.

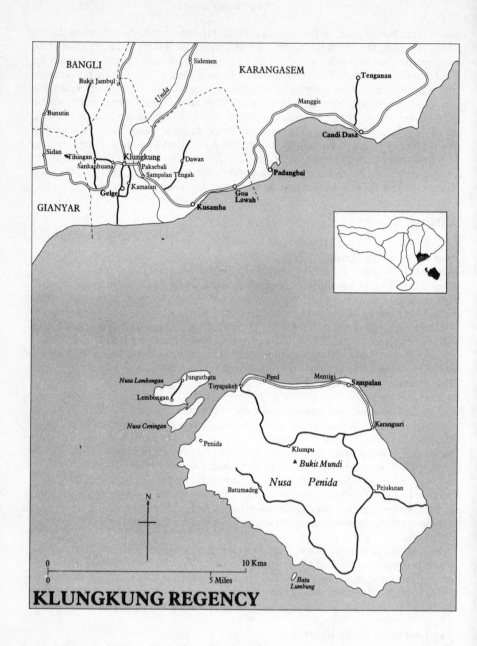

KLUNGKUNG REGENCY

234

They landed at Padangbai and proceeded to Kusamba, where, to the indignation of the Balinese, they desecrated a particularly sacred temple. The gods were to have their revenge. Incapacitated by dysentery, the Dutch were sitting ducks for a night-time attack led by the Dewa Agung's half-sister, Dewa Agung Isteri, which inflicted numerous casualties and fatally wounded their commander, General Michiels. The Dutch re-assembled and prepared to face a force of 33,000 gathered by the Dewa Agung of Klungkung, swelled by a further 16,000 troops raised by the Raja of Tabanan and the dynamic Danish trader, Mads Lange. This was a daring preemptive move by Lange: backed by this show of strength he was able to negotiate a peace between the Dutch and the Balinese that was to last another fifty years.

This period saw the gradual encroachment of the Dutch upon the traditional sphere of influence of the Dewa Agung who, meanwhile, continued his traditional squabble with the Raja of Gianyar, the Dewa Manggis. Eventually Gianyar turned to the Dutch for support, leaving the Dewa Agung Putra to pursue a policy of testy isolationism. The Dutch traveller, H. van Kol, who visited Klungkung in 1902, offers a picture of an impoverished rajadom, living in a mere shadow of its former glory, with a population of only 36,000 (Gianyar had 190,000).

When the Dutch launched their full-scale invasion of the south in 1906, it was the Raja of Badung, not the Dewa Agung, who was the focus of their attentions. After 1906, and the traumatic *puputan*s of the royal families in Denpasar, the Dutch controlled the entire island but for Klungkung and Bangli. Two years later, Dutch troops assembled outside the old *puri* of Klungkung and witnessed yet one more sickening *puputan* (see pp.88–89), which consumed the last in the line of the 600-year-old Majapahit empire.

Klungkung

Klungkung is the main town and the focus of administration for the regency. It is a hot, grubby, colourful place, with all the bustle and confusion of a market town and regional administrative centre, complete with its ancient *dokars* (pony traps). It is unlikely to strike you instantly as a town of architectural grandeur, suited to its glorious past. Only the **Kerta Gosa** provides historical interest: as you come into the main square you can see its spare lines and intricate decorations of traditional Bali, contrasting with the nondescript and exhausted architecture of the rest of the town.

Klungkung is not very big. It clusters around the noisy central crossroads and square. On one side is the Kerta Gosa and the **Pemedal Agung**, a surviving gateway to the old palace. On the other side is the new assembly hall for the regency, built on the site of the Dutch controleur's house, and which will soon boast a newly-erected monument to the *puputan*. To the east of the square is the short main street of three-storey buildings in modern Balinese style—some heavily decorated with carvings—where there are a few tourist art and antique shops amongst a number of local general stores.

As is usual in Balinese towns, people gather in the big open space where the buses and *bemo*s stop (**stasiun Klungkung**) to eat, drink, talk, buy and sell. The other gathering places are the bustling covered market, across the road from the *stasiun*, where you can buy handicrafts, and the night market (**pasar malam Senggol**) which springs up at dusk in the *stasiun*, alive with *warung*s selling Balinese food.

235

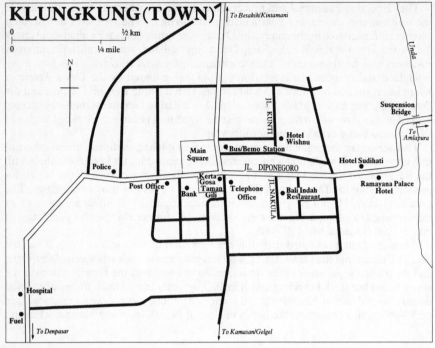

Klungkung Town

GETTING THERE

In Denpasar take a bus or *bemo* from Kereneng bus station, heading towards Amlapura (also known as Karangasem) or Candi Dasa. The fare is 600rp.

From Ubud take a *bemo* as far as the Sakah junction, then change. Expect to pay 200–300rp to Sakah and another 500rp to Klungkung. At Sakah take a left turn. Travelling time from Ubud is around one hour on public transport; it is much quicker if you have a motorbike or car.

Klungkung is the next town after **Gianyar**, 13 km (8 miles) further on the main Amlapura road.

Coming from the east, all buses and *bemo*s heading towards Gianyar, Ubud or Denpasar will take you to Klungkung. Travelling time from Candi Dasa is about 30 minutes and the fare is 500rp. It is worth checking that the *bemo* is going direct to Klungkung because some stop off at Padangbai to wait for ferry passengers.

TOURIST INFORMATION

There is no tourist office in Klungkung. The nearest tourist centres are Candi Dasa, 25 km (15.5 miles) to the east, and Ubud, approximately the same distance to the west.

There is a **post office** just to the west of the Kerta Gosa, and a Perumtel **telephone** office on the corner next to the Kerta Gosa. **Bank Rakyat Indonesia**, which is next to the Pemedal Agung, has a moneychanger.

236

There is a **petrol station** on the left-hand side of the road on the western approach to the town.

Taman Gili

Literally 'island garden', the Taman Gili complex is the only sizeable vestige of the **Semara Pura**, the great palace of the Dewa Agungs, to survive reasonably intact. It occupied the northeastern corner of the palace. The garden contains two large, open pavilions famous for their elaborately painted ceilings: the **Kerta Gosa** and the **Bale Kambung**.

The Semara Pura was built in or around 1710 by Dewa Agung Gusti Sideman when the court moved to Klungkung from Gelgel. It was built by the most skilled craftsmen of the day using the best materials available. Of the main palace buildings nothing remains but the gateway, the Pemedal Agung, to the west of the Taman Gili. The rest was destroyed by fire at the time of the Dutch aggression in 1908. Local stories have it that the fire responsible for much of the damage was started by disaffected citizens of Klungkung, who took advantage of the prevailing chaos to rebel against the raja.

The Kerta Gosa, Court of Justice, is raised above the level of the noisy street, in the northeast corner. In the centre of the garden stands the Bale Kambung, surrounded by a moat. In the northwest corner is a *kulkul* tower—a small, raised, open-sided building with two long wooden bells, or *kulkul*, hanging inside it.

Once open to passers-by, the Taman Gili has now been walled-in and an entrance fee of 200rp is payable in the car park opposite. The guides available on site are generally short on historical detail; for a reliable guide, make arrangements through a hotel or with one of the guides recommended by the tourist office in Denpasar (see p.141). Even then you will discover that there are conflicting accounts of the names of the buildings, which raja built them, and the dates of construction.

KERTA GOSA

The Kerta Gosa is to your left as you enter the walled garden. It is a rectangular open-sided pavilion, and is raised above street level by a short flight of brick steps with *naga*s acting as balustrades. From this height the raja could look down over gardens, the palace and the townspeople.

Most reports agree that the Kerta Gosa began as a meeting place for the princes and lords of Klungkung regency to discuss matters of general importance to the district and the island. *Kerta* were men of the Brahmana caste who acted as judges; Kerta Gosa means the place where the *Kerta* met. The raja would have met his ministers here, to study important *lontar* texts, and, in particular, to consider with them matters of justice too important to be left to village elders.

The building was badly damaged in 1908, but the Dutch controleur of Klungkung had it rebuilt along its original lines in 1920 to serve as a court dealing with *adat* law (i.e. local, not colonial justice). Criminals were summoned before a tribunal of six: the raja, or his representative, and his clerk; the controleur and his clerk; and a Brahman priest and lawyer. The finely carved wooden table and chairs date from this time.

THE KERTA GOSA CEILING

The panelled ceiling of this open-sided *bale* is decorated with fantastically rich and detailed paintings of the classical *'wayang'* school. This style of painting flourished under the patronage of the raja in the nearby painters' village of **Kamasan** at the time the palace was built in the early 18th century. Presumably the ceiling was first decorated then, probably under the supervision of I Gede Modara, a distinguished painter of the time who enjoyed royal patronage. He was held in such high esteem by the Kamasan villagers that he was worshipped as a deity and the foremost painters in the village today claim descent from him.

The paintings are first referred to in a *lontar* book dated 1842. We do not know if the content was the same then as it is now, for what you see today are copies of earlier versions. In the 1930s Walter Spies took a photograph of the Kerta Gosa ceiling, from which it is evident that the paintings were then similar to those we see today, but lacking in fine detail. They were probably those done by Pan Seken from Kamasan, who supervised major restoration work on the ceiling in 1930. In 1960 Pan Semaris, the son of Pan Seken, carried out further work, replacing the canvas or painted wood panels with fibrous cement sheets. The name of Pan Semaris can still be seen on one of the panels. Further restoration took place in 1982/3.

The paintings tell several stories on a series of panels rising to a central gilded wood lotus, surrounded by four doves. The first (outermost) small row of panels tells a series of five stories from the 'Ni Djah Tantri', the Balinese version of the Arabian *One Thousand and One Nights*, in which Tantri plays the part of Scheherazade.

The next two rows are devoted to the 'Bhima Swarga', the main story of the ceiling. The 'Bhima Swarga' (from *Bhima ka Swarga*, meaning 'Bhima goes to the home of the gods') is an off-shoot of the *Mahabharata*. This part tells the tale of Bhima, second of the Pandawa brothers, who goes to hell in search of the souls of his parents, in order to rescue them. In the top three rows of panels the story is continued: Bhima travels to heaven to gain the holy water of immortality (Amerta) from the gods, so that the souls of his parents might gain admission to heaven.

The story is interrupted between the third and fourth rows (between the visit to hell and the visit to heaven) by two other stories. The first row tells part of the Adiparwa, about the legendary Garuda bird of Vishnu, and the second has stories from the Balinese astrological calendar.

Bhima is recognizable by his dark skin, moustache, elaborate hairstyle and bejewelled club. You can also see the long curved nail of his right thumb, a sign of magical powers. The story starts at the far northeastern corner of the ceiling, and continues clockwise. In the first panel there are eight characters, critical to the story, four each side of the central tree. From left to right these are Mredah and Twalen, Bhima's faithful comical retainers, who accompany him on every stage of the journey; Yudhistira, the eldest of the Pandawa princes; and Kunti, the mother of the princes, recognizable by her elaborately dressed white hair and beautiful batik sarong. Facing Kunti on the other side of the tree is Bhima. Notice that he is darker than the other princes and does not have their wing-like epaulettes. This is because Bhima is a representation of physical strength, courage and aggression: he does not need the formal dress of his brothers. His sarong is of the black and white checked material (*kain poleng*) that you see wrapped around statues in Bali, believed to have magical properties of protection. Behind Bhima stand his other Pandawa brothers, the handsome Arjuna and twins Nakula and Sahadewa. These characters feature regularly in *wayang kulit* puppet shows and are familiar to all Balinese.

The Kerta Gosa is famous for its lurid portrayal of punishments carried out with great relish by the little demons called *buta*s in the Kingdom of the Dead. The artist has not spared us the gory details: this is a veritable Rabelaisian romp through torture. Moving around from the northeast corner, clockwise, look out for the following retributions for the various misdemeanours:

East side: disrespect for ones' ancestors, or disobedience to one's parents: being sawn in half.

South side: lust: a *buta* shakes daggers from a tree which cuts into offenders; for a woman failing to nurture children: a giant suckling caterpillar is attached to the breast; a multiplicity of crime: being boiled in a vat.

West side: aborting babies: walking over a rickety bridge suspended over flames (watched from beneath by the aborted foetuses); laziness: being beaten over the head; farting in public: having your intestines removed through the anus; breaking *banjar* rules: being beaten on the backside.

North side: stealing: having your fingers cut off with a knife; adultery: burning the genitals; male promiscuity: also burning the genitals; bestiality or homosexuality: being eaten by a pig; petty stealing: being crushed by a crab; prostitution: having flames applied to the vagina; witchcraft: having your tongue pulled out.

It is often suggested that these pictures illustrate models for traditional Balinese punishments. Whereas punishments by the rajas prior to the arrival of Dutch law could undoubtedly be extremely savage—mutilation being a notorious aspect of this—this proposition is fanciful. At best these pictures serve as reminders to the judges and the judged of the cosmic implications of misdemeanour of any kind. Traditional law in Bali is inseparable from obligations of social behaviour. Caring for children and treating older people with honour are not just desirable but obligatory. Not to do so is a serious offence, punishable by the law of Kharma in the next life. The consequences may be visited on your family for the next three generations.

BALE KAMBUNG

The Bale Kambung ('floating pavilion') is the open-sided building in the centre of the Taman Gili, surrounded by its own moat. Once filled with water-lilies, the water is now a violent green colour and strewn with litter. This pretty pavilion was the place where important guests were received and Brahmana judges from the Kerta Gosa withdrew here for relaxation and refreshment. It was enlarged during the Dutch occupation. (Since that time this building has been referred to as the Taman Gili—confusing, as this is also the name for the whole complex.) Note the playful statues of Dutchmen on either side of the entrance. Like the Kerta Gosa, the Bale Kambung also has wonderfully intricate painted ceiling panels, in the same natural colours.

Once again the date of the original paintings is not known. The last original work on the ceiling was done in 1945; restoration was carried out in 1983.

There are eight rows of narrative paintings. The first row at the bottom of the ceiling has Balinese astrology as its theme; the second illustrates the story of Pan Brayut, a children's tale of a couple who have 18 children (commonly featured in the 'primitive' woodcarvings of Pujung in Gianyar); all the rows above show stories about another character in local folklore, Sang Sutasoma, an old wise man.

Notice the scenes of everyday domesticity which remain unchanged in Bali to this day:

The punishment for abortion, from the Kerta Gosa ceiling

the preparation of *babi guling*; the man balancing heavy loads at each end of a pole twice as long as he is high; men fishing in the water-filled *sawah* for the tiny eels which the Balinese still like to eat crisp-fried.

PEMEDAL AGUNG

Standing to the west of Taman Gili, the Pemedal Agung is a huge stone gateway, all that remains of the main palace buildings of the Semara Pura. At the time of the Dutch the area behind this was used as a barracks and a prison, conveniently close to the court of justice.

The side doors, main door and supporting archway are elaborately carved and, rather oddly, decorated with a number of stone Dutchmen, top-hatted and formal, and decidedly ludicrous.

To the right, the old stones of the palace have been incorporated into the walls of Bank Rakyat Indonesia. In front, a brick platform marks the site of the old cockfighting arena.

Pura Taman Sari

As all Bali's temples, Pura Taman Sari is open to the sky. Its position on the side of Bali's most sacred mountain, and the spaciousness of the views, seem to have influenced its 17th century architect. The effect is a particularly gracious combination of *meru*s and ponds, a peaceful and tranquil retreat from the hot and busy town. 'Taman Sari' means 'flower garden'.

GETTING THERE

To get to Pura Taman Sari, head out of town 500 m (500 yards) on the north road, following the sign to Besakih. Pass the police station on a small turning to your right. Shortly afterwards turn right at a minor crossroads. A sign forbids you to enter this road, but ignore it; the police assured us an exception is made for visitors to the temple. Go straight along this road across another small crossroads. Ahead you will see the sign for the temple. Just outside the entrance is a big, beautiful, banyan tree.

240

Weaving

Klungkung and surrounding villages are noted centres for the production of *songket* and *ikat* (see pp.65–66). You can buy traditional *ikat* and *songket* pieces in Klungkung's market. Expect to pay upwards of 10,000rp for an *ikat* sarong (2.15 × 1m, 84 × 40 inches), at least twice as much for good quality *songket*. In **Toko Songket** on the main street, an *endek* sarong costs 17,000rp, a Javanese wedding batik sarong with gold overlay costs 20,000rp, and a fine *songket* sarong costs 50,000rp. At the cheaper end of the range is the distinctive blood-red *ikat* cloth imported from Nusa Penida. For *ikat*, see also Sampalan Tengah (p.245).

WHERE TO STAY

Klungkung is not a good place for overnight accommodation. There is really only one place to stay, and little choice of eating places. Better by far to base yourself in Ubud or Candi Dasa where you have a good choice of accommodation and restaurants.

If you do decide to stay, the **Ramayana Palace Hotel** is on the right of the road out to Amlapura, on the outskirts of the town, some 300m (300 yards) from the central crossroads. Though pleasant, it is nothing like as grand as its name suggests. The five large rooms are set in a typical Balinese garden, with shrubs, flowers, ponds ... and frogs which croak right through the night. The *mandi* is shared by all the rooms; there is no hot water. The price of 6,000/4,000rp does not include breakfast. There are no fans.

The more intrepid could stay at **Hotel Wishnu** in Jl. Kunti, or **Hotel Sudihati** on the Amlapura road, but we mention these for want of alternatives rather than as any sort of recommendation.

WHERE TO EAT

It is an extraordinary sign of the neglect of Klungkung as a travellers' destination that there is no decent restaurant in Klungkung centre other than that attached to the Ramayana Palace Hotel. Even this is nothing to get excited about. It serves a standard Indonesian tourist-style menu (*nasi goreng, mie goreng*, chicken steak) at standard prices (e.g. 2,500rp for *mie goreng*), and is open for breakfast.

There is also a Chinese *rumah makan*, **Bali Indah**, which doubles as a video cassette store; it is quite bearable, inexpensive and clean, though the chef is a little heavy handed on the monosodium glutamate. It is 20m (20 yards) off Jl. Diponegoro (the main throughroad) in Jl. Nakula, and is but two minutes' walk from the Kerta Gosa. The old man and his family are very friendly. Two doors down on the same side of this street is the **Sumber Rasa** restaurant with a standard Indonesian menu.

You could try *sate* at a *warung* in the night market (goat *sate* makes an interesting change from the usual tourist fare), with plenty of local atmosphere.

Otherwise the nearest options are **Rumah Makan Sederhana** (its name means 'simple'), on the outskirts of the town to the west, on the Gianyar road; or **Depot Makan Mini Agung** on a corner at Sampalan Tengah, 3 km (1.8 miles) outside Klungkung on the road east to Amlapura, beyond the long suspension bridge. These are both cheap, plain, down-to-earth places to eat, just a room with cement floors and formica-covered tables, but the traditional Balinese food is spicy and delicious. Look out for *srombotan*, a complex mixture of a variety of vegetables and spices, a speciality of Klungkung.

If you are heading north the nearest place to eat beyond Klungkung is the tourist restaurant at Bukit Jambul (see pp.242–43).

241

West of Klungkung

Tihingan

For a scene like something from an Old Master, go to see the blacksmiths at work making *gamelan gongs* in their tiny bronze foundries in the village of Tihingan (also known as Tahingan, or Tiyingan). (See pp.122–24 for an explanation of the *gamelan* instruments.) Blackened men sit half-naked round a roaring fire in a pit in the ground, assisting the master blacksmith. Bellows pumped by an apprentice bring the flames to the required heat, while another man holds the anvil, and another the water to plunge the bronze into.

The instrument makers are master craftsmen, clearly still held in respect by the other villagers. Once blacksmiths held a special position within the Balinese communities; known as *'pande'*, they had their own caste, and their own unique privileges.

In the centre of the village is the **Puri Penetaran Pande**, dedicated to the local blacksmiths' ancestral soul. Note the splendid *kulkul* tower, the roof columns of which are supported by *rangda*s, with a central painted *rangda* busy scoffing a child. In the open space in front of the temple there is a splendid stone statue of Twalen, the bulbous and comical retainer who features in the *Mahabharata* epic. Under the banyan tree is a statue of the goddess of the winds that feed the forges.

At last count there were 26 *gong*-making businesses in Tihingan, employing 140 craftspeople. The metal instruments are made here but the elaborately carved wood structures which hold them are made in Denpasar.

GETTING THERE
Tihingan lies 2 km (1.25 miles) along a small side road which leads away from a curve in the road at a hamlet called **Sankanbuana**, which is itself 2 km (1.25 miles) to the west of Klungkung. Coming from Klungkung, you leave the main Gianyar road and take the right-hand fork, what is effectively straight on. If you are coming here by *bemo*, you will probably have to get off here and walk. The junction is distinguished by a painted picture of a man with his arm thrust into the rear end of a cow—a promotion for artificial insemination.

North of Klungkung

The road north out of Klungkung is used by tour coaches going up to the **Besakih** temple. It has a good surface as far as the Besakih turn-off, spectacular views and a large tourist restaurant en route.

As it begins to wind up the lower slopes of Mt Agung you can see way back down the valley to the coast. Stop at **Bukit Jambul lay-by** opposite the restaurant for an exhilarating view of rice terraces atop rolling green hills which tumble down to a glittering sea. There is a feeling of immense space here.

The restaurant is similar to other big places used by tour buses on the well-established routes: geared to cater for large organized parties, bland food, high prices. It is redeemed only by the views. The menu is typical of such places with several varieties of *nasi goreng*, soup, omelettes, *sate*, fried chicken and some Chinese style seafood dishes. Prices for a main meal are around 4,500rp, plus drinks.

After Bukit Jambul the road climbs on up Mt Batur into Bangli regency.

South of Klungkung

Kamasan

This leafy, prosperous little village is the home of the *'wayang'* painters, and gives its name to the classical style of their paintings (see pp.62–63 for a full description of this). The most famous examples of their work are on the ceilings of the Kerta Gosa and the Bale Kambung. You can buy pictures here from the artists: the subjects are usually taken from the *Ramayana* and *Mahabharata* epics, but some artists also specialize in pictorial Balinese calendars. They can cost 10,000rp or less, though the top-quality paintings are now much sought after and worth a lot of money.

Kamasan was established by the Dewa Agung Dalam Ktut Ngulesir, supreme ruler of Bali, in 1380, during one of the periodic flourishes of Gelgel's artistic glory. It was originally a settlement for the court gold and silversmiths—Kamasan means 'place of the gold workers'. The local *banjar* is still called Banjar Pande Mas, the *banjar* of the goldsmiths, and a village temple is specifically consecrated for their use. Crowns and jewellery for the raja and his family were made here. Later Kamasan became better known as the home of sculptors and painters who decorated the palace buildings. In time the Kamasan artists were invited to decorate palaces in other regencies, so the style spread and was adapted. For example, Krambitan in Tabanan developed its own type of *wayang* painting in the late 19th century.

The distinctive Kamasan style nearly died out after the Dutch arrived, for now there was no longer the secure base of patronage on which it depended; but in the 1920s the Dutch commissioned the replacement of the Kerta Gosa paintings from a Kamasan family, and the art revived briefly. Later, in the 1960s, visitors to Bali created a new market for the paintings.

GETTING THERE
At the main Klungkung crossroads a small road goes down towards the coast; after 2 km (1.25 miles) it passes through Kamasan village, the main part of which is to the east of the main road. The village is not on the usual tourist track and is not well sign-posted, so keep asking.

Gelgel: ghost of a glorious past

Only the wide streets and spacious layout of the village and the temple give clues that it was once the site of the royal palace of Swecepura, established in the late 14th century by the Majapahit princes as the focus of the Hindu religion and culture they brought from Java. Its glory was the symbol of their power. The princes, priests, musicians, dancers and craftsmen who settled here made the court of Gelgel famous not only as a spiritual centre but also for the quality of its arts. The political power of the dynasty reached its peak at the time of Batu Renggong in the 16th century.

Descendants of the dynasty settled in other areas of Bali, establishing new rajadoms. Gradually they grew to rival the regency of Klungkung in political power. The Dewa Agungs continued to be looked to as spiritual leaders, but the supremacy of Gelgel was on the wane. In the early 18th century the palace was damaged in a feud between rival princes I Gusti Agung Meruti and Raja Dewa Agung Jampe, and in 1710 or thereabouts the son of Meruti, I Gusti Sideman, moved the court to the Semara Pura site in Klungkung.

There is now nothing much here for the tourist to see; all the resplendent finery of the court, its paintings, carvings and beautiful gardens—as witnessed in wonder by Arnoudt Lintgens in 1597—have now vanished. The gradual decay of the palace that began back in the 18th century was completed by the Dutch when they bombarded the town from the sea following the murder of agents of their opium monopoly here in 1908, events that preceded the final march on Klungkung (see p.89).

The outer courtyard of the **Pura Dasar temple** in the centre of Gelgel is said to occupy the site of the old palace; this temple remains an important one for the Balinese. It certainly has a royal scale. The outer courtyard is massive, as are its *bale*s, including a large *wantilan*, used for dance and drama performances. The inner courtyard is similarly spacious and contains two huge *meru*s, one with eleven roofs, one with nine. The *odalan*, held on the fifth day after the festival of Galungan, is very impressive.

The temple gate greets you with this admonition: 'IN ORDER TO KEEP THE CLEAN-NESS AND HOLINESS OF THE PURA WE ANNOUNCE TO THE VISITORS AND VIEWERS WHO IN UNCOMFORTABLE CONDITIONS (SUCH AS HAID, HAVING FAMILY DIED ETC) PLEASE DO NOT ENTER THE COMPLEX OF THE PURA.' (*Haid* means menstruation; see p.52.)

Further to the west, opposite the statue of Shiva on a pedestal in the middle of the road, is the **Pura Nataran**, with its splendidly eroded brick and stonework.

GETTING THERE

Gelgel is south of Kamasan. You can get there by turning south at the main crossroads in Klungkung, by the Kerta Gosa. It is 3 km (1.8 miles) to the left-hand turn for Gelgel. *Bemo*s travel this route. If your *bemo* is continuing south, it is a short walk from the stop-off point to the Pura Dasar.

Kampong Gelgel

Kampong Gelgel is a Muslim enclave within Desa Gelgel, a little to the east of the Pura Dasar. Visiting is a curious experience because the atmosphere is noticeably different from the surrounding Hindu Balinese villages, and is reminiscent more of Java. The children are much less shy, almost aggressively inquisitive. How this enclave comes to be here is related in a mixture of history and myth (see below).

Kampong Gelgel has a fine mosque with an old interior, including the *mihrab* (prayer niche) which faces distant Mecca. But note that if you try to enter, you are liable to cause consternation.

THE RAJA'S FORESKIN

Gelgel contains one of the three Muslim communities of Bali, founded during the

Majapahit era (somewhere between the 14th and 16th centuries). The other two are in Kusamba and Sarenjawa (in Karangasem). Tradition has it that they were established by the Dewa Agung to provide shelter for the families of Muslim missionaries sent from Java to convert the Balinese. When the missionaries failed, they felt unable to return home and so, to save them from an ignominious end, the Dewa Agung allowed them to stay.

The Muslims have their version of why Bali has remained Hindu. The Dewa Agung who founded Gelgel in the late 14th century had a brother in Java who converted to Islam. This brother wanted to spread the joys of Islam to his family in Bali, and so duly sent three missionaries to Gelgel. Now, the Dewa Agung had heard a great deal about Islam and was much intrigued by it. But one thing bothered him: don't all Muslims have to be circumcized? He listened carefully to the missionaries who told him the story of the Prophet Muhammad, and how the word of God had been dictated to the Prophet by the Angel Gabriel and was now contained in the holy *Koran*. All this the raja was quite willing to accept.

'But,' he said eventually, 'even if I accept that there is no God but Allah, and Muhammad is his Prophet, do I not have to be circumcized?'

'Ah!,' said one of the missionaries, 'it is nothing. We take a very sharp bamboo knife...'

'Show me the knife,' said the Dewa Agung.

So the missionaries produced a bamboo knife, of a kind the Balinese still use to slaughter livestock. The Dewa Agung tested it on a fingernail; the knife failed to make an impression. He then tried to cut the hairs on his arm with it; they remained intact. Unwilling therefore to submit yet more sensitive parts to such a blade, the Dewa Agung handed back the knife, and thus Bali remains Hindu to this day.

East of Klungkung

Immediately after Klungkung, on the road out towards Amlapura, you cross the new suspension bridge over the **Unda river**. Enjoy the view of the river valley and the weir. The wide valley has been gouged out of the foothills by torrential floods pouring down from the central mountains in the rainy season. The long bridge gives you a bird's eye view of the part played by rivers in the life of the Balinese.

Morning and evening villagers gather—as they have done for hundreds of years—to bathe in sociable groups, women and men separately. Nowadays they sometimes carry a towel and soap or shampoo, but often they come with only the sarongs they are wearing, which serve as towels in the traditional way. Men and boys bathe naked; in public view the women are more modest and cover themselves with their sarongs. In the daytime, women come to do the laundry, scraping and beating the washing against rocks to get it clean, while children help or play in the fast-flowing water.

A little beyond the bridge, **Paksebali** is a village famous for making ceremonial parasols and flags, which are on sale in small shops beside the road.

Sampalan Tengah is the next village, only 1 km (0.6 mile) further along this road. This is a centre for *ikat* weaving (see pp.65–66). Next to the Depot Makan Mini Agung is a small unpaved track leading to an *ikat* hand-weaving factory, with some truly stunning designs in cotton or pure silk. Prices vary from 10,000 to 13,000rp per metre for cotton to 25,000rp or more per metre for pure silk.

Shortly afterwards the road passes through an area covered by lava in the 1963 eruption of Mt Agung. Here, villagers excavate and sell sand, gravel and stones as building materials, compensating to some extent for the loss of income they suffered when the fertile rice-growing land was buried.

Dawan

Set back off the road at the foot of **Bukit Gunaksa**, the small, shady village of Dawan is the centre of production for brown palm sugar (*gula Bali*). This delicacy is served on black rice pudding, or with the mound of coconut on your breakfast fruit salad. It is to processed white sugar as the aromatic Balinese coffee is to Nescafé. Its rich brown flavour is reminiscent of the best maple syrup. It is made from *tuak*, the fresh palm wine drawn from the cut tip of the flower of palm trees. Each tree produces some 2 litres (about 4 pints) of *tuak* per day. The job of climbing the trees to collect the liquid must be done early in the morning, while the sap is rising.

The *tuak* is cooked with coral lime and the bark of the jackfruit tree to produce a sweet, rich, yellowish-brown sugar, which can be bought in the village *warung*s in rounded cakes moulded in coconut shells. The sugar is also used to cook strips of yam to make a light brown 'sugar cake' which is sold in small plastic bags in the markets, at 200rp a bag.

The other product of Dawan is the delicious caramel-flavoured, brown-skinned *sawo* fruit (*sabu* in Bahasa Bali). You see them growing on the dark-green-leaved trees which line the road to the village.

The *pedanda* (High Priest) of Dawan has a formidable reputation and is held by many in Bali to be the most powerful and knowledgeable priest on the island—'a man next to God', as one person put it.

These attractions apart, Dawan is far from a tourist village—you'll need your best Bahasa Indonesia to get very far here.

GETTING THERE
A small paved road goes off the main road to the left some 3 km (1.8 miles) after Sampalan, 7 km (4.3 miles) from Klungkung. Get off at the turning and walk if you're travelling by *bemo*. Dawan is 2 km (1.25 miles) north, nestling in the first foothills of Mt Agung.

Kusamba

Kusamba is a working fishing village, with a dirty black-sand beach and scruffy buildings, and a definite whiff of old fish in the air. Even the modern mosque (built 1948) looks run down. The population consists of Hindu and Muslim families, plus a large number of goats, which seem as much at home wandering around the village as their owners. The fact that it is known as Kampung Kusamba, as opposed to Desa Kusamba, indicates its history as a Muslim and Javanese community; Kusamba is one of the three original Muslim villages of Bali, established during the Majapahit era (see pp.244–45).

For the visitor, the attraction of the village lies in the brightly painted fishing *prahu*s pulled up on the beach. Take the turning towards the south at the Y-shaped junction in the town centre, where the market is held. Late in the afternoon the waves pounding on this beach give a desolate feel to the place: most suitable for the point of departure for the infamous **Nusa Penida**.

You can also get a boat for Nusa Penida, as well as neighbouring **Nusa Lembongan** (see pp.250–55), from the so-called 'harbour', though it is actually just another bit of black-sand beach—with a Hindu temple. It is down a short road, about 100m (100yards) from the main Klungkung–Amlapura road. The signpost, to **'Dermaga Penyebrangan Kusamba 200m'**, comes shortly after the market in the centre of Kampung Kusamba (as you travel east).

Kusamba is a centre for the production of salt. Further along the beach you can see the little thatched huts where the salt extraction takes place, surrounded by the curious raked terraces of black sand and their ranks of hollowed palm trunks (see below).

Kusamba is one of the few places in Bali where *krises* (the sacred curvy knives) are forged by specialist craftsmen, some of whom you may be able to visit, although this is a secretive art (see pp.68–69).

There is no *losmen* at Kusamba. The nearest places to stay are in Padangbai to the east, or the Ramayana Palace Hotel at Klungkung.

GETTING THERE
Kusamba stretches along the road, 8km (5 miles) east of Klungkung, at the point where the road meets the coast. It is on the main Klungkung–Amlapura road, served by regular *bemo*s (150rp from Klungkung).

Salt Production
In various coastal regions of Bali, notably Kusamba, but also the tidal marshlands south of Sanur, and Amed on the northern coast of Karangasem, salt production is big business. Large quantities can be extracted daily from the salt-rich black sand. This is spread out in flat terraces outside the salt-maker's hut, ready for processing. The sand will be scooped up into a large, roughly-hewn palmwood box inside the hut, then seawater will be strained through it, producing a clear, very salty water which is channelled into vats made out of hollowed-out palm trunks. From here it is transferred to shallow troughs made of thinner palm trunks, set in ranks on the beach under the full power of the blazing sun. The speed of evaporation is regulated by little palm-leaf roofs placed over the troughs towards the end of the process, or when rain threatens. Each trough will yield a large quantity of clean white coarse salt, perhaps as much as 2kg (4.5lb) in a day during the dry season. This is used for salting fish, rather than as culinary or table salt.

Salt production provides a very slender income, and the process seems to have a wearing effect on the families involved, making them a dour breed living on the margins of Balinese society. The salt turns everything grey, and they are surrounded by a landscape of black sand: there is a Dickensian grimness to this occupation, only occasionally brightened by a Balinese smile.

Goa Lawah
The road east from Kusamba leads along the coast and, after 3km (1.8miles), passes the entrance to the Goa Lawah, which means, literally, 'bat cave'.

Goa Lawah invokes curiosity for the repulsive. In the gaping mouth of this cave, plastered over the walls and ceiling in a thick, quivering layer of black fur and leather, are thousands upon thousands of bats, flitting about and tittering anxiously as they vie for a tiny clawhold in the throng, and all constantly adding to the generations of stinking black guano that lie beneath them.

There are legends attached to the cave. It is said to lead right into the heart of Bali and anyone brave enough to do so can, apparently, emerge at a so-called Pura Goa (Cave Temple) at Besakih some 30 km (18.6 miles) away—as the bat flies. The sacred serpent, or *naga*, called Basuki, custodian of cosmic equilibrium, is said to reside in the cave at Goa Lawah, feeding on the bats.

Goa Lawah is an important temple, with a row of delicate shrines in the mouth of the cave, each topped by its own crown of manure. It is believed to have been founded in the early 11th century by the great priest of Padangbai, Kuturan.

The carpark is surrounded by *warung*s and small shops, with a bevy of trampish young girls selling necklaces and postcards. Entry costs 100rp.

A hillside overlooking Goa Lawah is a popular spot for launching hang-gliders. (Ask for details at the Badung Government Tourist Office in Denpasar if you're interested in doing this.) On one occasion one of a group of hang-gliders got into trouble and had to come down on the beach, much to the alarm of worshippers at a large ceremony there, who were sent scattering with their offerings and parasols by the sudden intervention of a modern-day Garuda.

GETTING THERE
Goa Lawah is 3 km (1.8 miles) to the east of Kusamba on the main Klungkung–Amlapura road. It should be easy to find, since this is a major tourist attraction, visited by the busload, but in fact it is quite easy to miss if you are driving. There is no sign to the cave, only a couple of pictograms by the side of the road (in both directions), one of a bus, the other denoting a picnic area. From Klungkung the price of the *bemo* is 250rp.

Nusa Penida, Nusa Lembongan and Nusa Ceningan

The administrative district of Nusa Penida comprises three islands: Nusa Penida itself, the smaller Nusa Lembongan to the northwest, and tiny Nusa Ceningan sandwiched in between them. 'Ceningan' comes from the Balinese word *cenik* meaning small. *Nusa*, of course, simply means 'island'.

Nusa Penida covers 102 sq km (78 sq miles), a mere 3.6% of the total area of Bali; it has a population of 45,000. Its main town is **Sampalan**, on the north coast, with a port known as Sampalan Mentigi. It is a hilly, dry island, with rainfall very nearly as low as the north coast of Bali, and it is not suitable for rice-growing. Water has to be collected in concrete cisterns known as *cabangs*. The high white cliffs which can be seen from Sanur are limestone and the geology of the islands is similar to that of the Bukit peninsula on the mainland. The **Bukit Mundi** in the centre of the island is its highest point, 529 m (1,735 ft) above sea-level. The northern coast has low sandy beaches, as does the neighbouring Nusa Lembongan.

Rice and many other foodstuffs have to be brought from the mainland. Local crops are soyabeans, peanuts, cassava (manioc), corn and sweet potatoes. Island products exported to the rest of Bali include mangoes, sardines (*lemuru*), and a fruit known as *sawo Bali*, a large grape-like fruit that has nothing to do with the brown-skinned *sawo* more commonly seen in Bali.

There is one further crop which is of particular interest as it may hold the prospect of greater prosperity for these islands: seaweed. It is a particular variety of seaweed which can be processed into 'agar', a useful food substance with gelatin-like properties, much in demand by the food industry of Japan and, increasingly, Europe; it is also used in cosmetics.

The mythology of Nusa Penida is forbidding in the extreme (see below) while its history—as a penal colony and place of exile from the regency of Klungkung—combined with its hostile climate and topography are scarcely more inviting. In a manner typical to Balinese perspective and philosophy, the very scariness of the place constitutes its importance in their religion and attracts thousands of Balinese visitors to the island every year. School parties are organized to visit the temple which represents the evil power of Nusa Penida, the dwelling place of Ratu Gede Macaling, one of the most terrifying of the Balinese deities.

For the tourist, Nusa Lembongan offers the more Western-style attractions of beautiful white-sand beaches, hotels, restaurants, snorkelling, scuba-diving and surfing—although facilities are barely developed at present. This could be the perfect answer for the more adventurous hedonist.

Nusa Ceningan has the same kind of harsh, mountainous terrain as Nusa Penida. There are no inviting beaches and just a small settlement of fishing families who are now increasingly turning their hands to seaweed production. At low tide Nusa Ceningan can be reached on foot from Nusa Lembongan across a sandbar: otherwise it can only be reached by boat (no regular services).

HOW TO GET THERE

One thing you should know about Nusa Penida and the other two islands is that the strait which separates them from mainland Bali, the Selat Badung, is notoriously treacherous and a fair number of people are lost to it every year; indeed 40 or 50 people are said to have died in these waters in August 1988 alone. At certain times of the day the tides rip through the strait producing a bubbling cauldron of water which only the most powerful boat could hope to cross. Conditions are particularly bad at the change of seasons.

That said, many people do use the local *jukung*s and live to tell the tale, but those who prefer not to put their life on the line, and who can afford the price, can take a day trip organized by some of the major hotels, or go on one of the excursions offered by the watersports 'clubs' at Benoa village and by the Bali International Yacht Club at Sanur (see pp.254–55).

The *jukung*s are large motorized *prahu*s, about 1.2 m (4 ft) wide, with seats along the sides; some of them carry alarming quantities of cargo to and from the islands. Come prepared for a wet journey. You will probably have to help push the boat out, and you can expect some spray from the Kusamba surf. Wrap all belongings in plastic bags to be on the safe side.

To Nusa Penida

There are three possible points of departure:

From Kampung Kusamba (the beach of Kusamba village—see pp.246–47). This is the route used by most Balinese. The fare to **Toyapakeh**, the usual arrival point in Nusa Penida, is 2,500rp. The journey lasts around two and a half hours. Once in Toyapakeh a *bemo* to the capital, Sampalan, costs around 1,000rp, a 9-km (5.6-mile) journey.

The boats operate like *bemo*s and wait till they are full before making the journey. Go in the late afternoon to catch the people of Nusa Penida returning home.

From Kusamba Banjar Bias (the new 'harbour'). A short distance after the market place in Kusamba village on the main Amlapura road, there is a sign on your left pointing to 'Dermaga Penyebrangan Kusamba 200 m'. It is possible to get a boat here going straight to **Sampalan Mentigi** (the port of the main town of Sampalan). However, prices are rather higher here than at Kampung Kusamba and the wait for the boat to fill up will probably be longer.

From Padangbai. Boats leave from Padangbai direct to Sampalan, fare 2,500rp. Here, as everywhere, you have to wait for the boat to fill up before it will leave.

To Nusa Lembongan

From Kampung Kusamba. Some boats go from the beach at Kampong Kusamba direct to **Jungutbatu**, the landing place on Nusa Lembongan, for a fare of 2,500rp. More usually, however, you have to go via Toyapakeh on Nusa Penida. From here the journey to Jungutbatu takes about half an hour and costs 1,000rp.

From Sanur. There is a service from Sanur to Lembongan from the beach at the end of the road past the Bali Beach Hotel. It does not seem to be very regular though. Expect the fare to cost you more than the 6,000rp the local Balinese will pay. The journey from Sanur is 2–3 hours. It is essential to get there early in the morning. In the afternoon the waves get boisterous and the currents in the straits are strong.

CHARTERING

It is possible to cut your waiting time by chartering boats to Nusa Penida or Nusa Lembongan. From Kusamba beach expect to pay around 30,000rp for Toyapakeh or Nusa Lembongan, 40,000rp for Sampalan Mentigi. Roughly the same prices operate from the other Kusamba point of departure. You can also charter boats from Sanur to Nusa Lembongan.

RETURN JOURNEY

Unless you have your own chartered boat you are unlikely to be able to return direct from Nusa Lembongan to the mainland. The occasional boat that does make the journey leaves the beach at Jungutbatu on Lembongan at 4–5 am. Otherwise, take a *jukung* from the beach at around 6 am to Toyapakeh, to join the local people leaving for the mainland.

Note that it is too dangerous to leave Nusa Penida for Kusamba any later than around 1pm because of the waves and currents that build up in the late afternoon.

Nusa Penida

The journey itself from the mainland to the islands is exhilarating: approaching Nusa Penida from the southwest you see the sheer, white limestone cliffs that are visible from

Sanur. The north coast, however, offers mostly long sandy beaches with palm-fringed, coral shores—but alas most of these have now been disfigured by the offshore pens used for seaweed cultivation. The villages in the interior of the island have had little contact with Westerners.

Nusa Penida is usually referred to simply as Nusa by the Balinese. It has an eerie reputation for those who do not live there. The Balinese word for the island's mystical evil power is *angker*, and of all the places which might merit this label, there is one particular temple here which is the most forbidding. This is the temple **Pura Dalem Penataran Peed**, believed to be the dwelling place of fanged monster Ratu Gede Macaling, the source of disease, disaster and evil magic.

GETTING AROUND
For ways to get to Nusa Penida, see above.

There is paved road between Toyapakeh and Sampalan, and running on from Sampalan to a village called **Karangsari**, before looping back round to Toyapakeh via the village of **Klumpu**. You can get around by *bemo* on these roads; beyond them *bemo* travel is a real endurance test. It is possible to take a motorbike over on the boat from Bali. You can also arrange with someone local to take you around on their bike. There are good walks, but remember it is hot and dry here.

TOURIST INFORMATION
There is nothing of the kind; you're on your own here. In 1985 a radiotelephone contact with the Klungkung mainland was set up. Sampalan has a post office and a telegram office. Electricity is supplied by a diesel generator in the Sampalan area.

Pura Dalem Penataran Peed
You can find the temple just off the main road between Toyapakeh and Sampalan, about 4 km (2.5 miles) north of Toyapakeh, in Desa Peed. It is close to the beach.

This temple is outstandingly ugly. Its income comes from barren land, so there have been few resources to repair the buildings. The *paras* stone that is usual for the construction of Balinese temples has been mixed with local limestone blocks and patched with concrete. Its ill-fitting and patchy structure increases the sinister aspect of the place.

There are two courtyards, outer and inner. The important feature is the shrine for I Macaling, or Ratu Gede Macaling. This is the place of greatest evil power on the island—a shrine for practitioners of black magic, a place for offerings to the *leyak*s who draw their power from I Macaling.

The shrine is beyond the outer west wall of the temple. It is accessible from both courtyards. In the opposite wall of the second courtyard is another important shrine: that of Dalem Peed, or Dalem Dukut.

I MACALING AND KING DALEM DUKUT
The story of these infamous characters dates back to the arrival of the exiled Majapahit princes and their Hindu followers from Java. It is about the struggle between the existing (old Bali) ruler of Nusa Penida and the newly arrived ruler Batu Renggong whose kingdom was based in Gelgel. Almost certainly it deals in a mythological way with the real political power struggles of that time.

When the great priest Nirartha arrived in Bali in around 1550 to take up his role as adviser to Batu Renggong, an unfortunate misunderstanding in the north of the island led his daughter to place a curse on the villagers around Pulaki, turning them into the *wong gamang* or *bala samar*—invisible beings with supernatural powers (see pp.319–20). Some of these 'invisible ones' became followers of I Macaling. I Macaling may well have been a real character of significance on Nusa Penida but, being an opponent of the Majapahit, he has gone down in myth as a demonic being. At that time Nusa Penida was ruled by King Dalem Dukut.

Batu Renggong extended his rule over eastern Java, Lombok and Bali. Then he wanted to subdue Nusa Penida as well. However, the myth relates, King Dalem Dukut had the supernatural power of I Macaling and the *bala samar* at his disposal. Three times the forces of Batu Renggong came to fight the *bala samar*. On the third occasion the invading general had with him the tooth of one of the two sacred *naga*s who support the world turtle, and he used this weapon to destroy King Dalem Dukut. Before he died Dalem Dukut gave the *bala samar* and their leader, I Macaling, to the general as a kind of double-edged gift. If the king was given the proper cremation rites and I Macaling was treated with due respect and ritual, the power of the *bala samar* would help to protect the people and prevent sickness and bad luck. If not, the *bala samar* would constantly trouble the people with their evil ways.

Another tale relates how I Macaling was causing havoc and pestilence throughout Bali at some later point in history. In order to appease him a priest suggested that the Balinese offer him a wife. So they selected one Jero Luh, a dreadful harridan that matched her spouse point for point in ugliness. This was enough to satisfy I Macaling, who then withdrew back to Nusa Penida with his love, but always ready to return to the mainland if not paid proper respect by the people.

I Macaling shows up regularly in the folk traditions of Bali, appearing throughout the land as 'Barong Landung' in popular drama and in the festivals of Pura Dalems. Barong Landung is a huge black figure standing upright, unlike the usual dragon-like Barong. He is also known as Jero Gede and is accompanied by Jero Luh, his white-faced wife.

Hence the importance of the temple which enshrines both Dalem Dukut and Ratu Gede Macaling. Propitiating the evil spirits is an essential part of Balinese Hinduism. Good and evil stand in dynamic contrast to one another: and out of these opposing forces comes creativity.

Goa Karangsari

This is a cave near the village of Karangsari on the northeast coast, 6 km (3.75 miles) beyond Sampalan. It is not easy to find, since the entrance is just a small opening like a pothole. Seek out a helpful local to give you directions. The entrance leads to a series of chambers filled with bats and their droppings; there is a shrine in the middle of the caves where ceremonies are held. At the far end the cave opens out onto a spectacular view of a remote valley beyond.

WHERE TO STAY AND EAT

There is only one place for tourists to stay on the island. It is a 'homestay' called **Bungalow Pemda** in the main town of Sampalan, about 9 km (5.6 miles) from Toyapa-keh, where most of the boats land. You can get there by *bemo*. Bungalow Pemda has five bungalows with two rooms and a bathroom each. It costs around 4,000rp double, 3,000rp single, and is quite basic. There are no restaurants; the only food available is from the many local *warungs*.

A better option would be to stay on Nusa Lembongan and make a day trip to Nusa Penida.

Nusa Lembongan

Lembongan is 4 × 2.5 km (2.5 × 1.5 miles) in area—a low, sandy-shored island that lies 10.5 km (6.5 miles) from the Klungkung coast. Two factors have rescued the island from its previous obscurity: one is the development of tourism based on the attractions of white sandy beaches, clear sea, coral reefs and impressive surf; the other is the development of the seaweed industry.

If you come in directly to Nusa Lembongan from the mainland, the view from the boat is of a fairy-tale island of white beaches, palm trees and thatched beach huts, fronted by a reef bearing the rampant prow of a wrecked ship. Nusa Penida towers in the background.

Nusa Lembongan has two villages: the one where your boat will arrive, Jungutbatu, and Lembongan. The latter is a hot half-hour walk to the south. This is the centre for seaweed production, with a large bay, full of activity, smelling strongly of the local produce. It is an old and attractive village, with the usual temples; it's like stepping back thirty years.

The reasons for staying on the island are the watersports and the unspoilt scenery. The boat owners, known as 'captains', rent out surfboards and snorkelling gear as well as their boats. Prices vary with the season: July, August and September are the busy months. The captains know all the best spots for everything. The surfing can be excellent—both Australian and Japanese surfers come here (see p.46). The clarity of the water and the sea-life around the coral reefs make for some excellent snorkelling. It is not possible at present to arrange scuba-diving on the spot here; for this you have to make arrangements with the diving clubs on the mainland (see pp.46–47).

GETTING AROUND
For ways to get to Nusa Lembongan, see p.250.

Lembongan is too small for you to need any transport other than your own two feet—there is a rough road from Jungutbatu to Lembongan and that's all. There are only six motorbikes on the island, and one truck.

Boats arrive near the small police station on the beach front.

TOURIST INFORMATION
There is nothing official of this order here; the following points are worth noting.

There is no contact with the outside world from Nusa Lembongan other than by the boats. The nearest post office and a telegram office is in Sampalan on Nusa Penida. There is a bank (Bank Rakyat Indonesia) in Jungutbatu, but be warned, it is for local use only and does not change traveller's cheques; bring cash.

There is no mains electricity on the island; one or two places have their own generator. Expect romantic, lamp-lit accommodation.

There is just one craft shop on the island, in Jungutbatu on the road opposite the Bank

253

Rakyat Indonesia. It is owned by I Ketut Nyatra, a school-teacher, a friendly man who is a good source of local information.

WHERE TO STAY

The cheapest accommodation is to be found in Jungutbatu village, where there are several *losmen*s at 3,000rp double, 2,000rp single. They are not especially inviting.

The rest are on the beach front. **Johnny's** has six rooms at 6,000rp and 4,000rp, with Indonesian-style *mandi*s. This is a pleasant place to stay; Nyoman will help sort out any problems. When it opened in 1984, this was the only place to offer accommodation on the island.

Losmen Agung has some similar rooms at 7,000rp double, 5,000rp single, and also has a new bungalow for 15,000rp double or single.

The Main Ski Inn has ten rooms in five two-storey buildings, which are spacious and have decent bathrooms. These are 15,000rp double, 10,000rp single.

The best rooms on the island are to be found at **Nusa Lembongan Restaurant/Bungalows**. Here they have eight two-storey 'bungalows', new, smart and clean. The price is 20,000rp double or single, or 25,000rp for three people sharing. Unlike the other accommodation, here a breakfast of tea or coffee and a pancake is included in the price. This hotel has its own electricity.

Australians are involved in the running of Johnny's, the Main Ski Inn and Nusa Lembongan Restaurant/Bungalows, attracted here by the great surf.

WHERE TO EAT

As nearly all food supplies come from the mainland and there is no mains electricity for refrigeration, the range in the restaurants is limited. Most offer standard fare at prices equivalent to the mainland. The highlights of the menus are the fish.

Johnny's has standard food at cheap prices (e.g. *nasi goreng* at 800rp). There are three other restaurants grouped together by the beach, all of which have sand floors, giving a desert-island kind of atmosphere. The largest of the three—and the only one with (blaring rock) music—is the restaurant of the Nusa Lembongan Restaurant/Bungalows. There are a few Western dishes on offer, but it is still all pretty basic, certainly not expensive.

Prices of bottled drinks are noticeably higher here; a small bottled water is 750rp and a large beer 2,100rp.

DAY TRIPS TO THE ISLANDS

There are a number of ways to see these islands without having to commit yourself to a long stay, or to the mercies of the *jukung*-masters of Kusamba. Some of the watersports 'clubs' on the beach at Benoa village (see p.48) offer day trips to Nusa Penida and Nusa Lembongan, and you can make other arrangements through the major hotels.

The most luxurious day-trip, however, and probably the most interesting, is that run by the **Bali International Yacht Club** at Sanur (see p.48), which has a powerful boat seating up to 20 passengers that can rocket you comfortably across the straits. For the hefty sum of $56 US you will see the south of Nusa Penida (from the boat), and one of the other two islands.

Seeing the south of Nusa Penida like this is fascinating: in the first place you will have a splendid view of the cliff-faces that line the whole of the southern flank. The south of the island is virtually waterless, and the scattered villages depend on springs that emerge at the foot of these cliffs, just above the sea. In order to reach them, the villagers have to walk down long and precarious paths and ladders, and then up again with the water. Fishermen use similar routes to come down to the water's edge, where a few of them fish from curious nest-like constructions built onto the cliff walls. The trip will also take you to the little island called **Batu Lumbung**, thickly coated with large, brown fruit bats, which leave their perches and swirl about at a hoot of the boat's horn. You can snorkel in 'Crystal Bay' on the west side of the island, or take a walk through silent and peaceful woods to the village of Penida, not yet accessible to motorized transport. (There is talk of building 'homestay' bungalows here, and it would certainly be an outstanding location.) You also visit Nusa Ceningan or Nusa Lembongan, where you can see the seaweed 'farming' in progress. The price includes a good packed lunch and drinks, and the use of snorkelling equipment.

255

Part VIII

BANGLI REGENCY

Duck herding

The only regency in Bali without any coastline, and the most consistently mountainous, Bangli curls itself around the old crater of **Mt Batur**, with its strikingly beautiful lake and surrounding mountain peaks, and tails off to the lowland south in a wedge shape to a point just north of the town of Gianyar.

Bangli contains some of the island's most historic and memorable temples: at **Pura Kehen**, in the town of **Bangli** (the main town of the regency), and **Pura Tegeh Koripan** in Penulisan, you will find inscriptions and archaeological remains linking them with the era of King Udayana, in the late 10th and early 11th century. The old **Pura Ulun Danu**, on the shores of **Lake Batur**, is said to be one of the oldest temples on the island.

The southern part of the regency has the ease and relative affluence that characterizes all the southern fertile plains. The lower slopes of the mountains below Bangli provide good rice-growing country, decked with glossy green-blue terraces, clumps of bamboo and waving palms. Above Bangli the vegetation becomes dense as the climate becomes cooler. Here there are coffee groves and *salak* plantations, and the rice terraces give way to grass and open farmland. Further north, the road becomes closed in by taller trees and matted jungle, before it suddenly breaks out at the rim of the Batur crater, with startling mountain views all around.

Mt Batur is an extraordinary double volcano. First there is the huge outer rim rising to an average of around 1,300 m (4,264 ft) and up to 1,745 m (5,723 ft) at **Mt Penulisan**, to the northeast. This rim is dotted with villages along the perimeter road, the best known of which is **Kintamani**, also the name of the district and frequently used to refer to the whole area. From this rim you look down onto the crescent-shaped Lake Batur,

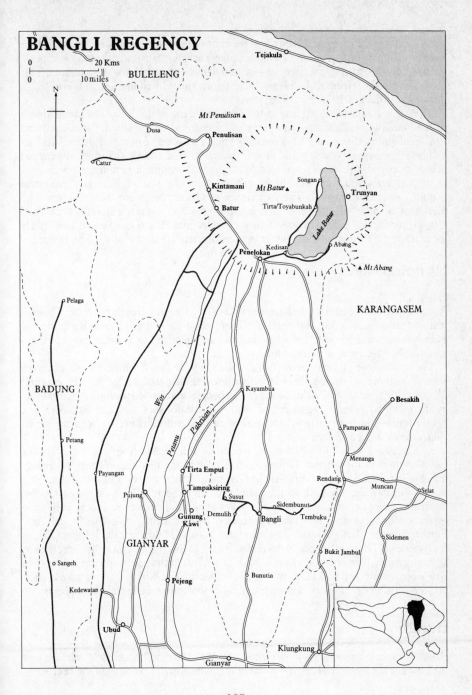

BANGLI REGENCY

0 ————— 20 Kms
0 ————— 10 miles

N

BULELENG

Tejakula

Mt Penulisan ▲

Dusa

Penulisan

Catur

Kintamani   *Mt Batur* ▲   Songan

Batur   Tirta/Toyabunkah   **Trunyan**

Lake Batur

Penelokan   Kedisan   Abang

▲ *Mt Abang*

KARANGASEM

Pelaga

BADUNG

Wos

Petanu   *Pakrisan*

Kayambua   **○ Besakih**

Pampatan

Petang   Menanga

Payangan   **Tirta Empul**   Rendang   Muncan   Selat

Pujung   **Tampaksiring**

Susut   Sidembunut

Gunung Kawi   Demulih   **Bangli**   Tembuku   Sidemen

GIANYAR

Sangeh   Bukit Jambul

Pejeng   Bunutin

Kedewatan

Ubud   Klungkung

Gianyar

257

sparkling along the easternmost edges of the crater a thousand feet below. And out of the floor of this huge crater, some 12 km (7.5 miles) across, thrusts another volcanic peak, younger, cruder, with its abrasive, lava-coated flanks dotted with rough scrubland. This is Mt Batur itself, rising to 1,717 m (5,632 ft), still active and menacing. It erupted to devastating effect in 1912 and 1926.

The air is cooler here, bracing even. The landscape in the lee of the mountains is clothed in alpine vegetation—pine trees and ferns, and, in the sunnier spots, red and flesh-pink poinsettias which have somehow made their way from their native Mexico.

This is spectacular country, and reveals yet another suit to Bali's hand. But its rugged beauty comes at a price. The people of the central mountain region are poorer and correspondingly rougher, sometimes criticized by the rest of Bali as '"mountain people", not to be trusted'. The experience of visitors bears out this criticism. The bleakness of their villages, and their harsh voices and expressions reflect the hard struggle for survival in the shadow of the great volcanoes. As a result, you are more likely to want to pass through the mountain regions of Bangli than stay any length of time.

Historical Notes

Bali Aga

According to the Indonesian archaeologist, Dr R. P. Soejono, Bangli can claim a human history that goes back 300,000 years. At Trunyan on the shores of Lake Batur, he has found stone axes and other tools believed to have belonged to a community of Homo erectus, the precursor of Homo sapiens.

Trunyan is one of Bali's most famous 'Bali Aga' villages, whose people claim an ancestry that precedes the influx of the Javanese-Hindu peoples after the 10th century. Literally, the term means 'Balinese mountain people' and is used somewhat pejoratively by the majority Balinese, who are not 'Bali Aga'. 'Bali Mula' (original Balinese), is a politer term—but these original Balinese tend to identify themselves with their own villages more than as a race apart.

As successive waves of newcomers arrived in the islands from the early days of Hinduization, so the original Balinese retreated into the mountain fastnesses, rigidly maintaining their ancient traditions. In fact, many of these pre-Hindu traditions still have a wide currency throughout the island and can be seen in life cycle rituals, taboos, marriage by elopement, tooth-filing, the belief in harmful demons and local spirits, the reverence for ancestors, and so on. So these are by no means exclusive to the Bali Aga. Furthermore, the Bali Aga have also adopted a gloss of Hinduism, albeit superficial, in the pantheon. Their difference to the rest of Bali is, in this respect, more by degrees than absolute. Such differences were probably less obvious in the past when most villages in Bali were remote and had their own separate identities; modern changes have eroded much of this, but reinforced the separateness of the conservative Bali Aga villages.

Bangli

Bangli is a quiet, spacious town, stretched out along the road up a hillside, with little of the bustle and commercial activity usual in the administrative centres of the regencies.

Like the other main towns, it was once the ruling seat of a kingdom. The old palace has an air of genteel decay, despite having been turned into a *losmen* in the late 1960s. The climate is cool and refreshing and there are excellent walks in the surrounding hills. It is a convenient base for visiting Besakih, or for getting an early morning start for the trip to the mountains further north. The best time to visit is when there is a festival at Pura Kehen, the impressive major temple of the town.

People here are friendly; there is none of the pressure associated with developed tourism. Accordingly, there are precious few amenities to cater for tourists either—no restaurant that panders to Western tastes, no nightlife, no tourist shops. It is a good place to come to get an untarnished picture of the culture, to stay quietly without being bothered.

Rather suitably for one of Bali's sanest, quietest areas, Bangli is home to the island's only lunatic asylum. It seems to operate more as an asylum—in the true sense of the word—than as a place of psychiatric intervention; in any case the mentally disturbed are

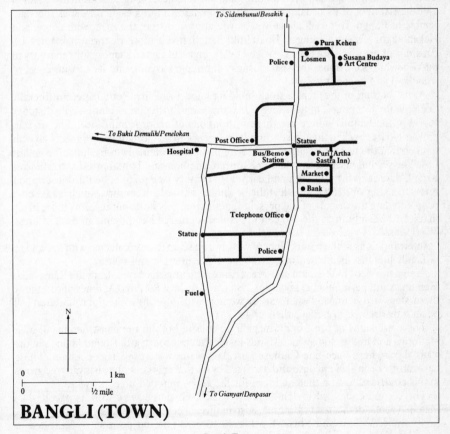

Bangli Town

tolerated more easily in Bali than in the West. Bangli features often in jokes among the Balinese because of this hospital: the townspeople must get tired of it.

GETTING AROUND

You will have no problems getting a *bemo* from Gianyar (300rp). The *bemo*s stop by the main crossroads, just opposite the old palace. *Bemo*s also go north to Kintamani from here (400rp).

Drivers should turn north off the Gianyar–Klungkung road about 2 km (1.25 miles) out of Gianyar. The road is signposted.

TOURIST INFORMATION

None. The **telephone** office (don't bother trying to make international calls) is on the road in from the south, the **post office** is on your right on the road out west.

Pura Kehen

This is something special, even among Balinese temples. Its age, its dramatic position and the richness of its ornamentation justify its fame and its exalted rank as the state temple of Bangli. It towers above you as you approach from the road, with a long and elegant flight of steps leading up Bukit [hill] Bangli. Inside there are three main terraces. An atmosphere of restful calm is evoked by the graceful carved shapes of the masonry in pinkish-white sandstone, the spaciousness of temple's layout, and its surroundings of woodland and coconut groves.

At the bottom of the steps a small building known as **Pura Penyimpenan** (literally 'Temple for Keeping Things') serves as a museum for the important inscribed stones found in the temple. There are three inscriptions of major significance. The first, in Sanskrit, dates back to the 9th century. Its reference to the 'lord of fire' connects up with the fact that the temple is said to have been dedicated originally to Brahma, the god of fire. The second inscription refers to Kuturan, an important Hindu priest at the time of King Udayana in the late 10th and early 11th century (see p.76). The third inscription refers to a king who ruled in Bali at the beginning of the 13th century, which leads some people to date the origins of the present temple from this time, but it seems more likely that it had been built in the 9th century and was enlarged at the time of each of these inscriptions.

Interpretations of the name 'Kehen' vary, but all seem to be connected with fire and so of family life, just as the hearth is symbolic of the home in our culture.

Lining the steps to the main gate are statues depicting characters from the Ramayana: Hanuman and his monkey army, Rama, Sita, and the evil Rawana. At times of ceremony these steps are a moving staircase of women with offerings, men and children, all beautifully dressed to honour their gods.

There are signs of pre-Hindu megalithic culture both in the constructions of high platforms and in the stone which stands inside the first courtyard. Round hollows in the walls show where once fine Chinese porcelain plates were used as decoration. These have mostly been shaken loose and damaged by earth tremors. A huge banyan tree grows in this courtyard, with a thatched roof for the *kulkul* perched in its branches.

The second courtyard is dominated by an eleven-tiered *meru* with its pagoda-like thatched roofs, dedicated to Brahma. Also in this corner is a *padmasana* with three seats, for Brahma, Vishnu and Shiva, the Hindu trinity. The top position is dedicated to Sanghyang Widi, the supreme god.

Art Centre

The **Sasana Budaya Art Centre** is a massive affair, just down the road from Puri Kehen, where dance and drama are staged. Bangli is said to have one of the largest *gamelan* orchestras in Bali: originally from Klungkung, it was moved to Bangli by the Dutch. There is no formal schedule of performances; the best way to find out what is going on is to ask locally, or at the Badung Tourist Office in Denpasar before you set out.

Bukit Demulih

This is a well-known viewing point, though not easy to find. Turn west at the main crossroads in the town in the direction of Tampaksiring. The turning to Demulih is signposted on your left about 3 km (1.8 miles) from this point. From here you have to walk. At the top of the hill is a small temple called **Pura Penataran Kentel Gumi**. From this vantage point you can see right back to the southern coast and the whole range of mountains over to the west.

Pura Langgar

Some 7 km (4.3 miles) to the south of Bangli on the Gianyar road lies the village of **Bunutin**. Here an unmarked turning to the east takes you to a temple built out over a lake, unusual because of its construction along the lines of a mosque. The story goes that, during the 17th century, a local Hindu prince once became seriously ill. His younger brother consulted a *dukun* (local healer) in his search for a cure, and was told to build a temple for the worship of the Islamic spirits of an ancestor, I Dewa Mas Wili. This ancestor had come from Blambangan, in Java, to join the court at Gelgel, and had been given the land at Bunutin by the raja.

Accordingly the younger brother designed a temple on Muslim principles, with four central pillars and four gateways in the direction of the four winds. It is a beautiful spot, with the lichen-covered temple buildings and dense palm groves reflected in the calm, lily-filled water of the lake. The sick prince duly recovered, and to this day the family refrain from eating pork in honour of their Islamic predecessor, and the temple is, unusually, a place of prayer for Muslims and Hindus alike.

WHERE TO STAY AND EAT

The best option is the old raja's palace in Bangli, not so glamorous as its formerly regal status implies, but quiet, with friendly people. It is called **Artha Sastra Inn**. Rooms here are very simple, but clean, with private bathroom and breakfast included for 5,000rp (double or single) a night. It is right opposite the bus/*bemo* station.

The other *losmen* in town is opposite the Pura Kehen, the rooms are small and dark.

At the moment there is really nowhere special to eat: the night market in the *bemo* station has plenty of *warung*s but that is about all. Eat early, for everything closes before 8 pm.

North of Bangli

GETTING AROUND

The main road north climbs from Bangli up the side of the ancient volcano of Batur to the rim of its crater—known as '*kawah kuno*' ('ancient crater') by the Balinese—some

20 km (12.5 miles) to the north. The road is good with a firm surface, the climb steady rather than steep. At **Penelokan** the road emerges to clear views of lake and mountains.

An alternative route is to turn right just north of the centre of Bangli, taking the cross-country route to **Rendang**, then turn north on to the main Besakih road. At the village of Menanga continue straight on instead of forking right to Besakih. The road this far is good—it is the route taken by the coaches. Beyond Menanga the population thins out and the road passes through dark, jungly forest. Further north, gaps in the vegetation give access to superb views of Mt Agung. During the rainy season the road surface suffers, potholes appear and driving becomes more demanding. Allow extra time and be prepared for a touch of seasickness. However, you don't have to worry about traffic: you may not even see another vehicle.

This road meets the crater rim at its southernmost point. Below you is the village of Kedisan, at the lakeside. To the northwest is the new Gunung Batur peak formed by volcanic action within the old crater. On a clear day the view across the lake presents a massive panorama in delicate pastel shades. Here, unlike further along the crater rim, you can enjoy the scene in peace and at your leisure, without flocks of persistent sellers or busloads of other visitors.

To reach this point by public transport, go to Penelokan, then walk.

TOURIST INFORMATION
There are no tourist facilities beyond restaurants and *losmen*s up here, either at Penelokan or at Kintamani, Batur or Penulisan.

There are regular *bemo*s from Tampaksiring (400rp) and from Bangli (600rp). There are also *bemo*s south from Singaraja (1,000rp). Some buses use this route between Denpasar and Singaraja, via Tampaksiring.

Gunung Abang

From the point where the Besakih road arrives at the rim of the crater a small road to the right leads through dense rainforest up towards the peak of **Mt Abang** (2,152 m; 7,058 ft). The area around Gunung Abang (the name means 'red mountain') is protected and you need permission from the PPHA authority in Denpasar (see p.41) to enter. The sign forbids fires and hunting. The climb to the windy peak and back takes about five hours. It is a slippery trail with not much to see until you reach the top where the views are magnificent. There is a temple there which may have been established when the ancient village of Abang was high up on the mountain, before it moved, because of land slips, to its present position down by the lake. There are still villages tucked away on the mountainside which survive by cultivating sweet potatoes and vegetables to exchange for fish at the marketplace at Abang.

Penelokan

As with all the villages around the Batur crater, Penelokan (1,450 m; 4,756 ft) has one outstanding attraction to outweigh several disadvantages. The good news is the view; indeed, Penelokan means 'place for looking'. This is sensational, quite unlike anything else in Bali in scale and rugged grandeur. It is best to get here early to get the clearest light: the clouds often descend after 8 or 9 am, and after midday it can become very misty. The sunrise can be magical. Be prepared for intense cold at that early hour.

The bad news is that the village itself, like Batur and Kintamani, is grimly unappealing. The buildings are drab, often with corrugated tin roofs, the roads littered, the *warung*s mean, vegetation sparse. Accommodation is generally damp, cold and dirty. The people are pushy and demanding and often downright dishonest. A five-minute pause by the roadside can make the best-mannered of tourists become abusive. It does no good: the clamour of the sellers increases in proportion to the fury of their victim. The craft wares on sale tend to be tacky, the fruit dry. The best strategy is to wait until a more gullible group of foreigners falls prey to these hordes, then to sneak out surreptitiously to steal a look at the landscape.

Even filling up with petrol can be risky here. A common complaint is that a swarm of young men is likely to descend on your vehicle and claim that this is faulty or that needs fixing immediately or that you must have oil/pump your tyres/completely renew your engine, and they are not above causing considerable damage just to charge you to put it right. Deal with this by filling up before your journey, and again by the lake if you go down inside the crater.

WHERE TO STAY AND EAT

In general, accommodation around here is just plain miserable. Prices are usually about 5,000rp (double or single) including breakfast, but apart from the views, the places are unattractive, and the poor standards of hygiene, the cold and the damp, make them unhealthy too. The best available in Penelokan is the **Caldera Batur Restaurant & Bungalows**, which is up behind **Homestay Lakeview** just before the turn down to the lake. There are no views of the lake here, and the accommodation is far from luxurious, but the place is clean and the rooms have private bathrooms and bamboo-style beds which do not seem to hold the moisture as much as the old solid wood beds. There are five identical rooms, all at 15,000rp a night, double or single. Bring your woollies and check that the blankets are dry.

In terms of food, the restaurant at **Caldera Batur** (on the right hand side on the road up from Bangli, just before you reach the view), is recommended in preference to the big tourist restaurants round the crater, such as the Rama and the Puri Selera, which aim to cater for coach parties from the hotels and agencies. The latter have great views over the south of the island but their size and the blandness of the food are off-putting. Homestay Lakeview has a terrace with a magnificent view up Lake Batur, but the food and the service are decidedly indifferent. Note that everything shuts around 7.30pm.

Lake Batur

This crescent-shaped crater lake is 1,000m (3,280ft) above sea level and some 12km (7.5 miles) from top to bottom. Serene, deep and mysterious, it is surrounded by shadowed mountains which from a distance appear to rise vertically from its edge. Its still surface takes on the colours of the sky, reflecting clouds and mountains and the stars at night. At the lakeside, small settlements cling precariously to the foot of the great mountains, dwarfed into absurdity by the monumental scale of the landscape. As with all the mountain lakes of Bali, Lake Batur is considered to be the headwater of numerous irrigation systems fed by the rivers that flow down the flanks of Mt Batur, and for this reason it is sacred.

The road hairpins down from Penelokan to the lakeside. Check the brakes beforehand. Vehicles go off this road at a fair rate: their skeletons remain as a warning to those who try to be smart.

Kedisan

This is the first lakeside settlement as you descend from Penelokan. Take the signposted right turn. From here the boats leave for Trunyan and its cemetery, Kuban. Apart from the landing-place there is nothing but a huge car park, a couple of *warung*s and some uninteresting souvenir shops. Day-trippers on their way to Trunyan should stop here to hire their boat (see pp.268–69). If you plan to stay in the area, take the left-hand turn leading northwards along the western side of the lake, before Kedisan.

WHERE TO STAY AND EAT
Just beyond the Kedisan turning, standing back from the road, is **Segara Homestay**. It is in the middle of nowhere in particular; it is a further 7 km (4.3 miles) to the hot springs at Tirta (see below). Nevertheless it is one of the better options for accommodation and food in the area. The rooms are pleasant and clean and have showers, but no hot water. They cost 6,000rp for a single person, 10,000rp for doubles. The restaurant is a viable alternative to the rather fly-blown *rumah makan* at the lakeside; the menu offers the standard fare.

Kedisan to Tirta: trip through a lunar landscape

The road winds on northwards and then follows the lakeside through some of the strangest country in Bali—a lunar landscape of black lava rocks and sparse scrub. This is where the 1926 eruption of Mt Batur spilled hot lava down to the lakeside, completely obliterating the cultivated land and the entire village of Batur. Hickman Powell, author of *The Last Paradise* (1930) quotes his friend who saw the eruption: 'Fire spouted to the very heavens … all its [Mt Batur's] slope burst out in craters.' The tragedy remains fresh in the mind as you bump along the switchback road.

The villagers who once lived here were no strangers to volcanic eruptions. In 1926 they refused to leave their homes because on a previous occasion, nine years earlier, the lava flow had stopped just short of their temple, built above the village on the mountainside. They interpreted this as a miracle indicating they were under the divine protection of the gods. In 1926 troops, under the command of the Dutch Resident, had to be brought in to move them. When the eruption eventually came to a halt, their village had been buried beneath 30 m (100 ft) of lava at a temperature of 900°C.

Following this event, the village of Batur was moved up to the crater rim where it is today, straddling the road beside its impressive new temple (see pp.270–71).

The road weaves, climbs and falls over grey lava mounds so abruptly you think you might be falling off the edge of a cliff at each summit. Use your horn! The few dwellings rebuilt along this stretch look pointless and misplaced. The thin layer of soil is used for growing some hardy vegetables and occasionally breadfruit trees. Before the village of Tirta a signpost points off to the left, marking one of the routes for climbing Mt Batur. Over another hillock you come upon Tirta. At a fork one road goes into the village, the other goes on to the art centre at **Toyabunkah**.

GETTING AROUND

There are *bemo*s down from Penelokan to Kedisan and Tirta, and up again. They are not frequent. The official price is 500rp but people often end up paying 1,000rp.

Of course your own transport enables you to get around in a shorter time. One piece of advice: do not attempt the return climb to Penelokan on a near-empty tank, because the steepness of the slope will drain the petrol from the engine. You can fill up at **Desa Songan** beyond Tirta if you are worried. Even quite sturdy jeeps sometimes have a problem getting out of the crater: the altitude seems to affect the engines on this very steep climb, causing unnerving 'pinking' and stalling. It is certainly not a journey for a clapped-out wreck. If you have to be bailed out of this region, it will cost you a small fortune.

Tirta: the hot springs

(Also known as Toyabunkah. Both *toya* and *tirta* mean 'holy water'.) For any claims it might have to the title of resort, Tirta boasts a few *warung*s and shabby *rumah makan*s, four very basic *losmen*s, stupendous views and a newly constructed public bathing place at Bali's best-known hot springs. There are several good walks and climbs: Tirta is a good base from which to climb Mt Batur. You can bathe in the lake or take a boat across it to Trunyan (see pp.269–70). The art centre just beyond the village is a unique attempt to connect Balinese traditional arts with the mainstream of Western culture (see below).

TOURIST INFORMATION

There are no official facilities for tourists. Help is at hand from Nyoman (or Norman!) Pangus, who runs the *rumah makan* on your right as you come into Tirta. He is friendly and helpful, and will even look after your transport if you want to climb the mountain. Do give him something for doing this (though he will not ask): it is an invaluable service. Nyoman will tell you most of what you need to know. What he cannot tell you, the art centre probably can.

The hot springs

The baths here have now been housed in a new brick complex of traditional architecture, and look very much more inviting than the dingy muddy pools of old. The water is hot—almost too hot to bear—and sulphurous; it is excellent for soothing muscular aches and pains, especially if you have just climbed the mountain.

Like most things in Bali the hot springs have a spiritual significance and are associated with the ritual cleansing of *mala*, polluting influences. According to pre-Hindu traditional thinking, holy water springs in Bali form a threefold hierarchy: the hot springs here are the 'Tirta Bungkah', the holy waters of the mountain; 'Tirta Empul' at Tampaksiring are the holy waters of the plain; and 'Tirta Selukat' at the coast near Medahan in Gianyar are the holy waters of the sea. A special ceremony known as *melukat* involves bathing in all three kinds of holy water, and is carried out particularly by women in early pregnancy and by people who have just recovered from a long illness. Around the edge of the lake volcanically heated water bubbles up into the lake water to make warmish baths. Local people bathe here; one area for women, one for men, and another where children gather to play. The water is not inviting because there is so much litter around. A swim can lead to a face to face encounter with an empty food can, or worse. Somehow the care that goes into nourishing the environment elsewhere in Bali is not extended to its holy lake.

Gunung Batur

The volcano is by no means dormant—sometimes it glows at night and ejects fumes and debris. It last erupted in 1963, spilling lava down the southeastern flank; there is a locally printed postcard of a dramatic night-time view of this.

It takes two to three hours to climb the 700 m (2,300 ft) to the summit from the old crater floor, starting from Tirta. You can hire a guide for 1,500rp or more, but most people do not bother. It is not hard to find your way; there are several paths, some of them marked, and no hidden obstacles.

It is a tough climb though. Start in the cool of the early morning. You get better views early in the day, as the mountains tend to gather clouds as the morning wears on. Take some money with you in case you do need to ask the way. People round here can be reluctant to help you without financial encouragement. Also there are places to buy drinks on one of the routes—the one starting just before Tirta on the road from Kedisan, clearly signposted 'Mt Batur 1,717 m' (5,632 ft). Once at the top it is possible to walk right round the crater rim, or down into the crater itself. The ground is warm in some places and steam wafts out from cracks in the rocky surface.

Balai Seni Toyabunkah: art centre

This project, founded in 1973, is the brainchild of a Sumatran professor and poet, Sutan Takdir Alisjahbana. It brings together artists and people interested in art theory, from Bali, Indonesia and all over the world, to consider problems and develop new ideas in an atmosphere of 'reflection and creation'. It is a serious project, attracting the interest of a group of Jungian psychologists from Geneva. The aim is to express international consciousness through the traditional medium of Balinese dance and music. Several new Balinese dances have been created here, on such universal themes as 'From Darkness to Light' and 'Woman at the Crossroads'. The centre only really comes to life when there is a visiting study group in residence; however, casual visitors can enjoy the small but interesting library, the restaurant and the guest bungalows (see 'Where to stay and eat', below).

Songan

Continue round the lake beyond Tirta and Toyabunkah to reach Songan, the largest of the lakeside villages. It is a good place to wander. Songan has an archaic feeling to it, due no doubt to the relatively undisturbed continuity of village life here. Children play naked beside the road, old people sit gossiping in the shade of the *warung*s.

Beyond the village is the cultivated flat land on which the people depend for their livelihood. The land is evidently much more fertile here than back at Tirta.

Pura Ulun Danu

At the end of the road is the Pura Ulun Danu, a temple dedicated to the god of the lake, a very ancient place of worship with animistic connections which go back well before Hinduism. (Note that the new temple of Batur is also called Pura Ulun Danu; the two are not to be confused.)

The old traditions continue here, including major ceremonies to honour and appease the god of the lake. Buffaloes, pigs, goats, geese and chickens are adorned with quantities of *kepeng*s, gold and other decorations, taken out into the middle of the lake in boats, and ceremoniously drowned. This event was witnessed with some horror by K'tut Tantri (Vannine Walker) before the last war and is described briefly in her powerful memoir *Revolt in Paradise* (1960). She was accompanied by the son of the Raja of Klungkung, Agung Nura, who made the dispassionate observation that the floor of the lake must be covered in the untold riches of generations of such sacrifices. This ceremony takes place every ten years: the last was in 1984, the next is scheduled for 1994. Not for followers of the Animal Liberation Front—but then little in Bali would be. Meanwhile the temple *meru* is undergoing repairs after earlier periods of neglect. It's a remote, peaceful, wild spot.

WHERE TO STAY AND EAT

By far the best place to stay by the lakeside is at the Toyabunkah art centre, **Balai Seni Toyabunkah**. Here the individual bungalows are attractive, furnished and well cared for, with their own verandah at the front. The attached restaurant serves breakfast (included in the price of a room) and has fresh lake fish on the menu. Prices for both rooms and restaurant are very reasonable considering the level of comfort: rooms with two beds and private bathroom with hot water are 15,000rp (double or single); a Western style bath puts up the price to 20,000rp and a family suite with three beds costs 40,000rp. You can book accommodation in advance by applying to Semadi Rent Company, Jl. Blanjong, Sanur.

The next best choice is **Losmen Amertha**, right next to the hot springs, which pumps up hot water for showers in the private bathrooms. Views of the lake are good here too. Prices are 6,000rp for doubles, 4,000rp for a single and may or may not include breakfast, so negotiate this. **Losmen Tirta Yatra**, **Nyoman Mawa** and the **Siki Inn** are in the same price range and have similar small, plain rooms, but without the advantages of Amertha.

Apart from the art centre, **Nyoman Pangus** and **Nyoman Mawa** both have restaurants of the enlarged *warung* variety, with standard menus and usual prices, with the extra bonus of fresh fish from the lake (*ikan mujair*), bony but tasty (3,000rp). Nyoman Pangus' book of comments makes lively mealtime entertainment.

Trunyan

Trunyan is a small 'Bali Aga' village (see p.258) which lies on the eastern shore of Lake Batur, and is usually reached by boat across the lake (although you can go by foot from Kedisan). It is undoubtedly a fascinating place for anthropologists, for the ancient traditions of the Bali Aga, with their numerous life-cycle rituals and taboos have provided, and continue to provide, a rich source of study. Here women give birth in traditional Balinese style, in a sitting position with their knotted hair clasped by a virgin girl, assisted by a male mid-wife and delivered by their husbands. Here the dead are not cremated, but left out in the open air to decay. Here, in other words, is a centuries-old tradition barely touched by the outside world.

For tourists, however, the appeal is considerably diminished. The village is an unattractive sprawl of old thatch and wattle houses, increasingly interspersed with modern bungalows of brick and concrete and corrugated iron. The people are renowned for their merciless and unceasing demands for extravagant sums of money at every turn. A visit here could cost you some 50,000rp (25,000rp for the crossing from Kedisan, 5,000rp for tourist registration at Kedisan, 5,000rp for tourist registration at Trunyan, 5,000rp as your temple donation, 5,000rp as a donation for the cemetery, 5,000rp for your 'guide' who will cling to you uninvited the moment you step ashore . . .). Of course, this is an absurd sum, but in the intimidating atmosphere of the place it is sometimes unavoidable.

Is it worth it? Certainly not; almost anywhere in Bali is more pleasant. Why do people go? Well, there is something of a challenge in this reputation, certainly. But to many people the big lure of Trunyan is its custom of leaving dead bodies unburied in the cemetery to rot and be eaten by maggots rather than pursue the Hindu rite of cremation. Some people seem to find this morbid attraction quite irresistible. But even they are disappointed, for the bodies are covered in cloth—and for some reason you can't even smell them.

The traditions of ancestor worship in Trunyan pre-date the Hinduization of Bali. The most important of their ancestors, Ratu Gede (or Sakti) Pancering Jagat (the Powerful God of the Centre of the Earth) has been incorporated into the Hindu religion by the name of Batara. A four-metre long statue of him, famous throughout Bali, is said to be concealed within a seven-tiered *meru* in the compound of the main temple, the Bali Desa Pancering Jagat Bali—and is said to be cleaned regularly by virgin boys using a mixture of chalk and honey. But since not even the villagers themselves are allowed to see the statue except on ceremonial occasions it is hard to attest this. Ratu Gede Pancering Jagat, so the story goes, married Ratu Ayu Pingit Dalam Dasar, the lake goddess (Dewi Danu to the rest of us), who was tempted down from heaven by the scent of the Taru Menyan tree, from which Trunyan is sometimes said to derive its name. This same tree is also a great lure to evil demons, who are, however, easily diverted by corpses—which is why, as legend would have it, the villagers do not bury their dead.

There is a more logical explanation: land is so scarce here there's just no place to bury them. Visitors are taken two minutes by boat to **Kuban**, a spot a little way to the north of the village, to see the cemetery. This is the *sema wayah*, the cemetery for married people, where there are somewhere between seven and eleven plots (no one seems quite sure) available to those villagers who die a natural death. Those who commit suicide or die of disfiguring diseases are buried. You will see a heap of bones by the shore and the odd artlessly arranged pile of skulls. Because there is a limited number of plots, the dead have to be shunted out of their resting place as soon it is required by another. After elaborate rituals, the naked body is laid in a shallow pit, covered with batik cloth and then protected from scavengers by a kind of triangular bamboo cage called a *tanjak*. The body is apparently reduced to a skeleton in a matter of three weeks.

A sideshow of the cemetery is provided by young boys in primitive dugout canoes who, at the sight of a tourist, will whip off their clothes and dive into the lake after 100rp coins. They get quite shirty if your aim is not helpful.

Trunyan does, undoubtedly, have a memorable setting, on a narrow stretch of flat land between the lake and the steep mountain behind, with spectacular views across the water of Mt Batur, which is often shrouded in low-lying mist. There is a massive *pule* tree in the centre of the village; its thicket of trunks lends credence to the claim that it is 1,100 years old. You can enjoy to some extent the unaltered pace of life here: women pounding the grain in giant mortars; the people clothed in their long *kains*, usually in the attractive muted colours of natural dyes. You may also see the great wooden carousel, like a fairground big wheel, erected in the centre of the village for ceremonial occasions (as in the other 'Bali Aga' village, Tenganan) upon which the local boys will throw themselves with reckless abandon.

But by and large life here is bleak and wrapped in arcane mystery. The hapless tourist receives rough treatment. Because the people are poor and their resources are few, a tradition has grown up of begging for rice from other communities, a tradition apparently sanctioned by a holy man in Trunyan during times of hardship in the past. No other Balinese will beg—at least not openly; and so the habit is frowned on but persists nonetheless.

If you do decide to go, a locally produced publication called *Life Cycle Ceremonies in Trunyan, Bali* (1985) by Professor James Danandjaja will give you a brief and accessible account of what is going on behind the scenes and will help lift the veil of mystery to some extent.

GETTING THERE
The situation at Kedisan for arranging a trip across the lake became so bad the government stepped in. There are now fixed prices for boat hire if you arrange it at the government office near the quayside. Official prices are between 7,500 and 9,000rp for a boat, with a maximum of eight passengers, plus 125rp per person. The price varies

Pounding rice in Trunyan

according to the number of destinations; trips usually include both Trunyan and the cemetery a little to the north.

This does stop you being assailed by a throng of boatmen and agents offering all kinds of alternatives. If you negotiate privately, the boatmen (who tell you the government office no longer operates and the fixed rate doesn't apply) will ask 25–35,000rp for the Kedisan–Trunyan–cemetery–Tirta–Kedisan trip. The Denpasar tourist office still receives numerous complaints about boatmen renegotiating the price when they have you halfway across the lake, or when you are stuck in Trunyan. Moreover it's risky leaving motorbike or car in Kedisan, where it can be tampered with. If you want to do the trip, our advice is either to join an organized outing, or to bring someone reliable from your hotel to guard your transport.

The crossing will take about 20 minutes. It can be decidedly chilly on the open water, even at midday: take a pullover. The boats are purpose built and have awnings to protect you from the sun.

You can also hire a boat to Trunyan at the hot springs at Tirta. There is no government office here, though, to protect you against leaky boats and shady boatmen.

Another way to reach Trunyan is by a path that runs round the lake from Kedisan. You can just about get by on a motorbike as far as Buahan village, after that you have to walk. Doing it this way will take around one and a half hours each way.

Batur and Kintamani

Back on the crater rim, the road continues north from Penelokan through Batur, Kintamani and Penulisan.

Batur and Kintamani have grown to be virtually indistinguishable. Batur is the newcomer, moved up here from the valley following the eruption of Mt Batur in 1926. Both suffer from the mountain blight: unattractive buildings and unfriendly people. The surrounding region is surprisingly fertile, making the early morning market a colourful and lively affair. The focal point of Batur is the new temple, **Pura Ulun Danu**, to which the shrine to the god of the lake was brought in 1926. The temple is a great deal better cared for than anything else around here.

GETTING AROUND
From Bangli, *bemo*s cost 700rp. The short journey from Penelokan is 100rp. *Bemo*s also run between Kintamani and Singaraja (700rp).

Pura Ulun Danu
The new temple of Batur is worth a visit for its striking architecture and its dramatic position. The tall gateways and thatched roofs of the *meru* shrines stand out against the black volcanic earth and the sky above the open, cleanly swept courtyards. It is all on a satisfyingly vast scale, producing the strange sense of release of walking on the top of the world.

Construction began in 1927 and is still underway. There is a mixture of the old and the new, with modern brick-and-stone architecture, typical of current Balinese practice, contrasting with the dark stone of older constructions, and setting off the bejewelled quality of the ornate sanctuary of the inner temple, with its gilded doors and stone reliefs, and the small group of brightly painted sculptures of animals and other figures.

Pura Ulun Danu is particularly sacred to all the rice farmers in the lands fed by the 37 rivers that rise from Mt Batur. This temple is considered to be at the summit of a great pyramid of sacred sites and temples attached to the tributaries, rivers, dams and irrigation systems that spread out between here and the sea in the south, and upon which hundreds of thousands of people depend for their livelihood. The priest of Pura Ulun Batur plays a vital role in this distribution of water, lending his authority to the choice of times for planting and harvesting and so on, as well as approving or otherwise any plans to alter watercourses.

Kintamani market
This is the other attraction of the area. Oranges, lemons, passion fruit, coffee beans and a wide variety of vegetables—grown on the more hospitable southern slopes of Mt Batur—change hands here.

You get a fine sense of the contradictions of these mountain people by visiting market and temple. Apparently absorbed in the rough business of scratching a living from a thin topsoil—or bullying it out of tourists—and bartering with attention to the last part of a rupiah, they nevertheless put all their hard-won resources into building a temple fit for a fairy story.

WHERE TO STAY AND EAT
The best option is **Hotel Puri Astini**, which is about 1 km (0.6 mile) off the main road at the northern end of Kintimani. Turn right before the radio tower. The *losmen* is much better constructed than most accommodation around here, important in the damp, cold air of the mountains. The rooms are comfortable, plenty of dry blankets are available, and the sitting room looks out over the volcano. Prices are 7,500rp for a single, 10,000rp for doubles, including a private bathroom and breakfast.

Of the tourist restaurants between Penelokan and Kintamani, the huge **Kintamani Restaurant** has the best reputation.

Sadly, the old government resthouse, once a popular stopover for visitors in the 1930s, is now empty and decaying.

Penulisan

Beyond Kintamani the road keeps climbing through a number of run-down settlements with a kind of weather-beaten charm, in the middle of the pine forests. Looking back you can sometimes see the whole range of mountain peaks lined up to the east.

Pura Tegeh Koripan
Up a soaring flight of stone steps is Bali's highest and most spectacularly positioned temple, overlooking mountains, lakes, wooded hillsides, fruit and coffee groves, ravines, coast and sea. Bukit Penulisan is 1,745 m (5,723 ft) above sea level.

In fact, several temples are grouped together as one here, all dedicated to Sanghyang Grinatha, a manifestation of Shiva as god of the mountains. The highest point of the temple, the tall shrine of Panerajon, is also the oldest, a representation of a mountain peak, symbolizing victory.

The temple site was used to honour the god of the mountains long before Hinduism arrived. There is archaeological evidence of a sanctuary here around 1500 BC. It seems the hill was used as a hermitage and place of meditation under the patronage of early royal dynasties. Megalithic stones from this period are kept in the temple. It was a place of worship for a religion that honoured the gods of three worlds, the upper world of the mountains, the middle world of the plains, and the lower world of the coast and sea deities. It is within this very ancient religious structure that the Penulisan temple is connected with Pura Pusering Jagat in Pejeng, a temple for the gods of the plains.

You will also see a pair of stone *lingam*s and a *yoni*, the male and female symbols associated with the cult of Shiva; in this context these symbols are also linked—on a splendidly massive scale—to Mt Agung (the *lingam*, the male aspect) and Mt Batur (the *yoni*, the female aspect).

The stone statues and friezes are from the period when Bali was part of the ruling empires of Java. The one showing a marriage is said to represent King Udayana and his Javanese princess, Mahendradatta, and to date from the 11th century. Another statue is named as Batari Mandul, wife of Anak Wangsa, one of Udayana's sons and a ruler of Bali, and is dated AD 1077. A further marriage scene represents Ratu Gung Kang and his wife: legend tells how this Balinese king (black) married a Chinese princess (white). In respect of this, the shrine is cared for by Chinese living in the area as well as by Balinese.

After Penulisan the road starts its long and winding descent to the northern coast. Above and below the road the hillsides are densely planted with a rich profusion of coffee trees, many types of citrus including oranges and the grapefruit-like pomelo (*jeruk Bali*), figs, *dapdap* trees, banana trees, clove trees and vanilla vines. The mountain falls away abruptly from the road, and you can see out over the wooded ravines to the waving palm trees and gleaming sea beyond.

Catur

Just beyond Pura Tegeh Koripan at Penulisan a mountain road goes off left to the village of **Catur**, on the side of the mountain of the same name. This and other villages are strung out along the watershed between the north and south of the island, and they preserve many features of their 'Bali Aga' heritage. The road is worth exploring for the scenery as well as for the villages, but you have to be prepared for a rough ride, and the possibility of finding the route quite unpassable.

Part IX

KARANGASEM REGENCY

The lagoon at Candi Dasa

Karangasem has an impressive range of moods. Within its 2,000 or so square kilometres (750 square miles) the steep rise from coast to mountain creates magical scenery like sets from a fantasy film. Dominating the district is **Gunung Agung** (3,142 m, 10,306 ft) (literally 'Great Mountain'), home of Bali's gods, who are prone to signify their displeasure by invoking the volcano to spew its rage over the surrounding countryside in molten lava and rocks. The last eruption was in 1963, as preparations were being made for the once-in-a-lifetime Eka Desa Rudra celebrations at Bali's mother temple, Pura Besakih. The eruption killed more than a thousand inhabitants, and changed forever the lives of thousands more (see pp.93–94).

The lava is now used to make breeze blocks and gravel as building materials, and with time and water it becomes wonderfully fertile soil. The southern and western slopes and foothills of the mountain produce two crops a year of best quality rice. But in the driest parts, in the northwest, nothing much grows besides cacti and kapok trees. The few settlements in this area live by fishing and subsistence farming, or by salt production. The name Karangasem means 'ground nut', a local product; you can see the straggly plants growing in the lowland fields, near Amed for instance.

One effect of the eruption has been the relatively slow spread of tourism here, but there are good places to stay on the south coast below **Amlapura**, Karangasem's principal town, chief amongst which is **Candi Dasa**. More recently, accommodation and restaurants have been established at **Padangbai**, where ferries leave for Lombok, and at **Balina Beach** near the small village of Manggis. There is also good accommodation at **Tirtagangga**, a quiet spot in the hills by the water palace of that name.

Historical notes

Karangasem and Lombok

In its past Karangasem has looked eastward to the island of Lombok, lying some 35 km (22 miles) off its shores, as much as to the rest of Bali. In the early 17th century the rajas of Lombok came increasingly under the influence of Islam, a by-product of flourishing trading links with the Bugis traders of Makassar. Karangasem meddled in Lombok's affairs until the decisive war of 1677–8 which gave the raja of Karangasem full control of the island. The Makassarese were expelled, and Karangasem installed four Hindu rajas of their own persuasion. From this time on, the story of Lombok concerns the way in which the small Balinese élite of the Karangasem family ruled over the mainly Muslim Sassak majority, and squabbled amongst themselves.

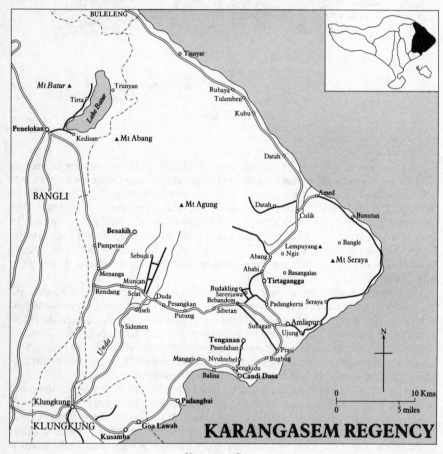

Karangasem Regency

274

By the 1830s Lombok was under the control of two rival rajas. One of these rajas was dominated by the daughter of the Raja of Karangasem, known simply by her title, the Cokorda; this faction was based in the port town of Ampenan and was supported by the powerful Danish trader Mads Lange, who was later to play a vital role in Bali's contest with the Dutch. The other faction centred upon the Raja of Mataram, a town but 4 km (2.5 miles) from Ampenan, who was supported by Mads Lange's trading rival, the Englishman George King. This story ends in bloody conflict: in 1838 the Raja of Mataram was killed at the moment of victory over the Cokorda, who carried out a *puputan*. Mads Lange fled to Bali. The Raja of Mataram was succeeded by his son, Gusti Ngurah Ketut Karangasem, who now controlled all Lombok and now sought to pursue his grievance with the Cokorda to the heart of her family Bali.

The Dutch—always concerned to protect their trading interests in Lombok—established good relations with the young raja. When, with their Third Military Expedition Against Bali in 1849, the Dutch finally succeeded in dislodging Jelantik's forces from Jagaraga and thus took control of Buleleng, they sought to follow up the initiative in the south of the island. Who better to help them tackle Jelantik's main allies, Karangasem, than the disgruntled Raja of Lombok? So it was that the Dutch landed 4,000 Lombok troops in Karangasem, whilst they themselves landed at Padangbai and moved westward.

It was to be a historic decision; for just as the Dutch, crippled with dysentery and licking the wounds inflicted by a night raid led by the Dewa Agung's sister, were about to make a humiliating withdrawal, news arrived that Jelantik had been ambushed by Lombok troops and killed, whilst the Raja of Karangasem, seeing unavoidable defeat, had committed *puputan* with his family.

In the wake of these traumatic events, Lombok was rewarded by the Dutch with the gift of power over Karangasem, which it ruled through a regent from 1849 to 1893.

The 1870s saw the rise of one of the most enigmatic figures of Balinese history: Gusti Gede Jelantik. Jelantik was the effective ruler of Karangasem, although his half-brother, Gusti Gede Putu, was in fact the regent. Around 1885, southern Bali was in upheaval, as the Dewa Agung, having imprisoned the Raja of Gianyar, set out to carve up his prisoner's territory between himself and Bangli. Jelantik raised an army of Lombok troops, mainly Muslim Sassaks, and waded into the fray on the pretext of pursuing Karangasem's dubious claim to Gianyar territory. It was a military disaster, and Jelantik had to return home with a bloody nose and mutinous troops.

From then on Jelantik was involved in a succession of military adventures. In 1891 the Sassaks of Lombok revolted against their Balinese overlords in the face of continued maltreatment, especially at the hands of a cruel ruler called Gusti Made, who was acting on behalf of the senile raja. Jelantik set forth to sort out the Sassaks. The Sassaks appealed to the Dutch who, embarrassed by the antics of their Balinese allies in Lombok, attempted to intervene, only to be rudely rebuffed by the raja. The Dutch now saw the prospect of losing control of Lombok; in 1894 they despatched the 'Lombok Expedition', consisting of some 2,200 troops, the majority of whom were, for once, European.

The Dutch, using Jelantik as an intermediary, landed in Lombok, where they were welcomed, treated respectfully, fêted even. They demanded that the cruel Gusti Made be delivered up to them; the Lombok Balinese procrastinated, and in the end said that Gusti Made had committed suicide with his wife. The Dutch demanded to see the bodies, and sent the controleur accompanying the expedition to verify the claim. Again the Balinese delayed, but eventually took the controleur to a courtyard of the palace of Cakranegara. There indeed lay the bodies of Gusti Made and his wife, but Gusti Made's body was still twitching. Quite what events led up to this moment remained a mystery.

The Dutch now continued their courteous occupation while the treaties were settled. All was smiles and jollities. But on 25 August the atmosphere turned. Jelantik, the intermediary, suddenly made himself 'unavailable'. During the night Balinese gathered and fell upon the Dutch with great ferocity, killing 98 of their troops.

This event, known as the 'Lombok Treachery', was answered by savage vengeance. The towns of Mataram and Cakranegara were razed by Dutch reinforcements, and there was a series of *puputan*s of the royal families.

Though never sure of Jelantik's innocence in the affairs of Lombok, the Dutch nevertheless decided to appoint him regent of Karangasem. It was a wise enough decision: he asserted his power effectively, living luxuriously in the eclectic palace of Amlapura until 1902.

The Lombok affair did much to colour the attitude of the Dutch to these islands in general, and goes some way to explaining the behaviour of the military during the invasion of Bali in 1906. Whereas many Dutch administrators took an academic and sympathetic view of the Balinese, there was a powerful lobby within the Netherlands Indies régime, especially among the military, to whom memories of what happened in Lombok remained very vivid. The humiliation of the Dutch troops in Lombok, and the distrust that this incited, cast long shadows.

Amlapura

The main town of the regency of Karangasem, Amlapura, is a pleasant, uneventful little market town set in the valley between Mt Agung and Mt Seraya, en route to nowhere at all. There is the usual bustle around the shabby central market building and the *bemo* station, but it is very subdued compared to Klungkung, Singaraja or even Gianyar. Most of the streets are green, flowery and residential. Even the telephone/telegram office is set in its own garden. Service is sleepy.

The town was badly damaged in the 1963 eruption, which wiped out the nearby village of **Subagan**; in one incident lava and mud swept through a mosque killing 170 Muslims who had gathered there to pray. It was at that time that the name of the town was changed from 'Karangasem' (as local people still call it) to Amlapura, in the hope of averting further disaster.

Amlapura has an interesting palace with relics of past glories, but little else. There are just two basic 'hotels' here, not the kind to attract you away from nearby Candi Dasa or Tirtagangga.

GETTING AROUND
Amlapura lies just off the main circular route around Bali's coast. If your bus or *bemo* is not coming directly to the town you will have to get off at the turning after Subagan and take another *bemo* into town (100rp): the main road goes up to Tirtagangga and the northeast. The *bemo* station by the market has buses and *bemo*s to Klungkung (700rp)

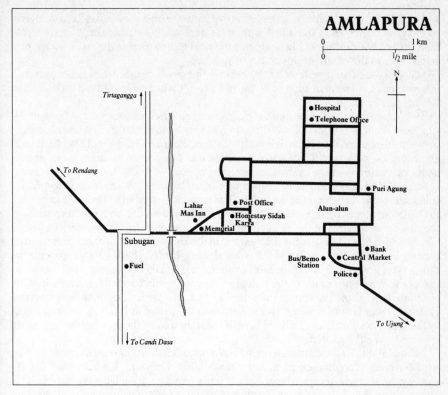

Amlapura Town

and Denpasar (1,250rp). Buses leave Amlapura to go north through to Tirtagangga (200rp), and around the coast to Singaraja (2,200rp).

TOURIST INFORMATION
There is no tourist office in Amlapura. The **post office** is on the one-way street as you enter the town just past the war-memorial statue, near the two hotels. The **telephone** office is on the right-hand side of the more westerly of the two roads leading to the north of the town. You can change **money** (but not travellers' cheques) in Amlapura, at the Bank Rakyat Indonesia in the market place by the *bemo* station.

There is a Pertamina **petrol station** in **Subagan**, to the west of Amlapura, on the Candi Dasa road.

Puri Agung Karangasem
The Puri Agung (also known as Puri Kanginan) is the nearest thing to a stately home in Bali. It was built by Raja Anak Agung Gede Jelantik, who ruled from 1902 to 1935. It is an attractive if rather eccentric palace, shaded by fruit trees and flowering shrubs which grow around carefully laid out pavilions.

The first courtyard of the palace is a narrow garden with a *candi gelung* (a high, tiered gateway) at either end, and filled with trees and shrubs—frangipani, 'flame' trees, hibiscus and bougainvillea. There are three big old lychee trees in the raja's family; one stands here in the centre of this courtyard.

You pay your entrance fee (200rp) beyond this first courtyard and collect printed information. A young man adopted by the raja's family is on hand to tell you anything else you need to know.

The Maskerdam reception building dominates the second courtyard. The name is supposed to derive from the word Amsterdam in honour of the close ralationships between the raja and the Dutch. It is built with something of the flavour of Dutch colonial architecture—some say it looks like a bandstand. The façade contains three superb doors carved by Chinese craftsmen imported specially for the task, and a decaying collection of pictures and photographs of the raja's family. A series of dingy, high-ceilinged rooms lie behind the verandah. Through the barred windows you can peer at the bedroom of the late raja—very Western in style—and his uniform; rooms containing the *gamelan* orchestras of the palace, one of them for *semar penulingan*, the love music which used to be exclusive to the palaces; and in the last room, a set of chairs presented to the raja by Queen Wilhelmina of the Netherlands (reigned 1890–1948), apparently in return for a generous birthday present from the raja of 20,000 florins.

Opposite the bedrooms are the toilet facilities, set behind a modern screen with an elaborate relief depicting scenes from the *Rajapala*. We are luckier these days than the Dutch traveller H. van Kol who visited Jelantik at the palace in 1902; he was impressed by the sophisticated tastes exhibited here, but flummoxed by the fact that the only toilet appeared to be the garden.

In front of the Maskerdam is an ornate building called the *bale pemandesan*, which was used for family ceremonies, particularly tooth-filing. Opposite this is the *bale lunjuk*, used by the *pedanda* during religious ceremonies. A water lily-filled moat surrounds a rather uninspired *bale kambung* (floating pavilion) or *gili*, a poor cousin of the *bale kambung* in Klungkung's Kerta Gosa. Here the palace held important meetings and dinners and entertained guests with the traditional dances and puppet shows.

To the south, east and north are more of the palace buildings still used as private residences by the descendants of the Karangasem royal family, said to number some 150; you may look through the gateways but do not wander. In the northern section another well-known building, the so-called *bale London*, houses furniture with a London crest, but it is not open to the public. A very old lady, the third wife of the old raja, still lives here amidst the chickens and the cooking pots in the crumbling splendour of the old buildings. Most of the younger members of the family have left to pursue more modern lives, as doctors, government officials and teachers in Denpasar or Sanur or abroad.

The private compound to the east contains a fine wedding house; and to the south among the small houses lived in by the family, is a large, rather desolate-looking *bale* used for staging public functions.

Further south are the **Puri Gede** and the **Puri Kertasura**; anyone wishing to visit these should write in advance. You can see the Puri Gede from the road (overlooking the *alun-alun*) now in a picturesque state of collapse with stucco reliefs peeling off their wire mesh bases, and carved and gilded doors swinging in the breeze.

WHERE TO STAY AND EAT

If you must stay here, **Lahar Mas Inn** (5,000rp single or double, including breakfast) is on the left of the road into town and possibly has the edge over **Homestay Sidha Karya** opposite the post office.

To eat, head for the central market where there are *warung*s and a *rumah makan*.

It is possible for groups to stay in some of the rooms in the southern part of the palace, the Puri Agung, but arrangements should be made in advance by writing to the family, or through the Badung Government Tourist Office in Denpasar. Costs are about 25,000rp for doubles for full board (which includes specially prepared Balinese food).

Around Amlapura

Ujung

Ujung, 3 km (1.8 miles) to the south of Amlapura, is the site of a royal water palace, now a mere skeleton of its former elegance, but worth visiting for the views alone. Known as the 'Floating Palace' for its moats, fountains, pools and pavilions, Ujung was built by the last of the rajas of Karangasem, Anak Agung Anglurah, and not completed till 1921. The raja was also responsible for the rather better maintained water palace at Tirtagangga. Most walls at Ujung are low, crumbling and covered in graffiti; none of the fountains works, the remaining stone carvings look sad and neglected. Part of the destruction was due to the earthquakes of 1963; the rest is due to the elements and three decades of neglect. Attempts to restore the palace in the 1970s were frustrated by another earthquake in 1979.

This was never a great architectural glory, more a curiosity. A Dutch guidebook of the 1930s says, 'The Water Castle . . . is of modern construction and has nothing about it typical of Balinese architecture: in fact, if the truth be told, it is typical of no architectural style at all.' It was in decline in 1963 when a nephew of the raja described it to Anna Mathews (author of an account of the eruption of Mt Agung, called *The Night of Purnama* (1965)): 'A great many pools and fountains. And life-sized animals in concrete, very gay, painted all sorts of colours, red and yellow and blue . . . they are decorated with little bits of mirror so that when the sun shines, everything flashes and the water sparkles . . . my uncle goes and sits in a little garden with his peacock and some flowers.'

The road out here, on the other hand, is well worth the trip: views are open and sweeping, the ricefields drop down to long stretches of black-sand beach beyond Ujung. A road now goes right round the eastern tip of the island to Amed on the northeast coast. The roughly hewn double peak of Gunung Seraya (1,175 m (3,854 ft) and 1,058 m (3,470 ft)) dominates the peninsula. The village, **Desa Seraya**, perched on its side, has beautiful views down to the sea, with its temple, **Pura Seraya**, high above it. This is a quiet, unspoilt part of Bali, where all the children rush out to say hello, and adults return smiles with that slightly bemused but friendly tolerance so characteristic of the village Balinese.

West of Amlapura

Candi Dasa

Early in the 1980s no one had heard of Candi Dasa. But after a decade of unplanned building along the shore, it stands alongside Lovina in the modest second rank of tourist development. It filled a very important need for Western visitors to the island—a seaside resort which didn't overwhelm with tourist trappings, a place where Bali is still Bali and not some kind of hybrid south of Spain for Aussies, and where cheap accommodation and food could be found similar to that in Ubud, but with a beach. Now its future hangs in the balance. Never really a village in its own right, Candi Dasa grew from a holy site of exceptional beauty (its name means 'temple of the 10 teachings') to a tourist resort centred on a small but picturesque beach. But the outlying coral reef which protected the shoreline was a source of livelihood for local people, who harvested the coral to make lime. Little by little through the 1980s visitors noticed the beach shrinking, as the erosion of the protective reef left it exposed to the predatory waves and currents. The government acted, but too late. By the time alternative sources of income had been found for the coral dredgers, Candi Dasa beach was nothing but a narrow strip of coral litter, revealed at low tide only. The ferocious pounding of the waves that now roared in without interruption has eaten away at the grounds of the *losmen*s which now cover every inch of the little bay, forcing *losmen* owners to invest in crude and unattractive sea defences. For a while it looked as if the peak of Candi Dasa's development was to coincide with the disappearance of the resort's raison d'être.

A new beach is now being built by the government. No one knows exactly how long it will take, what it will look like, or if it can literally turn the tide of Candi Dasa's misfortunes. In the meantime visitors keep coming, loyal to the inexpensive, traditional *losmen*, attracted by the good food, the peace and quiet, the rustle of the wind through the palms, and the drama of the pounding surf.

There are wonderful views to the hills across the bay to the west, often overshadowed by low brooding clouds. Out at sea there are four tiny rocky islands, mere dots clothed in determined vegetation, reminiscent of a Chinese ink painting. A lagoon lies at the eastern end of the beach, once one of Bali's most photographed landscapes, calm water reflecting palm trees and sky. *Prahu*s are pulled up where the fresh water runs into the sea. In the last few years the water level of the lagoon has dropped noticeably, so that, except at dusk, the place now looks dirty and abandoned.

Behind the lagoon, across the road, is a temple on two levels. At street level is the statue of the giantess Hariti, surrounded by her children. Childless couples come to Hariti to enlist her help. Beside the statue a long flight of steps leads up to a shrine on the hillside overlooking the bay. The shrine houses the remains of a stone *lingam*, symbol of Shiva, which is said to have the power to end a drought.

There is a Ghandian ashram to the west of the lagoon; it aims to keep a low profile, its first concern being the tranquillity of its setting.

Candi Dasa consists of a series of *losmen* and homestays strung out along the road for a distance of about 2 km (1.25 miles), though the 'centre', where the accommodation and restaurants are thickest, covers less that 1 km (0.6 mile). It's still a quite place. No one hustles to sell you anything. A disco which opened to the north of the coast road is usually deserted except for the odd hopeful Balinese youth looking for some action. There are few shops, few facilities of any kind apart from the restaurants. People come to Candi Dasa to swim, snorkel, walk, eat and read.

Tourist development is spreading along the bay, Labuhan Amuk, in both directions, and has already reached Balina Beach to the west (see pp.287–88).

GETTING AROUND
Buses and *bemos* heading east along the coast road from Klungkung to Amlapura all pass through Candi Dasa on a direct route from Kereneng bus station in Denpasar. If you are coming from Ubud, take any *bemo* going towards Denpasar and change at the Sakah junction. The journey by public transport from Denpasar or Ubud takes about three hours and involves a lot of stopping and starting. It costs 3,000rp from Sakah or Denpasar. If you drive, the journey takes about two hours.

In Candi Dasa, the **Pandawa Tour Information Centre** (opposite Sasra Bahu Homestay and near Lila Berata and the Pondok Bamboo Seaside Cottages) operates as a tourist office, where tours can be organized and cars, motorbikes and snorkelling gear rented. It is open from 8am (or earlier) to 6pm every day. There are four VW safari cars available for hire (the kind with the convertible tops and unreliable mechanics), one Toyota hardtop, and motorbikes.

On the opposite side of the road, to the west of Sasra Bahu, **P.T. Tri Ayu Graha** also has a couple of VWs to rent and organizes day trips for 7,500rp per person for a group of five. They will take you to the airport for 25,000rp. They also offer a four-day/three-night tour of Bali, stopping in Kintamani, Lovina and Ubud. The price is negotiable, depending on how many people are going and how many places you wish to visit.

There are other places with the odd car or motorbike to rent—look out for the signs. **Homestay Kelapa Mas** has some motorbikes, and **Sri Jati** has plenty of pushbikes to hire.

TOURIST INFORMATION
There is no official tourist office in Candi Dasa but Pandawa Tour Information Centre and P.T. Tri Ayu Graha should be able to solve most problems. They can arrange transport, rent snorkelling and diving equipment, organize tours (see below).

You will find a Perumtel **telephone** office just east of Sasru Bahu Homestay.

A **doctor** holds a surgery in the same building 2–4pm, and another, Dr Sindhu, has a surgery near the Tenganan turn-off from 4 to 6pm. Both are closed Sundays and holidays.

There is no **post office** but several shops, including ASRI in the Gusti Pub and Restaurant, sell stamps. ASRI also processes film. The *bis surat* (letter box) is outside Sanjaya Shop, near the telephone office. The shop sells stamps.

There are two **money changers** here, both of whom give acceptable rates for travellers' cheques.

Mr Nengah Gabiyuh at the Sasra Bahu gives **massages**. Expect to pay upwards of 5,000rp for an hour. Mr Gabiyuh is in his late 70s, but is as adept as ever. Besides giving an excellent massage, he is a *dukun* and a skilled healer.

Candi Dasa for the Restless
Candi Dasa is an excellent base for exploring east Bali. Local excursions include trips to the Bali Aga village of Tenganan; to Kusamba, where you can take the boat to Nusa Penida and Nusa Lembongan; to the 'bat cave' of Goa Lawah; to Amlapura, Ujung and

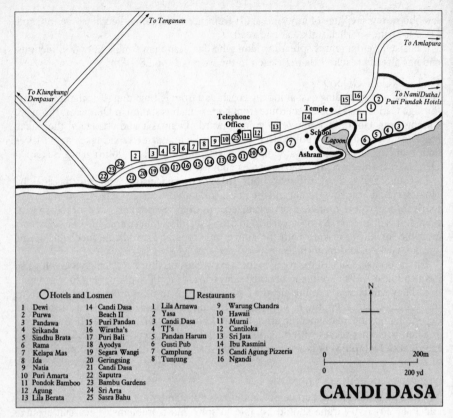

Candi Dasa

Tirtagangga. There are plenty of other places within a day's trip if you have your own transport.

In Candi Dasa itself the beach and the sea are the main attractions for swimming, sunbathing, snorkelling and boat trips. For scuba diving go round the bay to Balina (see below), where equipment and instructors are available.

Snorkelling around Candi Dasa can be rewarding, even if it is less spectacular than Lovina. The remains of the reef in front of Candi Dasa is not particularly good: the water is shallow and turbulent. It is better to sign on for an organized snorkelling trip. The Candi Dasa Book Store (in the middle of the village, on the north side of the road) offers a 'three locations' trip, departing 9 am or 12 noon, for 10,000rp. This takes you to three spots between Padangbai and Candi Dasa, travelling by *bemo* to Balina Beach and from there by boat. First, there is the 'shipwreck'—a large lump of scrap iron with an embryonic covering of coral; this is the least interesting of the three. Then there is the 'temple', meaning a coral stand lying near the shore on which stands a temple; pretty enough, but alas much of the coral is in poor repair. Lastly, there is the best dive of the three: the 'Blue Lagoon', an offshore pool surrounded by coral. This is also a favoured spot of scuba-diving lessons.

There is no great night-life at Candi Dasa. Two places now stage Balinese dances: **Lila Arnawa** restaurant, next to the lagoon, and **Pandan Harum**, next to Gusti Pub. *Legong, barong* and *kecak* dances are all shown here. Ask for the current programme from your *losmen*. Pandan has party nights with a 'Balinese buffet' (*babi guling* etc.), traditional dance and loud Western music to finish. Prices depend on what you choose to eat, but are reasonable.

WHERE TO STAY

There were 34 hotels and homestays or *losmen*s in Candi Dasa at the last count, all strung out along the one road. Stroll along and check them at your leisure; there are always rooms available since development raced ahead of demand.

By far the most sophisticated hotel is the **Candi Dasa Beach Bungalows II** (for reservations write to P.O. Box 270, Denpasar, tel (0361) 51205 or 51934; or telex 35199 IDA KUTA or 35515 ROSES). These are not bungalows at all but rather a two and three-storey hotel in traditional style, in two blocks on either side of the resort's only swimming pool. It is large by Candi Dasa standards (43 rooms); the rooms are spacious and well-furnished, the bathrooms positively luxurious. There is hot water and a fan in each room. Locally owned, it has the feeling of a Western-style hotel with Balinese charm. The restaurant serves Chinese and Western food at reasonable prices. Hotel rooms cost $25 US for doubles and $20 US for a single, including tax and service and breakfast—good value for this standard.

Nearby **Pondok Bamboo Seaside Cottages** is also good. The design is the more usual traditional Balinese bungalows, built round a pretty garden. Bathrooms are of the alfresco variety, with Western-style fittings; rooms have a small fan in each, and room service is available from 6 am–9 pm. The restaurant is right on the beach. Facilities include games, postal service, money-changer, safe deposit boxes and laundry service. Snorkelling, diving and fishing trips can be arranged, and there are pushbikes and motorbikes for hire. Rates are $12 US for a single, $14 US for doubles, and include breakfast but not tax or service. In the restaurant prices are comparatively high.

Puri Pandan Bungalows (for reservations write to P.O. Box No.6, Amlapura 80801, tel Amlapura 169) is also in this price bracket—10 cottages by the sea, pleasant rooms with attractive woven bamboo walls, laundry service, postal service, money-changer, bar and restaurant, car and bike hire.

In the middle price range are **Rama Bungalows**, next to the lagoon, and further east, **Sindhu Brata**. Rama has good two-storey thatched buildings with nice bathrooms for 12,000rp for a single, 19,000rp for doubles. Sindhu Brata has very big rooms with fans and splendid bathrooms for 15,000rp single or double.

The rest of the accommodation is mostly more basic. You get a small bare room with bed and table, a verandah with bamboo table and chairs, a *mandi* at the back and a good breakfast. Given the sun, the views, pretty gardens and the proximity to the beach, this is really not so spartan. Prices are from 4–6,000rp for a single, including breakfast, tea, taxes etc. Sometimes prices are higher for the beach-side rooms. Look for cleanliness and details which show care has been taken, such as rubbish bins being emptied, gardens swept, sheets the right size and so on, and try to get somewhere with a *mandi* as well as a shower in case the water supply gives out in the night. Not all places have electric lighting.

Kelapa Mas is one of the long-standing budget *losmen*s, and is recommended for its friendliness and its setting in a spacious grove of banana trees and coconut palms. The rooms are basic and not very well maintained, but if this does not bother you it is a good base from which to enjoy the sea and the air and the atmosphere of Candi Dasa. It boasts a small library and bookshop, and bikes for hire, and has a little restaurant ('**Warung Tambak**'). The people here are a good source of information about local temple festivals and walks.

To the west of Candi Dasa, near the Tenganan turn-off, there are a few places to stay, mostly basic. Just past the turn-off is **Bayu Paneeda Beach Inn**, with 12 good rooms in shared bungalows. As elsewhere, the beach here disappears at full tide but there is a platform for bathing off and a pleasant grassed sunbathing area with bamboo sun-beds. There is also a restaurant. Rooms are 12,000rp for doubles and 10,000rp for a single near the beach, 9,000rp and 7,000rp otherwise.

Further developments are taking place along the shore towards the headland to the east of Candi Dasa, beyond the lagoon. Accommodation here is similar to that of the rest of the village and is reached by following a very dusty, or alternatively muddy, track which leaves the main road as it sweeps left at about 100 m (100 yards) from the temple and lagoon. The track leads through a coconut and banana plantation past the very poor bamboo-screen homes of fishermen and the families who work the plantation. The *losmen*s are all on the sea front, buffeted by the breezes and with a feeling of remoteness from the gentle hubbub of Candi Dasa. There is precious little to do here beyond walking and contemplation: a damp and rocky beach is only revealed at low tide, when the retreating sea leaves pools inhabited by tiny tropical fish and hermit crabs. The sea is generally thought to be unsafe along this stretch. Nor are there any restaurants here at present, so you will have to make your way back along the dusty/muddy track to Candi Dasa for every lunch and dinner.

You could stay at the **Nani Beach Inn**: eight bungalows sturdily built to a high standard in concrete and glass under tiled roofs right by the sea. The prices are 10,000rp to 15,000rp per bungalow including breakfast. Next door is the **Dutha Guest House**, with traditional style bungalows if somewhat delapidated, but with a good position and similar prices. The best of this group, however, is **Puri Pundak**, with nine rooms at 10,000rp and four rooms at 15,000rp (including breakfast), stretching back from the sea and set in a pretty garden shaded by papaya, coconut and banana trees.

WHERE TO EAT

Candi Dasa has become renowned for its good, cheap food, from the traditional *nasi goreng*, *gado-gado* and fried chicken to the excellent local fresh fish (usually *kakap* or tuna).

Ibu Rasmini's *warung* near the lagoon is an old favourite—a proper *warung*, admirably resistant to fashion. **Warung Chendra** also has excellent Indonesian food, at bargain prices. For variation, **Hawaii**, **Tanjung Camplung**, and **Gusti Pub and Restaurant** are all worth a try. The original beachside restaurant **Puri Amarta** is still as good as any. **Restaurant Agung** has recently moved out to a new position by the

Tenganan turn-off, but the chips and the fried bananas with chocolate are as wonderful as ever.

Pandan Restaurant offers similarly eclectic fare: it also has cocktails and wine, plus a choice of three breakfast menus—Continental, American (with eggs) and Indonesian. For lunch and dinner they offer crab, and spaghetti Bolognese. The prices are reasonable for a good standard of food.

The in-place, however, is **TJs**—all very tasteful with its designer lily pool and a bridge to the higher eating level, cocktails and their own printed T-shirts. The fare is very much the same as in the Kuta branch of the same name, under the same ownership: whole food, salads and seafood as well as hamburgers and chips. Prices are reasonable for this type of place.

Tenganan

In a broad, flat, fertile valley at the foot of Mount Agung is one of the most extraordinary of Bali's tourist attractions. Tenganan is a strange place, with its own canon of legends and rituals. As you wander along the deserted grassy main street between two orderly rows of stone houses, you may wonder whether the entire village has become stage-managed for the benefit of gullible tourists. In fact, the village is home to the few surviving families of the Bali Aga (see p.258) community which once flourished here, and which still lives by rules and traditions handed down from pre-Hindu days when all of Bali was animistic, casteless, and all ownership of land and resources was communal. Tenganan is nearer to the coast than any of the other Bali Aga villages, yet it appears to have preserved its customs with more rigour. The village, hidden away at the end of its own road, has an isolated atmosphere, remote not just from the rest of Bali, but in time.

The people of Tenganan claim to be a community of chosen people founded by the Hindu god Indra. In legend, and as recorded in the ancient *lontar* chronicle, *Usana Bali*, Indra founded Tenganan before his great battle with the evil king Mahadanawa, an event which is associated with the victory of Javanese Hinduism in Bali. In other words, Tenganan ascribes to itself an earlier history than the rest of the island.

The laws of the village are aimed to preserve the purity of blood of its inhabitants, in honour of their sacred origins. Marriage outside this small community is forbidden; those who choose to break the rule are banished to the section of the village called Banjar Pande to the east and may not join in the endless round of sacred traditions and practices by which the village preserves the ancient order. Divorce and bigamy are also prohibited. In consequence, the population has shrunk to a mere 300 inhabitants, from 106 families. Incest taboos are strict and include first cousins (unlike Britain, for instance), but nonetheless the genetic spread is very narrow and an increasing number of marriages are barren.

Tenganan is a wealthy, landowning community with lands that cover some 1,000 hectares (2,500 acres). There is a legend that explains these comparatively vast territories. King Beda Ulu of the Pejeng dynasty, who was later to be defeated by the Javanese general Gajah Mada in 1343, had a famous horse which he loved dearly. One day the horse went missing. King Beda Ulu immediately sent out search parties, and promised a reward to anyone who found the horse. It was found near Tenganan, dead. The king, nevertheless, standing by his offer of reward, proposed that the local people should keep all the land around the place where the horse was found—as far as the smell of death extended. The king sent out an official to adjudicate. Surprisingly, the horse could be smelt over a vast area; seeing that the reward was getting out of hand the official eventually drew the line at the current boundaries. When he had gone, the chief of the villagers who had accompanied the official in his perambulation pulled open his sarong and revealed a lump of rotting horse flesh.

The wealth of the people of Tenganan has given them the leisure necessary to maintain their elaborate rituals. One tradition, with sacred connotations, has made Tenganan famous throughout the world. This is the cloth called *gringsing*, which is a unique form of double *ikat*, in which not just the weft threads but the warp threads as well are resist dyed before weaving, to form intricate patterns (see p.65). The cloth has distinctive colours of reddish brown, off-white and blue-black, and is decorated with abstract patterns of lozenges and squares, floral designs, and sometimes—most celebrated of all—images of the gods and figures from the *wayang* puppet plays. One such cloth can take five years to complete.

Gringsing, in the form of sarongs and sashes, is obligatory wear in many of the sacred rights of Tenganan. It is said to have magical protective qualities and is cherished throughout Bali; and it is also highly prized by textile collectors for its rarity. The tradition of *gringsing* weaving was threatened with extinction, but has been maintained with financial help raised by ethnologists in Switzerland and Japan. One of them, Urs Ramseyer, has written a short but detailed ethnographic study called *Clothing, Ritual and Society in Tenganan Pegeringsingan* (1984), which is available locally.

It may be possible to see weavers at work in their homes. Don't bother to attempt to buy this cloth unless you are a serious collector prepared to spend serious money. You are more likely, in the rather surly atmosphere of the village, to be palmed off with something grotesquely inferior to the real thing.

Because of the declining population, many of the traditions of Tenganan are gradually fading away. There are two surviving ones which you might come across. If you visit the village during the especially sacred fifth month of their lunar-solar year, which coincides with the winter solstice, you may see a primitive kind of ferris wheel made of wood, which forms a part of the ceremonies and represents an ascent to heaven to receive blessings. But in recent years the ceremony has been cancelled because there were not enough young people to take part. Another is *perang pandan*, a theatrical fight staged between two men or boys armed with clubs made up of thorny pandanus leaves and woven shields. These weapons inflict bloody scratches, which are taken in good heart as a form of ritual bloodletting.

It is as well to point out that some people, especially women, feel strangely enervated and out of sorts at Tenganan. This is sometimes ascribed to the effect of the journey up from sea level, but the Balinese from outside the village—who are never very complimentary about Tenganan—say it is the hostile spirit of the place.

GETTING THERE
Tenganan lies 5 km (3.1 miles) inland and uphill to the north of a turning 1 km (0.6 mile) to the west of Candi Dasa; it is clearly signposted. Since this road leads only to Tenganan, there is not much traffic. You can hitch a ride with any passing vehicle in exchange for a few hundred rupiah, or you can walk—an agreeable amble through the plantations and the smaller neighbouring villages of **Nyuhtebel** and **Pasedahan**.

For refreshments there is a small *warung* at the southern end of the village, next to a shop selling cloth; but there is nowhere to stay or eat a meal here. The nearest accommodation is Candi Dasa.

Mendira Beach

Some 3 km (1.8 miles) to the west of Candi Dasa is a small beach development in the village of Sengkidu. A big sign on the road directs you to **'Anom Beach Bunga-lows—500 m'**. The beach is white sand, with fine views of the bay. Anom's has 10 spacious fan-cooled rooms with attractive bathrooms for 25,000rp for doubles, 15,000rp for a single. There is a restaurant. **Amarta Putra** is also on Mendira Beach, seven rooms with bathrooms at 15,000rp, doubles or single.

The problem here is lack of facilities, and the prices are steep for such an isolated position.

Balina

The name of this small beach just around the bay from Candi Dasa is **Buitan**, but the tiny resort is usually referred to as Balina after **Balina Beach Inn**, the first hotel here. 'Ina' means 'pleasure', as also in 'Lovina'.

Balina is unusual in having been developed by the people of the nearby village of Manggis as a cooperative venture in an attempt to ensure that tourist money stays in the area and benefits the local community. There is a space put aside for villagers to set up stalls selling local produce during the day, complete with little wooden stands. Villagers come to the beach at the end of the day, wandering along the sand or chatting in groups while the children play or swim. Here you get a sense of the pageant of Balinese life, and need never be bored. That said, it is a fairly isolated spot, without the range of facilities offered by Candi Dasa; it is better if you have your own transport.

The beach itself is a narrow sweep of soft white sand in a wide open bay sheltered by headlands and the Padangbai promontory. Lovely open views and, at night, the twinkling lights of the fishing *prahu*s out in the bay make this an attractive spot, often invigorated by a stiff salt breeze and the sound of pounding surf. The beach is scruffy, with bits of sea vegetation and stones scattered on it, but the swimming is fine here, with clear, warm water and no dangerous currents. The *prahu*s of the Manggis villagers are pulled up on to the beach in the day time. They go out in the late afternoon and bring back fresh fish, which you can have cooked for your supper.

GETTING AROUND
The beach is down a short road off the main coast road between Padangbai and Candi Dasa. As you go east, the signposted turning comes just after the village of Manggis, unmistakable for its monument with a large painted stone mangosteen (*manggis* in Indonesian) atop.

*Bemo*s and buses run along the coast road between Klungkung and Amlapura. Pay 500rp from Klungkung, and 100rp on to Candi Dasa.

There is a jeep for hire at the Balina Beach Hotel and other cars, motorbikes and pushbikes are available in Candi Dasa.

TOURIST INFORMATION
Balina specializes in diving facilities, snorkelling and fishing (see below) but there is not much else here. The nearest place with any general amenities is Candi Dasa, 3 km (1.8 miles) round the bay to the east (see pp.280–85). The Balina Beach Hotel will sell you stamps, arrange for letters to be posted, rent you a jeep and organize local tours. They also have safe deposit boxes for your valuables.

Diving
The **Balina Beach Diving Centre** offers instruction and equipment for scuba diving and boats are available to take you all round the island for diving and snorkelling trips. Note that no certificate is required for scuba diving; you can learn here, but none of the diving is controlled by international diving club regulations. Prices range from a local trip to the 'Blue Lagoon' ($5 US snorkelling, $25 US scuba diving) to a trip to Nusa Penida ($20 US snorkelling, $45 US scuba diving), or all the way to Menjangan Island on Bali's northwest tip for ($25 US snorkelling, $50 US scuba diving). The Balina Beach Diving Centre has a representative in Sanur: contact Balipro, 129 Hyatt Road, Sanur 80227, tel (0361) 88777 or 88451.

WHERE TO STAY AND EAT
There are just two hotels in Balina and as many restaurants. The newest is called **Puri Buitan Cottages** (P.O. Box 444, Denpasar), though nothing resembling a cottage is in sight. The two-storey buildings are built on an absurdly crowded ground plan to second rate international style; there are 20 rooms, 16 standard and 4 suites, all with Western-style bathrooms. Prices are $25 US for a single, $30 US for doubles, plus 15.5% tax and service. The restaurant occupies the central court, fronting a small swimming pool, with the sea just beyond.

The **Balina Beach Hotel** has been open for several years, and has a pleasant settled feel to it. There are 41 rooms, mostly in small bungalows with a variety of standards and rates, ranging from $13 US for a single or $15 US for doubles for a small twin-bed room with bathroom and verandah, to a more luxurious $22 US for a single, $25 US for doubles. There are bungalows for $30–35 US and a 'family unit' for $35 US. Extra beds are $5 US. Rates include tax and room service and breakfast. All rooms are clean and well cared for. Rooms can be booked through travel agents; for reservations contact PT Bali Nusa Granada, Jl. Batu Jimbar 129, Sanur 80227, tel (0361) 88451, telex 35307 SANUR IA BANUGRA, fax (021) 3101832.

The Balina Beach Hotel restaurant is right beside the beach; fresh fish is a speciality. The bar is open all day. Lunch boxes are made up for guests going on diving trips or outings.

Padangbai

Not far from the Klungkung border a small turning off the main coast road takes you down a picturesque, leafy lane to the scruffy port of Padangbai, where the ferry leaves for Lombok.

Padangbai is important for its position in a neat curve of the well-sheltered bay, where international cruise boats sometimes lower anchor, for the ferry which docks at its small quay, and for its fishing industry. It is an unassuming little town. Some travellers looking for less tourist-ridden places to relax in head for the *losmen*s around the bay, where you can swim in clear water, lie on the white sand and watch the fishermen with their *prahu*s.

In the mid-1980s Padangbai was home to a curious vessel, pulled up on the beach under its own thatched canopy. This long, hand-worked wooden boat was built in the Philippines in the style of hundreds of years ago and bound for Madagascar, following the route of the first traders from the East to Africa. It was the project of an energetic part-time resident of Padangbai, Bob Hobman, an Englishman based in Australia, and was designed to prove how people in traditional craft could travel widely across the oceans. In a similar vein, in 1988 Padangbai hosted a motley crew of international adventurers bound for Australia in 'The Great *Jukung* Race' taking 10 local sailing boats (*jukung*s) along the islands 2,250 km (1,400 miles) to Darwin. To cater for these and other visitors, accommodation has sprung up at the far end of the beach, along with restaurants and car-hire facilities. Bob Hobman's impressive-looking house can be seen on the hillside beyond this. It must have a wonderful view: this is an appealing bay, a perfect crescent of sparkling blue, bounded by ageless olive hills and backed with waving palms. The accommodation is bound to increase in the next few years.

The port itself boasts little but a main street of unimportant *warung*s, cramped dark *losmen*s and frontless *rumah-makan*s, leading down to the large parking area and small concrete quay for the Lombok ferry. The buildings lining the street were notorious for the plague of rats which sported in the rafters, in blatant contempt for the hapless human diners beneath, impatient to get at the leavings. At the moment the main street is undergoing radical renovation.

Padangbai is said to have been the home of Empu Kuturan, the great 11th-century priest who introduced the caste system to Bali at the time of King Udayana and Erlangga. Way out on the promontory which guards the bay on the north side, a well-loved and cared-for temple, **Pura Silayukti**, is said to mark the place where Kuturan lived.

As with many of Bali's coastal towns there is a Muslim community here, some 50 Lombok families nestling around a shabby mosque near the dock. The call to prayer echoes across the bay, broadcast by loudspeaker in concert with the thousands of mosques throughout the archipelago.

GETTING AROUND
*Bemo*s operate along the road down to Padangbai from the main Klungkung–Amlapura route. Get a *bemo* direct to here from Klungkung, or get off at the turning and wait for one coming south. Fares are Klungkung–Padangbai 400rp, Padangbai–Candi Dasa 500rp.

There is a car rental service advertised at the end of the beach offering a Suzuki jeep. This is about the sum total of Padangbai's tourist services.

TOURIST INFORMATION
There is no tourist office here, and nowhere to change money (the nearest places are in Candi Dasa or Klungkung). There should be a **post office** on the main street if it survives current renovations; and there is a Perumtel **telephone** office at the entrance to the dock.

Details of the **ferry services** are printed on the side of the port building. The main service is to Lembar in Lombok, which leaves three times a day, at 9 am, 2 pm and 4 pm. The journey takes 3½ hours, and single fares are as follows: first class adult 4,775rp; economy class adult 3,325rp; motorbike 3,300rp; jeep 38,500rp; car 49,000rp; cow, buffalo, horse 3,000rp; pig, goat 1,500rp. A service connecting with Surabaya (Java) and Ujung Pandang (Sulawesi) also calls by here, once a fortnight in each direction.

WHERE TO STAY AND EAT

The most attractive places are all at the far end of the beach along 'Silayukti Street', a turning just north of the town which takes you round the back of the residential area and past a Chinese graveyard.

At **Homestay Padangbai Beach Inn**, the original *losmen* here, are 12 quiet, unpretentious rooms with attached *mandi*s for 5,000rp double or single, including breakfast. It has a friendly, homely atmosphere.

Sedana Kerthi Beach Bungalows has some old-style rooms with bathrooms for 6,000rp doubles or single, and some new thatched two-storey buildings in the rice-barn style, bathroom below and bedroom above, for 15,000rp double or single.

The smartest of the three, **Rai Beach Inn**, has nine lovely two-storey rice-barn style houses each with its own little garden; the ground floor is the sitting room, the upper floor the bedroom. You rent the whole house for 15,000rp.

None of these places has hot water or even electricity, which has yet to be brought down to this end of the beach—but there is a certain romance about the oil lamps.

Rai Beach Inn has an inviting restaurant serving Indonesian and Western food at very reasonable prices.

There is another restaurant here, on the edge of the beach, **Restaurant Celagi**, serving good food, painstakingly prepared, including fresh seafood. Again, prices are very reasonable.

There is also accommodation on the main street, near the ferry quay, such as **Losmen Madya**—not very enticing, especially in the vicinity's current state of decay.

North of Amlapura

Tirtagangga

Once a lovely water-palace, with fountains, carvings and clear fresh pools, Tirtagangga sits in the hills below Mt Agung amongst panoramic views of ricefield terraces, little rice temples and the sea glittering way below. The openness and coolness here after the tropical heat of Amlapura, 7 km (4.3 miles) to the south, make it an excellent place to stay a while to enjoy its tranquil beauty. You can swim in the palace pools and enjoy pleasant walks in the surrounding countryside.

The palace is much more recent than it looks. It was built in 1947, unbelievably, in the midst of national and international crises, by Anak Agung Anglurah, the last Raja of Karangasem. It suffered damage in the 1963 eruption of Mt Agung and then fell into disrepair. Little now remains of the original complex beyond the formal layout of the six large pools, and the soothing spirit of the place. The *losmen* and restaurant here provide a good base from which to explore the eastern coastal region and the slopes of Mt Agung.

GETTING THERE

There is a sign on the road from Candi Dasa just before Amlapura, for Tirtagangga, 5 km (3.1 miles). Turn left here. This is the main route to the northeast, and all *bemo*s going to the northeast coast and round to Singaraja pass through Tirtagangga. From Amlapura the fare is 200rp and the journey takes about 20 minutes. You can't miss the site of the pools, prefaced by the usual *warung*s and fruit stalls.

TOURIST INFORMATION

Apart from the *losmen*s, restaurants and a few local *warung*s, there are no facilities of any kind at Tirtagangga. The nearest post office, telephone and money changer (not travellers' cheques) are in Amlapura.

Swimming in the water-palace costs 500rp (children 300rp) for the top pool and 300rp (children 100rp) for the lower pool; there is a place to change inside the grounds. You pay at the entrance gate.

WHERE TO STAY AND EAT

A new *losmen* has been built actually inside the walls of the water-palace. It sits on the hillside with a wonderful view of the pools and the ricefields beyond. Called **Tirta Ayu** ('Beautiful Holy Water'), it has decent-sized rooms for 15,000rp for doubles, 10,000rp for a single, arranged in small bungalows at different levels. The price includes breakfast and also the cost of swimming. The rooms could do with another coat of paint, but the setting and the gardens could hardly be bettered. There is a restaurant in the hotel which looks directly over the water-palace. Service is poor, and the food is not exceptional, but prices are reasonable.

An old favourite at Tirtagangga is **Dhargin Taman Inn**, just outside the water-palace entrance. It is an attractive old *losmen*, well arranged in beautiful gardens, with very friendly management. The cheapest rooms here are still only 4,000rp for doubles, 2,000rp for a single. The better rooms have their own broad verandahs, still at reasonable prices. There is a restaurant here too, in a lovely open *bale*.

The other *losmen*s are across the road. **Homestay Rijasa** has standard cheap rooms. Further down the hill, **Taman Sari** has 25 rather uninspired but clean rooms, and a pretentious restaurant, all coloured lights and artificial grottos. They do, however, serve fresh fish which you can choose yourself from the little pool.

Kusamajaya is the other *losmen* here, also cheap, about 300 m (300 yards) up the road and a long steep flight of steps up the hillside. The view is terrific, but the rooms are nothing special. Strictly for the energetic.

Tirtagangga to Tianyar: the northeast coast road

Beyond Tirtagangga the road continues to wind up the mountainside with the rice paddies like a living blue and green quilt far below. As the ricefields come level with the road there is a rice temple out in the fields, where all the stages of rice growing are celebrated. Just after this, to your left, a small turning in the village of **Ababi** takes you through quiet rural villages to join the Bebandem–Sibetan road (see p.294).

The main road continues round the side of Mt Agung. At the village of **Abang** a signpost marks a turning left to Dam Andong—up a bumpy track leading to the higher slopes. To the right a small road leads up to **Ngis, Puraya** and **Basangalas**. This is the best point of departure for a tough but spectacular walk to **Pura Lempuyang**, which is one of nine directional temples (*kayangan jagat*) of Bali (see p.116). The temple is nothing special, but is sited on the summit of **Gunung Lempuyang** (768 m, 2,520 ft), otherwise known as Gunung Bisbis in imitation of the noise made by raindrops on the leaves of the trees. There are several paths up to Pura Lempuyang, but the one from Basangalas pursues a gentler gradient. The very energetic could continue on to the remote village of **Bangle** before descending to Bunutan on the northern coast—a total of some 20 km (12.5 miles).

Not long after Abang a sudden bend reveals some particularly beautiful rice terracing. The curves of a hilly promontory, carved with the grace and ease of a master-sculptor, juts out over the flat valley like a ship becalmed up-river. Beyond, the foothills of the mountain are terraced too. It is a perfect study in blue-green peace and reflected light. Around the next bend the scene changes abruptly. A great, brown-fleshed, Star-Wars monster of a ridge hunches over the plain below, its skin falling in folds pockmarked with elephant grass and black lava outcrops. It broods over the gentle, fertile valley, a primeval mass hinting darkly of the power of the volcano above it.

The road descends now towards the sea. **Culik** village is strung out for a couple of kilometres around the junction with the coast road to Amed (see p.293). Culik looks poor when you come from Amlapura, but decidedly wealthy when you reach it from the other direction.

Shortly afterwards there is another left turn which takes you up the mountainside. The road surface on this turning is very bad indeed. Beyond **Datah** village the bends become sharp and steep and the drops outrageous. You might just manage it with a four-wheel-drive jeep. The road winds around Mt Agung and continues on all the way to Gunung Abang—so the villagers told us. We didn't care to try. This is excellent walking and climbing country, and the villagers of Datah are friendly and helpful. School stopped on our arrival and all the children came out to pose unasked for a photo, while their teachers practised their English.

The coastal plain brings a great contrast to the fresh green landscape of the valley above. After Culik the colours are the burnt umber of sun-scorched earth, and the black of lava rocks, set against a very blue sea dotted with the sails of a mass of fishing *prahu*s. Strange-looking palm trees grow here, dwarf fronds sprouting untidily from bare elongated trunks. The coastal villages of **Datah** and **Kubu** are just a scattering of poor houses, depleted by transmigration. Wild-looking children, skin burnt dark by the relentless sun, will pop up and ask for money, friendly enough but with the hardened look of deprivation.

From here Mt Agung has a savage face, soaring monumentally from the foothills over which its debris is strewn. Not much grows on the parched land except cacti, some dusty specimens of the ever-present poinciana trees, and plantations of kapok. The odd patch of maize and vegetables struggles beside the village houses. Where water is available, white grapes are grown. At 3 km (1.8 miles) beyond Kubu is Tulamben.

Tulamben and the Wreck of the *Liberty*
There is a sign for Tulamben in the middle of nowhere, no houses or *warung*s, only goats and a small kapok production hut. The road winds on to the sea. You pass a fairy-tale

tree, like a dead dinosaur left behind in the evolutionary race. This is a cotton tree, its fin-like roots, with the texture of elephant skin, in folds round its trunk. In October its large pods split, showering the landscape with their silky filling.

The wreck of the *Liberty*, a merchant ship sunk by the Japanese is 1942, lies offshore a little to the west of the two *losmen*s here (see below). This is a popular diving spot for the watersports clubs. There is no equipment available locally and most people who come to dive here are on day trips from Balina or Sanur.

Tulamben is the place to come to if you really want to get away from it all—but stuck out here in this bare and merciless landscape, you could also be getting away from everything you came to Bali for. Some people will tell you that Tulamben is the 'new Candi Dasa': ask them if they have ever been here.

After Tulamben the road follows the coast closely through the local market village of **Rubaya** and then on to Tianyar and Buleleng regency.

WHERE TO STAY
Signposted and fronting on to Tulamben's beach of black pebbles there are two homestays more or less side by side. The **Bali Timur** is the better of the two, with fair rooms at 15,000rp for a double, 13,000rp single, with Western-style bathrooms—though the baths are not much of an asset since there is no hot water—lockable wardrobes and verandahs. Prices include breakfast.

The **Paradise Palm Beach Bungalows** next door hardly lives up to its name on any count, but is pleasant enough. Its four bungalows (8 double rooms) are basic but well looked after, clean, with their own bathrooms. Prices are 12,000rp for doubles, 8,000rp for a single, and include breakfast. There is a restaurant for guests here, offering fresh tuna bought from the fishing *prahu*s which come into a nearby beach.

Amed
Back at Culik, on the road from Abang, a right-hand turn leads you down through groundnut fields to Amed, home to a small, mostly Muslim community living off fishing and salt production. All along the beach, as far as the eye can see, are row upon row of salt pans—hollowed palm trunks in which the salt is dried. The salt is collected in baskets like up-ended ice-cream cones. This place is not accustomed to tourists. Show a camera here and people will down tools and hurdle the salt-pans with babies in their arms in search of an easier way to pay for their evening meal.

The road continues on to Bunutan, and right round the eastern peninsula to join the road from Seraya (see p.279). At present it is a bone-shaking, tooth-breaking surface of pebbles in a bed of dust, but it is due for improvement in the near future.

Northwest of Amlapura

The Mountain Road: Sibetan, Putung, Selat, Rendang

The roads above Amlapura towards Klungkung and Bangli, along the side of Gunung Agung, are among the most beautiful in all Bali. This route is a picturesque alternative to the main coast road and an attraction in its own right.

Several roads lead up to this route: those in best condition are between Candi Dasa and Amlapura. Turn north at Prasi or Subagan. More picturesque are the smaller roads at Padangkerta, 3 km (1.8 miles) south of Tirtagangga (the turning has no sign but is on a sharp corner in the village), and Ababi, 1 km (0.6 mile) north of Tirtagangga. The latter turning comes just after the ricefields level out with the road as you drive north; you see a temple in the ricefields on your right and turn left shortly afterwards.

The last two roads bump you through peaceful rural villages, where you share the road with rice farmers and women walking with heads piled high with produce; children playing, dogs, ducks, cattle; and the inevitable *bakmi* man, calling out his wares as he trundles his small glass-sided barrow. There is a feeling of quiet prosperity and the continuity of tradition. A loop in the road takes you to **Budakling**, said by some to have Buddhist connections, and below it, the village of **Saren Jawa**. Here a rather ugly mosque bears witness to the fact that this is one of the three original Muslim communities in Bali, whose origins go back to the Muslim priests who came from Java in Majapahit days to convert the Dewa Agung at the court of Gelgel (see pp.244–45).

The road goes on through the market village of **Bebandem**, and on through **Telaga**, **Putung**, **Pesankan** and **Duda**. Along the way the jungle presses in on either side, restrained by bamboo fences, interrupted only by village buildings and clearings. Banana trees, bamboo, *salak* and coconut palms crowd together, intertwined with a myriad of creepers, an illustration of the extraordinary fertility of Bali's lava enriched soil. Any destruction wrought by the 1963 eruption has long since been hidden by the fast-growing greenery. The road is narrow but serviceable.

At Putung a sign 'Putung Bungalows 600 m' directs you to the edge of a ridge. From here there is a magnificent view that takes in Manggis and Balina Beach directly below, the glistening blue straits of Badung. You can stay in this magnificent spot in two excellent new two-storey 'bungalows'—recommended. The *losmen* also has three large old rooms, almost colonial in style, that are clean and acceptable, though in need of redecoration. Rooms are 7,000rp for a single, 9,000rp for doubles. There is a restaurant here too.

It is said that Putung is a favourite haunt of *leyak*s (see pp.106–7), which appear at night floating around the hills and cliffs that run down to the coast.

Beyond Duda, a left-hand turn goes down to Klungkung via **Iseh** and **Sidemen** (see below). The mountain road continues on to **Selat** and **Rendang**, opening out onto the beautiful ricefields for which the area is famous—terracing fringed with coconut palms, hills, forests, dramatic ravines, and beyond them the central mountains: this is Bali's best. Don't miss it.

Two roads lead northwards up Mt Agung from here, one about 1 km (0.6 mile) beyond Duda, the other in Selat itself. These roads take you into the villages that were the most seriously hit by the eruption of Mt Agung in 1963 (see pp.93–94). **Sorga** (or Sorgre) (the name means 'heaven') is the starting point for a two-day climb to the scarred crater of Mt Agung (3,142 m, 10,305 ft), staying one night on the mountainside, usually at a place just below the tree line called Tirtha Mas, where holy water is collected. This involves a hard and fairly dangerous walk; you need good weather and trekking experience. Consult an expert guide; ask, for example, at the Badung Government Tourist Office in Denpasar. And remember that this is Bali's most sacred place; any Balinese who accompanies you will demand the correct attitude, and will want to carry out all the necessary propitiations to the gods.

South to Klungkung: Iseh and Sidemen

Just after Duda and before Selat, a left turn at a small monument in the centre of the road takes you down the mountain following the fertile Unda river valley. This is another exceptional route for views. The road clings to the steep east side of the valley, and bumps, winds and changes camber with the rapidity of a rollercoaster.

This road takes you through Iseh, where Walter Spies came to live in 1932, later followed by fellow artist Theo Meier. It is also where Anna Mathews and her husband came to live in August 1962, and from here they witnessed the eruption of Mt Agung from its earliest rumblings in February 1963, through its most terrifying violence. She describes this experience very vividly in her book *The Night of Purnama* (1965). Looking at this landscape today, it is hard to imagine the extent of desolation that it suffered during the eruption.

At 4 km (2.5 miles) beyond Iseh is Sidemen, an attractive market town. **Homestay Sidemen** perches on the mountainside above the road, overlooking the valley, with a view that stretches down to the sea and beyond to Nusa Penida. There are two huge rooms here; one has a massive four-poster as well as a single bed. For some reason they only do full-board, which makes it rather expensive at 25,000rp per person. The bar overlooks the valley and is a great place to stop for a drink—if you can face the climb (steps, no road).

There is a big dam on the river before you get to Klungkung. You join the road at **Paksebali**, just before the bridge. Turn right for Klungkung and Gianyar.

Besakih

Besakih is Bali's 'Mother Temple', the most sacred of all its temples. It is remarkable more for its location than for any intrinsic beauty—an austere mass of stonework

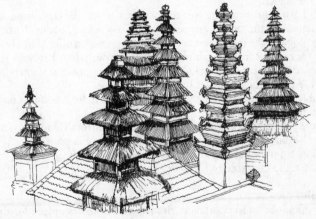

Merus at Besakih

295

decorated with umbrellas and pendants and the thatched roofs of a multitude of *meru*s, reaching to the sky in competition with the peak of Gunung Agung, on the flanks of which the temple lies. At 950 m (3,120 ft) above sea level, it is frequently doused in damp cloud that rolls down the mountain. It is not a joyous place: you get an uncanny impression of the darker sides of Balinese Hinduism and its burden of forever struggling with forces that dwarf all human concerns.

There are conflicting accounts of its origins. The site as a place of worship no doubt predates the arrival of Hinduism in Bali, set up in honour of the holy mountain. This is glossed over by the theory which claims that the temple was founded by the 8th-century missionary priest Danghyang Markandeya as a place of meditation. Markandeya is said to be the one who introduced the concept of the single god (Sanghyang Widi Wasa) to Bali, and to have created the tradition of daily offerings (*bebali*). His son, Empu Sang Kulputih, became the temple's first high priest. As a reward for these signs of devotion, so the legend goes, Shiva sent a son, Mahadewa, and a daughter, Dewi Danu (goddess of water) to the island and had transported there a part of the holy mountain of the gods, the Mahameru, to form Mt Agung. The evil king of Bedulu, Mahadanawa, set about spoiling the fun at Besakih's service of dedication, so Sang Kulputih appealed to Mahadewa and Dewi Danu to intervene. They in turn pleaded for the help of more senior gods, namely their father, Shiva, and Indra. Thus began the great battle between Indra and Mahadanawa which raged all over Bali before being settled bloodily on the slopes of Mt Batur (see Tampaksiring, pp.218–19).

By the 11th century Besakih was acknowledged as the major Hindu temple of Bali, according to inscriptions found on the site. Later it was the state temple for the Gelgel/Klungkung dynasty. Over the years new temples were added in honour of the great array of Hindu gods and various holy men and ancestral figures. Its position on Mt Agung establishes it as the home of the gods and the centre of the entire cosmos, according to Bali's sacred texts. It is now the state temple for Bali, of national significance, and is maintained with financial support from the government.

GETTING THERE
If you don't have your own transport the best way to visit Besakih is on an organized day-trip from any of the tourist centres: Candi Dasa, Ubud, Sanur, Kuta, Nusa Dua, Lovina. It is probably the most common of all the day-trips on offer. The cost depends on where you are coming from and how many are in your party: between 10,000rp and $20 US! Try to find a trip that includes some of the magnificent scenery on the lower slopes of Mt Agung, such as Bukit Jumbul.

It is possible to get to the temple by *bemo*, from Bangli or from Klungkung (400rp), but be prepared for some long waits.

If you have your own transport, take the road north from Rendang. The turning is about 3 km (1.8 miles) further, on your right. The surface is good.

The walk up from the parking area is a steep one; you may be glad of the motorcyclists who are on hand to take you up for 200rp or so.

The Temples
Despite its grandeur and importance, Besakih is not an easy place for the tourist to appreciate. It comprises a large and confusing array of temples, each with its own

significance to those that worship there, but obscure to outsiders. The complaint of visitors through the years is that you are badgered for 'donations'—for parking, entering, hiring a scarf. This is one of several places in Bali where brusque officials taking entrance donations add noughts to the figures entered into the books by donors and point angrily at these when anyone tries to give less. The recommended minimum is 500rp. Besakih reminds you that for the Balinese the temple itself is not significant, merely the place where the gods come to visit. Only when the gods are in residence does the building become holy.

There are about 200 structures arranged into 40-odd temples and shrines, in a series of courtyards. There are said to be seven terraces, seven being a significant number in religious mythology, but only six are apparent. The main temple at the centre is **Pura Penataran Agung**, which itself consists of more than 50 smaller temples and shrines. Pura Penataran Agung represents Shiva, the Destroyer, and is decorated with white banners. It is also the home of the *padmasana* (the high, tiered 'lotus throne') for Sanghyang Widi Wasa, the supreme god. The other two members of the *Trimurti* (the Hindu Trinity), are represented by **Pura Batu Madeg** (Temple of the Standing Stone) for Vishnu the Preserver, which has black banners, and **Pura Kiduling Kreteg** (Temple of the South of the Bridge) for Brahma the Creator, hung with red banners.

Every regency in Bali has its own temple here: for example Karangasem is responsible for Pura Kiduling Kreteg and Bangli for Pura Batu Madeg. Other temples in Bali are also represented by shrines at this site, so that the *odalan* of, say, Pura Luhur Batukau, can be celebrated here at the appropriate shrine by those unable to make the journey west to Batukau.

Because so many different gods, regions and temples are honoured here, there always seems to be some kind of ceremony going on. The main temple festivals, however, are Tawur Kesanga which takes place every year of the Balinese *saka* calendar; the Panca Wali Krama ceremony, every ten years (in theory, at least—but the only ones recorded are 1933, 1960, 1978 and 1989); and, most important of all, Eka Desa Rudra, approximately every hundred years. The last Eka Desa Rudra was held successfully in 1979 after the 1963 ceremony was annulled. These major ceremonies involve massive animal sacrifice to placate the evil spirits.

Surprisingly, given its position, Besakih suffered comparatively little damage from the eruption of Mt Agung in 1963. As everywhere else it was coated in a thick layer of ash and a number of wooden structures collapsed; and the main gate was toppled in the subsequent earthquakes.

Part X

BULELENG REGENCY

A stone relief at Pura Maduwe Karang, Kubutambahan

Buleleng district sprawls over the full length of Bali's north coast, hot, dry, fringed with dramatic black sand beaches and coconut palms. It meets Karangasem on the northeast coast not far from Tianyar, dips down to take in the southern slopes of the central mountains, and includes a good chunk of the jungle territory of Bali's National Park in the west.

This is the region that has been the most exposed to foreign influences in the past. **Singaraja,** its capital city, was a port for trading boats coming east on the route to the Spice Islands, and where Chinese, Arab and Bugis merchants—as well as wayward Europeans—came to exchange opium, arms and *kepeng*s for Balinese rice, fruit, cattle, pigs, fowl and slaves in the days before the Dutch asserted their control.

Singaraja—or to be more precise, its adjoining port, called Buleleng—was the chief means of entry right up to when the first Western tourists started to arrive on the island, long before there were any plans for an international airport down south. The city was the capital for the Dutch during their time on the island; Bali and all the Lesser Sunda Islands to the east (called collectively Nusa Tenggara), were governed from here until 1953. It has a completely different atmosphere to the new capital, Denpasar: the colonial influence is still evident in its residential perimeters with their wide streets, ample bungalows, unhustled pace of life.

The narrow northern coastal strip is the driest region of all Bali. Only on the slopes of the mountains is there sufficient rainfall for fruit trees and spices to flourish, alongside the dark green coffee trees that provide one of the regency's chief exports. Other exports are cattle, raised on the coastal plain, and copra. You can see grapevines and orange trees on the lower slopes and on the plains. There is much less rice cultivation than in the rest of Bali: because of the dry heat maize is the main cereal crop.

Without the rice terraces that are such a dominant feature of the landscape in the south, the north looks different; and the general absence of the *subak* (rice council) structure in the villages seems to give them a different atmosphere—less contained, less cohesive. But perhaps this is just the spirit of place in this open, arid landscape.

Buleleng regency has some excellent beaches, each with its own character, also plenty of places of interest to visit should sand and sea pall. Most of these are within day trips of the **Lovina** beach area, which has a good choice of accommodation and places to eat. Lovina is not like the other resort areas of Bali: perhaps because it is less accessible it has remained quieter, cheaper, less touristy, attracting long-term 'back-packers' and impoverished hedonists. But as everywhere in Bali, standards of comfort and prices are edging upwards to meet the needs of increasingly well-heeled visitors.

Historical notes

The first Dutch regency

Throughout history, and really up to the first decade of the 20th century, the history of Bali has tended to follow two geographic channels: one runs along the top of the island from Karangasem, through Buleleng to Jembrana; the other concerns the tangle of rajadoms to the south, which centred upon—and owed stronger allegiance to—the Dewa Agung at Gelgel and Klungkung. This division was exploited by the Dutch, and it was the swathe of land north of the mountains that first came under their direct control, following their three military expeditions in 1846, 1848, and 1849 (see pp.84–86).

The Dutch now had control of northern Bali and its principal port. At first Buleleng was placed under the rajadom of Bangli, but in 1854 Buleleng rebelled against this arrangement and the Dutch, at the request of Bangli, intervened.

Thereafter, Buleleng was ruled by the raja, who took 'advice' from a Dutch controleur. In 1882, Bali and Lombok were made into a combined Residency, and Singaraja became the headquarters.

In 1864 a powerful *punggawa* (head of a district) named Ida Made Rai returned uninvited from exile in Java, and managed to establish a more or less independent enclave around the village of Banjar, near Seririt, to the west of Singaraja. This provoked the Fifth Dutch Military Expedition in 1868, which was swiftly successful. Ida Made Rai was once more sent into exile, but not before establishing his mark as a hero of the north, where he is remembered not just for his rebellion but also for his exploits in love and his ruthlessness in dealing with his rivals in all fields of his activities.

Colonial rule worked its way slowly into the landscape of Buleleng. The Dutch built roads, improved irrigation, and allowed a number of plantations to be developed in the hills, primarily in coffee. Also, fearing an unwholesome influence on the Dutch troops and administrators, the authorities required all women to cover their breasts in public, introducing them to the *kebaya*—the short, long-sleeved jacket seen at temple ceremonies today.

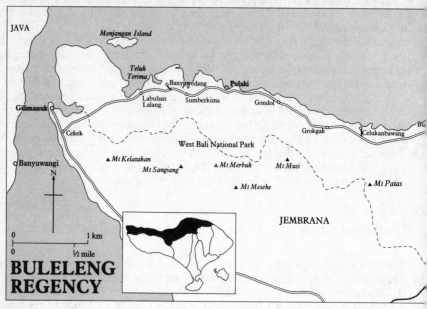

Buleleng Regency

The dawn of tourism

With Singaraja the capital of Dutch interests in Bali until the Second World War, the regency of Buleleng prospered, and in the early decades of this century it was the entry point for the new breed of visitors to Bali, the tourists. Arriving at the port of Buleleng on the KPM cruise ships, they would travel through the Arab and Chinese quarters to reach Singaraja, where they could book accommodation at the island's seven Government Rest Houses.

Tourism attracted an exotic array of residents. One enigmatic character of this time was a Persian-Armenian called M.J. Minas, who ran a cinema in Singaraja and, in the 1920s, went from village to village with a travelling film show. In about 1924 he was joined by an American traveller, photographer and cineaste, André Roosevelt, who became the representative of American Express and Thomas Cook, provoking KPM into building an office in Buleleng. André Roosevelt was responsible for encouraging the American journalist Hickman Powell to write *The Last Paradise*, the first book written in English about the island, published in 1930.

Another notable character of these early days of tourism was the flamboyant Mah Fatimah (or Patimah—the Balinese cannot accommodate Fs). She is described by Covarrubias as a 'gay and dignified middle-aged Balinese "princess"' who 'married a henpecked Mohammedan, changed her religion and became the prosperous owner of a silver and brocade shop and of a fleet of fine motor-cars for hire'. To engender trade she was rowed out to the liners brandishing a bottle and a bunch of flowers to greet the new

300

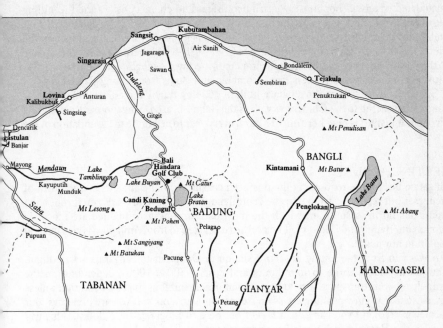

Buleleng Regency

arrivals. She was said to have belonged to the household of the Dewa of Klungkung, but happened to be out of town on the day of the great *paputan* in 1908, and so survived to take up her pioneering role in Bali's new era of tourism, celebrated by visitors as some kind of curiosity.

The Japanese used Singaraja as one of their two headquarters during the Second World War; but, on their return to the island after the war, the Dutch transferred the administrative centre to Denpasar, nearer the airport and the greater concentrations of population. With the development of tourism focussing primarily upon the south, the regency of Buleleng has quietly slumbered, content perhaps to be at some remove from the sharp end of Bali's changing profile.

Singaraja

The residential part of this capital city of Buleleng regency has an orderly, quietly prosperous, European bourgeois atmosphere, quite different from other Balinese towns. Here you can really feel the legacy of the Dutch. Those tidy-minded administrators are still present in spirit in the colonial style bungalows, the white-painted house of the governor, the broad streets.

Downtown Singaraja has everything you would expect a large town to have—shops and markets, cinemas, *warung*s, the occasional *rumah makan* and hotels plus the usual dilapidated concrete shophouses, garish neon signs and cinema posters and the stifling fug of exhaust fumes. As well as the bungalows there are new, expensive-looking houses built in the colonial style. Its population of 15,000 is noticeably more mixed than in the south; this is where Bali's more prosperous Chinese live, and there is plenty of evidence of the Arab traders of old in the appearance of the town's inhabitants. There are also Muslim communities of settlers from Lombok, and Bugis from Ujung Pandang.

Singaraja owes its name to a palace built in 1604 by Raja Panji Sakti. 'Singa' means lion, a beast sacred to the Chinese as well as the Balinese, as in 'Singapore'. 'Raja' speaks for itself. A festival is held here on 30 March every year to celebrate the foundation of the town.

GETTING AROUND

Singaraja lies on the road along the northern coastal strip of Bali, almost due north of Denpasar but separated from it by the central mountains. Several roads run through the mountains north to south, of which the most used and best maintained are those via Kintamani/Bangli and Bedugul. The northeast coast road from Amlapura is also in good condition nowadays.

*Bemo*s run from the Ujung bus/*bemo* station in Denpasar to Singaraja via Bedugul. The journey takes three to four hours and costs 1,500–2,100rp, depending on the antiquity of your transport. Try to find a comfortable minibus in good condition unless you particularly enjoy pushing *bemo*s on steep mountain slopes. If you are breaking your journey in Bedugul you can take a *bemo* from here to Singaraja for 1,000rp. This trip ends in the **Banyuasri** bus station, from where you can catch a *bemo* westwards to **Lovina**, the main location of places to stay in these parts.

You can also take a *bemo* direct to Singaraja from Kintamani in the mountains by Lake Batur. You go via Kubutambahan on the north coast. The journey takes around two hours and costs 1,000rp; the bus arrives at **Kampung Tinggi** bus station. If you are going on to Lovina you will have to cross Singaraja to Banyuasri bus station for the west.

*Bemo*s and buses travel right along the northeast coast regularly, from Amlapura via Tirtagangga, Tianyar, Tejakula and Yeh Sanih. From **Amlapura** the fare is 1,750rp. Start early if you are coming this way; the journey takes around three hours and you will have to cross from one bus station to the other in Singaraja if you want to go on to Lovina for the night.

Travelling west, the *bemo* fare to Lovina is 350rp; all the way to Gilimanuk costs 1,500rp.

In Singaraja itself the main means of public transport is still the *dokar* (pony and trap). There are also many small and smelly mini-*bemo*s (*tiga roda*) as in Denpasar; it costs 150rp to cross the city in one of these.

TOURIST INFORMATION

There is a tourist office on Jl. Veteran, next door to the Gedong Kirtya—at least, there is a building with a sign proclaiming 'Tourist Information', but in three out of three visits during office hours we could find no one around.

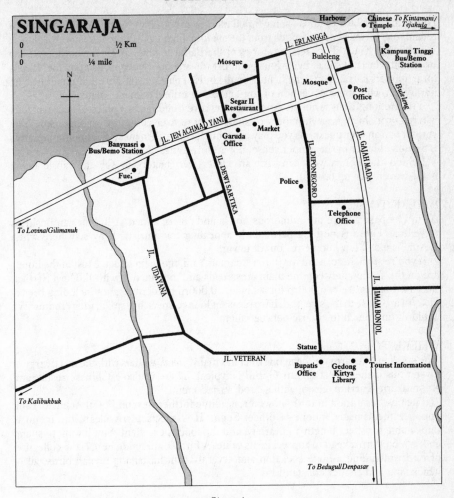

Singaraja

The **post office** is on Jl. Gajah Mada directly opposite the junction with the main road. Further south, betwen Jl. Imam Bonjol and Jl. Ngurah Rai, is the **telephone and telegraph** office. International calls can be made here, but the line is not very clear.

There is a **Garuda Indonesia** airline office on Jl. Jen Achmad Segar.

Gedong Kirtya

Singaraja remains a centre for study in Bali, particularly for traditional learning. The Gedong Kirtya (situated at the eastern end of Jl. Veteran) is a library founded by the

Dutch in the 1920s to house some 3,000 old *lontar* books; these are books made up of rectangular strips of dried fronds from the *lontar* palm on which the text, in the Balinese script, is inscribed. They tell the stories of the Balinese religion, lay down the *adat* law (traditional laws of social behaviour), and list the ancient remedies used by the *dukun*s (practitioners of traditional medicine) for all kinds of physical and spiritual ailments. The library also contains a collection of royal edicts inscribed on metal plates.

The Gedong Kirtya, not an especially attractive building, is a place of serious study where surprisingly large numbers of students pore over copies of original texts. The curator can answer questions you may have, but it is as well to make an appointment; this is a public library in the proper sense, not a tourist attraction.

Behind the library you can visit an *endek* (*ikat*) factory to see the fabric being hand-woven (see pp.65–66).

WHERE TO STAY

As in Denpasar, there are numerous hotels and *losmen* aimed at Indonesian business travellers. There is nothing particularly appealing for tourists. Why stay here when Lovina is just a few kilometres out of town?

If you're stuck here, head for Jl. Jen Achmad Yani, the main street. Most of the hotels are on the section between the main crossroads and the junction with Jl. Dewi Sartika. Standard prices are 5/6,000rp for a single, 10,000rp for doubles, not including break-fast. All are close to the street, all have pleasant lounge areas, but small, dingy rooms. We couldn't find much to choose between them.

WHERE TO EAT

The small market area on the main street has many *rumah makan*s with the usual array of mysterious dishes. **Restaurant Gandi** is typical. There is also a Chinese restaurant, **Restaurant Kartika**, clean, with a good, varied menu.

The best restaurant in town, however, is a little further west on Jl. Jen Achmad Yani, opposite the Garuda Indonesia office: **Segar II** is spectacularly clean, the menu is unbeatable for sheer length and variety, and the food is excellent. You'll want to spend about 5/6,000rp a head to appreciate its value. A further attraction here is the collection of birds, including a huge cockatoo and several beautiful talking mynah birds, all of which sing and chatter constantly.

East of Singaraja

The northern temples

To the east of Singaraja are some interesting temples, situated conveniently near to one another so you can see them all in a day. They are notable for the stone carvings which decorate their walls. In these northern temples the pinkish sandstone used is as soft as, but more durable than, the *paras* (volcanic deposit) stone used for temples in the south. Maybe the durability has encouraged the even more elaborate carvings. Especially curious to Western eyes are such non-religious details as bicycles, an aeroplane, two Europeans in a car being held up by a man with a gun, and other oddities.

You will notice many of the northern temples are set out to a pattern that is rather different from those in the south. In the north all the buildings in the inner courtyard tend to be grouped together, on a single base, rather than being scattered around. Some centre upon an arrangement of stepped pedestals, reminiscent of the Mayan temples of Central America.

Sangsit

At 6 km (3.75 miles) to the east of Singaraja lies Sangsit, where Bali's most ornate temple, **Pura Beji**, is to be found. To reach it, turn off the main coast road at the second of two small crossroads, and walk 500 m (0.3 mile) down towards the sea.

Pura Beji is a *subak* temple, dedicated to the rice goddess, Dewi Sri, and cared for by the local *subak*. Its style is typical of the north: a series of platforms rising from a stone base. The decoration is exceptionally lavish. Floral motifs intertwine with monsters and demons of all kinds—a storehouse of Balinese images, appealing because of the freshness and humour of the fine detail. The carvings cover the front panels and the inside wall of the temple. Two *naga*s (serpents) guard the entrance. There is a huge shady frangipani tree inside the spacious inner courtyard.

Beyond Sangsit another temple at **Bungkulan** is worth a visit for its unusual *kulkul* decorated with carved wooden heads.

Jagaraga

Back on the main road take the next right turn for the village of Jagaraga which lies 5 km (3.1 miles) inland.

The village of Jagaraga and its surroundings were the scene of fierce resistance against the Second and Third Dutch Military Expeditions in 1848 and 1849 (see pp.85–86). It was here that Jelantik assembled his men, armed with bamboo lances, and with rifles and cannon brought to Singaraja by British traders out of Singapore. On both these occasions, Jelantik had fortified the village well, setting up barricades in all the approaches; in 1849 a massive trench 8 m (9 yards) wide blocked off the main access route from the plains. But it was in vain; a lethal attack during the night of 15 August by the Dutch troops put an end to the long resistance of Jagaraga in a carnage that cost the Dutch 33 lives, the Balinese uncounted thousands.

The temple of Jagaraga is about 2 km (1.25 miles) beyond the village on the left-hand side. It does not look very striking from a distance so it is easy to miss. Take a look at the stone panels inside and outside the front walls. In amongst the flowers and alien figures of gods and demons are some very familiar European images: a man on a bicycle; a single-propeller aeroplane plunging into the sea; a European character fishing; someone else flying a kite; two men paddling a canoe; a house with a European sitting on the verandah; an open-sided car with a long-haired driver and two back-seat passengers (one with a neat, pointed beard); and the often reproduced open-topped T-Ford convertible with two Europeans being held up at gunpoint by a third man. They are witty, decorative, unexpected—and thoroughly Balinese.

A short walk onwards (south) along this road brings you to other temples with oddities of their own. There is a man holding a pistol and a seated European facing a man with a hoe on one; two men dressed in jackets and trousers carrying guns, accompanied by a dog, apparently threatening a monkey up a tree on another (the date on the gateway here is 1933). Another temple on the right-hand side of the road is decorated with a variety of fish and fishermen.

Sawan
Lying 1 km (0.6 mile) further to the south is the village of Sawan where instruments for the *gamelan* orchestras (or *gong*s) of northern Bali are made. The village is old, peaceful, lovely, tucked away in the foothills of Mt Batur on a road that leads nowhere in particular.

Turn right in the village for the *gong* makers: there is a sign. The villagers are very friendly, not much used to tourists, and they will be glad to show you around. Visit in the morning when everyone is at work. You can see the craftsmen casting the metal instruments, and others carving the elaborate wooden frames that support them.

Kubutambahan: A Man on a Bike
The road from the Central Mountains via Batur and Kintamani joins the coast road at Kubutambahan, about 11 km (6.8 miles) east of Singaraja. **Pura Maduwe Karang**, the biggest of the temples of the northern coastal region, is a further 1 km (0.6 mile) east of this point. It is a peaceful agricultural temple, elegantly laid out, with several fine stone carvings. To gain access, you may have to address yourself to the lady in the shop opposite the entrance to the temple: she has a key and will collect your donation. Pura Maduwe Karang means 'Temple of the Owner of the Land'; its purpose is to protect unirrigated land and crops such as the fruit, coconut, maize and coffee. The remains of temple offerings are buried by local farmers to ensure the fertility of the soil.

There is a much drawn and photographed carving on the base of the stone pedestal in the inner courtyard; it depicts a man on a bicycle with elaborately flower-decorated wheels riding through an explosion of floral design. Europeans have been interested in this carving since the beginning of the century. A 1904 picture shows a much simpler version: the ornate flowers on the wheels and decorating the man's sarong were added later during restoration after an earthquake. When we last saw the carving someone had added a real flower, freshly picked, tucked behind the rider's ear—a nice piece of Balinese-style visual wit.

Kubutambahan to Tianyar

The beauty of this road eastwards was appreciated by the Dutch, who called it the 'Balinese Corniche'. In the 1930s it went no further than Tejakula. Nowadays the surface is comparatively good right the way along the coast, although you may have to negotiate the odd muddy ravine to bypass roadworks and in the wet season you may have to ford several small rivers.

The road follows the shoreline, but as with most coast roads in Bali the sea is only rarely, and tantalizingly glimpsed. One reason for this is that the road is lined virtually the entire way with tall tamarind (*asam*) trees, forming a beautiful, dappled avenue, sheltering you from the fearsome glare of the arid landscape on either side. Whoever planted these trees, however, did not know the merits of variety. You will follow them for mile after mile after mile. They line the road to the west of Singaraja too.

This is, nonetheless, a delightful road: quiet, unspoilt, agreeably remote. The people here look genuinely welcoming—the children hello-helloing, adults waving, oncoming cars and *bemo*s giving way to let you pass. No one will try to force a sarong or a wooden chess-set on you here.

In the dry season the landscape looks thirsty and unforgiving, with tattered mountains to the south rising above fields of red earth. The lack of rain is signalled by the number of wells where villagers have to draw their water. Grapes grow in rocky terraces on the lower slopes near the villages; cattle graze amongst the coconut groves.

The coast is bordered by outcrops of rough volcanic rock dotted with clumps of cacti. Here and there are small bays of black sand where brightly-painted *prahu*s are drawn up beyond the reach of the tide. In the late afternoon farmers bring their cattle to the shore to bathe them in the sea.

The road passes through **Air Sanih**, with its freshwater pools, **Tejakula**, the main town of the district, and on through a few small settlements and villages to Tianyar.

Air Sanih

This small and beautiful oasis next to the sea, 7 km (4.3 miles) east of Kubutambuhan, makes an ideal stopping off point if you are exploring the temples of the north coast. (It is also known as Yeh Sanih, by the way: *yeh* and *air* both mean water, but *yeh* is Balinese and *air* is Indonesian.)

Air Sanih derives its name from the cool, clear, natural springs which feed the freshwater pools here, around which lies a pretty garden shaded by palm trees and overlooked by a pleasant hotel and restaurant.

Local people come to bathe and wash their clothes in the stream which runs from the pools to the sea. This is a lovely spot for cooling down from the north coast heat, refreshing on the eyes as well as the body. You pay 150rp at the entrance for the pleasure of swimming in the crystal clear water of the pools, accompanied by freshwater fish, frangipani blossom and the odd weed or two. The pools have been renovated recently and now have well-made edges and borders. Afterwards you can stretch out on the raised platform of one of the covered wooden *bale*s set up in the garden for this purpose. Or you can lie on the black-sand beach a stone's throw away. There are also tennis courts nearby, attached to the hotel but available to the public.

WHERE TO STAY AND EAT
The **Puri Sanih Bungalows** are in two groups. Those nearest the restaurant on the western side of the pools are the oldest, and show it. They have the benefit of their garden setting, with views through the palm trees to the sea, but there is a tawdriness about them. Given this, prices here are rather high: 8,000rp for doubles, 6,000rp for

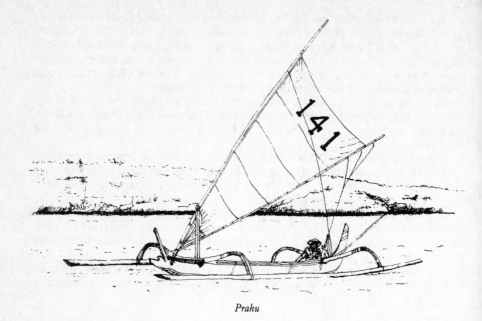

Prahu

singles for a fair-sized room with a shared bathroom; or 15,000rp for a double in a two-storey building with bathroom.

There are also newer rooms to the east of the pool, which are rather better, if somewhat soulless, with Western-style bathrooms. The best ones are very close to the sea and cost 25,000rp for doubles. Prices in both sections of the hotel include a simple breakfast; hotel guests, furthermore, do not have to pay to swim in the pools.

The other place to stay is **S.S. Beach Bungalows**, 200 m (200 yards) up the road, with five largish rooms at 7,000rp double or single, not including breakfast.

WHERE TO EAT
Up 33 steep steps opposite Puri Sanih Bungalows, the **Puri Rena Bar and Restaurant** has a splendid view over the pools and out to sea. The food is standard, at standard prices.

The other restaurant is part of the hotel. With a similar menu including fresh fish, it is rather over-priced, but it has a pleasant position overlooking the springs.

Sembiran

Some 10 km (6.25 miles) on from Air Sanih an unmarked turning to the right leads to Sembiran. The narrow road, just passable for cars, climbs precipitously up to this quiet mountain village perched on the hillside with the sea visible far below it, the view marred only by the tin roofs of the houses. The village is an interesting comment on the story of the Bali Aga, the original inhabitants of Bali. Like Trunyan and Tenganan, Sembiran was known as a traditional Bali Aga village (see p.258), and was described as such in government guides until recently. However, whereas the other two villages are well-known and well-frequented tourist spots, Sembiran seems to have all but forgotten its Bali Aga traditions. On the mountain to the back of the village stands the old temple, similar to that of Tenganan, just a group of rough stones on the edge of a ravine. In Covarrubias' day the dead were left out near the ravine with offerings, to be devoured by wild animals.

You'd be lucky to get anyone to take you there. The villagers here only laugh when you try to talk about the Bali Aga. Nowadays cremations take place here as elsewhere, and marriage restrictions are no greater than in other ordinary villages. It seems that Sembiran does not need tourists and has decided to merge with the rest of Bali. Presumably the same has happened to other Bali Aga villages in these mountain districts.

Tejakula

Just after the Sembiran turning, around 15 km (9.3 miles) beyond Air Sanih is Tejakula, the principal town of the *kecamaten* (administrative district) and the local market town. It has a modest, out-of-the-way charm but no particular distinction other than being the site of a famous horsebath. This is a very prosaic, and now unused, area near the sea where horses and cows were scrubbed down adjacent to the usual separate baths for men and women, still very much in use. Apparently the baths were built at the time of the Dutch. Tejekula is also famed for its *gamelan*, the *gong Tejakula*, which has its own unique sound.

South of Singaraja

The road leading directly south from Singaraja rises up through the valley of the Buleleng River. This is a beautiful route with great views of the mountains **Catur** (2,096m, 6,875 ft) and **Batukau** (2,276m, 7,465 ft). The road winds perilously; the scenery is breathtaking. Coffee and fruit trees grow in rich profusion on the upper slopes, behind you palm trees wave in the distance and there are views all the way down to the sea beyond Singaraja.

Gitgit waterfall

At about 35 km (22 miles) south of Singaraja, just before **Gitgit** village, you will pass the sign for Air Tejun on your right. The waterfall is reached by a walk of nearly 1 km (0.6 mile) through the ricefields and woodlands in the fresh, cool air of the hillside. It's about 15 m (50 ft) high, more dramatic than Singsing on the north coast. This is a pleasant place to visit if you are looking for somewhere to break your journey or have a picnic. You can swim in the pool at the foot of the falls.

Lake Buyan and Lake Tamblingan

Continuing up this road, Lake Buyan will appear below you on your right as you reach the top of the ridge. Soon after this, and before the **Bali Handara** golf course and hotel (see below), there is a small turning on your right which meets the main road at a sharp angle, taking you round Lake Buyan and the smaller Lake Tamblingan to join up with the road to Munduk and Kayuputih, and on to the main Pupuan–Seririt road.

This road remains high, affording glimpses of the lakes below through dense vegetation; the landscape is pretty sparsely populated, with scattered groups of houses. It is excellent walking country, and indeed you need to walk to enjoy the lakes fully. Shortly after the turning off the main Singaraja road, there is a track that leads down to the southern shore of Lake Buyan, but in the wet conditions of the mountains this may not be passable in a vehicle.

Beyond Lake Tamblingan the Kayuputih road drops rapidly, winding down a series of violent bends that demand great caution. The views over the north of the island are spectacular.

The village of **Munduk** once boasted a *pasangrahan*, or Government Rest House (since disappeared), with a covered swimming pool, and was a popular stopping place for early tourists, mainly on account of the views, but also for the air and the walks. Munduk is famous for its tradition of communal cremation—massive affairs which take place once every ten years or so.

Near Munduk is the site of a recent archaeological dig by an Indonesian team which unearthed a mass of Chinese ceramics, believed to be from the Sung (960–1279) and Ming dynasties (1368–1644) and earlier, also metal rings and pots and evidence of blacksmiths at work. It seems that a village on the shores of Lake Tamblingan was a religious, cultural and administrative centre between the 10th and 14th centuries AD, but the full story has yet to be revealed.

After Kayuputih the road continues towards **Mayong**, dropping down through coffee plantations and rice terraces built along deep gorges where the rivers have carved out their route from the central mountains to the sea. After Mayong you join the Seririt–Pupuan road.

The Bali Handara golf course
'Yesterday, paradise was just a dream. Tomorrow it will be a true dream', says the publicity of the Bali Handara Kosaido Country Club—a little hard for Westerners to grasp but one gets the drift. This is indeed a stunningly beautiful spot, and a 'true dream' for golfers. It is situated on the Singaraja–Bedugul road, just north of the border between Buleleng and Tabanan. The course, designed and maintained to very high standards, has an exceptional mountain setting, which will be appreciated by non-golfers as well. The green fee for the golf course is $33 US (less 25% if you are staying at the hotel); the hire of clubs $14 US, and a caddy $3.50 US.

WHERE TO STAY AND EAT
The Bali Handara Kosaido Country Club incorporates a first class hotel. It is not a great pleasure to behold, but it contains everything one might expect, and more: tennis courts, fitness centre, an excellent restaurant (with Japanese food) and bungalows with open

fires to fend off the chill mountain nights. Room rates range from $49 US (for a standard 'cottage') to $280 US for the Presidential Suite. Lunch and dinner cost between $12 US and $20 US. All prices are subject to the standard 15.5% tax and service charge. (Reservations: P.O.Box 324, Denpasar, tel (0361) 28866, (0362) 41646.)

Other accommodation and restaurants are available nearby, around Lake Bratan (see pp.336–37).

West of Singaraja

Lovina

Some 6 km (3.75 miles) to the west of Singaraja is the area known as 'Lovina Beach', which centres on the villages of **Anturan** and **Kalibukbuk**. Lovina in fact comprises a whole string of beaches, all with black sand, all baking hot, three of them with accommodation. The name was given to this stretch of coastline by the last Raja of Buleleng, Anak Agung Panji Tisna, a famous Balinese author who built a leisure retreat here (he died in 1978). The general purpose of his retreat can be deduced from the name he gave it: 'Lovina' derives from 'love' and '*ina*', which means pleasure (a modern, more prim explanation claims that '*ina*' is short for Indonesia).

The beaches were used by the people of Singaraja for recreation before they were discovered by Western visitors. In 1970 the same Anak Agung Panji built a hotel here, 'Tasik Madu'; a few years later the area was developing fast as a destination for travellers. From the start it seemed to attract a different sort of visitor from Sanur or Kuta. Accommodation here is mostly inexpensive, pleasant but basic, the food is good and cheap—no frills.

There is a definite 'Lovina scene'. The people you meet here all seem to have come for one or two nights and ended up staying several weeks. These are often long-term travellers, back-packers mellowing out after a few months travelling on the India/ Thailand trail. Here you encounter beachcombers Bali-style, beautiful young men who take Westerners snorkelling and much else besides. There are also Javanese prostitutes, here more for the holiday than with the expectation of meeting rich punters. The places where these colourful characters and their current mates hang out constitute Lovina's 'night-life'. It's all very relaxed and friendly. Someone plays a guitar, others sing or dance.

But it is not to everyone's taste. Those in search of unadulterated Balinese charm could be disappointed: traffic on the road that runs through this zone has become heavy and noisy; many of the homestay hotels are now owned by absentee landlords and are run by people without personal interest. Their indifference no doubt reflects the indifference of the increasing numbers of tourists who arrive here with only the beach, the sun and alcohol in mind. Those on the other hand who must have comfort will not appreciate the generally rudimentary quality of the accommodation. Yet this is due to improve: as the *atap* roofs of the bungalows reach the end of their lives many owners are pulling down the old buildings and replacing them with rooms of a much higher standard, and a much higher price. But is Lovina really the place for the wealthier tourist? The next few years will tell if Lovina can preserve its special charms.

311

GETTING AROUND

Lovina is a good place to base yourself for exploring the north coast. You can travel by the *bemo*s which ply regularly along the north coast, but a better way to get around in this region may be to hire a car and driver between three or four of you and take day trips. You can also make an arrangement with any motorbike owner who may be happy to take you around for the day for a fee of 8/10,000rp. There are motorbikes to hire informally, and pushbikes. Ask at your *losmen* or ask **Abdullah** at **Martha's Warung**—Abdullah is friendly, knowledgeable, and speaks good English. Pushbikes cost around 1,500–2,000rp a day. Don't forget it gets hot here, and the roads inland can be steep.

There are no regular car-hire places in Lovina. If you want to rent a self-drive car, approach any car owner to negotiate. The available cars are all old VW Safaris with the

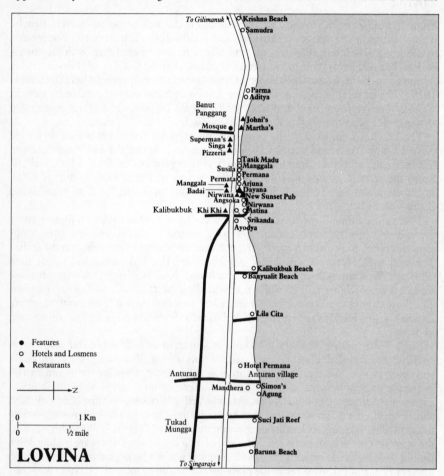

Lovina

exception of Simon's (of Jati Reef and Seaside Cottages) Suzuki Jeep. Again, ask your *losmen* or at Martha's Warung if you need advice. Expect to pay rather less here than the 30,000rp per day down south. But be warned: you are unlikely to find anyone with an insurance arrangement to cover you.

TOURIST INFORMATION

There is a small tourist information cabin in Lovina, opposite **Badai Restaurant**, which has a few ancient pamphlets on places of interest in the region, such as Pulaki and Teluk Terima. These are not visible on the counter, and requests for information meet with some surprise. No one understands much English.

There is no **post office** here but the **Manggala** *losmen* has a 'postal agent' where they sell stamps at slightly more than face value. The orange *bis-surat* for posting letters is about 50 m (50 yards) west of Manggala.

You can make **telephone** calls from the Perumtel telephone/telegram office at Kalibukbuk. International calls are channelled through Singaraja so it can take for ever to get a line, and it may not be clear when you do get it.

There is a **money changer** by the telephone office, and another one between **Permana Homestay** and **Arjuna Homestay**, open 8 am–4 pm. The latter becomes a **doctor's surgery** in the evenings. Rates of exchange are noticeably poorer here than at Kuta.

Beach and Sea

Most people come to Lovina to laze, swim and snorkel. It's a fine place for all of these. Despite the disconcerting look of them, the black-sand beaches are cleaner than beaches in the south, and they extend for ever, romantically fringed with coconut palms. To some extent these are working beaches, the *prahu*s are drawn up onto the sand. **Anturan** is a fishing village. You can see the *prahu*s being prepared for the fishing trip in the late afternoon. Kerosene lamps are hung round the boats. When the sun sets the lamps are lit and you can see them twinkling out across the blackness of the sea, calm within the protection of the coral reef.

Fishing trips can be arranged for late afternoon. The cost is 3–5,000rp according to season for a two or three hour trip. In the season (September and October in particular) you can hire a motorized *jukung* to take you out into the bay to watch **dolphins**. It means getting up before dawn (5 am) and heading out to sea in the last, soft hour of darkness. As dawn comes up over the volcanoes behind Lovina and mist hovers in the palms along the shoreline, as many as 200 dolphins will assemble in small schools and surface in gentle arcs around the boats, occasionally leaping into the air. The trip will cost around 7,000rp (including 'breakfast'—a cup of tea and a couple of fried bananas) and lasts about three hours. Ask in any of the popular restaurants.

The **snorkelling** off Lovina is excellent, over the great coral reef which extends along the shelf that lines the coast. It is best in the early morning. Snorkelling, like fishing, can be arranged through your *losmen*. Otherwise, catch the boatmen as they return from trips in the morning. The prices are as for fishing, 3,000 to 3,500rp for about three hours in the low season, 5,000rp per person at the popular holiday times. There seems to be a kind of unofficial association which maintains these prices. Snorkelling is less good during the rainy season, which affects the visibility.

It is very, very hot at midday in Lovina. Lying on the black-sand beach between 11 am and 4 pm is not recommended. These hours are best spent in the shade with a drink and a good book. For sightseeing get up and go out early. Things close up early at night, so early rising should not be a problem.

The night-time gathering places vary. Wander along the road to see where the action is. Sadly there no longer seems to be *legong* dancing at the **Rama Restaurant** on Saturday nights, but check in case it is reinstated.

Bull racing

Well, cow-racing, to be precise. *Sapi gerumbungan* is one of the great spectacles of Buleleng, although for some reason it receives much less notice than the Negara bull-races (see p.343). Those involved will tell you with some pride that the Negara races are all to do with speed, whereas the Buleleng races are judged primarily on elegance.

The races normally take place in the village of **Kaliasem**, part of the Lovina group of villages, on the day after the annual festival of Galungan, and on 16 August (the day before Independence Day), and sometimes on special occasions as well. The water-buffaloes—many of which are specially bred for the purpose—are finely decked out, with their horn and yokes decorated with leather crowns, pompoms, tassles, ribbons, flowers and banners, and with massive wooden bells slung around their necks. They are driven in pairs in front of a small wooden plough-like sled, usually by local farmers who not only have to control their team as they rush around the course of about 500 m (550 yards), but have to do so whilst performing graceful dance-like gestures.

WHERE TO STAY

There are no luxury class hotels, but *losmen*s are strung out along three beaches: Happy Beach, Lovina, and Kalibukbuk. Nearly all them are on the north side of the road next to the sea. The cheapest cost as little as 2,000rp (less if you stay a long time), the most expensive 30,000rp.

The chief disadvantage of the cheaper places is their proximity to the road. Several old favourites are now nearly deserted because of the increasing traffic.

Expensive

Samudra is inconveniently out to the west, but it has the attraction of being the only hotel in Lovina to have air conditioning and hot water in the rooms. The rooms are fine, but the prices of 25,000rp for doubles and 20,000rp for a single are steep for Lovina.

Moderate

Agung, Astina and **Jatur's** all have attractive gardens and cost 7,500rp for double or 5,000rp for a single. **Hotel Perama Beach Inn, Srikanda, Aditya** and **Lila Cita** are the same price: of these Lila Cita has the edge, being right on the beach. **Mandhera Beach Inn** is the same price, close to the fishing village of **Anturan** which is untouristy and interesting. **Suci Jati Reef** is just before Anturan, down a track through the cornfields. It has some insect-ridden rooms for 5,000rp (double or single) above the restaurant, but also some bungalows in the field behind the beach, which are excellent value for 10,000rp double or single. There are four neat white bungalows, each with four decent-sized rooms, garden bathrooms and private verandahs; fans, tea and towels included in the price. Suci Jati Reef has its own (basic) restaurant. The owner, Simon, also owns **Simon Seaside Cottages** at Anturan. Here there are eight lovely rooms, four upstairs at 30,000 rp double or single, four downstairs at 25,000 rp, with balconies front and back, set in spacious grounds. There is, however, no hot water.

Bunyualit Beach Inn is further west on Kalibukbuk. It has rooms from 8,500rp upwards, and a large restaurant: good value here. Still further west on a turning down to the beach, **Nirwana** is one of the oldest and largest of Lovina's *losmens*—33 rooms ranging from 'standard' rooms through 'superior' bungalows to two-storey, traditional style houses facing the sea, costing from 4,000rp for a single in the cheapest rooms to 30,000rp double or single for the houses. It even has a telephone, tel (0362) 41288. Given the rather shoddy state of the rooms and the very indifferent food in the restaurant the price is high.

Budget

The budget class accommodation clusters around the Lovina Beach area. From east to west are **Angsoka Cottages** (this one is off the main road), **Arjuna Homestay, Permana Homestay, Susila Beach Inn I & II, Manggala, Permata,** and well out to the west, **Krishna Beach Inn. Ayodya,** just before Arjuna Homestay, was described back in the early seventies as 'the best value in Bali'—now the road past is so busy it is hard to get a good night's sleep. But it is still the best of the budget places, with its traditional atmosphere preserved. You pay around 3/4,000rp. Prices in Lovina do not usually include breakfast, so ask about this.

Good Value

Our recommendation is to go to the **Kalibukbuk Beach Inn.** Kalibukbuk is both near enough to restaurants and right by the beach. It has over 20 rooms from 8,000rp to 15,000rp for a single, 20,000rp for doubles. The better rooms were exceptionally good value, attractive, well cared for, with fans and a good breakfast included in the price. Alternatively, go to the **Puri Tasik Madu** (Tasik Madu means, 'Sea of Honey'), recently re-opened and offering six fine rooms for 10–15,000 rp, single or double, with good bathrooms, fans, and breakfast included. This *losmen* is still run by the family of the last Raja of Buleleng, Anak Agung Panji Tisna.

WHERE TO EAT

Although Lovina cannot boast a great variety, the the food is good and fresh and very reasonable. Where presentation is lacking, good humour abounds.

Most places have their own restaurants so you can get something to eat on the spot if you're some distance from the main road. Menus are standard but a few places stand out as worth a visit. These are all around the Lovina Beach area. Nearest the Singaraja end on the left is the **Khie Khie Restaurant.** Kitchens are reassuringly in full view and it's an excellent place for fish. Just opposite is the **Srikanda Hungarian Restaurant,** which has a long-standing reputation for good food with a genuinely Hungarian touch to it. Further along on the same side of the road, **Nirwana's** open-sided two-storey restaurant is an essential stop for early evening cocktails. Sit upstairs and watch the spectacular sunset with a gin and tonic for that colonial touch: this is as glamorous as you'll get in Lovina.

In the road behind Nirwana is **Tony's Bar**, which claims to have 'the best food between Tahiti and Singapore'. This is a friendly place, which may not quite live up to its boast.

A short walk on the opposite side of the main road takes you to **Badai Restaurant**, easily the most popular eating place in Lovina. The atmosphere is strictly informal, with seating at long communal tables. This is a lively, convivial place to spend the evening; the food is fine, prices low.

The other most popular places are **Martha's Warung** and **Johni's Restaurant** next to it. Martha's (or Marta's) is run by the friendly Abdullah, source of tourist information for Lovina. Abdullah was born in Bali, but his parents come from Sulawesi. There are 13 varieties of the ubiquitous *nasi goreng* here, starting at 350rp, and altogether 150 items on the menu. Juices are good, and the banana, honey and coconut pancake worth the pilgrimage (350rp).

Johni's Restaurant also has a long menu but the food is not as good. There are always people here though; it's a good place later in the evening, for music and general entertainment.

Manggala and **Dayana Restaurants** have made attempts to smarten up and add variety to their menus, boasting European cuisine and clearly attempting to go up-market. The **Khi Restaurant** offers a superb range of food, specializing in fish cooked to Balinese or Chinese recipes, crab and lobster, frogs' legs and a range of standard Balinese dishes. The prices are reasonable for food of this quality.

For lunch near the beach, or just a drink after swimming, there are a couple of places open right by the beach. One is the old **Nirwana** restaurant by Nirwana Cottages, the other is the **New Sunset Pub** nearby.

Breakfasts can be a problem in Lovina if not provided by your *losmen*: independent restaurants tend to stay closed in the mornings. Ayodya's restaurant is open for everyone however, not just guests. Good value, but service and presentation are rough.

Around Lovina

Singsing waterfalls

You reach these by turning inland exactly 1 km (0.6 mile) after Samudra, coming from the east. There is a blue and white sign, on the beach side of the road, which could hardly be smaller and on the corner is a large shop selling bamboo. At about 500 m (500 yards) up the road is a sign which reads 'Singsing Air Tejun', translated poetically as 'Daybreak Waterfalls'. By the sign is a parking space.

You walk alongside the stream which runs down from the waterfalls for a further 500 m (500 yards). The path is easy, with fields to the left, forest to the right. In the morning and late afternoon local people come to the stream to bathe. The first cascade is about 15 m (50 ft) high, not spectacular, but it's a pleasant place to sit around on the rocks or swim in the pool (not clear water here though) or watch the Balinese boys hurl themselves into the water from a tree above the pool.

There is a **Singsing Air Tejun II**, a little bigger, which you reach by a steep climb up the rocks to the left of the first falls. The mud baths up here are reputedly very therapeutic for the skin.

GETTING THERE

If you don't have your own transport you can take a *bemo* to the turning off the main road, and walk from there. Or you can walk out from Lovina. It's a tough expedition in the heat of the day though—better leave early, especially if you want to catch a *bemo* back. As with all *bemo* routes there's not much available after 4 pm. Bring your own food and drink.

Buddhist monastery

The **Brahma Vihara Arama** ('vihara' means monastery in Indonesian) and the hot springs at **Banjar Tega** (see below) are about 2.5 km (1.5 miles) uphill and inland from **Dencarik**, which is on the main coast road at 9 km (5.6 miles) from Kalibukbuk. Both are beautiful tranquil spots, close enough together to be enjoyed on a day trip—a highly recommended excursion.

Some 20 years old, this Buddhist monastery was established by a local man as a study centre for Buddhism, combining both Theraveda and Mahayana traditions (i.e. those associated with, for example, Thailand on the one hand and Tibet on the other); the monks here come from all over the world. It sits high on the hillside looking down to the sea. Its dazzlingly white walls, contrasting with the orange roofs, orange-painted Buddha statues and orange-robed monks going quietly about their business, differentiate this place of religion from the usual Balinese temples. There are Balinese touches in the woodcarvings, but all in radiant technicolour.

There is a small *warung* outside the entrance where you can buy cold drinks—very welcome if you climbed up on foot.

GETTING THERE

You can take a *bemo* to Dencarik. There is a brightly painted sign pointing to the left on the main coast road. The road inland is very steep indeed: if you don't have your own transport your best bet is to use the motorcyclists who are on hand to buzz you up the 2.5 km to the monastery. They charge around 200 rp one way. You pass through **Banjar Tega**, where there is a turning to the hot springs.

Banjar Tega Holy Hot Springs

After the monastery the perfect place to rest is the shady tree-filled area around the pools fed by hot springs. The pools (entrance 300 rp) are beautifully laid out in a peaceful, green, shady wood, with plenty of places to sit and enjoy the peace and quiet of it all—unless your visit happens to coincide with the increasingly frequent tour buses. There is also a restaurant.

There are two pools: a shallow upper pool fed by eight ornamental 'naga' waterspouts, which in turn feeds through five spouts into a larger lower pool, which slopes away to a depth of 2 m (6.5 ft) and is big enough to swim in. The water is pleasantly warm, clean and refreshing. The upper pool is the hotter. Near the baths is a small pool where water, channelled through bamboo, drops some 2 m (6.5 ft) like a shower, but with such force as to act as a sort of painful massage.

These are the best hot springs in Bali. The installations have been built, or at least renovated in the recent past. There are now toilets and half a dozen changing rooms— you will need your swimsuit. And no soap may be used in the pools. The restaurant serves good Indonesian food; it is a little more expensive than those in Lovina but has a good view over the pools.

The nearby village of **Banjar** is the place where Ida Made Rai set up his virtually autonomous state in 1864 before being crushed by the Fifth Dutch Military Expedition Against Bali in 1868.

GETTING THERE
If you are walking down from the monastery, turn left at Banjar Tega to cut across to Banjar.

If you are going direct to the hot springs from the coast (by motorbike or car), continue along the road beyond the Banjar Tega turn-off until you reach Banjar (you can buy fruit at the market here to eat at the hot springs). It's a short way uphill from Banjar to the 'Air Panas' (literally 'Hot Water') sign, and a further 1 km (0.6 mile) along a dirt road to a parking place (small charge) by the pools.

There are *dokar*s available at Banjar to take you to the hot springs if you are on foot. They will also take you back to the main coast road for 250rp.

Lovina to Gilimanuk

As with the road east of Singaraja, the road to Gilimanuk follows the coastline, but the sea remains out of sight for most of the way. The road has a good surface all the way through to Gilimanuk. This again is something fairly new: during the Dutch period a good road (lined with the now-rather-too-familiar tamarind trees) went as far as **Seririt**, and a poorer road continued as far as **Pulaki**. To the people of Buleleng, Pulaki was the end of their world; beyond lay the unknown. This is an arid region, much of which is flat and sunbaked, with the roughly forested hills behind.

There is, however, a charm to this emptiness. There is a sense of space; the road is quiet and rural, the air balmy. There are coconut groves, fields of maize and terraces of grapevines, and also plantations of kapok trees with their strange, angular branches like electricity pylons. The villages are strung out intermittently along the road, with un-pretentious modern concrete bungalows interspersed with very poor traditional housing of wattle and thatch. They are distinguished from the browns and faded greens of the rest of the landscape by exuberant and untidy clumps of red and orange bougainvillea, hibiscus and poinciana. There would seem to be almost as many mosques as temples, but then their height and silver domes draw the eye more readily.

The mountains to the south of this road, from about Seririt onwards, comprise the **West Bali National Park**. The perimeters of this drop down to the coast a little to the west of **Sumberkima**, after which you enter a rather different world of forest and scrubland, variously luxuriant and denuded, depending on the season. This corner of Bali is undoubtedly remote, but it could be perfect for those in search of tranquillity surrounded by little else but nature.

Seririt

About 12 km (7.5 miles) beyond Lovina a main road turns off south over the central mountains by way of **Pengastulan** and **Mayong** (see p.310 for details of this road). At the junction is the unexpectedly large town of Seririt. This seems to be the name given to the whole area which covers Seririt itself on the coast, **Bubunan** on the main road, and Pengastulan which lies slightly further inland. There are plenty of shops here, a central market and an odd mosque that resembles a water-tower. The streets are a jumble of *dokar*s and bicycles, and there is not a tourist in sight. The area is notable for its grapes—vineyards stretch for miles around—from which they produce a sherry-like wine.

For the Seririt–Pupuan road, see p.346.

There is a Pertamina **petrol station** just to the west of the town.

Some 15 km (9.3 miles) further along the coast is **Celukanbawang**, which is billed by some as the main port of North Bali. It is hard to see what justifies this claim: a turning off the coast road leads down to a wharf. A couple of fishing boats lie at anchor in the bay. Maybe the place comes to a feverish pitch of activity every *other* day; we saw no sign of it.

There is now a more or less uninterrupted drive of 25 km (15.5 miles) to **Pura Pulaki**. At **Gondol**, 8 km (5 miles) short of Pulaki, there is a splendid deep bay of black and yellow sand inhabited by poor fishermen and the families living among the palms in wattle-and-thatch houses and supplementing their income with lime-kilns.

Pura Pulaki

Pura Pulaki is a temple that commands special reverence throughout Bali. Set into the base of a rugged cliff-face overlooking the road and the sea beyond, the temple is home to a large band of energetic monkeys, and the site of a legend about a Shivaist priest who landed at Pulaki from Java in the days of the Majapahit Empire.

It was near here that Danghyang Nirartha (also called Danghyang Bau Rauh, 'the holy newcomer', see p.183) arrived in Bali with his daughter Ida Ayu Swabhawa in around 1550. He came in the role of adviser to the ruler of Bali at that time, the celebrated Dewa Agung Batu Renggong, and was due to travel to the Raja's palace at Gelgel near Klungkung.

The priest parted from his daughter at a nearby village, promising to return in three days. After waiting seven days, Ida Ayu set out southwards to look for him, asking everyone she met for news of her father, but no one seemed to know anything about him. Frightened and angry, she inflicted a curse upon the villagers of the area, rendering them invisible. These invisible people, the '*wong gamang*' or '*bala samar*' are said to have special powers and are held in considerable awe: they feature in many of the legends, such as the story of the conquest of Nusa Penida (see pp.251–52).

Ida Ayu also became invisible. Later a new shrine was built on the site where Ida Ayu is said to have issued her curse, and this became known as Pura Pulaki.

Another version of the same legend tells that the priest and his daughter arrived at Gelgel but were forced to flee the court because the king wished to marry the beautiful Ida Ayu; but she was a Brahmana and he was of the lower Ksatria caste. Nirartha took refuge in Pulaki by making the city and its people invisible to the eyes of the pursuing king and his army.

There is something peculiarly lovely about this remote spot. The temple itself has undergone heavy renovation (completed 1983) and now boasts a series of terraces with brand new gates in black volcanic stone, and temple houses in newly varnished wood. They contrast strikingly with the tumble-down rocks of the cliffs to which the shrine clings. Sea-breezes rush around the empty spaces and rustle through the massive trees that shade the flat ground at the foot of the cliffs. To the west is the open sea, and in the distance the impressive silhouettes of the three volcanoes at the eastern tip of Java.

Just outside the perimeter walls to the east of the temple, there is a peculiar little squat, cross-shaped building of red lava. The interior has an odour of ancient primitiveness. This is a shrine to the *wong gamang*; look up to the cliffs above this and you will see the caves from which they are said to emerge to descend to the shrine during ceremonies.

There is a vastly over-optimistic car park next to the temple, signposted 'Short Stopover'; this is flanked by some forlorn *warung*s. The people are pleasant, only shyly insistent, not yet brutalized by tourism.

The troop of monkeys seems friendly enough, but show interest in them only at your own risk: temple monkeys are notoriously unpredictable. If you come by car, make sure the windows are firmly closed when you park: even then, you may have difficulty getting back in if a monkey decides it rather fancies it. Anyone who comes in an open-top jeep can expect a real party.

Banyuwedang

Just after the extended village of **Sumberkima** (called **Sumberkerta** on most maps), some 10km (6.25 miles) after Pulaki, the road splits. A sign to the right indicates 'Air Panas', which is the hot and sulphurous spring of Banyuwedang, well-used by local people for their medicinal value, but not inviting as a tourist spot. Water is almost too hot to touch; it collects below a concrete building on the seaward edge of a swampy bay lined with mangroves. The water on the upper level is drunk by the villagers, washing takes place on the lower level. It is said to be good for skin complaints—by which one assumes that it cures them rather than promotes them.

WHERE TO EAT
There are very few eating places along this whole stretch of road. There is a friendly *warung* next to the temple above the hot springs at Banyuwedang, good for a standard (but tasty) *nasi goreng* or *campur*. Alternatively you can retrace your steps to Sumberkima where the *rumah makan* 'Depot Mini' **Indrasari** on the north side of the road is run by a friendly family who offer excellent *nasi goreng* at a reasonable price. **Indrayani**, the owner's daughter will try out her English and teach you some Indonesian.

Teluk Terima and the West Bali National Park

Taking the left-hand fork just after Sumberkima, you enter the National Park (the Taman Nasional Bali Barat). The road takes you through impenetrable scrubland, dotted with one or two very poor villages, to a place called **Labuhan Lalang** on the bay of Teluk Terima, with groves of tall coconut palms and splendid views over the sea to the towering volcanoes of eastern Java.

Once a port of entry into Bali for traders, Labuhan Lalang and the nearby settlement called Teluk Terima are now the point of entrance to the West Bali National Park. Under an ambitious plan for tourist development, Labuhan Lalang is destined to become an up-market resort, to provide facilities for naturalists and walkers, and also for divers wishing to explore the depths around **Menjangan Island**, where Bali's best diving is to be found (see below). Teluk Terima will provide more primitive and low-budget accommodation for longer-term guests doing specialist studies.

There are nature trails through the park but for the majority of visitors it remains a mysterious and impenetrable region, home of such rare creatures as the *jalak putih*, the blue-faced white starling, and the wild *banteng*, near-extinct ancestor of Balinese household cows. No tigers have been seen here since the 1940s when the park was created.

If you want to walk in the National Park, apply first to the **PPHA** (a helpful abbreviation of the long translation for Directorate General of Forest Protection and Nature Conservation (see p.41) office, either at Jl. Suwung 40, PO Box 320, Denpasar, or at the one at the road junction at Cecek just south of Gilimanuk. There is also a PPHA office at Teluk Terima, but it is not always manned. Otherwise some travel agencies will make arrangements for you. For example, **Tunas Indonesia Tours & Travel** in the arcade of the Hotel Bali Beach Hotel offer a 'Safari' of two days and one night which includes a trek through the forest and overnight accommodation with food. The cost depends on the size of the party: $130 US each for two people, down to $60 US each for a group of 11–14.

Menjangan Island

Pulau Menjangan (Deer Island) is a small, low-lying island just to the north of the bay at Teluk Terima on which a herd of deer still roams amongst the wind-torn scrub. The reef around this island provides Bali's best location for scuba diving and snorkelling. The coral is protected by the government from the coral gathering (to make lime) that has done so much damage elsewhere. The water is crystal clear; there is shallow water for snorkelling, and the reef drops off precipitously on both north and south shores of the island—excellent for scuba diving (see pp.46–47). It is possible to make arrangements yourself for a boat with local boat owners, but most people based in the south of the island come here on special trips organized through tour agencies. These provide transport and equipment and will arrange overnight accommodation—the drive out from the Denpasar area is a lengthy 4 hours out and the same back again, really too much for a day trip.

The Shrine of Jayaprana

Just to the west of Labuhan Lalang, and a 10-minute walk up a stepped path, is the **Makam Jayaprana**, the memorial to Jayaprana, a great Balinese hero. Jayaprana features in several dance/dramas and puppet shows and his story is familiar to all Balinese. You will often hear it referred to as the Balinese 'Romeo and Juliet' (see below).

The path to the memorial is clearly marked, rising to the left of the road, opposite a parking place and *warung*. The memorial is said to be on the site of Jayaprana's death (his burial place is in **Kalianget**). It is a quiet spot, with wonderful views over the bay of Teluk Terima. It is also a marvellous cocktail of taste. Inside the brightly painted shrine are images of Jayaprana and his wife Leyonsari in a glass box, with *rangda*-like figures on either side, and several clocks. A separate *bale* is adorned with no fewer than 18 clocks of all kinds, some of which actually tell the time, and garish tapestries and paintings.

These are offerings donated by devotees eager to propitiate favour for a new enterprise, either in business or in love. For Jayaprana, although a secular figure, is said to exert a strong protective force on both these activities. His name cannot be taken in vain: it is said that no commercial venture called Jayaprana has ever succeeded. Every full moon there is a large ceremony at the Makam Jayaprana, and the *odalan* draws gift-bearing crowds from all over Bali and even from Java.

JAYAPRANA AND LEYONSARI

Jayaprana was orphaned as a baby by an epidemic which struck his native village, Kalianget. When he was seven he was brought to the palace and grew up under the king's protection. He was hard-working, handsome and kind, loved by the people and a favourite of the old raja.

When he reached the age of twenty, the old king told Jayaprana he should be married. To the surprise of all, Jayaprana did not choose one of the young women in the palace but went out into the village and chose Leyonsari, a beautiful young girl who sold fruit in the market. They fell in love and were married.

Unfortunately as soon as the old raja saw Leyonsari he too fell in love with her, and determined to have her for his wife. He began to think of ways to get rid of Jayaprana. He devised a plan to send him into the forest with a small troop to fight some rebellious villagers. Meanwhile he bribed his *patih* (Prime Minister), I Saunggaling, to murder him. This I Saunggaling did.

Leyonsari was told that Jayaprana had been killed by a tiger. She managed to evade the old raja's advances and one night had a dream that told her the truth of Jayaprana's death. On waking she killed herself, and the couple were buried together.

There is another version that provides an additional twist. Jayaprana is said to have been protected by a magical *kris*. When the *patih* received the king's instructions, he could not bear to kill one so popular as Jayaprana, and so told him what he had been ordered to do. Jayaprana, however, like a true knight, could not contradict the sanctity of his king's wishes, and so handed over his *kris* to his would-be assassin. While Jayaprana was putting down the rebellion, he was ambushed and, no longer protected by his magical *kris*, was killed.

According to a *lontar* book in the Gedong Kirtya library in Singaraja, these events took place around 1642.

WHERE TO STAY AND EAT

At the time of writing Teluk Terima is going through a transformation under the watchful eye of the Italian-German partnership of Ermanno Re and Edwin Bergmann, who also run Mandara Cottages in Kuta. They have been retained as consultants by the Balinese Government to oversee the development. This land was given to the veterans of the Independence struggle in Bali, the Margarana Association, to provide income for pensions from the copra plantations; it is now their wish to see it developed for the benefit of those wanting to make proper use of the Park. Labuhan Lalang is the site of an attractive and spacious 35-room development of medium price range, directly over-looking the bay, with full watersports facilities and a restaurant.

At Teluk Terima, a little to the west, the existing, rather simple accommodation called **Menjangan Cottages** (8 rooms at present) will be upgraded, but will retain its agree-able, low-budget character. New cottages will be built in the *lumbung padi* (rice-barn) style. This place will have a note of more serious study than the more tourist-oriented Labuhan Lalang, with rather longer-term guests. To find Menjangan Cottages watch out for the sign pointing right from the main road, and follow it down a rough track through a coconut plantation.

The restaurant at Menjangan Cottages consists of a shaded verandah in front of the main bungalow. It serves good Indonesian and European food at a reasonable price.

The road to Gilimanuk

As the road from Teluk Terima cuts inland towards Gilimanuk, the landscape under-goes a rapid change. Suddenly we emerge from a rocky, arid landscape into the lush, damp greenery of the south, with ricefields and neat villages. The road meets the southern road at Cecek: turn right for Gilimanuk, left for Negara and Denpasar.

Part XI

TABANAN REGENCY

Pura Ulun Danu, Candi Kuning

'Bali', began a leading article in the local tourist magazine, 'is very potential.' And nowhere is Bali more potential than in the regency of Tabanan. Just west of Badung, stretching from a coastline of massive black rocks and sandy bays up to the central mountains, Tabanan is a beautiful and unspoilt part of Bali. It is also richly fertile. It contains the best agricultural land in the island, which brings peace and prosperity to its villages, and until now has kept them out of the scramble for tourist revenue. That the situation is about to change fast has been made public and official by the establishment in 1988 of a government body, a 'Diparda', with the specific aim of developing tourism in Tabanan and neighbouring Jembrana. The project has already attracted investors from France, Italy and Japan.

In the northwest, Tabanan runs into dense forest, part of the wild, mountainous and unpopulated West Bali National Park (Taman Nasional Bali Barat). East of the National Park is an area of outstanding beauty on the slopes of Mt Batukau ('Coconut Mountain') (2,276 m, 7,465 ft) and Mt Catur (2,096 m, 6,675 ft). There is a well-maintained road north from Denpasar to Lake Bratan which lies at the heart of this region, and several not so good roads to the west of it, up to Jatuluwih and Pura Luhur. Both these parts are well worth visiting, Jatuluwih for its spectacular views and Pura Luhur for its brooding mystery; Lake Bratan for its lakeside resort of Bedugul, for the Botanical Gardens, the fruit and flower market at Candi Kuning, and the lovely Ulun Danu Temple, which appears to float on the lake in ethereal beauty.

The main road west, to the Gilimanuk ferry, runs inland through Tabanan and on to Antosari, where there is another turning north, and then drops down to the coast with glimpses of sea and small inlets. All round Tabanan is fertile agricultural land, similar to the plains of the east, covered in terraced ricefields, clumps of bamboo and waving palm trees, intersected by deep gorges carved out by rivers racing down from the mountains.

Only in one spot by the coast has tourism hit Tabanan in a big way: the coastal temple of Tanah Lot, perched on black rocks with its high roofed *meru*s standing out against a backdrop of deep blue ocean, is a perfect subject for picture postcards or for snaps for the folks back home, freshly discovered at sunset every day by throngs of people bussed in for the purpose. The coastal area just north of Tanah Lot has been earmarked for the next major tourist development in Bali, the focus of interest for those foreign investors in 'potential' Bali.

An aspect of Tabanan currently being promoted for tourism is the old *puri* of Krambitan, where guests can stay for a weekend of Balinese hospitality and culture within the palace itself. Tabanan prides itself on its traditions of dance and *gamelan*. The town of Tabanan (or rather a village just outside it) was the home of a great Balinese dancer and choreographer Mario (or Marya), who was an important figure in the 1920s and 1930s when dance traditions were undergoing a renaissance. Mario is known particularly as the creator of the *kebyar trompong* dance, in which a single dancer performs the larger part of the dance in a sitting position. In the early 1950s, John Coast (author of *Dancing out of Bali*, 1954) sought out Mario, then in his fifties, working in a government office in Tabanan and pursuing a passion for cockfighting. At John Coast's behest, Mario came out of retirement to create a new dance for the leaders of the dance troupe from Peliatan, which was about to embark on a world tour. The result was the charming *oleg tambulilingan*—the now famous 'bumblebee dance'. Mario's pupil, I Gusti Agung Ngurah Supartha, now continues the Tabanan tradition by creating new dances at the Arts Centre of Denpasar, of which he is the director.

Historical notes

Suttee

Throughout the latter part of the 19th century the Dutch presence on the island was becoming increasingly noticeable; their officers would tour the island, paying visits to the various rajas, negotiating borders and petty treaties. One of the Balinese traditions which particularly offended Dutch sensibility was the Hindu practice of *suttee*, whereby widows would immolate themselves on the funeral pyre of their dead husband—a controversial practice even in Bali. In the distant past, it appears Balinese *suttee* involved fairly extensive incineration, consuming not only wives but their numerous servants as well, who were stabbed to death before cremation. By the late 19th century the practice was on the wane. *Suttee* was banned by the Dutch in Buleleng in 1859, and pressure was put on the southern rajas to follow suit. By and large they seem to have done so.

In 1903, however, Raja Ngurah Agung of Tabanan died, having ruled since 1844. He left two ancient wives, brought up in the old tradition who declared that they would commit *suttee* at the cremation, which was scheduled to take place in great style seven months later, a lapse of time which allowed the prospect to be exhaustively aired in the Dutch press. The Dutch tried to persuade the new raja to restrain his father's wives but he insisted that the Dutch had no jurisdiction in the matter since all pre-dating treaties precluded the Dutch from interfering in the rajas' domestic affairs.

Despite the presence of two Dutch battleships off the coast, the cremation and the *suttee* took place; the old women, beautifully dressed in white, walked along a specially constructed bridge and flung themselves into the flames in the prescribed manner. It was to be the last public *suttee* in Bali. The next year the Dutch Resident declared the practice illegal, though it did continue to take place covertly for a while afterwards.

The events of 1903 caused the Dutch much embarrassment and irritation. It was in this atmosphere of tension that the Chinese merchant ship, *Sri Kumala*, ran aground in

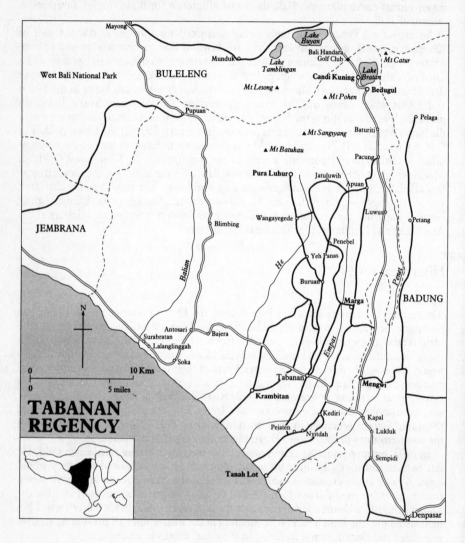

Badung in 1904, to be plundered by wreckers, a practice which the Dutch in Indonesia had repeatedly attempted to stamp out through numerous treaties with the rajas.

The people of Tabanan were somehow seen to be implicated in the plundering of the *Sri Kumala*, and when, in 1906, the Dutch invaded the south and took Badung, they next marched on Tabanan. Whereas the Rajas of Badung and Pemecutan had led their people in ritual *puputan*s, the Raja of Tabanan sued for peace, against the advice of his high priest. Accompanied by his son and heir the raja made his way to Denpasar, where he met the Dutch and proposed that they make him regent of Tabanan, to be assisted by a Dutch controleur—as in the other Dutch-controlled provinces. But the Dutch took him and his son prisoner and threatened them with exile. On seeing themselves thus dishonoured, and their cause lost, they committed suicide. The Dutch then moved into Tabanan and demolished the palace, reputed to have been the finest in all Bali.

Tabanan

The main town of the regency, Tabanan, is quiet and unmemorable. Because the area has grown wealthy from its agriculture, the government offices are housed in more than usually attractive buildings, but the rest of the town is unappealing, modern, dusty and traffic-ridden. A one-way system through the town, sweeping traffic on its course between Denpasar and points west, does little to alleviate the problem of through traffic.

If you ask people what Tabanan is famous for, likely as not they'll say *gondo* (also *gonde*), a spinach-like vegetable grown locally in between the rice plants, for which people will apparently make pilgrimages, arranging Sunday outings in order to buy some. It sometimes appears on the menu as *sayur pelecing*.

Tabanan makes no concessions to tourism. There is nowhere to stay here, and though there are several *rumah makan*s, nowhere special to eat. The only place of interest to the visitor reflects the preoccupations of the region: the **Subak Museum**, which presents the story of rice cultivation, irrigation and the *subak* system.

As you enter the town there is a large monument to two heroes of the 1946 War of Independence, I Gusti Debes and Wagimin, who died there.

GETTING THERE
Tabanan lies 21 km (13 miles) to the northwest of Denpasar, on the main road to Gilimanuk. As this suggests, it is well served by public transport. *Bemo*s leave regularly from Ubung station in Denpasar (350rp).

TOURIST INFORMATION
Tabanan has a tourist office on Jl. Gunung Agung. This publishes its own brochure, proclaiming the wonders of the regency. But you are likely to be better served by the Badung tourist office in Denpasar, whose former 'chief', I Gusti Ngurah Rai Girigunadhi, comes from Krambitan in Tabanan and has done much to promote the standing of the regency as a place of interest for tourists.

Museum Subak
The museum is situated on the south side of the eastern approach road to Tabanan, about 500 m (0.3 mile) from the town centre.

One of eight museums in Bali, this is the only one to focus on agriculture, in particular on rice cultivation and the social organizations that govern it. It contains models of a *subak* compound and of the irrigation system, and an interesting collection of tools used in rice cultivation (see 'rice', pp.101–103). There's also a model of a typical Balinese kitchen which shows the utensils used for preparing rice. The information leaflet at present available in the museum has some very confusing English but the attendants can answer questions and act as guides. Opening hours are 8–2 Mon–Thurs, 8–11 am on Friday and 8–12.30 pm on Saturday. There is no formal entrance fee but a donation is expected.

WHERE TO STAY AND EAT

There is virtually nowhere to stay in Tabanan, and little reason why you should want to. As for eating, you will have to make do with one of the modest *rumah makan*s of the town. Try **Budi Jaya** on the south side of the main road west, rudimentary but with tasty food, including *gondo*, all of which is prepared in conditions not recommended to the faint-hearted.

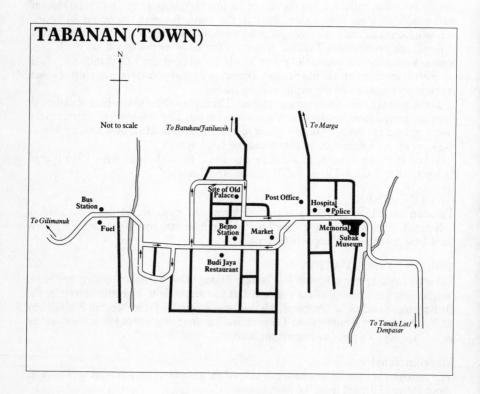

TABANAN (TOWN)

South of Tabanan

Pejaten: Ceramics

Until recently ceramics have been somewhat neglected as objects of interest to tourists in Bali, and this makes an interesting exception. To reach the pottery village of **Pejaten**, turn south off the main Denpasar–Tabanan road at **Kediri**. It's signposted to **Tanah Lot**. After 2 km (1.25 miles) the Tanah Lot road veers left, but you keep straight on. This turning is not signposted. Pejaten is 4 km (2.5 miles) south of Kediri, beyond the village of **Nyitdah**. The route is distinguished by heaps of pottery roof tiles that line the road. The main pottery is 3 km (1.8 miles) beyond Pejaten, reached by following signs with red arrows on a white background.

The actual name of the enterprise is Ceramics Project **'Banjar Pamesan'**—ask for this if you get lost. It produces some really lovely work of various kinds, including ware in white china clay glazed in grey-green celadon colours and light blue, and also unglazed earthenware plates, bowls and ornaments, including the spectacular decorations for the apex of thatched roofs called *jambangan*.

The project was founded with the help of funds from Holland and now employs some 45 people, including a guide who speaks English to deal with the comparatively few visitors who make the trek here.

This is a friendly visit, interesting and relaxing. You can buy pieces of pottery from the gallery (5,000–65,000rp), and you can enjoy a drink with a view across the ricefields.

Tanah Lot

The striking image of the black thatched-roof *meru*s clustered on this rocky little island is often used in promotional literature on Bali and may be familiar, but that does not detract from the drama of the real thing. Even the tacky little stalls surrounding the car park and along the road to the sea, have not quite succeeded in destroying the magic of the place. The shabby little sign that told tourists 'Take Sunset Photos Here' was removed at the time of the visit of a Jakarta dignitary and not replaced, but most of the clutter that surrounds recognized tourist sites in Bali remains. You'll be asked for donations every few steps of your way—for viewing the cave of the magic snake on the sands, for hiring a temple scarf, and for entering the area around the temple itself. But the beat of the waves on the jagged rocks sends up an impressive spray, and its splendid position makes this still one of the best temples to visit. Only at low tide can you walk across to the rock on which the temple is built; at high tide it is cut off from the beach, so that it resembles a ship at sea. Or rather it used to, but now the 'ship' has been moored to the mainland by a crude bridge for the use of worshippers. This is the subject of local controversy: there are those who agree that a bridge is necessary so that ceremonies can cater for the huge numbers that gather, without the added problem of negotiating the tide, but others feel that the bridge is not only an eyesore, but destroys the very charm derived from the temple's relationship with the elements. Still more offensive to the eye, however, are the huge concrete tetrapods that have been dropped into the sea (by helicopter) in order to prevent the erosion that threatened to destroy this famous site. Tanah Lot has been the

329

focus of a restoration plan, aided by the West German government at a cost of some 1.5 billion rupiah, and is now nearing completion. The World Bank provided funds for improving the access road.

The coastline to the north of Tanah Lot has been earmarked for tourist development—a series of medium-range tourist hotels, with a Japanese-funded golf course. Tanah Lot already suffers from the pressures of mass tourism, bussed in daily from afar, which detracts from its essential quality of peaceful isolation. It is hard to imagine that its charms can survive extensive tourist development on its doorstep.

'Tanah Let' means 'ancient land'; it is not clear whether the name derives from this or from 'Tanah Lod', which means 'land to the south'. Its history has to do with the legends surrounding the 16th-century Javanese priest Danghyang Nirartha, who arrived in Bali at Pulaki on the north coast, and went on to spread his teachings round Bali, founding some of the island's most scenically sited temples as he went. It is said that he was already old when he interrupted his teachings at Rambut Siwi temple to follow a mysterious light eastwards along the coast. The radiance emanated from a fresh water spring, which is still to be found on the sands beneath the rock, just east of Tanah Lot. The rock on which Tanah Lot was built was known to the local people as 'Gili Beo', meaning 'bird rock', because of its shape and it is said to have originally been attached to the land. Here, on the beach below **Beraben** village, Nirartha settled to meditate and preach to the people. As he gathered disciples the local holy leader, the Bendesa Beraban Sakti, became angry at the desertion of his own followers and demanded that Nirartha leave. Nirartha then used his meditative powers to move the rock on which he sat into the sea, hence another possible origin for the name of Tanah Lot—'Tengah Lot', meaning 'land in the middle of the sea'. He also transformed his scarf into snakes, to guard his refuge.

Some time later, the Bendesa Beraben became converted to Nirartha's teachings. As he headed off to the place of his final transcendance, Ulu Watu on the Bukit peninsula, Nirartha left his holy *kris* with the village headman as a sign of gratitude. The *kris* is known as 'Jaramenara', and is still kept in the Puri at Kediri, specially honoured and celebrated at the Kuningan festival every year.

The best time to visit Tanah Lot is at sunset, when the sky behind the temple *meru*s lights up in red and gold splendour. Take your camera and join the throngs. The *odalan* of the temple is held every 210 days on *Rebo Kliwon Lankir*, the Wednesday after Kuningan. Dances are performed on the beach below the rock. The Balinese flock to this ceremony, which is splendid indeed. Inside the temple itself, the three-tiered *meru* is dedicated to Nirartha, or Ida Pedanda Bau Rauh ('newly arrived holy man') as he is sometimes called, and the five tiered *meru* is dedicated to Sanghyang Widi Wasa, the Supreme Deity. Nirartha himself, however, founded the temple in the name of the god of the sea.

There are good walks all round this coastal area, and it is a lovely spot for picnics.

GETTING THERE

Most tour agencies in the resorts run minibuses to Tanah Lot. There are *bemo*s too, but it means waiting at the top of the turning, on the Denpasar–Tabanan road, and there is no guarantee of a return journey. The *bemo*s do not run after mid-afternoon, so if you want to see the sunset, you must go with a tour or use your own transport. The access road is good, and well signposted. Tanah Lot is 12 km (7.5 miles) southwest of the main road, and 31 km (19 miles) from Denpasar. *Bemo*s from Denpasar's Ubung bus station to the top of the turning cost 300rp and it's a further 200rp south to Tanah Lot.

WHERE TO STAY AND EAT
There are numerous little restaurants around the car park at Tanah Lot and overlooking the temple itself, all much of a muchness. **Dewi Sinta**, a large tourist restaurant by the car park, specializes in seafood, as well as serving Indonesian, Italian, Chinese and Japanese food, of medium prices and in agreeable surroundings.

There is nowhere to stay in the immediate locality at present, since most visitors are on tours, or come by hired transport, for the sunset.

Krambitan

Krambitan is an attractive little village, full of flowering shrubs and friendly people. It has a strong reputation as a centre for traditional arts and dancing. Indeed the name is said to derive from the Sanskrit *karawitan*, meaning 'art, music and dance'. The style of painting here is similar to that of Kamasan—the *wayang* style, with figures in semi-profile, in red, black and ochre, usually depicting scenes from Hindu mythology. The great Krambitan painters of the 1920s and 1930s, especially Gusti Wayan Kopang and I Macong, were nearly the last of the Krambitan tradition, but in the 1980s the traditional skills of this kind of painting were revived by the young painters in the village. Krambitan's traditions of art and dancing are now actively maintained by its two palaces, Puri Anyar and Puri Gede.

GETTING THERE
Karambitan lies about 8 km (5 miles) to the southwest of Tabanan. It is served by regular *bemo*s, but you are more likely to come here with your own transport or with an organized tour. The best road to Krambitan is a turning with a sign for 'Jalan Garuda', just after the huge red Gudang Garam hoarding as you round a bend outside Tabanan.

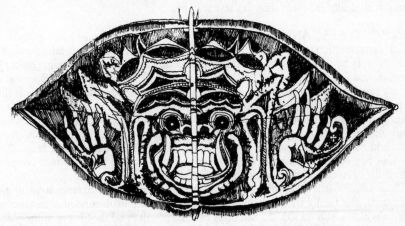

The face of Boma on a championship kite, Puri Anyar, Krambitan

Puri Anyar and Puri Gede

These two palaces date to the 17th century. They are both full of treasures: paintings, woodcarvings, antiques of all kinds, beautifully preserved, in lovely old buildings, set in tranquil gardens. These are not so much museums as places to stay and from which to observe and take part in a variety of cultural events and studies—dance, painting, even kite-flying and *lontar*-reading.

The twin brothers, Pak Oka (Anak Agung Ngurah Oka Girigunadhi is his full title) and Pak Rai, who now live in the palaces are the 9th generation descendants of Puri Gede's founder.

THE PURI NIGHT

Apart from their accommodation facilities (see below), these palaces offer special events for which visitors come from the resorts for an overnight stay and are treated to the best of Balinese hospitality and culture. The palace is beautifully decorated, and everyone dresses up for the occasion, which may be attended by many of the villagers. Guests are met in the street with a *janger* dance, and led into the first courtyard, where they are given *brem* (Balinese rice wine). Then there is a *joged bumbung* dance, in which Balinese girls extend their scarves to members of the audience, who then must partner them in the dance—to the best of their ability.

In the second courtyard a feast is meanwhile prepared around the central *cempaka* tree, with the lawn below it decked out in flowers. A second *gamelan* orchestra accompanies the meal, which is brought in by a procession of servers. The food is delicious, and offers a real insight into the palatable side of Balinese cuisine.

After a tour of the *puri* comes the final entertainment, a version of the *calonarang*, the eternal battle between good and evil, to the accompaniment of an excellent *tektekan* bamboo orchestra. This is a trance dance, a serious event during which visitors must not take flash photographs for fear of bringing harm to the participants.

The whole event is well organized and has the feel of a real celebration, involving villagers and guests, nothing like the rather distant 'tourist dances' put on at the big hotels, technically excellent though these may be.

WHERE TO STAY AND EAT

The accommodation is all in the Puri Anyar, and must be arranged in advance through a tour agent, or by contacting the Denpasar tourist office, or Rai Girigunadhi (office: Jl. Surapati no. 7, Denpasar, tel (0361) 23399 or 23602). There are only 12 rooms of varying standards and sizes, but all are clean and spacious, with a definite family feel to them. Some have the style of a Balinese palace, richly ornate, with a four-poster bed. Or, if you want to be really Balinese, you can sleep on a splendid four-poster in an open *bale*. The rooms are in the process of being modernized so that each has a private shower, hot water and a fan. Accommodation is with full board, including real Balinese feasts. You can also buy soft drinks and beer. The service is traditional Balinese too: everyone beautifully dressed and discreet, with wonderful smiles.

The brothers will take you round the *puri* and explain the arrangement of the courtyards, the family temple (which has numerous shrines decorated with Chinese porcelain plates, still intact), the offerings and ceremonies and the history of the place. Famous visitors have included Princess Lilian and Prince Bertil of Sweden, King

Hussein, Mick Jagger and David Bowie. Prices are by negotiation, according to your length of stay, but are reasonable by the standards of the international hotels.

The coast

To the west of the turning for **Antosari**, the main road to Gilimanuk turns south towards the coast and the surfing beach at **Soka**. The scenery here is magnificent: huge open expanses of ricefields roll away to meet the jungle-covered lower slopes of **Mt Batukau** and the forests of West Bali National Park. It is on a scale you do not see elsewhere in Bali. The miles and miles of water-filled terraces are interspersed with little clumps of palms and fruit trees round neat, tiled houses.

As you head south you see the blue expanse of sea above the tops of the palm trees. Beneath the palms are perfect picnic places on the grassy banks of little sandy coves, protected by the black rocks on which the surf pounds and sprays. Two pieces of advice for picnickers: do not sit right under a coconut palm, and keep an eye open for snakes if you're in long grass.

Balian Beach Club

This is the only accommodation along this stretch of coast; it is just to the east of the village of Lalanglinggah, near **Surabratan**. It is owned by Australian surf enthusiasts, as one might guess from the 'biscuits and vegemite' on the menu, and has a lovely view of the peaceful blue-green inlet below the coconut grove in which it is set. Non-surfers stay here to find peace and quiet in a beautiful spot, and to explore West Bali. Guests can rent a Suzuki Jimny jeep or a motorbike. There's a mechanic to fix them here too!

Most of the little bungalows built on the grassy hillside are very basic. You get bare boards and an open top bathroom for 10,000rp double or 6,000rp single, including breakfast. The new house is slightly more sophisticated, 17,000rp double or 15,000 single. There is an additional 5% service charge.

The restaurant here is not bad, and moderately priced. The fare is a pleasant mix of Western and Indonesian: specialities are pâté, homemade coleslaw, and curried chicken in coconut cream. There are also small fresh fish, whenever someone manages to catch any.

North of Tabanan

Marga and Candi Margarana

The village of **Marga**, 5 km (3.1 miles) to the northwest of Mengwi, was the site of a heroic last stand against the Dutch at the time of the War of Independence, by the hero I Gusti Ngurah Rai and his loyal platoon of freedom fighters. The Indonesians were in the process of marching into the mountains, hoping to draw the Dutch after them, and distract attention from the arrival of fresh troops from Java on the coast of Jembrana. They were hopelessly outnumbered by the Dutch, who also had air cover. On 20 November 1946 the final struggle took place, with the Indonesians making a valiant last stand and then fighting to the death—a last re-enactment of the dreadful *puputans* at the beginning of the century. Ngurah Rai is also commemorated by a fine statue on the approach road to the airport at Tuban, which is named after him. At Marga, in a rather forlorn area of open ground, a *candi* has been built in honour of the fallen, on the site of the battle. The visitor is greeted by a statue of the battle, in the usual infelicitous modern style; but note how some of the men are armed with *bambu runcing*, sharpened bamboo poles, which was all that many of them had as there were not enough guns (left over from the Japanese occupation) to go round.

The memorial was built in 1954, and on 20 November 1960 was officially declared a national monument on the anniversary of the battle. It is called the Margarana Monument (Margarana means 'the battle at Marga').It is 17 metres high, to commemorate 17 August, the date of the Declaration of Independence. The eight roofs indicate the month of August, while the four stairways and five pillars represent 1945. The pillars are inscribed with the symbols of Pancasila, the founding philosophy of the Indonesian nation (the star: god; the chain: democracy; the bull: nationalism; the banyan tree: humanity; rice and cotton: social justice).

Each of the inscribed insets around the walls of the *candi* itself contains a section of the final letter of defiance issued by Ngurah Rai to Lieutenant Colonel Termeulen, commander-in-chief of the Dutch troops in Denpasar. Ngurah Rai complains about the Dutch causing instability and economic distress to Bali. He requests that the Dutch address themselves to the central Indonesian government in Java for negotiations, requests the Dutch to leave, and then proclaims that his men will fight to the death. The letter ends with Ngurah Rai's battle cry '*Merdeka atau mati!*' ('Freedom or death!')

Behind the *candi* there is perhaps the most moving sight of this memorial, reminiscent of the war graves of northern France. In neat rows of *stupas*, all of the participants of this last *puputan* are commemorated. These monuments symbolize the unity of religion in the struggle: the tops represent the onion-shaped domes of mosques; the tiered roofs, the Hindu *candis*; and the base of each is marked with the religion of the individual which the monument celebrates—swastika for the Hindus, crescent and star for the Muslims, and cross for the Christians. There were five Japanese among the 96, who are given Balinese names, but whose monuments also bear Japanese inscriptions. A further six Japanese who died in the struggle elsewhere on the island are commemorated here too.

There is a small, modern museum nearby containing mementos and documents relating to the Margarana (open 8–12, closed Sunday); it is mainly designed for the education of local parties.

The monument is felt by the Balinese to be a symbol of pride in their fight for freedom, and the anniversary date is always celebrated by a mixture of religious and military ceremonies, involving the families of the dead war heroes.

GETTING THERE

There is a turning to Marga north off the main Denpasar–Tabanan road. Or you can turn left off the north road to Bedugul. If you are travelling by *bemo* you will need to get off at the junction on the north road and walk 2 km (1.25 miles). Note that there is nowhere to stay or eat in the vicinity.

Lake Bratan, Bedugul and Candi Kuning

The area round Lake Bratan is one of the most beautiful parts of Bali. It is approximately 1,240 m (4,070 ft) above sea level, so the climate is more temperate than in other parts of the island. Visit it for the outstanding beauty of the landscape, the temple **Ulun Danu** on the lake, the richly colourful fruit and flower market, Bali's botanical gardens and for the water sports facilities at the south end of the lake. Just to the north of the lake, but in the regency of Buleleng, is one of the island's most luxurious hotels, the Bali Handara, beside the international-standard golf course, (see pp.310–12).

GETTING THERE
*Bemo*s from Ubung bus station in Denpasar cost 2,000rp and take around three hours to cover the 48 km (30 miles). These sites are also on fairly well-trodden tourist routes, so you could join a party; or use your own transport.

If you are driving up from the south, the first sign for Bedugul is misleading. The right turn here takes you only to the Taman Rekreasi, where you have to pay to enter and then again to park, only to find that the temple and village are somewhere else entirely. Ignore the sign and keep to the left; this takes you up to the Botanical Gardens, the fruit and flower market, the villages of Candi Kuning I and Candi Kuning II and the lakeside temple. The whole area is referred to as Bedugul.

Lake Bratan

The lake itself has become a recreation area, by far the best place in Bali for water-skiing. Follow the sign to Bedugul at the south end of the lake to find the **Taman Rekreasi** ('leisure park'), entrance 200rp. Here you will find water-skiing training facilities and equipment for hire. Parasailing costs 12,500rp for five minutes, including equipment; water-skiing is 25,000rp for half an hour. You can hire a motorboat to go out on your own for 30,000rp an hour, or small wooden *prahu*s for rowing, 5,000rp an hour. If you want to fish off the bank it costs 500rp for a day, plus the cost of the equipment. There are also tours of the lake, at 2,000rp per person, minimum three people, or 14,000rp for eight people hiring together.

Apart from the buildings of the Taman Rekreasi there are only a few souvenir shops and the **Hotel** and **Restaurant Bedugul** down this road to the lakeside. There is no actual village here.

Some 5 km (3.1 miles) further north, on the Singaraja road is Bali's best golf course, up to international tournament standards: the **Bali Handara Golf Club** (see Where to Stay, below).

Botanical Gardens

South of the market are the botanical gardens, the **Kebun Raya** which stretches over 130 hectares (320 acres) of hillside, including a densely forested area on the lower slopes of **Mt Pohon** ('tree mountain') (2,065 m, 6,773 ft) to the west. The gardens contain 668 different species of tree, and 459 species of orchid in the orchid nursery. It is a great place for walking and for picnicking. The trees are labelled with their Latin names, but the notices are all in Indonesian. The only map is at the entrance, on a board. There are seats, walkways and toilets inside the park. It costs 250rp to go in and is open daily from 8–4.30.

Fruit and Flower Market, Candi Kuning

The market at the lakeside village of Candi Kuning is full of luscious fruits and masses of flowers that are not seen much elsewhere in Bali. You'll find it if you follow the road to the left, north of the Bedugul turning. Outside it is a comical modern statue of a corn on the cob sitting on a giant cabbage. The market is vivid with the colour of the local produce and the traditional clothes of the market women. It is hard to come away empty-handed from the stands overflowing with orchids and begonias and fern-like pot plants, or from the great piles of mouth-watering rambutan and mangosteen, sawo and watermelon, apples, pineapples, mangoes, durian, papaya, grapes, salak and the small, delicious, wild strawberries.

Pura Ulun Danu

The lakeside temple at Candi Kuning is another popular subject for picture postcards. It is beautiful in real life too. It appears to float out over the lake, and parts of it are only accessible by boat. Apart from when the tour buses arrive it is a very peaceful spot. You can take a dinghy out onto the lake to fish or just to contemplate the views of the green hills and the cloud-covered mountains surrounding the lake; or you can walk round the edge of the lake from here. A huge banyan tree shades the entrance to the temple and there are lovely gardens all around it. Outside the temple gate is a Buddhist shrine, with delicate carved stonework, to remind you how close the links often are in Bali between the Buddhist influences of the past and the more commonly recognized Hinduism of today. The temple was consecrated in 1633, having been founded by the first Raja of Mengwi. The *meru* with three roofs houses a large *lingam* and is dedicated to Shiva; the one with 11 roofs is dedicated to Vishnu; the one with seven roofs to Brahma. Dewa Ulun Danu is the god of the lakes, a manifestation of Vishnu.

WHERE TO STAY

The lakeside area has been a popular place for Westerners to relax since Dutch colonial times. Now, however, the hillsides around Bedugul and Candi Kuning are becoming increasingly populated with holiday homes for wealthy Balinese, to which to escape from the coastal heat. There are also several new places to stay overnight, and at which to eat.

The most luxurious accommodation in the area is further north, at the **Bali Handara Kosaido Country Club** (or Golf Club); it is in fact in Buleleng regency but is very much a part of the Bedugul landscape (see pp.310–12).

Just south of the Golf Club, still high above Lake Bratan, is the **Pancasari Inn**. Newly completed, this has a family orientation, with very well-furnished family suites for $50 US a night, complete with fireplaces for log fires to ward off the chill of the nights. There are also singles for $20 US. There is a restaurant here, tennis courts and a children's play area.

Down by the lake, the Hotel at Bedugul, next to the water sports complex, has rooms from 12,500rp single up to 35,000rp, at which price you get hot water and, incredibly, TV. There are two restaurants, one right on the lake.

On the bend of the road, up a steep driveway, **Lila Granda** is a former government resthouse which has accommodation in a pleasant old building perched on the hillside, looking down over a jungly valley but with no view of the lake. Rooms here have hot water, with attractive, well-equipped bathrooms and cost 30,000rp double or 20,000rp single, including breakfast.

A new place to stay— or just to visit for the lovely hillside gardens— is the **Ashram Candi Kuning** ('Losmen and Taman Rekreasi'). The entrance of the rocky driveway is just past the entrance of Lila Granda as you come from the south, on the opposite side of the road. The Ashram has been converted from old school buildings, and is aimed at groups, but individuals are welcome too. The eight rooms are two sets of four, each four sharing two rather basic bathrooms. For 15,000rp, double or single, a good breakfast is included.

Cheaper rooms are available at **Losmen Mawar Indah** on the road to the botanical gardens. The rooms are small, but pleasant, with their own bathrooms but no hot water: singles are 7,500rp and doubles 10,000rp. There is a pleasant restaurant, rather more expensive than you would expect though. The real budget accommodation in the area is attached to the place selling petrol, next to **Pelangi** restaurant in Candi Kuning I. The rooms here are basic but clean, and cost 5,000rp single, or 7,000 double, sharing a bathroom, without breakfast except for tea or Balinese coffee.

WHERE TO EAT

There are two restaurants by the lake at Bedugul near the water sports complex, one rather grandiose, another looking over the lake and the moored boats. The latter is good value. Pancasila Inn has its own restaurant, Bali Handara does too, of course, so does Lila Granda. Near the market are a few *rumah makan*s and *warung*s, plus a reasonable Chinese restaurant called **Pelangi**. The best *nasi campur* is at **Bogasari**, a *rumah makan* near the junction with the road to the Botanical Gardens. Try the Balinese red rice tea. The 'tea room' near the temple sounds appealing but is unfortunately not worth bothering with. We recommend you to stop for a drink at the open lakeside *bale* attached to the Ashram Candi Kuning (see above). A series of stepping stone paths up the hillside takes you up and around a treat of a floral display, and the view is lovely. There's a restaurant here too, certainly worth trying.

Pura Luhur Batukau and Jatuluwih

Gunung Batukau, or Batukaru, ('coconut mountain') is not much written about in the tourist literature, since it is much less accessible than Gunung Batur or Gunung Agung. At 2,276 m (7,465 ft) it is the second highest mountain in Bali, after Mt Agung. Its attraction is the wild beauty of the jungle scenery by the temple and the views from Jatuluwih.

GETTING THERE

You need your own transport for this journey, and preferably a jeep in good order, or a motorbike (but be prepared to get wet!). Some tour operators do visit Pura Luhur, however.

Turn north in Tabanan town itself for 13 km (8 miles), until you come to the small village of **Buruan**. Here there is a sign for **Yeh Panas** ('hot springs'). Turn left at the next junction, with no sign, and you come to a 'Yeh Panas - 300m' sign. At this point the road is little more than a track. The hot springs bubble into a rather murky pool beside a dilapidated building, and the stream flows from the pool down the hillside. The water is said to be healing, but it does not look especially inviting. There is a **warung** by the car/bike park. The place is not easy to reach except by your own transport, and really not worth any great effort.

Continue northwards a further 10 km (6.25 miles) to reach Pura Luhur in the village of Batukau. The road goes through many small villages unused to tourists.

Pura Luhur

When Tabanan was an independent kingdom, Pura Luhur was the state temple. It is very old and mossy, surrounded by dense, humid jungle. Rare orchids and butterflies flourish here. The rainfall, 700 m (2,300 ft) above sea level, is the highest of any place in Bali. Mythical tigers are said to roam in the forest, invisible except in spirit form manifesting themselves in a trance dance particular to the *odalan* of this temple.

Though remote, the temple is one of the most sacred for the Balinese, representing the spirit of the mountain upon which it is built. Some people find the atmosphere here quite uncanny.

An account of its history is recorded in an ancient *lontar* book. The site is said to have been founded by the Javanese Hindu holy man, Kuturan, who arrived in Bali in AD 1005. Further evidence came from the researches in 1925 of the great Dutch scholar of Bali Dr Roelof Goris, who made an archaeological exploration of a nearby bathing area. He found statues similar to those of Goa Gajah in Gianyar regency, which dates from the 11th century.

The temple buildings were destroyed by the raja of Buleleng, Ki Ngurah Panji Sakti, in 1604 in the course of the power struggle. According to legend, the raja and his troops were immediately attacked by millions of bees. They fled, believing they were being punished for their sacrilege. The temple was not rebuilt until 1959, though the local people continued to worship here among the ruins.

There are several shrines in the temple complex, some hidden well away in the surrounding jungle. There is also a lake with a shrine in the centre. The main temple is dedicated to the god of Gunung Batukau, Mahadewa, who is honoured by a seven-tiered stone shrine, with seven *meru* roofs. The shrines on each side of that to Mahadewa are to Shiva in the female aspect of Layang Petak, spirit of prosperity, and also to the Raja Ki Ngurah Panji Sakti, to ask for him to be forgiven for the destruction of the temple.

There are also shrines to the gods of the three lakes, Bratan, Buyan and Tamblingan, shrines representing the other major temples of Bali founded in the Majapahit era, and, in its own little compound, the temple of Gaduh in honour of Dewi Sri, rice goddess, where you can see two small shrines in the shape of rice barns.

From Pura Luhur you can see over the jungle to the mountains, Batukau, Sangiyang (2,093 m, 6,865 ft) and Pohon (2,063 m, 6,766 ft), on the sides of which are the **Botanical Gardens** of Bedugul.

Jatuluwih

From Pura Luhur to Jatuluwih (which means 'truly marvellous') the roads are very bad, and are frequently impassable. If you plan to make your way east to Jatuluwih from the turning at Pacung on the main Denpasar–Bedugul road, prepare to be disappointed. Heavy rains in this region frequently wipe out great segments of the road, or destroy the bridges.

The scenery from Jatuluwih is spectacular though. Rice terraces curve away down the hillside and up again into the clouds beyond. It is well worth enduring the bumpy ride. Jatuluwih also has a temple, curiously surrounded by carved and painted stone mythical creatures, similar to the statues outside Chinese temples.

Barong dance

The nearby villages of **Apuan** and **Pacung** are renowned among the local Balinese for their Barong dances at the time of the temple *odalan*. These are some of the most spectacular of Balinese dramas, not to be missed if you are in Bali at the time of their performance. As many as 60 Barongs visiting from other temples all over the island may be present. The temples concerned are **Pura Natar Sari** at Apuan, and **Pura Bukit Kembar** at Pucung. For information about times ask locally or in the tourist office in Denpasar.

Antosari to Pupuan

This is a little-known road north, the most westerly of the roads in Tabanan, passing through beautiful rice terracing and small villages. On the higher land is the principal spice-growing area of Bali. There is a wonderful smell of cloves in the air: you'll see vanilla pods ripening and cloves laid out to dry beside the road.

Around Pupuan is the main coffee-growing region of the island.

Part XII

JEMBRANA REGENCY

Bull-racing, Negara

Jembrana is the least known region of Bali, scarcely visited by tourists, little populated except along the main road west along which lorries and buses thunder to Gilimanuk and the Java ferry. Most of the regency is covered by the densely forested highlands of Bali's National Park. The flatter southern region is rice-growing country. Miles of gently curving countryside are carved into the contours of the rice terraces, with here and there a small settlement, fringed with coconut palms. Along the coast the streams which water the terraces on their way down from the central hills meet the sea in a succession of tiny coves and marshy deltas. The road crosses some sluggish rivers overhung with greenery. Cows graze beside the road in the more open areas, from which you get glimpses of sea and sandy beaches.

Villages have a prosperous air, partly due to the mass of flowering shrubs which almost obscure the neat little houses. It is sad that most people who see the peaceful countryside and inviting coastal bays of Jembrana do so from the grimy windows of crowded buses, speeding along this road to and from Gilimanuk.

The major fishing port of Bali, **Pengambengan**, is in Jembrana, 10 km (6.25 miles) southwest of **Negara** (capital of the regency). Pengambengan is the centre of a large sardine industry; the fish are caught in Selat Bali, the narrow straits between Bali and Java. You can see the fishermen's large motorized *prahu*s come in to the beach here, and there are several canneries. A small prawn-breeding industry based in this area may be extended to supplement reductions in catches due to overfishing.

Otherwise Negara's income derives primarily from coconut plantations on the land cleared of jungle on the southern edge of the national park, coffee plantations near the border with Tabanan, cloves and, increasingly, vanilla.

340

There is talk of developing Jembrana as a tourist region, but, meanwhile village life for the regency's few inhabitants continues, its rural traditions undisturbed.

Historical Notes

Hindus, Christians, Muslims

Jembrana has always been isolated and largely unaffected by events in the rest of the island: the road that now forms its main artery, carrying traffic from Java to Denpasar, was only completed in the 1930s when the Gilimanuk ferry was inaugurated.

Jembrana has looked west as much as to the rest of Bali, and in certain respects continues to do so. Its history is largely tied to that of Buleleng to the north; after the Dutch had successfully overrun Buleleng in 1849, they assumed control of Jembrana as well. Jembrana's isolation accounts for a sequence of events in the 1930s, when both it and neighbouring Tabanan were the target for a sudden spurt of activities by Christian missionaries.

Until then, the Dutch actively discouraged the presence of missionaries. In the 1930s, however, an American fundamentalist sect sent an Indonesian Chinese by the name of Chang to work among the Balinese Chinese. The Dutch Resident turned a blind eye and before long Chang had converted a fair number of Balinese, largely through introductions by the Balinese wives of his Chinese converts. Chang would address himself

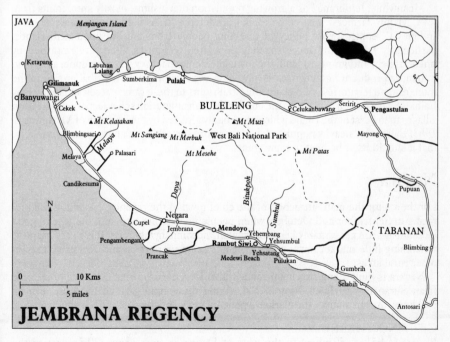

341

to the most oppressed of the lowest *sudra*, and promise them freedom from taxes, from obligations of labour, and even relief from disease if they converted. Many were disappointed, but Chang succeeded in exploiting antipathy between the castes and converts were ostracized from their villages.

In 1932 Chang declared that he had made 300 converts, but he paid dearly for his boast. Back in Holland the various missionary societies were furious that the Resident, whilst keeping them at bay, had allowed another Christian church — and a fundamental- ist American one at that — unfettered access. The Resident responded quickly by having Chang removed, but he faced continuing pressure from the Dutch missionaries. In the end he allowed one missionary each from the Catholic and the Protestant church to come to Bali, but on the strict conditions that they did not evangelize. They duly arrived, and behaved with discretion, but nonetheless the number of Christians in Bali continued to rise throughout the 1930s.

Meanwhile the pressures faced by the converts from their fellow villagers did not diminish. Revilement by their fellows, and the paltry rewards of Christianity against what they had been promised, caused many to revert to Balinese Hinduism. Others, however, persisted. To ease the ensuing tensions, the Dutch set aside two parcels of land in a remote spot on the edge of the jungle and beneath the mountains some 25 km (15.5 miles) northwest of Negara. One was for the Protestants, who against great odds have carved out the village of **Blimbingsari** for themselves, and who now number some 1,700; the other is **Palasari**, 5 km (3.1 miles) away, a village of 1,500 Catholics.

Meanwhile, Jembrana has a growing population of Muslims, mostly immigrants from Java. Mainly farmers, they come to Bali under the 'transmigration' scheme. This is Indonesia's controversial policy of directing people from the overpopulated islands, particularly Java, to the more sparsely populated territories. They are rewarded by financial help and grants of land, the principle being that they will turn underused land into more productive enterprises — not, however, a view shared by tribal groups in the more remote territories, who claim ancestral rights to these same parcels of land. Many Balinese have moved to other islands under the transmigration scheme, particularly from villages to the east of the island which were badly affected by the eruption of Mt Agung in 1963. Bali is very heavily populated; it is therefore something of an irony, and a mystery, that it should itself be host to immigrants.

Negara

For the visitor the main attraction of the chief town of the regency, Negara, is the bull racing in September and October, when people flock to the area, and the several good local *losmen*s are presumably kept going by the accompanying trade. It is a very friendly, welcoming little market town, and the people seem more open and accessible than in other rural areas.

Negara is built along two main roads, Jalan Diponegoro, which extends to become Jalan Surapati, and Jalan Ngurah Rai. Along these roads are all the usual official buildings, the bus station, the market, a petrol station, and the post and telephone offices.

GETTING THERE
Negara is 95 km (59 miles) to the west of Denpasar, and 33 km (20.5 miles) to the

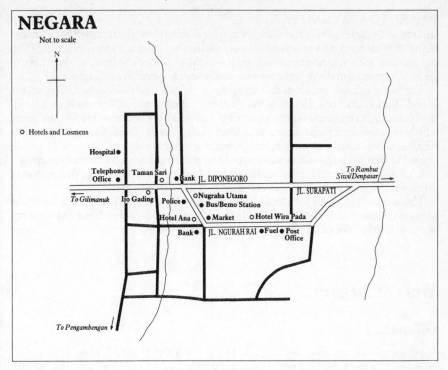

Negara Town

southeast of Gilimanuk. This road is one of Bali's busiest, and the surface is for the most part well maintained. But this is no motorway: allow around four hours to get from Denpasar by rented car or motorbike. The swiftness of the journey by public transport (bus or *bemo* from Ubung station in Denpasar) will depend on the number of stops; if you don't want it to take forever, try to catch one of the evening buses on its way to Gilimanuk and Java beyond. The fare will be around 1,250rp.

The bull races

'Bull' races are held on a track in the fields outside Negara, usually in September and October, to celebrate the end of the rice harvest. The dates vary from year to year; ask at the tourist office in Denpasar for further information. In fact it is water buffaloes which run the races. Unlike the Buleleng bull races, the winning factor here is speed as much as elegance, but that doesn't stop farmers decorating their beasts with style. The drivers career around a dusty 2 km (1.25 mile) course on little two-wheeled carts pulled by a yoked pair of buffaloes, which are said to reach 80 kph (50 mph). The atmosphere at these events is very festive and they are well attended. Your hotel will be able to arrange transport if you have come independently. Many visitors come on a package arrangement from the main resorts.

343

WHERE TO STAY AND EAT

At 1 km (0.6 mile) east from the town is a sign for **Cahaya Matahari**, which lies a further 800 m (800 yards) along a poor road. The rooms here are good and spacious for 10,000rp double or single, including breakfast, but it is in the middle of nowhere, so you'd have to go into Negara or make do with the tiny local *warung*s for an evening meal.

The other choices are all in the town, along the two roads mentioned. The best is **Hotel Wira Pada**, with 25 rooms from 10,000rp double or 7,500rp single to 7,500rp double and 5,000rp single for the 'economic' rooms. All are above average for the price, which includes breakfast. There is a large *rumah makan* there too, with generous helpings of the usual *nasi campur, nasi goreng, ayam goreng* etc.

Ijo Gading is also excellent value—its 18 large rooms have a traditional setting and cost 5,000rp double or single without breakfast. **Taman Sari** is the same price, with over 20 rooms, friendly people, and an excellent *rumah makan* attached.

The two budget places are **Hotel Ana** and **Nugraha Utama**. The latter is the better of the two, small rooms at 4,000rp double or 3,500rp single including breakfast—but not worth it for the sake of saving a couple of thousand rupiah.

West of Negara

Gilimanuk

Right at the westernmost tip of Bali, 16 km (10 miles) beyond Teluk Terima, lies Gilimanuk. This is the port from which the ferry leaves to cross the 'Selat Bali' or Bali Straits to Java. It is dominated by the view of Java's three easternmost volcanoes which loom impressively out of the haze across the water. Around the bay at Gilimanuk are extensive mangrove swamps, with their odd pre-historic beauty.

The ferry was started by two Germans in the 1930s, who were the first to create a regular service across a notoriously difficult stretch of water. Things cannot have changed all that much. In loading and unloading, vehicles have to run the gauntlet of an approach over sand and have been known to be left there, embedded, as the ferry sails away.

Apart from the ferry, there is not much to bring the tourist to Gilimanuk. It is barely a town at all, more a ribbon development along the road east, albeit with an open and friendly air. There is a market by the bus station in the centre, around 1 km (0.6 mile) from the ferry port. *Dokar*s will take you to and from the port for 200rp each way. There is a Pertamina petrol station on the outskirts of town on the Denpasar road.

WHERE TO STAY AND EAT

If you need to stay here, there are four homestays and one *rumah makan*, all near the bus station and market, and within calling distance of the large new mosque. The brightest of the homestays is **Gili Sari**, at 5,000rp (double or single), no breakfast; but there is little too choose between the four in comfort or price. The **Rumah Makan Padang** is passable. There are several *rumah makan*s and *warung*s down by the port.

East of Negara

Rambut Siwi

The temple of Rambut Siwi is the main tourist site of the area. Even so, it is hardly overrun with visitors except at festival time. It is a special sort of place, peaceful, beautiful, full of hidden nooks of great significance to the Balinese who come to pray here. It is set in rice fields right by the sea, perched above the narrow sandy beach on a high black rock. The surf pounds in from the Indian Ocean, threatening the survival of the most seaward of the temple buildings. In 1988 the Bali government provided funds to shore up the rock against erosion.

Pura Rambut Siwi is 18 km (11 miles) east of Negara, near the town of **Mendoyo**, between the villages of **Yehembang** and **Yehsumbul**. You see it on an otherwise deserted stretch of road because of the pull-in place and *warung*s opposite the entrance. Lorries stop here to be blessed. This is a fertile, fruit-growing region, and bananas, durian, rambutan, sawo, pineapples, jackfruit, mangosteen and oranges can all be bought here in season. You can drive in through the carved gateway, down to the temple itself.

The temple is another monument to the religious powers of holy man Nirartha (see also Pulaki and Tanah Lot), who came from Java to reinforce the Hindu religion in Bali against the encroaching influence of Islam in the 16th century. He came to Rambut Siwi after leaving the court of Dewa Agung Batu Renggong at Gelgel. He first went to **Pura Peranca**, 6 km (3.75 miles) east along the coast, and is said to have founded Pura Rambut Siwi in 1546. The temple gets its name from the legend that Nirartha left his hair (*rambut*) here, to be a symbol of worship to his Hindu followers. Nirartha is sometimes known by the Balinese name given to him on his arrival, Bhatara Sakti Bau Rau ('the holy man newly arrived') and some of the shrines in the inner courtyard of the temple are dedicated to him under this name.

The temple buildings are of lovely mellowed red bricks and stone, beautifully carved and laid out, with stone *naga*s and boars guarding the entrance. There are shrines to the rice goddess, known here as Rambut Sedana, and to Saraswati, the goddess of learning, who is represented here with her symbolic goose. There's some oddly crude new painting on some of the inner temple buildings. Notice an unusual stone carving by the gate of the second courtyard of a holy man being swallowed by a *naga*. The whole temple smells sweetly of frangipani, and in September and October of *cempaka* flowers from the trees outside, which attract huge, brightly coloured butterflies.

The small shrine to the goddess of fertility, Dewi Melanting, out on the rocks is especially frequented by people praying for good business. Below it, on the sands, are two holy places in caves. **Goa Hariman**, the Cave of the Tiger God, has five chambers, the first of which is mysteriously clean, despite being the haunt of bats and swallows. The second, **Goa Tirta**, is a holy water cave, where priests come to pray for holy water at times of festival. The spring is supposed to appear only at these special times. Snakes live in these caves, revered as holy, protecting the caves. All along the edge of the cliff offerings (*sajen-sajen*) have been placed under the low overhang of the black rock. A remote, mysterious atmosphere is promoted by the din of the surf beating on the sands and the curious white quality of the light, here, as elsewhere along this stretch of coastline.

Below the main temple just to the east is another smaller temple down on the rocks, **Pura Penatarah**.

Medewi Beach

Between Yehsumbul and **Pulukan**, 25 km (15.5 miles) east of Negara, **Medewi** is one of the garden villages of Jembrana. Decorative shrubs line the roads and the only local traffic is schoolchildren on high bicycles and women carrying their burdens from the rice harvest. Houses stand discreetly back from the road, screened by yet more flowering shrubs and trees; villagers stand and gossip in their colourful front gardens.

A sign to the beach, picturing a faded surfer, stands at the head of the stony track down to the sea. There is a concrete promenade in the shade of a spectacular banyan tree, a few sleepy fruit and drink sellers, but not a lot else. The surf is said to be good here, and there's a strip of brownish sand to bathe off. *Prahu*s with colourful striped sails line the beach and dot the sea.

There are other good surfing beaches nearby on this road, at **Selabih**, for example, to the east.

WHERE TO STAY AND EAT

If you're serious about staying here there is a hotel and *rumah makan* beside the main road just outside Medewi. A room with private bathroom costs 8,000rp double or 5,000rp single, but may not be spectacularly clean. The restaurant is pleasant enough though.

North from Pulukan

This road joins the north–south Seririt–Antosari road at Pupuan, in Tabanan regency. En route is some more good scenery where the hills have been terraced for rice. At one point you actually pass right through the centre of a huge banyan tree, which grows in an arch over the road. As on the Antosari road you will see spices drying beside the road as you climb higher and enter the coffee-growing region around Pupuan.

CHRONOLOGY

*c.*3000 BC onwards	Movement of Malay peoples throughout the archipelago
First millennium BC	Bronze age in Southeast Asia
*c.*100 BC–AD100	Beginning of use of iron in region. Trade with China. Beginning of wet-rice cultivation
2nd and 3rd centuries AD	First encounters with Hinduism in the region through Indian traders
9th century AD	Evidence that Hinduism has reached Bali. Bali ruled by kings of the Warmadewa dynasty
Late 10th century/early 11th century	Bali conquered by King Dharmawangsa of Java. His sister, Mahendradatta marries Balinese King Udayana. The priest Kuturan reforms Balinese Hinduism. Udayana's son, Prince Erlangga, becomes ruler of eastern Java (Kediri) (*c.*1010–49)
1284	King Kertanegara of the Javanese Singasari dynasty reconquers Bali
1293	Foundation of the Majapahit empire in Java. Bali ruled by the Pejeng dynasty. Late 13th century: Islam arrives in northern Sumatra
1343	Conquest of Bali and defeat of Pejeng dynasty by Majapahit forces under Gajah Mada. New palace set up at Samprangan under Javanese nobleman Kapakisan
Late 14th century	Palace moved to Gelgel, probably by Kapakisan's grandson
15th century	Gradual disintegration of the Majapahit empire under pressure from surrounding Islamic states
1509	First European traders (Portuguese) enter the region. 1511: Portuguese conquest of Malacca
1515–20	Final collapse of the Majapahit empire in Java in the face of the rising Mataram empire; evacuation of the courts to Bali
1550–1600	Golden Age initiated by Dewa Agung Batu Renggong, raja of Gelgel *c.* 1550–70. Territory increased to include east Java (Blambangan), Lombok and Sumbawa. Religious reforms undertaken by the high priest Nirartha
1597	Bali visited by three ships under the Dutch navigator Cornelis de Houtman. Four members of crew visit palace at Gelgel
1601	Expedition under Jacob van Heemskerck results in trading agreement which forms basis for Dutch claim to Bali hereafter. 1602: foundation of Dutch East India Company. 1619: Dutch found Batavia (now Jakarta) as their regional capital

Late 17th/early 18th century	Gradual decline in power of Gelgel dynasty and rise of rajadom of Buleleng. *c.*1710: Dewa Agung's palace moved to Klungkung. Development of trade in foodstuffs, slaves and opium with Europeans
Mid-18th century	Rise of rajadom of Karangasem, now controlling Lombok; it conquers Buleleng and Jembrana
1811–17	Britain takes over Dutch East Indies during Napoleonic War, appointing Raffles as Lieutenant-Governor. Raffles visits Bali. 1814: brief British military expedition to northern Bali under Major-General Nightingale. 1817: Indonesia returned to Dutch
1820s and 1830s	Dutch make vain attempts to control Bali through treaties with the rajas. 1826: they set up recruiting station in Kuta. 1836: Danish trader Mads Lange sets up trading post in Kuta, outshining Dutch efforts to break into the market. Series of official Dutch missions to Bali in effort to seal trading treaties and prevent Balinese practice of plundering wrecks
1844–50	1844: Dutch arrive in Buleleng to finalize treaty and are rebuffed. 1846: First Dutch Military Expedition to (northern) Bali ends in settlement which is not honoured by Balinese. 1848: Second Expedition repulsed in bloody ambush at northern hill-town of Jagaraga; Balinese led by Jelantik. 1849: Third Expedition results in victory for Dutch at Jagaraga. The Dutch now control northern Bali. 1850: attempts by the Dutch to advance on Klungkung from the south fail and a treaty is agreed through the intercession of Mads Lange
1880s	Chaotic period in southern rajadoms ends with the annihilation of the old rajadom of Mengwi
1894	Dutch troops are massacred in the 'Lombok Treachery', in answer to which the Dutch conquer Lombok and take over control of Karangasem, which had been under Lombok control since 1850
1900	Gianyar, under continuing threat from Klungkung, agrees to accept Dutch rule in return for protection
1903–4	*Suttee* (burning of widows) takes place in Tabanan against Dutch instructions and causes international scandal. The wreck of the Chinese schooner *Sri Kumala* is plundered; the Dutch sue the Raja of Badung for compensation, which he ignores
1906	The Dutch decide to enforce their claim by invading Badung at Sanur. In Denpasar the courts of the Rajas of Badung and Pemecutan commit *puputan* (suicidal fight to the death). The Raja of Tabanan commits suicide. Only Klungkung and Bangli remain outside direct Dutch control

1908 — After the murder of Dutch agents of the opium monopoly at Gelgel, Dutch troops march on Klungkung. The Dewa Agung and his court commit *puputan*. The Dutch now control all Bali

1908–41 — Period of paternalistic colonialism. Beginnings of tourist trade through Buleleng/Singaraja (the capital). 1930s: the arrival of numerous Western artists, writers, dancers, anthropologists. Beginnings of renaissance of Balinese art

1942–5 — February 1942: Singapore falls to advancing Japanese armies; they capture Bali unopposed in the same month. Japanese occupation forces not noticeably more oppressive to the Balinese than the Dutch until the last years of the war. 1945: Japanese surrender and evacuate

1946 — Dutch return to Bali. Ngurah Rai and 96 men fight to the death at Marga, resisting the Dutch in the name of Indonesian independence. Bali forms part of the Dutch-controlled Republic of East Indonesia

1949 — At the Round Table Conference in The Hague the Republic of the United States of Indonesia is created with Sukarno as President. Bali now a part of independent Indonesia

1957–65 — Deteriorating political and economic situation throughout Indonesia. 1963: eruption of Mt Agung devastates the eastern part of Bali, causes some 2,000 deaths and makes 100,000 homeless. 1965: attempted coup in Jakarta ignites massive revenge against the Communist party throughout Indonesia. Estimated that 40,000 people die in Bali as old scores are settled

1968–present — 1968: Suharto formally takes over Presidency. Indonesia opens up to Western investment. Period of political stability and economic growth backed by oil revenue. 1970s: rapidly growing tourist trade in Bali, transforming the southern part of the island. 1980s: opening of five de luxe hotels in major complex of Nusa Dua; continuing annual rise in tourism

LANGUAGE

Bahasa Indonesia: A Traveller's Vocabulary

Bahasa Indonesia is the primary language of communication used throughout Indonesia. For a description of Bahasa Indonesia, how it functions, rules of pronunciation and grammar, see pp.31–38. This is not the place to give you a basic course in Indonesian, but if you take the trouble to go right through this list you will soon see how phrases and sentences are built up by bringing together simple components. For example, *pagi* is 'morning', *makan* is 'to eat': *makan pagi* is breakfast.

Greetings

please	1. *tolong* when asking a favour: e.g. *Tolong bantu saya*, please help me.
	2. *silakan* when offering something: e.g. *Silakan duduk*, please sit down
thank you	*terima kasih* (lit., 'receive my love')
you're welcome (in response to thanks)	*kembali* (lit., 'return')
yes	*ya*
no	*tidak* (or *bukan* for nouns and pronouns, e.g. *bukan dia*, not him)
Good morning	*Selamat pagi* (used until about 11 am)
Good afternoon	1. *Selamat siang* (used from about 11 am to 3 pm)
	2. *Selamat sore* (used from about 3 pm until nightfall)
Good evening/night	*Selamat malam*
Sleep well	*Selamat tidur*
Goodbye (when you are leaving)	*Selamat tinggal* (lit., greetings on your staying)
Goodbye (when someone else is leaving)	*Selamat jalan* (lit. greetings on your going)
Welcome	*Selamat datang*
Bon appetit!	*Selamat makan!*
Please come in	*Silakan masuk*
Please sit down	*Silakan duduk*
Excuse me (May I?)	*Permisi*
I am sorry	*Maaf*
How are you?	*Apa kabar?*
good/fine	*baik*
It doesn't matter	*Tidak apa apa*
already	*sudah*
not yet	*belum*

350

later	*nanti saja*
in a while	*sebentar*
not now	*tidak sekarang*
Be careful!	*Hati-hati!*
Look out!	*Awas!*

'Please' and 'thank you' are generally used much less than in English.

Before someone starts to eat they will ask permission, '*Permisi?*', to which the polite reply is '*Silakan*', i.e. please go ahead, followed by '*Selamat makan!*', i.e. Bon appetit!

When you say goodbye temporarily, someone may add, '*Sampai bertemu lagi*' or '*Sampai berjumpa lagi*' = 'Till we meet again'.

When you are walking along the street or in the ricefields, people may call out, '*Mau kemana?*' or just '*Kemana?*', which means 'Where are you going?' This is not persecutory or even unwarranted curiosity, but just a habit common in village society where everyone generally knows everyone else's business. It is a good idea to tell them exactly where you are going unless you have some reason for hiding it, because you will very likely learn something about where you are going, the time you need to be there, a quicker route, or vital information about the state of the road, etc, etc ... If you know exactly where you are going and have no wish to discuss it further, just smile and say, '*Kemana mana*' = 'Wherever', or '*Jalan-jalan saja*' = 'Just wandering around'.

Basic Chat

Outside the tourist resorts, where hotel staff are well trained not to ask questions, everyone wants to know your personal details. It can drive you nuts after a while, but it is a good way to learn some basic language because you hear the questions and use the answers so often.

What's your name?	*Siapa nama anda?*
My name is Wayan	*Nama saya Wayan*
Where do you come from (Miss/Sir)?	*Asal dari mana (Nyonya/Tuan)?*
I come from London/New York	*Saya dari London/New York*
I am English/American/ Australian	*Saya orang Inggeris/Amerika/Australi*
Where do you live?/Where are you staying?	*Di mana tinggal?*
I live in/am staying at ...	*Saya tinggal di...*
How old are you?	*Berapa umur anda?*
I am twenty-one years old	*Umur saya duapuluh-satu tahun*
Are you married/single?	*Sudah kawin/masih sendiri?*
Do you have a family?	*Sudah berkeluarga?*
wife	*isteri*
husband	*suami*
family	*keluarga*
father	*bapak*
mother	*ibu*

351

friend	*teman*
child	*anak*
son	*anak laki-laki*
daughter	*anak perempuan*
older brother/sister	*kakak*
younger brother/sister	*adik*
How many children?	*Berapa anak-anak?*
Do you like Bali?	*Senang di Bali?*
Yes, I like it	*Senang*
What is your occupation?	*Kerja apa?*
How long have you been here?	*Berapa lama di sini?*
I have been here one week/two days	*Saya sudah di sini satu minggu/dua hari*
Do you speak English?	*Bisa bahasa Inggeris?*
I don't understand	*Saya tidak mengerti*
I don't speak Indonesian	*Saya tidak bisa bicara Bahasa Indonesia*
Slowly!	*Pelan-pelan!*
I don't know	*Saya tidak tahu*
I think so	*Saya kira begitu*

Nationalities

nationality	*kebangsaan*
country	*negeri*
England/English	*Ingerris*
USA/American	*Amerika*
Canada/Canadian	*Kanada*
Australia/Australian	*Australi*
New Zealand/New Zealander	*Selandia Baru*
South Africa/South African	*Afrika Selatan*
France/French	*Perancis*
West Germany/German	*Jerman*
The Netherlands/Dutch	*Belanda*
Belgium/Belgian	*Belgia*
Switzerland/Swiss	*Swis*
Austria/Austrian	*Austria*
Italy/Italian	*Italia/Itali*
Spain/Spanish	*Spanyol*
Denmark/Danish	*Denmark*
Sweden/Swedish	*Swedia*
Norway/Norwegian	*Norwegia*
Finland/Finnish	*Finlandia*
India/Indian	*India*
Japan/Japanese	*Jepang*
China/Chinese	*Cina*

Constructions using the names of countries should include the word *negeri*, country. Thus, England is *Negeri Ingerris*. Similarly, the word for a person is *orang*, so a Frenchman (or woman) is *orang Perancis*.

Questions

What?	*Apa?*
Who?	*Siapa?*
Where?/Where is?	*Dimana?*
Where?/Where to?	*Kemana?*
When?	*Kapan?*
How?	*Bagaimana?*
Why?	*Mengapa/kenapa?*
Which one?	*Yang mana?*
How much/many?	*Berapa?*
Examples:	
How much does it cost?	*Berapa harga(nya)?*
How much is the fare?	*Berapa ongkos(nya)?*
What is the time?	*Jam berapa?*

Useful Words and Phrases

beautiful	*indah*
very agreeable	*bagus* (*Bali bagus!*)
young	*muda*
old	*tua* (person); *lama* (thing)
correct	*betul*
wrong	*salah*
broken	*rusak*
and	*dan*
with	*dengan*
this	*ini*
that	*itu*
perhaps	*barangkali*
very	*sekali*
boy/male	*laki-laki*
girl	*perempuan*
age	*umur*
religion	*agama*
profession	*pekerjaan*
to want	*mau/ingin* (*ingin* is more polite)
to give	*memberi/beri*
to speak	*berbicara/bicara*
No entry	*Dilarang masuk*
No smoking	*Dilarang merokok*

Time and Numbers

minute	*minut*
hour	*jam*
day	*hari*

353

week	*minggu*
month	*bulan*
year	*tahun*
date	*tanggal*
now	*sekarang*
today	*hari ini*
tomorrow	*besok*
yesterday	*kemarin*
morning	*pagi*
afternoon (about 11 am to 3 pm)	*siang*
late afternoon/evening (about 3 pm to nightfall)	*sore*
night	*malam*

One	*satu*
two	*dua*
three	*tiga*
four	*empat*
five	*lima*
six	*enam*
seven	*tujuh*
eight	*delapan*
nine	*sembilan*
ten	*sepuluh*
eleven	*sebelas*
twelve	*duabelas*
thirteen	*tigabelas*
fourteen	*empatbelas*
twenty	*duapuluh*
twenty-one	*duapuluh satu*
twenty-two	*duapuluh dua*
thirty	*tigapuluh*
thirty-eight	*tigapuluh delapan*
forty	*empatpuluh*
seventy-five	*tujuhpuluh lima*
one hundred	*seratus*
two hundred and forty nine	*duaratus empatpuluh sembilan*
one thousand	*seribu*
two thousand	*duaribu*
ten thousand	*sepuluhribu*
one million	*satu juta/sejuta*
half	*setengah*

What is the time?	*Jam berapa sekarang?*
eight o'clock	*jam delapan*
half past eight	*setengah sembilan* (lit., half to nine)

354

twenty past eight	*jam delapan lewat duapuluh*
twenty to nine	*jam sembilan kurang sembilan*
Sunday	*Hari Minggu*
Monday	*Hari Senin*
Tuesday	*Hari Selasa*
Wednesday	*Hari Rebo*
Thursday	*Hari Kemis*
Friday	*Hari Jumat*
Saturday	*Hari Sabtu*

Shopping

to buy	*beli*
to pay	*bayar*
money	*uang*
market	*pasar*
handicrafts market	*pasar kerajinan tangan*
art market	*pasar seni*
shop	*toko*
stall/small shop/small restaurant	*warung*
open	*buka*
closed	*tutup*
how much (is it)?	*berapa harga (nya)?*
expensive	*mahal*
too expensive	*terlalu mahal*
cheap	*murah*
more	*lebih*
less	*kurang*
approximately	*kira-kira*
price	*harga*
another one	*satu lagi*
enough	*cukup*
strong	*kuat*
better quality	*lebih halus*
I want to buy one kilo	*Saya mau beli satu kilo*
I only want half a kilo	*Saya mau setengah kilo saja*
I don't want to pay that price	*Saya tidak mau bayar harga itu*
Is that your lowest price?	*Apa itu sudah yang paling murah?*
I like (it)	*Saya senang (nya)*
Do you give a discount?	*Apa ada potongan?*
I will come back again tomorrow	*Saya kembali lagi besok*
Yes I'll buy it	*Ya saya mau belinya*
Thank you very much	*Terima kasih banyak*
Sorry, I don't have any money	*Maaf, saya tidak ada uang*

Clothing and Handicrafts

skirt/dress	*rok*
trousers	*celana*
shirt/blouse	*baju*
hat	*topi*
shoes/sandals	*sepatu*
socks	*koas kaki*
watch	*arloji/jam*
earrings	*anting-anting*
bag	*tas*
jacket	*jaket*
sarong	*sarong*
material	*kain*
tablecloth	*taplak meja*
cushion cover	*sarong bantal*
bedcover	*tutup tempat tidur*
handicrafts	*kerajinan tangan*
woodcarvings (wooden things)	*ukiran (barang-barang kayu)*
statue	*patung* (wooden)/*arca*
mask	*topeng*
gold	*emas/mas*
silver	*perak*
painting	*lukisan*
basket	*keranjang*
leather	*kulit*
shadow puppets	*wayang kulit*
stone	*batu*

Colours

colour	*warna*
light	*muda*
dark	*tua*
black	*hitam*
white	*putih*
blue	*biru*
red	*merah*
pink	*merah muda*
yellow	*kuning*
green	*hijau*
grey	*abu-abu*
brown	*cokelat*
purple	*ungu*

Size

size	*ukuran*
short	*pendek*

356

long	*panjang*
big	*besar*
small	*kecil*
May I try it on?	*Boleh saya coba?*
It does not fit/suit me	*Tidak cocok*

Stationery/Photography/Pharmacy

book	*buku*
dictionary	*kamus*
map	*peta*
newspaper	*surat kabar*
pen (ballpoint)	*bolpoin pena* (or use *alat tulis*, lit., 'writing instrument')
(writing) paper	*kertas (tulis)*
envelope	*amplop*
stamp	*perangko*
(camera) film	*filem (untuk kamera)*
colour/black & white film	*filem berwana/hitam putih*
film developing	*cuci filem*
one print	*satu cetak*
toothpaste	*pasat gigi*
razor	*pisau cukur*
shampoo	*shampoo* (sometimes written *syampo*, also *sabun rambut*)
soap	*sabun*
tampons	*tampon*
sticking tape	*plester*
antiseptic	*antiseptis*

Bank/Moneychanger

I want to change money	*Saya mau tukar uang*
Can you cash travellers' cheques?	*Apa bisa tukar travel cek?*
Do you have change?	*Ada uang kecil?*
Please give me large notes/bills	*Tolong beri uang besar*
What is the exchange rate for sterling/dollars today?	*Berapa milai pon Inggeris/dollar hari ini?*

Hotel and *losmen*

small hotel	*losmen*
room	*kamar*
to take a bath/shower	*mandi*
bathroom	*kamar mandi*
toilet (room)	*kamar kecil* or *WC* (pron., 'way-say')

357

to sleep	*tidur*
bed	*tempat tidur*
table	*meja*
fan	*kipas*
hot water	*air panas*
mosquito coil	*obat nyamuk*
bed sheet	*seprei*
blanket	*selimut*
towel	*handuk*
candle	*lilin*
electric light	*lampu listrik*
toilet paper	*kertas kloset*
wet	*basah*
dry	*kering*
dirty	*kotor*
to wash	*cuci*
clean	*bersih*
empty	*kosong*
Do you have a room?	*Ada kamar kosong?*
I need a room for just one night/a week	*Saya perlu kamar untuk semalam saja/satu minggu*
How much does this one cost?	*Berapa harga ini?*
Does it include breakfast?	*Apa dapat makan pagi?*
I would like to see the room	*Saya mau lihat kamarnya dulu*
Have you a bigger/better/cheaper room?	*Ada kamar lebih besar/lebih baik/lebih murah?*
Is there hot water?	*Ada air panas?*
Are tax and service included?	*Apa sudah termasuk pajak dan servis?*
Please wake me at eight in the morning	*Tolong bangunkan saya jam delapan pagi*
I'd like to stay one week. Is there a discount?	*Saya mau tinggal satu minggu. Apa ada potongan?*
The door doesn't lock	*Pintunya tidak bisa dikunci*
I can't find my key	*Saya tidak bisa menemui kunci saya*
There's no electricity. Do you have a paraffin lamp/candle?	*Listrik mati. Ada lampu/lilin?*

Food and Drink

General Words

to eat	*makan*
restaurant	*rumah makan/restoran*
breakfast	*makan pagi*
lunch	*makan siang*
dinner	*makan malam*
sugar	*gula*

milk	*susu*
salt	*garam*
chilli sauce (strong)	*sambal*
hot (chilli)	*pedas*
sweet (adj.)	*manis*
sweet and sour	*asam manis*
soy sauce (sweet)	*kecap manis*
hot chilli peppers	*cabe/lombok*
ginger	*jahe*
bread	*roti*
toast	*roti panggang*
cheese	*keju*
butter	*mentega*
fried	*goreng*
boiled	*rebus*
sauce	*saus/bumbu*
soup	*soto*
meat	*daging*
beef	*daging sapi*
steak	*bistek*
chicken	*ayam*
duck	*itik*
lamb	*domba*
goat	*kambing*
pork	*daging babi*
liver	*ati*
fish	*ikan*
prawn	*udang*
shrimp	*udang kecil*
lobster	*udang karang*
crab	*kepiting*
rice	*nasi*
plain boiled rice	*nasi putih*
rice flour noodles	*bakmi*
wheat flour noodles	*mie*
rice gruel	*bubur*
egg	*telur*
vegetables	*sayur*
onion	*bawang*
garlic	*bawang putih*
potato	*kentang*
tomato	*tomat*

Fruit

fruit	*buah*
apple	*apel*

orange	*jeruk manis*
lemon/lime	*jeruk nipis/limau*
banana	*pisang*
pineapple	*nenas*
water melon	*semangka air*
coconut	*kelapa*
grapes	*buah anggur*
mango	*mangga*
papaya/pawpaw	*papaya*
avocado	*apokat*

With other local fruit you are more likely to encounter the Indonesian word in the first instance:

manggis	mangosteen
sawo	sapodillo
belimbing	starfruit/carambola
sirsak/zurzat	custard apple/soursop
nangka	jackfruit
durian	durian
jeruk Bali	pomelo/grapefruit
rambutan	rambutan
salak	salak
jambu air	water apple/rose apple
jambu batu	guava
anggur Bedugul	a large kind of passionfruit
asam	tamarind

Drinks

to drink	*minum*
hot/cold drink	*minum panas/minum dingin*
ice	*es*
coffee	*kopi*
black coffee	*kopi Bali*
white coffee	*kopi susu*
instant coffee	*nescafé*
tea	*teh*
tea with lemon	*teh pakai jeruk nipis*
orange/lemon juice	*air jeruk/air jeruk nipis*
beer	*bir*
rice wine	*brem*
drinking water	*air minum/air putih*

In the Restaurant

menu	*daftar makanan*
I'd like to see the menu	*Saya mau lihat daftar makanan*

fork	*garpu*
knife	*pisau*
spoon	*sendok*
cup	*cangkir*
plate	*piring*
glass	*gelas*
I haven't got a fork	*Saya belum ada garpu*
Please bring another glass	*Tolong membawa sebuah gelas lagi*
Is that very hot (chilli)?	*Apa itu pedas sekali?*
I am not used to eating spicy food	*Saya belum biasa makanan pedas*
We are ready to order now	*Kami mau memesan makanan sekarang*
How much is a large beer?	*Berapa harganya satu bir besar?*
Is it cold?	*Apa itu dingin?*
No ice please	*Tolong tanpa es*
No sugar please	*Tolong tanpa gula*
What kind of fish do you have today?	*Yang mana ikan ada hari ini?*
Another one please	*Satu lagi*
The bill/check please	*Minta notanya/billnya*
We're ready to pay now	*Kami mau bayar sekarang*
That was delicious	*Enak sekali*

On the Menu

See pp.18–19 for a description of Indonesian and Balinese cooking. Here is a list of the most common dishes on the menu:

nasi goreng	fried rice with added vegetables, meat, fish etc
nasi campur	steamed or boiled rice with vegetables, meat, fish and *krupuk*
krupuk	rice or cassava crackers, usually prawn-flavoured
bakmi goreng	rice-flour noodles with added vegetables, meat, fish etc
mie goreng	wheat-flour noodles with added vegetables, meat, fish etc
sate	small kebabs of meat or fish served with a spicy peanut sauce
gado gado	raw or steamed vegetables served with a spicy peanut sauce
capcai	Chinese-style stir-fried vegetables
ayam goreng	fried chicken
opor ayam	lightly curried chicken cooked in coconut milk
rendang	fiery-hot dried-cooked beef
ikan pepes	fish wrapped in a banana leaf and steamed
kare udang	curried shrimps
babi kecap	pork cooked with sweet soy sauce

babi guling	spit-roast pork
betutu bebek	smoked duck
tempe	deep-fried tofu (soya bean 'cheese')
pisang goreng	fried banana
rijsttafel	a gourmand's selection of Indonesian dishes

Directions and Places

here	*sini/disini*
there	*sana/disana*
north	*utara*
south	*selatan*
east	*timur*
west	*barat* (Westerner: *orang barat*)
right	*kanan*
left	*kiri*
turn left/right	*belok kiri/kanan*
straight on	*terus*
here	*disini*
from	*dari*
to	*ke*
up/above	*atas/diatas*
down/below	*bawa/dibawa*
opposite	*dimuka/didepan*
beside	*disebelah/disamping*
near	*dekat*
far	*jauh*
address	*alamat*
road/to walk	*jalan*
sea	*laut*
harbour	*labuhan*
airport	*lapangan terbang*
aeroplane	*kapal terbang*
ship	*kapal laut*
bus	*bis*
car	*mobil*
bicycle	*sepeda*
motorbike	*sepeda motor*
bus station	*stasion bis*
police	*polisi*
petrol/gas station	*pompa bensin*
post office	*kantor pos*
swimming pool	*kolam renang*
temple	*pura*
palace	*puri*
entrance	*masuk*

exit	*keluar*
I am lost/I don't know the way	*Saya kesasar/Saya tidak tahu jalannya*
I want to go to the market	*Saya mau ke pasar*
Please show me the way to the post office	*Tolong jalanmana menuju kantor pos*
What street (village) is this?	*Jalan (desa) apa ini?*
How far is the temple?	*Berapa jauhnya pura?*

Dance and Drama and Temple Festivals

ticket	*karcis*
temple scarf/waist band	*selandang*
What time does it start?	*Jam berapa mulai ini?*
What time does it finish?	*Jam berapa selasai ini?*
Where is the Barong dance?	*Dimana menari Barong?*
Will there be seats?	*Apa ada kursi?*
Do I pay?	*Apa saya harus bayar?*
Can I buy a ticket?	*Apa saya bisa beli karcis?*
Is there a *bemo* to that place?	*Ada bemo ke sana?*
How long will it take to get there by *bemo* (walking)?	*Kalau naik bemo (kalau jalan) berapa lama ke sana?*
Must I wear a sarong/scarf?	*Apa harus pakai sarong/selendang?*
May I take photos/use a flash?	*Boleh saya ambil photo/memakai blitz?*

Health

doctor	*doktor*
dentist	*doktor gigi*
pharmacy	*apotik*
painful/unwell	*sakit*
hospital	*rumah sakit*
I am sick	*saya sakit*
head	*kepala*
stomach	*perut*
tooth	*gigi*
ear	*telinga*
throat	*kerongkongan*
I have a headache/stomach ache/toothache/ earache	*Saya sakit kepala/perut/gigi/telinga*
medicine/drugs	*obat*
a cold	*pilek*
flu	*flu*
diarrhoea	*mulas*
infection	*infeksi*
I need medicine for a cold/flu/ diarrhoea/throat infection	*Saya mencari obat pilek/plu/mulas/infeksi kerongkongan*
to vomit	*muntah*
constipation	*sembelit*

GLOSSARY

adat	the traditional code of laws and social behaviour
agung	great
alang-alang	a kind of elephant grass used for thatching
aling-aling	the wall behind a gateway that prevents evil spirits from passing
alun-alun	an open piece of common ground or square in a town
arak	distilled alcohol, usually from palm wine, but sometimes from rice wine
atap	palm leaf thatching
bale	a raised pavilion, usually open or only partially enclosed
bali	small offering of rice or grain to the gods
Bali Aga	slightly pejorative term for traditional clans who relate back to a pre-Javanese Hindu ancestry
balian	Indonesian word for *dukun*
banjar	the local village community, or division within a village; also applied to the committee in charge of this community
banten	temple offering
Barong	common term for the *barong ket*, the sacred dragon-like animal that represents good in the battle against the evil witch Rangda
Batara	the title given to a deity or deified ancestor
batik	fabric printed by a dye-resist method using wax
batu	rock or mountain
bemo	general term for a minibus or enclosed pick-up truck used for public transport
Brahmana	the priestly caste
brem	rice wine
bukit	hill
buta	demonic spirit
candi	shrine, usually in a tall, tiered form
candi bentar	split gate
cili	doll-like motif, usually representing the rice goddess
dalang	puppeteer
danghyang	title given to the great spiritual leaders
desa	village
destar	a man's folded cloth headdress
dewa/dewi	god/goddess
Dewa Agung	the ruler of Gelgel and Klungkung, traditionally the most important raja in Bali
dokar	pony trap
dukun	native doctor, faith healer, herbalist, dealer in spells and counter-spells
empu	literally, 'master craftsman', honorific title also given to holy men, philosophers *et al.*
endek	Balinese for *ikat*
Galungan	major 10-day festival held once every 210-day year
gamelan	traditional Balinese percussion orchestra, composed mainly of xylophone-like instruments

gong	the instrument, but also used to indicate the whole of a *gamelan* orchestra
gunung	mountain
homestay	family hotel or *losmen*
ibu	mother (of)
ikat	woven cloth in which the pattern is created by dye-resist binding prior to weaving
jalan	street (often abbreviated to *Jl.* or *Jln*)
jukung	outrigger (sailing or motorized boat)
kabupaten	Balinese term for regency
kain	piece of cloth, worn as a long style of sarong
kaja	towards the mountains (opposite of *kelod*)
kala	demonic spirit
kampung	village or community (Indonesian word)
Kawi	old Javanese, still used in poetry, theatre and religious chants
kebaya	a woman's formal long-sleeved, tight-fitting jacket
kelod	towards the sea (opposite of *kaja*)
kepala desa	village headman
kepeng	Chinese coin pierced with a square hole
klian	head of a *banjar* or rice council
kretek	cigarette flavoured with crushed cloves
kris	sacred dagger, usually with a curvy blade
Ksatria	the princely caste
kulkul	large wooden bell made of a hollowed tree trunk, hung vertically
Kuningan	the festival on the eleventh day after Galungan
lamak	a flat palm-leaf temple hanging
legong	common term for *legong kraton*, or the young girl dancers who perform this
leyak	ever-present evil spirits associated with witchcraft
lingam	phallic-like symbol associated with cult of Shiva
lontar	a palm with wide, fan-shaped fronds that are used to make the long, thin 'leaves' of *lontar* books
losmen	hotel accommodation at the cheaper end of the scale
lumbung padi	traditional thatched rice barn
mandi	Indonesian-style shower/bath
mantra	arcane chant of sacred significance
meru	pagoda-like temple structure
naga	mythical serpent
nusa	island
Nyepi	day of silence, second day of the New Year celebrations
odalan	ceremony held once every 210-day year in every temple
om swastyastu	religious formula used as a welcome greeting (usually written)
padmasana	the 'lotus throne', the empty stone throne reserved for the highest god at any temple
padu raksa	temple gateway (not a split gate)
pande	smith
pasar	market

365

pawukon	the Balinese calendar with a year of 210 days
pedanda	Brahmana priest ('high priest')
pemangku	village priest
penjor	tall bamboo pole hung with decorations, used to line the streets at Galungan
perbekel	village headman
pondok	small shelter at the edge of a ricefield
prahu	outrigger (sailing or motorized boat)
punggawa	leader of a district (historical)
puputan	'the end', suicidal fight to the death when defeat is inevitable
pura	temple
pura dalem	temple of the dead
pura desa	village temple
pura puseh	'temple of origin', for the founders of the village
puri	palace
purnama	full moon
putri	princess
raja	ruler
Rangda	the evil sorceress, Queen of the *leyak*s
rattan	tough vine used in basketwork
rumah makan	restaurant of a modest kind
saka	the Balinese lunar calendar
sakti	having great spiritual powers
sanggah	family shrine in household temple
sanghyang	a title given to any deity or being of great spiritual standing
sarong	piece of cloth wrapped around the waist like a long skirt, worn by men and women
sawah	ricefield
segehan	small offering placed on the ground to appease evil spirits
sirih	the betel nut chew
songket	patterned woven cloth, usually incorporating gold or silver thread
subak	rice council
Sudra	the lowest caste, the caste of common people
taman	park
tiga roda	small three-wheeled taxi
tilem	new moon
tirta	holy water
triwangsa	the three senior castes, Brahmana, Ksatria and Wesia
tuak	palm wine
wadah	cremation tower
wantilan	large pavilion used for performances and cockfights
warung	small food stall or restaurant
wayang kulit	shadow puppet theatre
Wesia	the warrior caste

FURTHER READING

Baum, Vicki, *A Tale from Bali*, translated from the German and first published in English in 1937; reissued by Oxford University Press in their 'Oxford in Asia Paperback' series, 1973. A highly readable and well-researched novel describing the events leading up to the Dutch invasion of Bali in 1906.

Covarrubias, Miguel, *The Island of Bali*, first published in 1937, reissued in paperback by Routledge & Kegan Paul in their 'Pacific Basin Books' series, 1986. The classic account of Balinese culture, written with great energy and understanding; despite being 50 years old, much of the information is relevant today.

Dalton, Bill, *Indonesia Handbook*, Moon Publications, Chico, California, new edition 1985. An impressively researched guide to the whole of Indonesia: if you are travelling to other islands besides Bali, this is the book to take.

Djelantik, A.A., *Balinese Paintings*, 'Images of Asia' series, Oxford University Press, 1986. A small volume, concise, authoritative and well illustrated.

Eiseman, Fred, *Bali, Sekala and Niskala*, published privately in two volumes, 1985, 1986 (available in Bali). A series of very detailed but accessible articles on a wide variety of aspects of Bali: very rewarding reading for the Bali enthusiast.

Leuras, Leonard, and Lloyd, Ian, *Bali, the Ultimate Island*, Times Editions, 1987. A stunning, large-format, richly illustrated by excellent photographs, with an informative text; the ultimate glossy book.

Mabbett, Hugh, *In Praise of Kuta*, January Books, Wellington, New Zealand, 1987. An interesting and witty assessment of what makes Kuta tick, and how the real Bali still lurks there, somewhere.

Mabbett, Hugh, *The Balinese*, January Books, Wellington, New Zealand, 1985. A series of essays about all aspects of Balinese life and culture, with plenty of well observed anecdote: one of the best introductions to Bali.

Mathews, Anna, *The Night of Purnama*, first published 1965, reissued by Oxford University Press in their 'Oxford in Asia Paperback' series, 1979. A powerful, well written eye-witness account of the eruption of Mt Agung in 1963 (the author endured two hellish months living below the volcano, in Iseh).

McPhee, Colin, *A House in Bali*, first published 1944, reissued by Oxford University Press in their 'Oxford in Asia Paperback' series, 1979. A personal account of Bali in the 1930s by this American composer who set up home in Sayan, near Ubud; delightful.

Moerdowo, R.M., *Reflections on Balinese Traditional and Modern Arts*, Balai Pustaka State Publishing and Printing House, Jakarta, 1983 (available in Bali). An excellent survey of Balinese art, music and dance by this Javanese doctor of medicine and painter who has been Chairman of Fine Arts at Udayana University, Denpasar, as well as its Professor of Internal Diseases.

Powell, Hickman, *The Last Paradise*, first published in 1930, reissued by Oxford University Press in their 'Oxford in Asia Paperback' series, 1982. A personal account of a journey in Bali in the 1930s which paints an interesting picture of the island in this period of Dutch colonialism.

Tantri, K'tut, *Revolt in Paradise*, first published in 1960, reissued by Gramedia Paperbacks (available in Bali) 1988. A passionate account by an American woman of a Manx family (Vannine Walker) who travelled to Bali in the 1930s, helped set up one of the first hotels in Kuta, suffered appalling treatment by the occupying Japanese forces in Java, and went on to help the cause of Indonesian Independence by broadcasting in English on behalf of the Republicans, for which she earned the nickname 'Surabaya Sue' from the British and Dutch troops; absorbing reading, and something of a puzzle.

de Zoete, Beryl, and Spies, Walter, *Dance and Drama in Bali*, first published in 1938, reissued by Oxford University Press in their 'Oxford in Asia Paperback' series, 1982. Very thorough, but readable; a key source book for aficionados of Balinese dance.

INDEX

Note: Page numbers printed in *italics* refer to maps and illustrations.